Youth and the Law

NEW APPROACHES TO CRIMINAL JUSTICE AND CHILD PROTECTION

Third Edition

Susan Reid

Rebecca Bromwich

Sarah Gilliss

emond

Toronto, Canada
2015

Emond Montgomery Publications Limited
60 Shaftesbury Avenue
Toronto ON M4T 1A3
http://www.emp.ca/highered

Printed in Canada.

We acknowledge the financial support of the Government of Canada through the Canada Book Fund for our publishing activities.

Emond Montgomery Publications has no responsibility for the persistence or accuracy of URLs for external or third-party Internet websites referred to in this publication, and does not guarantee that any content on such websites is, or will remain, accurate or appropriate.

Publisher: Mike Thompson
Managing editor, development: Kelly Dickson
Director, editorial and production: Jim Lyons
Developmental editor: Nora Rock
Assistant developmental editor: Sarah Fulton
Copy editor: Rodney Rawlings
Production editor: Laura Bast
Permissions editor: Derek Capitaine, MRM Associates
Indexer: Paula Pike
Text and cover designer: Tara Wells
Cover image: Gettyimages.ca / aurumarcus

Library and Archives Canada Cataloguing in Publication

Reid, Susan, 1958-, author
    Youth and the law : new approaches to criminal justice and child protection / Susan Reid, Rebecca Bromwich, Sarah Gilliss. — Third edition.

Includes index.
First edition: Youth and the law : new approaches to criminal justice and child protection /
    Laurence M. Olivo and David Goldstein with Ralph Cotter.
ISBN 978-1-55239-477-9 (pbk.)

    1. Juvenile justice, Administration of—Canada—Textbooks.   2. Juvenile delinquency—Canada—Textbooks.   I. Bromwich, Rebecca, author   II. Gilliss, Sarah, 1984-, author   III. Olivo, Laurence M., 1946- .   Youth and the law.   IV. Title.

KE9445.O55 2014   364.360971   C2014-906444-6
KF9780.ZA2.O55 2014

To our students.

—*S.R. & S.G.*

To my children, soon to reach their own adolescence.
May they know their rights and responsibilities.

—*R.B.*

Contents

PART I

The Context of Youth Justice in Canada

PART II
Legislation

PART III
Policing and Criminal Procedure

PART IV
Meaningful Consequences

PART V

Ongoing and Emerging Social Issues

Preface

In *Youth and the Law*, you will be introduced to the complexity of the issues facing young people in conflict with the law and will acquire a foundational understanding of their experience within the youth criminal justice system. While only a small percentage of Canadian youth are actually involved in criminal behaviour, the opportunity to respond to their challenges before they become enmeshed in the adult criminal justice system is important. Because youth do not have the same capacity as adults, there are important safeguards and protections for them. This book will help you understand the characteristics unique to the youth justice system. While it is important to hold youth accountable when they break the law, we must also recognize that their level of culpability is less than that of adults, and therefore we must always consider alternative ways of imposing meaningful consequences.

When members of law enforcement encounter young suspects, they must have a full understanding of the enhanced procedural processes to be utilized. Also, if you choose a career as a police officer in the future, it is important for you to understand the alternatives that may prevent further misconduct, since you will have the front-line responsibility to make such choices. Even if you do not choose a career in policing, the community has a responsibility to help young people grow up, and how you decide to deal with a youth who has broken the law might change his or her life.

This text has five parts. Part I, The Context of Youth Justice in Canada, comprises Chapters 1 and 2. Chapter 1 introduces you to the demographics of Canadian youth and discusses youth crime rates using official statistics and self-reported methodologies. With an understanding of the reported youth crime rate, the chapter examines public perceptions of crime and analyzes the role of the media in educating the public on youth crime in Canada.

Chapter 2 considers the most common offences committed by young people. In order to understand youthful offending more fully, the chapter applies theoretical explanations of human nature. Finally, the chapter describes the five theoretical models of youth justice, which help explain the various intervention options when a youth contravenes the law.

Part II, Legislation, includes Chapters 3 and 4. Chapter 3 provides an overview of the separate criminal justice system for youth. This system has undergone many changes as the guiding legislation has changed from the *Juvenile Delinquents Act* to the *Young Offenders Act* and finally to the legislation in use today, the *Youth Criminal Justice Act*. The explanation of the YCJA's major provisions and guiding principles will give you a better appreciation of the distinct features of the youth justice system.

Chapter 4 examines provincial legislation relevant to youth beyond the *Youth Criminal Justice Act* and the *Criminal Code*. Child welfare matters, including the provisions for children in need of protection who may be involved in the foster care system, are discussed. Liquor laws, highway traffic laws, and other provincial laws provide offences with which youth may be charged. Although the material in Chapter 4 is based primarily on examples from Ontario, related legislation from other provinces and territories is also presented.

Part III, Policing and Criminal Procedure, comprises Chapters 5 to 7. Chapter 5 describes the procedures followed when youth have committed a criminal offence. The provisions of the *Canadian Charter of Rights and Freedoms* extend to young people; additional safeguards are found in the YCJA. Before the decision is made to charge or arrest a youth, alternatives outside the formal criminal justice system, in the form of extrajudicial measures, must be considered.

Chapter 6, which covers the pre-trial period, outlines what occurs when an extrajudicial measure is considered insufficient for holding a young person accountable. When a charge is laid, the decision must be made whether to hold the youth in pre-trial detention or release the youth on bail. Provisions in the YCJA guide this decision, but special considerations under the United Nations Convention on the Rights of the Child may also be important.

Chapter 7 focuses on formal youth court proceedings: the components of first appearance, plea, trial, and adjudication. The roles of the Crown, defence counsel, and judge are described and a youthful accused's right to counsel is explained. Specialized courts such as drug courts and mental health courts are examined, and specific safeguards built within the YCJA for Aboriginal youth are addressed.

Part IV, Meaningful Consequences, consists of Chapters 8 and 9. Chapter 8 focuses on sentencing options. The question always paramount in the youth criminal justice system is how best respond to a young person convicted of a criminal offence. The 2012 amendments to the YCJA, which introduced the principles of deterrence and denunciation as guidelines for sentencing youth, have made the answer to the question more complex than before.

Chapter 9 examines "what works" with regard to both the prevention of youth crime and the rehabilitation of young people. The guiding principle of the YCJA recognizes the importance of reserving the most serious sentence (incarceration) for the most serious offenders. In order to be able to implement this principle, it is necessary to understand risk and protective factors and to match programs to the youth's criminogenic risks and needs. In recent years, Canada has been promoting the need to implement evidence-based programs that respond to these risks and needs. Some of these intervention options are explored in this chapter.

Part V, Ongoing and Emerging Social Issues, consists of Chapter 10. The chapter considers special issues facing young people today and what the future may hold for youth growing up in Canada. Among the topics explored are the overrepresentation of Aboriginal youth in the criminal justice system, the changing demographics of youth in Canada, gender, poverty, and social media.

Since the second edition of this textbook, the landscape of youth criminal justice in Canada has changed, most notably as a result of amendments to the YCJA introduced by Bill C-10, the *Safe Streets and Communities Act*, in 2012. This legislation, passed by the Conservative government, included recommendations from the Nunn Commission regarding the pre-trial detention of young offenders. The amendments, with their focus on public safety, have made the youth criminal justice system more similar to the adult criminal justice system. Among other things, youth are now subject to the adult sentencing principles of specific deterrence and denunciation, and adult sentences can now be considered for some violent offences. In view of these changes, it is essential to understand what works in the prevention, rehabilitation, and reintegration of young persons who come in conflict with the law, in order to ensure that the spirit and the intent of the YCJA remain intact.

The format of the third edition of *Youth and the Law* has been completely revised. Chapters now include scenarios that encourage you to apply the theory and content of the text to real-life examples. Other features delve into particular aspects of the discussion in more detail, and touch on notable cases, such as Ashley Smith and Omar Khadr, and youth programs from across Canada. Also new to this edition are critical thinking questions throughout, questions that give you the opportunity to explore the material more fully. As you progress through the material, you will be challenged to tackle many of the same issues facing front-line professionals within the youth criminal justice system every day.

It is our hope that you will continue to ask the difficult questions that have faced juvenile justice practitioners and policy-makers over the past century. In considering how to respond to young people who commit offences, we hope you will more fully understand the concept of mitigated accountability and the need to retain a separate and distinct system of youth justice in Canada in the years to come.

Note to Readers

Under the *Youth Criminal Justice Act*, the term that refers to a youth who violates the criminal law is "young person." However, throughout the text, the terms "young offender" and "young person" are used interchangeably.

Acknowledgments

The authors gratefully acknowledge the generous help of Jim Lyons in guiding this text to its conclusion. The efforts of Kelly Dickson, Nora Rock, Laura Bast, and Rodney Rawlings were very much appreciated. The ongoing dialogue with Anthony Rezek, Vice President, Publishing, allowed for the various voices to be heard throughout the entire process and provided us with much-needed support to complete the project.

For the young persons we have met through the years in the youth criminal justice system, we hope that this text will honour the education that we received first-hand in our work with you, and that students who pursue careers in the youth justice field will be better equipped to deal with the complexities of the lives they will guide and assist.

About the Authors

Susan Reid is a full professor of criminology and criminal justice at St. Thomas University in Fredericton, New Brunswick. She is also the director of the Centre for Research on Youth at Risk, which is the eastern hub of the Students Commission of Canada/Centre of Excellence for Youth Engagement at St. Thomas University. Her research interests include youth justice, youth at risk, youth voice, and youth engagement. She has been actively involved in promoting adult–youth research partnerships and being an adult ally to youth through the New Brunswick network *Youth Matters*. She has written a number of publications on youth justice and in 2014 was inducted into the New Brunswick Crime Prevention Hall of Fame for her community outreach and service.

Rebecca Bromwich is a lawyer and legal academic. She teaches courses relating to youth and the law at the University of Ottawa Faculty of Law and at Carleton University, and is currently finishing her PhD in the Carleton University Department of Law and Legal Studies. She has taught in the Police Foundations and Social Service Worker programs at Fanshawe College and the University of Western Ontario, as well as at the University of Cincinnati, among others. She also works as a staff lawyer, Law Reform and Equality, at the Canadian Bar Association.

Sarah Gilliss is an instructor in the Police Foundations and Criminal Justice programs in the Social Sciences Department of the New Brunswick Community College (NBCC) in Miramichi, New Brunswick. She has had experience on the front line as a correctional officer and youth worker, working with youth in the youth criminal justice system. Co-founder of *Youth Matters*, she is currently running weekly groups with the *Youth Matters* chapter inside the New Brunswick Youth Centre as part of a national project and in collaboration with a group of her students from NBCC.

PART I

The Context of Youth Justice in Canada

Youth Crime: Perceptions and Realities

1

LEARNING OUTCOMES

After completing this chapter, you should be able to:

- Critically assess media portrayals of youth crime and consider the role of the media in creating public anxiety or "moral panic" about youth crime.

- Understand the concept of "hidden delinquency" and what it means for the reporting of official statistics.

- Understand how youth crime is counted through the Uniform Crime Reporting Survey and various self-report and victimization surveys, and identify strengths and weaknesses of each reporting method.

- Conduct an elementary analysis of uniform crime report statistics to identify apparent trends and patterns of youth crime.

- Understand the usefulness of the Crime Severity Index in terms of reporting various types of violent crime.

- Consider the role played by police perceptions about youth crime in the reporting of official statistics.

Introduction

How we come to understand youth crime depends on a number of factors. Where do we learn about young people who offend? What influence does the media have on our perceptions of the reality of youth crime? What is similar or different about youth crime today compared with earlier periods in history? What influence do US television and media sources have on our understanding of the youth justice system? This section will outline the various ways we measure and explain youth crime, and will examine Canadian interpretations of the way youth are dealt with under the *Youth Criminal Justice Act*, the law that governs Canada's youth justice system. As the book unfolds, you will gain more insight into the finer details of the youth justice system, but it is important to understand the broad terms and ideas that have helped frame youth justice policy and practices today.

What is your understanding of youth crime in Canada? Is the rate of youth crime on the rise? What factors can you think of that might account for rising crime rates among youth? Are young people who commit crimes today different from youth from previous generations? After you think about these broad questions, review the following statements and decide whether they are true or false. We will come back to consider these at the end of this chapter.

- The news media accurately shows us that the increase in the **crime rate** in Canada is directly related to the increase in youth crime.
- If young people are going to act like criminals, we should treat them like criminals. We don't need to have a separate system of youth justice.
- Young people are much more likely to victimize and hurt older people.
- Most young people today are involved in criminal gangs and commit serious crimes.
- The kinds of crimes that young people commit are becoming much more serious than in the past.

---

crime rate
ratio of police-reported crimes in an area to the population of that area

For a variety of reasons, adding the adjective "youth" to any media report of a violent incident introduces an extra measure of shock value into reports of crime in the news.

As former youth, and perhaps as parents of young people, our expectations of how the young should behave are influenced by personal and family experience. Whether we view youth as vulnerable and innocent or as threatening and troublesome, or some combination of both, accounts of youthful involvement in violence either confirm or challenge our personal beliefs. Much fear is rooted in misunderstanding, and as we struggle to understand youth, it is sometimes easier to simply believe what we have been told by our parents, friends, or colleagues, or what we have read in the news media.

Are offences by young people really on the rise? Has there been any significant change in the rate of youth violence? It is perhaps telling that these questions are the source of continued debate, and that something as apparently straightforward as the crime rate is so misunderstood.

If we hope to effectively measure the success of legislation, programs, and procedures designed, at best, to improve the lives of youth generally and prevent youth criminality or, at worst, to control and punish youth who have violated our criminal laws, we must grapple with these unresolved questions. We must accept the limitations of the data available to us, rationally consider the extent to which forces such as the media distort that data, and come to our own informed conclusions. Only after we have completed this process can we make a credible assessment of current initiatives and offer suggestions for how they might be improved.

A Profile of Canadian Youth

Demographics

- There were approximately 35,158,300 people living in Canada as of July 1, 2013 (Statistics Canada, 2013a).

- Of these, there were 1,251,354 young people between the ages of 15 and 18 (approximately 4 percent of the total population).

- According to Statistics Canada, young people between the age of 12 and 17 years represent just over 7 percent of the Canadian population, while youth aged 18 to 24 years account for 10 percent (Allen & Boyce, 2013).

- By 2026, the non-native population of individuals under the age of 25 is predicted to be only 6 percent higher than it was in 2001, while the First Nations youth population is predicted to be 37 percent higher (National Crime Prevention Centre, 2012). This means that there will be significantly more First Nations young people in Canada.

- According to the most recent crime statistics, approximately 104,000 youth were accused of a *Criminal Code* offence in 2013, about 22,000 fewer than in 2012 (Boyce, Cotter, & Perreault, 2014).

Age–Crime Relationship

Data from both Canada and the United States indicates that the arrest rate rises through adolescence, peaks at age 19, and then falls off in a person's 20s. See Figure 1.1. Those in their teen years seem to commit mostly property crimes, while the extent of violent crime rises among those in their 20s.

FIGURE 1.1   Persons Accused of Crime, Age 12 to 65, Canada, 2011

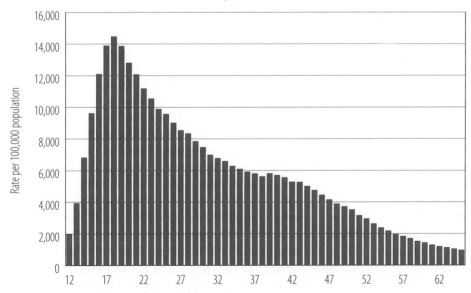

SOURCE: Based on data from Brennan (2012, p. 20, chart 15).

Looking at Figure 1.1, what is the age range of those responsible for most of the crime being committed in Canada?

If one looks at the breakdown by age of youth accused of different types of offences (see Table 1.1), it is clear that older youth (that is, 16- and 17-year-olds) are committing more offences than their younger age peers. What factors do you think might be influencing older youth to commit more offences than younger youth?

TABLE 1.1   Cases Completed in Youth Court by Offence Category and Age of Accused, Canada, 2011–2012

	Total cases	12–15 years old		16–<18 years old		Other*	
Offence category	Number	Number	% of total	Number	% of total	Number	% of total
Total *Criminal Code* offences	37,996	15,602	41	21,605	57	757	2
Crimes against the person	13,095	5,722	44	7,135	55	215	1
Crimes against property	17,240	7,354	43	9,647	56	236	1
Administration of justice	5,233	1,637	31	3,355	64	243	5
Other *Criminal Code*	2,428	889	37	1,468	61	63	2

* "Other" age refers to cases in which the accused was older than 17 at the time of the offence as outlined in ss. 136 to 139 of the *Youth Criminal Justice Act*, or where the age was not known.

SOURCE: Statistics Canada, CANSIM Table 252-0064.

ADMINISTRATION OF JUSTICE OFFENCES AND "OTHER"

Youth law-breaking behaviours are most often classified in four categories: crimes against the person, crimes against property, administration of justice offences, and other *Criminal Code* offences. Crimes against the person and property are self-explanatory, but the other two categories require more explanation. Looking at Table 1.1, you will see that "other *Criminal Code* offences" totalled 2,428 cases, or less than 1 percent of cases completed in the youth justice courts of that year. The category of "other" includes offences such as traffic violations, impaired driving, and drug offences. One of every six court cases is an administration of justice case. These tend to be about behaviours that are offences only because they involve violation of a court order. Examples are: failure to appear (for a court date), breach of probation, being unlawfully at large, and failure to comply with an order. These types of offences are also the ones most likely to lead to the detention of a youth.

SOURCE: Department of Justice (2013). © Her Majesty the Queen in Right of Canada, represented by the Minister of Justice and Attorney General of Canada, 2013.

QUESTION

Do you think youth should be sent to custody (jail) for administration of justice offences?

When we think about the relationships between age and crime, it is important to look at the nature and type of offences that are being committed by young people as well as at the processes used for detecting and counting crime. We must also consider the factors that influence whether an offence comes to the attention of the authorities, such as the perception of community members, the policies and programs available in the province, and the influence of the media on public perceptions of youth crime. In some cases, it may be that despite an overall falling crime rate, there is a community belief that youth crime is much worse than it was in the past, and this has a dramatic impact on how youthful misbehaviour is interpreted.

The Role of Media in Understanding Youth Crime

People are understandably concerned about crime in general, but there seems to be elevated concern about youth crime in particular. Opinion polls consistently reveal that the public is very concerned about crime, particularly violent crime. A large part of this concern is focused on youth crime. Statistically, most of us are never the victims of youth crime, so our perceptions of it often come from somewhere other than our own experience. For most of us, the primary source of information is the media. Newspaper, television, and radio reports feature a constant stream of stories about violence in schools, home invasions, gang slayings, robberies, assaults, and drug-related offences. Accompanying these accounts are the comments of editorial writers, politicians, police officials, social workers, and other commentators.

But is there more youth crime than previously? Are the types of crimes more vicious and serious than they used to be? Are youth gangs on the increase? Is the fabric of society under more stress as a result of youth crime?

Consider these actual newspaper headlines:

Student Shoots Teacher in the Leg

Another Outbreak of Street Gang Fighting Has Reawakened Citizens to the Extent of the Problems That These Young People Present

This kind of reporting probably sounds familiar to you. However, the shooting incident referred to occurred in 1901, on the day Queen Victoria died. It was reported on the front page of the *Toronto Globe*, but thanks to Queen Victoria's demise it got less space than it otherwise might have. The gang-fighting incident was reported in the Toronto *Globe and Mail* in 1949 (Tanner, 1996, pp. 1–2). It involved a gang called the "Junction Boys," whose activities included car theft, breaking and entering, liquor offences, street brawling, and inciting riots in neighbourhoods outside their own district. This behaviour was attributed to broken homes and "declining moral standards" (Tanner, 1996, pp. 1–2). Clearly, the past was not as peaceful as we'd like to think.

Media reports about youth tend to exaggerate and sensationalize, often presenting atypical situations as representative of youth in general. Both the news and the entertainment industry frequently portray uncommon crimes or criminal justice events as much more common than they are. Factors that influence crime news selection include: the seriousness of the offence, "whimsical" or unusual elements of the crime, sentimental or dramatic aspects of the offence or the criminal, and the involvement of famous or high-status individuals (Ericson, Baranek, & Chan, 1989). Media reporting reinforces the "validity of law" as purported through crime myths and further delineates for the general public who is a criminal and what is a crime (Robinson, 2000, p. 139). The media presents criminality as a choice of the individual offender, which implies that other social, economic, or structural explanations of the crime phenomenon are irrelevant. Further, the frequent use of a "vocabulary of force" such as referring to police as "crime fighters" leaves the public with a clear message that crime must be "fought" rather than "solved," "eliminated," or "prevented" (Gorelick, 1989, p. 429). The message that the public gets is that the solution to crime is in the expansion of the present criminal justice system through harsher punishments and more law enforcement.

CRIME MYTHS AND MORAL PANIC

crime myth

distorted conceptions of issues related to crime and criminal justice policy that have come to be accepted because they have been relied on in public forums, debates, and personal conversations

Crime myths can be defined as distorted conceptions of issues related to crime and criminal justice policy that have come to be accepted because they have been relied on in public forums, debates, and personal conversations. The concept of **moral panic**, as coined by the criminologist Stanley Cohen (1972), is the idea that societal outrage can be directed against certain groups within a society through the presentation of negative images of them in the media. These negative representations often create a public outcry that then justifies harsh and oppressive treatment of those persons on whom the panic is focused. Bell (2011, p. 32) suggests that a moral panic about youth crime is produced through "continual and sensationalized" crime reporting, which is reinforced through the "selective reporting" of public outrage not only about "out-of-control youth," but also about the legislation that is failing to control crime—which is characterized as the cause of the problem. Four indicators characterize a moral panic:

moral panic

extreme social response to the belief that the moral condition of society is deteriorating rapidly; may be directed against targeted groups to justify harsh and oppressive treatment

- increased concern over the behaviour of the group and the consequences for society
- an increased level of hostility toward the group responsible for the behaviour
- a widespread consensus that the threat from this group's behaviour is serious
- public concern about the behaviour that is disproportionate (excessive) in view of the actual harm

Some moral panics simply subside, while others become entrenched and a matter of routine. An example can be found in what have become known as "school shootings." High-profile media reports about the rare acts of school violence can lead to what has been referred to as the "Columbine Effect," in which, as in the case of the horrific events at Columbine High School near Littleton, Colorado, schools feel pressured to enhance school safety measures (Muschert & Peguero, 2010).

Howells (2013) analyzed a total of 2,497 news items from over 20 years of articles from the *Globe and Mail* and another southern Ontario newspaper (from January 1, 1990 to December 31, 2010). The results showed that existing trends of reduced rates of school violence were not reported in the articles. Rather, there were three distinct periods of time during which high numbers of articles were published about school crime—and these mirrored the implementation of safe-school initiatives at the school board level in 1992–1994, the Columbine shooting in 1999, and the Virginia Tech shooting in 2007. Howells suggests that the media was not intentionally trying to suggest that schools were becoming increasingly less safe, but rather that the press was responding to these newsworthy items in an episodic fashion, which resulted in the creation of "crime waves." The news reporting of these rare events—which did not reflect the actual rates of school crime and violence—was likely to mislead readers into thinking that the rate of violent events was much higher than it actually was.

When the media presents disproportionate reports about school crime and violence, schools are pressured to respond by implementing policies that will have the appearance of keeping young people safe. Unfortunately, some of these policies (for example, armed uniformed officers, more frequent locker searches, and increased surveillance and monitoring) may alter the school climate, making it feel uncomfortable for many students who would not have engaged in crime or violence in the first place.

QUESTIONS

1. What news stories have you read recently that have provided you with something to think about in a way that you hadn't before? Were these stories about something that you already knew about, or a new area of discovery? Think about how much of the news article provided you with fact-based information. Do you remember whether you agreed or disagreed with the news reporter?

2. As you read articles in the media, think about the sources provided and who is called upon as an expert witness. What kinds of stories about young people seem to be predominant in the news media?

As you will learn later in this chapter, youth who commit offences are most likely to commit property offences (in particular shoplifting). However, in previous studies of newspaper coverage of youth crime, less than 7 percent of news articles reported on property offences (Reid, 2004). The coverage of youth crime in print news is much more likely to be printed within the first 15 pages of the newspaper, occupy a greater "newshole" space, and have substantially larger headlines than stories about youth who may be participating in more **pro-social** activities such as sporting, school, or cultural events. This distorted portrayal of youth crime does little to explore the reality of the lives that youth are living and promotes a general misunderstanding of the entire youth justice system.

Some news commentators have argued that "[i]t is not the newspaper's job to tell people what to think, but rather to tell people what to think about" and "it is a reader's responsibility to use the information as a stepping stone to further participate in the democratic process" (Seskus & Mofina, 2000, p. 140). However, the news media has the power to create a story, determine that it is within the realm of "youth crime," speculate about the causes of the event, and then propose a variety of social, political, and cultural solutions to the "problem" they are reporting (Herda-Rapp, 2003).

While the news media cannot determine what readers will perceive or believe to be true, journalists can suggest to their audiences what they should be thinking about and how they should be thinking about it; consequently, they are able to influence the importance of certain issues that eventually become the focus of public opinion and dialogue. While research has shown that exposure to news media can provide important factual information, the way information is emphasized and presented can influence the perceived importance of the topic under consideration. One must question how many readers actually critically evaluate the information being presented in the newspapers they read. Since very few people have had any direct experience with the youth justice system or with young people who commit criminal offences, they have no basis for observing crime rates beyond what is reported. The result is a picture of youth that is distorted and misleading, which in turn affects people's perceptions.

pro-social
intended to help others; a characteristic of behaviours

Collecting and Analyzing Crime Data

One of the many difficulties in discussing "youth crime" is that the term itself leads to considerable misunderstanding. People often use shorthand language that has very precise meaning to some people, but is taken to mean something much broader by others. When people talk about the "youth crime rate," for instance, their discussion is rarely based on actual statistics about the incidence of crime by youth in a community. Usually, it is based on statistics about arrests or cases that come before the courts.

How does the perception of youth crime generated by the media actually square with the reality as revealed by official statistics and other forms of investigation? The media, politicians, and lobbyists on youth issues all rely on statistical information to make their arguments. For objective analysis, you need to know what kind of information is out there, how it is collected, what it shows, and what its limitations are.

In Canada, the courts and the police keep statistical records on crime, and the crime rate is reported every July by the Canadian Centre for Justice Statistics. Since 1962, Statistics Canada has been conducting the **Uniform Crime Reporting (UCR) Survey**, which collects information on all criminal incidents that have been reported to and substantiated by Canadian police forces. The UCR Survey, originally developed in the United States, was designed to provide comparable and consistent crime statistics in order to compare trends over time and across jurisdictions.

Uniform Crime Reporting (UCR) Survey
system for classifying reported incidents by type of crime, on the basis of crime detected by police and reported by the public

Contrary to what some people may believe, the crime rate has been steadily decreasing over the past few years. The crime rate (for both adults and youth) was at its highest level in 1991 and has generally declined. In 2012, the crime rate was at its lowest level since 1972 (Perreault, 2013).

Perhaps a look at the number of cases in which youth have been accused of the most serious offence of homicide will help illustrate issues flowing from the impact of the media reporting of high-profile cases. Figure 1.2 shows the actual number of youth accused of homicide from 1974 through 2012. Despite three different pieces of federal legislation to deal with young people who commit crimes (the *Juvenile Delinquents Act*, 1908–1983; the *Young Offenders Act*, 1984–2002; and the *Youth Criminal Justice Act*, 2003–present), there is enormous variability from year to year in the number of youth accused of homicide. One might argue that if youth crime were becoming more serious, there would be a higher incidence of homicide in more recent years. While it is true that the highest number of homicides was reported in 2006 (84 youth accused), the lowest number over the past 38 years was reported in 2012, with only 34 youth accused of homicide.

FIGURE 1.2   Youth (12–17) Accused of Homicide, 1974–2012, Canada

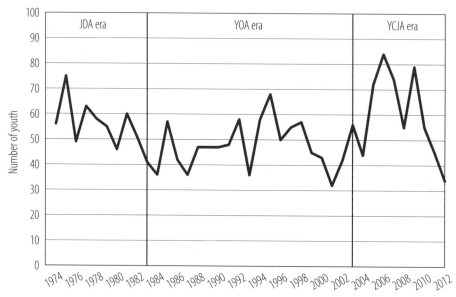

SOURCE: Based on data from Statistics Canada (2013b, c); Boyce & Cotter (2013).

We must remember when we look at these numbers that even though 34 murders may seem high, we are speaking of 34 youth out of a possible four million in Canada! Homicides are very rare, even though they appear in the newspaper as frequent occurrences.

Regarding the level of youth crime over the same period, Figure 1.3 shows the rate of youth charged both for all crimes and for violent and property crimes. Unlike the data related to the actual number of youth who committed homicide as shown in Figure 1.2, the rates of youth accused of crime are displayed as a rate per 100,000 population so that those provinces with smaller populations could be compared to larger populations. As shown in Figure 1.3, the rate of youth crime has been steadily declining over the past 20 years.

In 2013, there were approximately 22,000 fewer youth accused of *Criminal Code* offences than in 2012. This means that the rate of youth accused of crime per 100,000 youth population decreased to 4,346 youth per 100,000. This decrease shows a 16 percent decline from the year previous and a 40 percent lower rate than 2003, the year the YCJA came into force (Boyce, Cotter, & Perrault, 2014, p. 22).

FIGURE 1.3   Youth (12–17) Charged by Police, 1992–2012, Canada

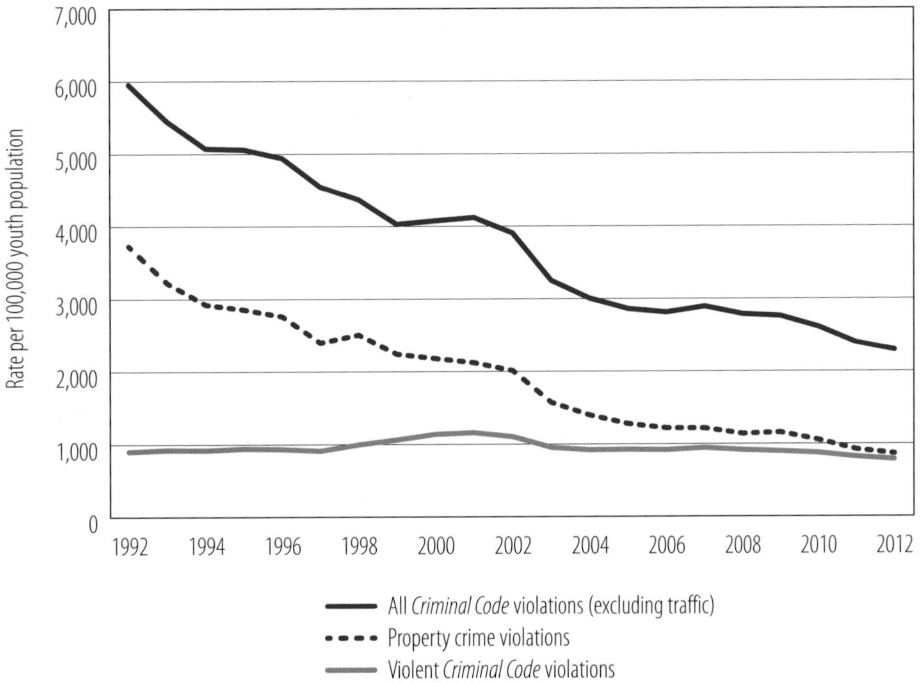

Legend:
- —— All *Criminal Code* violations (excluding traffic)
- ••• Property crime violations
- —— Violent *Criminal Code* violations

SOURCE: Statistics Canada (2013c).

The most likely violent offence for youth in 2012 was **assault level 1**. There was a considerable reduction in the number of youth accused of the more serious violent crimes of assault levels 2 and 3, showing a 10 percent decrease from the previous year (see Figure 1.3).

Canada's violent crime rate for both youth and adults has generally declined since 1990, after increasing throughout most of the previous three decades. The higher rates prior to 1990 probably reflect the presence of "baby boomers" occupying the youth and young adult age cohorts most likely to be involved in crime. The decline after 1990 probably has more to do with smaller numbers of young people in the relevant age cohorts than with an outbreak of **pacifism**.

Table 1.2 provides an overview of the actual number of incidents, the rate per 100,000, and the percentage change from the previous year for each province and territory. As you look at this table, find your particular province and see how it compares with the national numbers presented under the category "Canada." Note also that some percentage increases may not point to trends of real significance; a 2 percent increase in one year in a category of crime with a very low rate compared with other categories does not necessarily indicate a significant crime problem.

assault level 1
assaults that cause little to no physical harm to victims; can include such acts as pushing and shoving

pacifism
ideology or movement that consists in being opposed to war or violence

1. Which province or territory had the highest rate in 2012? Is the crime rate consistent across all types of offences (violent, property, other)? What factors might account for this variation?

2. Which province had the biggest decrease in 2012? What might account for this change?

TABLE 1.2 Police-Reported Youth Crime Rate, by Province and Territory, 2012

Province or territory	Total crime (crime rate)			Violent crime		
	Number	Rate	% change in rate, 2011–12	Number	Rate	% change in rate, 2011–12
Alberta	7,642	2,805.8	−7.04	2,062	757.08	−10.73
British Columbia	3,874	1,280.68	−9.93	1,515	500.83	−9.51
Manitoba	4,606	4,596.07	−2.64	1,697	1,693.34	−0.69
New Brunswick	1,286	2,575.45	−8.85	421	843.13	−2.2
Newfoundland and Labrador	758	2,276.69	−8.2	287	862.02	−6.65
Northwest Territories	197	5,560.26	−18.35	55	1,552.36	−24.8
Nova Scotia	2,115	3,398.03	−5.8	637	1,023.42	−13.88
Nunavut	246	6,077.08	1.95	81	2,000.99	−14.84
Ontario	18,408	1,920.68	−9.97	7,064	737.05	−9.86
Prince Edward Island	213	1,947.87	3.88	77	704.16	59.41
Quebec	8,914	1,722.81	22.85	3718	718.58	16.56
Saskatchewan	6,618	7,996.23	−10.69	1,220	1,474.07	−7.46
Yukon	128	5,295.82	40.05	46	1,903.19	25.15
Canada	**5,505**	**2,291.81**	**−4.26**	**18,880**	**786.64**	**−4.36**

Province or territory	Property crime			Other *Criminal Code* offences		
	Number	Rate	% change in rate, 2011–12	Number	Rate	% change in rate, 2011–12
Alberta	3,290	1,207.94	−8.83	2,290	840.79	−0.51
British Columbia	1,391	459.84	−8.76	968	320	−12.19
Manitoba	1,407	1,403.97	−2.66	1,502	1,498.76	−4.74
New Brunswick	510	1,021.37	−8.71	355	710.95	−15.81
Newfoundland and Labrador	307	922.09	−14.87	164	492.58	4.02
Northwest Territories	89	2,512	−7.23	53	1,495.91	−26.58
Nova Scotia	823	1,322.26	−5.11	655	1,052.34	2.61
Nunavut	128	3,162.06	11.17	37	914.03	19.21
Ontario	6,651	693.96	−12.32	4,693	489.67	−6.59
Prince Edward Island	113	1,033.38	−13.81	23	210.33	−10.26
Quebec	3,568	689.59	23.45	1,628	314.64	38.46
Saskatchewan	2,444	2,952.97	−18.75	2,954	3,569.18	−4.2
Yukon	39	1,613.57	57.03	43	1,779.06	44.28
Canada	**20,760**	**864.97**	**−6.26**	**15,365**	**640.19**	**−1.31**

SOURCE: Statistics Canada (2013b).

How Is Youth Crime Counted?

There are two main ways of collecting information on crime in Canada: (1) the Uniform Crime Reporting Survey (UCR) and (2) the General Social Survey (GSS) on Victimization. The UCR is reported every year and is a compilation of police-recorded crime. The GSS is administered every five years to a sample of Canadians over the age of 15. One of the advantages of the GSS on victimization is that it captures crimes not reported to police. However, it only collects selected information on a subset of criminal offences (sexual assault, robbery, assault, break and enter, theft, and vandalism).

Police record two categories of crime: those detected by the police themselves and those reported to them by victims and members of the public. Only about 10 percent of recorded crimes are in the first category. This dependence on the public leads to selective reporting and statistical distortions in a variety of ways. The most obvious distortion is underreporting. Victimization surveys consistently show that those surveyed know of illegal acts that were not reported. In the 2009 General Social Survey on Victimization, only 31 percent of offences were reported to the police (Perreault, 2013). The reasons for non-reporting vary: the offence might seem trivial; the act might not be seen as illegal; the victim might not trust the police or believe they will be effective; or the victim might fear or know the perpetrator and would rather deal with the matter informally. Similarly, the police might note an incident and deem it too trivial to justify an arrest or charge; they might find it more useful to deal with the problem informally or, depending on the circumstances, not proceed with a charge if the complainant does not want to. Statistics on crimes detected by the police might also be distorted by policy decisions about whom or what to police. For example, a "war on drugs" is likely to feature many more charges for drug offences than would otherwise occur.

Another issue with counting crime lies in the manner in which the crime rate is actually counted. The traditional police-reported crime rate is calculated by dividing the number of criminal incidents reported to police by the population and is usually expressed as a rate per 100,000 population. A criminal incident consists of one or more related offences (up to four) committed during a single event. For serious offences, if someone is accused of assault on three victims at the same time, this would therefore be counted as three incidents. However, in cases of minor offences that occur with *relatively* more serious ones, the most serious is the one counted. This can affect the crime rate when, for example, there is a reduction in incidents in which the most serious offence is theft of $5,000 or under, which tends to be one of the most common offences. The reduction in the volume of these cases may show a sharp reduction in the crime rate, even when the number of more serious incidents (for example, homicides, robberies) increases.

In order to combat this problem, the **Crime Severity Index (CSI)** was created. The CSI assigns a higher weight to offences that are more severe on the basis of the **custodial sentences** handed down by the courts for each type of offence. The more severe the average sentence, the higher the weight assigned for the offence. There is a CSI for all crimes, including *Criminal Code* violations, traffic offences, and drug offences, and a separate index for violent and non-violent offences. Figure 1.4 shows the crime severity indexes for youth from 2002, the year before the *Youth Criminal Justice Act* came into effect, to 2012.

Crime Severity Index (CSI)
system for measuring the severity of police-reported crimes each year, and the change in severity year to year; created to alleviate some of the problems in determining the crime rate

custodial sentence
a judicial sentence that requires a term of either open or secure imprisonment of the offender

FIGURE 1.4   Police-Reported Youth Crime Severity Indexes, 2002–2012, Canada

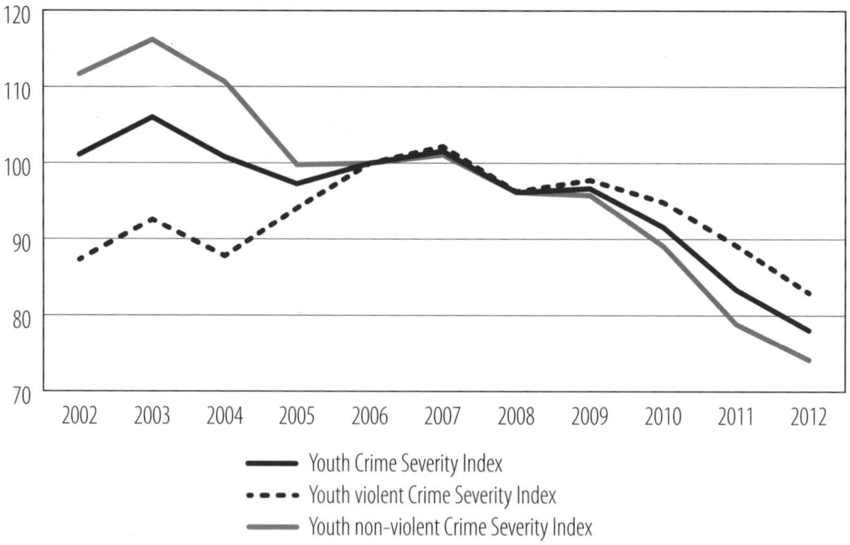

SOURCE: Perreault (2013, table 8b).

What surprises you about Figure 1.4? Compare this figure with Table 1.3, which outlines crime severity indexes by provinces and territories, and look for patterns within your own jurisdiction. How does your province compare with the national Crime Severity Index? What factors might account for this?

TABLE 1.3   Police-Reported Youth Crime Severity Index, by Province and Territory, 2012

Province or territory	Crime Severity Index		Violent Crime Severity Index		Non-violent Crime Severity Index	
	Index	% change, 2011–12	Index	% change, 2011–12	Index	% change, 2011–12
Alberta	81.52	−3.31	72.88	−6.77	87.28	−1.14
British Columbia	57.38	−6.52	55.64	−7.67	59.07	−5.74
Manitoba	144.46	−8.86	166.07	−16.70	128.53	−0.26
New Brunswick	80.01	−2.81	61.22	−3.21	92.96	−2.62
Newfoundland and Labrador	65.07	−10.96	50.49	3.74	75.11	−16.59
Northwest Territories	393.35	6.31	246.05	14.44	495.96	3.72
Nova Scotia	111.08	−7.93	100.41	−14.59	118.15	−3.39
Nunavut	321.24	6.55	238.96	40.21	378.10	−3.78
Ontario	68.94	−9.11	83.24	−9.57	58.50	−8.65
Prince Edward Island	69.06	9.90	58.56	85.61	76.19	−10.08
Quebec	63.88	−2.68	74.88	−2.05	55.81	−3.28
Saskatchewan	206.30	−7.93	162.55	3.83	236.37	−12.74
Yukon	181.90	21.49	146.91	55.96	205.88	9.28
Canada	**78.05**	**−6.38**	**82.97**	**−7.02**	**74.23**	**−5.86**

SOURCE: Statistics Canada (2013b).

The Crime Funnel

Our knowledge of what is actually happening in terms of youth crime is shaped by (1) what information is collected and (2) at which point in the youth justice process we examine the information. The term **crime funnel** refers to a reduction in the number of individuals involved at each stage in the operation of the criminal justice system: detection, reporting, prosecution, and punishment. The degree to which numbers get smaller depends on the factors we have been discussing:

- the public (when they call the police)
- the police (what the police do when they are called and what types of crimes they are actively pursuing according to police directives)
- federal government (laws that provide for police discretion, diversion of youth)
- provincial governments (their policies about diverting youth out of the formal system through **extrajudicial measures** [EJM] or **extrajudicial sanctions** [EJS])
- Crown attorneys (whether there are formal EJS programs for diversion in the province)
- legal aid (availability of financial resources to provide lawyers to youth who may wish to pursue a trial and not plead guilty)
- courts (judges' decisions about guilt or innocence and sentencing practices)
- provincial governments (provision of services in communities for alternatives to custody sanctions, presence of custodial facilities in proximity to the young person, other issues of concern for the young person such as access to mental health services, addiction counselling)

crime funnel
the reduction in the number of individuals involved at each stage of the decision-making process in the criminal justice system

extrajudicial measure
a way of dealing with offenders outside the formal justice system

extrajudicial sanction
a more formal counterpart of extrajudicial measures

The crime funnel is pictured in Figure 1.5. At the mouth of the funnel are all the young people in a community. Many of those young people, at some point in their youth, do things that might be seen as "criminal." For example, many youth will shoplift, but only some of those actions will come to the attention of authorities. Some merchandise won't be missed from the stores. Some merchandise will be missed, but only during inventory counts. Some youth will actually get caught shoplifting. Some of them will just be warned by the shopkeeper. For others, the police will be called. In some communities, when the police are called, a first-time shoplifter will just get a lecture. Some will be formally cautioned by the police.

In other communities, the shoplifter may be referred to a community program that explains the repercussions of shoplifting for the store and the rest of the community.

In Figure 1.5, notice that in the total incidents reported to the police (153,552), 57 percent of the youth (85,392) are not formally charged. Note also that another 13 percent (19,331) are diverted out of the formal youth justice system through extrajudicial sanctions following their initial charge. As you will learn throughout this book, the *Youth Criminal Justice Act* provides a number of strategies outside of the youth court to deal with the problems facing young persons who commit offences. The numbers of young people in the system keep getting smaller the further along in the process we go.

There are variations from one province to another in how extrajudicial measures and sanctions programs are administered. For example, in Halifax, say there were 900 youth caught shoplifting in a particular year. Of those 900, about two-thirds would be cautioned by the police. The remaining third would be referred to an anti-shoplifting program offered in the community. In this example, none of the youth were formally charged. However, in Calgary, the opportunity to participate in an anti-shoplifting program is not

FIGURE 1.5   The Crime Funnel: Youth Crime, 2012

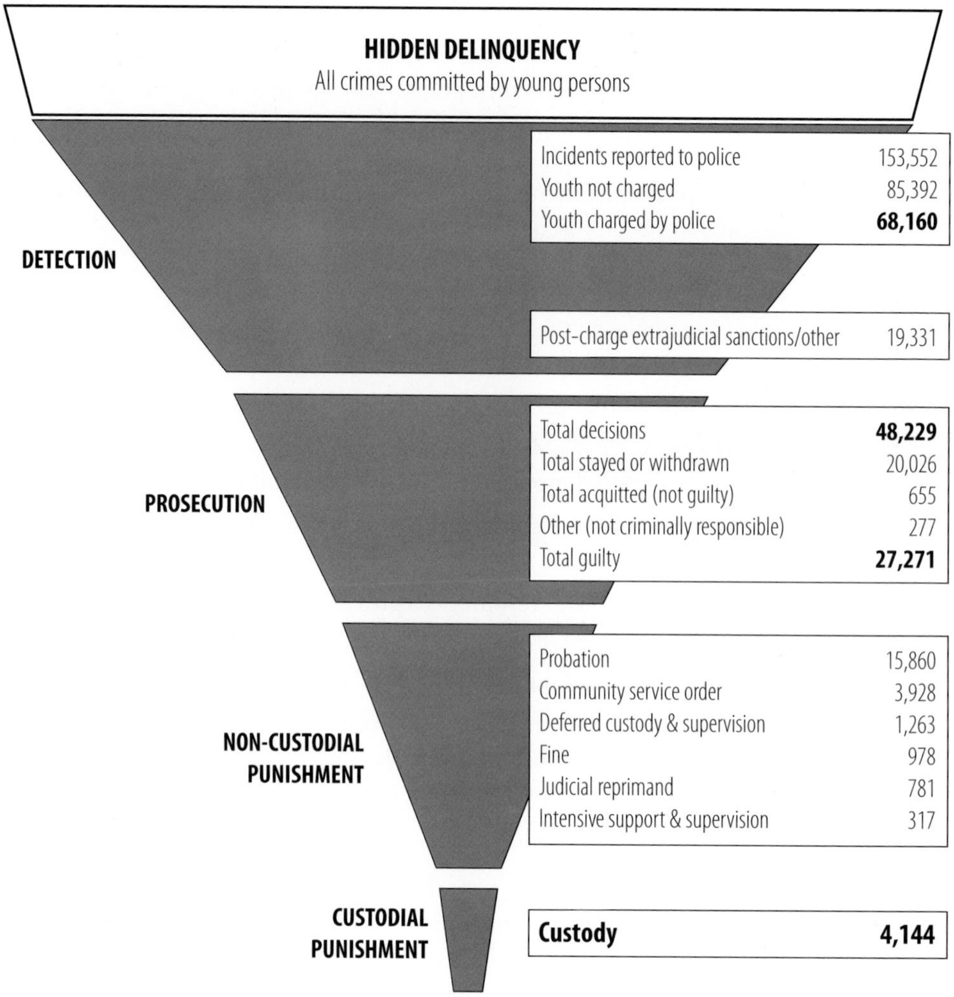

HIDDEN DELINQUENCY
All crimes committed by young persons

DETECTION

Incidents reported to police	153,552
Youth not charged	85,392
Youth charged by police	**68,160**

Post-charge extrajudicial sanctions/other	19,331

PROSECUTION

Total decisions	**48,229**
Total stayed or withdrawn	20,026
Total acquitted (not guilty)	655
Other (not criminally responsible)	277
Total guilty	**27,271**

NON-CUSTODIAL PUNISHMENT

Probation	15,860
Community service order	3,928
Deferred custody & supervision	1,263
Fine	978
Judicial reprimand	781
Intensive support & supervision	317

CUSTODIAL PUNISHMENT

Custody	**4,144**

SOURCE: Adapted from Statistics Canada, CANSIM tables 252-067, 252-0051gov.

available, and if the police wish to hold the young person accountable, they may need to formally lay a charge.

The dynamics of the funnel change all the time. Policy changes by government, police, and community agencies have an impact on which behaviours get included in "youth crime."

Official statistics almost always underestimate the volume of crime, so it is difficult to speak accurately of the extent of youth crime. It is not easy to say whether increases or decreases in recorded youth crime are real or just apparent. Increased efficiency may lead to more charges while the actual rate of occurrence remains unchanged. Also, public willingness to report crime may artificially increase the crime rate.

As was noted in the earlier section on the media influence on youth crime, the public, fed a steady dose of news coverage focusing on sensational youth crime cases, may believe youth crime is on the increase; and this can lead to a greater likelihood of increased reporting. Even policy decisions may change the incident rate. The decision by some school boards to implement a "zero-tolerance" policy on violence in the schools may lead to charges for relatively trivial assaults on school premises that previously would have been handled informally or internally through the school administration. Anything from spitting and verbal threats to punching to the use of weapons may get lumped into the category of "violent crime." With a zero-tolerance policy, behaviours that were regularly happening in schools and group home settings are now being handled through formal police intervention, thereby showing an increase in violent crime.

Similarly, the number of youth arrested by police for certain kinds of offences will also depend on police and political priorities. Over time, the policing emphasis on certain kinds of crimes (for example, drug crime) may change due to shifting political priorities. Certain groups of youth may get more or less attention from the police and other justice authorities. There may be a push to "clean up" certain neighbourhoods, which may increase the police presence and therefore increase the likelihood of crimes being detected and processed. This runs in sharp contrast to more affluent neighbourhoods, where the police are less likely to be called in, and where, when police do get involved, they react less harshly and are more tolerant of certain kinds of behaviours among middle-class youth.

THE CREATION OF A "YOUTH GANG"

Three youth with too much leisure time on their hands hang around their housing complex in a public courtyard. They look "tough" in their clothing and demeanour. They tease some vulnerable people in the neighbourhood as they enter the complex. They are what might be called "ruffians," but not a serious youth gang. Nobody takes them seriously enough to actually confront them about their behaviour. A neighbour receives a brochure about the rising number of youth gangs in her community and starts to talk about the three youth as a "youth gang." Neighbours start to see the group as the cause of all manner of crime in their neighborhood and the police get called regularly. The "ruffians" start to take their gang label seriously and conflict escalates.

QUESTIONS

1. What do you think will happen to the violent crime rate in this community?

2. Would the same thing happen if a neighbour received a brochure about youth gangs in a more affluent neighborhood? Why or why not?

3. Would this example meet the criteria to be called a moral panic? How would a moral panic affect crime statistics?

Gender, Peer Violence, and Other Violations

Male and female youth have very different patterns of offending behaviour. The majority of arrested youth are males. In 2012, 77 percent of all cases heard in youth court were cases of young men (Dauvergne, 2013). Although the evidence shows that offending behaviour in both males and females is related to having been a victim of violence or abuse, the relationship between abuse and crime is stronger for girls (Corrado, Odgers, & Cohen, 2000). As has been pointed out in the literature, girls sentenced to probation are often given more conditions than their male counterparts in order to provide additional "supervision" (Chesney-Lind & Shelden, 1998; Sprott & Doob, 2009; Sprott, 2012). If a girl violates conditions, she is more likely to receive an additional criminal offence, and cases involving failure to comply with an order account for a larger portion of cases for girls than for boys, particularly as the case proceeds to additional charges leading to custody (Sprott & Doob, 2009). More about the distinction between conditions for male and female youth will be discussed in Chapter 3.

Most crimes of violence committed by young people are directed against other young people. Assaults by youth on adults are relatively unusual. Only 2 percent of victims of violent crimes by young offenders in 1998 were 55 or older. In the 2009 General Social Survey, people between the ages of 15 and 24 years were almost 15 times more likely than those aged 65 and older to report being a victim of a violent victimization (Perreault & Brennan, 2010). For children under the age of 6, the majority of police-reported physical assaults were committed by someone known to the victim, with six in ten assaults being perpetrated by a family member. Older children (9 to 17 years) were most likely to be assaulted by an acquaintance. In the majority of assaults by youth, the offender and the victim knew each other.

In addition to *Criminal Code* offences, a number of charges arise from provincial liquor legislation and regulations and from other federal statutes, principally the *Controlled Drugs and Substances Act* (1996). The most recent statistics on drug-related charges indicates an 8 percent decrease in youth charges from 2011. Sixty-three percent of all drug charges for youth were for cannabis possession in 2012; 82 percent of all accused in possession cases in 2012 were males.

Counting Youth Crime Using Self-Report Measures

To compensate for distortions or inadequacy in uniform crime report statistics, other data collection methods have been developed. The best-known and most frequently used of these other methods is **self-report studies**. Respondents are asked to answer a series of questions, either in a personal interview or through a questionnaire, on a range of activities that would be classified as offences for which they could be criminally charged, whether or not those offences were reported or detected by the police. The self-report survey has been seen as useful in uncovering what has been referred to as the **dark figure of crime**, or in the case of young people, **hidden delinquency**. The self-report methodology is important because

- it provides information on how many times a person has engaged in behaviour that would be deemed criminal; and
- it records the acts of those who have not been categorized as offenders as well as the acts of those who have, thereby permitting some comparisons between the two groups.

Self-report data have generally proven to be accurate guides to all but the most serious delinquency.

In the case of young people, self-report surveys are easier to administer than in the adult offender population because youth are required by law to attend school until they are at least 16 years of age, and in some provinces there is mandatory education until the young person reaches the age of 18.

Self-reporting is important because official statistics record only a small proportion of actual offenders and may over- or underrepresent some types of offenders, reflecting police biases or discretionary practices in laying charges: visible minority or poor youth may be overrepresented while white middle-class youth and females generally may be underrepresented among those charged.

Self-reporting has been criticized as containing its own biases and built-in inaccuracies:

- Respondents may be reluctant to accurately report incidents that might land them in legal difficulties, particularly if the incident involves serious crime. Despite assurances from those responsible for administering the survey that the young

self-report studies
method of data collection that relies on self-administered surveys or questionnaires given to a target group in order to obtain a group profile of the identified behaviours in which the researcher is interested

dark figure of crime
the number of crimes that do not come to the attention of the criminal justice system

hidden delinquency
undetected rule-breaking behaviour

person's responses will be held in confidence, youth who may have already had experience in the youth justice system are aware of the impact of record-keeping on the kinds of options available to them in the future.

- Respondents may forget or disregard some of the incidents.

- Respondents may brag about, exaggerate, or invent incidents because they feel the need to fit in with their same-age peers or simply because they see it as an opportunity to "mess with" adult authority figures with little chance of being caught.

One of the earliest self-report studies on youthful crime was conducted in the 1960s, when both Canada and the United States had an all-encompassing definition of youth deviance known as delinquency. Delinquent behaviour is much broader than criminal conduct and includes offences that only young people can be charged with, known as **status offences** (for example, truancy/skipping school).

When reading reports that refer to delinquent behaviour of youth, it is important to consider how the term is operationally defined. In these early self-report studies, it was found that youth from lower socio-economic classes were much more likely to report engaging in delinquent acts and doing so with more frequency and severity than their middle-class counterparts (Vaz, 1966). This trend has most recently been noted in the second International Self-Report Study of Delinquency (ISRD-2) administered in 30 cities around the world (Junger-Tas, 2012). However, it has not been shown consistently in the self-report literature, and whether class is a variable distinguishing the involvement of young people in the criminal justice system is open to debate. It may be that working-class youth are charged more often and watched more closely by the police, reflecting a societal bias in the official statistics, or that the two measurement methods may be recording different things (a more likely explanation). Self-report surveys target students in attendance at high school. This means that young people who skip class or drop out are underrepresented in the sample. It is possible that the class truants and dropouts are more likely to be involved in serious delinquency, so this type of delinquency is underreported on the self-report surveys.

In a Canadian sample of 3,200 Toronto youth who participated in the ISRD-2, over one-third of the students indicated that they had engaged in one or more acts that would have been a violation of the *Criminal Code* (Savoie, 2007). Slightly less than one-quarter of the youth reported that they had engaged in some form of violent behaviour ever in their life. The most common offences reported were participating in group fights (16 percent) and carrying a weapon such as a stick, chain, or knife (10 percent). It did not appear that this kind of behaviour was repetitive in nature, with two-thirds reported committing only one type of violent behaviour over their lifetime. About one-third of the students reported committing a property offence in their lifetime; incidents of shoplifting and vandalism during the previous 12 months were most frequently reported by youth.

With increasing use of computers and technology, it is not surprising to find out that these students were involved in illegally downloading music or movies (14 percent). Twenty percent reported purposely accessing adult sites to view sexually explicit material. Only 3 percent had sent pornographic pictures over the Internet. One of the risk factors for committing offences is the lack of a capable guardian, and youth reporting that they had committed offences were more likely to indicate that they were without consistent adult supervision. Among different family types, the prevalence of delinquent behaviour was lowest among respondents who were living with both parents (18 percent) and significantly higher among those from lone-parent families (25 percent) and step-families (35 percent) (Savoie, 2007).

Other findings from the international study have provided support for the idea that victims and offenders may be more alike than we had previously expected. In a study of all

status offence
a genre of criminal offence that is based not on the committing in the past of a particular prohibited action or inaction but on the allegation that the offender has a certain personal condition or is of a specified character

30 countries involved in the ISRD-2, an analysis of the responses of the 52,000 youth showed that individuals who had earlier been victims of violent offences were more likely to be violent offenders. This correlation had previously been shown in academic literature related to adult offenders, but has now been shown to be consistent for youth. Additionally, this research extended our previous knowledge on the relationship between victims and offenders in that there is such a relationship in cases not only of violent offences, but also of property offences. Youth reported that if they had been a victim of theft, they were much more likely to commit a theft-related offence (Posik, 2013). Among Toronto youth, it was found that about 40 percent reported being a victim in the previous 12 months. About 28 percent stated that they had been victims of a theft, while 21 percent reported being victims of bullying at school. The issue of bullying has received national attention in recent years as a result of a number of sensational cases in which victims have committed suicide after repeated bullying and harassment. This issue will be further discussed in Chapter 10.

Health Canada administered the Canadian Alcohol and Drug Use Monitoring Survey (CADUMS) in 2010. According to the survey, youth aged 15 to 24 years ($n = 3,989$) were approximately six times more likely than adults (25 years or older) to report problems with their physical health, home life, and friendship and social life; legal problems; or work/school issues due to illicit drug use in the past year.

The general findings from self-reporting can be summarized as follows:

- Youth crime is more common than the official statistics indicate.
- A majority of respondents revealed participation in delinquent behaviour for which charges could be laid, although most of the identified behaviours of "unofficial" delinquents were relatively minor and trivial—for example, trivial shoplifting (a candy bar) or alcohol and drug consumption.
- More serious delinquency is relatively rare. Most who report serious illegal acts are likely to be identified as "official" criminals and show up in crime report statistics.
- There are some differences between those who are involved in trivial delinquency and those who are involved in more serious incidents—serious delinquents are predominantly older males.
- Female adolescents report engaging in fewer incidents than their male counterparts, which is consistent with the official statistics.
- Compared with youth who are not engaging in delinquent acts, youth involved in delinquency are more likely to have consumed alcohol and drugs, and report having friends who are also involved in delinquent activities.

Self-report studies are indispensable for testing and developing criminological theories because they provide an opportunity for researchers to ask young people specific questions about the causes of youth crime and look at their responses to determine links between the various concepts thought to predict criminal behaviour. However, caution must be exercised in relying too much on the data received from such surveys, because a lot depends on how the questions are asked and whether the young person is being asked specific questions.

Similarly, if specific rather than general questions are asked, youth may have difficulty remembering events they may have participated in. For example, the question "Have you ever caused damage to property?" may lead to fewer responses than a question that asks whether you have ever broken a window on someone else's property.

While these self-report measures provide an opportunity to further delve into our understanding of youth crime, we must be cautious about the kinds of results that are achieved.

List a number of other situations or factors that might complicate accurate responses to a self-report survey.

Victimization Surveys

Crime may also be measured by reference to **victimization surveys**, which are based on reports by victims who have suffered from crime. It seems that victimization surveys are better suited than self-report studies to describe the level of crime, because they do not suffer from the problem of underrepresenting chronic offenders (Junger-Tas, 2012) and because they are less affected by having the participants respond in a socially desirable way.

Victimization surveys are useful in that they show, perhaps surprisingly, that the profiles of victims are quite similar to those of offenders—that is, victims are disproportionately young, male, and working-class. Despite perceptions that other, more seemingly vulnerable groups (women, the elderly) are at particular risk for victimization, these surveys have shown that youth are at comparatively high risk for victimization, and that crimes against youth are often underreported, due in part to reduced access to police or to victimization by important (and intimidating) adults in the youthful victims' lives (Taylor-Butts, 2010).

In Canada, the General Social Survey is administered every five years to a representative sample of all Canadians over the age of 15 years. Respondents are asked to provide information about their own personal account of criminal victimization for eight types of crime: sexual assault, robbery, physical assault, break and enter, motor vehicle/parts theft, theft of household and personal property, and vandalism. As was discussed earlier, it is not very likely that an older person will be the victim of a violent crime, and this was found in the GSS, where younger Canadians (age 15–24 years) were almost 15 times more likely than those aged 65 and older to report being a victim of a violent victimization (Perreault & Brennan, 2010).

In 2000, a victimization survey was conducted with over 3,000 Toronto high school students regarding their criminal victimization and beliefs and involvement with gangs (Wortley & Tanner, 2006). Eighty-nine percent of the students reported that they had never been a member of a gang, with only 5 percent indicating that they had ever been in a gang or were currently a gang member. Street youth were also surveyed ($n = 3,960$) and 74 percent of those youth indicated they had never been in a gang, 10 percent reported being former gang members, and 16 percent said they were current members of a gang. When asked what kinds of activities they participated in as a member of a gang, the large majority (over 80 percent) indicated they were part of a gang for social reasons, to play sports together or to party and go to clubs.

When the researchers separated out those individuals who were actively pursuing criminal behaviour, the results showed that only 4 percent of the high school students and 15 percent of the street youth were in what might be classified as a "criminal gang." With respect to violence, 91 percent of criminal gang members reported that they had been in a physical fight in the past year, compared with only 27 percent of what were classified as "social gang" members and 26 percent of students who did not belong to a gang. Further, about 80 percent of criminal gang members reported that they had been physically assaulted in the past year in contrast to only 35 percent of non-gang youth (Wortley & Tanner, 2006). This data adds further evidence of the self-report studies discussed above about the likelihood that offenders have also been victims at some point in their lives.

victimization surveys crime surveys based on incidents of crime (either reported to police or unreported) as described by self-identified victims

Police Perceptions and the Impact on Youth Crime

The perceptions of police personnel with respect to crime rates are especially important for two reasons. First, police in regular contact with youthful offenders might be expected to have a much more accurate perception of variations in the rate of crime than the rest of us. Second, as the ones who lay charges against youth, police are those most likely to translate perceptions of growing violent and non-violent crime into formal charges.

In terms of the official police-reported crime rate, it is important to recognize the characteristics of the police that impact on a decision to lay a charge or divert the youth into an extrajudicial measures or sanctions program. In a 2008 Canadian study, police officers said that the seriousness of the offence committed by the young person was the primary factor that influenced their decisions, followed by the youth's prior criminal record and his or her demeanour or attitude at time of arrest (Marinos, 2008).

In one research study of police involvement in referring youth to community agencies, some officers reported that they would be unlikely to consider a referral to a community agency as an extrajudicial measure if the youth displayed a "bad attitude," because they believed that the referral system had "no teeth" if the young person failed to show up to the program (Vogt, Cohen, & Czeck, 2012, p. 9).

> How would these kinds of police perceptions affect the official crime statistics?

The makeup of the police department also affects how youth cases are handled. In a study of police forces that had specialized youth officers, it was found that the officers were much more likely to rely on alternatives under extrajudicial measures and sanctions initiatives, and to refer youth to community agencies. Police departments without such resources were 14 percent more likely to lay a charge (Schulenberg, 2004). This may also influence the number of youth who come to the attention of the more formal court system.

Conclusions: Is Youth Crime on the Increase?

Let's return to the statements that you considered at the beginning of this chapter:

- The news media accurately shows us that the increase in the crime rate in Canada is directly related to the increase in youth crime.
- If young people are going to act like criminals, we should treat them like criminals. We don't need to have a separate system of youth justice.
- Young people are much more likely to victimize and hurt older people.
- Most young people today are involved in criminal gangs and commit serious crimes.
- The kinds of crimes that young people commit are becoming much more serious than in the past.

By now you should realize that all of these statements are false.

Because uniform crime reports underreport the actual volume of youth crime, and because there are distortions in the statistics arising from policy and legislative changes, societal biases about who should be charged, and changing enforcement patterns, it is difficult to accurately determine whether the behaviour of young people is deteriorating.

Court and police statistics could only be presumed to be a valid representation of change over time if attitudes of the public and the police toward laying charges remained unchanged. Clearly, public attitudes, public policy, and police activity do change over time, which makes it more difficult to determine whether more offences are being committed or whether the increase is due to more charges being laid.

Other information-gathering techniques can provide data that gives insight into the official crime statistics, though these other techniques have problems of their own. Self-reporting tracks minor infractions relatively well, but it underreports serious offences. It also tends to miss the activities of those who are not in school and who are more likely to be involved in serious youth crime.

Despite problems with data-gathering techniques, the information available from them gives us a reasonably accurate view of youth crime generally. Media reports of youth crime, on the other hand, do not provide a basis for accurate generalizations about criminal behaviour of young people. The media has been pushing panic buttons on the subject of youth crime since the Victorian era. Therefore, it is probable that the problem of youth crime is less a cause for alarm than the media image and public perception may suggest.

It is difficult to convince the public that there is no youth crime crisis, however. As Freiberg (2001, p. 274) has argued:

> The key to countering the myths of law and order must lie in the ability of programs
> to help overcome the sense of helplessness and insecurity that crime engenders.

As you continue to consider the finer details of the causes of youth crime, the prevention, control, and rehabilitation of offenders, and the legislative provisions for youth who come in conflict with the law, think about how you are learning about the way to overcome the "compassion fatigue" that Freiberg describes.

CHAPTER SUMMARY

Statistical and other data on youth crime reveals some common perceptions about youth crime and certain realities about it.

The problem of youth crime is not new. It was a matter of public concern 100 years ago, just as it is now. It was perceived by the media at the turn of the 20th century, and thus by the public, in much the same way as it is perceived now. Persistent media themes have been that youth crime is getting worse, that it is more violent, that more punishment is needed to control it, and that things were better 20 years ago. Because the public gets its information from the media, these perceptions become the public's.

The reality of youth crime is measured by uniform crime reports, which provide official statistics of crime, and by self-report studies, which provide information about youth crime and delinquent behaviour missed by the official statistics. The data collected by the two methods complement each other, providing a more detailed picture of the reality of youth crime. Each method, however, has limitations that result in distortion of the data and prevent us from having a perfectly accurate picture of the reality of youth crime. Notwithstanding these limitations, the picture of youth crime that emerges is quite different from that described in the media. Youth crime rates do not change a great deal over time, although probably more crime occurs than is revealed by official crime statistics. Youth crimes generally are property offences, rather than crimes of violence, and are generally directed toward other youth rather than adults. Serious crimes of violence are probably not increasing, and the most serious—murder—has been and continues to be relatively rare.

Even with the emergence of new varieties of crime and despite media reports to the contrary, the reality of youth crime appears to be less a cause for alarm than public perceptions suggest.

KEY TERMS

assault level 1, 11
crime funnel, 15
crime myth, 8
crime rate, 4
Crime Severity Index (CSI), 13
custodial sentence, 13
dark figure of crime, 18
extrajudicial measure, 15
extrajudicial sanction, 15

hidden delinquency, 18
moral panic, 8
pacifism, 11
pro-social, 9
self-report studies, 18
status offence, 19
Uniform Crime Reporting (UCR) Survey, 9
victimization surveys, 21

REFERENCES

Allen, M., & Boyce, J. (2013, July 11). Police-reported hate crime in Canada, 2011. *Juristat*, p. 14. Retrieved from http://www.statcan.gc.ca/pub/85-002-x/2013001/article/11822-eng.pdf.

Bell, S. (2011). *Young offenders and juvenile justice: A century after the fact* (4th ed.). Toronto: Nelson Thomson Learning.

Boyce, J., & Cotter, A. (2013). Homicide in Canada, 2012. *Juristat*, 33(1).

Boyce, J., Cotter, A., & Perreault, S. (2014, July 23). Police-reported crime statistics in Canada, 2013. *Juristat*. Ottawa: Canadian Centre for Justice Statistics. Retrieved from http://www.statcan.gc.ca/pub/85-002-x/2014001/article/14040-eng.pdf.

Brennan, S. (2012). Police-reported crime statistics in Canada, 2011. *Juristat*. Ottawa: Canadian Centre for Justice Statistics. Retrieved from http://www.statcan.gc.ca/pub/85-002-x/2012001/article/11692-eng.htm.

Chesney-Lind, M., & Shelden, R.G. (1998). *Girls, delinquency, and juvenile justice*. Los Angeles: West/Wadsworth.

Cohen, S. (1972). *Folk devils and moral panics*. London: Paladin.

Controlled Drugs and Substances Act. (1996). SC 1996, c. 19.

Corrado, R.R., Odgers, C., & Cohen, I.M. (2000). The incarceration of female young offenders: Protection for whom? *Canadian Journal of Criminology and Criminal Justice*, 42(2), 189–207.

Criminal Code. (1985). RSC 1985, c. C-46, as amended.

Dauvergne, M. (2013). Youth court statistics in Canada, 2011–2012. *Juristat*. Catalogue No. 85-002-X. Retrieved from http://www.statcan.gc.ca/pub/85-002-x/2013001/article/11803-eng.pdf.

Department of Justice. (2013). *The Youth Criminal Justice Act: Summary and background*. Ottawa: Department of Justice and Attorney General of Canada. Retrieved from http://www.justice.gc.ca/eng/cj-jp/yj-jj/ycja-lsjpa/pdf/back-hist.pdf.

Ericson, R.V., Baranek, P.M., & Chan, J.B.L. (1989). *Negotiating control: A study of news sources.* Toronto: University of Toronto Press.

Freiberg, A. (2001). Affective versus effective justice instrumentalism and emotionalism in criminal justice. *Punishment & Society, 3*(2), 265–278.

Gorelick, S. (1989). Join our war: The construction of ideology in a newspaper crime-fighting campaign. *Crime and Delinquency, 35,* 421–436.

Herda-Rapp, A. (2003). The social construction of local school violence threats by the news media and professional organizations. *Sociological Inquiry, 73,* 545–574.

Howells, S.A. (2013). *In search of a culture of fear: Understanding the gap between the perception and reality of school dangers* (PhD dissertation). McMaster University, Hamilton, ON. Open Access Dissertations and Theses, Paper 7665.

Junger-Tas, J.I. (2012). *The many faces of youth crime: Contrasting theoretical perspectives on juvenile delinquency across countries and cultures.* New York: Springer.

Marinos, V.A. (2008). Factors influencing police attitudes toward extrajudicial measures under the Youth Criminal Justice Act. *Canadian Journal of Criminology and Criminal Justice, 50*(4), 469–489.

Muschert, G.W., & Peguero, A.A. (2010). The Columbine effect and school antiviolence policy. In M. Peyrot & S.L. Burns (Eds.), *New approaches to social problems treatment: Research in social problems and public policy, Vol. 17* (pp. 117–148). Bingley, UK: Emerald.

National Crime Prevention Centre (NCPC). (2012). *A statistical snapshot of youth at risk and youth offending in Canada.* Ottawa: Public Safety Canada.

Perreault, S. (2013, July 25). Police-reported crime statistics, Canada 2012. *Juristat.* Catalogue No. 85-002-X.

Perreault, S., & Brennan, S. (2010). Criminal victimization in Canada. *Juristat, 30*(2).

Posik, C. (2013). The overlap between offending and victimization among adolescents: Results for the second International Self-Report Delinquency Study. *Journal of Contemporary Criminal Justice, 29*(1), 106–124.

Reid, S.A. (2004). Youth crime and the media. In K. Campbell (Ed.), *Understanding youth justice in Canada* (pp. 134–152). Toronto: Pearson.

Roberts, A., & Garton Ash, T. (Eds.). (2009). *Civil resistance and power politics: The experience of non-violent action from Gandhi to the present.* Oxford: Oxford University Press.

Robinson, M. (2000). The construction and reinforcement of myths of race and crime. *Journal of Contemporary Criminal Justice, 16*(2), 133–156.

Savoie, J. (2007, September). Youth self-reported delinquency, Toronto, 2006. *Juristat, 27*(6).

Schulenberg, J.A. (2004). Police discretion with apprehended youth: Assessing the impact of juvenile specialization. *Police Practice and Research, 10*(3), 3–16.

Seskus, T., & Mofina, R. (2000). Young offenders and the press. In J.A. Winterdyk (Ed.), *Issues and perspectives on young offenders in Canada* (pp. 131–150). Toronto: Harcourt Canada.

Sprott, J.B. (2012). The persistence of status offences in the youth justice system. *Canadian Journal of Criminology and Criminal Justice, 54*(3), 309–332.

Sprott, J.B., & Doob, A.N. (2009). *Justice for girls? Stability and change in the youth justice systems of the United States and Canada.* Chicago: University of Chicago Press.

Statistics Canada. (2013a, July 1). Canada's population estimates: Age and sex. *The Daily.* CANSIM Table 051-0052.

Statistics Canada. (2013b). Canadian Centre for Justice Statistics, Uniform Crime Reporting Survey. Catalogue No. 85-002-X. CANSIM Table 252-0051.

Statistics Canada. (2013c, December 19). Homicide survey, number and rate per 100,000 population, Canada, province and territories. CANSIM Tables 253-001–007.

Tanner, J. (1996). *Teenage troubles: Youth and deviance in Canada.* Scarborough, ON: Nelson.

Taylor-Butts, A. (2010). Where and when youth commit police-reported crimes—2008. *Juristat, 30*(2).

Vaz, E. (1966). Middle class adolescents: Self-reported delinquency and youth culture activities. *Canadian Review of Sociology and Anthropology, 2,* 52–70.

Vogt, A., Cohen, I.M., & Czeck, J. (2012). *"Measuring up": A self examination of police receptivity to the Extrajudicial Measures Database.* Abbotsford, BC: University of the Fraser Valley, Centre for Safe Schools and Communities.

Wortley, S., & Tanner, J. (2006). Immigration, social disadvantage, and urban youth gangs: Results of a Toronto-area survey. *Canadian Journal of Urban Research, 15*(2), Supplement, 18–31.

Youth Criminal Justice Act. (2002). SC 2002, c. 1.

EXERCISES AND REVIEW

Review Questions

1. Are young people committing more crime today than in years past?

2. What problem does the Crime Severity Index (CSI) help combat?

3. How does the media generally describe youth crime?

4. What does the media say causes youth crime?

5. What is a moral panic?

6. How is data collected for uniform crime reports?

7. How is data collected for self-report studies?

8. What are the strengths of the Uniform Crime Report System? What are its weaknesses?

9. What are the strengths of the self-report system? What are its weaknesses?

10. At what age does the arrest rate peak for young people?

11. Is it true that older people are often the victims of crime by young people?

12. How can the disparity in extrajudicial measures opportunities affect the crime funnel?

Discussion Questions

1. Using an Internet search engine, search for "youth crime" and review the first ten results that deal with youth for a specified period that post-dates the proclamation of the *Youth Criminal Justice Act* (after 2003). Analyze the articles in terms of whether the article is concerned with, mentions, or cites the following:

   a. gang activity

   b. poverty

   c. other economic circumstances

   d. social values

   e. adequacy of the law

   f. need for stricter punishment

   g. violence

   h. positive or negative views about youth

   j. whether the story relies on police reports

   k. the perspective that the story is being told (police, victim, community, legal professionals, or young person)

2. Using the data in Tables 1.1 to 1.3, indicate what the data tells you about:

   a. whether youth crime is increasing or decreasing

   b. whether crimes of violence by youth are increasing or decreasing

   c. whether there are more crimes of violence than there are crimes against property by youth

   d. whether the proportion of violent crimes that can be classed as serious violent crime is rising or falling for youth

3. On the basis of the data available from the uniform crime reports and from self-report studies as described in this chapter, answer the following questions:

   a. What is the picture of contemporary youth crime that emerges from the data?

   b. How does the picture of youth crime drawn from the data in (a) differ from the picture of youth crime that appears in the media?

4. Pacifism is a movement that can be traced back to the beginning of the 20th century (Roberts & Garton Ash, 2009). This ideology is grounded in anti-war and anti-violence beliefs. Though initially founded on religious principles of treating others with dignity and respect, in more modern times pacifism has aligned with the principles of world leaders such as Mahatma Gandhi and Martin Luther King Jr. Gandhi's famous teaching "An eye for an eye only ends up making the whole world blind" exemplifies the pacifist movement's dedication to living in a world that does not use violence as a mechanism for progress. The most notable symbol associated with the pacifist movement is the peace sign.

   What are some recent attempts that you have seen reported that relate to a movement opposed to violence?

Youth Crime: Offences, Risk Factors, and Models of Youth Justice

2

LEARNING OUTCOMES

After completing this chapter, you should be able to:

- Identify the most common types of crimes that young people commit.

- Be able to explain gender and youth criminality with a particular focus on the gendered nature of administration of justice offences.

- Understand the premise of conflict theory, functionalist theory, and symbolic interactionist theory and the application of these theories to youth criminality.

- Understand the underlying risk factors and protective factors related to crime.

- Identify the theoretical models of youth justice and understand how they assist in our understanding of youth justice processes.

What Types of Crime Do Youth Commit?

In Chapter 1, we examined the frequency and extent of youth crime and, in doing so, we made some observations about what sorts of crimes are commonly committed by young people. We now examine these in more detail.

If we take a closer look at the actual offences committed, a pattern does emerge, with certain types of offences characteristic of youth crime. It also becomes clear that even though certain types of crimes are committed by both adults and youth, youth criminal involvement may be a result of factors quite different from those associated with adult behaviour. As we will see in later chapters, this difference in motivation may explain why traditional crime-reduction strategies such as deterrence and custodial sentences seem less effective for youthful offenders.

Let's begin by looking at the most common offences committed by young persons. As was pointed out in Chapter 1, youth are most likely to commit property offences, with the most common being shoplifting, as shown in the high number of youth accused of theft under $5,000. According to the most recent official statistics, more than half of all youth accused of crimes were accused of theft of $5,000 or under, mischief, level 1 assault, or cannabis possession (Perreault, 2013) (see Figure 2.1).

Vandalism

vandalism
destruction of, or damage to, private property

Statistics generally describe **vandalism** as "mischief to private property" (*Criminal Code*, s. 430). Broadly speaking, vandalism involves destruction of, or damage to, property. Many acts of vandalism are directed against schools and private residences, but may also be done in other more public places such as shopping malls.

Common behaviours that may lead to a mischief charge from vandalism include

- spray-painting another's property with the purpose of defacing
- "egging" someone's car or window
- keying or scratching paint off someone's car
- defacing public property (mail boxes, park benches, etc.) with graffiti
- altering or knocking down street signs
- slashing someone's tires.

Communities are responding to this type of behaviour by passing bylaws and setting up task forces that address graffiti cleanup. Police are actively involved in these initiatives with more vigilance in laying charges or referring youth to anti-graffiti programs.

On May 1, 2006, London, Ontario's city council passed a bylaw that made it illegal for persons under the age of 18 to purchase spray paint or permanent markers in the city. The London Police responded in kind by appointing a special constable as "graffiti investigator" to monitor graffiti occurrences, track and identify graffiti trends, establish suspects, investigate occurrences, and target highly victimized areas. The Toronto Police Service has a designated graffiti officer in each of its 17 divisions to implement strategies to reduce graffiti under the Toronto Anti-Violence Intervention Strategy (TAVIS). In addition to surveillance of highly victimized areas, the Toronto Police Service is engaged in crime prevention and education using police cautions and referrals under the *Youth Criminal Justice Act* to divert youth charged with mischief to arts programs and community organizations that educate, coach, and mentor youth. Activities include assisting in graffiti removal, creating public murals, and attending art forums. In Fredericton, New Brunswick, an initiative of a police crime prevention officer was implemented called "Spray No to Violence,"

FIGURE 2.1   Youth (12–17) Accused of Crime, Canada, 2012

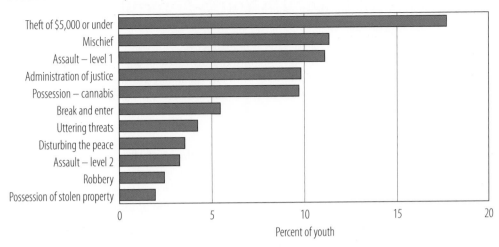

SOURCE: Perreault (2013).

in which youth accused of graffiti and mischief were diverted into a program where they were given the responsibility for creating canvases with spray paint with crime prevention messages.

EDMONTON'S GRAFFITI "BRUTE"

The city of Edmonton, Alberta takes the issue of graffiti very seriously. In 2012 the city recorded 1,116 incidents of graffiti, down only 1.5 percent from 2011. On January 21, 2013 one of the individuals known to police as an active participant in the city's graffiti problem was arrested. The youth, age 17, cannot be identified as per the *Youth Criminal Justice Act*, but is known locally as "Brute." The "Brute" tag has been spotted throughout Edmonton since 2010 and in over 250 locations. The police stopped the teen riding on his bicycle close to 5 a.m. and noticed paint residue on his face, hands, and clothes with spray cans on his person. After searching his residence they found additional evidence linking him with the tag. The youth is now facing 151 counts of mischief in connection with his graffiti vandalism, making this the most counts against given to a youth in the city.

QUESTIONS

1. Could "Brute's" love of graffiti be harnessed to create something positive for the city he vandalized? Why do you think vandalism is a problem for communities?

2. Have a look at your own community and see which areas seem to have the most graffiti. What initiatives are in place in your community?

3. What do you think is the best way to handle the problem of vandalism?

Chapter 1 noted that as technology changes, crime is changing with it. Vandalism is no exception. We can now include under the category of vandalism computer **hacking**, in which a young person who is a proficient computer user can breach database security systems and destroy or badly damage information by introducing a computer virus into the data system. In a self-report study of Toronto high school students, 27 percent of respondents admitted that they had hacked a computer at some point in their lives (Tanner & Wortley, 2002). It has become commonplace among young people to indicate in a status update on Facebook or Twitter that they have been "hacked" when a friend accesses their account, often to write something outlandish on their status.

hacking
a breach of a database security system to destroy or damage information by introducing a computer virus into the data system

***Criminal Code*, Mischief in relation to data**

430(1.1) Every one commits mischief who wilfully

(a) destroys or alters data;

(b) renders data meaningless, useless or ineffective;

(c) obstructs, interrupts or interferes with the lawful use of data; or

(d) obstructs, interrupts or interferes with any person in the lawful use of data or denies access to data to any person who is entitled to access thereto.

***Criminal Code*, Causing disturbance, indecent exhibition, loitering, etc.**

175(1) Every one who

(a) not being in a dwelling-house, causes a disturbance in or near a public place,

(i) by fighting, screaming, shouting, swearing, singing or using insulting or obscene language,

(ii) by being drunk, or

(iii) by impeding or molesting other persons,

(b) openly exposes or exhibits an indecent exhibition in a public place, [or]

(c) loiters in a public place and in any way obstructs persons who are in that place ...

is guilty of an offence punishable on summary conviction.

Disturbing the peace may also be treated as a form of mischief, and is quite common among young people. As is noted in the *Criminal Code* box here, the kinds of behaviour that constitute disturbing the peace range from shouting and screaming to simply loitering. Many youth do not have a place to meet their friends and are often asked to "move along" when standing in a group in a restaurant or in a coffee shop parking lot. The rate per 100,000 at which youth were charged for disturbing the peace in 2012 was 17.5, compared with 24.1 in 2007. This decrease may be evidence of the police using sections of the *Youth Criminal Justice Act* whereby police administer a caution or warning under the provisions for extrajudicial measures rather than laying a charge.

Arson

***Criminal Code*, Arson—damage to property**

434. Every person who intentionally or recklessly causes damage by fire or explosion to property that is not wholly owned by that person is guilty of an indictable offence and liable to imprisonment for a term not exceeding fourteen years.

One form of vandalism that needs to be considered separately is arson, which, as can be seen in the *Criminal Code* box here, is a serious offence. While arson only accounts for 2.1 percent of property offences, in 2012 there was a 21 percent increase in the number of youth accused over the previous year. Further, 2012 also had the highest percentage of property offences due to arson in ten years. In the data from 2011 to 2013, the 2012 increase in arson (18.2 per 100,000) appears to be an anomaly, with the rate per 100,000 of youth charged in 2013 (15.2) returning to a rate similar to that found in 2011 (14.8) (Boyce, Cotter, & Perreault, 2014). These fluctuations may be due to a change in police charging practices, the influence of a number of key media reports of sensational cases, or other environmental factors such as an enhanced relationship between the police and fire prevention agencies. One media report from Winnipeg indicated that a 17-year-old street gang member would receive the maximum punishment for arson that left 40 apartment dwellers homeless and caused over $1 million in damages (Turner, 2012).

There are a number of reasons why children and youth set fires. Of particular interest and concern is fire-setting by youths who seem to be fascinated by the act itself. This kind of arson is often perceived to indicate some degree of mental illness or disturbance. The following types of youth fire-setters have been described by the American Psychological Association (Dittmann, 2004):

- *Curiosity/accidental.* Non-pathological fire-setters. The most common type; they often do not understand the consequences of fire-play and tend to be 5 to 10 years old.
- *Cry-for-help.* Children who consciously or subconsciously use fire to draw attention to a stress in their life. Common problems underlying this type are depression, attention deficit hyperactivity disorder, and family stress.
- *Delinquent.* Fire-setters who often show little empathy for others but tend to avoid harming others. Typically 11 to 15 years old, they cause significant property damage and often show common aggression and conduct problems.
- *Severely disturbed.* Children with a fixation on fire, including paranoid and psychotic children who may want to harm or kill themselves.
- *Cognitively impaired.* Developmentally disabled or impaired children. They tend to lack good judgment but avoid intentional harm; significant property damage is common.
- *Sociocultural.* Children who set fires primarily for support from peers or community groups, such as those fires set during riots or in religious fervour.

> Looking at this list of types of fire-setters, what do you think is the best kind of intervention for each type? Does the seriousness of the punishment outlined in s. 434 of the *Criminal Code* apply to the majority of these cases?

Break and Enter

Breaking into private premises is closely related to vandalism. However, the rate of break and enter was 43 percent lower in 2012 than ten years earlier and the number of youth charged was 4.4 percent lower than in 2011. Uniform crime reports had shown that in 1995 and for roughly three years thereafter, 40 percent of all break-and-enters were committed by young offenders (Kong, 1997). This trend started a downward decline in 1998 as shown in Figure 2.2, so that by 2012 youth accused accounted for less than a quarter of all the break-and-enters in Canada.

Historically, break-and-enters have accounted for about one-quarter of all property crimes reported to the police. According to the General Social Survey (GSS), fewer citizens reported break-and-enters to the police as self-reported in the 2009 survey than in the 2006 survey. Reasons victims gave for not reporting the incident to the police included that they felt the incident was too trivial to report or the police could not do anything about it (Perreault, 2010).

> Do you think that there has been an actual decline in break-and-enter offences committed by youth, or do the numbers reflect the public not calling the police?

FIGURE 2.2   Percentage of Cases with a Youth Accused, Break and Enter, Canada

(bar chart; y-axis: Percentage of youth cases, 0 to 40; x-axis: years 1998 to 2012)

SOURCE: Statistics Canada (2013).

Motor Vehicle Theft

"Officer Root will never believe the car was stolen. He knows we have four teenagers!"

© 2009 Steve Delmonte. www.CartoonStock.com.

> ***Criminal Code,* Taking motor vehicle or vessel or found therein without consent**
>
> **335**(1) … [E]very one who, without the consent of the owner, takes a motor vehicle or vessel with intent to drive, use, navigate or operate it or cause it to be driven, used, navigated or operated, or is an occupant of a motor vehicle or vessel knowing that it was taken without the consent of the owner, is guilty of an offence punishable on summary conviction.

Car theft is and has long been a common offence committed by the young. While adult car theft is often for financial gain, and frequently forms part of a sophisticated and complex operation, car theft by the young, like vandalism, often occurs for other reasons. In fact, the *Criminal Code* has long included the offence commonly known as "joyriding" (s. 335) in which, typically, a car is stolen and driven around and then abandoned. In a 2008 self-report study of high school students in British Columbia, about one in four indicated that they had either thought of or engaged in auto theft behaviours (Dhami, 2008).

> 1. What value would charging the son/daughter criminally have in the case of the cartoon shown here?
> 2. How often do you think joyrides turn into **car surfing**?

car surfing

a thrill-seeking activity consisting in riding the exterior of a moving vehicle while another person drives; the term was introduced in the mid-1980s

In 1996, approximately 43 percent of all motor vehicle thefts were by young offenders (Sauve, 1997). However, it appears that the rate at which car theft is committed has been falling. According to the most recent crime statistics, youth charged with motor vehicle theft account for 29 percent of all youth charges. Further, the rate of motor vehicle theft in 2012 was 57 percent lower than ten years earlier, and the number of youth charged with motor vehicle theft was 4.2 percent lower than in 2011 (Perreault, 2013).

Controlled Substances Offences

Some people have argued that substance abuse among youth is at or near an "epidemic" in Canada. However, statistics seem to show a recent decline in the use of certain illicit drugs. For example, in 1990 approximately one in four students in grade 10 had used cannabis at some point in their lives, and by 2002 this had doubled for boys and increased to two in five for girls. However, by 2010 the rates of cannabis use had declined by approximately 40 percent for both boys and girls (Freeman, 2011). It is good to keep in mind that the likelihood of being charged for any offence, including possession of cannabis, is much higher if you are a young person, as shown in Figure 2.3.

FIGURE 2.3   Youth and Adults Charged with Possession of Cannabis, 2008–2012

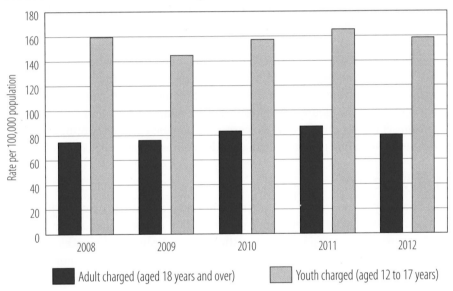

SOURCE: Statistics Canada, CANSIM Table 252-0051.

The possession, production, distribution, importation, and exportation of illicit drugs is prohibited under the *Controlled Drugs and Substances Act* (1996). In 2012, of the more than 100,000 drug-related offences, less than 17 percent involved youth; and in more than 67 percent of those that involved youth, charges were not laid. Sixty-three percent of all charges laid against youth for such incidents involved possession of cannabis, and 18 percent were for the trafficking, production, or distribution of cannabis. By contrast, possession of cocaine accounted for just 2.3 percent of charges (Statistics Canada, 2013).

TO POT OR NOT?

In Canada today there appears to be a divergence between legislation governing marijuana possession, production, and distribution and what the people want. According to an Angus Reid poll, 57 percent of Canadian adults not only support decriminalization, but are in support of the legalization of marijuana (Geddes, 2013). Is it time for the legislation to be adjusted to match the beliefs of the majority of Canadians? Justin Trudeau, leader of the Liberal Party of Canada, thinks so—he has called for the legalization of marijuana. He is not alone in re-examining this issue. The Canadian Association of Chiefs of Police passed a resolution in the fall of 2013 to lobby the federal government to allow them to ticket individuals found in possession of small amounts of marijuana, rather than proceed with criminal charges, because in their view these charges put an unwarranted burden on the resources of the Canadian criminal justice system.

Marijuana use and possession is still firmly prohibited under Canadian criminal law, but the legalization debate remains open.

QUESTIONS

1. Should the law reflect the majority's position on an issue?
2. How might the legalization of marijuana affect youth crime statistics?

Administration of Justice Offences

administration of justice offence
violation of court-ordered conditions such as curfew, non-association with criminals, attendance at school or mandated treatment, showing up in court, etc.

Administration of justice offences include failure to appear in court, failure to comply with conditions of bail or probation terms, or violations of provisions in the *Youth Criminal Justice Act* (such as being late for curfew or consuming alcohol). Perhaps the most surprising aspect of these types of offences is how often Canadian girls have been charged with them in the past two or more decades. Sprott and Doob (2009) found that while girls are more likely to receive additional charges due to breaches of conditions of their release, they are also likely to receive more conditions of release than their male counterparts. Even for non-violent offences, they found that girls were given additional requirements to attend mandatory counselling. In 2011–2012, 61 percent of female cases of administration of justice charges were for failure to comply with an order, compared with 57 percent for males.

Crimes of Violence

Despite the relatively stable rate of violent crime in Canada, many people feel there has been an increase in the rate of violent crime committed by young women and girls. Caution must be taken when making such a suggestion, because gender differences related to crime are often pathologized—meaning that, despite lack of evidence to support such an assertion, differences are tied to what are seen as weaknesses in females' biological and psychological chemistry (Artz, Stoneman, & Reitsma-Street, 2012). Police statistics about female offending suggest that, although involvement in recorded crime by females has increased in recent years, the increase has occurred mainly in less serious assaults and in victimless crimes such as offences against the administration of justice. In 2011–2012, less than one-quarter of all cases completed in youth court involved females (23 percent). Females were most likely to commit fraud, failure to appear in youth court, and disturbing the peace (Dauvergne, 2013).

Assault

Criminal Code, Assault
265(1) A person commits an assault when
(a) without the consent of another person, he applies force intentionally to that other person, directly or indirectly;
(b) he attempts or threatens, by an act or a gesture, to apply force to another person, if he has, or causes that other person to believe on reasonable grounds that he has, present ability to effect his purpose; or
(c) while openly wearing or carrying a weapon or an imitation thereof, he accosts or impedes another person or begs.

There are three levels of assault, with level 3 being the most serious. *Level 1* assaults are by far the most common among young people and include contact such as pushing and shoving where there is very little harm to the victim. *Level 2* assaults, or assault with a weapon or causing bodily harm, are those that involve carrying, using, or threatening to use a real or imitation weapon. This category also includes incidents that involve injury to a person that interferes with their health or comfort and is more than merely transient or trifling in nature. *Level 3* assaults, also referred to as *aggravated assaults*, constitute those in which a victim is wounded, maimed, or disfigured or whose life is endangered.

There was a dramatic increase in the number of youth charged with assault level 1 when schools introduced zero-tolerance policies prohibiting violence in any form. The impact of these policies meant that behaviour that had previously been dealt with by school personnel (principal, vice-principal) was now being dealt with through more formal processes by calling the police. There may not have been any more assaults by young people than previously, but they were being counted for the first time in official statistics.

In 2012, the majority of assaults charged against youth were level 1 (66 percent). Level 2 assaults accounted for 31 percent, while assault level 3 accounted for less than 3 percent of all assaults (Statistics Canada, 2013).

Serious violence by youth is still a relatively rare event.

Guns and Weapons Offences

Some high-profile cases involving gun violence have given rise to a great deal of public concern about the increase in the use of guns and the proliferation of youth gangs in Canada. Much of this concern has resulted from media reports about incidents in Toronto. The year 2005 came to be known as "the year of the gun," but since 2003 only 16 young people have been killed by guns.

In 2012, youth charges accounted for 16 percent of all weapons violations. However, the rate per 100,000 people with respect to firearms violations among youth has increased from 3.95 in 2008 to 5.42 in 2012, and includes using a gun in the commission of an offence, pointing a firearm, and discharging with intent (Statistics Canada, 2013).

Gun violence has been blamed on the availability of guns, an alleged cultural celebration of guns and violence, and violence in entertainment, such as television and movies, video games, and war toys. The impact of the media on violence will be considered in more detail in the next section.

Effect of Violent Media Exposure on Youth

The potential effects of violent media on aggressive tendencies among young people has been studied for many years, and the results show that there is an effect on physical aggression (Anderson, 2007). How this happens is related to both the psychological and the physiological responses that occur after repeated exposure that desensitizes youth to the violence, making it seem normal and mundane. Such desensitization leads to a decreased perception of injury severity and decreased sympathy for victims of violence, and to simply less attention being paid to the violent events portrayed. The result is fewer pro-social and more anti-social behaviours including aggression.

While a number of analyses have shown this link, there has been considerable controversy about the link to violent video games or watching violent media generally. Those who disagree with the evidence suggest that playing video games is part of being an adolescent and that the violent media exposure has no identifiable effect on delinquency. Scholars have reported that any links between video games and aggression are merely the byproduct of other processes occurring in the life of the child and that there is virtually no evidence media violence is related to serious or criminal violence (Ferguson, 2007).

In a recent study of incarcerated youth, researchers found that for youth who were very interested in playing violent video games, there was a strong relationship to measures of delinquency. Perhaps this can be explained by the number of hours the youth reported playing video games. Other researchers (Weiss, 2011) have suggested that the majority of young people consume about three hours of electronic media per day, whereas youth who are in the psychiatric population have levels that are roughly double this (six hours). In the study of youth in the correctional facility, they reported a range of electronic media use between 10 and 40 hours a week (DeLisi, 2013).

---

1. Judging on the basis of your own experience, what do you think about the link between violent video games and aggression?
2. What does this research suggest in terms of working with young people in custody?

FATAL FANTASY

When it comes to gaming culture, there is much debate about whether virtual violence breeds real-life violence or whether gamers are drawn to violent games to meet their pre-existing violent urges. However strong this debate, there is one thing both sides can agree on: violence in video games and the media has increased. The year 2013 was a banner year in this respect, with the release of *Call of Duty: Ghosts*, and *Grand Theft Auto 5*. The *Call of Duty* series, a militaristic, first-person-shooter game, has received criticism, most notably for *Call of Duty: Modern Warfare*, which allowed players to kill civilians in the infamous "airport massacre scene" (Etengoff, 2009). Jackson Katz, anti-sexist male advocate, criticized the media attention surrounding the *Call of Duty* series, which used Hollywood actors Jonah Hill and Sam Worthington to promote one of its editions, in his documentary *Tough Guise 2: Violence, Manhood & American Culture* (Earp & Jhally, 2013). *Grand Theft Auto 5* has also received harsh criticism for its extreme violence, misogynistic depictions of sex, and most notably inclusion of the mission called "By the Book"—in which players are tasked with getting information from a fugitive using torture instruments provided to them.

QUESTION

Even if the correlation between video-game and real-life violence is still a matter of debate, have the games gone too far in the name of fantasy?

---

conflict theory
an approach to how societies work that emphasizes conflict, power relations, differences among groups, and social change resulting from group conflict

functionalist theory
an approach to how societies work that emphasizes the way various parts of society function and interact to produce social harmony or equilibrium

Theories of Youth Criminality

There are almost as many theories and explanations about why young people commit offences as there are people studying and thinking about the matter.

Conflict theory seeks to understand social relationships by identifying social groups that are engaged in conflict and by studying that conflict. From this perspective, society is presumed to be composed of various groups in conflict with one another, with each group seeking to improve its position at the expense of another group. The goals, norms, and values of one group often clash with those of other groups.

Functionalist theory sees society as being composed of coherent social systems in which all the system parts work harmoniously and contribute to the well-being of society. When social systems are working well, they are stable or in equilibrium. When they do not work well, there is strain between the society's goals and values and an individual's ability to achieve those goals and internalize those values.

Conflict and functionalist theories both hold that shared values are required for society to function. Conflict theorists see shared values as the result of coercion, believing that some groups force their values on others and on the society's institutions; they see youth crime as an expression of resistance to the imposition of "mainstream" social values, often by relatively powerless working-class or minority youth. Functionalist theorists, in contrast, see youth crime resulting from some youth imperfectly learning the society's value system due to dysfunctional families, mental illness, poverty, inadequate schools, or poor neighbourhoods. (For a more detailed introduction to these two theories and some of their key social theorists, see Johnson & Bauer, 2004, pp. 4–5 and chap. 1 generally.)

Labelling theory suggests that individuals will "live up to" stereotypical labels ascribed to them by others. A child labelled a "delinquent" will, in response to being labelled that way, behave as society expects juvenile delinquents to behave, and will come to believe he or she is truly deserving of the label.

Symbolic interactionist theory focuses on individual interaction, often in small groups, and assumes that an analysis of why people behave as they do can only be understood in the context of interactions with others. For symbolic interactionists, people are not simply victim to their social circumstances (such as being born into a life of poverty) but play an active role in creating their own experience. From the standpoint of symbolic interactionism, the argument can be made that youth should be accorded the same rights as adults in the criminal justice system: if youth are actively creating their own experience, they must have a voice in the process.

Social learning theory gives emphasis to the importance of considering various individual traits or psychological attributes within the moderating environment of a shared social context (Andrews & Bonta, 1998). This social psychological theory endorses the risk–needs system for assessing individual risk for recidivism or dangerous behaviour.

labelling theory
a subtheory of symbolic interactionism that suggests that individuals will "live up to" stereotypical labels—e.g., "delinquent"—ascribed to them by others

symbolic interactionist theory
an approach that holds that individual behaviour is influenced by people's interaction with others, and that self-image is constructed by a conscious reading of the symbolic meaning of these interactions

social learning theory
a social psychological approach that holds that behaviour is learned by observing and modelling those around one

THEORETICAL EXPLANATIONS OF CRIMINALITY

Jessica is a young person who has been in trouble with the law numerous times. The majority of her interactions with the criminal justice system have occurred because of thefts that she committed around her community. Jessica lives in a low-income area of the city where poverty is common and where there are very limited opportunities for employment, especially for youth. Growing up, Jessica's mother was arrested many times for theft; and each time her mother explained that she did so to feed her family.

The three theoretical paradigms—conflict, functionalist, and symbolic interactionist—can be used to assist in understanding the roots of Jessica's offending, which, in turn, can help suggest effective approaches to correcting it. Each approach will examine Jessica's case using its own set of assumptions to explain her behaviour.

QUESTIONS

Now it's time for you to practise behavioural analysis. Examine Jessica's social reality and crime from each perspective to answer the question "What is the root cause of Jessica's criminality?"

1. How would a conflict theorist explain Jessica's behaviour?

2. How would a functionalist explain Jessica's behaviour?

3. How would a symbolic interactionist explain Jessica's behaviour?

The value of understanding these broad theories is that they reveal the assumptions that guide our policies and interventions with young people who commit crime, and our strategies for prevention. Beliefs about what causes young people to commit crime vary from one person to the next, and are often tied up with ideological assumptions about the best ways to intervene, redirect, or punish. **Ideology** is defined as a set of general and abstract beliefs or assumptions about the correct or proper state of things, particularly with respect to the moral order and political arrangements, that shape one's position on specific issues. Models based on these varying perspectives can be helpful in sorting out the distinctive ways the youth justice system might operate. These models will be discussed later in this chapter. Before moving to that discussion, let us now outline the various factors shown to correlate with greater risk of youth committing offences. It is important to recognize that no single risk factor on its own is indicated as *causing* crime. The more risk factors a young person displays, however, the higher the likelihood they do engage in criminal behaviour (Reid-MacNevin & Waddell, 2005).

ideology
a set of general and abstract beliefs or assumptions about the proper state of things that shapes one's position on specific issues

Risk and Protective Factors and Youth Crime

Attempts have been made to blame crime on everything from diet and TV violence to different skull shapes and sizes. Each of these theories has been limited by the absence of convincing data. There is, however, growing and consistent evidence that poverty, unemployment, abuse, and family or school problems correlate to crime. While one cannot say with any certainty that these factors are causes of crime, they certainly are causes of disadvantage and many of these youth are referred to as *disenfranchised*. The concern lies in the fact that those individuals who are most disadvantaged socially, emotionally, and personally and who lack financial and personal resources are often left behind, and they are the people most likely to come into conflict with the criminal justice system.

No single **risk factor** or set of risk factors is powerful enough to predict with certainty that youth will come into conflict with the law. For example, doing poorly in school is an individual risk factor, but by no means will all young people who perform poorly in school become violent offenders. Similarly, many are exposed to a multitude of risks in the community, family, and school, but not all will get involved in criminal behaviour or violence. **Protective factors**, those circumstances and experiences that tend to shield young people from involvement in behaviours that would be damaging to themselves and to others, may be operative. Protective factors might come from the interaction of environmental processes (neighbourhood, school, peer group, community groups), family processes (family resources, parental characteristics, parental behaviour), and individual characteristics (self-beliefs, cognition).

risk factors
negative influences or circumstances in the lives of individuals, groups of persons, or communities that may increase the presence of crime, victimization, and/or fear of crime in a given community

protective factors
circumstances and experiences that tend to shield people from involvement in behaviours that would be damaging to themselves and to others

The following section will outline some of the key risk and protective factors known to be related to youth crime. They are grouped into broad categories based on individual, family, school, peers, neighbourhood/community, and environment.

Individual Factors

Individual risk factors include characteristics such as gender, age, and physiological, biological, and psychological traits. The most powerful individual predictors of youth crime are gender and age: youth crime is most prevalent among boys in late adolescence and young adulthood, as has been shown in Chapter 1. Individual risk factors include a tendency toward risk-taking, poor social skills, limited attention span, hyperactivity, and restlessness. In addition, some adolescents with specific disabilities (for example, emotional disturbances, attention deficit disorder, and some learning disabilities) are more likely to display anti-social behaviour. Attitudes and beliefs also have an effect on youth crime. Those young people who hold anti-social beliefs and have pro-violence and hostile attitudes are more likely to be aggressive and engage in crime.

FETAL ALCOHOL SPECTRUM DISORDER

The number of children and youth who were exposed to alcohol prenatally and who develop fetal alcohol spectrum disorder (FASD) is estimated to be 9 in every 100,000 people (Mills, 2006). FASD is characterized by anomalies in the neurophysiological development of the brain, nervous system, and endocrine system; and anomalies in psychosocial development, including personality formation, social conduct, and capacity for relationships. There is also a stronger likelihood that individuals with FASD will experience cognitive deficits and emotional disorders. This constellation of problems increases the risk that an individual will become involved in criminal behaviour.

QUESTION

Look further into the problems that children and youth face who have FASD. What kinds of programs exist to assist children and youth with this problem?

A growing and diverse body of research (Lipsey, 2009) has concluded that youth who are involved in the youth justice system have significantly more mental health and substance abuse problems than other youth. However, it is important to recognize that although these studies have found a correlation between mental disorders and youth crime, the correlation doesn't imply a causal relationship. There are many other factors related to the individual, family, school, and community that create a social context that may either heighten the risk of offending or reduce the effects of any single risk factor. The more cognitive, emotional, social, and relational competencies a young person has, the less likely he or she is to engage in youth crime.

Table 2.1 summarizes the main individual risk and protective factors.

TABLE 2.1   Main Individual Risk and Protective Factors for Youth Crime

Individual risk factors	Individual protective factors
• History of violent victimization	• Active, positive engagement and participation in family, school, and community activity
• Early socialization supportive of criminal behaviour and anti-social beliefs and attitudes	• Pro-social values (caring, respect, equality, social justice, responsibility)
• Mental health issues (poor behavioural controls, deficits in social cognitive or information processing abilities, high emotional distress)	• Social age-appropriate competencies (problem-solving skills, conflict resolution skills, emotion management, positive coping skills, interpersonal skills, resistance skills)
• Inability to plan for future	• Optimism, hope, and self-efficacy

Family Factors

The greater the number of challenges a family has, the greater the likelihood a young person will get involved in problem behaviour. Structural factors such as poverty and unemployment are often out of the control of family members. These factors increase the risk of family disruption, overcrowding, stress, and depression.

Risk factors that predict early onset of problems as well as chronic patterns of anti-social behaviour in youth include harsh and ineffective parental discipline, lack of parental involvement, family conflict, parental criminality, child abuse and neglect, and witnessing domestic violence. Children who experience maltreatment are nearly twice as likely to report emotional and behavioural disorders as children and youth who do not report being abused or maltreated by their parents. Using the data from the Canadian National Longitudinal Survey on Children and Youth, Dauvergne and Johnson (2001) point out that children who witnessed family violence were nearly three times more likely to be involved in physical aggression at school, and twice as likely to be involved in indirect aggression (excluding others, spreading gossip, etc.), as their peers who did not experience family violence.

It is often assumed that coming from a home where the parents have separated or divorced is closely associated with youth crime. However, research has shown no relationship unless the separation involved family conflict and disruption. There are other features of family life that have also been found to correlate with children involved in official delinquency. Low parental supervision and control, low family cohesiveness, high parental conflict, infrequent family recreation, large family size, high family criminality, and lower social class all seem to be associated with delinquent behaviour (Latimer, 2001). However, if the parents did not engage in criminality, were in stable marital relationships, and had higher-than-average intelligence, it seemed to buffer the problems that might have been created by lack of family recreation, conflict in the family, and large family size.

Table 2.2 shows the main family risk and protective factors.

TABLE 2.2   Main Family Risk and Protective Factors for Youth Crime

Family risk factors	Family protective factors
• Child abuse, neglect	• Supportive family environment (prenatal through to transition to adulthood)
• Criminally involved parents/siblings	• Positive family role models and healthy behaviours
• Single-parent household	• Affectionate ties or bonds with a family member (parent, grandparent, sibling)
• Lack of parental involvement	• Parental engagement in young person's development (involvement in schooling, sports, recreation)
• Lack of effective parenting strategies (authoritarian child rearing; harsh, lax, or inconsistent disciplinary practices)	• Family explains clear, age-appropriate behavioural expectations and consequences, and monitors child's activities

School and Peer Factors

A successful non-violent social adjustment at home increases the likelihood of, but does not guarantee, a successful non-violent adjustment to school. As children mature into adolescence, the direct impact of family factors on their behaviour is largely overshadowed by school and peer influences. Young people bring into the classroom their family environments, their experiences in the neighbourhood, their attitudes about how to handle frustration, and their views of the world. Teachers and school administrators can play a role in assisting youth exposed to multiple risks through the provision of safe learning environments and setting high yet achievable academic and social expectations.

Youth who do poorly in school are more likely to engage in crime. Students on modified learning tracks have been found to be about twice as likely to be convicted of a crime as their more academically engaged peers. School is a primary arena for the dynamics of competition for status, and when schools put academically poor students in the same classes as aggressive troublemakers, delinquent peer groups tend to emerge. Feelings of anger, rejection, and alienation are mutually reinforced in these groups.

Children who do not do well in school are also more likely to be truant or to stop attending school altogether. The opportunity for engaging in crime is significantly greater than it would be if the youth were attached to school and attending on a regular basis. In 2009–10, 10 percent of young men and 7 percent of young women were school dropouts. Young Aboriginal people were more likely to drop out than non-Aboriginal people. From 2007 to 2010, the dropout rates among off-reserve First Nations, Métis, and Inuit were 23 percent, compared with 9 percent for non-Aboriginal young people (National Crime Prevention Centre, 2012).

Unsafe environments in schools can contribute to a difficult school experience for some students, especially for a subgroup who experience frequent physical and verbal harassment. These youth are more likely to exhibit problems in high school, including aggressive behaviours, choice of anti-social peer associates, alcohol use, and psychological distress (for example, low self-esteem, insecurity, depression, anxiety, and suicide) (Leschied, 2011).

School-related risk factors include, for the student, low school involvement and academic or social failure. School staff who lack clarity and follow-through on rules and policies, have inconsistent and inequitable disciplinary practices, provide inconsistent administrative support, and make few allowances for individual differences create situations of risk for young people.

There is considerable overlap between school and peer dynamics. Schools bring peers together. For some youth, the only reason they attend school is to see their friends. Positive peer relationships are strongly correlated with positive school attitude, attendance rates, and high academic performance. Having peers who disapprove of delinquent behaviour may inhibit later delinquency and violence, while having anti-social peers contributes to the spread of delinquency and criminal behaviour (Loeber & Farrington, 2003). Adolescents who are not involved in conventional social activities and are unpopular at school are at higher risk of becoming involved in youth criminality because often the only acceptance they can find is with an anti-social peer group (Dembo & Schmeidler, 2003).

Table 2.3 provides a summary of the risk and protective factors related to peers and schools.

TABLE 2.3   Main Peer- and-School-Related Risk and Protective Factors for Youth Crime

Peer- and school-related risk factors	Peer- and school-related protective factors
• Poor academic performance, low commitment to school, and school failure	• Friends and schools that promote academic engagement
• Anti-social peers	• Friends who model pro-social responsible behaviour
• Social rejection by peers	• Positive peer influence
• Inadequate attention and resources paid to school environments	• Caring, respectful school environment that provides clear expectations, rules, and consequences
• Lack of economic opportunities	• Development of academic apprenticeships
• Enrollment in schools that are unsafe and fail to address student's academic, social, and emotional needs	• Schools that work to ensure a culture of respect, inclusivity, diversity, and student engagement

Neighbourhood/Community Factors

Community factors that increase risk of youth offending include the physical environment, economic and recreational opportunities, existing social support, and the presence or absence of a network of community organizations. Some communities lack opportunities that help prevent anti-social lifestyles, such as before- and after-school programming, recreational opportunities, and pro-social adult mentors. Like an influential family member, a community mentor can be helpful in teaching a child strategies for avoiding trouble and interacting positively with others.

Youth are at higher risk of coming into conflict with the law when their neighbourhood or community has high rates of crime, violence, and drug activity. Adolescents who are exposed to violence in their neighbourhood often feel vulnerable and unable to control their lives. These feelings can lead to helplessness and hopelessness. Such young people may turn to crime and violence as a way of asserting control over their surroundings.

Criminality risk increases when the community offers not only few part-time job opportunities, but also few after-school activities such as organized sports or youth groups. Some studies suggest that unemployment and lack of money are not as directly linked to youth crime as formerly assumed, and it has been argued that youth crime is likely the result of idleness and boredom. Those with time on their hands are simply more likely to get into trouble, particularly when this idleness is combined with immaturity.

Generally speaking, the oppression and reduced opportunities that result from poverty, racism, and sexism increase the impact of risk factors both in terms of involvement in youth crime and the potential of being victimized. Environmental factors involve larger social issues such as social values, prevailing ideologies, poverty, racial/ethnic discrimination, social policies, and the impact of the media. For example, if a young person of colour lives in a small community with little racial diversity, he might have greater difficulty building social relationships in that community, which puts him at risk for criminality.

The general disenfranchisement of young people in our society also contributes to youth crime. Our culture has largely failed to recognize youth as a valuable asset. As a result, many youth find it difficult to engage in meaningful relationships with adults both individually and within the larger community. This lack of connection may contribute to youth feelings of isolation, alienation, and disassociation from mainstream society, thus increasing the risk for delinquent and/or violent behaviour (MacKenzie, 2006).

Table 2.4 summarizes the risk and protective factors related to the community.

TABLE 2.4   Main Community Risk and Protective Factors for Youth Crime

Community risk factor	Community protective factors
• Lack of connection to community	• Positive adult role models and other supportive adult relationships
• Community disorganization leading to lack of acceptance of youth	• Community attitudes/action that respect and value identity, diversity, and equality
• Disenfranchised youth	• Community attitudes and actions that value children and youth
• Youth non-participation in community affairs	• Strategies that support child and youth engagement and participation
• Poverty	• Opportunities for youth economically and socially
• Lack of cultural, recreational, and aesthetic infrastructure	• Opportunities for self-expression through recreation and culture

Theoretical Models of Youth Justice

When the juvenile court was created in 1908, the prevailing practice for dealing with youth crime was to provide as much intervention as possible to treat the young person. This perspective was based on the **medical model** of intervention suggesting that youth crime was due, not to an individual's free will or choice, but rather to factors that pushed the young person to commit offences. The way to deal with this behaviour was to provide treatment dispositions to attend to the needs of the young person for as long as was necessary to "cure" him or her.

Concerns about long treatment dispositions handed out in juvenile courts during the 1960s were raised by legal scholars; they argued that juvenile offenders should also be protected with the due process provisions of the adult system. This **justice model** still focuses on the protection of society through deterrence principles; however, in view of possible human error in the discovery and subsequent findings of guilt, those upholding this model believe young people should be accorded the same rights to legal protection as adults. Rather than seeing young people as in need of treatment regardless of guilt or innocence, the justice model emphasizes the right to legal counsel and the legal protections of innocence until proven guilty.

There are five possible models that can help us understand juvenile justice procedure: crime control, justice, welfare, community change, and restorative justice, which fall loosely on a right-to-left ideological continuum—that is, a continuum in which the right represents more conservative values and the left more liberal values (Reid & Zuker, 2005). Table 2.5 provides a comparison of the five models in terms of the main elements of the theoretical perspectives.

The **crime control model**, at the extreme right, is largely concerned with the protection of society and with assuring the public that crime will not be tolerated, and that once discovered it will be severely punished. In the middle is the **welfare model**, which stresses the importance of looking after the needs of the offender to ensure that his or her problems are treated so that crime will not recur. At the far left is the **community change model**, which stresses the importance of the broader community in looking after members of the community and addressing some of the root causes of crime, such as poverty, to ensure that all people have an opportunity to do well. Within this left end of the continuum is the **restorative justice model**, which includes accountability of the young person to the community for his or her crime but also reflects the community's responsibility for successful reintegration of young offenders.

The right end of the continuum is largely based on the philosophy of **deterrence**, and the idea that individual offenders choose to commit crime on the basis of their own personal gain. The left end of the continuum offers an explanation for criminal behaviour as being outside the individual and due to either individual, family, or community factors that push the young person into committing an offence. A great deal of criminological research has pointed up the strong positive correlation between poverty and other adverse societal and environmental factors and crime (as discussed in the previous section). The community change model suggests that disadvantage and the lack of access to resources for some members of society are underlying contributors to crime. From this perspective, all members of the community have an ongoing responsibility for prevention and rehabilitation of young people who come in conflict with the law.

The approach commonly referred to as restorative justice is based on some tenets of the community change model. Restorative justice puts the emphasis on healing relationships broken by conflict and crime. Viewed this way, crime is not simply an offence against the state, but also a violation of human rights and relationships and a disruption of the peace

---

medical model
a model of justice that focuses on intervention based on the belief that criminal behaviour is a sign of illness

justice model
a model of justice that focuses on the protection of society through deterrence principles; those upholding this model believe young people should be accorded the same rights to legal protection as adults

crime control model
a model of justice that is largely concerned with the protection of society and with assuring the public that crime will not be tolerated, and will be severely punished

welfare model
a model of justice that stresses the importance of looking after the needs of the offender to ensure that his or her problems are treated so that crime will not recur

community change model
a model of justice that stresses the importance of the broader community in looking after members of the community and addressing the root causes of crime to ensure that all people have an opportunity to do well

restorative justice model
an approach to justice that characterizes crime as harm done to people and relationships, and that encourages responses to crime that help repair that harm

deterrence
a philosophy of justice that holds that individual offenders choose to commit crime on the basis of their own personal gain

of the community. The approach encourages the participation of victims, offenders, and the community affected in finding solutions that will achieve reconciliation and restore harmony. It uses measures outside of the criminal justice system to respond to the crime, and recognizes the importance of engaging the community in meaningful dialogue about the best way to repair the harm and work toward a beneficial solution for both victim and offender, one that will ensure that the latter understands the impact of his or her behaviour.

As will be discussed in more detail in the chapters that follow, the elements of each of these models can be found in the legislation designed to deal with young persons who

TABLE 2.5   Comparison of the Theoretical Models of Criminal Justice

LEFT ← → RIGHT

	Restorative justice	Community change	Welfare	Justice	Crime control
Main idea	Commission of a crime affects not only the victim and the offender, but the wider community as well.	All of society is responsible for the promotion of the welfare of its citizens and must work together to prevent crime and delinquency.	The treatment needs of the individual offender and his or her family must be seen as a priority.	Any interference with an individual's freedom is limited with procedures based on consent by all parties as much as possible.	It is the responsibility of the state and the courts to maintain order in society.
How the causes of crime are viewed	All citizens have a role to play in the prevention and repair of the harm done when a crime is committed.	Criminal behaviour is seen as being determined by life consequences (e.g., poverty, lack of opportunity).	Behaviour is seen as being determined by social (e.g., family, peers, school) and psychological factors (e.g., individual problems).	Individual chooses to commit offences and the behaviour may be seen inaccurately due to human error of authorities.	Individual chooses to commit offences and authorities know how to deal with this using deterrence.
Individual or collective response	*Collective*: families, victims, and the community are involved to the greatest extent possible in rehabilitation, community safety initiatives, and holding offenders accountable.	*Collective*: Focus on society rather than the individual offender as being responsible for criminal conduct.	*Individual*: Focus on criminal conduct as part and parcel of other social events affecting the individual who needs rehabilitation or treatment (family dysfunction, alcohol/substance abuse, victim of family violence).	*Individual*: Focus on the repression of crime with a qualification that there is a high probability of error in informal fact-finding (i.e., need to have legal safeguards that protect individual liberty and rights).	*Collective*: Repression of criminal conduct through punishment, **denunciation**, and individual and general deterrence.
Criminal justice response	Individual is required to face the personal harm his or her behaviour has done to the victim and the wider community; **restitution, victim–offender mediation**, and community service form part of the restoration of the victim, the offender, and the community.	Focus on changing social processes (e.g., reduce poverty, enhance opportunities for recreation) that lead young people to engage in criminal conduct, and on improving the quality of life for all citizens.	Focus on an evaluation of the whole youth and his or her life circumstances; the person is brought to court to be aided and assisted to reduce risk factors that brought him or her to court.	Focus on formal adversarial system of justice; key is the protection of rights, legal safeguards, due process rights, right to a lawyer, right to appeal, right to legal representation at all stages of proceedings.	Focus on a screening process that diverts the innocent out of the courts (i.e., only the guilty go to court); no need for legal safeguards when young person brought to court; punishment based on deterrence.

come in conflict with the law. In order to be able to critically evaluate the provisions of the law, it is important to have an understanding of the theoretical orientations that are the basis of these legislative provisions.

FIRE SETTING: EXPLANATIONS, VICTIMS, AND INTERVENTIONS

Four boys were loitering outside a community centre watching the other young people come out after they had finished their swimming lessons or other organized sporting activity. They recognized some of the young people from school as they came out of the building and they came over to hang out. One of the youth, Jordan, decided to light up a cigarette. While he was lighting up he decided it might be fun to also light the cushion of the old couch they were sitting on, which had been left outside to be picked up by a local anti-poverty organization. The rest of the youth watched and thought it was pretty cool, and that it might be even more fun to set the whole couch on fire. Some of the youth who had left the community centre didn't think it was such a good idea and left. The four boys set the couch on fire, but it got out of control quickly and soon there was a grass fire. Because it had not rained lately, the flames spread across the lawn and started to engulf the community centre. The fire department was called, and it managed to put out the fire; but the centre was damaged and needed to be closed for renovation for six months.

QUESTIONS

1. Think about the models outlined above and determine how this scenario might be dealt with by each of the perspectives. What do you think are the main causes of the arson committed by the youth?

2. When thinking about this scenario, consider all of the victims that might be affected by the fire. See if you can add to the list below:
   - the families of the four boys, who are ashamed of their actions
   - youth who play sports in the centre
   - elementary school children who use the centre for games after school
   - adults who use the centre
   - parents who use the centre's daycare to mind their children while they are at work
   - seniors who use the centre to play bingo and cards
   - firefighters who had to put the fire out
   - community centre staff who are now temporarily laid off from work
   - the other kids who were with the boys, who feel ashamed that they did not do something when those four started playing with fire

3. What kind of reconciliation or intervention would you suggest for each of these victims and the four boys? Which model did you consider when you were thinking of the ways that you might design such an intervention? What would be different in the way you approached this case if you considered it from the standpoint of each of these models: crime control, justice, welfare, community change, restorative justice?

individual response
focuses on factors and behaviour related to a single person (e.g., mental illness)

collective response
focuses on broader issues in society that affect an individual (e.g., poverty)

denunciation
a way to communicate disapproval of a young person's actions as "wrong" through punishment

restitution
financial reparations owed by an offender to a crime victim who suffers a financial loss as a result of the crime

victim–offender mediation
negotiation between a victim and an offender, facilitated by a trained mediator, with the goal of resolving the conflict and constructing their own approach to justice as it relates to the specific crime

CHAPTER SUMMARY

A close look at the actual offences committed by young persons reveals a pattern of offences characteristic of youth. It was noted that not only are the offences different, but the risk factors and theories to explain youth crime are very different from those associated with adult offenders. Traditional crime reduction strategies such as deterrence and custodial sentencing used in the adult system appear to be less effective when applied to young people.

The most common youth offences continue to be property-related, with more than half of accused youth being found guilty of theft of $5,000 or under, mischief, and disturbing the peace. A common form of mischief is vandalism, often directed against schools, private residences, and shopping malls. Computer hacking, another form of vandalism, is also fairly common, with one self-report study of high school students reporting that 27 percent of respondents admitted that they had hacked a computer at some point.

Arson, a more serious form of mischief, has shown an increase in recent years. Children and youth set fires for various reasons: fascination with the act itself, curiosity or accident, a cry for help, delinquency, severe disturbance, cognitive impairment, and socio-cultural motivations.

The crime of break and enter by youth has been declining from 1998 to 2012, as has motor vehicle theft. While there are specific provisions within the *Criminal Code* to address "joyriding" by youth, the data indicates that motor vehicle theft in 2012 was 57 percent lower than 10 years earlier, and 4.2 percent lower than in 2011 for youth offenders.

Substance abuse of certain illicit drugs among youth seems to be in decline, with the most common offence still being possession of cannabis. In 2012, less than 17 percent of drug-related crimes involved youth; more than 67 percent were not charged. Most of the charges involved possession of cannabis. Possession of cocaine accounted for just 2.3 percent.

There are three levels of assault, with level 3 being the most serious. When youth commit violent offences, it is likely to be at the lowest level. Level 1 offences of youth dramatically increased when schools introduced zero-tolerance policies, under which behaviour previously dealt with by school personnel was now dealt with through more formal means such as calling police. Serious violence by youth is still relatively rare.

Despite the fact that many feel there has been an increase in violent crime committed by females, the increase in recent years has been recorded mainly in less serious offences such as those against the administration of justice. Girls are more likely to have additional charges laid against them for breaches of release conditions, and are more likely to be required to fulfill additional conditions of release than their male counterparts.

High-profile cases have caused much public concern about guns and youth gangs in Canada. Among the factors blamed have been availability of guns, alleged celebration of guns and violence in the culture, and violence as depicted in entertainment media. The effects of violent media on young people have been studied for many years. However, there has been controversy, with some suggesting that video games are part of growing up and any links to aggression are a byproduct of other processes in the life of the child.

Youth crime may be viewed from any of several perspectives: conflict theory, functionalist theory, labelling theory, symbolic interactionist theory, and social learning theory. The value of such perspectives is that they reveal assumptions that guide policies, interventions, and strategies for prevention.

There is growing evidence that poverty, unemployment, abuse, and family or school problems correlate to crime. Certainly they cause disadvantage, and those who are disadvantaged and lack resources are most likely to come into conflict with the criminal justice system. Key factors known to be related to youth crime can be grouped into the categories of individual, family, school, peers, neighbourhood/community, and environment.

Five models of youth justice procedure are helpful in sorting out the various processes employed in the youth justice system relative to theories of crime causation. While traditionally one may consider either crime control (deterrence and punishment) or welfare (treatment and guidance) in the youth system, there are variations of these models incorporating due process provisions (justice) and elements of community engagement (community change and restorative justice). Each of these models is embodied in the *Youth Criminal Justice Act*, and a good understanding of the provisions of each of these models is helpful in understanding the various legal provisions.

KEY TERMS

administration of justice offence, 34
car surfing, 32
collective response, 45
community change model, 43
conflict theory, 36
crime control model, 43
denunciation, 45
deterrence, 44
functionalist theory, 36
hacking, 29
ideology, 38
individual response, 45

justice model, 43
labelling theory, 37
medical model, 43
protective factors, 38
restitution, 45
restorative justice model, 43
risk factors, 38
social learning theory, 37
symbolic interactionist theory, 37
vandalism, 28
victim–offender mediation, 45
welfare model, 43

REFERENCES

Anderson, C.A. (2007). *Violent video game effects on children and adolescents: Theory, research, and public policy.* New York: Oxford University Press.

Andrews, D.A., & Bonta, J. (1998). *The psychology of criminal conduct* (2nd ed.). Cincinnati, OH: Anderson.

Artz, S., Stoneman, L., & Reitsma-Street, M. (2012). Canadian girls and crime in the twenty-first century. In J.A. Winterdyk & R. Smandych (Eds.), *Youth at risk and youth justice: A Canadian overview* (pp. 131–155). Don Mills, ON: Oxford University Press.

Boyce, J., Cotter, A., & Perreault, S. (2014). Police-reported crime statistics in Canada, 2013. *Juristat, 34*(1).

Controlled Drugs and Substances Act. (1996). SC 1996, c. 19.

Criminal Code. (1985). RSC 1985, c. C-46, as amended.

Dauvergne, M. (2013, June 23). Youth court statistics in Canada, 2011/2012. *Juristat.* Catalogue No. 85-002-X.

Dauvergne, M., & Johnson, H. (2001). Children witnessing family violence. *Juristat, 21*(6).

DeLisi, M.M. (2013). Violent video games, delinquency, and youth violence: New evidence. *Youth Violence and Juvenile Justice, 11*(2), 132–142.

Dembo, R., & Schmeidler, J. (2003). Classification of high risk youths. *Crime & Delinquency, 49*, 201–230.

Dhami, M. (2008). Youth auto theft: A survey of a general population of Canadian youth. *Canadian Journal of Criminology and Criminal Justice, 50*(2), 187–209.

Dittmann, M. (2004). Types of fire setters. *Monitor on Psychology, 35*(7), 42.

Earp, J. (Producer/Director), & Jhally, S. (Producer). (2013). *Tough Guise 2: Violence, manhood & American culture* [Motion picture]. Northampton, MA: Media Education Foundation.

Etengoff, A. (2009, November 20). Modern Warfare scriptwriter defends airport "massacre" scene. *TG Daily*. Retrieved from http://www.tgdaily.com/games/44742-modern-warfare -scriptwriter-defends-airport-massacre-scene.

Ferguson, C.J. (2007). The good, the bad and the ugly: A meta-analytic review of positive and negative effects of violent video games. *Psychiatric Quarterly, 79*, 309–316.

Freeman, J.M. (2011). *The health of Canada's young people.* Ottawa: Public Health Agency of Canada.

Geddes, J. (2013, August 28). Justin Trudeau and the politics of pot. *Maclean's*. Retrieved from http://www2.macleans.ca/ 2013/08/28/justin-trudeau-goes-to-pot.

Johnson, G., & Bauer, K. (2004). *Sociology and Canadian society* (2nd ed.). Toronto: Emond Montgomery, 2004.

Kong, R. (1997). Breaking and entering, Canada 1996. *Juristat, 18*(1).

Latimer, J. (2001). A meta-analytical examination of youth delinquency, family treatment, and recidivism. *Canadian Journal of Criminology, 43*(2), 237–253.

Leschied, A. (2011). The correlates of youth violence: Evidence from the literature. *International Journal of Child, Youth and Family Studies, 2*(1), 233–262.

Lipsey, M.W. (2009). The primary factors that characterize effective interventions with juvenile offenders: A meta-analytic overview. *Victims and Offenders, 4*, 124–147.

Loeber, R., & Farrington, D. (2003). *Child delinquents: Development intervention and service needs.* Thousand Oaks, CA: Sage.

MacKenzie, D.L. (2006). *What works in corrections? Reducing the criminal activities of offenders and delinquents.* Cambridge: Cambridge University Press.

Mills, R.M. (2006). Mental health and other service use by young children with fetal alcohol spectrum disorder. *Journal of Fetal Alcohol Syndrome, 4*, 1–11.

National Crime Prevention Centre. (2012). *A statistical snapshot of youth at risk and youth offending in Canada*. Ottawa: Public Safety Canada.

Perreault, S. (2013, July 25). Police-reported crime statistics, Canada 2012. *Juristat*. Catalogue No. 85-002-X. CANSIM Table 252-0051.

Perreault, S.A. (2010). Criminal victimization in Canada. *Juristat, 30*(2).

Reid, S.A., & Zuker, M.A. (2005). Conceptual frameworks for understanding youth justice in Canada: From the Juvenile Delinquents Act to the Youth Criminal Justice Act. In K.M. Campbell (Ed.), *Understanding youth justice in Canada* (pp. 89–113). Toronto: Pearson.

Reid-MacNevin, S., & Waddell, D. (2005). *Youth justice in Canada: A resource manual*. Toronto: Canadian Training Institute.

Sauve, J. (1997). Motor vehicle theft in Canada. *Juristat, 18*(1).

Sprott, J., & Doob, A. (2009). *Justice for girls? Stability and change in the youth justice systems of the United States and Canada*. Chicago: University of Chicago Press.

Statistics Canada. (2013). Canadian Centre for Justice Statistics, Uniform Crime Reporting Survey. Catalogue No. 85-002-X. CANSIM Table 0252-0051.

Tanner, J., & Wortley, S. (2002). *The Toronto and Youth Leisure and Victimization Survey: Final report*. Toronto: University of Toronto.

Turner, J. (2012, October 4). Youth gets max for apartment arson. *Sun News*. Retrieved from http://www.sunnewsnetwork.ca.

Weiss, M.D. (2011). The screens culture: Impact on ADHD. *Attention Deficit Hyperactivity Disorder, 3*, 227–334.

Youth Criminal Justice Act. (2002). SC 2002, c. 1.

EXERCISES AND REVIEW

Review Questions

1. What is the most common offence with which youth are charged?

2. Why is it important to consider the motivations for youth arson when determining an appropriate approach to preventing this for young people?

3. Describe the factors that distinguish assault levels 1, 2, and 3.

4. How are patterns of criminal behaviour of young females different from those of young males? How are they similar?

5. How might a functionalist theorist explain the relationship between lack of access to a good-quality educational environment and youth crime?

6. In what ways might being poor make a person more likely to be charged with a criminal offence?

7. What is the role of the school in ensuring that youth make a healthy transition from adolescence to young adulthood? What factors increase the risk for offending?

8. In what ways can family interaction positively and negatively affect youth crime?

9. What role does the peer group play in preventing or increasing the likelihood of involvement in criminal activities?

Discussion Questions

1. What role do risk factors play in helping an individual interested in designing a program to prevent youth crime? How might you go about designing such a program and what components would you like to have in place to address these factors?

2. Choose four factors that you think are most closely associated with causing someone to turn to youth crime. Explain why these factors are important and how they influence behaviour.

3. Imagine you are a criminal justice theorist who believes strongly in the labelling theory of youth offending. Consider various approaches to youth justice (denunciation, deterrence, restorative justice, and welfare model approaches) in turn, and explain which are most and which least likely, in your view, to exacerbate the labelling effect.

4. Why might a community change approach to youth justice be more complicated to implement than a crime control model?

PART II

Legislation

Legislative Framework: Criminal Offences

3

LEARNING OUTCOMES

After completing this chapter, you should be able to generally understand the purposes, structure, and contents of the *Youth Criminal Justice Act* (YCJA), specifically including an ability to:

- Appreciate similarities and differences between the current YCJA and earlier laws that sought to address youth crime in Canada.

- Understand where each of Canada's historical and current approaches fits along a spectrum of possible approaches to youth crime, and have an appreciation of some of the advantages and disadvantages of each approach.

- Understand the principles and objectives of the YCJA.

- Explain the overall structure and main sections of the YCJA.

- Identify the age jurisdiction of the YCJA.

- Define "extrajudicial measures" and what these mean in the context of the YCJA.

- Understand how the YCJA makes use of pre-trial detention.

- Know how the YCJA deals with privacy issues relating to publication and records.

- Appreciate ways in which the YCJA has changed as a result of the amendments made to it in 2012.

Introduction

This chapter provides an overview of the *Youth Criminal Justice Act* (YCJA), and puts the Act into historical context so that you can understand how the treatment of youth in conflict with the law in Canada has evolved over the years. Beginning with a historical overview of the treatment of young people who commit offences and a brief overview of the first youth criminal law in Canada known as the *Juvenile Delinquents Act*, the chapter discusses the differences in how the justice system treats adult and youth offenders.

A review of the introduction of the *Young Offenders Act* (new legislation created after a 25-year consultation) follows, and then an overview of the key provisions of each section of the *Youth Criminal Justice Act*.

Finally, the chapter looks at criticisms that have been made of the current law and how this law has evolved—and continues to evolve—over time.

In situating the current law in historical and theoretical context, this chapter shows how the current legislation both differs from and is similar to previous laws that dealt with criminal conduct by youth in Canada, and it explores how all those approaches might be understood as falling in different places along a spectrum of possibilities.

Fuller details about the sections of the YCJA and how the provisions are applied in practice are provided in later chapters; for example, Chapter 5 deals with the investigation of offences, Chapter 6 with the pre-trial period, Chapter 7 with trials, and Chapter 8 with sentencing. For ease of reference, the full text of the *Youth Criminal Justice Act* appears in Appendix A to this book, and you will be asked to refer to this from time to time as you delve deeper into the issues presented throughout these chapters.

The Range of Responses to Youth Offending: History and Possibility

The *Youth Criminal Justice Act* has not been in force for very long. Before it was enacted, two very different laws governed criminal offending by youth in Canada. First, the *Juvenile Delinquents Act* (JDA) (1970) was the guiding legislation for youth criminal justice for three-quarters of a century, from 1908 until the implementation of the *Young Offenders Act* (YOA) in 1984. The *Young Offenders Act* enjoyed a shorter tenure and was repealed by the *Youth Criminal Justice Act* (YCJA) in 2003. In turn, the YCJA came under strong criticism as soon as the Liberal government that enacted it lost power when Conservative Stephen Harper was elected prime minister in 2006. Calls to reform the legislation were made as early as 2006. By 2012, it had been amended significantly. Each legislative regime has been a creature of its time and a response, in part, to criticisms and the strengths of its precursor. To thoroughly understand the current legislation and its political and social context, it is useful to learn about the philosophies behind the prior statutes, and to understand the criticisms that led to their replacement.

Going back to the writing of Hebrew and Greek philosophers, we find evidence that in ancient times, children were not held to the same degree of responsibility for the commission of crimes as their adult counterparts. According to Aristotle, children were seen as being able to act voluntarily, but like animals and the insane, children did not possess the capacity for premeditation, and so could not be considered morally responsible for their acts. The legal doctrine of *mens rea* (guilty mind) can be traced to the moral philosophy of these early writers. The concept of "free will" or the ability to act on your own volition is the cornerstone of the principle of responsibility for crime. Throughout history, there are many accounts of children not having the ability to form intent for the same reason that "fools" could not be held responsible because of their inability to choose "good" over "evil" (Reid, 2013, p. 334).

Minimum and Maximum Age Jurisdiction in the Juvenile Justice System

Doli incapax is the notion that a child of tender years (under age seven) was incapable of an unlawful act because he or she was incapable of evil intent. This doctrine formed the basis of the first minimum age jurisdiction for criminal responsibility. Puberty was traditionally seen to be reached at age 14 in males and 12 in females. Children between the ages of 7 and 14 were considered accountable for their actions, but only if the proof of their intention to act was clear and certain.

Since April 1, 2003, the criminal prosecution of people in Canada who are aged 12–18 has been governed by the *Youth Criminal Justice Act*. Section 2 of the YCJA sets out its "age jurisdiction": only people aged 12 years or older and who are younger than 18 at the time of committing an alleged offence are covered by the law. After being found guilty, adolescents who were 14 to 17 at the time of the alleged offence may be sentenced as adults under certain conditions, as described later on in the Act and explored later in this text. People younger than 12 when they commit what would otherwise be considered a criminal offence cannot be prosecuted under Canadian criminal law, but, as is discussed in the next chapter, they are dealt with under the provisions of provincial child welfare legislation. People over age 18 are dealt with under the *Criminal Code*.

The separate and distinct treatment of adolescent offenders under the YCJA was affirmed by the 2012 amendments to the law. These amendments, while arguably making the law harsher for the most serious offenders, also provide that youth are to be kept in youth facilities (and not adult prisons) at least until they turn 18, even if they are serving an adult sentence.

doli incapax
a Latin term for the notion that young children are not capable of distinguishing between right and wrong

1. How do the ages in the current minimum and maximum age jurisdiction of youth court reflect the philosophy of the *doli incapax* doctrine?

2. What would be the rationale for increasing the lower age limit of youth court?

3. Is there any evidence in support of increasing the upper age limit to, say, 21 years of age?

In thinking about these questions, consider that during the 17th, 18th, and early 19th centuries, the "good and evil" test continued to be paramount in cases involving children. In the 19th century, the "classical" school of thought came to dominate criminology. This philosophy was premised on the assumption that people are rational beings capable of comprehending all consequences of their actions. The punishment for any deviation from the norm was proportionate to the seriousness of the offence committed. Thus, classical criminologists put emphasis on clear and precise laws, process, and dispositions, with few protections for the accused (Bolton et al., 1993).

THE DETERRENCE DOCTRINE

penology
the study of corrections and control of criminal offenders

Deterrence has recently been introduced into youth justice legislation with the amendments of the YCJA, but it is not a new philosophy in **penology**. It was developed by philosophers Cesare Beccaria and Jeremy Bentham, and has been a guiding philosophy of our criminal justice system since the 18th century.

These theorists believed that people in society had free will to choose criminality, and that the best way to deter them from committing crimes was to exploit would-be criminals' fear of punishment. Today, two types of deterrence are used in the criminal justice system: specific and general. *Specific deterrence* involves handing down punishments to individuals who have committed crimes to deter them from committing further crimes; *general deterrence* involves influencing would-be criminals by demonstrating that those who do offend are punished severely.

QUESTIONS

The effectiveness of general deterrence requires that would-be criminals be aware of the sentences handed down to other offenders.

1. Where do you think youth get their information about criminal sentences?
2. Is this information communicated to youth well enough to make deterrence effective?

By the end of the 19th century, there was growing dissatisfaction with the classical approach to criminology. A social movement led primarily by social workers and church workers mobilized in response to a perceived increase in juvenile crime rates and poor treatment of children in reformatories and industrial schools. These reformers sought to decrease the use of institutionalization, favouring a home-environment approach (Leon, 1977). If parents were unable to control their child's behaviour, probation officers and social service workers could be called on to provide support and encouragement in his or her home. In this way, the state could manifest its control over the delinquent child within the family.

positivist school of thought
a branch of social sciences that argues that human behaviour is a product of social, biological, or psychological forces

paradigm
a pattern to explain phenomena

In criminology, the **positivist school of thought** dominated the period between the late 19th century through the middle of the 20th century. While the classical approach emphasized rationality as the root of both adult and youth behaviour, the positivist **paradigm** allowed greater recognition of social ills as a cause. This new theory characterized crime prevention as a responsibility of society in general and sought to prevent crime by promoting the welfare of the population, shifting the emphasis from a punitive to a rehabilitative response. Unlike classical thinkers, positivists believed crime was caused not by a deliberate act, but by forces, such as societal and/or parental failure, that were out of the individual's control. Much like a patient suffering from a medical illness, a criminal should be "treated" and reintegrated into society. This approach, applied to youth criminality, set the stage for implementation of the JDA, which has been described as a product of a diverse social reform movement dedicated to "saving" or "rescuing" children from what were seen as undesirable and harmful aspects of life in the increasingly urbanized and industrialized society of the 19th and early 20th centuries (Leon, 1977).

CHILD SAVERS

The creation of the first juvenile justice system in Canada occurred during a time of great social change. The 19th century was a time of industrialization and urbanization, and few protections were in place for youth who got into trouble with the law; they would be prosecuted within the adult justice system and imprisoned in adult facilities. By the mid-19th century, there was a growing concern about the treatment and welfare of youth, and the group responsible for this shift in concern was known as the "child savers." These child savers, predominantly women, sought to bring awareness to society about children and youth at risk. Rather looking upon youth the same as adults, they argued that youth delinquency was a moral problem that required the state to step in and act as a parent to help reform the child. They believed wayward youth could be corrected with the appropriate interventions. It was the child savers who sparked change and the eventual creation of a separate juvenile justice system.

QUESTIONS

1. Why do you think it was Victorian women who led the movement to create the first juvenile court?

2. What was happening during that era that drew the women's attention to the plight of children?

The Juvenile Delinquents Act

The positivist approach was highly influential in the drafting of the JDA. Through this "welfare model" legislation, the drafters sought to integrate an approach based on the "best interests" of children, and a framework to address "delinquency" or misbehaviour. Children were not to be perceived as "criminal," but rather "misguided" and "misdirected."

PHILOSOPHY OF THE JUVENILE DELINQUENTS ACT

Section 3(2) of the *Juvenile Delinquents Act* provided:

> Where a child is adjudged to have committed a delinquency he shall be dealt with, not as an offender, but as one in a condition of delinquency and therefore requiring help and guidance and proper supervision.

Because of its welfare focus, the youth justice system created by the JDA was closely tied to social services. Lines between redress for adolescent offending and provision of social services for youth in need were blurred. The court's role was similar to that of a parent, intervening in the place of parents who were not able to effectively guide the child into adulthood. Section 38 stipulated that

> the care and custody and discipline of a juvenile delinquent shall approximate as nearly as may be that which should be given by his parents, and that as far as practicable every juvenile delinquent shall be treated, not as criminal, but as a misdirected and misguided child. ...

QUESTIONS

1. What is attractive about this approach to dealing with young people in conflict with the law?

2. How does this philosophy address some of the root causes of youth crime discussed in the previous chapter?

The JDA system was modelled on the ***parens patriae*** approach that dominated the English Chancery Court. *Parens patriae*, loosely translatable as "state as parent," is a legal doctrine or concept that emphasizes state protection of the property and lives of vulnerable persons. It implies a connection between flawed care and control (that is, usually "poor" parenting) and juvenile criminality. Reitsma-Street (1989, p. 512) noted:

> [I]f young persons committed crimes, it was evidence that a different combination of care and control by the family group or a state representative was needed to promote the young person's best interests.

parens patriae
the doctrine that the state has the responsibility to look after the well-being of vulnerable persons, such as youth, and to step in as parent if necessary

Hence, the same theorists who advocated at the end of the 19th century for *An Act for the Prevention of Cruelty to and Better Protection of Children* (1893) in Ontario lobbied hard for the welfare-oriented JDA. The common purpose of the two pieces of legislation was to protect "misdirected" young persons from their own "evil tendencies" and from becoming criminals, and to save them from wilful neglect and the prospect of "idle, dissolute, immoral lives" (Reitsma-Street, 1989, pp. 514–515). Even at the turn of the 20th century, there was an understanding that children's need for protection from corrupting tendencies was best achieved through early intervention: the age jurisdiction of the JDA extended from ages 7 to 16 or 17 years.

The court's structure under the JDA was procedurally informal. The purpose of this informality was to allow for ample flexibility in the design of rehabilitation programs suited to individual needs. Judges had almost infinite discretion to impose any disposition for an indeterminate length of time. The legislation specified little if any procedural rights for the alleged delinquent child. The court processes were "informal and speedy, not subject to the discipline of public scrutiny in the courts or in the press, judicial appeal, or **due process** procedures. Discretion and informality were promoted, despite the potential for coercive action" (Reitsma-Street, 1989, p. 515). Children had no explicit right to legal representation, and appeals were extremely limited. The court took a paternalistic stance, with the assumption that it knew what was in the child's best interests. The positivist philosophy underlying the JDA remained unchallenged for the first half of the 20th century.

A juvenile could be found to be "in a state of delinquency" for offences that were relevant only to youth, known as **status offences** (for example, truancy or skipping school, sexual impropriety). The juvenile court judges controlled the movements and decision making of young persons until such time as they were no longer "delinquent." Providing treatment and rehabilitation to these "wayward" youth often meant that long periods of custody in a "training school," "industrial school," or "reformatory" were imposed on children and youth who may not have committed any criminal offence, but had been seen to be incorrigible, truant, or otherwise disruptive to the maintenance of an orderly community (Reid-MacNevin & Kappell, 2003).

However, in the mid-20th century, women, racial minorities, and youth made remarkable gains toward recognition of their rights under law. This "rights revolution" and other socio-political influences of the late 1960s inspired an increase in critical writing on youth justice. The new research reflected a growing dissatisfaction with the JDA's paternalistic approach to youth criminality. Competing theories began to cast doubt on the effectiveness of rehabilitation for juvenile delinquents. Further, in response to the limited rights afforded to children under the JDA, many critics advocated due process in the administration of youth justice (Bolton et al., 1993).

Advocates for due process pushed for reform to the JDA. By the late 1960s, social workers and lawyers grew increasingly uneasy about the vast discretion given judges who sit in the juvenile courts. They argued that children should be accorded, at minimum, the same legal rights as adults. In the light of children's lack of sophistication and experience with the court system, many even advocated for *additional* rights.

The principle of due process requires that young people be regarded as persons, entitled to a minimum number of social goods because they are individuals and citizens (Reitsma-Street, 1989). Unlike the paternalistic approach of the JDA, a rights approach requires that criminal justice officials justify their control over an alleged delinquent. A shift toward children's rights was accompanied by a shift toward increased accountability in the recognition of society's rights to protection. When there is justification for intervention, the due process principle suggests, the state should impose the least restrictive means in balancing the interests of the individual criminal and society's need for protection.

due process

the doctrine that the state must respect all rights owed to a person under the *Canadian Charter of Rights and Freedoms*

status offence

a genre of criminal offence that is based not on the committing in the past of a particular prohibited action or inaction but on the allegation that the offender has a certain personal condition or is of a specified character

Supreme Court decisions in the United States set the stage for due process advocacy in Canada. Although a similar line of cases did not follow in Canada, a due process movement developed that sought reform through legislation.

US CASE LAW PAVES WAY FOR A NEW YOUTH JUSTICE REGIME

While the United States is a separate and distinct legal jurisdiction, decisions reached south of the border certainly influence the creation of Canadian legislation. Below are three examples of US cases processed under juvenile delinquency legislation in the 1960s that had a profound effect on the creation of new Canadian youth justice legislation.

The 1966 case *Kent v. United States* concerned a 1961 incident in which a youth, Kent, allegedly broke into a woman's home, stealing from her and then raping her. Upon arrest he was interrogated for seven hours, during which time he admitted his involvement in the incident. The judge simply moved the case to adult court where the accused was found guilty and sentenced to 30 to 90 years. After being upheld upon appeal, the case reached the US Supreme Court, which ruled that Kent was not afforded due process, and in fact did not receive some basic legal rights guaranteed to adults—namely, the right to have counsel present during interrogation and the right not to self-incriminate. It was held that *parens patriae* could not override procedural justice and that, while the court may be attempting to act as a "kindly parent" to address the "best interests" of the youth, the rules of the court must not be arbitrarily applied.

Just one year later, another due process case made its way to the US Supreme Court. *In re Gault* (1967) concerned a 15-year-old youth alleged to have made lewd phone calls to his neighbour. The complainant stated that she received a phone call in which she was asked questions such as "Are your cherries ripe today?" At the adjudication hearing, the complainant was not present and the proceedings were never recorded. This led to much disagreement among those present as to whether Gault admitted to making the phone call. Even though it was never really determined whether Gault had made the call (which would establish legal guilt), he was sentenced to an industrial school until age 21. For this same offence, an adult might get a minor fine or a maximum of two months' imprisonment. The issue that formed the basis of the appeal in Gault's case was that he was not advised of his rights, nor was he ever instructed about his right to counsel. He was found to have been denied the right against self-incrimination and the right to confront witnesses. In addition, his parents were denied notice of the proceedings. The US Supreme Court overruled the conviction, once again criticizing the *parens patriae* approach. Again, the idea that trying to assist a troubled youth would negate fundamental rights was seen as contrary to a first principle that due process rights are an essential aspect of the law for *all* accused persons.

A final noteworthy US case that drew attention to juvenile justice rights was *In re Winship* (1970). Winship was accused of theft after a woman discovered money had been stolen from her purse and saw Winship fleeing from a store. Neither she nor the store employees witnessed the youth take the money. At the hearing, he was found guilty on the basis of a "preponderance of evidence" (similar to the civil court usage of "balance of probabilities") as opposed to the "beyond a reasonable doubt" standard used in adult courts. The trial judge even admitted that there was reasonable doubt with the evidence but stuck to his initial ruling. Winship was sentenced to up to six years in a training school. Upon appeal to the US Supreme Court, the main issue raised was due process, and whether it could be obtained without using the standard of "beyond a reasonable doubt." Once again, the philosophy of youth justice courts was called into question: Was the primary goal to step in and save youth or to give them a fair trial? The court ruled that "beyond a reasonable doubt" must be the measure used in all criminal proceedings.

These cases, while American, demonstrate the evolution of fundamental rights for youth. With insights gleaned from *Kent*, *Gault*, and *Winship*, Canadian legislators insisted that due process be a cornerstone of the *Young Offenders Act*.

QUESTIONS

1. As we saw in Chapter 2, a great deal of youth crime is in the form of mischief, much like that of the case of Gault. Do you believe that due process rights are afforded young people in cases of mischief today? Why or why not?

2. What issues do you anticipate a young person might have in ensuring that he or she is able to instruct counsel on his or her wishes? How might these issues be remedied?

3. Do you think that *parens patriae* has a place in the youth justice system today? Why or why not?

The Young Offenders Act

The road from criticism of the JDA to enactment of the YOA was a particularly long one. In response to criticism levelled at the JDA, the federal government, in 1965, appointed a committee of the Department of Justice to research the problem of juvenile delinquency and offer its recommendations for legislative reform. The result was a lengthy report (Department of Justice, 1965) that led to a draft bill (Department of the Solicitor General, 1967) to replace the JDA. This was followed, in 1970, by Bill C-192, which died after second reading. As a result of the bill's failure, a solicitor general's committee was established to evaluate the proposed reforms. This eventually led to Bill C-61 (1981), which came into force as the *Young Offenders Act* in 1984.

Bolton et al. (1993) point to three important developments that contributed to successful reform in the late 1970s and early 1980s. First, empirical studies demonstrated that rehabilitative techniques consistent with the *parens patriae* system had been ineffective in preventing recidivism (recurrence of offending behaviour). Second, academics and professionals increasingly emphasized the potential of diversion programs, and more and more of these were becoming available. "Diversion" encompasses anything from community absorption plans to police screening, pre-trial diversion, and alternatives in sentencing (Law Reform Commission of Canada, 1975, p. 1). Third, Canadians were becoming more "conservative" in their ideological preferences, and this was reflected in their exaggerated perceptions of juvenile involvement in crime. The new legislation was a way the government could demonstrate its response to the public's various concerns.

To some extent, the resulting legislation incorporated a shift backward to the classical approach to juvenile justice that existed before the implementation of the JDA. This corresponded with a shift from a purely rehabilitative to a more punitive response to juvenile crime.

In breaking from a purely *parens patriae* approach, the YOA incorporated not only a rights-based framework but also elements of crime control. Although it sought to balance the rights of the child with the rights of society, the former were intended to be paramount; and, though to a lesser extent than under the JDA, "protection of young people and promotion of their best interests [were] still part of the philosophy of the YOA" (Reitsma-Street, 1989, p. 519). While many reformers wished to de-institutionalize the juvenile justice system and to introduce community-based treatment programs, others wanted to make youth more accountable and to introduce more protections for society from juvenile crime (Bolton et al., 1993).

This uneasy compromise was reflected in an internally contradictory declaration of principle (s. 3; see the discussion in the next section) that set the stage for abuse of judicial discretion (Reid-MacNevin, 1991). It is not difficult to see how a judge might interpret the YOA in a way that suited his or her own values. A judge who was biased toward "protecting society" might impose a lengthy custodial sentence in the name of "rehabilitation." By contrast, a judge with a bias toward "minimal intrusion" in a child's life might rely on s. 3(f) to justify no custody at all for a similar conviction. In *R v. T.(V.)* (1992), the Supreme Court of Canada commented on the disparity of approaches within the principle of the Act, concluding that it was not sufficient to have a singular approach to deal with the complex nature of youth criminality. Justice L'Heureux-Dubé held (at para. 29, quoting Bala & Kirvan, 1991, pp. 80–81):

> The YOA does not have a single, simple underlying philosophy, for there is no single, simple philosophy that can deal with all situations in which young persons violate the criminal law. ... The underlying philosophical tensions in the YOA reflect the very complex nature of youthful criminality. ... Judges and the other professionals who work with young persons who violate the criminal law require a complex and balanced set of principles. ...

Recalling the five models of youth justice discussed in the previous chapter (crime control, justice, welfare, community change, and restorative justice), what do you think the value is of having all of these models represented in a philosophy of youth justice? Might any unintended outcomes be expected as a result of a criminal justice worker having so many models to select from within the youth justice system?

Ironically, the YOA was widely accepted by all major political parties, academics, criminal justice officials, and the public at its inception in 1984. But shortly after its proclamation and for the ensuing years until its ultimate repeal, it attracted continual calls for reform, from two major schools of opposition: the "punitive response" critics argued that young offenders were getting away with overly lenient sentences, while the "rehabilitation" critics argued that the legislation did not go far enough in providing for meaningful rehabilitation and called for a return to legislation more similar to the JDA.

The punitive response critics argued that crime had increased since the enactment of the YOA and sought reform calling for tougher, longer sentences and provisions making it easier to have a young offender transferred to adult court. However, many "get tough" advocates failed to acknowledge that, under the YOA, there was actually a substantial increase in custodial sentences (though typically for shorter durations than those ordered under the JDA) (Bala, 1994), and the prevailing criminological research demonstrated that a more punitive approach to youth criminality was not likely to act as an effective deterrent (Leschied & Vark, 1989).

The rehabilitation critics, on the other hand, argued that since enactment of the YOA the rehabilitation ideal had been forgotten (Leschied & Gendreau, 1986). Many mental health professionals expressed concern about the legislation's original requirement, under s. 22, of consent on the part of those young offenders who are "detained for treatment." This prevented many youths from obtaining necessary treatment because a majority would not provide consent. The movement toward the requirement of young people to give their consent to medical procedures spilled over into the youth justice system and is perhaps the best example of the impact of the rights of young people being observed. Even in terms of a medical or psychological assessment that might determine an effective course of treatment by a professional, s. 22 of the YOA required young offenders to give consent. Some argued that the requirement of informed consent by a young person regarding assessment increased the likelihood that he or she would not be appropriately assessed (Awad & Perillo, 1988; Awad, 1991). However, others argued that "the real obstacle to the provision of rehabilitative services to young offenders [was] not s. 22, but rather the reluctance of provincial governments to provide adequate resources" (Bala, 1994, p. 248).

Other criticisms of the YOA were directed at what was perceived as its "overboard" response to calls for due process rights for youth. Many reformers, recognizing the great expense of our criminal justice system, fought to eliminate the YOA's guarantee of a lawyer at the state's expense. Many also believed that the standard for police questioning was too high because it often led to the exclusion of important evidence in circumstances in which the youthful accused was most likely guilty. These critics argued that judges should have been given the discretion to admit statements in circumstances of a good-faith effort on the part of police personnel to comply with the statute (Bala, 1994).

In a study of Miranda warnings (the US equivalent of *Canadian Charter of Rights and Freedoms* rights), it was found that the warnings given youth were too long, and given at a level sometimes above a grade 12 reading and comprehension level, making it difficult for young people to comprehend (Goldstein, Condie, Kalbeitzer, Osman, & Geier, 2003; Abramovitch, Peterson-Badali, & Rohan, 1995; Rogers et al., 2012). In a Canadian study of young offenders' ability to comprehend their right to legal counsel and right to silence, similar difficulties emerged. An earlier study showed that when looking at the relationship between age, IQ, and whether the individual had special education requirements, and the likelihood of a false confession, the only significant variable was age. This suggests that, given the age and stage of maturity of young people, it is important to recognize the possibility of false confessions from youth who may not understand their rights.

Considerable debate developed over the provisions dealing with access to information about the young offender. The first time the media was allowed in the youth court proceedings was with the advent of the YOA. Prior to this, under the JDA, proceedings were private. The opportunity to present some information about youth crime to the general public through news sources meant that the public, given a taste of the story for the first time in history without the identity of the offender, were thirsty for more. In its original form, the YOA restricted any public access to information about the offender. Many reformers argued that this denied the public the ability to ensure protection from offenders who were released. In 2000, the *Hamilton Spectator* published the name and young-offender record of a 19-year-old offender who was at large. The argument that was made by the newspaper was "the limitations of the Young Offenders law do not provide people with an understanding of the offender's past and potential threat" (CBC News, 2000). The publication led to criminal charges against four employees of the newspaper.

> What do you think of the publication of information about young people who come into conflict with the law? What might be the benefit to the general public? Are there any potential benefits for a young person?

In response, amendments to the YOA were made in 1986 to allow for greater access to information about the identity of young suspects and offenders in special circumstances. As will be discussed later in this chapter, this area has continued to be expanded under amendments made to the YCJA in 2012.

Despite this and numerous other amendments in the late 1980s and early 1990s, pressure to reconsider the entire system led to reform discussions and formal hearings and presentations as early as 1996. But the new *Youth Criminal Justice Act* followed a passage into law as rocky as that of its predecessor. A first attempt to pass it, in 1998–99, was unsuccessful. A second attempt, in March 1999, was similarly unsuccessful. When Parliament adjourned in June of that year, the bill died on the order paper. It was reintroduced as Bill C-3, but prior to its third reading an election was called and it again died on the order paper. In February 2001 the YCJA was introduced for a third time, as Bill C-7. Finally, after lengthy debate, on February 4, 2002 the House of Commons passed the *Youth Criminal Justice Act*.

Overview: Mapping Out the Youth Criminal Justice Act

preamble
an introduction that explains the intent and philosophy of a piece of legislation

While the YCJA describes how a young person is supposed to be dealt with when he or she is alleged to have committed a crime, many parts of the process of dealing with that young person still require people like police, lawyers, judges, and probation offers to rely on their judgment, make decisions, and interpret how the law should apply in any particular case. For this, the YCJA itself provides a great deal of guidance throughout, but general interpretive guidance is most significantly provided in its **preamble** and the declaration of principle (at s. 3). The preamble is not binding like other aspects of the legislation; it is intended only to be helpful in describing the values upon which the legislation is based.

Protecting the rights and freedoms of young persons is an inherent goal of the *Youth Criminal Justice Act*. This is reflected in the inclusion of the United Nations Convention on the Rights of the Child (UNCRC) as part of the preamble. Article 40 of the UNCRC requires that children who have violated the penal law be treated in a manner consistent with the child's age and with an eye to the desirability of the child's reintegration and his or her taking up a constructive role in society. The UNCRC urges diversion from criminal proceedings to extrajudicial solutions and socio-educational intervention, and consideration of imprisonment only as a last resort. (For ease of reference, the full text of the UNCRC appears in Appendix B to this book.)

UN CONVENTION ON THE RIGHTS OF THE CHILD

The United Nations Convention on the Rights of the Child (UNCRC) is the world's most ratified international convention. This legally binding international agreement first came into effect in 1989, and since that time 193 countries around the world have ratified it, Canada doing so in 1991. The UNCRC promotes the principle that all children have the right to a basic quality of life. Its 54 articles address such matters as: the right to be protected from abuse and exploitation; the right to education and health care; and the right of children to have a voice in matters that concern them. The convention has four guiding principles: non-discrimination; devotion to the best interests of the child; the right to life, survival, and development; and respect for the views of the child. In ratifying the UNCRC, the Canadian government committed to reflect these principles in its legislation, including the *Youth Criminal Justice Act*.

IN-CLASS DISCUSSION

Take a brief tour of the articles of the United Nations Convention on the Rights of the Child, and highlight with your peers three rights that you were not aware of prior to reading the document. Are you surprised that the rights you selected are protected in an international agreement?

Principles and Objectives of the Youth Criminal Justice Act

The YCJA is distinct from most legislation because an exceptional amount of information intended to guide its interpretation is provided throughout its text, in the preamble, the declaration of principle, and the sentencing principles.

Traditionally, the preamble to a piece of legislation serves as a guide to its legal intention, providing information about the values of the legislators and the objectives of the law. Of course, in interpreting a provision judges are required to look first to the wording of the provision itself. But where there is ambiguity, or doubt about the application to a situation, judges may look to the preamble for clues about the intent of the law's creators.

The preamble to the YCJA provides guidance about what is most important under the law: "[The YCJA] reserves its most serious intervention for the most serious crimes and reduces the over-reliance on incarceration for non-violent young persons." This statement epitomizes the philosophy of the YCJA and its practical effect—namely, the reduction in the use of incarceration for young people in general and non-violent ones in particular.

The balance of the preamble refers to general concepts such as "societal protection" and "effective rehabilitation." The concept of "accountability" through "meaningful consequences" gets particular new emphasis, reflecting widespread criticism that, historically, youth criminal justice legislation did not go far enough to ensure that offenders were held accountable.

Section 3 of the YCJA contains a declaration of principle intended to provide direction to professionals within the youth criminal justice system. As a numbered section, this declaration of principle, while similar philosophically to the preamble, is directly and specifically binding upon decision-makers. This is in contrast to a preamble, which is more of an aid to interpretation.

The drafters of the YCJA sought to remedy the lack of **statutory prioritization** by identifying, in s. 3(1), four primary principles. However, those principles were amended in 2012 (see the quotation below) to clearly indicate that the protection of the public should be emphasized as a primary goal of the legislation. Consequently, police and Crown prosecutors are asked now to consider protection of the public as paramount at the time of arrest and during youth court proceedings. This also limits their discretion to consider other factors.

> **3**(1) The following principles apply in this Act:
>   (a) the youth criminal justice system is intended to protect the public by
>   (i) holding young persons accountable through measures that are proportionate to the seriousness of the offence and the degree of responsibility of the young person,
>   (ii) promoting the rehabilitation and reintegration of young persons who have committed offences, and
>   (iii) supporting the prevention of crime by referring young persons to programs or agencies in the community to address the circumstances underlying their offending behaviour;

To summarize, the YCJA has articulated goals of

1. the long-term protection of the public;
2. a system separate from the adult system with special rehabilitative, procedural, and timeliness emphases;
3. culturally sensitive sentencing that promotes respect and reparations "within the limits of fair and proportionate accountability"; and
4. "special considerations" applicable to young persons, including full civil rights, sensitivity to victims, and support for parental involvement.

Each principle is followed by a list of sub-principles, such as rehabilitation, **reparation**, meaningful consequences, enhanced procedural rights, timely intervention, and notice to victims and parents. These sub-principles are designed to support the primary principles.

Although the drafters intended to clarify their message, it seems the considerable judicial discretion that has existed in the past will continue. Judges with differing personal values, for example, might view the means to the end differently. One may see rehabilitation as the best way to protect society, while another might see tougher sentencing as the answer. Further, young persons in conflict with the law require specialized treatment that reflects their individual histories and backgrounds. Judicial discretion, as a result, is an important part of the system's response to individual cases.

The declaration of principle specifies, at s. 3(1)(b), that the criminal justice system for youth must be separate from that of adults. This principle recognizes the reduced level of maturity and greater dependency of young persons, which in turn justifies the need for measures that ensure "proportionate accountability" for harm done.

As was discussed earlier, the philosophy of youth justice legislation changed from the singular focus of *parens patriae* under the *Juvenile Delinquents Act* to a multiple focus under the *Young Offenders Act*. The principles stated by the YOA contained all the models of youth justice procedure, and this created problems of lack of consistency across jurisdictions and variations in interpretation, perhaps sometimes due to the ideological biases of actors within the system. Unfortunately, the YCJA, when introduced, did not provide clear and uniform language to rank priorities. Even within the principles of s. 3, there are competing models of youth justice procedure, as shown here:

(a) the youth criminal justice system is intended to protect the public **{crime control}** by

(i) holding young persons accountable **{crime control}** through measures that are proportionate to the seriousness of the offence and the degree of responsibility of the young person, **{justice}**

(ii) promoting the rehabilitation **{welfare}** and reintegration of young persons who have committed offences, and

(iii) supporting the prevention of crime by referring young persons to programs or agencies in the community to address the circumstances **{community change}** underlying their offending behaviour; ...

Consider other subsections of s. 3 of the YCJA and determine whether the wording reflects one model or multiple models.

Principles of YCJA and Models of Youth Justice Procedure

The YOA was criticized because the philosophy and principles section had contradictory models and there was no rank order to the principles. This meant that, depending on the ideology or perspective of the youth justice professional, his or her own preferred model of intervention could be accommodated when making a decision about how to deal with a young offender. The YCJA attempted to respond to this problem by laying out a set of principles not only in s. 3, but also before the section on **extrajudicial measures** and sanctions (s. 4) and before the section on sentencing (s. 38).

Section 3 lays out a set of principles that are meant to govern how the Act is to be interpreted. In Chapter 2, we discussed models of youth justice procedure—namely, crime control, justice, welfare, community change, and restorative justice. As you go through each of these subsections here, you will note that even within a phrase more than one model of youth justice is sometimes exemplified:

extrajudicial measure
a way of dealing with offenders outside the formal justice system

---

3(1) The following principles apply in this Act:

(a) the youth criminal justice system is intended to protect the public **{crime control}** by

(i) holding young persons accountable through measures that are proportionate to the seriousness of the offence and the degree of responsibility of the young person, **{justice}**

(ii) promoting the rehabilitation **{welfare}** and reintegration of young persons who have committed offences, and

(iii) supporting the prevention of crime by referring young persons to programs or agencies in the community to address the circumstances **{community change}** underlying their offending behaviour;

(b) the criminal justice system for young persons must be separate from that of adults, must be based on the principle of diminished moral blameworthiness or culpability **{justice}** and must emphasize the following:

> (i) rehabilitation **{welfare}** and reintegration,
>
> (ii) fair and proportionate accountability **{justice}** that is consistent with the greater dependency **{welfare}** of young persons and their reduced level of maturity, **{welfare}**
>
> (iii) enhanced procedural protection **{welfare}** to ensure that young persons are treated fairly and that their rights, including their right to privacy, are protected, **{justice}**
>
> (iv) timely intervention **{crime control}** that reinforces the link between the offending behaviour and its consequences, **{crime control}** and
>
> (v) the promptness and speed **{crime control}** with which persons responsible for enforcing this Act must act, given young persons' perception of time; **{welfare}**
>
> (c) within the limits of fair and proportionate accountability, **{justice}** the measures taken against young persons who commit offences should
>
> (i) reinforce respect for societal values, **{crime control}**
>
> (ii) encourage the repair of harm done to victims and the community, **{restorative justice}**
>
> (iii) be meaningful for the individual young person given his or her needs and level of development **{welfare}** and, where appropriate, involve the parents, the extended family, the community and social or other agencies **{community change}** in the young person's rehabilitation and reintegration, and
>
> (iv) respect gender, ethnic, cultural and linguistic differences and respond to the needs of aboriginal young persons and of young persons with special requirements. ... **{welfare}**

---

1. What did you find surprising about the range of models present in s. 3?
2. Were there any other phrases that might be reflective of differing models that were not highlighted?
3. Were any highlighted words or phrases categorized as a specific model that you don't agree with?
4. If you were given only the principles section of this legislation, would you know how to intervene in the lives of young people in conflict with the law?

According to the Department of Justice, the 2012 amendments to the YCJA changed the principle section to: (1) "highlight the protection of the public as a key goal of the youth justice system" and (2) recognize a fundamental tenet of justice identified by the 2008 Supreme Court case *R v. D.B.* (discussed more fully in Chapter 8) that the youth justice system must be based on the "principle of diminished moral blameworthiness or culpability of young persons."

Do you think that these amendments have made it clear which model of youth justice procedure is to be followed when dealing with young persons in conflict with the law?

Part 1: Extrajudicial Measures and Extrajudicial Sanctions

Part 1 of the YCJA authorizes the use of *extrajudicial measures*—ways of dealing with offenders outside the formal justice system—with respect to youth who commit offences. Section 4(d) states that such measures are appropriate if "they are adequate to hold a young person accountable for his or her offending behaviour." Extrajudicial measures may include pre-charge diversion—including the administration of **police (or Crown) cautions** and referrals to community mental health facilities.

Section 6 requires the police to consider, before laying a criminal charge, the following options: (1) take no action, (2) warn the young person, and/or (3) refer the young person to a community-based program. These measures are discussed in greater detail in Chapter 5—along with more onerous extrajudicial **sanctions**, which consist of a type of extra-judicial sentence (usually, attendance at a community program or performance of community service).

The most formal type of extrajudicial measures (formerly called *alternative measures*) may be administered either pre-charge or post-charge, and require the young person to accept responsibility for the behaviour that precipitated the police involvement. Accepting responsibility is not the same as pleading guilty, but the police must show that there is sufficient evidence to proceed with a charge. If the young person fails to complete the requirements set out in the extrajudicial sanction, the case may continue to the court process. It is important to note that extrajudicial sanctions are intended only to be used when a caution, warning, or referral is not suitable.

The line between the informal processes of extrajudicial measures and more formal procedures in court has become more blurred by the 2012 amendments to the legislation. As of 2012, police are required to keep records of youth's participation in extrajudicial measures programs. Further, the YCJA now allows for the imposition of a **custodial sentence** on a youth who has failed to complete extrajudicial sanctions and is subsequently convicted of the offence.

Part 2: Organization of the Youth Criminal Justice System

Section 13(1) provides for provincial courts and judges with specific jurisdiction over YCJA proceedings. These courts, designated *youth justice courts* or simply *youth courts*, have exclusive jurisdiction over youths in conflict with the law under the YCJA. Section 14 states that "a youth justice court has exclusive jurisdiction in respect of any offence alleged to have been committed by a person while he or she was a young person."

Trial by Judge and Jury

Under the YCJA, unlike under earlier laws, there is no provision stating that all offences shall be treated as summary conviction offences. This means that the separate procedures for **summary conviction** and **indictable offences** that exist under the *Criminal Code* also apply to offences under the YCJA. This introduction of more formal procedures for serious offences is intended to bolster and support the expressed principle in the YCJA that youth have rights, including procedural rights under the criminal law. Thus, for certain indictable offences, youth in conflict with the law are, like adults, entitled to a trial by jury. For summary conviction offences, the youth is tried by a judge alone and does not have the right to a trial by jury.

Part 3: Judicial Measures

The first provision (s. 23) in this part allows the attorney general to establish a "program of pre-charge screening" that sets out circumstances in which his or her consent must be obtained for prosecutions in the jurisdiction to which the program applies. Where such a program is established in a jurisdiction, police officers will need to abide by its rules when considering a charge against a young person.

police (or Crown) caution

an extrajudicial measure that consists of a formal warning, which might include a letter to the youth (and parents) and/or a dedicated meeting at a police station to discuss the incident

sanction

a penalty that requires a young offender to accept responsibility for the act that forms the basis of the offence and to comply with certain terms and conditions, failure to comply with which can result in prosecution of the offence

custodial sentence

a judicial sentence that requires a term of either open or secure imprisonment of the offender

summary conviction offence

a minor offence carrying a maximum penalty of six months in jail, or a fine

indictable offence

the most serious of offences, which carries a maximum penalty of life imprisonment

The Right to Counsel in the Youth Court Process

Youth in conflict with the law have the right to consult counsel (that is, lawyers; s. 25). This right is guaranteed to all persons under s. 10(b) of the *Canadian Charter of Rights and Freedoms* rights, which states that everyone has the right to retain and instruct counsel without delay upon arrest or detention, and to be informed of this right. The right to consult with a lawyer arises early, even if the youth has not yet been charged, including "before and during any consideration of whether, instead of starting or continuing proceedings against the young person under this Act, to use an extrajudicial sanction to deal with the young person" (s. 25(1)).

The right to counsel includes the right to be informed of that right without delay, and the right to an opportunity to exercise the right. This means that to comply with this right, police must not only provide youth with information but also take steps to ensure that he or she can make use of it. There are also special "enhancements" of the right to counsel that adult suspects do not have, such as special notice provisions (including mention of the right to counsel in notices to parents in s. 26 and elsewhere) and a court's power to order that a youth be represented by counsel independent of counsel for the parents.

It is important to recognize that a young person's right to counsel is a personal right. In other words, the young person has the right to instruct counsel regardless of the wishes of his or her parents.

Parental Involvement in the Youth Court Process

Parental involvement in a youth's case is of particular concern, especially because many parents pay their child's legal costs. Most parents are very helpful to their children in such a crisis. However, many who are angry with or embarrassed by their child put pressure on their child and his or her lawyer to plead guilty as a form of punishment and to get on with the process. They press for such initiatives on their own against the child's wishes and even the child's best interests. For this reason, s. 25(8) empowers a youth court judge to order legal representation independent of the child's parents.

The YCJA contains provisions dealing with parental notice of a child's arrest. Section 26(1) requires that an officer in charge must, as soon as possible, give notice to parents of their child's arrest "stating the place of detention and the reason for the arrest." Furthermore, s. 27(1) authorizes a youth court to order a parent's presence "if in its opinion the presence of the parent is necessary or in the best interests of the young person." Section 27(4) enables a court to hold a parent in contempt if he or she fails to appear following an order. Unlike adults, young people also have the right to contact and consult with their parents or with a responsible adult before being questioned by police. That right is in addition to their right to consult counsel before providing a statement to police.

WHAT ROLE SHOULD PARENTS PLAY?

In a study of parental involvement in the youth justice system, Varma (2007) concludes that parents are an underutilized resource, acting mainly as bystanders in the court proceedings unless invited to speak or act as a surety in a bail hearing or supervise their son or daughter upon release.

In a few cases, parental presence in the courtroom was acknowledged by the judge as a mitigating factor in sentencing. In one case, where the youth was convicted of theft under $5,000, the judge stated: "Your parents are here and I appreciate them coming. They're hard working people and I don't think they want to be here. Let's make this the last time you're here."

In other cases, the victim was also the parent. In a case where a mother was assaulted and had her credit card stolen by her 13-year-old son, the mother was asked by the judge whether the attacks had been provoked, to which she replied that they had been arguing. In this case, the judge stated, "I have a problem with a conditional discharge. Two violent attacks on the mother … so … this is contrary to public interest." Even though the mother had indicated her willingness to support her son, the judge felt compelled to impose a stricter sentence (Varma, 2007).

QUESTION

What kind of role do you think parents might play as active participants in the youth justice system?

Detention of a Young Person Before Sentencing

For many youths charged with committing an offence, pre-sentencing detention is the first time they have been placed in a facility outside their community. The experience can be extremely traumatic and intrusive in their lives, because they are separated from their friends, families, and schools. For these reasons, there are numerous restrictions on the use of pre-trial detention. However, in 2012, the YCJA was amended to allow for pre-trial detention in expanded circumstances.

Medical and Psychological Reports

Section 34 of the YCJA empowers a youth court judge to order a psychological assessment of a young person by a "qualified person." The purposes for which an assessment may be ordered are listed in s. 34(2) and include the need to make a decision with respect to pre-trial release, the imposition of an adult sentence, and the making or review of a youth sentence. In certain appropriate cases, a youth may (under s. 34(4)) be **remanded** (ordered to be held) in custody for a period not exceeding 30 days for a psychological assessment, but there is a general presumption against remand for this purpose.

remand

to put (a defendant) on bail or in custody, especially when a trial is adjourned; committal to custody

The final medical and/or psychological report must be given to the youth, his or her attending parents, the youth's counsel, the prosecutors, and any parent of the young person who has an active interest in the proceedings and who was not present in court. Under s. 34(10), disclosure of the final report may be withheld from the young person, from his or her parents, or from or a private prosecutor, if it could impede the young person's rehabilitation, or physically or mentally endanger another person. This is qualified, however, where "the interests of justice make disclosure essential" (s. 34(11)).

WHERE THERE IS CONSENT

When the YOA was introduced in 1984, one of its central guiding principles was that youth must have the same legal rights accorded to adults and the same protections guaranteed by the *Canadian Charter of Rights and Freedoms*. An area that received much attention was s. 22(1), which required a youth court judge to obtain a youth's consent before referring him or her to treatment. This requirement continues under s. 42(8) of the YCJA. Consider the mandate of consent in the following case study, described by Leschied and Jaffe (1986).

S. was a 14-year-old ward of the state when she was charged with theft over $2,000. The incident was her third offence, which she committed while on probation. She was found guilty and sentenced to secure custody, where she was also referred for an assessment. The assessment revealed that she had been self-harming, had expressed suicidal thoughts, and had had a history of running away. It was also revealed that S. had had a traumatic childhood and was now suffering from depression. After a short time in the closed custody facility, staff determined that S. had psychological needs that required more vigorous intervention than was available at the institution, and upon review the judge recommended a five-month stay at a treatment facility. S. reluctantly agreed to enter the in-treatment program, but just four days into her placement she ran away. When apprehended after running away, S. said, "All right, fine then, I will do your stupid treatment if you promise to let me go afterwards."

For consent to be valid, it must fulfill four conditions. It must be

1. given voluntarily
2. given by a patient who has the capacity to give it
3. specific to the treatment and the provider
4. informed

The first condition, voluntariness, requires that a youth must have made a decision without "undue influence" or threat of repercussions.

For a young person to have the capacity to consent, he or she must be able to understand the information relevant to a decision about treatment, and appreciate the foreseeable consequences of consenting or choosing to withhold consent.

It is of utmost importance that the relevant details about the treatment plan be provided before consent is accepted. Many argue that for the condition of specificity to be met, even the person providing the treatment must be named.

Informed consent involves ensuring that the young person is given all the relevant information prior to deciding to consent. This can include but is not limited to

- a description of the treatment
- the benefits of the treatment and the likelihood of achieving such benefits
- whether the treatment is necessary or elective
- the urgency of the treatment
- the risks during the treatment and the likelihood of each risk materializing
- alternative available treatments and related risks
- the consequences of refusing treatment
- the consequences of receiving the treatment
- the recommendations of the physician regarding whether the treatment should be given or not
- any information the patient specifically requests

QUESTIONS

1. Looking back to the case of S., work through each of the four aspects of consent to see if they have been fulfilled in her case.

2. Now that you have a fuller appreciation of the concept of consent in the Canadian legal context, can a young person ever meet the qualification of valid consent?

Referral to Child Welfare Agency

Section 35 of the YCJA allows the youth court, "[i]n addition to any order that it is authorized to make," to refer a young person to a "child welfare agency for assessment to determine whether the young person is in need of child welfare services." This option was not included in the previous legislation and was drafted in response to critics who believed that judges, for lack of a suitable alternative, were sending some young persons into custody to get them out of difficult living circumstances or in the hope that rehabilitative programs would help them. The inappropriateness of this approach is condemned in s. 29(1):

29(1)   A youth justice court judge or a justice shall not detain a young person in custody prior to being sentenced as a substitute for appropriate child protection, mental health or other social measures.

However, unless appropriate child welfare funding is available to support such referrals, scarce resources will limit the benefit of the common sense and good intentions behind the provision.

THEFT OF PEPPERONI: NO LONGER A YOUTH COURT MATTER

In a decision of the Nova Scotia Supreme Court on January 20, 2004, K.D., a 14-year-old girl, had been charged in December 2002 with theft of "pepperoni." Subsequent to the initial charge a number of breaches related to undertakings related to curfew, living where directed, and going to school were laid. Despite recommendations against a custodial sentence, the young person was remanded for approximately one month awaiting trial, at which the sentencing judge imposed a period of custody for 90 days. The Court of Appeal quashed the custodial sentence, and in reviewing the sentencing judge's decision found that there had been a number of errors in law; the Nova Scotia Supreme Court went so far as to say that the sentencing judge had "misinterpreted or misapplied each of the sections she referred to" (at para. 12).

The issue before the sentencing court was that the young person was a troubled 14-year-old unable to return home to live with her parents, and it was believed that she was living on the streets. It was clear that the issues presented by the young person were more child welfare matters, and that the use of custody as a substitute for child protection, mental health, or other social measures was in violation of s. 39(5) of the YCJA. This decision clearly underscored and corrected many of the problems under the YOA, whereby young people who would have been better served through social services were being incarcerated due to the lack of appropriate child welfare services. The judge remarked that "the entire series of events started with the primary offence where this troubled young person took a piece of pepperoni" (at para. 24).

Further, "a young person who has committed a relatively minor offence but has serious psychological needs that seem to have contributed to the behaviour should receive a sentence that reflects the seriousness of the offence and not the seriousness of the psychological needs" (at para. 15). This decision underscores the move away from the welfare model that underpinned the *Juvenile Delinquents Act*.

QUESTIONS

1. Thinking back to the discussion of whether *parens patriae* has a role in youth justice today, how does this case affect your opinion?

2. What kinds of services do you believe are integral for the prevention of youth crime such as that found in this case?

Part 4: Sentencing

Because youth are subject to the same criminal law as adults, it is important to return to the preamble of the legislation in order to more clearly understand the intent of the legislation:

> AND WHEREAS Canadian society should have a youth criminal justice system that commands respect, takes into account the interests of victims, fosters responsibility and ensures accountability through meaningful consequences and effective rehabilitation and reintegration, and that reserves its most serious intervention for the most serious crimes and reduces the over-reliance on incarceration for non-violent young persons …

> On the basis of this passage only, what kinds of sentences do you anticipate the YCJA might impose? How would you use the models of youth justice to assist you in making sentencing decisions? Which elements would you want include in your dispositions to ensure that you were addressing the needs of victims?

Some have argued that the sheer number of provisions that speak to sentencing in the YCJA suggests it is primarily a sentencing statute. Provisions relating to sentencing and the administration of youth custody and supervision are covered by 72 of the YCJA's over 200 provisions. Section 42 alone, which sets out the range of sentences available, is more than 2,500 words long. Not only are these provisions very complex; they have proven controversial and have gone through a number of amendments since the law was enacted.

Prior to the enactment of the YCJA, Canada was criticized for having one of the highest youth custody sentence rates in the world. In an attempt to remedy this problem, the YCJA has a guiding provision, s. 38, which establishes the purpose(s) of sentencing in the youth court system:

> **38**(1) The purpose of sentencing … is to hold a young person accountable for an offence through the imposition of just sanctions that have meaningful consequences for the young person and that promote his or her rehabilitation and reintegration into society, thereby contributing to the long-term protection of the public.

Section 38(2) outlines sentencing principles in addition to the overriding principles in s. 3 of the YCJA, which can be summarized as follows:

- *No greater than adult punishment.* A young person should not receive a punishment greater than that of an adult convicted for the same offence in similar circumstances.
- *Regional consistency.* The sentence must be similar to sentences imposed on young persons found guilty in the same region of the same offence in similar circumstances.
- *Proportionate to offence and responsibility.* The sentence must be proportionate to the seriousness of the offence and the degree to which this particular young person was responsible. (For example, the question might be considered whether there was a co-accused or some "ringleader" this young person was following along with.)

- *Priority to non-custodial sanctions.* For all young persons, and especially Aboriginal youths, custody is a last resort. This means that all available sanctions other than custody are to be considered before a custodial sentence is imposed.

- *Rehabilitation/reintegration.* The sentence must be one likely to rehabilitate the young person and reintegrate him or her into society, and to promote a sense of responsibility and an acknowledgment of the harm done to victims and the community.

As will be discussed later in this book, the YCJA's sentencing regime has been expanded in terms of how it deals with the most serious offences. When first enacted, it did not allow for deterrence and denunciation to be used as principles in sentencing. However, in 2012, Bill C-10, the *Safe Streets and Communities Act* (an omnibus crime bill), was passed. It made sweeping changes to many facets of Canada's criminal law, including establishing specific deterrence and denunciation as sentencing principles for youth. It also expanded the definition of a "dangerous violent offence" to include reckless behaviour endangering public safety (s. 167). There is also provision for adolescents aged 14 or over who have committed very serious offences to be sentenced as adults once a guilty finding has been reached. As of 2012, Crown counsel now have to indicate before a trial commences that they will be seeking an adult sentence.

Sentencing will be covered in greater detail in Chapter 8.

CASE IN POINT

R v. K.D., [2003] NSJ No. 165 (SC)

In *R v. K.D.* (2003), one of the first reported cases under the YCJA from the Nova Scotia Supreme Court, Justice Lynch gave a **judicial reprimand** to a 15-year-old girl who had been charged with assault and uttering threats while she was being restrained at her group home residence. The young girl had eight prior findings of guilt related to uttering threats (*Criminal Code*, s. 264.1) and assault (*Criminal Code*, s. 266) committed under similar circumstances whereby she received community service work caring for animals as a sentence. The pre-sentence report indicated that she had had a "horrendous" background and had been the victim of physical abuse and neglect, including being locked in cupboards (at para. 2). Since the age of nine, the youth had been living in the Children's Response Program, which is part of the I.W.K. hospital in Halifax. Her psychiatric and psychological assessment reports prepared for the court indicated a number of behavioural problems and mental health conditions (ADHD, oppositional defiant disorder, conduct disorder, posttraumatic stress disorder, and attachment disorder).

    K.D. acted out in an aggressive manner when a physical restraint was put on her for disciplinary measures. The doctor who had been treating her for the previous six years wrote in the pre-sentence report: "K.D. is a young adolescent who requires specialized care within a nurturing environment in an attempt to undo the effects of institutionalized behaviour patterns" (para. 7). Further, the team leader of the Child Response Program wrote: "The child has been failed by the system. A lot of her behaviours in the past two years have been out of despair and institutionalization" (para. 10).

    In her statement of reasons, the judge discussed meaningful consequences in the context of the young person's multiple psychological and psychiatric diagnoses and her limited cognitive abilities. The judge made it clear that the agencies responsible for assisting this young girl were not to offload their responsibility onto the justice system: "The requests that have been made in the presentence report with regard to why I should sentence her to probation or why I should sentence her to community service work are, as I said, not the job of sentencing. They are the job of the Department of Community Services and the

judicial reprimand
a stern warning from a judge

Department of Health. They are to provide those opportunities to her" (para. 17). The pre-sentence report indicated that there had been some success with a change in medication and the completion of anger management programs and that she had had fewer incidents of being removed to a secure unit at the I.W.K. hospital. The judicial reprimand to the youth was as follows (paras. 20–21):

> I understand that the situation is not a good one at this point, but I want you to understand that those people do not deserve to be physically assaulted by you. Do you understand that? You have to use your best efforts, as it appears you have been trying to, to keep your anger under control. … [Y]ou have a history of this type of behaviour and I have to take that into account. I have to take into account the fact that the description of your last six years at the Children's Response Pro-gram, the fact that it has not been an appropriate placement for you, but I think that you have to bear in mind that the people that work with you do not deserve the behaviour that you have shown to them. I want you to keep that in mind.

The sentencing option of a judicial reprimand was new to youth justice legislation when it was introduced with the *Youth Criminal Justice Act*. With this, a youth is given a lecture by the judge when it is believed that the reprimand will suffice in holding the youth account-able for his or her offence(s). This form of diversion is unique to the youth justice system—it is not an option with adult offenders. Should this provision remain in the legislation as a method to deal with youth who have broken the law?

Let's now examine this case through the lens of each model of youth justice procedure.

QUESTIONS

1. Using the welfare model, how would the judge have handled this case?

2. What if the judge had used the justice model?

3. Finally, would the outcome for K.D. have been different if the crime control model had been utilized?

4. Looking at this case from a legislative perspective, K.D.'s case occurred under the YCJA. How would the outcome have been different if she had been living in the 1970s when the JDA was in force? in the 1980s when the YOA was in force?

Part 5: Custody and Supervision

Part 5 of the YCJA contains provisions dealing with the administration of custodial sen-tences, including the appointment of youth workers, programs for reintegrating offenders into the community, the review of custodial sentences, and facility choices and/or transfers (open or secure custody, youth or adult facility, and so on). These issues are dealt with separately from the sentencing provisions, largely because post-sentencing decisions are often made not by the youth court (although certain decisions do require court approval or involvement) but by administrators in the youth custody system, who have considerable discretion with regard to how a court-imposed sentence will be carried out.

The purpose of youth custody and supervision is set out in s. 83 of the YCJA, which states that this system is designed to contribute to the protection of society through safe, fair, and humane measures while at the same time assisting the young person to be re-habilitated and reintegrated into society.

For custody to be considered, a youth's case must meet at least one of the following four criteria:

- The youth has committed a violent offence.
- The youth has failed to comply with two or more previous non-custodial sentences.
- The youth has a "pattern of findings of guilt" (that is, two or more previous occasions) *and* the offence is one in which an adult would receive a sentence of more than two years.
- It is an "exceptional" case, in which the aggravating circumstances make it impossible to provide a non-custodial sanction.

If all four criteria are met, the length of the custody imposed is determined by the offence and the degree of responsibility of the young person, and is not to be determined by such factors as the time needed to treat the youth in a custodial program. Some evaluation research has suggested, for example, that it might take more than six months of drug rehabilitation in a residential facility, which might be longer than an appropriate sentence for the type of offence committed. (Remember, under the JDA, juveniles might be kept in custody until their 21st birthday, regardless of the offence.) All offences except the most serious ones (known as "presumptive offences") are considered to receive one-third custody and two-thirds community/reintegrative supervision orders.

Part 6: Publication, Records, and Information

Restrictions on the disclosure of youth records have long been an important part of Canada's laws in relation to the criminal responsibility of youth. Such restrictions have been intended to protect the privacy of youth in conflict with the law. It has been thought that minimizing stigmatization or "labelling" would increase the likelihood of rehabilitating these youths.

There are extensive provisions in the YCJA relating to when it is—and isn't—permissible to publish identifying information about young persons in conflict with the law. Section 110(1) of the YCJA establishes that "no person shall publish the name of a young person, or any other information related to a young person, if it would identify the young person as a young person dealt with under this Act." However, the ban is not absolute.

Section 110(2) contains three major exceptions: (a) a case where a young person is subject to an adult sentence; (b) a case where a young person is subject to a youth sentence for a "presumptive offence" (see definition in s. 2—certain violent offences) or is designated a "violent offender"; and (c) a case where the publication of information is "made in the course of the administration of justice, if it is not the purpose of the publication to make the information known in the community." For example, the police may be required to publicize identifying information about a young person at large if it will aid them in their search for and ultimate arrest of an alleged offender. In all three of these cases, the ban on publication does not apply.

The general ban on publication of identifying information also applies to victims and witnesses under 18 years of age and involved in youth court proceedings (s. 111(1)). Once the victim or witness turns 18, he or she is entitled to publish or "cause to be published" such information.

However, new exceptions to the general ban on publishing identifying information about youths were introduced by the 2012 amendments to the YCJA. Now the names of youth convicted of violent offences may be published (*Safe Streets and Communities Act*, ss. 185 and 189, amending YCJA, ss. 75 and 110(2)(b)).

PUBLICATION BANS AND FACEBOOK

As you have learned, there is a ban on the publication of the identity of any youth dealt with under the YCJA. Despite strict regulations, in the age of social media new questions have emerged about what constitutes a publication violation. One of the social media sites at the centre of this discussion is Facebook.

In 2008, four teenagers in Camrose, Alberta were charged after it was discovered that they had broken into a neighbour's home and killed a family cat in the microwave. Shortly after the crimes became known, a Facebook page appeared that not only posted the identity of the teens, but also accumulated many threats to their safety. The police eventually shut the web page down for being in violation of the YCJA and commented that the page would infringe on the youth's right to fair trial.

Another example, also occurring in 2008, involved the publication of the name of a youth victim, which is also a violation under the YCJA. In this case, a 13-year-old girl was stabbed to death by a 17-year-old boy and a 15-year-old girl on New Year's Day in Toronto. For 24 hours after the girl's death, a publication ban was in place so that authorities could first secure consent from the victim's parents to release the name. Despite this ban, a memorial Facebook page was posted identifying the victim. In this particular case the web page was allowed to remain, the police stating they would only remove it if a complaint were lodged by the victim's parents.

Both cases illustrate the challenges faced by legislation such as publication bans in an era of increasingly accessible information through social media.

QUESTIONS

1. What is your opinion about the use of social media to transmit information about criminal events?

2. Does Facebook constitute "publication" of news?

3. How do provisions in the Charter apply to social media (for example, freedom of expression)?

Access to Youth Records

Sections 114 to 124 of the YCJA specify who may keep or have access to youth records. A youth justice court, a review board, or any other court may keep a record of any case that comes before it. A record of any alleged offence may be kept by any police force that participated in the investigation of a young person. These police records may also be kept by the Royal Canadian Mounted Police in a central repository for the purpose of keeping criminal history files. The government or any agency of the government may keep records for the purpose of investigating an alleged offence, for use in youth court proceedings, for determining sentencing and the appropriateness of extrajudicial measures, or as a result of the administration of extrajudicial measures. A person or organization that helps implement an extrajudicial measure may also keep a record.

Similar provisions apply to providing others access to records about young persons. Section 118(1) orders that no access should ever be given unless authorized under the YCJA. This does not apply, however, to youth subject to adult sentencing. Section 119(1) provides an extensive list of individuals, agencies, and institutions that may have limited access to court and/or police records about young persons (for example, a person carrying out a criminal record check for government employment purposes).

Section 119(2) provides limitations on the period available for the access to records that depend on the sentence imposed on the young person. If extrajudicial sanctions are imposed, access to records is terminated two years following the imposition of sanctions. If the young person is acquitted of the offence, the access ends two months after the time to appeal expires. If an **absolute discharge** is ordered, the period ends one year after a finding of guilt. In the case of a **conditional discharge**, access to records will be denied three years after the verdict. When there is a finding of guilt for a summary conviction offence, the period lasts three years after the sentence has been completed. Finally, in the case of an indictable offence, an authorized individual may be provided access to records up to five years after completion of the sentence.

Even if the authorized period of access to records about young persons expires, the interests of justice may require some flexibility. Accordingly, s. 123(1) provides exceptional circumstances under which an individual may acquire access to a record beyond the prescribed the time period. Furthermore, a young person to whom a record relates may have access to the record at any time.

Certain individuals and institutions may receive information contained in a record. A police officer, for example, may disclose such information to any person if this is necessary in the course of an investigation (s. 125). As under the YOA, schools and other institutions and professionals working with young persons may also obtain such information. Here, disclosure must be necessary to ensure compliance with probation or conditional sentencing, to ensure the safety of others, or to help rehabilitate the young person. However, if information is indeed accessed for these purposes, it must be kept separate from any other records about the young person, no one else may be permitted access, and the information must be destroyed once the purpose for which it was obtained has been achieved. Information cannot be disclosed after the period for access to records has expired.

Section 127(1) empowers the youth court to enable the provincial director, a peace officer, or the attorney general to disclose information about a youth record to anyone. The applicant must demonstrate to the court that the young person has caused serious personal injury and continues to pose a serious risk to others. The applicant must also prove that disclosure is necessary to avoid such risk. The youth court must give the young person, the parent of the young person, and the attorney general an opportunity to be heard before rendering its decision. An application for disclosure can be made in the absence of a young person if all reasonable efforts have been made to locate him or her.

absolute discharge
a type of judgment of a criminal case, in which a finding of guilt is obtained but no conviction is registered and no conditions are imposed

conditional discharge
a type of judgment of a criminal case, in which a finding of guilt is obtained but no conviction is registered, but a set of conditions is imposed in the form of a probation order

ACCESS TO YOUTH CRIMINAL JUSTICE RECORDS

Who can *retain* a youth record?

- a youth justice court
- a review board (for example, a custody review board)
- any other court that hears a youth's case
- a police force that investigated an alleged offence by a youth
- the RCMP central repository, even if the RCMP did not investigate
- a government or government agency that acquired the record by
  - investigating an alleged offence
  - determining sentencing
  - deciding about extrajudicial measures
  - administering an extrajudicial measure
- any person or organization that was involved in implementing an extrajudicial measure

Who can *gain access* to a youth record?

- A person or agency listed in s. 119(1) of the YCJA (for example, a person carrying out a criminal reference check for government employment purposes).

- A police officer who requires the information for use in an investigation (under s. 125).

- Staff at schools and other institutions working with the young person, or professionals working with the young person, but only for particular purposes: assisting rehabilitation, protecting the safety of others, or ensuring compliance with sentences. Strict rules apply to how and for how long the information is retained.

- Any other person to whom access is given by the provincial director, a peace officer, or the attorney general to disclose information, after authorization by a youth court (see s. 127).

The legislation contains rules about how long a record can be retained, under what circumstances it can be disclosed, and how those who have access to the information must protect its confidentiality. See ss. 110 through 127 of the YCJA for full details.

QUESTIONS

1. What do you find surprising about who can access youth records?

2. Do you think that these provisions protect a young person's rights?

Part 7: General Provisions

This part deals with procedural issues such as the disqualification of judges after a change of plea, exclusion of certain individuals from the courtroom (including the young person himself or herself, under certain circumstances), and out-of-province transfers of jurisdiction. It makes it an offence to help a youth escape custody, to interfere with a youth's compliance with sentence conditions, or not to comply with the publication ban (s. 138).

Part 7 also establishes the general applicability of the *Criminal Code* to the youth criminal justice system, subject to certain exceptions "with any modifications that the circumstances require" (ss. 140 to 142).

Sections 146 to 153 deal with evidence in the youth justice system.

Finally, s. 157 authorizes the Attorney General of Canada or a minister designated by the lieutenant governor in council of a province to establish certain "community-based programs":

> (a) programs that are an alternative to judicial proceedings, such as victim–offender reconciliation programs, mediation programs and restitution programs;
>
> (b) programs that are an alternative to detention before sentencing, such as bail supervision programs; and
>
> (c) programs that are an alternative to custody, such as intensive support and supervision programs, and programs to carry out attendance orders.

1. What programs are available in your community for each of the types outlined above?

2. Do you think there are a lack of programs or too many services in your community? Why do you think this way?

Experience Under the YCJA

The past decade or so has seen both change brought by and made to the YCJA. Most significantly, the goal of reducing Canada's overreliance on courts and jails for dealing with wayward youth has been successful to a large extent. Since the YCJA came into force, police diversion of cases through extrajudicial measures has increased significantly. Further, formal court proceedings have been used less often under the YCJA even where extrajudicial measures are not used.

However, not all experiences under the YCJA are success stories. Although the law was intended to reduce overuse of pre-trial detention, rates of detention before trial for youth for non-violent offences were actually higher in 2009–10 than before the YCJA came into force. Common offences giving rise to detention included breach of condition or failure to appear—that is, administration of justice offences, not violent offences. This is troubling considering the law was supposed to ensure that Canada's youth were no longer incarcerated so often.

Further, some key aspects of the YCJA have recently been amended in ways that arguably take away from the internal rationality of it as a law that reflects the principles in s. 3 and the values in its preamble. As discussed earlier in this chapter, the sentencing principles of the law have been altered to allow for denunciation and deterrence; the meaning of "violent offence" under the law was expanded in 2012 to include a broader range of offences; and records of youthful offenders' identities can now be published in more cases. These amendments seem to indicate a major shift from the approach taken in 2003. With the 2012 amendments, it is arguable that Canada is dealing again with a fundamentally changed regime for youth criminal justice, even though the name of the law remains the same.

CHAPTER SUMMARY

The *Youth Criminal Justice Act* is a lengthy and complex piece of legislation. It is divided into several parts. These parts deal with extrajudicial measures, organization, judicial measures, sentencing, custody and supervision, publication of records, and general provisions. Some of the most important issues addressed by this legislation are the legislation's age jurisdiction, its provision for parental involvement, the entitlement of youth to rights including the right to counsel, and sentencing principles.

The guiding principles of the legislation are expressed in s. 3. In comparison with the approaches in Canada's prior criminal laws that dealt with youth, the YCJA attempts to balance welfare and law and order considerations and articulate a justice model for dealing with youth. That the protection of the public is the paramount principle for courts to consider in making decisions under the Act is newly clarified by the 2012 amendments. It is made clear in this chapter that the YCJA is an attempt to address the criticisms of the YOA and to improve upon Canadian youth justice, as will be discussed in the following chapters.

Youth who come into contact with the criminal justice system have special protections that prevent the release of their name, except in specific circumstances such as when a youth is given an adult sentence. Similar protections are in place for a youth's record. The record can only be retained by those who have direct involvement with investigation or implementation of measures. A record can only be accessed by criminal justice agencies or those working specifically with the youth. Access will be granted in other instances as well, but it must be authorized by a youth court.

In 2012 major amendments were made to the YCJA. Overall, they made the law more strongly punitive for the most serious offences and allowed for the incarceration of more youth both before and after trial. Although the YCJA now allows for more use of custody, it remains to be seen how judges and Crown prosecutors will interpret the amended provisions. It is evident that the law dealing with youth who are alleged to have committed criminal offences in Canada is always controversial and perpetually changing.

KEY TERMS

absolute discharge, 75
conditional discharge, 75
custodial sentence, 65
doli incapax, 53
due process, 56
extrajudicial measure, 63
indictable offence, 65
judicial reprimand, 71
paradigm, 54
parens patriae, 55

penology, 54
police (or Crown) caution, 65
positivist school of thought, 54
preamble, 60
remand, 67
reparation, 62
sanction, 65
status offence, 56
statutory prioritization, 62
summary conviction offence, 65

REFERENCES

Abramovitch, R., Peterson-Badali, M., & Rohan, M. (1995). Young people's understanding and assertion of their rights to silence and legal counsel. *Behavioural Science and the Law, 17*, 455–465. Retrieved from http://www.deepdyve.com/lp/wiley/young-people-s-experience-of-the-canadian-youth-justice-system-0sCfClaX9B.

An Act for the Prevention of Cruelty to and Better Protection of Children. (1893). SO 1893, 56 Vict., c. 45.

Awad, G. (1991). Assessing the needs of young offenders. In A. Leschied, P. Jaffe, & W. Willis (Eds.), *The Young Offenders Act: A revolution in Canadian juvenile justice* (pp. 173–185). Toronto: University of Toronto Press.

Awad, G., & Perillo, C. (1988). The court as a catalyst in the treatment process. *American Journal of Psychotherapy, 42*, 290–296.

Bala, N. (1994). What's wrong with YOA bashing? What's wrong with the YOA? Recognizing the limits of the law. *Canadian Journal of Criminology, 36*, 247–248.

Bala, N., & Kirvan, M.-A. (1991). The statute: Its principles and provisions and their interpretation by the courts. In A.W. Leschied, P.G. Jaffe, & W. Willis (Eds.), *The Young Offenders Act: A revolution in Canadian juvenile justice* (pp. 71–113). Toronto: University of Toronto Press.

Bill C-61. (1981). *Young Offenders Act*, 1st Sess., 32nd Parl.

Bill C-192. (1970). *An Act Respecting Young Offenders and to Repeal the Juvenile Delinquents Act*, 3rd Sess., 28th Parl.

Bolton, J., Caskey, J., Costom, S., Fowler, R., Fox, S., Hillman, K., Taylor, M., & Yarin, R. (1993). The Young Offenders Act: Principles and policy—The first decade in review. *McGill Law Journal*, *38*, 939–945.

CBC News. (2000, February 9). Identity of young offender published. *CBC News*. Retrieved from http://www.cbc.ca/news/canada/identity-of-young-offender-published-1.237432.

Criminal Code. (1985). RSC 1985, c. C-46.

Department of Justice. (1965). *Report of the Department of Justice Committee on Juvenile Delinquency*. Ottawa: Queen's Printer.

Department of the Solicitor General. (1967). *First discussion draft: An Act Respecting Children and Young Persons*. Ottawa: Queen's Printer.

Gault, In re. (1967). 387 US 1.

Goldstein, N.E.S., Condie, L.O., Kalbeitzer, R., Osman, D., & Geier, J.L. (2003). Juvenile offenders' Miranda rights comprehension and self-reported likelihood of offering false confessions. *Assessment*, *10*(4), 359–369.

Juvenile Delinquents Act. (1970). RSC 1970, c. J-3.

K.D., R v. (2003). [2003] NSJ No. 165 (SC).

Kent v. United States. (1966). 383 US 541.

Law Reform Commission of Canada. (1975). *Diversion*, Working Paper No. 7. Ottawa: Queen's Printer.

Leon, J.S. (1977). The development of Canadian juvenile justice: A background for reform. *Osgoode Hall Law Journal*, *15*, 71–81.

Leschied, A., & Gendreau, P. (1986). The declining role of rehabilitation in Canadian juvenile justice: Implications of underlying theory in the Young Offenders Act. *Canadian Journal of Criminology*, *28*, 315–322.

Leschied, A.W., & Jaffe, P.G. (1986). Implications of the consent to treatment section of the Young Offenders Act: A case study. *Canadian Psychology*, *27*(3), 312–313.

Leschied, A., & Vark, L. (1989). *Assessing outcomes of special need young offenders*. London, ON: Family Court Clinic.

Reid, S. (2013). Thinking about youth justice: Historical roots and contemporary approaches. In K. O'Regan & S. Reid (Eds.), *Thinking about criminal justice in Canada* (pp. 333–354). Toronto: Emond Montgomery.

Reid-MacNevin, S.A. (1991). A theoretical understanding of current Canadian juvenile justice policy. In A. Leschied, P. Jaffe, & W. Willis (Eds.), *The Young Offenders Act: A revolution in Canadian juvenile justice* (pp. 17–36). Toronto: University of Toronto Press.

Reid-MacNevin, S.A., & Kappell, A. (2003). *Youth justice in Canada*. Toronto: Canadian Training Institute.

Reitsma-Street, M. (1989). More control than care: A critique of historical and contemporary laws for delinquency and neglect of children in Ontario. *Canadian Journal of Women and the Law*, *3*, 510–530.

Rogers, R., Blackwood, H.L., Fiduccia, C.E., Steadham, J.A., Drogin, E.Y., & Rogstad, J.E. (2012). Juvenile Miranda warnings: Perfunctory rituals or procedural safeguards? *Criminal Justice and Behavior*, *39*(3), 229–249.

Safe Streets and Communities Act. (2012). SC 2012, c. 1.

T.(V.), R v. (1992). [1992] 1 SCR 749, 71 CCC (3d) 32, 1992 CanLII 88.

UN Convention on the Rights of the Child (UNCRC). (1989, November 20). 1577 UNTS 3.

Varma, K.N. (2007). Parental involvement in youth court. *Canadian Journal of Criminology and Criminal Justice*, *49*(2), 231–260.

Winship, In re. (1970). 397 US 358.

Young Offenders Act. (1985). RSC 1985, c. Y-1.

Youth Criminal Justice Act. (2002). SC 2002, c. 1.

EXERCISES AND REVIEW

Review Questions

1. Does the *Criminal Code* have any application to people aged 12 to 17? Why or why not?

2. Why is an extrajudicial sanction more serious/onerous than a police caution?

3. How did the YCJA's introduction of indictable procedure for some offences committed by youth increase the protection given to youth rights? Give an example.

4. Which (two) new sentencing principles were introduced into the YCJA in 2012? Explain these two principles.

5. What are the three exceptions to the rule against publishing information that would identify a youthful offender?

6. Explain why an informal and speedy procedure for prosecution of youth offences was consistent with the *parens patriae* philosophy underlying the *Juvenile Delinquents Act*.

Discussion Questions

1. Describe the purpose of s. 3 of the YCJA: the declaration of principle. Identify three provisions in the legislation that you feel reflect the principles stated here, and explain why.

2. The YCJA incorporates both general principles (like those described in s. 3) and sentencing principles. The expectation is that judges applying the legislation will consider and balance these principles when they use their discretion to impose sentences on youth. Why do you believe the drafters of the legislation chose this formula—principles plus judicial discretion—to frame how youth should be dealt with, when they could have imposed a more objective system—for example, specific sentences for specific offences?

3. Although the age jurisdiction of the YCJA is a very narrow six years (12–17), human beings experience very significant developmental changes during those years. How might the developmental differences between a 12-year-old and a 17-year-old pose challenges for the drafters of youth justice legislation?

4. The YCJA in its current form seems to recognize that many youth in conflict with the law are in need of social welfare services. However, the legislation makes it clear that the justice system is not to be used as a means of getting youth into social welfare programs. Do you agree that child welfare and youth justice should be kept separate? What would be the downside, for example, to allowing police to arrest youth "for their own safety"?

5. In this chapter, you learned that although the YCJA is intended to limit the custodial detention of youth, youth are often kept in detention not for violent offences, but for administration of justice offences, such as breach of probation or failure to appear for trial. Why do you think judges tend to impose custodial sentences for these kinds of offences? Do you agree with these reasons? Why is it difficult to come up with effective sentences for administration of justice offences that do *not* include detention in custody?

Legislative Framework: Provincial Offences and Child Protection Matters

4

LEARNING OUTCOMES

After completing this chapter, you should be able to:

- List and describe provincial statutes that provide offences with which youth may be charged.
- Review the general purpose and structure of the Ontario *Provincial Offences Act*, and how it is enforced with respect to youth.
- Compare sentences applicable to youth found guilty of a provincial offence with sentences applicable to adult offenders.
- Understand the principles and purposes behind other youth-related provincial legislation.
- Summarize the paramount purpose of Ontario's *Child and Family Services Act* (CFSA).
- List the signs or criteria that, if observed in relation to a child, could trigger a duty to report that the child might be at risk of abuse or neglect.
- Explain the method set out by the CFSA for dealing with a child under the age of 12 who is suspected of having committed an act that is a crime under the *Criminal Code*.
- Describe the process for taking a child suspected to be in need of protection into care pending proceedings.

Introduction

Chapter 3 presented a detailed examination of Canada's youth criminal justice system as it applies to young people today. It is also important to put the youth criminal justice system within the broader context of laws affecting youth in Canada. For purposes of this text, we will restrict our discussion to a review of selected statutes that directly address the circumstances of children and youth. The examples are mostly drawn from Ontario legislation; however, examples and tables pointing to other provincial and territorial jurisdictions are included to encourage you to consider similarities and differences across the country.

Many statutes (such as the Ontario *Family Law Act* and other provincial equivalents) have a considerable effect on the lives of children and adolescents within families. Ontario's *Child and Family Services Act* (CFSA), *Provincial Offences Act* (POA), and *Education Act* deal with youth as individuals in their own right, separate from the family unit, and govern their interactions with the state and society. In regulating such interactions, the statutes (to varying extents and for different purposes) acknowledge the differences between children or adolescents and adults. Further, they convey, both explicitly and implicitly, community and state expectations with respect to the role of youth in society, and the responsibility of other members of society with respect to youth.

By taking the time to review this general legislative context, we will be better prepared to understand the subcontext of the youth criminal justice system.

What Is a Provincial Offence?

In Chapter 3 you read about the legislative provisions for young persons under the federal *Youth Criminal Justice Act* (YCJA). The YCJA influences the interpretation of the *Criminal Code* of Canada as it applies to youth. The Code is a product of the federal government's authority over criminal matters. Not all offences in Canada are listed in the federal *Criminal Code*. There are also many offence-creating statutes enacted by the provincial and territorial legislatures. An "offence" under a provincial offences act is defined as "an offence under an Act of the Legislature or under a regulation or by-law made under the authority of an Act of the Legislature" (POA, s. 1). The offences created under these statutes are often referred to as "provincial offences" (even though some occur under territorial legislation). Municipalities, exercising powers delegated to them by the provinces, can also create regulatory offences.

Examples of provincial offences with which youth may be charged include those under the *Highway Traffic Act*, the *Liquor Licence Act*, the *Fish and Wildlife Conservation Act*, and the *Occupational Health and Safety Act*. (Each of the other provinces has legislation similar to that mentioned for Ontario.)

Although provincial offences do not carry the same stigma as *Criminal Code* offences, they can still have very serious consequences: several provincial penalty provisions allow provincial courts under the *Provincial Offences Act* to impose significant financial penalties.

Procedural Legislation for Prosecuting Provincial Offences

Each province has a statute that regulates the procedure for prosecuting provincial offences. In Ontario and in Newfoundland and Labrador, the regulatory statute is called the *Provincial Offences Act*; in Nova Scotia and Prince Edward Island, the *Summary Proceedings Act*; in Alberta and New Brunswick, the *Provincial Offences Procedure Act*; in Manitoba and Yukon, the *Summary Convictions Act*; in Quebec, the *Code of Penal Procedure*; in Saskatchewan, the *Summary Offence Procedure Act*; in British Columbia, the *Offences Act*; and in Northwest Territories and Nunavut, the *Summary Conviction Procedures Act*.

The Ontario *Provincial Offences Act*, unlike the *Criminal Code*, does not primarily create offences. Instead, it regulates the prosecution of offences contained in various other provincial statutes. The enactment of the Ontario POA in 1979 represented a major change in the way offences created under provincial statutes were treated. In creating that law, one of the main purposes was to replace the summary conviction procedures common in many other provinces for the prosecution of provincial offences with one that would distinguish between provincial offences (created by provincial statutes) and criminal offences (created by the *Criminal Code*) (POA, s. 2(1)).

Table 4.1 presents an overview of the manner in which each province and territory has developed provincial offence legislation as provided by the consolidation of provincial laws and regulations. (When an amendment is made to a piece of legislation, an "amending" act or regulation is required. For example, when amendments are made to the federal *Youth Criminal Justice Act*, the provincial and territorial enabling legislation must also be amended to provide the new changes. A consolidated act or regulation is one that has been updated and incorporates the amendments into the original text.)

TABLE 4.1 Applicable Legislation for Provincial Offences by Province and Territory

Province/territory	Applicable provincial/territorial legislation
Alberta	• *Provincial Offences Procedure Act*, RSA 2000, c. P-34 • *Procedures Regulation*, Alta. Reg. 233/1989
British Columbia	• *Offence Act*, RSBC 1996, c. 338 • *Victims of Crime Act*, RSBC 1996, c. 478
Manitoba	• *The Summary Convictions Act*, CCSM c. S230 • *The Victims' Bill of Rights*, CCSM c. V55
New Brunswick	• *Provincial Offences Procedure Act*, SNB 1987, c. P-22.1 • *Provincial Offences Procedure for Young Persons Act*, SNB 1987, c. P-22.2 • *Victims Services Act*, SNB 1987, c.V-2.1
Newfoundland and Labrador	*Provincial Offences Act*, SNL 1995, c. P-31.1
Northwest Territories	*Summary Conviction Procedures Act*, RSNWT 1988, c. S-15
Nova Scotia	• *Alternative Penalty Act*, SNS 1989, c. 2 • *Summary Proceedings Act*, RSNS 1989, c. 450 • *Victims' Rights and Services Act*, SNS 1989, c. 14 • *Youth Justice Act*, SNS 2001, c. 38
Nunavut	*Summary Conviction Procedures Act*, RSNWT (Nu) 1988, c. S-15
Ontario	• *Provincial Offences Act*, RSO 1990, c. P.33 • The rules of court made under the *Courts of Justice Act*, RSO 1990, c. C.43
Prince Edward Island	• *Summary Proceedings Act*, RSPEI 1988, c. S-9 • *Victims of Crime Act*, RSPEI 1988, c. V-3.1 • *French Language Services Act*, RSPEI 1988, c. F-15.1
Quebec	*Code of Penal Procedure*, CQLR c. C-25.1
Saskatchewan	*The Summary Offences Procedure Act*, 1990, SS 1990-91, c. S-53.2, c. 37
Yukon	*Summary Convictions Act*, RSY 2002, c. 210

SOURCE: Application of Provincial Laws Regulations Consolidation, SOR/96-312, current to November 26, 2013, available at http://laws-lois.justice.gc.ca.

Look at some of the other provincial offence acts and consider whether the provisions based in the Ontario *Provincial Offences Act* are the same or different. What might it mean for young people who commit offences under both a provincial offence act and the *Criminal Code*?

The Role of Intent in Provincial Offences

There are important differences between provincial offences and the federal offences created by the *Criminal Code*. When an individual is found guilty of a Code offence, the result is a criminal record, but this is not true of a conviction under a provincial or territorial statute. These offences are also generally less serious in nature than crimes listed in the *Criminal Code* and, theoretically, do not "stigmatize" the accused with a criminal record.

To commit a criminal offence in violation of the *Criminal Code*, a person has to not only do the prohibited thing (*actus reus*) but also intend to do it, or have a guilty mind (*mens rea*). While the crimes under the Code often reflect the intent to do harm, provincial offences often describe acts that are prohibited because they represent conduct that is disorderly or undesirable for practical or logistical reasons, but that are not generally condemned as "immoral." In some cases, a person can commit a provincial offence without any specific intent at all. Offences that can be committed without intent are called **absolute liability offences**. Prior to the Supreme Court decision in *R v. Sault Ste. Marie* (discussed in the box below), people accused of public welfare regulatory offences such as liquor law offences, pollution, misleading advertising, and traffic infractions were convicted simply if the Crown was able to prove the accused committed the act or omission described in the offence. The absolute liability rendered it nearly impossible for the accused to defend themselves against such charges. If the offence had occurred, one was judged guilty, regardless of whether or not the individual had taken reasonable precautions to prevent the offence from occurring.

absolute liability offence
an offence of which an accused can be found guilty if the prosecution proves that the accused committed the act or omission that constitutes the offence, regardless of the presence or absence of intent or of any particular state of mind

CASE IN POINT

R v. Sault Ste. Marie, [1978] 2 SCR 1299, 1978 CanLII 11

In this case, the City of Sault Ste. Marie had hired a contractor to dispose of the city's waste. The contractor's disposal site bordered on a creek with freshwater springs flowing into it. The disposal contractor submerged the springs and disposed of the waste. Unfortunately, the waste seeped through the artificial barrier created by the disposal company and eventually ran into the nearby river. The river flowed into a lake that supplied municipal water to the residents of Sault Ste. Marie. The city and the disposal company were charged with pollution of the creek and the river under s. 32(1) of the *Ontario Water Resources Commission Act*, which stipulated that "every municipality or person that discharges, or deposits, or causes, or permits the discharge or deposit of any material of any kind into any water course, or on any shore or bank thereof, or in any place that may impair the quality of water, is guilty of an offence." The trial court found that the City of Sault Ste. Marie had had nothing to do with the operations of the independent contractor and that the city employees were not employees of the disposal contractor.

Justice Dickson created the category of **strict liability offences** as a halfway point between full *mens rea* and absolute liability, recognizing the different standards of proof according to the three categories of offences. (See Table 4.2.)

strict liability offence
an offence that does not require proof of intent, but to which the accused may have a defence (e.g., the defence of due diligence)

TABLE 4.2   The Requirement of Mens Rea According to Type of Offence

Criminal Code crimes	Wide range of regulatory offences	
Full *mens rea*	Strict liability	Absolute liability
Proof of a guilty act committed with full intention beyond a reasonable doubt	• *Prima facie* proof of commission of the offence • Due diligence defence	• Commission of offence proved • *Mens rea* assumed; no defence on basis of lack of intention

SOURCE: Bowal & Iss (2013).

QUESTION

Consider the case of the Walkerton Tragedy (2000), in which more than 2,000 people became sick and seven died from drinking contaminated water. Strict liability as defined by *Sault Ste. Marie* required the Town of Walkerton to show that it had taken reasonable preventive measures to ensure the safety of the drinking water for the residents. Do you believe the town would have taken different precautions if the contamination of drinking water were deemed an absolute liability offence?

Driving-related strict liability offences include failure to remain at the scene of an accident, driving with a suspended licence, and failure to wear a seat belt. An example of a strict liability offence is towing a trailer that doesn't have an operating taillight system. The trailer may *have* a taillight system, and it may been turned on, but for some reason that the driver is unaware of, the system may have failed between the time the driver set out and the time the vehicle was pulled over. The burden of proof is put on the defendant to show that he or she took all reasonable actions to prevent the offence from happening—that is, the defendant exercised **due diligence**. In this kind of case, if the driver can prove he or she checked to make sure the system worked when setting out, he or she may have a defence and avoid a ticket.

due diligence
the taking of reasonable steps to avoid committing an offence

Youth and Provincial Offences

The authority for police to arrest for provincial offences is found in each provincial act being enforced. Age generally becomes a factor only after officers charge someone. An example of the overlap between federal criminal law and provincial regulatory law might be best illustrated by the following scenario.

YOUTH AND LIQUOR OFFENCES

Kyle (age 19), Jordan (age 21), Sarah (age 15), and Margaret (age 18) were driving home from a party. Margaret was the designated driver and had not been drinking. The other three had been drinking quite heavily, and Kyle and Sarah were both still drinking a beer in the back seat of the car. They were pulled over.

QUESTIONS

1. What are the possible charges and relevant legislative provisions for these young people?

2. Kyle is of legal drinking age, but with open liquor in the car he would be charged with a provincial offence under the *Liquor Licence Act* and would likely be fined. If the group had not had a designated driver, and one of them had decided to drive after drinking, that person would be charged under the *Criminal Code* and get a fine, suspension of driving privileges for a minimum of one year, and a criminal record. Sarah is a young person in this situation according to both provincial and federal law. What would be the implications for her?

The Ontario Provincial Offences Act: A Closer Look

Introduction

The Ontario Court of Justice hears virtually all provincial offence matters and offences against municipal bylaws. Examples of such cases are:

- *Highway Traffic Act* charges such as speeding or traffic violations;
- municipal bylaw charges relating to excessive noise, animal control, or garbage disposal; and
- charges laid under provincial legislation such as the *Environmental Protection Act*, the *Occupational Health and Safety Act*, the *Dog Owners' Liability Act*, or the *Trespass to Property Act*.

Different types of charges that might apply under the *Provincial Offences Act* include: (1) under the *Highway Traffic Act*, speeding or driving while suspended; (2) under the *Compulsory Automobile Insurance Act*, failing to have insurance on a car you are operating; (3) under the *Trespass to Property Act*, being present on private property without authorization by the lawful owner; (4) under the *Liquor Licence Act*, having open liquor in a car, snowmobile, or boat; (5) under the *Dog Owners' Liability Act*, having your dog found to "pose a menace" if a complaint is made about its behaviour.

Under a memorandum of understanding, municipalities administer courts where most provincial offence cases are tried, and also prosecute many of these cases on behalf of the Ministry of the Attorney General.

Structure of the POA

The Ontario POA is divided into eight distinct parts. The first three parts set out the processing options for the different types of offences. Part I regulates proceedings for offences commenced by a **certificate of offence**. Part II applies to proceedings for parking infractions that are commenced by a **certificate of parking infraction**. Part III deals with proceedings for offences commenced by the laying of an **information** and the issuing of a summons. These are relatively more serious charges (but generally not as serious as a criminal offence).

There is a broad range of sentencing options for Part III offences, including imprisonment, probation, and restitution.

Part IV of the POA governs trials and sentencing. Part V contains miscellaneous provisions—for example, with respect to defences available, recording of evidence, and the use of interpreters. Part VI, which is the most important part for the purposes of this text, deals with the treatment of young persons under the POA. Part VII deals with appeals, and Part VIII pertains to arrest, bail, and search warrants.

Charging and Arresting Youth Under the POA

Generally, a young person cannot be arrested for a provincial offence without a warrant. Section 106 of the POA, however, enables a police officer to arrest a young person without a warrant in two situations. First, where there are "reasonable and probable grounds to believe it is necessary in the public interest" to establish the identity of the young person,

certificate of offence
an unsworn, formulaic document (in a specific format and with specific content) prepared for proceedings having to do with less serious offences

certificate of parking infraction
a parking ticket or "tag"

information
a statement sworn, typically before a justice of the peace, for the purpose of laying a more serious charge

an arrest may be made without a warrant. Second, if the purpose of the arrest is to prevent the continuation or repetition of an offence that seriously endangers the young person or the person or property of another and there is no time to obtain a warrant, a valid arrest without a warrant may be made.

TEEN PICNIC GOES WRONG

Samantha and Joanne were shopping at a mall on a Saturday afternoon. They ran into four of their friends, who asked them to come along for a picnic and go four-wheeling in a nearby forest. The girls joined in, and as the girls and boys climbed into the vehicles, they found they did not have enough helmets for everyone. Even so, Samantha and Joanne stayed on and they all drove to the woods.

The group decided to stop near a stream and go for a swim. Leaving the vehicles at the side of the stream, they drank some beers and then jumped into a deep quarry. While they were swimming, a park ranger came along, saw the vehicles unattended, and called down to them. It turned out that two of the young men were violating probation orders requiring them not to associate with one another.

QUESTION

What charges might arise out of this scenario?

A police officer is required to release a young person from custody after arrest "as soon as practicable" unconditionally or upon service of a summons (POA, s. 107(2)). The officer is permitted not to do so in two situations: (1) where he or she has reasonable and probable grounds to think it is in the public interest to detain the young person in order to identify him or her (POA, s. 107(2)(a)); or (2) to prevent the continuation or repetition of an offence that seriously endangers the young person or the person or property of another (POA, s. 107(2)(b)).

1. List some scenarios you believe might establish grounds for police detention of a young person.

2. What are the rights of a young person kept in detention?

Where the investigating officer believes it is necessary to continue to detain a young person after arrest, he or she is required to deliver the person to the officer in charge (POA, s. 107(3)). If the officer in charge does not release the youth, the officer is required to notify the youth's parents as soon as possible (POA, s. 107(4)). Section 107(6) requires that, when a detention order is made, the young person is not to be detained in a place where adults are also detained.

Section 95 of the Ontario POA provides that a young person cannot be issued an offence notice under Part I. Therefore, a young person who commits a provincial offence must be given a summons to attend court.

One of the issues worthy of considering is that under the Ontario POA, a young person is defined under s. 93 as follows:

"young person" means a person who is or, in the absence of evidence to the contrary, appears to be,

(a) twelve years of age or more, but

(b) under sixteen years of age. ...

Therefore, the minimum age for the POA is the same as that for the federal YCJA, but the upper age limit is lower.

1. What does the lower upper-age jurisdiction for the Ontario *Provincial Offences Act* mean in practice?
2. How might this affect young people who commit both criminal offences and provincial offences?

Trials and Sentencing for Youth Under the POA

Section 98(1) of the POA requires a young person to be present in court during his or her trial unless the court is satisfied that the reason for not attending is appropriate. In extreme cases, in which a young person is required to attend court and fails to do so, the court may issue a warrant for his or her arrest (POA, s. 98(4)).

Like the federal YCJA, the POA recognizes the importance of protecting the identity of young persons involved in proceedings. Section 99(1) of the POA stipulates that the identity of a young person may not be published in connection with an offence or alleged offence. Any person who breaches this provision has committed an offence and could be fined as much as $10,000 (POA, s. 99(2)). This is one of the few offences created under the POA itself.

CAMPFIRE POSTER IDENTIFIES YOUTH

A group of young people in a provincial park are detained by a park ranger for lighting a campfire contrary to the regulations governing activities in the park. In a bulletin subsequently handed out to campers upon entry into the park, these same youth are pictured in a poster indicating that such behaviour will not be tolerated.

QUESTION

Would this bulletin meet the criteria set out in s. 99(1) as a breach of the rules requiring the protection of identity?

Section 97 outlines the sentencing options applicable to a young person found guilty of committing a provincial offence, in a proceeding commenced by a certificate of offence. The court may impose a maximum fine of $300 or suspend the passing of sentence and put the young person on probation. Section 101.1 sets out the penalties when the proceeding has commenced by way of information and provides for a maximum fine of $1,000. In both types of proceedings, the maximum term of probation is 90 days instead of two years, which is the maximum term for adults (POA, s. 97(2)). The court also has the option of granting an absolute discharge under s. 97(1)(b). Unlike under the federal YCJA, no conditional discharges are available under the Ontario POA.

1. What benefit does a conditional discharge confer on young persons?
2. What benefit does an absolute discharge have for a young person?

A young person may not be imprisoned except upon conviction for a breach of probation under s. 75, and if he or she is imprisoned the maximum penalty is 30 days. Section 103 requires the place of incarceration to be an "open facility" such as a group home. Despite the change in federal legislation from the *Young Offenders Act* to the *Youth Criminal Justice Act*, which no longer has provisions for "open" and "secure" custody, the Ontario POA states that youth shall be placed in an open facility:

Where a young person is sentenced to a term of imprisonment for breach of probation under clause 75(d), the term of imprisonment shall be served in a place of open custody designated under section 24.1 of the *Young Offenders Act* (Canada), whether in accordance with section 88 of the *Youth Criminal Justice Act* (Canada) or otherwise.

1. What might happen if Ontario decides not to continue to operate "open" custody facilities?
2. What do other provinces/territories suggest regarding the incarceration of young persons found guilty of breach of probation under their provincial or territorial legislation?

Other Provincial Legislation Relevant to Youth

Highway Traffic Act

Every province has legislation governing the conduct of motor vehicle traffic. These statutes are similar to Ontario's *Highway Traffic Act* (HTA), which sets out the regulatory offences related to the operation of motor vehicles, including age restrictions. Young persons who drive before the age of 16 are often charged with "driving without a valid driver's licence." They may also be charged with "being in possession of an altered driver's licence" if the date of birth on the document has been altered to state that the youth are older than they really are (often 19 or more years, so that they can also legally buy alcohol). As with the *Education Act*, young people convicted of these offences often face a probation order under the jurisdiction of the POA. The consequences of breaching such an order are described below.

In many cases, young people who commit driving offences are also charged with a criminal offence. For example, one who takes a vehicle without permission may be charged with "taking a motor vehicle or vessel without consent" under s. 335(1) of the *Criminal Code*. If the youth flees from police, he or she may be charged with "failing to stop the vehicle" under s. 249.1(1).

In addition, the Ontario Ministry of Transportation can generate a driver's licence number even for a person under the age of 16 who is charged with certain driving offences, so that if the offence includes a point reduction, the points can be taken off the licence he or she later obtains.

NOVICE AND YOUNG DRIVERS: GRADUATED DRIVER'S LICENCES

It has long been customary in Canada for young people to go through two stages to become fully licensed drivers of motor vehicles. Starting at age 16, upon completion of a written test, the young person would be issued a "beginner's" or "learner's" permit that stipulates he or she must drive only with another licensed driver. The person would practise for the road test and, once he or she had passed, get a full licence and be able to drive unaccompanied anywhere an adult licensed driver could.

These laws came under scrutiny several years ago, after the release of research citing the relationship between the inexperience of young drivers and collisions and fatalities. Provinces have since introduced new licensing rules for young people, such as graduated driving laws and a longer period between the passing of a written test and allowing new drivers to drive on their own.

Further research has shown that the later in the day it is, and the more passengers in a vehicle, the higher the collision risk. This has led to the introduction of limits on the time of day during which a young person may drive and restrictions on how many passengers may ride with a new driver.

In Ontario, someone with a G1 or G2 licence (or an M1 or M2 motorcycle licence) is referred to as a **novice driver**; a **young driver** is anyone under the age of 22, regardless of his or her class of licence. Drivers holding a G1 licence have successfully completed a written exam and are eligible to drive when accompanied by a fully licensed driver with at least four years of driving experience. After successful completion of a road test, holders of a G2 licence are able to drive without an accompanying driver, but restrictions on who is allowed to be in the vehicle apply. Initially, G2 drivers 19 years of age or under can carry only one passenger aged 19 or younger. After the first six months and until the G2 driver earns a full G licence or turns 20, they can carry only three passengers aged 19 or younger.

In New Brunswick, Level 1 drivers are those who have completed a written test and are eligible to drive with a supervising driver of three years' or more experience. A Level 1 driver cannot drive between midnight and 5 a.m. and must wait 12 months before taking a road test and passing into Level 2. (The wait time is reduced to 8 months for those who have passed a certified driver training course.) Level 2 drivers have completed a road test and are permitted to drive alone with up to three passengers. They are only allowed to drive between midnight and 5 a.m. if driving with a supervising driver of three years' experience, driving to or from work or school.

As of this writing, half of Canada's provinces (Ontario, New Brunswick, Manitoba, Nova Scotia, and Quebec) have a zero-tolerance policy for alcohol for young drivers under their respective provincial legislation. For any person aged 21 and under, there is a zero blood alcohol concentration (BAC) rule while driving, regardless of which level of licence he or she has. If caught with any alcohol in the blood, such a person will get an immediate 24-hour licence suspension and will likely be charged with impaired driving under s. 253(1)(a) of the *Criminal Code*. If convicted, he or she can be fined between $60 and $500 and the licence can be suspended for 30 days. If the BAC is between 0.05 and 0.08 or higher, the person can be charged with driving under the influence and with another offence under s. 253(1)(b). If the person is a G1 or G2 licence holder, he or she may be returned to the start of the graduated licensing system, having to retake the written test and go through the time required driving with an experienced driver all over again.

novice driver
in Ontario, someone who has a G1 or G2 licence (or an M1 or M2 motorcycle licence)

young driver
any driver under the age of 22, regardless of his or her class of licence

QUESTIONS

1. What are the provisions for graduated driving licences in your province?

2. Do you think most young people are aware of the consequences of violating any of these provisions?

3. What kinds of educational tools do you think might be useful in making sure young people are made aware of the driving rules and regulations?

The Liquor Licence Act

Just as every province has a law equivalent to the *Highway Traffic Act*, every province has a law equivalent to the *Liquor Licence Act* (LLA). While many offences are created as a result of the regulation of the sale and consumption of liquor, the most pertinent for young people is the legal drinking age, which in Canada is 19, except for Quebec, Alberta, and Manitoba, where it is 18. Those who consume liquor underage are in violation of the LLA, and if convicted are subject to sentences ranging from fines to probation.

DRINKS AT A BBQ

Julie and her friends are attending an open-air barbeque at a friend's house where the hosts are handing out beer and coolers to the guests.

QUESTIONS

1. Do the hosts need to have a liquor permit to serve alcohol at their home?

2. What if the party were held at a neighbourhood park? Who is responsible for determining whether Julie and her friends meet the legal age for consumption of alcohol?

3. What are the repercussions of serving alcohol to a minor?

4. Who is responsible for ensuring a safe ride home for the guests who have consumed alcohol?

The Education Act

Every province and territory has legislation equivalent to Ontario's *Education Act*. The purpose of the legislation is to govern the operation of schools and the delivery of educational programs. The interplay between the education systems and the youth justice systems is often shaped by school attendance requirements up to a certain age. So, in addition to being subject to the youth justice system under the YCJA, young persons have legal obligations to attend school for a certain minimum time period.

One of the earliest rationales for laws compelling school attendance appeared as the value in terms of future employment, opportunities for advancement, and economic gain. Oreopoulos (2005) reports that research has shown school compulsion to reduce crime and improve health and involvement in civic affairs.

Table 4.3 presents the legal school-leaving ages by province or territory.

Looking at Table 4.3, consider the discrepancies across the country and outline the value of a lower or higher school-leaving age with respect to the impact it might have on youth crime.

Part II of the *Education Act* in Ontario deals with this mandatory requirement of children's attendance in schools. Section 21(1) sets out the general rule requiring all children to attend school between the ages of 6 and 18 years. Children are excused from the requirement only if their attendance has been excluded for one of the reasons listed in s. 21(2): satisfactory instruction at home, illness or other unavoidable cause, insufficient transportation, suspension or expulsion, and religious holy days. Section 21(5) puts a positive duty on the parent or guardian of the child to enroll the child in school.

Section 30 of the *Education Act* creates offences with respect to a child's non-attendance at school. A parent whose child is absent from school for a reason other than those listed in s. 21(2) may be found guilty of a provincial offence and, on conviction, is liable to a fine of not more than $200. Similarly, a person who employs a child between the ages of 6 and 18 during school hours may be found guilty of an offence and, on conviction, is liable to a fine not exceeding $200. These are examples of provincial offences created by a provincial statute.

TABLE 4.3   School-Leaving Age by Province and Territory

Province/territory	School-leaving age
Alberta	17
British Columbia	16
Manitoba	18
New Brunswick	18
Newfoundland and Labrador	16
Northwest Territories	16
Nova Scotia	16
Nunavut	16
Ontario	18
Prince Edward Island	16
Quebec	16
Saskatchewan	16
Yukon	16

WORKING AT PART-TIME JOB VERSUS ATTENDING SCHOOL

Bill has a part-time job at a restaurant after school. The owner of the restaurant calls him before school one day, saying that a full-time staff member has called in sick and asking if he is willing to work during the day. Bill asks his parents if it is okay, and they agree as long as he keeps up with his homework.

Section 30(5) of the *Education Act* creates an offence for children of school years who have failed to attend school without a legal excuse. It states:

> **30**(5) A person who is required by law to attend school and who refuses to attend or who is habitually absent from school is, unless the person is 16 years old or older, guilty of an offence and on conviction is liable to the penalties under Part VI of the *Provincial Offences Act* …

QUESTIONS

1. Who would be in violation of s. 30 of the *Education Act* in this situation?

2. Do you think s. 30 is a good provision?

The authority of police officers established by the *Education Act* is applicable here to arrest a child, a parent, or an employer who has committed an offence under the Act.

truancy
not attending school (without a legally acceptable excuse) when school attendance is required by law for a child of the truant's age in the truant's province

Truancy remains an ongoing issue for young people, their families, and school officials. When the *Juvenile Delinquents Act* was in force, young people who skipped school would be found to be in a state of "delinquency" and treated as offenders. With the proclamation of the *Young Offenders Act* in 1984, only *Criminal Code* offences applied to this legislation, meaning that young people in violation of provincial acts such as the *Education Act* were not held to be criminal. This meant that the provincial and territorial legislative provisions for education were the only recourse to deal with youth who were truant.

Young persons are regularly put on *Provincial Offences Act* probation orders as a result of failure to attend school. This in itself is not problematic as long as he or she complies with the order. Unfortunately, young persons often do not. As a result, they may face POA s. 75 "breach of probation" charges, which creates problems for the court when it comes to sentencing. The YCJA makes it clear that a young person cannot have custody imposed on a first conviction of breach of a YCJA-based probation order. However, as noted previously, because the breach is a violation of a POA order, sentencing for it falls under the jurisdiction of the POA, and therefore the court can impose a period of open custody.

1. What do you think of this provision to impose a term of open custody on a young person for truancy?

2. Do other provinces or territories provide for this option in cases of truancy?

Child Protection

Introduction

Child protection laws aim to do just that: provide a mechanism by which the state can ensure that children and young people grow up free from abuse and neglect. Legal protections for children can be found in both the common law and statute law.

Child Protection Under the Common Law

Three legal principles (Wilson, 2011, p. 1) derived from common law apply to the issue of child protection:

- **Fiduciary duty** means that there is a higher standard of care demanded of adults entrusted with the responsibility of protecting children.
- *Parens patriae* refers to the state's power to step in as a "parent." Courts are obliged to listen to and assist young people in need of help. If no statutory remedy applies to the circumstances, the courts can provide a remedy under the common law.
- **Procedural fairness**, a general legal principle, exists to support children and youth to exercise their rights regardless of what others might assert to be in their best interests.

The main responsibility for the well-being of children in Canada rests with the parents. It is recognized, however, that sometimes others have to intervene. When a caregiver is unable or unwilling to provide a minimum standard of care, the state, through provincial child protection law, steps in.

Constitutional Basis of Intervention on Behalf of Children

The law recognizes the right of parents to care for and control their children. This right to "security of the person" is protected under s. 7 of the *Canadian Charter of Rights and Freedoms*. It can only be infringed upon in accordance with the principles of fundamental justice. The *Constitution Act* grants provinces and territories the authority to operate child welfare systems to intervene when necessary and to set legislation to govern those systems. The purpose of provincial and territorial child welfare systems is to protect the safety and well-being of children. To the extent that these laws are based on the principles of fundamental justice, they can permit, in certain circumstances, certain infringements on parents' rights.

The Criminal Code

Child welfare legislation assumes that children are dependent on adults for the necessaries of life until they reach the age of majority. Section 215 of the *Criminal Code* requires parents of children under the age of 16 to provide them with the necessaries of life, which include food, acceptable shelter, and necessary medical treatment. Provincial statutes further this through child welfare acts, which require parents to provide appropriate care, supervision, and protection. Provincial education acts also require parents to enroll children in school and ensure their attendance. Other adults responsible for the care of children such as teachers, daycare workers, and guardians stand *in loco parentis* ("in place of the parent") and are required by law to adhere to the standard of care a parent would provide.

The Child and Family Services Act

The *Child and Family Services Act* is the most important child protection legislation in Ontario. Every province in Canada has similar legislation, and much of it originated near the beginning of the 20th century.

Around that time, there was a lot of overlap between the federal *Juvenile Delinquents Act* (JDA) and provincial child protection legislation. As has already been discussed, a young person who committed a criminal offence under the JDA was not to be considered as a "criminal," but as a "delinquent" in need of protection and guidance.

fiduciary duty
the duty of adults to meet a higher standard of care when entrusted with the responsibility of protecting children

parens patriae
the doctrine that the state has the responsibility to look after the well-being of vulnerable persons, such as youth, and to step in as parent if necessary

procedural fairness
a general legal principle that exists to help children and youth exercise their rights regardless of what others might assert to be in their best interests

In implementing the JDA, the provinces did not distinguish between children and youth who came to court for criminal behaviour and those who were there due to neglect, abuse, or misconduct such as truancy. The *Young Offenders Act*, which came into force in 1984, marked a change in how young people were dealt with, and those in court for criminal matters and those in family court for child welfare matters were clearly separated.

This section considers the provincial legislation that deals with children under the age of criminal responsibility (12 years) and those under age 18 who receive services under what is known as "child welfare."

The Child Welfare System

"Child welfare" describes a set of government agencies, non-government agencies, and private services designed to protect children and help families stabilize after an event that puts them under the care of the state. Canada's provinces and territories all have child welfare agencies that can be contacted by the public 24 hours a day to report a **child in need of protection**, or to access services.

child in need of protection
legal definition/ determination, based on an established set of criteria and evidence, that forms the basis of a protective order in child welfare proceedings

These agencies ensure the safety of children who, for a variety of reasons, may not be safe in their homes. The main aim of child protection services is to safeguard children from abuse and neglect by investigating allegations made by members of the public or law enforcement personnel. Child welfare services also include arranging and supervising foster care placements, arranging adoptions of children who require new permanent homes, and offering support, education, and guidance to families so that they can stay intact and raise their children successfully.

Guiding Principles

Although there are differences from one province or territory to another, the child welfare systems throughout Canada all have the primary mandate of ensuring that children are safe. The various provincial and territorial systems operate according to several common underlying principles:

duty to report
a statutorily or legally explicit (as opposed to moral/ethical) requirement to report qualifying incidents or observations

best interests of the child
a guiding principle of the UNCRC that, in all matters affecting children, care must be taken to consider what decision would best protect the child's physical, psychological, and emotional safety, security, and well-being

- they all make it clear that everyone has a **duty to report** child abuse and neglect;
- the **best interests of the child** must be considered when a child is found to be in need of protection;
- the parents' primary responsibility for child-rearing is respected;
- it is acknowledged that continuity of care and stability is important for children;
- the views of children are important to take into consideration when decisions are being made that affect their futures;
- cultural heritage should be respected, especially for Aboriginal children.

Although Aboriginal children represent less than 6 percent of the child population in Canada, they make up an estimated 26 percent of children placed in out-of-home care during a child protection investigation. The percentage of Aboriginal children in child welfare systems reaches 60 percent to 78 percent in some provinces and territories (Vandna & Kozlowski, 2013). According to the 2011 National Household Survey, almost half of all children under the age of 14 in foster care were Aboriginal children (48.1 percent). Fewer than 1 percent (0.3 percent) of all non-Aboriginal children were placed in foster care, compared with nearly 4 percent of all Aboriginal children (Statistics Canada, 2013).

KEY TERMINOLOGY RELATED TO ABORIGINAL PEOPLES IN CANADA

Aboriginal peoples of Canada is a collective name for all of the original peoples of Canada and their descendants. It is defined in the *Constitution Act*, 1982, s. 35(2) as including the Indian, Inuit, and Métis peoples of Canada.

There is no single term commonly used to describe indigenous peoples throughout the world. According to the National Aboriginal Health Organization (NAHO, 2014), the following guidelines are helpful in understanding the different terminology in use today to describe indigenous peoples in Canada:

- *Aboriginal Nations.* This term was used in the final report of the Royal Commission on Aboriginal Peoples to refer to a "sizeable body of Aboriginal people with a shared sense of national identity that constitutes the predominant population in a certain territory or collection of territories."

- *First Nations.* The term came into common usage in the 1980s to replace "Indian," which some found offensive. Despite its widespread use, there is no legal definition for the term in Canada. Some communities have adopted "First Nations" to replace "band." It is important to recognize that the term is not a synonym for "Aboriginal Nations" because it does not include Inuit or Métis.

"Aboriginal identity," as defined in the National Household Survey, refers to whether the person reported being an Aboriginal person (that is, First Nations or North American Indian, Métis, or Inuit) and/or being a registered or treaty Indian (that is, registered under the *Indian Act*) and/or being a member of a First Nation or Indian band.

SOURCE: Erasmus & Dussault (1996).

The federal government typically pays for child welfare services in First Nations communities, while the provinces pay for child welfare service delivery in places that are not on reserves. Child welfare services provided to Aboriginal children will include the Aboriginal community as an important element in the lives of children. For example, they will often consult with elders, band members, and extended family members when making decisions about the "best interests of the child." Many child welfare issues in Aboriginal communities are hampered by poverty, community isolation, lack of social services infrastructure, and higher living costs.

HAND IN HAND: NEW BRUNSWICK FIRST NATIONS CHILD WELFARE

In 2009, Child and Youth Advocate Bernard Richard conducted a review of child welfare services on the 11 First Nations communities in New Brunswick. Richard reported that First Nations children in New Brunswick are six times more likely than other children to be taken from their homes and placed in foster care, are four to five times more likely to be charged as young offenders, and may be at greater risk of health issues such as obesity and fetal alcohol spectrum disorder. The report recommended that all levels of government in the province take new approaches to housing, job creation, economic development, drug monitoring and treatment, and law enforcement as it related to Aboriginal children and youth in the province.

One approach that emerged from the implementation of the report was the creation, in collaboration with the Department of Justice, of a "healing to wellness court" in Elsipogtog First Nation. This community-driven initiative seeks to address the underlying causes of criminal behaviour among First Nations youth and adults, and to make the justice system more responsive to the needs of Aboriginal people. A model is being developed jointly with the New Brunswick Department of Social Development and First Nations communities to deliver child welfare services in a culturally appropriate manner. (The Elsipogtog Healing to Wellness Court is also discussed in Chapter 7.)

QUESTIONS

1. In the light of the statistics showing a disproportionate number of children and youth from First Nations communities in both child welfare and youth justice systems, what kind of successes would you hope for in a new model of delivery service?

2. How might the health to wellness court assist Aboriginal youth in conflict with the law?

Children's Aid Organizations and Supporting Legislation

Provincial and territorial child welfare legislation carries out its protective mandate by empowering various authorities to intervene where parents have not lived up to their duty of care in protecting and supervising their children. In Ontario, under s. 15(2), the services are designated to be offered by a children's aid society.

There are 46 children's aid societies in Ontario. Six serve the Aboriginal population, two the Catholic population, and one the Jewish population. Children's aid societies have direct responsibility for child protection. The activities undertaken by the societies include investigating reports of abuse and neglect and, if necessary, taking children into care and supervising their placement in foster and group homes. The Ontario Ministry of Child and Youth Services financially supports and regulates the societies, develops policies to assist the child welfare program, and is responsible for setting standards for group and foster homes.

In other provinces, government ministries are usually designated to offer the child protection services. Table 4.4 lists the legislation for each of the provinces and territories and the agencies responsible.

Purposes of the Child and Family Services Act

The "paramount purpose" of the Ontario *Child and Family Services Act* (CFSA) is "to promote the best interests, protection and well being of children" (s. 1). The CFSA defines "child in need of protection" as any child who is or who appears to be in danger of physical, sexual, or emotional abuse; neglect; or harm.

Other purposes of the CFSA, which must be interpreted in a way "consistent with the best interests, protection and well being of children" (Canadian Coalition on the Rights of the Child, 2014), are as follows:

1. To recognize that while parents may need help in caring for their children, that help should support the autonomy and integrity of the family unit and, wherever possible, be provided on the basis of mutual consent.

2. To recognize that the least disruptive course of action that is available and appropriate in a particular case to help a child should be considered.

3. To recognize that children's services should be provided in a manner that

    a. respects children's needs for continuity of care and for stable family relationships, and

    b. takes into account physical and mental developmental differences among children.

4. To recognize that, wherever possible, services to children and their families should be provided in a manner that respects cultural, religious, and regional differences.

5. To recognize that status Indian and other native people should be entitled to provide, wherever possible, their own child and family services, and that all services to

Indian and native children and families should be provided in a manner that recognizes their culture, heritage, and traditions and the concept of the extended family.

Purposes 1 and 2 show the high value the legislation puts on the "autonomy and integrity of the family unit," and require that child protection approaches minimally disruptive to that unit be given due consideration. Ideally, the approaches will involve parental participation and will be provided with their consent. The remainder of the purposes section of the CFSA is dedicated to ensuring that any services provided are sensitive to the family's background.

> Look at two other provincial or territorial child welfare statutes and compare and contrast the stated purposes with those found in the Ontario CFSA. Do you notice particular ideologies or models present (crime control, justice, welfare, community change, restorative justice) within each of the acts? Is there one dominant ideology in the differing statutes?

Prescriptive and Proscriptive Standards with Respect to Children

Legislation for child protection includes what are referred to as prescriptive and proscriptive standards. A **prescriptive standard** outlines things a parent or legal guardian is required to do; a **proscriptive standard** outlines things that are prohibited. Table 4.5 provides an overview of prescriptive and proscriptive limits for parenting.

prescriptive standard with respect to child welfare, a standard that requires a person responsible for a child to do something (e.g., provide shelter)

proscriptive standard with respect to child welfare, a standard that prohibits a person from doing something to or in respect of a child (e.g., selling tobacco to him or her)

TABLE 4.4 Provincial and Territorial Child Welfare Legislation and Relevant Government Agency Responsible for Child Protection

Province/territory	Child welfare legislation	Government agency responsible
Alberta	• *Child, Youth and Family Enhancement Act*, RSA 2000, c. C-12 • *Drug-Endangered Children Act*, SA 2006, c. D-17 • *Protection of Sexually Exploited Children Act*, RSA 2000, c. P-30.3	Ministry of Children and Youth Services
British Columbia	*Child, Family and Community Service Regulation*, BC Reg. 527/95	Ministry of Children and Family Development
Manitoba	• *The Child and Family Services Act*, CCSM c. C80 • *The Child and Family Services Authorities Act*, CCSM c.C90	Department of Family Services and Housing
New Brunswick	*Family Services Act*, SNB 1980, c. F-2.2	Ministry of Social Development
Newfoundland and Labrador	*Children and Youth Care and Protection Act*, SNL 2010, c. C-12.2	Department of Health and Community Services
Northwest Territories	*Child and Family Services Act*, SNWT 1997, c. 13	Department of Health and Social Services
Nova Scotia	*Children and Family Services Act*, SNS 1990, c. 5	Department of Community Services
Nunavut	*Child and Family Services Act*, SNWT (Nu) 1997, c. 13	Department of Health and Social Services
Ontario	*Child and Family Services Act*, RSO 1990, c. C.11	Ministry of Children and Youth Services
Prince Edward Island	*Child Protection Act*, RSPEI 1988, c. C-5.1	Department of Social Services and Seniors
Quebec	*Loi sur la protection de la jeunesse (Youth Protection Act)*, CQLR c. P-34.1	Ministère de la Santé et des Services sociaux
Saskatchewan	• *The Child and Family Services Act*, SS 1989-90, c. C-7.2 • *Emergency Protection for Victims of Child Sexual Abuse and Exploitation Regulations*, RRS c. E-8.2, Reg. 1	Ministry of Children and Youth Services
Yukon	*Children's Law Act*, RSY 2002, c. 31	Yukon Health and Social Services

TABLE 4.5   Responsibilities of Adults to Children: Prescriptive and Proscriptive Standards

Prescriptive standards (required actions)	Proscriptive standards (prohibited actions)
Providing the necessaries of life (s. 215 *Criminal Code*)	Adults prohibited from engaging in sexual activity with children (sexual interference s. 151 *Criminal Code*; invitation to sexual touching s. 152 *Criminal Code*; incest s. 155 *Criminal Code*)
Facilitating enrollment in public or approved school (*Education Act*)	Adults prohibited from exposing children to corrupting influences such as sex, gambling, violence (corrupting children s. 172 *Criminal Code*) (provincial theatre ratings)
Facilitating immunization and providing appropriate health care for sick and injured children (s. 215 *Criminal Code*) (provincial health act, *Immunization of School Pupils Act*)	Adults prohibited from selling or granting children access to dangerous goods, such as alcohol, tobacco, controlled substances, weapons (*Criminal Code*, *Controlled Drugs and Substances Act*, *Firearms Act*) (provincial liquor licence act, *Tobacco Act*, *Drug-Endangered Children Act*)
Providing economic support from both parents, including the non-custodial parent, in the event of divorce or separation (federal *Divorce Act*, provincial family law acts)	Adults and corporations prohibited from employing children of mandatory school attendance age during school hours; underage children employable outside school hours only in limited contexts (federal *Canada Labour Code*, provincial employment standards)

SOURCE: Rock (2005, pp. 8–9).

HANGING OUT AT THE COFFEE SHOP

Evan and a group of his friends like to go for a coffee at the local Tim Hortons and then hang out in the parking lot to socialize. While there are quite visible signs posted that Tim Hortons will not tolerate loitering and that patrons are allowed to stay no longer than 20 minutes, the group frequently ignore this rule. On the night in question, Evan and his friends were loitering in the lot after midnight. The police came and told them they needed to get in the cruiser; then they were taken home.

CHILD AND FAMILY SERVICES ACT, SECTION 79

Allowing child to loiter, etc.
    (5) No parent of a child less than sixteen years of age shall permit the child to,
        (a) loiter in a public place between the hours of midnight and 6 a.m.; or
        (b) be in a place of public entertainment between the hours of midnight and 6 a.m., unless the parent accompanies the child or authorizes a specified individual eighteen years of age or older to accompany the child.

Police may take child home or to place of safety
    (6) Where a child who is actually or apparently less than sixteen years of age is in a place to which the public has access between the hours of midnight and 6 a.m. and is not accompanied by a person described in clause (5)(b), a peace officer may apprehend the child without a warrant and proceed as if the child had been apprehended under subsection 42(1).

QUESTIONS

1. What are the possible consequences for the young person of being driven home by the police?
2. What are the consequences for the parent?
3. Do you think this is a criminal matter, a child protection matter, or something else?
4. If you were one of the police officers in this situation, what would you do?

Offences Under the CFSA

A person who neglects a child or subjects a child to physical or sexual abuse can be found guilty of an offence under s. 85(2) of the CFSA. (Such a person also, obviously, faces the risk of a charge under the *Criminal Code*.)

Child abuse for purposes of the CFSA offence is defined in s. 79 as "a state or condition of being physically harmed, sexually molested or sexually exploited" (s. 79(1)) and **neglect** is broadly defined to include lack of supervision; failure to treat a mental, emotional, or developmental condition; and allowing a child to loiter late at night. If a child is found in a public place between midnight and 6 a.m. unaccompanied by a parent or designated adult, under s. 79(6) a police officer may, without a warrant, apprehend the child. One example of such a situation would be a child left outside a bingo hall, casino, bar, or other establishment that doesn't allow children while the parent is inside. In all such circumstances, police could lay a charge against parents under s. 85(2). Parents convicted under this section may face a fine of up to $2,000 or a prison term of up to two years, or both. Note, however, that such a charge would not result in a criminal record.

child abuse
physically harming, sexually molesting, or sexually exploiting a child

neglect
failure to meet a child's basic needs, such as health care, supervision, and nutrition, and psychological, educational, or housing needs

Duty to Report Abuse or Neglect

In cases of abuse and neglect, a child's life may be in danger. Troubled parents, dealing with problems of their own, might not recognize that their child is being harmed. However, physical or verbal abuse may escalate to the point where it becomes obvious to people outside the home. For example, the child may exhibit marked changes in behaviour, or may show up at school with unusual bruises. Police may be called to the home in response to a reported disturbance, or at the request of neighbours who suspect young children are wandering unsupervised or are being left at home while the parents are out.

The CFSA requires that perceived child abuse or neglect be treated, not as a private family problem, but as society's problem. This being so, certain provisions of the CFSA require the public in general, and in particular people who work with children, to report suspected abuse or neglect. The duty to report provisions under s. 72(1) provide that a person making the relevant observations is required to report as soon as he or she has reasonable grounds to suspect that harm has occurred, is occurring, or is threatened. Such harm may include:

1. physical harm through abuse or neglect;
2. sexual molestation or exploitation either directly or by not being protected;
3. deprivation of necessary medical treatment;
4. emotional harm through abuse or neglect;
5. deprivation of treatment for emotional or developmental problems, whatever the cause of the problems;
6. abandonment;
7. deprivation of services or treatment designed to prevent the child (under 12) who has killed or seriously injured someone from doing so again; and
8. a risk of doing serious harm to a person or property as a result of encouragement by another person or through insufficient supervision, if the child is under 12 (Rock, 2005, p. 110).

Section 72(1)6 of the CFSA specifically lays out behaviours that might be noticed in a child who is being abused or neglected:

> 6. The child has suffered emotional harm, demonstrated by serious,
>   i.   anxiety,
>   ii. depression,
>   iii. withdrawal,
>   iv. self-destructive or aggressive behaviour, or
>   v.   delayed development,
>
> and there are reasonable grounds to believe that the emotional harm suffered by the child results from the actions, failure to act or pattern of neglect on the part of the child's parent or the person having charge of the child. …

WHO ARE THE PERPETRATORS OF CHILD ABUSE?

In February 2012, two grandparents were found guilty of failing to provide the necessities of life to their 3-year-old granddaughter who had been living with them for two years because her mother was addicted to drugs (Polischuk, 2012).

In February 2013, a 41-year-old RCMP officer and his 34-year-old wife were charged with several counts of aggravated assault, assault with weapon, aggravated sexual assault, forcible confinement, and failing to provide the necessaries of life. The investigation was launched after an 11-year-old child was discovered wandering in a residential neighbourhood in Ottawa. Police sources report that it is believed handcuffs were used to keep the child in the basement of a house for months (Canadian Press, 2013).

In June 2014, Scott Stanley, aged 30, a former Scouts Canada leader and City of Ottawa lifeguard and swim coach, pleaded guilty to ten counts of sexual interference, three counts of luring, and three counts of invitation to sexual touching. The boys involved were between the ages of 12 and 15 at the time of the abuse, which began in 2012 and continued for a year and a half (CBC News, 2014, June 26).

In June 2014, "Operation Snapshot" led to the rescue of five preteen children (two from British Columbia and one each in Ontario, New Brunswick, and Quebec), and to more than 150 people being charged with over 340 counts of child sex assault, luring, and possessing, distributing, and making available child pornography (CBC News, 2014, June 19).

QUESTION

Given the social roles of the accused in these examples, what challenges might exist for police and other social service workers in their duty to report suspicions of child abuse?

Reporting Child "Criminality"

While the majority of the incidents requiring a report of a child who may be potentially in need of protection relate to child abuse, neglect, or abandonment, it is important to underscore ss. 72(1)12 and 13, which require a report on children under the age of 12 who have committed acts that might support a criminal charge, if the child were old enough to be charged:

> 12. The child is less than 12 years old and has killed or seriously injured another person or caused serious damage to another person's property, services or treatment are necessary to prevent a recurrence and the child's parent or the person having charge of the child does not provide, or refuses or is unavailable or unable to consent to, those services or treatment.
>
> 13. The child is less than 12 years old and has on more than one occasion injured another person or caused loss or damage to another person's property, with the encouragement of the person having charge of the child or because of that person's failure or inability to supervise the child adequately.

Under s. 42(1), a peace officer who suspects that a child under 12 years of age has committed an act that, if proven, would otherwise constitute an offence, may apprehend that child without a warrant, and on doing so

> (a) shall return the child to the child's parent or other person having charge of the child as soon as practicable; or
>
> (b) where it is not possible to return the child to the parent or other person within a reasonable time, shall take the child to a place of safety to be detained there until the child can be returned to the parent or other person.

If the police officer has reasonable grounds to believe that returning the child to the parent may put the child at risk, the police officer can take the child to a place of safety instead. A group home made available by child welfare authorities or perhaps even the home of a relative might constitute a place of safety.

Children apprehended for the reasons above are put in detention pending a child protection hearing. There are provisions to ensure a quick resolution. Section 46 decrees that, within five days of the detention, a plan is to be decided upon—either court proceedings commenced, the child returned home, or temporary care arrangements made.

Section 47 deals with the child protection hearing. Regardless of the child's age at the time of the hearing, a hearing will proceed if the child was under 16 years of age at the time of apprehension or the commencement of the proceedings. At the hearing, the judge will decide whether there is need of protection; if not, the child will be returned home.

Child Protection Orders

If the child is found to be in need of protection, the court will make one of four orders, as provided by s. 57:

1. A supervision order can be made whereby the child is returned home, subject to the society's supervision for 3 to 12 months.

2. The child can be made a **ward** of the Children's Aid Society. In this case, he or she is kept away from home and put in the society's care and custody for a period not exceeding 12 months.

3. In the most serious cases, the child can be named a ward of the Crown. Here, the child is put in the custody of the society until the child attains the age of 18 or marries, or a successful application to terminate the **wardship** is brought under s. 64 (by the child himself or herself, by the society, by a parent or guardian, by a foster parent, or, in the case of a First Nations child, by a community or band representative).

4. Consecutive orders of society wardship and supervision may be made whereby the child is made a society ward for a specified period and then returned home under supervision for a combined period not exceeding 12 months.

When making one of these orders, the judge must consider the written plan for the child's care that has been prepared by the society. The required features of such a plan are set out in s. 56. In considering the plan and the proposed order, the judge must prefer "less disruptive" care alternatives, including placement in the child's community with extended family, a neighbour, or a member of the child's band or First Nations community (CFSA, ss. 57(3), (4), and (5)); but the court must be convinced that the chosen alternative is sufficiently protective of the child. Under s. 58, the parents may also be granted access to the child if the court determines this would not put him or her at risk.

ward
a legally protected individual, usually either a child or an incapacitated person

wardship
the legal status of an individual that consists of being a ward of the state

CROSSOVER YOUTH

Crossover youth are youth who move between the child welfare and juvenile justice systems, or who are known to both at the same time. This group generally requires a range of services not offered by either the youth justice or the child welfare system considered separately. Research has shown that being placed into the services of child welfare is, in itself, not associated with an increase in offending for youth. Rather, the trauma of neglect, maltreatment, and witnessing domestic violence and other attachment disruptions in the context of the family are precursors to offending behaviour. In a series of interviews with crossover youth in Ontario, Finlay (2003) reports that one of the most salient features of these young lives is the negative impact of multiple, increasingly restrictive placements. The average number of different out-of-home placements for these youth was over 12, with a range of 6 to 18. Considering that the youth being interviewed were still under the age of 18, this is an incredible burden placed on young people already experiencing difficulties. A number of the youth expressed that group homes were a "gateway to jail," because, they felt, the foster parent system had given up on them and there was no place left to go.

A crossover youth by definition is involved with a multitude of agencies, each responsible for some aspect of the youth's well-being. It is not uncommon for a crossover youth to have had an assessment or "file" with child welfare, youth corrections, mental health services, substance abuse services, special education services, and so on. And rather than sharing information, each agency tends to work as a "silo," seemingly all too eager to hang on to its own files and assessments. This does nothing to enhance the service delivery to the young person, and in most cases lengthens the time before he or she actually receives an intervention.

QUESTIONS

1. What are some of the issues that you can predict for a young person who is both a ward of the state and a young person under the YCJA?

2. Where would a crossover youth be released during the reintegration phase of his or her sentence?

Bala, De Filippis, and Hunter (2013) report that Ontario police, prosecutors, and courts do not currently screen for child welfare involvement when a youth gets caught up in the youth criminal justice system, and suggest that to ensure appropriate and timely intervention police should screen for such involvement early in the process.

In New Brunswick, two sites are being evaluated for the feasibility of rolling out a province-wide Integrated Service Delivery system that would reduce the prevalence of "silos" by creating a coordinated service plan (Government of New Brunswick, 2014). While sharing resources and information under the mantra "one child, one file" seems useful in principle, working out the details of inter-agency cooperation is proving time-consuming.

Figure 4.1 provides an overview of the overlap between the child welfare system and the youth criminal justice system and where different categories of crossover youth might fall.

FIGURE 4.1   Which Statute Applies?

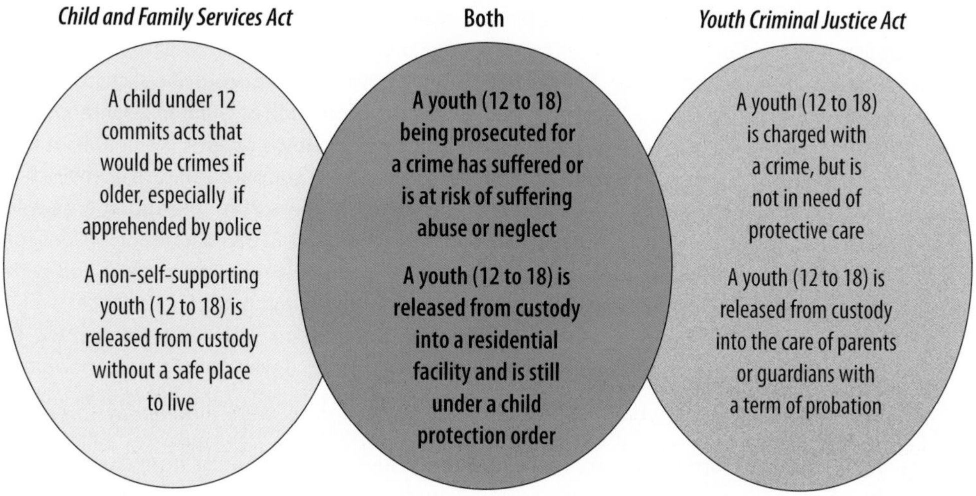

Child and Family Services Act   **Both**   *Youth Criminal Justice Act*

A child under 12 commits acts that would be crimes if older, especially if apprehended by police

A non-self-supporting youth (12 to 18) is released from custody without a safe place to live

A youth (12 to 18) being prosecuted for a crime has suffered or is at risk of suffering abuse or neglect

A youth (12 to 18) is released from custody into a residential facility and is still under a child protection order

A youth (12 to 18) is charged with a crime, but is not in need of protective care

A youth (12 to 18) is released from custody into the care of parents or guardians with a term of probation

SOURCE: Adapted from Rock (2005, fig. 6.1, p. 68).

HOW TO CREATE A CRIMINAL

If you were interested in creating a criminal you would have a pretty good chance if you took a young person from a seriously troubled home, put them into a series of foster and group homes, changed their primary worker on a regular basis, let them run away from "home" at any early age, allowed them to drop out of school and enabled them to develop a drug and/or alcohol addiction. Your chances would improve if, somewhere in their lonely and painful existence, they had been sexually, physically, or emotionally abused. If in those few instances that they sought help, you would ensure that there were no accessible services, that the workers they encountered were rushed and overwhelmed by heavy caseloads, and that they would be seen first and foremost as trouble, rather than troubled, is it surprising then that these young people would become perpetrators or victims of crime? (National Crime Prevention Council, 1997)

In 1997, a group of young people gathered to discuss the issue of crime prevention in Ottawa. The excerpt above was written by a former youth in care. Following the publication of the report called *Young People Say*, this excerpt was made into a video called *Bad Kids: How to Create a Criminal* (Atlantic Mediaworks, 2012).

QUESTIONS

1. Judging from what you have read about child protection, what kinds of things is this young person recommending to prevent youth criminality?

2. Think back to what you learned in Chapter 2 about the risks for criminality. What risks are identified by this young person?

3. The excerpt was written more than 15 years ago. What do you think has changed in the child protection and criminal justice systems today to ensure that young people will not face these challenges?

CHAPTER SUMMARY

Many provisions in the provinces and territories deal with offences committed by youth that are not listed in the *Criminal Code*. Youth, like adults, are subject to being charged with provincial offences—offences created by the provincial legislatures under numerous and varied pieces of legislation such as the *Education Act*, the *Highway Traffic Act*, and the *Liquor Licence Act*. The procedure to be followed in prosecuting provincial offences is set out in an administrative statute, the *Provincial Offences Act* in Ontario, and some variation of this in other provinces and the territories. This Act, like the federal youth criminal justice legislation, creates special procedures for dealing with young people, including notice of detention to parents, restrictions on place of detention, protection of suspect/offender identity, and reduced penalties on conviction.

Under the *Juvenile Delinquents Act* (1908–1984), all matters related to provincial offences, municipal bylaw infractions, and issues arising due to the neglect or abuse of children were handled under one all-encompassing law. It did not matter, for example, whether a child was in "need of protection" or had committed a provincial offence or a criminal offence; all "delinquents" were handled in the same manner as a misguided and misdirected child. With the division of criminal matters for young people into the *Young Offenders Act* (1984–2002) and the more recent *Youth Criminal Justice Act* (2003–present), provinces and territories have had to concern themselves with how to manage child protection cases and those young people who violate provisions under the *Education Act*.

The *Child and Family Services Act* is the provincial child welfare legislation that directs the protection of children in Ontario. This legislation focuses on cases in which parents are unable or unwilling to provide the necessary support and care to their children, and sets the legislative framework for the apprehension of children in need of protection. The CFSA includes provisions for dealing with children who suffer abuse and neglect and with those under the age of 12 who commit criminal offences.

Aboriginal youth in Canada are vastly overrepresented in child welfare systems. Many social welfare issues in Aboriginal communities are affected by systemic problems such as lack of infrastructure. Cultural practices must be incorporated and community members such as elders must be included in all processes addressing the needs of these youth. Crossover youth are those who are both wards of the state and young persons under the YCJA. Because they fall into both categories, child welfare services tend to be offered by many different organizations, each independently of the other. This tendency is problematic for youth; inter-agency cooperation is needed. For both Aboriginal and crossover youth, there must be partnership and communication between agencies in order to navigate these youth away from the youth criminal justice system.

KEY TERMS

absolute liability offence, 84
best interests of the child, 94
certificate of offence, 86
certificate of parking infraction, 86
child abuse, 99
child in need of protection, 94
due diligence, 85
duty to report, 94
fiduciary duty, 93
information, 86
neglect, 99

novice driver, 90
parens patriae, 93
prescriptive standard, 97
procedural fairness, 93
proscriptive standard, 97
strict liability offence, 84
truancy, 92
ward, 101
wardship, 101
young driver, 90

REFERENCES

Atlantic Mediaworks (Producer). (2012). *Bad kids: How to create a criminal* [Video]. Retrieved from http://www.youtube.com/watch?v=g7ZO7afg158.

Bala, N., De Filippis, R., & Hunter, K. (2013). Crossover youth: Improving Ontario's responses. Retrieved from http://www.afccontario.ca.

Bowal, P., & Iss, L. (2013). *Whatever happened to … R. v. Sault Ste. Marie: The due diligence defence*. Retrieved from http://www.lawnow.org/whatever-happened-to-r-v-sault-ste-marie-the-due-diligence-defence/.

Canadian Charter of Rights and Freedoms. (1982). Part I of the *Constitution Act, 1982*, being Schedule B to the *Canada Act 1982* (UK), 1982, c. 11.

Canadian Coalition on the Rights of the Child. (2014). Best interests of the child. Retrieved from http://rightsofchildren.ca/wp-content/uploads/Best-Interests-of-the-Child.pdf.

Canadian Press. (2013, February 15). Ottawa abuse case: Child allegedly handcuffed in basement; RCMP officer, wife charged. *The Huffington Post*. Retrieved from http://www.huffingtonpost.ca/2013/02/15/ottawa-child-abuse-handcuffs-rcmp-officer-charged_n_2692373.html.

CBC News. (2014, June 19). Child porn bust: 5 children saved, RCMP lay 343 charges. *CBC News*. Retrieved from http://www.cbc.ca/news/canada/nova-scotia/child-porn-bust-5-children-saved-rcmp-lay-343-charges-1.2680508.

CBC News. (2014, June 26). Ex–Scouts Canada leader pleads guilty to sexually abusing 4 boys. *CBC News*. Retrieved from http://www.cbc.ca/news/canada/ottawa/ex-scouts-canada-leader-pleads-guilty-to-sexually-abusing-4-boys-1.2688667.

Child and Family Services Act. (1990). RSO 1990, c. C.11.

Criminal Code. (1985). RSC 1985, c. C-46.

Education Act. (1990). RSO 1990, c. E.2.

Erasmus, G., & Dussault, R. (1996). *Report of the Royal Commission on Aboriginal Peoples*. Vol. 5. Ottawa: Royal Commission on Aboriginal Peoples.

Family Law Act. (1990). RSO 1990, c. F.3.

Finlay, J. (2003). Crossover kids: Care to custody. *Ontario Office of Child and Family Service Advocacy*, 1–28.

Highway Traffic Act. (1990). RSO 1990, c. H.8.

Government of New Brunswick. (2014). Integrated Service Delivery (ISD) for at-risk children and youth—Demonstration sites. Retrieved from http://www2.gnb.ca/content/gnb/en/corporate/pr/isd.html.

Liquor Licence Act. (1990). RSO 1990, c. L.19.

National Aboriginal Health Organization (NAHO). (2014). Terminology guidelines. Retrieved from http://www.naho.ca/publications/topics/terminology.

National Crime Prevention Council. (1997, January). *Young people say*. Final Report of the Youth Consultation Initiative.

Oreopoulos, P. (2005). *Canadian compulsory school laws and their impact on educational attainment and future earnings*. Analytical Studies Branch Research Paper Series. Ottawa: Statistics Canada.

Polischuk, H. (2012, January 17). Grandparents on trial charged with failing to provide necessities of life. *Leader Post* (Regina, Saskatchewan). Retrieved from http://www.oacas.org/news/12/jan/17child.pdf.

Provincial Offences Act. (1990). RSO 1990, c. P.33.

Rock, N. (2005). *Child protection and Canadian law: A service perspective*. Toronto: Emond Montgomery.

Sault Ste. Marie, R v. (1978). [1978] 2 SCR 1299, 1978 CanLII 11.

Statistics Canada. (2013). Aboriginal peoples in Canada: First Nations people, Métis and Inuit (analytical document). National Household Survey, 2011. Catalogue No. 99-011-X2011001.

Vandna, S., & Kozlowski, A. (2013). The structure of Aboriginal child welfare in Canada. *The International Indigenous Policy Journal*, 4(2), 1–21.

Wilson, J. (2011). *The law's treatment of youth and children*. Toronto: LexisNexis.

EXERCISES AND REVIEW

Review Questions

1. What part(s) of the *Provincial Offences Act* deal(s) specifically with youthful offenders?

2. Can a youth be arrested on suspicion of having committed a provincial offence? If so, under what circumstances?

3. List the sentences available to a judge when a youth is found guilty of a provincial offence.

4. Where will a youth given a custodial sentence under the POA be sent to serve his or her time?

5. What do you think happens when a child under the age of 12 is found committing what would be considered a provincial offence?

6. What is the age jurisdiction of the *Child and Family Services Act*?

7. Which agencies administer the protective services mandated by the CFSA?

8. What typically happens under the CFSA if a child under the age of 12 is suspected of having committed a serious crime?

9. When a child has been made a ward of the Crown, what rights do biological parents have (that is, can the parents visit with the child)?

10. Where might a child live once child protection proceedings have been commenced?

Discussion Questions

1. Part VI of the Ontario POA, which governs the legislation's application to youth, defines "young person" as a person between the ages of 12 and 16 years. What do you think of the disparity between provincial offences legislation age jurisdiction and criminal age jurisdiction? Is there a common problem regarding age jurisdiction for other issues such as driving, school-leaving age, and drinking alcohol?

2. In view of the patterns of youth criminality discussed in Chapter 2, under which provincial statutes do you think youth are most often charged?

3. Review the three scenarios below. Has the duty to report under s. 72 of the CFSA been triggered? Discuss or defend your answer.

   a. A gym teacher notices that, while many of the six-year-olds in her grade 1 class have bruises and scrapes on their legs and elbows, one little boy in particular routinely has bruises of various colours on his upper arms and shoulders. He behaves normally, seems cheerful, and interacts well with teachers and the other children.

   b. An architect who works at home notices that the two children who live next door, ages seven and nine, arrive home from school around 4 p.m. Their mother does not get home from work until about 5:30, and no other adult appears to be in the home between 4 and 5:30 p.m. Most of the time the children watch TV indoors or roughhouse in the backyard. They usually seem fine, but yesterday the younger one sat crying on his back porch for nearly 20 minutes.

   c. An elementary school principal has been having problems with the mother of one of the students. She refuses to send her daughter to school on days when compulsory standardized tests are conducted. Last year, when half the grade 2 class had contracted head lice, this mother had refused to administer the scalp treatment the school required as a condition of readmission. This year, another parent reported that this mother had lied about her daughter's vaccination status on the registration form, and that the child had, in fact, not been vaccinated against measles, mumps, and rubella. The principal feels that this mother is irresponsible and is not acting in her child's best interests.

4. In cases where a child under the age of 12 commits an act that would be a crime under criminal law, the CFSA empowers a peace officer to temporarily detain that child to determine whether he or she might be a "child in need of protection." What, if anything, does this method of dealing with underage criminality imply about families, or about child behaviour? Do you see any problems with this mechanism? If so, can you suggest an alternative mechanism?

PART III

Policing and Criminal Procedure

Extrajudicial Measures, Charging, Arrest, and Interviewing

5

LEARNING OUTCOMES

After completing this chapter, you should be able to:

- List and give examples of strategic decisions that have to be made by police personnel during initial contacts with a youthful suspect.

- Describe the requirements to comply with s. 146 of the *Youth Criminal Justice Act* (YCJA) and identify when the first point of compliance takes place.

- Describe the elements necessary to comply with both the *Canadian Charter of Rights and Freedoms* and the expanded information about rights under the YCJA.

- Explain police responsibilities regarding notice and access to parents upon the arrest and charging of a young person.

- Describe the features of a young suspect's valid waiver of the right to silence and the right to counsel.

- Define "spontaneous statement" for purposes of the YCJA.

- Discuss the research that supports the use of diversion outside of the formal youth court process.

- Explain extrajudicial measures and extrajudicial sanctions, and outline the differences between the two with examples.

- Outline the changes to extrajudicial measures and extrajudicial sanctions brought about through the *Safe Streets and Communities Act* (2012).

Introduction

The detention, questioning, and arrest of adolescents suspected of committing criminal offences in Canada is governed by three major sources of legislation: the *Canadian Charter of Rights and Freedoms*, the *Criminal Code*, and the *Youth Criminal Justice Act* (YCJA). (There are also some limited powers of arrest/detention with respect to provincial offences; these are prescribed in Ontario by the *Provincial Offences Act*, discussed in Chapter 4.)

The Charter and the Code apply to both adults and young persons. The YCJA guarantees special rights and protections to young persons in addition to those applicable to adults. These additional rights are prescribed on the basis of an understanding that adolescents are more vulnerable and generally less mature and sophisticated than adults, and are not as well informed about their procedural rights or the justice system in general.

Besides these enhanced procedural rights, certain provisions of the YCJA are intended to promote parental involvement throughout the process, as a means of providing youth with adult guidance and much-needed emotional support during what is often a difficult time.

WHEN A POCKETFUL OF CANDY DRAWS ATTENTION

Read the following case study and consider the questions at the end. As you move through this chapter you should be able to identify, think through, and discuss the different aspects of John's case. By the end of the chapter you should be able to answer all of the questions.

John and two of his friends, Rashid and Suzette, are hanging around outside a high school at 4:30 p.m. on a Monday afternoon. Two police officers, driving by with their windows down and smelling an odour of marijuana, stop to question the three. Rashid and Suzette run away, but John is halted.

He seems quite young and has no ID on him. As one officer speaks to John, the other notices a small hand-rolled cigarette on the ground and picks it up—it does look to him like marijuana. Startled, John blurts out that, in fact, it is, and he did take a drag of it, but that it belonged to one of his friends. "I'm really sorry, I'm only 14 and I've never been in trouble before. My mom is expecting me home … I'm going to be in so much trouble!"

Then John pulls his large coat close around him and the officers see bulges. He is put under arrest and searched. The officers find nothing illegal—the bulges are bags of candy.

After being taken to the police station, John provides a phone number where he says his mother can be reached. There is no answer at that number, however. John is brought to an interview room and informed of his rights. The police clearly state that before he answers any questions he has the right to summon a lawyer and have his mother or another responsible adult with him. John says that he understands, but that he is willing to answer the questions now. Under questioning, he admits the joint was his, and continues to apologize. While John is still in the room with the officers, his mother arrives, and he spends some time talking to her.

Returning to the interview room, the officers decide that the best option for John would be to use an extrajudicial measure, for a number of reasons: this is John's first run-in with the law; the offence is not serious; John seems remorseful; and the police believe he will benefit from an extrajudicial measure. They proceed to explain to John and his mother the steps required to complete the extrajudicial measure.

QUESTIONS

1. At what point was John "detained"?

2. Since John had no ID on him, how did the police proceed with assumptions regarding his age?

3. When John blurted out his confession, would this be considered a spontaneous statement?

4. Was the search of John's person lawful?

5. Was it a problem for the police to question John without his mother present?

6. What would be an appropriate extrajudicial measure (what activities might be included in the measure) for John?

Age, Detention, and Arrest

A Suspect's Age

The YCJA makes it clear that being under 18 years of age triggers special requirements for handling suspects and witnesses.

Police officers must keep in mind that at the first contact with a young person, it is important to be aware of the additional safeguards for youth provided in the YCJA. These provisions explain how to ensure that the rights of youth are respected; and from a police perspective, compliance with rights requirements (for example, with respect to search) increases the likelihood that evidence gathered at and around the time of detention and/or arrest will be admissible in court if the incident leads to a charge.

Physical and Psychological Detention of Young Suspects

Contrary to what most people believe, a police arrest is not usually the first contact an accused has with the youth criminal justice system. Police can detain, question, and search a suspect for the purpose of the investigation prior to making an arrest. Any time an officer stops someone of any age, it is considered a **detention**.

While a young person is delayed or kept waiting for questioning, Charter rights under ss. 9 and 10 do not apply, provided that there is no significant physical or psychological restraint. As outlined by Justice LeDain in *R v. Therens* (1985), detention includes not only *physical* but also *psychological* restraint, as when the individual believes he or she is "not free to refuse to comply." Even routine traffic stops amount to a detention. If an officer needs to conduct a more thorough investigation (longer than 15 minutes), the officer can detain a suspect or possible suspect up to 24 hours. This can be stretched to 36 hours under reasonable circumstances—for example, on long weekends or when no justice of the peace is available to decide whether the youth, if charged, should be released before trial.

When there is a link between the young person stopped and a recent or ongoing criminal offence, the police encounter becomes an investigative detention. Again, in *R v. Therens*, it was determined that a detention occurs when the police officer "assumes control over the movement of a person by a demand or direction which may have significant legal consequence and which prevents or impedes access to counsel."

With young people, police must be mindful not only of s. 9 of the Charter (the right not to be arbitrarily detained) and s. 10(b) (the right to retain and instruct counsel), but also of additional safeguards required because of the age and stage of maturity of the young person. The suspect's age as well as his or her responses and conduct must be taken into account by the police when they decide how to interact with the suspect and which words to use. Younger suspects will not have the same degree of understanding of legal rules as more seasoned young persons who may have previously been detained by the police. In *R v. Grant* (2006), a case about whether police questioning can be considered an unreasonable search, the court considered what the police officers said and did, including the questions asked

detention
being stopped by police on the basis of a reasonable suspicion; includes not only physical but also psychological restraint, as when the individual believes he or she is not free to go

and whether the young person was told by the officers that he was free to go. Evidence was also presented about the young person's responses to the questions and whether he clearly knew it was up to him to decide to stay in the discussion.

Case in Point

R v. M.E., [2006] OJ No. 1657 (CJ)

There is a fine line between a reasonable detention of a youth and one considered arbitrary (without reasonable grounds). The case of *R v. M.E.* (2006) demonstrates just how fine this line can be.

The accused in *R v. M.E.* was found asleep at a computer in an Internet café by three police officers and was informed he was going to be charged with trespassing. An officer asked the 17-year-old his name and date of birth, and whether he was wanted on any charges. One comment made to the youth was of particular importance. An officer informed the youth that if he did not provide this information he would be arrested. The youth then answered the questions. The police ran a Canadian Police Information Centre (CPIC) search, which led to the finding that the youth was wanted on a warrant. He was arrested and searched, and found to be in the possession of marijuana and ecstasy.

The question during trial was whether the youth had been arbitrarily detained. Justice Murray ruled that the officers involved did not have grounds to ask the youth for information to run a CPIC and could have written a ticket with less information. Further, by telling the youth that if he did not provide the information he would be arrested, the officers created a scenario in which the youth would have felt "psychologically compelled to submit to the officers' questioning." What had occurred had constituted detention, and moreover the youth had not been granted his s. 10 Charter right to know the reasons for detention. Justice Murray excluded the evidence and the youth was acquitted.

QUESTIONS

1. Explain what Justice Murray meant by "psychologically compelled."

2. How could the effect of psychological compulsion be intensified by the fact that the accused was a youth?

Pre-Arrest Questioning and Statements

Where a person is under age 18, the YCJA imposes special requirements with respect to questioning and the admissibility of statements. If the suspect looks to be possibly under the age of 25, officers should err on the side of caution to be in compliance with the Act. Where officers mistake suspects for adults, or where youthful suspects misrepresent their age as 18 or older, the YCJA provides a remedial provision under s. 146(8). Where a young-looking suspect cannot or will not produce proof of age, the age may ultimately be proven in court by means of parental testimony; until that time, investigators should treat him or her as a person under age 18.

spontaneous statement
a statement offered by a youth without his or her being prompted by police questions or comments, and before police have had a chance to advise the youth of his or her s. 146 rights

Another early issue investigating officers must consider is whether a young person being questioned about an incident is a witness, a victim, or a suspect (or any combination of these). It is always possible that a witness might make an incriminating **spontaneous statement**. Section 146(3) of the YCJA addresses this concern. It states that when questioning young persons, officers must make a reasonable effort to inform them of their protections under that section. However, if a witness suddenly blurts out something incriminating, the statement will be admissible in court if the officer did not realistically have time to point out the protections.

Another factor with respect to spontaneity is whether the officer prompted the statement. If an officer asks a question, however innocent, and it occasions an incriminating response from the youth, the statement is not "spontaneous." The appropriate test, then, is whether the utterance is "blurted out" without the prompting of a police officer in circumstances in which there is no opportunity to follow the appropriate procedures (Hanson, 1987, p. 199).

In any event, the case law demonstrates that the spontaneity of statements will be construed narrowly—that is, where there is any doubt, the issue will be decided in favour of the young person, and not the person seeking to admit the statement.

To Arrest or Not? Decision to Arrest

During an investigative detention, when police ask questions of a youthful suspect they are attempting to determine whether there are reasonable and probable grounds to lay a criminal charge. If there are, the police must make a decision to either arrest the suspect and lay a charge or handle things through extrajudicial measures.

According to Keenan (2013, p. 104), an **arrest** occurs when an officer assumes control over the movement of a person by some demand or direction. The authority of the police to make an arrest is granted under the *Criminal Code* and provincial statutes (for example, the *Highway Traffic Act*). An arrest can be made in order to prevent the commission of a criminal offence, to end an offence against public order (for example, causing a disturbance), or to compel attendance of the accused in court.

Police have the power to arrest a person without a warrant under s. 495(1) of the Code when they find someone committing an indictable criminal offence, or if they have **reasonable grounds** to believe a warrant of arrest is in force within the jurisdiction in which the person has been found. Section 495(2) requires police officers to obtain a warrant for arrest for summary conviction offences and hybrid offences unless it is necessary to arrest the young person to establish his or her identity, to secure evidence of or relating to the offence, or to prevent the continuation or repetition of the offence. If the police decide to arrest a suspect, they must tell the individual that he or she is under arrest, and identify the specific charge.

As is mentioned elsewhere in this chapter, detention of a young person triggers a range of police obligations under the YCJA: to further explain accused's rights in age-appropriate language; to arrange for detention separate from adults (s. 30(3)); and to immediately try to contact the parents (s. 26(1)).

The Charter protects the rights of individuals who have been detained or arrested. These rights are described in Charter ss. 8–10:

arrest
police control of the movement of a person by some demand or direction on the basis of probable cause, in order for the person to answer for a criminal charge

reasonable grounds
facts or circumstances, used as justification for police action, that to a reasonable person are beyond mere suspicions

> *Canadian Charter of Rights and Freedoms*
> **8.** Everyone has the right to be secure against unreasonable search and seizure.
> **9.** Everyone has the right not to be arbitrarily detained or imprisoned.
> **10.** Everyone has the right on arrest or detention
> (a) to be informed promptly of the reasons therefor;
> (b) to retain and instruct counsel without delay and to be informed of that right; and
> (c) to have the validity of the detention determined … and to be released if the detention is not lawful.

In addition to the Charter protections that are triggered by any arrest, the evidence provisions of s. 146 of the YCJA must be considered when the person under arrest is an adolescent.

Searches and Charter Rights at the Time of Arrest

The police can search any person who has been arrested, at the time of the arrest, in order to preserve evidence that might otherwise be lost and to ensure the officer's safety. So long as the arrest was lawful, anything discovered in the search can generally be used as evidence against the individual in court. However, a search incidental to arrest must be performed for a valid reason, such as to secure or preserve evidence, ensure the safety of the officer or the suspect, and prevent escape. Police may also perform warrantless searches when an individual voluntarily consents to it, waiving his or her constitutional rights. This is particularly important to note with young persons, because it is necessary to show that the suspect truly understood that the police would be able to use anything uncovered in the search in a subsequent prosecution. A summary of the law about adult warrantless searches is found in *R v. Wills* (1992, para. 69), where the court provided the following guidelines for establishing whether consent to a search had been given:

1. there was consent, expressed or implied;
2. the person had the authority to give consent;
3. the consent was voluntary and was not the product of police oppression, coercion, or other external conduct, which negated the freedom to choose;
4. the person was aware of the nature of the search being requested;
5. the person was aware of his or her right to refuse to permit the police to engage in the search; and
6. the person was aware of the potential consequences of giving the consent.

It is important to remember that the rules covering consent to a search after arrest are different from those covering a person's questioning in an investigative detention. In the leading Supreme Court of Canada case (*R v. Mann*, 2004, para. 45), it was stated that if an officer has reasonable grounds to believe that his or her safety or the safety of others is at risk, he or she may engage in a "protective pat-down search of the detained individual." However, such a search cannot be merely a "fishing expedition" for evidence.

Case in Point

R v. J.D., [2007] OJ No. 1365 (CJ)

In 2004, two police officers encountered three youth walking down a Toronto street late at night in a known high-crime area. The youth were all dressed in dark colours with hoodies. While the police did not know any of them, and were not looking for any specific individual, they stopped the group to ask a few questions, asked them to remove the hoodies and keep their hands in sight, and requested names and dates of birth in order to run CPIC searches. They were not notified of their legal right not to answer questions.

The CPIC queries revealed that one of the group, J.D., was in violation of a bail condition (by being in that area), and he was arrested on the spot. A search of his person turned up an imitation handgun, resulting in an additional charge of possession of burglary tools. J.D. was notified of his legal rights under s. 10 of the *Charter of Rights and Freedoms*.

QUESTIONS

1. When the police officers had begun speaking to the youth, were they then being detained?

2. Although the youth had a legal right to refuse to answer police questions at the beginning of their meeting, this had not been conveyed to them. If it had, might it have changed the outcome of the encounter?

When J.D.'s case went to trial, the court identified two Charter violations. By asking J.D. to remove his hoodie and keep his hands visible, the police officers had been detaining him—arbitrarily, since all three youth had been stopped without reasonable grounds. Also, long before the pat-down of J.D., a search had occurred by means of the CPIC, although the officers had purposely not advised J.D. about his right to refuse to answer questions. Therefore, the CPIC search had been unlawful, and any subsequent evidence obtained as a result (such as the imitation gun) was inadmissible.

The Role of Parents

The YCJA explicitly provides for a role for the parents of youth in trouble with the law—for example, by requiring that police contact parents when a young person is arrested. Under s. 146(2)(c) of the YCJA, a young person can elect to consult with both counsel and a parent. The legislation further specifies that, if a parent is unavailable, the young person may consult with an adult relative. In the absence of an adult relative, the youth may consult with any other appropriate adult who is not a co-accused or under investigation for the same offence.

The rules about parental involvement are designed to allow youth the benefit of adult guidance, emotional support, and assistance with practical matters like obtaining legal counsel. Case law has established that if a youth whom the police want to question expresses a desire to see a parent, the police must permit a meeting as soon as a parent is available (*R v. P.(S.)*, 1991, p. 317). Even if a youth is arrested but not detained pending trial, the police officer or Crown prosecutor must notify the parent in writing of the date of the youth court hearing.

Involving parents can sometimes create unique legal and practical problems. The views and wishes of parents and young people will not always be the same, which can create legal complications (such as a conflict of interest) when parents get involved with hiring (and especially paying for) legal counsel. Some well-meaning parents who are present during police questioning and do not know the particulars of the investigation against their children may unwittingly harm their child's case. Recognizing this, the law requires police officers to provide an opportunity for the parent and youth to meet alone before questioning. Before the meeting, the police should fully inform the parent of the charges and the nature of the investigation.

It may also be that problems in a young person's family life, including abuse by parents, are a factor that led to the young person's involvement with police. Young persons whose parents are unable or unwilling to support them during an investigation and prosecution can be at a significant disadvantage. The YCJA does contemplate this predicament and affords youth a chance to contact a "responsible person" if a parent is not available, or if contacting a parent would be inappropriate for some reason. When a youth is a Crown ward (has been removed from the care of parents by the state), a child protection worker or foster parent is considered a parent for purposes of the investigation. That is, all the procedural requirements regarding parents will apply.

In a study of police officers' views on the role of parents in the youth justice system, responders reported that in their experience there was not much of a role for a parent at the police station. In fact, they expressed concern about parents worsening the situation by getting into conflict with the child over the incident, increasing the child's stress and interfering with the ability of police to do their job. When officers were asked what they felt the ideal role for parents should be, they said it was socialization—helping the young person follow police conditions and take responsibility for his or her actions, and encouraging the child not to get into such trouble again (Peterson-Badali & Broeking, 2010).

The Admissibility of Youth Statements

Once a decision to charge has been made, protecting the value of investigative evidence, especially statements by the accused, becomes extremely important. Interviewing young suspects requires careful compliance with the protective provisions of the YCJA, such as confirming the youth's age, and informing him or her about the right to retain and instruct counsel without delay, the right to silence (and waivers to give up that right), and the right to consult with parents and/or another responsible person.

The right to counsel under s. 146(2)(c) includes the right to be informed of that right (s. 146(2)(b)(iii)). Full compliance with this section requires police to provide access to a phone and privacy to make the initial call(s); (ideally) a local list of criminal defence counsel; and information about the availability of legal aid and the relevant phone number.

Confessions and other statements are probably the most important source of evidence in the trial of a youth.

Commentators have noted that youth tend to perceive the justice system differently from the way adults do. Youth's understanding of guilt and innocence tends to be rudimentary, and they may believe that there is no hope for them (and no reason to exercise their rights, such as the right not to make a statement) if they are guilty in the factual—and not necessarily legal—sense of the word. In other words, they are less likely than adults to understand that a conviction depends not only on "the facts" but also on the prosecution's ability to present strong and admissible evidence, and to overcome defences that may be available to the accused. Conversely, youth are more likely than adults to believe that something might be gained—leniency, for example—through cooperation with the investigation and disclosure (for example, answering questions) to a degree not necessarily consistent with their best interests.

The YCJA puts the onus on the prosecution to prove that police personnel complied with the requirements. This must be proved beyond a reasonable doubt, making it very difficult for a statement to be admitted and requiring a very high standard of compliance on the part of police personnel. This is consistent with adult criminal law, where the onus is also on the prosecution to establish, beyond a reasonable doubt, the voluntariness and admissibility of any statement to be tendered.

Inadmissibility, of course, is the biggest threat to statement evidence.

If a police officer violates an accused's rights (to be free from self-incrimination or to acquire counsel, for example) under the Charter, the youth's statements may be inadmissible in court. In addition, any evidence subsequently discovered as a result of the statement during the investigation can be ruled inadmissible. For example, suppose police believe they saw a young man discard something out a car window as they approached. If the man's rights are violated in the arrest process, and he makes a statement about the location of the discarded item, it may later be ruled inadmissible as evidence because it was only discovered as a result of the inadmissible statement.

In making a determination of admissibility under the Charter, a judge considers whether "having regard to all the circumstances, the admission ... would bring the administration of justice into disrepute" (s. 24(2)). This involves an assessment of the seriousness of the infringement of rights and a consideration of whether the police officer was acting in "good faith." The essential elements of the law pertaining to Charter violations in the context of the discovery of evidence were confirmed by the Supreme Court of Canada in the case of *R v. Rodgers* (2006).

Youth Criminal Justice Act

General law on admissibility of statements to apply

146(1) Subject to this section, the law relating to the admissibility of statements made by persons accused of committing offences applies in respect of young persons.

When statements are admissible

(2) No oral or written statement made by a young person who is less than eighteen years old, to a peace officer or to any other person who is, in law, a person in authority, on the arrest or detention of the young person or in circumstances where the peace officer or other person has reasonable grounds for believing that the young person has committed an offence is admissible against the young person unless

(a) the statement was voluntary;

(b) the person to whom the statement was made has, before the statement was made, clearly explained to the young person, in language appropriate to his or her age and understanding, that

(i) the young person is under no obligation to make a statement,

(ii) any statement made by the young person may be used as evidence in proceedings against him or her,

(iii) the young person has the right to consult counsel and a parent or other person in accordance with paragraph (c), and

(iv) any statement made by the young person is required to be made in the presence of counsel and any other person consulted in accordance with paragraph (c), if any, unless the young person desires otherwise;

(c) the young person has, before the statement was made, been given a reasonable opportunity to consult

(i) with counsel, and

(ii) with a parent or, in the absence of a parent, an adult relative or, in the absence of a parent and an adult relative, any other appropriate adult chosen by the young person, as long as that person is not a co-accused, or under investigation, in respect of the same offence; and

(d) if the young person consults a person in accordance with paragraph (c), the young person has been given a reasonable opportunity to make the statement in the presence of that person.

Exception in certain cases for oral statements

(3) The requirements set out in paragraphs (2)(b) to (d) do not apply in respect of oral statements if they are made spontaneously by the young person to a peace officer or other person in authority before that person has had a reasonable opportunity to comply with those requirements.

Waiver of right to consult

(4) A young person may waive the rights under paragraph (2)(c) or (d) but any such waiver

(a) must be recorded on video tape or audio tape; or

(b) must be in writing and contain a statement signed by the young person that he or she has been informed of the right being waived.

Waiver of right to consult

(5) When a waiver of rights under paragraph (2)(c) or (d) is not made in accordance with subsection (4) owing to a technical irregularity, the youth justice court may determine that the waiver is valid if it is satisfied that the young person was informed of his or her rights, and voluntarily waived them.

> *Admissibility of statements*
>
> (6) When there has been a technical irregularity in complying with paragraphs (2)(b) to (d), the youth justice court may admit into evidence a statement referred to in subsection (2), if satisfied that the admission of the statement would not bring into disrepute the principle that young persons are entitled to enhanced procedural protection to ensure that they are treated fairly and their rights are protected.

Suspect Age and Validity of Waivers of Rights

According to s. 146(2), the officer must have explained to the young person his or her rights in "language appropriate to his or her age and understanding." This requires that the police officer assess the level of understanding of the young person before obtaining the statement, a requirement unique to the youth context and absent from the Charter rules or from the *Criminal Code*. In *R v. C.G.* (1986), the judge described some of the evidence required to establish a youth's "age and understanding," including educational level, language and vocabulary skills, and emotional state. Making an effort to build rapport with the young person will help the officer ascertain this information.

An investigating officer must use greater diligence in dealing with accused who are young or who have no previous experience with the criminal justice system. Learning disabilities and behavioural problems will be weighed by the court. The officer, when testifying, must be prepared to comprehensively explain how he or she formed an opinion about the young person's level of understanding.

Once the officer has formed this opinion, he or she must state the young person's rights in language appropriate to that level of understanding. In practice, it might be a good idea for the officer to ask the youth to repeat, or even transcribe, in his or her own words, the rights conveyed. Case law has demonstrated that a "high standard of performance" is expected of the investigating officer in this regard (*R v. P.B.*, 1984, p. 27).

waiver
the oral or written giving up or dispensing with the exercise of a legal right

When a youth makes the informed decision to waive his or her right to silence, there is a formal process that must occur in which the **waiver** is recorded and signed by the youth. In a study by Ontario researchers Abramovitch, Higgins-Biss, and Biss (1993), (innocent) male and female students in grades 6, 8, 10, and 12 (that is, aged about 11 to 17 years) were asked to imagine that they had been arrested for shoplifting and were administered a police-sanctioned caution including portions designed for youth. The youth were then given a typical youth waiver document in the form shown below (see the box). They were then asked whether they would sign the waiver.

TYPICAL YOUTH WAIVER

Waiver:

I, _____, understand I have the right to call a lawyer or call my parents or some other relative or some other adult. I also understand I can have any of these persons present with me now if I wish.

I do not want to call anyone or have anyone here with me now.

Dated the _____ day of _____ 19____.

Signed _____

Witnessed _____

Afterward, the students were questioned by the researchers about their understanding of the effect of the waiver. The study determined that, while the majority (61 percent) of the students understood the waiver form, *the LESS a student understood about the form, the MORE likely he or she was to sign it*. Further, while a majority of students understood the basic meaning of the waiver, fewer than 50 percent understood that if they signed the waiver, police questioning would follow.

LEGAL COUNSEL FOR ALL YOUTH

Upon arrest or detention, a youth must be informed that he or she has the right to obtain or instruct a lawyer and must understand this right. But what if the youth or family cannot afford a lawyer? There are provisions in Canada for this problem. While the availability of options is different across provinces, most provinces offer legal aid support to youth who cannot obtain a lawyer for financial reasons. For example, in British Columbia a lawyer is appointed to a youth by the Legal Services Society regardless of the youth's or family's income (Justice BC, n.d.). In other provinces, legal counsel is available through an agency such as the Newfoundland and Labrador Legal Aid Commission (n.d.) for youth who meet the requirements. In Canada, no youth will be denied the right to a lawyer because he or she cannot afford one.

QUESTION

While legal counsel is provided for all Canadian youth when they cannot afford it, the qualifications for such support vary across the country. Should all provinces adopt the same method for providing legal counsel?

As mentioned above, a young person may waive the right to consult with counsel and a parent under s. 146(4). However, the investigating officer has to meet a high standard of evidence for the waiver to be recognized. The young person should fully understand the right he or she is waiving and the consequences of doing so. Further, the officer might even be required to advise the young person of the reasons why he or she might wish such a consultation and of the fact it is in his or her best interests. The judge in *R v. M.A.M.* (1986, p. 573) explained the test for a valid waiver as follows:

> There should be a genuine endeavour by the person in authority to describe the function of the lawyer and the benefits to the young person of having a lawyer, or parents or relatives or an adult friend present. That endeavour should be designed to lead to an appreciation on the part of the young person of the consequences of the choices that he makes.

Who Is a "Person in Authority"?

Section 146(2) provides that the rules about statements apply in circumstances in which a youth is liable (whether spontaneously or in response to questions) to make a statement to a **person in authority**. A "person in authority," for the purposes of the provision, is any person that a reasonable young person might perceive as an agent of the criminal justice system. "Peace officer" is specifically included in the section and, therefore, the section applies to all police officers.

Whether individuals other than police officers can be persons in authority is a more complicated issue. While parents often have considerable influence over their children, the legislation makes it clear (s. 146(9)) that they are not ordinarily persons in authority for the purposes of s. 146, which means that theoretically (putting aside the issue of hearsay

person in authority for the purposes of the YCJA, any person a reasonable young person might think to be an agent of the criminal justice system

for a moment) a parent to whom a youth has confessed will be able to testify about that confession and it is admissible. However, if a parent were called to testify against a youth, the defence would almost certainly argue that the parent is or has become a person in authority.

Teachers and school personnel can occasionally be found to be persons of authority. For instance, if the police call on a teacher to assist directly in an investigation (for example, drug dealing on school premises), the teacher may be considered a person of authority if the matter leads to criminal justice proceedings.

Voluntariness

Section 146(2)(a) requires that, in order to be admissible, a statement by a youth must be voluntary. Although "voluntary" can be easily defined in ordinary usage, the legal concept of "voluntariness" is very complicated and has been built up over decades through layers of evolving case law.

Essentially, a youth's statement is voluntary if it is made

- freely by a youth
- who understands and has been made aware of his or her rights and
- who is competent, sane, and capable of understanding the consequences of making the statement;
- in the absence of promise of favour;
- in the absence of threat of (further) sanctions or other negative consequences; and
- in an atmosphere free of oppression, intimidation, or other discomfort.

Even when these requirements are met, lawyers and judges argue that voluntariness is still a subjective matter, and depending on the circumstances a statement can be involuntary despite the satisfaction of all these conditions. A review of the case law behind this "definition" is well beyond the scope of this text; suffice it to say that voluntariness must be informed and uncoerced, and is even more controversial than usual in the youth context.

From a practical standpoint, however, doing one's best to ensure the voluntariness of a youth's statement requires sensitivity. The interviewer should be specially trained in speaking with youth. The youth should be thoroughly informed of his or her rights, any waiver should be properly recorded, and all other elements of s. 146 should be satisfied.

Extrajudicial Measures and Extrajudicial Sanctions

Extrajudicial measures—and their more formal counterpart, extrajudicial sanctions—are an important feature of the unique focus of the YCJA, which requires police to consider using such alternatives to the formal justice system when dealing with youth.

The exercise of police discretion to use such measures will in some cases be very informal: the investigating officer may decide not to charge the youth at all, dismissing him or her with a simple verbal warning to stay out of trouble.

Police exercise discretion with adult suspects as well; but when dealing with adults, a decision not to charge is more commonly based on the officer's determination that the evidence available does not constitute the necessary "reasonable grounds." When dealing with youth, on the other hand, there is explicit provision in the legislation for the choice not to charge even if reasonable grounds do exist. When an investigating officer has grounds to support a charge, but is considering exercising his or her discretion to forgo resort to the judicial process, the case falls squarely into the realm of "extrajudicial measures."

Before starting any judicial proceeding against a young person, a police officer is *required* by the Act (s. 6(1)) to consider whether it would be sufficient to:

1. *Take no further action.* Generally, the police officer decides it is not necessary to do anything further because the parents, school officials, and in some cases the victim have taken measures to hold the young person accountable.

2. *Warn the young person.* Usually this is a one-on-one lecture by the officer explaining the possible outcomes if the behaviour is repeated and comes to the attention of the police again.

3. *Administer a caution.* This is a more formal warning by the police, generally put in writing in a letter, which may be issued in person in the presence of parents so that they are aware of the caution. The letter states that the police believe the young person has committed a crime and that he or she is not going to be charged at this time, but might be if he or she shows similar conduct in the future.

4. *With the consent of the young person, make a referral to a community program (for example, drug addiction program, homework program).* This may help the youth avoid committing further offences (Reid, 2009).

Although s. 6(2) provides that the failure of police to consider extrajudicial measures (sometimes known as "diversion") does not invalidate a subsequent charge, it is clear that the intent of the legislature is for such measures to be automatically considered in *every* case. To comply, police departments throughout the country have incorporated into their charge packages a section for police to fill out with details about why they are laying criminal charges rather than resorting to extrajudicial measures.

How Do the Police Feel About Extrajudicial Measures?

Research that has asked police about their feelings and decisions to "divert" or charge has shown that, in general, the seriousness of the offence, the youth's prior contacts with police, and the youth's attitude are the most influential factors in their decision-making about whether to charge or to employ extrajudicial measures (Doob & Cesaroni, 2004).

Consider the following scenario. A youth, Kalven, has been caught spray-painting graffiti in his community. This is not Kalven's first run-in with the law; he had been caught doing the same thing six months ago and had been accorded extrajudicial treatment. Should he get the same treatment now, or be charged? What if he had been previously picked up for shoplifting rather than spray-painting? Would this cause police to rule out extrajudicial treatment?

Similar scenario-based questions were posed to 70 police officers in Ontario during a study concerning police attitudes about extrajudicial measures (Marinos & Innocente, 2008). The purpose of the study was to determine which factors influence a police officer to use a diversion method.

The YCJA clearly provides that extrajudicial measures are "often the most appropriate and effective way to address youth crime" (s. 4(a)), but the practical application of these measures occurs on a case-by-case basis between an individual police officer and a youth that has allegedly broken the law.

The researchers found that officers consider three factors when dealing with a youth. First and foremost was the seriousness of the offence: Would an extrajudicial measure be an appropriate response to the offence committed? A secondary consideration was a youth's past contact with police. Many felt that if a youth had had past contact and had previously been granted an extrajudicial measure, there should be some escalation of response the second time. They argued that the youth must not have learned from the first extrajudicial measure, and needed a more severe intervention. Finally, the youth's attitude was cited as a consideration. Most police questioned felt that youth should demonstrate remorse for the actions or, even better, make an admission of guilt.

So what would this mean for Kalven? When surveyed, these officers reported that if Kalven was caught spray-painting a second time, they would likely charge him. However, if the offence were different (a prior of spray-painting, now for shoplifting), they would recommend diversion. The study concluded: "[I]t appears that each extrajudicial measure is conceptualized as ranked along a continuum of severity, and the use of one measure in the past prohibits its use again."

The most positive finding in the research was that police officers have relatively affirmative opinions about extrajudicial measures and their effectiveness. One commented, "I think the whole idea of the YCJA is benefitting and rehabilitating the youth, so those are things you have to take into consideration when holding youth accountable" (Marinos & Innocente, 2008, p. 482). Since the introduction of the YCJA, the use of extrajudicial measures has steadily increased, and with continued police training and beliefs of their effectiveness, they will become even more widespread.

In an analysis of diversion programs, Wilson and Hoge (2013) found that those programs that primarily called for police cautions were most effective in reducing recidivism for low-risk offenders, compared with programs that involved some form of intervention. They reported that "low-risk youth referred to caution programs were 2.44 times less likely to reoffend," while the same youth referred to an intervention program were only 1.49 times less likely to reoffend.

In gauging the success of applying the extrajudicial measure provisions, it is instructive to examine Figure 5.1, which provides an overview of the changes in police charging practices over a ten-year period.

FIGURE 5.1   Rates of Youth Apprehended by Police, Charged, and Diverted, Canada, 2000–2012

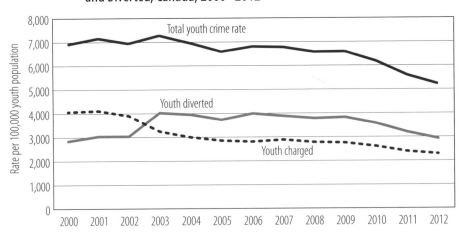

SOURCE: Statistics Canada, CANSIM Table 252-0051.

Bala (2014) argues that the decline in charges against youth in the years leading up to the enactment of the YCJA in 2003 reflects the fact that, prior to its implementation, considerable federal money had been invested in police training on the new provisions of the legislation that emphasized the value of diversion.

While police did embrace the concept of extrajudicial measures, some expressed concern about whether youth were at times being referred to community programs that, assuming the incident had proceeded without a charge, would not involve any consequences for their misbehaviour. The Ottawa Police Service was the first to embrace the science of risk–needs–responsivity discussed in Chapter 2 with reference to the "risk–needs system" and known as the *Youth Level of Service/Case Management Inventory—Screening Version* (YLS/CMI) (Hoge & Andrews, 2004). In this approach, scores are assigned to eight domains of the longer assessment: criminal history, family circumstances, education and employment, peer group association, substance use, leisure or recreation, personality or behaviour, and attitudes or criminal orientation. After receiving training, officers considering an extrajudicial measure complete the brief survey to ensure that only youth who meet the threshold of medium to high risk are being referred to more intensive measures while the low-risk offenders are given simple warnings or cautions.

In New Brunswick, the RCMP has created Youth Intervention and Diversion committees, made up of community service providers and others, who conduct broad risk assessments and develop recommendations related to intervention and diversion plans for young persons referred by a member of the RCMP, under the mandate of s. 18 of the YCJA (youth justice committees).

The *Safe Streets and Communities Act* amended the YCJA by adding to it a provision (s. 115(1.1)) that requires police to keep records whenever they impose extrajudicial measures. The amendment was in response to criticisms raised by police that youth were receiving too many cautions and warnings and there was no way to ascertain whether previous extrajudicial measures had been imposed in other jurisdictions. While the intent of the legislation is clear that an additional offence does not preclude another extrajudicial measure, the amendment was made to ensure that "police will be better informed of any past allegations of offending so that they can take appropriate action in respect of any subsequent offence allegations against a particular young person" (Department of Justice, 2013.)

A CHARTER FOR DIVERSION: A NEW BRUNSWICK EXAMPLE

The province of New Brunswick takes the matter of extrajudicial measures and sanctions very seriously. An important objective is consistency in the application of diversion possibilities for every youth who meets the criteria. In response to this mandate, the Attorney General, the Minister of Public Safety, the New Brunswick Association of Chiefs of Police, and RCMP "J" Division came together to develop the *Charter for Improvements to Diversionary Practices for Youth in New Brunswick* (New Brunswick, 2012). The mandate of this charter is to make diversion "provincially consistent." It will also help to increase stakeholder involvement. The guiding principles of the charter include: that diversion programs will strive to "provide meaningful, fair and appropriate consequences," to "reinforce societal/community values," and to repair any harm caused to a victim. But the charter also addresses the underlying causes of crime, and encourages respect for gender, cultural, racial, and linguistic differences and special needs. This charter was the first of its kind in Canada, signalling to the country that New Brunswick was committed to full implementation of the YCJA legislation regarding diversion.

QUESTIONS

1. Do you think such a charter will improve the consistency of diversion practices?

2. Should policing organizations in other provinces and territories develop their own charters to improve diversionary practices?

Extrajudicial Sanctions

The more onerous type of consequence outside the justice system is the extrajudicial sanction, established by s. 10 of the YCJA. If the police believe a warning, caution, or referral is insufficient to hold the young person accountable for his or her offence, the case is referred to the Crown, who has the option of using extrajudicial sanctions developed as part of a provincial program. If such a sanction is used, the YCJA requires that parents be notified and grants victims the right to be told what sanction was given. The Act also lays down when an extrajudicial sanction may be used (s. 10):

- It must be seen as an appropriate response with regard to the needs of the young person and the interests of society. This is in keeping with the concept of meaningful consequences.

- There must be, in the opinion of the Crown, sufficient evidence to justify proceeding with the prosecution.

- The young person must first accept responsibility for the act or omission that forms the basis of the offence. Before consenting, a young person must be advised of his or her right to legal representation and be given the opportunity to consult with counsel. The young person must not at any time have expressed the wish to have the charge dealt with by the court.

- No admission of guilt by a young person as a condition of being dealt with by an extrajudicial sanction is admissible as evidence against a young person in any criminal proceeding. However, if the youth does not complete the extrajudicial sanction and is later tried and convicted of the offence, the fact that the young person did not complete the extrajudicial sanction may be raised during sentencing.

Sanctions can be used on either a pre- or a post-charge basis—that is, a sanction can be imposed before a youth is charged (often with the condition that a charge will be laid if the sanction is not complied with), or after a charge is laid (often with the promise that the charge will be dropped if the sanction is complied with)—and most provinces have a policy about this, as well as eligibility guidelines. In Ontario, a charge is generally laid first, and police personnel make recommendations to the Crown where they believe that extrajudicial measures may be appropriate (or the Crown may make this decision independently). The Crown then typically refers the youth to a program, and a meeting is called with the youth (and sometimes the parents, the victim, or others) to develop a proposal for the sanction. If the sanction is acceptable to the youth and is complied with, the charge is dropped. In New Brunswick, there is a pre- and post-charge referral program. Sanctions can proceed on a post-charge basis as in Ontario, or can be imposed in lieu of charges for young persons deemed to be non-violent and low-risk offenders.

This approach is in keeping with a recent analysis of 29 studies indicating that more juvenile justice system processing led to higher rates of recidivism. The researchers looked at the impact of juvenile justice system processing over a 35-year period in studies that included 7,300 juveniles, and concluded that not only does formal processing of juveniles appear not to control crime, it actually seems to increase it on all measures studied (Petrosino, Turpin-Petrosino, & Guckenburg, 2010).

Although youth and parents who go through the sanction process often report satisfaction, some critics warn that these programs are not necessarily in the best interests of youth because the programs are delivered without the youth having been found guilty by a court, and may actually result in more onerous "penalties" than would be imposed by the court after a youth's conviction.

A young person's participation in an extrajudicial sanction may have implications for the youth in later court proceedings. Failure to complete a program can result in a charge, and evidence of any participation is admissible in court for certain purposes—for example, sentencing for a later offence. Pursuant to s. 123, records relating to extrajudicial sanctions are kept for two years from the date that the young person consents to become involved in the program.

Amendments to the YCJA, brought about by the *Safe Streets and Communities Act*, permit courts who are weighing eligibility for a custodial sentence to consider extrajudicial sanctions, in addition to findings of guilt, as indicative of a pattern of offending. This may make it easier to order a youth into custody, and may therefore conflict with the aim expressed in the legislation to reduce the high rate of incarceration that had existed under the *Young Offenders Act*.

POCKETFUL OF CANDY REVISITED

Now that you have read the chapter and understand police procedures for working with youth, let's revisit the case of John. If you recall, John was caught with marijuana. When the police questioned him, he confessed that it was his. Because of the factors in this case, the officers decided to use an extrajudicial measure to deal with John's behaviour.

QUESTIONS

1. At what point was John "detained"?

   The first question asked you to identify the moment when John was detained. Detention occurs when an individual is stopped by an officer. Detention may be physical, with the individual being immobilized, or psychological, with individual feeling compelled to stay and comply with police. So, in this case, John was detained when he was stopped and asked to show ID.

2. Since John had no ID on him, how did the police proceed with assumptions regarding his age?

   This question addresses the very important question of age jurisdiction. John had no ID on him to confirm his age, but on the basis of his demeanour and stature the police reasonably assumed that he was a youth and proceeded with the protections provided to John under the YCJA. When in doubt, this is the safest assumption.

3. When John blurted out his confession, would this be considered a spontaneous statement?

   Spontaneous statements are addressed in s. 146(3) of the YCJA. Was John's outburst confession spontaneous? At first glance it might seem that way, but in this case it was not. Because it was very clear that John was being stopped and questioned regarding the odour of marijuana, his confession was not spontaneous.

4. Was the search of John's person lawful?

   When the police searched John, they had reasonable grounds to do so. They had smelled the marijuana that led to the detention; John had confessed; and he was searched after being read his rights. Whenever reasonable grounds are present, police have the right to search a person, and in this case there were plenty of reasons.

5. Was it a problem for the police to question John without his mother present?

   The police have an obligation to inform a young person's parent(s) when their child is arrested, but what happens when they can't reach the parent? In this case the police had taken all reasonable steps. They had called the number provided by John. Prior to questioning John, they had informed him of his rights (which would include the right not to self-incriminate, the right to have a parent present, and the right to counsel), but of equal importance is ensuring that the youth *understands* his or her rights. If an officer believes so, and would like to proceed, questioning may take place. In this case, the officers chose to proceed.

6. What would be an appropriate extrajudicial measure (what activities might be included in the measure) for John?

John is a great example of a youth who would benefit from extrajudicial measures, because going through the formal criminal justice system may serve only to further label and stigmatize him, which might have very harmful consequences. What extrajudicial measure did you decide the police should use? Different options are available, but in this case a warning would likely be best. From this, John might learn the possible consequences of reoffending and this might set him on a crime-free trajectory.

CHAPTER SUMMARY

An investigator has to make several strategic and legal determinations in the course of a first encounter with a young suspect, and rely on his or her own judgment and knowledge of the law. He or she has to determine, for example, the young person's approximate age and his or her status as suspect or witness. Decisions include whether to warn or caution, whether to charge and/or arrest, and whether to refer (or to recommend referral) to an extrajudicial measures program or to the Crown for a possible extrajudicial sanction.

Compliance with the law and good judgment are important for those investigating young accused. Mistakes in law or judgment when arresting and/or cautioning—including acting on misunderstandings about voluntariness, age-appropriate explanations, the right to counsel, the right to consult with parents, and the requirements for a valid waiver—can lead to violation of the accused's rights and consequent exclusion of evidence at trial.

Police attitudes to extrajudicial measures are generally positive, and scientific evidence supports the diversion of low- to medium-risk offenders. A risk assessment tool, such as the that used by the Ottawa Police Services and the RCMP in the Atlantic region, may help ensure that the right service intervention is targeted at the right young person. Despite evidence in support of diversion, the *Safe Streets and Communities Act* introduced amendments to the YCJA that might curtail its use, with profound implications for youth who continue to commit minor offences.

KEY TERMS

arrest, 113
detention, 111
person in authority, 119

reasonable grounds, 113
spontaneous statement, 112
waiver, 118

REFERENCES

Abramovitch, A., Higgins-Biss, K., & Biss, S. (1993). Young persons' comprehension of waivers in criminal proceedings. *Canadian Journal of Criminology, 35*(3), 309–322. Retrieved from https://www.ncjrs.gov/App/publications/abstract.aspx?ID=144206.

Bala, N. (2014, June 25). Responding more effectively to youth crime in Canada: The legal context. Paper presented at Canadian Youth Justice Conference, Toronto.

C.G., R v. (1986). [1986] 16 WCB 323 (Ont. Prov. Ct.).

Canadian Charter of Rights and Freedoms. (1982). Part I of the *Constitution Act, 1982*, being Schedule B to the *Canada Act 1982* (UK), 1982, c. 11.

Criminal Code. (1985). RSC 1985, c. C-46.

Department of Justice. (2013). Recent changes to Canada's youth justice system. Retrieved from http://www.justice.gc.ca/eng/cj-jp/yj-jj/ycja-lsjpa/sheets-feuillets/amend-modif.html.

Doob, A.N., & Cesaroni, C. (2004). *Responding to youth crime in Canada.* Toronto: University of Toronto Press.

Grant, R v. (2006). 81 OR (3d) 1, 209 CCC (3d) 250, 2006 CanLII 18347 (CA).

Hanson, J. (1987). Youth confessions: Section 56 of the Young Offenders Act. *Canadian Journal of Family Law, 6*(2), 191–210.

Hoge, R.D., & Andrews, D.A. (2004). *Youth Level of Service/Case Management Inventory (YLS/CMI)—Screening version.* Toronto: Multi-Health Systems.

J.D., R v. (2007). [2007] OJ No. 1365 (CJ).

Justice BC. (n.d.). Right to a lawyer. Retrieved from http://www.justicebc.ca/en/cjis/youth/rights/accused/lawyer.html.

Keenan, K. (2013). The legal powers of the police. In K. O'Regan & S. Reid (Eds.), *Thinking about criminal justice in Canada* (pp. 99–128). Toronto: Emond Montgomery.

M.A.M., R v. (1986). 32 CCC (3d) 566, 1986 CanLII 1196 (BC CA).

M.E., R v. (2006). [2006] OJ No. 1657 (CJ).

Mann, R v. (2004). 2004 SCC 52, [2004] 3 SCR 59.

Marinos, V., & Innocente, N. (2008). Factors influencing police attitudes towards extrajudicial measures under the Youth Criminal Justice Act. *Canadian Journal of Criminology and Criminal Justice, 50*(4), 469–489.

New Brunswick. (2012). *Charter for improvements to diversionary practices for youth in New Brunswick.* Province of New Brunswick.

Newfoundland and Labrador Legal Aid Commission. (n.d.). Can I get legal aid? Retrieved from http://www.legalaid.nl.ca/eligible.html.

P.B., R v. (1984). 44 CR (3d) 24 (BCPC).

P.(S.), R v. (1991). 44 OAC 316 (CA).

Peterson-Badali, M., & Broeking, J. (2010). Parents' involvement in the youth justice system: Rhetoric and reality. *Canadian Journal of Criminology and Criminal Justice, 52*(1), 1–27.

Petrosino, A., Turpin-Petrosino, C., & Guckenburg, S. (2010). Formal system processing of juveniles: Effects on delinquency. *Campbell Systematic Reviews*. Retrieved November 5, 2014 from http://www.campbellcollaboration .org/lib/download/761/Review_System_Process_Effect _Juvenile_Delinquency_100129.pdf.

Reid, S.A. (2009). *125 warnings: A review of extrajudicial measures and extrajudicial sanctions for youth in New Brunswick*. Fredericton: New Brunswick Department of Public Safety.

Rodgers, R v. (2006). 2006 SCC 15, [2006] 1 SCR 554.

Safe Streets and Communities Act. (2012). SC 2012, c. 1.

Therens, R v. (1985). [1985] 1 SCR 613, 1985 CanLII 29.

Wills, R v. (1992). 7 OR (3d) 337, 70 CCC (3d) 529, 1992 CanLII 2780 (CA).

Wilson, H.A., & Hoge, R.D. (2013). The effect of youth diversion programs on recidivism: A meta-analytic review. *Criminal Justice and Behavior, 40*(5), 497–518.

Youth Criminal Justice Act. (2002). SC 2002, c. 1.

EXERCISES AND REVIEW

Review Questions

1. Why must an officer establish a suspect's age at the earliest opportunity?

2. If a youth is not necessarily in criminal trouble, but is in a risky situation, how might police deal with him or her (name the legislation)?

3. Does receiving a s. 6 caution give a youth a criminal (youth court) record?

4. How many s. 6 cautions can a youth receive before police are forced to lay a charge?

5. If a young woman confesses before police have a chance to advise her of her rights, will the statement be admissible in court?

6. How soon after detaining a youth must the police contact a parent? What if a youth has no available parent?

7. How must police record a youth's waiver of the right to counsel?

8. What if, unbeknownst to police, the recording technology fails while recording a waiver?

9. Must a detained youth choose between contacting a lawyer and contacting a parent?

10. Is a school principal a person in authority for purposes of s. 146? Why or why not?

11. Why might a youth wish to consult counsel before participating in a (pre-charge) extrajudicial sanction program?

Discussion Questions

1. This chapter introduced community diversion (as an alternative to charge/conviction) and prevention programs designed to reduce youth crime, but did not describe the specifics of these programs, because their availability varies from community to community. In your particular community, research the availability of diversion and prevention programs, and answer the following questions:

   a. Are there any formal diversion or "extrajudicial measures" community programs in your community? List and describe them.

   b. How and when do youth typically get referred to these programs?

   c. What is the typical profile of youths referred to this type of program? Are they first-time or repeat offenders? What kinds of offences do they typically commit? How old are they?

   d. How are local diversion programs funded? How did they start?

2. Find out how extrajudicial measures are administered in your community. Are referrals typically made at the pre- or post-charge stage? What is a typical extrajudicial sanction in your community?

3. What kinds of physical detention or interrogation conditions might invalidate the voluntariness of a youth's statement?

4. Draft the wording of a sample youth caution for each of the following cases. Make sure you take into account appropriate level of language and other factors such as temperament, learning styles, and abilities for the explanation in each situation.

   • a typical 17-year-old suspect

   • a crying, 12-year-old suspect who is in grade 5

5. Should police be required to explain to an arrested youth why contacting a lawyer is in his or her best interests? Defend your answer.

6. In a review of extrajudicial measures and extrajudicial sanctions in New Brunswick, one of the conclusions from a focus group participant led to the title of the final report *125 Warnings*. One participant stated: "The use of 'warnings' by the police should not ever be limited as in the case of a 'three strikes law'. If it can bring a young person back on track, then they should be used as much as is necessary to help turn around a young person and 'keep them out of the court room.'" What is your opinion on this?

The Pre-Trial Period

6

LEARNING OUTCOMES

After completing this chapter, you should be able to:

- Describe the show-cause hearing and the factors considered in decisions about judicial interim release.

- Explain the purpose of release conditions for young persons receiving bail and the consequences of failure to comply.

- Explain the role of police with respect to youth on bail.

- Outline the requirements for a surety in judicial interim release.

- Describe the principles of restorative justice that apply to conferences at the bail stage of the youth justice process.

- List the grounds for pre-trial detention under the current *Youth Criminal Justice Act* (YCJA).

- Critically assess the extent to which the YCJA regime for pre-trial detention has been put into practice so far and what may happen now that major amendments have been made.

- Discuss the provisions within the YCJA that prohibit the temporary detention of young persons for child protection matters.

- Describe the YCJA rules with respect to where a young person may be placed for pre-trial detention.

Introduction

As explained in Chapter 5, the *Youth Criminal Justice Act* (YCJA) sets out parameters for employing alternatives to the more formal court process whenever possible. Even when an extrajudicial measure or sanction is not sufficient to hold a young person accountable for an offence, and the incident results in a charge, contact between police and youth usually ends in the release of the youth on his or her recognizance. This occurs after the police have served the youth with a document compelling the youth's appearance in court—for example, a promise to appear. In more serious cases, police will need to consider whether it is appropriate to hold the young person in pre-trial detention while awaiting a decision on judicial interim release (bail).

The YCJA aims to discourage the use of custody as a sanction and to reserve it for the most serious cases, both at the pre-trial stage and after sentencing. The Act incorporates the holding preconditions expressed in the *Criminal Code* under s. 515 and, in addition, further limits the use of pre-trial custody by setting additional conditions under s. 39(1).

This chapter provides an overview of the provisions governing pre-trial detention and how they relate to young persons. The principle of "innocent until proven guilty" is viewed in the context of pre-trial detention and is considered from an international perspective. In each of these topics, the primary question considered is whether holding a youth in detention pending trial is reasonable in light of the international rules governing the treatment of children.

The chapter moves on to a discussion of the implementation of the YCJA, highlighting the disparity between the legislation's stated goal of reducing the use of incarceration and the increasing use of remand (pre-trial detention). While amendments introduced by the 2012 *Safe Streets and Communities Act* were designed to slow down the rate at which young people are being held in pre-trial detention, the conditions of release for some of them are very difficult to abide by. The breach of bail conditions then results in an additional criminal charge to be answered by the young person.

The Right to Be Presumed Innocent

Section 11(d) of the *Canadian Charter of Rights and Freedoms* provides that someone charged with an offence has the right "to be presumed innocent until proven guilty according to law in a fair and public hearing by an independent and impartial tribunal." From this, one might conclude that punishment for an act will not be imposed unless the person has been found guilty. But when we put people in pre-trial detention, we are indeed imprisoning them prior to finding them guilty.

MODELS OF CRIMINAL JUSTICE

1. Of the five models of criminal justice (crime control, justice, welfare, community change, and restorative justice), which might promote adherence to the principle of "innocent until proven guilty"?

2. Which model might suggest that holding an alleged offender in pre-trial detention would be acceptable?

Recall that the preamble to the YCJA sets out "special guarantees of [young persons'] rights and freedoms" and underscores the importance of reserving the "most serious intervention for the most serious crimes" in order to "reduce the over-reliance on incarceration for non-violent young persons." Prior to the 2012 amendments, pre-trial detention was presumed unnecessary if the young person, upon being found guilty, could not be committed to custody. However, the 2012 amendments introduced provisions surrounding pre-trial detention to ensure the protection of the public, including any witness to the offence (s. 29(2)(b)(ii)). In deciding whether to hold a young person in pre-trial detention, the court must be convinced that a release would "offer adequate protection to the public from the risk that the young person might otherwise present" and ensure the maintenance of "confidence in the administration of justice" (ss. 29(2)(c)(ii), (iii)).

As discussed in Chapter 1, the media tends to sensationalize crime, which fosters fear and misinformation in the minds of the public. Because most crime stories published in newspapers refer to the first stage of the process, in which an individual has simply been charged, it is clear that the public are invited to make judgments about people not yet found guilty. Similarly, when the public learns an offender has been remanded to a detention centre, they might make premature judgments of guilt.

Take a look at the online news source *Toronto Sun* (www.torontosun.com/news) and find a crime news story that indicates the offender has been remanded pending trial. Look at the language used by the reporter and ask yourself whether an untrained reader would keep in mind the principle of innocent until proven guilty.

In *R v. McDonald* (1998), an adult case, the court held that despite the official *preventive* purposes of remand to ensure that an accused shows up for trial and does not continue on a path of further offending, it is *punitive* as well. Holding an accused in jail deprives the individual of liberty, punishes him or her before a finding of guilt, and, in the case of a young person, may run contrary to the stated purpose of the legislation to reserve custody for the most serious offenders. As pointed out in *R v. Wust* by Madame Justice Arbour, "while pre-trial detention is not intended as punishment when it is imposed, it is, in effect, deemed part of the punishment following the offender's conviction" (at para. 41). The pre-trial detention of convicted offenders is a mitigating factor in sentencing and, as suggested, is in effect punitive.

TREATING GIRLS

In the Canadian criminal justice system, the idea that everyone should be treated equally before and under the law is paramount. But does that always play out in the courtroom?

A 2010 study that sought to examine the bail conditions imposed on male and female youth discovered that girls may be being treated differently. Under the *Juvenile Delinquents Act* (1908–1984), there was a category of "status offences" with which girls were often charged when they acted outside of gender norms (for example, when they were found to have exhibited "promiscuity"). When the JDA was repealed, status offences were abandoned; however, certain ideas underlying these offences have, according to some critics, been reflected in bail conditions imposed on girls (Sprott & Doob, 2009). Researchers studied 242 youth cases (195 boys and 47 girls) in courts in Toronto and found very few differences in the conditions imposed on the two genders, with one salient exception: treatment programs. Girls were much more likely than their male counterparts (51 percent as against 35 percent) to be required to attend a treatment program while on bail, especially when the alleged crime was non-violent. Today's YCJA makes it very clear that youth cannot be sentenced to custody for child welfare, mental health, or other social reasons, but the same limitation is not put on bail conditions. There is concern on the part of researchers that this disparity stems from previous gendered practices of responding to female criminality with treatment-based responses. Reflecting on this disparity, researchers said, "we suspect the use of treatment programs as a condition of release is a remnant of the paternalistic concern and care that youths—especially girls—have historically received in the youth justice system" (Sprott & Doob, 2010, p. 438).

QUESTIONS

1. What other practices have you noticed that appear to be paternalistic toward girls within the youth justice system?

2. Do you think that girls are treated differently from boys?

appearance notice
a notice given to an accused
by police after being charged,
telling him or her to appear in
court on a specific day/time to
answer to a criminal charge

promise to appear
a notice signed by an accused
promising that he or she will
appear before the court for
trial on the specific date

undertaking
conditions set out on a promise
to appear or a recognizance
when the youth agrees to
such things as a curfew,
parental supervision, or
other such requirement(s)

recognizance
a formal agreement by
an accused after being
charged that requires an
acknowledgment of a debt
to the Crown for an amount
up to $500, which may
require a deposit, in order to
be released prior to trial

responsible person
an individual willing and able
to exercise control over a young
person in order for him or her
to be released prior to trial

show-cause hearing
another name for a bail or
judicial interim release hearing;
the burden of proof is on
the Crown to "show cause"
why the accused should be
detained pending trial

judicial interim release (bail)
pre-trial release of an individual
accused of a crime after he or
she has appeared before the
court in a show-cause hearing

Crown brief
the document or file that
contains the important
information about a charge
(for what offences, name
of accused, summary of
evidence, details of prior
criminal record, etc.)

The Decision to Detain for a Show-Cause Hearing

In most cases in which the police initiate a formal process against a young person (as opposed to using extrajudicial measures or sanctions), he or she is released on an **appearance notice** followed by a summons issued to appear in court, a **promise to appear**, an **undertaking**, or a **recognizance**. In each of these situations, the young person is released to the care of his or her parents or a **responsible person**. If the youth has not been arrested, the police are likely to issue an appearance notice, which is later confirmed by a justice of the peace when the charges are laid. If the youth has been arrested, the decision by the police to continue to detain him or her is set out in ss. 497–498 of the *Criminal Code*. Under these provisions, factors that might justify detention include the need to establish the identity of the accused, the need to secure or preserve evidence relating to the offence, the need to prevent the continuation or repetition of the offence or the commission of another, and the need to circumvent the problem of the accused failing to attend court.

Factors that may prompt police to hold a young person long enough to bring him or her for a show-cause hearing include:

- symptoms or behaviour that suggest a need to seek a court-ordered medical or psychological assessment under s. 34 of the YCJA;
- the need to make arrangements for placement "into the care of a responsible person" under s. 31;
- an offence involving violence;
- a breach of probation or of conditional supervision;
- the commission of a serious offence (for which an adult might receive a sentence of two years or more) combined with a record of prior convictions; and
- a serious offence combined with a history of failure to attend at trial.

If at least one of the factors above is present, police may consider, instead of detention, placement of the youth in "the care of a responsible person" pending trial under s. 31. This measure is far less onerous, because the youth can remain within the community. Section 31 does not limit the definition of "responsible person" to the youth's parents. It simply stipulates that the person must be "willing and able to take care of and exercise control over the young person." Both the youth and the responsible person must consent in writing to the arrangement. At all times, the youth court judge has the discretion to dissolve this arrangement and issue an arrest warrant.

The Show-Cause Hearing

Once a decision has been made to detain a youth, police personnel will prepare a *Crown package*, which contains any police evidence that might be useful to the Crown prosecutor at a **show-cause hearing**, where he or she has to "show cause" why the accused should be detained. The YCJA rules contained in ss. 28–29 for pre-trial detention, show-cause hearings, and **judicial interim release (bail)** incorporate the same rules as those for the adult system found in the *Criminal Code* under s. 515. The package includes the **Crown brief**, a document with all the important information about the charge (the offence, the accused, the evidence, etc.). This must be done within 24 hours of the arrest as set out in s. 515 of the *Criminal Code*. For practical purposes, because of long weekends and other factors (particularly in remote areas), if a youth is arrested late in the week, he or she may not appear before a judge until Monday morning.

There are also implications for detention in remote areas where there may not be a youth detention centre in close proximity, which may mean that a young person is housed in a facility with adults. Such a practice is in violation of the United Nations Convention on the Rights of the Child under article 37, which states that children who commit criminal offences must be housed in separate facilities. Canada has consistently entered a **reservation** on this particular article, claiming that the geographic disparity in Canada precludes the ability to abide by it, particularly in cases of pre-trial detention. This is changing to some extent, because courts now sometimes conduct show-cause hearings remotely, by either videoconference or audio tape.

At the show-cause hearing, the judge hears from both Crown and defence, and makes a determination about whether the youth should continue to be detained pending trial or be released back to his or her community until the trial date. The burden of proof is on the Crown prosecutor to "show cause" why the accused should be detained pending trial. However, in certain circumstances, as set out in s. 515(6) of the *Criminal Code*, it will be up to defence counsel to show cause why the young persons should be released. Examples of such **reverse onus** situations include the young person's being charged with failing to attend court, breach of an undertaking or recognizance, or serious indictable offences including weapons offences. Perhaps the most common situation related to youth in a reverse onus situation occurs when the young person is under release for an indictable offence and then charged with a new indictable offence.

reservation
a statement made to the United Nations that limits how the government accepts a part of a treaty or convention (e.g., the UN Convention on the Rights of the Child)

reverse onus
the burden of proof being shifted from the Crown to a defendant in either a criminal offence or tort claim; e.g., the burden of proof resting on defence counsel to show cause why a youth should be released

---

Criminal Code, Judicial Interim Release

515(1) Subject to this section, where an accused who is charged with an offence … is taken before a justice, the justice shall, unless a plea of guilty by the accused is accepted, order, in respect of that offence, that the accused be released on his giving an undertaking without conditions, unless the prosecutor, having been given a reasonable opportunity to do so, shows cause, in respect of that offence, why the detention of the accused in custody is justified … .

(2) Where the justice does not make an order under subsection (1), he shall, unless the prosecutor shows cause why the detention of the accused is justified, order that the accused be released

(a) on his giving an undertaking with such conditions as the justice directs;

(b) on his entering into a recognizance before the justice, without sureties, in such amount and with such conditions, if any, as the justice directs but without deposit of money or other valuable security;

(c) on his entering into a recognizance before the justice with sureties in such amount and with such conditions, if any, as the justice directs but without deposit of money or other valuable security;

(d) with the consent of the prosecutor, on his entering into a recognizance before the justice, without sureties, in such amount and with such conditions, if any, as the justice directs and on his depositing with the justice such sum of money or other valuable security as the justice directs; …

(3) The justice shall not make an order under any of paragraphs (2)(b) to (e) unless the prosecution shows cause why an order under the immediately preceding paragraph should not be made.

The least onerous form of release is to be presumed appropriate, unless the Crown can show cause why a more onerous one is warranted. Although the Crown has to meet a high standard of proof to get an order for detention, the rules of evidence are relaxed in a pre-trial detention hearing. This means that evidence that would not be admitted in a trial is admitted at a pre-trial detention hearing as long as it is "credible and trustworthy" (s. 518(1)(e)).

In the course of a show-cause hearing, or at any other stage of the proceedings, if the court deems it necessary, it can issue an order that the young person undergo a medical or psychological assessment. The order must be made with the young person's consent—or, if there is no consent, only when certain statutory criteria are met. The report of the assessment can be admitted and considered for purposes of the detention or release decision.

Requiring a Surety

In 1972, the *Bail Reform Act* legislated that an accused should be released on bail without conditions, a monetary bond, or a surety unless the Crown prosecutor can prove a need for a more onerous type of release. According to s. 515(2) of the *Criminal Code*, in proving this the Crown must prove the need for restrictions on release sequentially, demonstrating why each form of release, starting with the most lenient, is unsuitable before recommending a stricter one (Trotter, 2010).

surety
a person who agrees to vouch for the accused's return to court for a trial, and to pay a certain sum if the accused does not show

A **surety** is a person who agrees to vouch for the accused's return to court for a trial, and to pay a certain sum if the accused does not show. In the context of the presumption of innocence, requiring a surety seems very punitive. In a study of 4,085 adult court case appearances in Canada, when accused persons appeared before a justice of the peace for a full bail hearing, the requirement of a surety was found to vary from 63 to 100 percent of cases (Myers, 2009). In a study of 199 youth bail hearings across four Toronto courts, 87 percent of youth released on bail were released with a surety. Moreover, the assumption that a surety would be required seemed almost automatic, as evidenced by the surety being called to the stand without discussion of any alternative or of less onerous conditions (Myers & Dhillon, 2013). Apparently—in view of the use of multiple conditions of release and the additional requirement of a surety to ensure that the youth abides by the rules—the principle that the least onerous form of release available ought to be used in youth cases is not being followed consistently (Doob & Webster, 2012).

Restorative Justice and Judicial Interim Release

The YCJA integrates significant restorative justice principles and practices into its approach to most matters, including at the pre-trial detention stage.

Restorative justice characterizes crime and conflict as harm done to people and relationships. Processes based on restorative justice are intended to provide supportive, safe opportunities for voluntary communication between those affected by and those accused of crimes. These processes, which involve offenders, victims, and community members, encourage not only remedies and accountability but also more subjectively experienced things like understanding, healing, and a sense of closure.

As was discussed in Chapter 2, restorative justice processes are unlike formal court proceedings: they are not adversarial or retributive and they involve non-expert citizens (Correctional Service Canada, 2012). You may recall that this approach incorporates the following concepts:

- provision of fair and proportionate accountability for young offenders that reinforces society's values;

- encouragement of decision-makers to craft responses that try to repair, where possible, harm caused by crime; and
- encouragement of decision-makers to craft responses in individual cases that are meaningful to the offender.

Conferences, which are provided for in s. 19 of the YCJA, can be used at the bail stage of the youth criminal justice process. A **conference** is a group of people called together to give advice to, or to assist, someone named as a decision-maker under the YCJA. Conferences are often very useful at the bail-hearing stage, because the involved parties (defence counsel, Crown, judge, parents, and sometimes child welfare workers) can shed their formal roles to work together at finding an appropriate placement for an at-risk young person. The parties can also suggest measures to stabilize the young person's life and ensure that he or she will not reoffend while awaiting trial.

Conferences at the bail stage can be particularly valuable for brainstorming creative solutions for runaways, for those who have had placement problems, or for those who find it hard to follow court orders to the point where further charges are laid against them. Further, in allowing for the prospect of release to a "responsible person," the conference encourages community involvement, which is consistent with restorative justice–based approaches. One Calgary police officer, who had been using conferencing in a number of the schools to which she had been assigned, said that instead of doing "a lot of finger wags where you say, 'don't do it again,'" the conference "allows a structured format that we can follow … I can see it being an extremely useful tool in the future for the police department" (Green & Healey, 2003, p. 53).

conferences

meetings that can occur at various stages of a criminal matter that bring together interested parties (judge, accused, lawyers, parents, others) in an attempt to resolve an issue related to the charge or trial

Assigning Conditions of Release

A justice (justice of the peace or judge) who decides to release a youthful accused has the discretion to impose controls on the youth's behaviour while in the community. Conditions of release, which apply to adult as well as youth accused, are covered in s. 515(4) of the *Criminal Code*. Typical examples are a requirement to report to a police officer, to remain in the jurisdiction, and to avoid people or places connected with the alleged offence. In the case of youth, there is sometimes a condition that he or she attend school.

In a recent study of adult bail courts that observed 718 cases over a 44-day period in five provinces (British Columbia, Manitoba, Nova Scotia, Ontario, and Yukon), the median number of bail conditions was 6.5. The Yukon court routinely imposed nearly twice as many as other provincial jurisdictions; however, the range of bail conditions imposed in Ontario was between 1 and 34 conditions (Deshman & Myers, 2014). While the average number of conditions is lower than what was observed in the youth sample by Sprott and Myers (2011), the range of conditions imposed in the adult study suggests that an increasingly punitive stance is being taken by Canadian courts with respect to conditions of release.

The more conditions that are put on a young person, the more likely he or she will breach one of them, resulting in an additional criminal charge of non-compliance. Further, the longer the youth has to wait on bail before trial, the more likely a breach will occur as well. Given that one of the stated purposes of the YCJA is to enforce meaningful consequences, conditions having little connection to the alleged offence might run counter to the stated purpose. Youth charged with shoplifting might not need to have their cellphones taken away to be held meaningfully accountable. Conditions sometimes seem to have been imposed for social welfare or punitive purposes, and sometimes they look borrowed from the standard practice for adult bail conditions without much thought about their application to youth. For example, if a young person is under the legal age to drink alcohol, having a prohibition on alcohol as a condition of an order may lead to two additional criminal charges if the youth is caught drinking alcohol (breaching the condition and drinking underage, instead of just drinking underage).

Once a youth has been released into the community, the police are responsible for ensuring that bail conditions are complied with and for responding appropriately if they are not. They have the authority, under s. 524 of the *Criminal Code*, to arrest and return the young person to custody for breach of a condition.

IS SHOPPING AT SHOPPERS DRUG MART A CRIME?

In 2013 a study was conducted about youth bail practices in four Toronto courts. The researchers wanted to explore the connection between offences committed by youth and the bail conditions imposed upon them. The purpose of setting a bail condition, according to s. 515 of the *Criminal Code*, is to ensure that the youth appears in court and that public safety is protected pending trial. The legislation provides that the least burdensome conditions of release that achieve these ends must be used.

What the researchers found instead was a practice of imposing bail conditions without consideration of the nature of the offence. For example, setting a condition to "abide by house rules" might conceivably put a youth in pre-trial detention for not cleaning his or her room.

Three types of connections were used to classify bail conditions: clear connection, in which the relation between the condition and the alleged offence was clear; ambiguous connection, in which there was a reasonable relationship between the two; and finally, no apparent connection, in which there no relationship could be found.

To illustrate how the study worked, consider one of the cases included. A 16-year-old youth appeared before the court on a charge of theft at Shoppers Drug Mart: he had allegedly stolen $14.19 worth of products from the store. At the time, he had been on bail for theft and robbery charges. He was granted release with a surety, and the release conditions included residing with his surety, abiding by house rules, following a curfew, not possessing any weapons, not entering any Shoppers Drug Mart stores in the province, and not communicating with or associating with the victim. Some of these conditions had clear connections: for example, not entering the Shoppers where the crime occurred. Conditions with an ambiguous connection included the curfew (only clearly connected if the theft had been committed at night). Finally, a condition with no apparent connection was the order not to possess weapons, because the offence had not involved the use of a weapon.

If the youth had violated the no-weapons bail condition, he could have been charged with two offences: one for the weapon (if it were prohibited), and another for a bail violation.

Another condition with no apparent connection was the order not to enter *any* Shoppers stores. It is clear why the youth was not permitted to go back to the scene of the crime, but the condition not allowing him to be at any other locations was not connected. If the fear was that the youth had a habit of stealing from pharmacies, the order should have imposed a ban that included all pharmacies in the area.

What this case demonstrates is a courtroom culture in which conditions of bail are imposed on youth that may have no logical connection to the alleged crime. "Rather than a mechanism for ensuring youths return to court and do not commit further offences, bail conditions seem to have developed into a tool that has little to do with their legal purpose" (Myers & Dhillon, 2013, p. 208).

QUESTION

If you were the judge in the case of this 16-year-old, what bail conditions would you impose?

It seems to be common sense that keeping young people in school will enhance their likelihood of success, so requiring school attendance as a condition of release is a standard option in most youth cases. Mayer (2005) suggests that juvenile arrests that result in conditions that mandate school attendance might strengthen attachments to education and lessen the likelihood of dropout. However, Kirk and Sampson (2013) in their study of juvenile arrests found that 73 percent of those arrested later dropped out of high school and that all of the youth in the sample who had spent any days in a detention centre dropped out. Part of the reason may be an adverse reaction by school staff following the arrest, which might lead to exclusionary policies of expulsion or assignment to alternative education sites (as discussed below). These reactions may weaken a student's bonds to school and facilitate association with more anti-social peers as role models. Hirschfield (2009) suggests that time spent moving through the youth criminal case process may lead to high rates of absenteeism from school that, in turn, leads to failing grades. Pager (2003) suggests there is convincing evidence that contact with the criminal justice system, even when arrest results in acquittal, dramatically limits employment opportunities, and that this, coupled with educational failure, is a further predictor of problems into young adulthood.

ALTERNATIVE EDUCATION SITES: A SASKATOON EXAMPLE

When youth are granted judicial interim release, it is at the judge's discretion to impose conditions. One often imposed is mandatory attendance at "school." But what if a youth can no longer return to his or her former school (for example, because of a previous expulsion)? In some cases, depending on where the youth lives, there might be opportunity to attend an alternative education site such as Core Neighbourhood Youth Co-op (CNYC, www.cnyc.ca) in Saskatoon. CNYC, which opened its doors in 1996, allows youth between the ages of 15 to 21 to complete their academic credits while developing skills in areas like carpentry, arts programming, and urban gardening. Promoting the values of "cooperation, sustainability, leadership skills, environmental principles, and youth initiative in a safe and respectful environment," CNYC aims to inspire agency in participating youth. Since 80 percent of the youth at CNYC are involved with the criminal justice system, the organization is working with those youth most in need of innovative educational approaches.

QUESTIONS

1. Do some investigating to find an organization like Core Neighbourhood Youth Co-op in your area. Are there any similarities between that organization and CNYC?

2. What benefits are there for neighbourhoods that have these types of organizations?

The police are entitled, under s. 125(6) of the YCJA, to share information with school officials about the involvement of a young person in the justice system if it is necessary to ensure compliance with bail conditions or to ensure the safety of other students or staff. Such information must be kept separate from other information about the student, and access to it is restricted to necessary staff. (Section 119(n)(ii) states that an individual responsible for the supervision and care of a young person may have access to the young person's record.) Any record of information about a student who has had involvement with the youth court system must be destroyed by school officials when it is no longer required.

In a study of a large Ontario youth court, Sprott and Myers (2011) found that imposition of a bail condition that told youth they needed to sign a consent form so that a treatment provider, principal, or teacher could monitor their attendance and progress at school increased from 1 percent of cases in 2003, when the YCJA was proclaimed, to 28 percent of cases in 2008. The increased surveillance on young people adds to the possibility of additional negative reaction from school staff. Given that relations between teachers and school staff is strongly correlated with positive student outcomes such as academic engagement and achievement (Kirk & Sampson, 2013), this enhanced surveillance may contribute to poor outcomes for the arrested youth.

Guidelines for Pre-Trial Detention

Section 515(10) of the *Criminal Code* provides for three grounds to consider in making an order for pre-trial detention of an accused:

1. *Primary ground.* Detention is necessary to ensure the accused's attendance in court.
2. *Secondary ground.* Detention is necessary for the protection and safety of the public.
3. *Tertiary ground.* Detention is necessary in order to maintain confidence in the administration of justice.

Although a young person's detention is justified on the same grounds as detention of an adult, the YCJA makes two stipulations:

- if a young person is detained, he or she must be held separately from adult offenders (YCJA, s. 84); and
- a young person must not be detained as a substitute for appropriate child protection, mental health, or other social measures (YCJA, s. 29(1)).

The Prohibition on Detention for Child Welfare Purposes

Under s. 29(1), a young person cannot be denied bail and kept in pre-trial detention as a substitute for appropriate child protection, mental health, or other social measures. For example, the YCJA does not specifically allow police to temporarily detain a street youth just because he or she has nowhere to go, unless there are reasonable and probable grounds to suspect the youth has committed an offence warranting detention. You may recall *R v. K.D.* (2004), discussed in Chapter 3, in which the justice wanted to send a young person who had stolen pepperoni to an open custody group home because she had no place to live, and that this was not allowed.

Some provinces have legislation that allows for the detention of vagrant youth, but not for mere homelessness. For example, in 2013 Alberta enacted the *Protection of Sexually Exploited Children Act*, which permits police or a child protection worker to detain children in a "safe house" for a maximum of five days without charging them. Proponents of the legislation argue that this allows the youngsters to escape from their pimps and enables them to receive medical, psychological, and addiction counselling and special legal services. Critics decry the legislation as a further abuse—and violation of the rights—of marginalized teenaged girls, one that will further alienate them from mainstream society.

PROTECTION OR VIOLATION?

In 2013, Alberta introduced the *Protection of Sexually Exploited Children* to help youth found to be victims of sexual exploitation and abuse on the streets of the province. This new legislation replaced the *Protection of Children Involved in Prostitution* (1999) after much criticism arguing that the old law was based on the false premise that youth chose to enter into prostitution. The new legislation approached the issue with the recognition that children and youth involved are being sexually exploited and regularly sexually abused.

The legislation focuses on removing children from situations of exploitation or abuse and providing services. For those seeking a way out, there are volunteer community services including medical assistance, drug and alcohol counselling, psychological services, educational programming, placement resources, and life skills support.

What is unique about the 2013 legislation is that it provides these services for youth up until the age of 22, whereas most such services end at 18. However, not all youth involved in prostitution will leave of their own volition, so provisions have been included for those who won't. These youth can be taken, involuntarily, by police or child protection workers to a "protective safe house" for a period of five days, during which time they can receive emergency treatment and assessment, with the ultimate goal making a plan to help the youth escape prostitution. While the intent of this involuntary placement is to protect the best interests of the youth, there is disagreement among critics about what those interests are.

QUESTION

Recall the discussion in Chapter 4 concerning provincial offences. There are times when youth can be held in remand custody for violation of provincial offences, as in the instance above. Even though these youth are not being charged, what harm might there be in placing them in remand custody to "help" them?

Place of Pre-Trial Detention

Certain provisions of the YCJA protect the young person who is detained pending trial. Section 30(3), for example, mandates that a young person be held in custody in a separate facility from adults. This protection is qualified, however, when the young person will pose a risk to himself or herself or others while there. In addition, if there is no place of detention for young persons within a reasonable distance, the youth may be placed in an adult facility.

As discussed earlier regarding the police detention of young persons, the UN Convention on the Rights of the Child (UNCRC) under article 37(c) states that "every child deprived of liberty shall be separated from adults unless it is considered in the child's best interest not to do so." Canada is a signatory to the UNCRC and ratified it in 1991. In order to comply with the UNCRC, a country is required to ensure that its laws are in conformity with the treaty. The YCJA, which entered into force in 2003, mentions the UNCRC in the preamble and throughout the legislation specifically refers to Canada's commitments under the convention. Despite this, countries are able to register a reservation to specific articles in the UNCRC when it is difficult to comply. Canada has registered such a reservation: "The Government of Canada accepts the general principles of article 37(c) of the Convention, but reserves the right not to detain children separately from adults where this is not appropriate or feasible" (UN Treaty Collection, 2014). Despite being advised to remove the reservation, even after the most recent review in 2012, Canada continues to stand on the reservation (UN Committee on the Rights of the Child, 2013).

1. What are the implications for the young persons of having to share a facility with adults?
2. What are the issues for the institution?

Criticisms of the Pre-Trial Detention Regime

The pre-trial detention regime under the original YCJA was heavily criticized for being ineffective and confusing. The Nunn Commission found that it was difficult for police and Crown prosecutors to apply both the YCJA and the *Criminal Code*, and recommended that Crown prosecutors be trained to use a consistent approach to pre-trial detention (Nova Scotia Public Prosecution Service, 2006).

THE NUNN COMMISSION OF INQUIRY

On October 14, 2004, Theresa McEvoy, mother of three, was killed when her vehicle was struck by another. The other vehicle was being driven by 16-year-old Archie Billard, who had stolen the vehicle and was driving at high speed. The seriousness of this case allowed the Crown prosecutor to seek an adult sentence, and when that was successful, the privacy provisions to keep the name of young persons charged under the YCJA no longer applied and the young person's name was released.

While tragic regardless of the circumstances, this accident garnered national attention when it became public that Billard had been, just days before, released from custody due to administrative error and miscommunication, despite having 38 outstanding charges against him (many for car theft and reckless driving).

Justice Merlin Nunn was charged with conducting an in-depth public inquiry into the circumstances surrounding Billard's release. His 2006 report contained 34 recommendations for improvements to Nova Scotia's youth criminal justice programs, the YCJA, and community youth services (Nunn Commission of Inquiry, 2006). Not only were all of Nunn's recommendations accepted (Nova Scotia Public Prosecution Service, 2006), but they went on to influence changes to the YCJA.

QUESTION

Prior to the accident that killed Theresa McEvoy, Archie Billard had broken the law numerous times. What might have been done, long before this accident, to help rehabilitate this boy?

The 2012 amendments to the YCJA included provisions that were taken directly from the recommendations of the Nunn Commission. The provisions for pre-trial detention under s. 29(2) were clarified to include cases in which a young person has been charged with a **serious offence** or has a criminal history that shows a pattern of either outstanding charges or findings of guilt. In order to maintain confidence in the administration of justice, the amendments also added "exceptional circumstances" as a valid reason for pre-trial detention. Such circumstances under s. 29(2)(b)(iii) might be the apparent strength of the prosecution's case, the gravity of the offence, certain facts about the offence (including whether a firearm was used), or whether the young person would be liable to a potentially lengthy custodial sentence upon conviction (Department of Justice, 2013).

Continuing with the overriding assumption that young persons are to generally be released, with conditions, amended s. 29(2)(b) clarifies the conditions that have to be met for a judge to continue detention:

serious offence
any indictable offence for which the maximum punishment for an adult is imprisonment for five years or more, including violent offences, some property offences (e.g., auto theft), and offences that might endanger the public (e.g., dangerous driving, murder)

(c) … that no condition or combination of conditions of release would …

(i) reduce, to a level below substantial, the likelihood that the young person would not appear in court when required by law to do so,

(ii) offer adequate protection to the public from the risk that the young person might otherwise present, or

(iii) maintain confidence in the administration of justice.

These provisions incorporate the principle that when public confidence in the justice system is lost, it can bring the administration of justice into disrepute. What does this mean?

If the youth is ordered detained and the trial date is not in the near future, the *Criminal Code* requires periodic rehearing of the detention decision. Rehearings are held every 30 days for a summary conviction offence and every 90 days for a hybrid or indictable offence. Also, s. 33 of the YCJA allows the detained person to apply to a youth court for early release from detention.

If either the Crown or the accused is displeased with a decision to release or to detain a young person in custody, either party may appeal.

Although the YCJA was intended to reduce rates of both custodial sentences and pre-trial detention, it succeeded only in reducing the numbers of young persons held after a finding of guilt. As for youth held before trial, their numbers actually increased significantly (Bala & Anand, 2013, pp. 316–318). See Figure 6.1.

FIGURE 6.1 Youth Remand Rate, 2001–2012

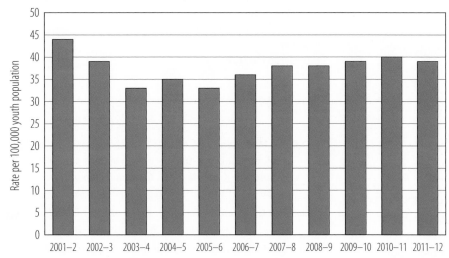

SOURCE: Adapted from Statistics Canada (2014b).

A report by the Washington, DC Justice Policy Institute (2011) studied the use of pre-trial detention for both youth and adults in Western countries. It showed that Canada, compared with other countries, had the highest percentage of the total incarcerated population being held in pre-trial detention (36 percent). Australia was the next-highest (21 percent), followed by the United States (20 percent), Finland (17 percent), Germany (16 percent), and England (15 percent). The United States has a much higher rate of incarceration generally than Canada, but when populations held in custody are compared, it seems Canada puts more people in custody before being actually convicted of a crime than the United States does. This runs contrary to the fundamental principle of justice requiring individuals accused of crime to be presumed innocent, and is in direct opposition to the preamble of the YCJA.

CHAPTER SUMMARY

The provisions for adults with respect to judicial interim release apply to young persons with additional options included within the YCJA. A key difference in application appears to lie in the number of conditions of release and the frequency with which youth are required to provide a surety compared with their adult counterparts. Canada has the dubious distinction of having the highest percentage in the Western world of its incarcerated population in pre-trial detention; and despite the express aim of the YCJA to reduce the use of custody for youth, the data do not show a reduction in use of custody at the pre-trial stage. One of the reasons for this is related to the percentage of youth who violate their conditions of release and receive additional criminal charges, allowing them to be eligible for consideration under the three grounds of pre-trial detention.

The recommendations of the Nunn Commission were incorporated into the amendments to the YCJA, which made pre-trial detention decisions less cumbersome.

In most cases, the onus is on the Crown to prove that a young person should be detained. Usually, as required by the UN Convention on the Rights of the Child and the YCJA, young persons are to be detained separately from adults. Such practices as using detention for youth for prevention or to assist with child welfare matters are prohibited under the YCJA.

For young persons being dealt with under the YCJA, pre-trial detention is intended as a last resort rather than an option—unless there is violence, breach of probation, the combination of a serious offence and a criminal record, or serious concern about failure to appear that cannot be remedied by releasing the young person into the care of a responsible person. Restorative justice principles and processes are incorporated into the pre-trial detention regime, including the availability of conferences under s. 19.

KEY TERMS

appearance notice, 132
conferences, 135
Crown brief, 132
judicial interim release (bail), 132
promise to appear, 132
recognizance, 132
reservation, 133

responsible person, 132
reverse onus, 133
serious offence, 140
show-cause hearing, 132
surety, 134
undertaking, 132

REFERENCES

Bail Reform Act. (1970–71–72). SC 1970–71–72, c. 37.

Bala, N., & Anand, S. (2013). *Youth criminal justice law*. Toronto: Irwin Law.

Canadian Charter of Rights and Freedoms. (1982). Part I of the *Constitution Act, 1982*, being Schedule B to the *Canada Act 1982* (UK), 1982, c. 11.

Correctional Service Canada. (2012). Restorative justice backgrounder. Retrieved from http://www.csc-scc.gc.ca/restorative-justice/003005-0004-eng.shtml.

Criminal Code. (1985). RSC 1985, c. C-46.

Department of Justice. (2013). Recent changes to Canada's youth justice system. Retrieved from http://www.justice.gc.ca/eng/cj-jp/yj-jj/ycja-lsjpa/sheets-feuillets/amend-modif.html.

Deshman, A., & Myers, N. (2014). *Set up to fail: Bail and the revolving door of pre-trial detention*. Canadian Civil Liberties Association and Education Trust. Retrieved from http://ccla.org/wordpress/wp-content/uploads/2014/07/Set-up-to-fail-FINAL.pdf.

Doob, A.N., & Webster, C.M. (2012). Back to the future? Policy development in pre-trial detention in Canada. In K. Ismaili, J.B. Sprott, & K. Varma (Eds.), *Canadian criminal justice policy* (pp. 30–57). Toronto: Oxford University Press.

Green, R.G., & Healy, K.F. (2003). *Tough on kids: Rethinking approaches to youth justice*. Saskatoon: Purich.

Hirschfield, P. (2009). Another way out: The impact of juvenile arrests on high school dropout. *Sociology of Education, 82*, 368–93.

Justice Policy Institute. (2011). Fact sheet: Pretrial detention and remand to custody. *Finding direction: Expanding criminal justice options by considering policies of other nations*. Retrieved from http://www.justicepolicy.org/uploads/justicepolicy/documents/pretrial_detention_and_remand_to_custody.pdf.

K.D., R v. (2003). [2003] NSJ No. 165 (SC).

Kirk, D.S., & Sampson, R.J. (2013). Juvenile arrest and collateral educational damage in the transition to adulthood. *Sociology of Education, 86*(1), 36–62.

Mayer, S. (2005). *Educating Chicago's court-involved youth: Mission and policy in conflict.* Chicago: Chapin Hall Center for Children.

McDonald, R v. (1998). 40 OR (3d) 641, 127 CCC (3d) 57, 1998 CanLII 13327 (CA).

Myers, N. (2009). Shifting risk: Bail and the use of sureties. *Current Issues in Criminal Justice, 21*(1), 127–147.

Myers, N.M., & Dhillon, S. (2013). The criminal offence of entering any Shoppers Drug Mart in Ontario: Criminalizing ordinary behavior with youth bail conditions. *Canadian Journal of Criminology and Criminal Justice, 55*(2), 187–214.

Nova Scotia Public Prosecution Service. (2006). Youth Criminal Justice Act prosecutions—Nunn Commission recommendations. Practice Memorandum. Retrieved from http://www.gov.ns.ca/pps/publications/ca_manual/ProsecutionPolicies/YCJApolicyNunnRecsMTSwpd.pdf.

Nunn Commission of Inquiry. (2006). *Spiralling out of control: Lessons learned from a boy in trouble: Report of the Nunn Commission of Inquiry.* Halifax: Province of Nova Scotia.

Pager, D. (2003). The mark of a criminal record. *American Journal of Sociology, 108*, 937–75.

Protection of Sexually Exploited Children. (2012). RSA 2000, c. P-30.3.

Safe Streets and Communities Act. (2012). SC 2012, c. 1.

Sprott, J.B., & Doob, A.N. (2009). *Justice for girls? Stability and change in the youth justice systems of the United States and Canada.* Chicago: University of Chicago Press.

Sprott, J.B., & Doob, A.N. (2010). Gendered treatment: Girls and treatment orders in bail court. *Canadian Journal of Criminology and Criminal Justice, 52*(4), 427–441.

Sprott, J.B., & Myers, N.M. (2011). Set up to fail: The unintended consequences of multiple bail conditions. *Canadian Journal of Criminology and Criminal Justice, 53*(4), 404–423.

Statistics Canada. (2014a).Youth correctional services, average counts of young persons in provincial and territorial correctional services. CANSIM Table 251-0008. Retrieved November 13, 2014 from http://www5.statcan.gc.ca/cansim/a26?lang=eng&retrLang=eng&id=2510008&paSer=&pattern=&stByVal=1&p1=1&p2=37&tabMode=dataTable&csid=.

Statistics Canada. (2014b). Youth custody and community services (YCCS), admissions and releases to correctional services. CANSIM Table 251-0010. Retrieved November 13, 2014 from http://www5.statcan.gc.ca/cansim/a26?lang=eng&retrLang=eng&id=2510010&paSer=&pattern=&stByVal=1&p1=1&p2=37&tabMode=dataTable&csid=.

Trotter, G.T. (2010). *The law of bail in Canada* (3rd ed.). Toronto: Carswell.

UN Convention on the Rights of the Child (UNCRC). (1989, November 20). 1577 UNTS 3.

UN Treaty Collection. (2014). Chapter IV, Human rights: Convention on the Rights of the Child. Retrieved from https://treaties.un.org/Pages/ViewDetails.aspx?mtdsg_no=IV-11&chapter=4&lang=en#EndDec.

UN Committee on the Rights of the Child. (2013). List of issues concerning additional and updated information related to the third and fourth combined periodic reports of Canada (CRC/C/CAN/3–4). Addendum: Written replies of Canada, Sixty-First Session, 17 September–October 2012, UN Doc. CRC-C-CAN-Q-3-4, Add. 1, 21 January. Retrieved from http://daccess-dds-ny.un.org/doc/UNDOC/GEN/G12/413/56/PDF/G1241356.pdf?OpenElement.

Wust, R v. (2000). 2000 SCC 18, [2000] 1 SCR 455.

Youth Criminal Justice Act. (2002). SC 2002, c. 1.

EXERCISES AND REVIEW

Review Questions

1. What is meant by the presumption of innocence and how does this apply in decisions about release or detention?

2. What steps are to be considered by the Crown in determining more onerous release conditions during a bail hearing?

3. What is the difference between a surety and a responsible person?

4. What impacts did the Nunn Commission report have on the pre-trial detention decision process?

5. When can a youth be detained awaiting trial?

6. What role can police officers play when youth are ordered back to school while awaiting trial?

7. When can a youth be housed in the same facility as adults?

8. What differentiates restorative justice practices from formal courtroom proceedings?

Discussion Questions

1. What do you think the changes made in 2012 to pre-trial detention requirements will mean with respect to the number of youth being held in pre-trial detention?

2. In the pre-trial process, how might a police officer help guide a young person at risk toward positive life choices? Discuss.

3. Trevor was charged with vandalism after spray-painting the side of his neighbour's house. Through the restorative justice process, during a conference called at his bail hearing he was able to speak with his victim about the financial and emotional toll his crime took. What value will this have in terms of Trevor's release?

4. Listed below are 16 actual bail release conditions given to young persons in Toronto-area courtrooms. As you read in this chapter, youth receive an average of about 9 conditions of release. Select 9 of the 16 here and describe how you would adhere to them while managing your current daily routine. Assume that the co-accused is one of your friends and the victim is someone who lives in your neighbourhood.

   - residence condition to reside with surety
   - abide by the "house rules"
   - no drugs/alcohol
   - weapons prohibition
   - attend school each and every day and attend each and every class
   - attend counselling and take treatment/medication/see doctor
   - curfew of 7 p.m. on weeknights and 9 p.m. on weekends
   - boundary conditions not to travel farther than a certain number of blocks from residence
   - not to apply for a firearms acquisition certification (FAC)
   - not to possess break-and-enter instruments (such as lock picks)
   - not to possess a cellphone
   - carry bail papers on person at all times
   - not to attend any [named] store in the province
   - not to be where co-accused lives, works, or happens to be
   - not to be where victim lives, works, or happens to be
   - non-association order—not to be in the community with anyone with a criminal record

5. The seven graphs in Figure 6.2 show the percentage of youth sentenced to custody or held in remand custody from 1997 to 2012. The first graph is for all Canada; the others are for Ontario, Nova Scotia, New Brunswick, Saskatchewan, Alberta, and British Columbia.

   Analyze the trends in the data and consider why there are differences from one province to the other. Describe the main trends with respect to youth in sentenced custody as against youth in pre-trial custody. (We will return to this discussion when we consider sentencing in Chapter 8.)

FIGURE 6.2   Average Counts (Percentage) of Young Persons in Remand and Sentenced Custody

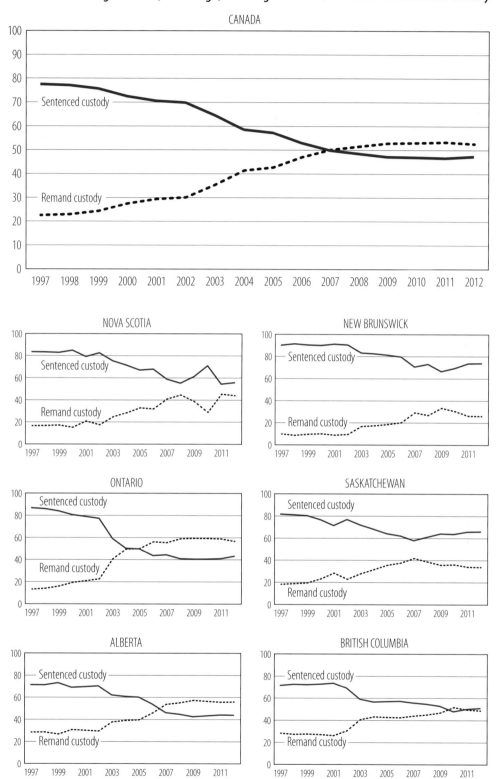

SOURCE: Adapted from Statistics Canada (2014a).

CHRIS: SIMPLE SCHOOL FIGHT LEADS TO CHARGE

Chris is a 15-year-old who has been charged with aggravated assault. After a show-cause hearing, he was released pending trial into the care of his parents, with whom he lives.

The alleged assault took place at his high school, where he got into an argument with another 15-year-old named Victor. The argument got heated and witnesses say Chris pushed Victor. Victor fell down some stairs and fractured both legs. His recovery took several months and involved his participation in rehabilitation programs and physiotherapy. Chris had been previously charged with assault against another boy, Imran, and had been on probation at the time Victor was hurt.

Chris is adamant that he had not pushed Victor and that, if he had made contact at all, it was an accident and not a "push." He has entered a plea of not guilty to the charge of aggravated assault. After entering the plea, Chris and his lawyer got into an argument and fired him, giving the reason that "the man couldn't be trusted." So now as he prepares for trial, Chris also has to find new legal representation.

As you read through the steps in the trial process set out in this chapter, consider the experiences Chris will go through.

Introduction

As was explained in Chapters 5 and 6, the *Youth Criminal Justice Act* (YCJA) provides many exit points from the more formal court process from the time of the first police contact through the use of extrajudicial measures and sanctions. Pre-trial procedures described in Chapter 6 included the release of young persons on bail or into the care of a responsible person. This chapter concerns itself with those young people being dealt with by way of charge who have not been diverted to some other program outside the formal process and will be proceeding to court. Procedures explained in this chapter are first appearance, deciding on a plea, the trial, and adjudication (the judge or jury's rendering a decision). Sentencing will be discussed in Chapter 8.

Jurisdiction of the Youth Court

As was discussed in an earlier chapter, some provisions in law are substantive and others are procedural. When adults are charged under the *Criminal Code*, both the substantive offences and the procedures are found within the Code. In the case of youth courts, there is a separate procedural code in the YCJA. As is pointed out by Davis-Barron (2009, p. 179), this gives young persons enhanced procedural protections, which allows for more informal and expeditious proceedings that are appropriate to the accused's age and stage of development and provides a court in keeping with the young persons' "best interests."

youth justice court
(1) a court specifically constituted for the purpose of hearing youth trials; (2) an existing adult court designated (temporarily or permanently) for that purpose

Section 13 of the YCJA provides for the establishment, in each province of Canada, of **youth justice courts**. Such courts deal with all matters in which a young person is charged with an offence under the *Criminal Code* or with another federal offence. A youth justice court can be a separately constituted court reserved only for the purpose of hearing youth cases, but it is often an existing court that is also "designated" or permitted to serve as a youth justice court. For purposes of appeals, however, youth courts are generally considered equivalent to the second-lowest criminal court level (for example, the Ontario Court of Justice level in Ontario).

If an existing court is simply "designated" a youth justice court for those occasions in which the accused is a young person, do you think it is likely to be as effective in offering youth-specific services as it would be if it were a separately constituted court, such as a family court?

"Young person" for the purpose of youth court **jurisdiction** is defined in s. 2 of the YCJA:

> "young person" means a person who is or, in the absence of evidence to the contrary, appears to be twelve years old or older, but less than eighteen years old and, if the context requires, includes any person who is charged under this Act with having committed an offence while he or she was a young person or who is found guilty of an offence under this Act.

jurisdiction
the scope of authority of a court; can be based on a defined territory (Ontario court), a defined age range (youth court), a defined class of offences (small claims court), a defined area of law (family court), and so on

As was discussed in Chapter 6 regarding bail and places of temporary detention, the age jurisdiction of the youth court is important, because if a young person is being held pre-trial and turns 18, he or she may be moved from a youth to an adult facility. However, if a young person is charged with an offence while under the age of 18, even though at the time of the trial she or he is over 18, the case will still be heard in youth court.

While maintaining the adversarial approach of the adult court, the youth justice court is governed by YCJA procedural provisions that take into account the lack of maturity of accused and provide enhanced safeguards for young persons' rights. As in adult court, the parties involved are Crown counsel, representing the province, and defence counsel, representing the accused. However, the youth court judge is required to remind the young person of his or her right to counsel throughout the process and ensure that he or she understands this, using language that is both age-appropriate and appropriate for the developmental level of the individual.

A CAREFUL BALANCE

In Canadian criminal court rooms, whether adult or youth, a careful balance needs to be struck between procedural justice and substantive justice. Both are required to ensure both fair treatment of the accused and to serve justice with respect to an outcome from the perspective of society at large.

Procedural justice focuses on fair processes: the rules that govern our courts must be followed impartially and applied consistently so that their decisions are unbiased. For example, procedural justice in a youth court would require that a youth be made aware of all of his or her rights and have legal representation. **Substantive justice**, on the other hand, is more concerned with the guilt or innocence of the accused: the focus is on the criteria used to prove facts and prove guilt, and the appropriateness of sanctions.

Substantive justice ensures that the law is fair. Procedural justice ensures that it is fairly applied.

procedural justice
ensures that the administration of justice and fair processes are upheld in the courtroom

substantive justice
ensures that the application of law is fair and just

QUESTION

What sort of differences would you expect there might be between adult court and youth court in terms of procedural and substantive justice?

Role of Judge in Youth Court: First Appearance

When an indictment is laid against a young person, he or she must appear before a youth justice court judge, who reads the information or indictment to him or her, and if the young person is not represented by legal counsel, informs him or her of the right to retain and instruct counsel. Further, as per s. 32(1)(c), if the person is charged with an offence for which an adult sentence could be imposed, he or she must be advised of the rights that arise from this. If the judge is not convinced the young person understands the matters that have been explained to him or her during the first appearance hearing, and the youth is not represented by counsel, the judge must direct that the young person be represented by counsel in those cases in which a youth might receive an adult sentence. In other cases, in which the youth justice court is not satisfied that the young person understands the charge, the court must enter a plea of not guilty and proceed with the trial.

Pleas in Youth Justice Court

When a youthful accused pleads not guilty, a trial will be held. When the accused pleads guilty, and the court is satisfied that the facts (as read in by the prosecutor) support the charge, the accused will be convicted.

As in adult courts, justices presiding in youth criminal justice court are required to conduct a *plea inquiry* before entertaining a plea of guilty. This requires that the court make inquiries of the young person to ensure that the plea is voluntary, and that the accused understands that he or she is admitting the essential elements of the offence and that the court is not bound by any plea agreement that might have been negotiated between the defence counsel and prosecutor (*Criminal Code*, s. 606(1)).

However, there is further provision for "second-guessing" a guilty plea if it is made by a young person. If the court is *not* satisfied that the facts support the charge, according to s. 36(2) of the YCJA a trial will proceed anyway. This is a difference between the adult and youth systems. The "second-guessing," intended as a special, additional protection for youthful accused, is carried over from the historical *parens patriae* philosophy of the youth court.

Preliminary Motions

preliminary motions and applications
mini-hearings, separate from the main trial, to resolve preliminary, usually procedural, issues

Preliminary motions and applications involve issues raised by the defence or the Crown before the commencement of the trial. These motions often involve procedural matters and, occasionally, Charter applications. Some of the most common preliminary motions are change of venue, joinder/separation of counts or accused, and disclosure orders. Preliminary motions are less common in youth criminal justice proceedings than in adult proceedings.

Preliminary Inquiries and Electing Mode of Trial

To understand the difference between jury trials and trials by judge alone, it is also important to understand the difference between a summary conviction offence and an indictable offence under the *Criminal Code*. When an adult is charged with a crime, he or she is accused of either a summary conviction offence or an indictable offence. Some offences, called

hybrid offences under the Code, can be dealt with either summarily or by indictment at the discretion of the Crown. Note that for arrest purposes, police treat all hybrid offences as indictable. A summary conviction offence is simply a less serious offence, and the court procedure is less formal. In this way, the court system can run more efficiently by conserving its resources for more serious cases. Specifically, all summary conviction offences are heard before a judge alone with no option of a jury.

In contrast, indictable offences, such as murder, are far more serious. Because there is the possibility of much more being at stake for the defendant and for the state, the trial process is more comprehensive, with extensive preliminary inquiries and many witnesses. The trial of an indictable offence may be heard before a judge and a jury.

Regardless of whether a youth is charged with a summary conviction or an indictable offence, the procedural rules followed in youth court are those for summary conviction offences as laid out in part XXVII of the Code. As Bala and Anand (2012, p. 354) have noted, the proceedings are much shorter, more informal, and less complex than those for indictment in the adult court. They further point out that this helps ensure that the court is not so intimidating to the young person. However, indictable offences still carry stiffer penalties.

Section 11 of the *Canadian Charter of Rights and Freedoms* guarantees all persons the right to a jury trial if the offence they are charged with carries a maximum penalty of five years or more. The same provisions dealing with summary conviction and indictable offences under the *Criminal Code* apply to offences under the YCJA. This means that, for many indictable offences, youth in conflict with the law are, like adults, entitled to a trial by jury. For summary conviction offences, the youth is tried by a judge only. Jury trials are available to youth charged with indictable offences for which the penalty on conviction is five years or more in total custody and supervision time. A youth can elect to be tried by judge alone or by a judge and jury. The YCJA also establishes the right of a young person to elect his or her mode of trial by requesting a preliminary inquiry.

In both adult and youth courts, accused persons can change their mind about the mode of trial they have selected after a preliminary inquiry (s. 561 of the Code). This is another area in which young people, due to their age and stage of development, have been given maximum flexibility in terms of election and re-election provisions for their mode of trial. As decided in *R v. K.P.H.* (2007), youth courts should normally agree to such a request.

hybrid offence
a type of offence that can be dealt with either as a summary conviction offence or as an indictable offence, at the discretion of the Crown; for arrest purposes, police treat all hybrid offences as indictable

---

Criminal Code, **Aggravated Assault**
268(1) Every one commits an aggravated assault who wounds, maims, disfigures or endangers the life of the complainant.
(2) Every one who commits an aggravated assault is guilty of an indictable offence and liable to imprisonment for a term not exceeding fourteen years.

CHRIS, REVISITED (I): ELECTING MODE OF TRIAL

1. Is aggravated assault an offence that offers the young person the opportunity to elect a mode of trial?
2. What are the advantages and disadvantages of a trial by judge alone and trial by a judge and jury for the accused young person?
3. What about for the society at large?

Youth Justice Committees and Conferences

Even if formal charges, including serious ones, have been laid, the YCJA allows some use of informal mechanisms to resolve the situation. Section 18 provides that each province may establish one or more "youth justice committees" made up of "citizens" who support various aspects of the youth justice system by

- giving advice on the choice of extrajudicial measures;
- "supporting" victims and facilitating victim–offender reconciliation;
- arranging for community support services and mentoring relationships for the young person;
- coordinating the interaction of child protection agencies and the youth criminal justice system;
- monitoring government compliance with the YCJA and advising government about improvements; and
- planning public education campaigns about the youth criminal justice system.

Because the responsibility for the establishment and administration of provincial youth justice committees lies with the provinces, the availability of these committees is quite varied across Canada, and the activities they undertake also varies provincially.

Youth justice committees are also authorized to "act as a conference" for purposes of s. 19, which provides in part:

> **19**(1) A youth justice court judge, the provincial director, a police officer, a justice of the peace, a prosecutor or a youth worker may convene or cause to be convened a conference for the purpose of making a decision required to be made under this Act.
>
> (2) The mandate of a conference may be, among other things, to give advice on appropriate extrajudicial measures, conditions for judicial interim release, sentences, including the review of sentences, and reintegration plans.

A conference (also discussed in Chapter 6) may be called by a youth justice court judge, the provincial director (a representative of the Probation Services department), a police officer, a justice of the peace, a prosecutor, or a youth worker (youth probation officer). Advice may be sought on appropriate extrajudicial measures, bail conditions, sentences, review of sentences, and reintegration.

Different types of conferences may be convened. One is a case planning conference, which brings together a team of professionals to discuss programs and services that may be available for the young person within his or her community; such conferences can take place at any stage in the YCJA process. Another is a restorative justice conference, whose purpose is to hold the young person accountable for his or her actions and to help promote reparation for the harm done to the victim and to the community.

The mandated conferencing provisions allow for a creative, innovative, community-based approach to the problem of youth crime. The effectiveness of this concept lies in the development of links between the young person, the justice system, and community agencies and counselling services. Thus, through conferencing, a truly multidisciplinary approach to youth crime is achieved. The use of conferencing varies widely throughout the country.

Even when a youth appears in youth court, however, the judge still has the opportunity to deal with the matter outside of the formal process by ordering a **stay of proceedings** and referring the youth to an extrajudicial program or restorative justice initiative.

stay of proceedings
a dismissal of further legal proceedings

Restorative Justice Initiatives

Restorative justice processes include but are not limited to victim–offender mediation, restorative conferencing, and "circle" processes. While the techniques used in each form may differ, the ultimate goal remains the same: repairing and restoring severed relationships and enabling healing. Restorative justice programs recognize that a relational rift occurs when a wrong is committed—a rift between the offender and the victim, the victim's family, the broader community, and lastly the offender's own family. Restoring the broken relationships between offenders and victims—and not the criminal sanction imposed by the state—is the critical element.

Restorative justice programs are based on the belief that the best way to deal with people affected by crime is to bring them together to discuss how their lives have changed in the wake of the incident in an equal and flowing dialogue. The dialogue process serves as the starting point to bring about other restorative justice outcomes (Walgrave, 2006). The outcomes hoped for are (1) reconciliation, (2) reparation, and (3) transformation.

When a young person offers an apology to the victim and to the community at large, there is an opportunity to engage in a process of reconciliation and to give reparation or to "make good" through restitution or some form of community service. The final outcome—transformation—relates to the sense of liberation from the conditions that perpetuate the cycle of violence. It occurs because the process reduces fear among the community members by reassuring them that the youth has been held accountable, and it provides them with a greater awareness of the conditions that led the young person to commit the crime.

The RCMP is championing a specific restorative justice process known as *community justice forums*. These forums are facilitated by a trained restorative justice leader and include the police, other community members, the victim, the offender, and the families of those involved. The environment is a safe, controlled space, where the group discuss the offence and how they have all been affected, and then collaboratively come up with a plan to correct what has occurred.

The restorative justice process in the community justice forums provides an opportunity for young people to accept responsibility for their actions and to understand the impact of their behaviour on others. Such a realization often brings about deep feelings of remorse and empathy and assists the offender in understanding the consequences of his or her behaviour. When victims are able to express how they have been affected by what has happened and then see and hear genuine expressions of remorse, they are more likely to accept and to forgive. This enables everyone to return to the community with a sense of closure and optimism for the future.

There are provisions within the YCJA to hold conferences; in some jurisdictions across the country these are referred to as *family group conferences* (FGCs). The focus is similar to that offered in the RCMP community justice forum, with an added focus on the families of the offender and the victim following the model developed in Australia (Hayes & Daly, 2003). Proponents of FGCs suggest the following reasons why it might be a more appropriate process than the more formal criminal justice system for certain crimes (Foley, 2013):

- It gives families the opportunity to participate in decision-making and care of their children.
- It offers a collaborative, strengths-based, culturally sensitive approach to helping families.
- Neutral facilitation is provided by community service agencies.
- It creates plans that are realistic, achievable, and long-lasting.

- It enables youth to strengthen relationships and vital attachments with family, community, and culture.
- It restores balance and harmony for families and promotes understanding.

Research on youth who had been referred to restorative justice processes showed that the young people were less likely to have further police contact than their peers who were processed through a traditional court process. For those youth who did have further police contact, there was a longer delay before reoffending than for their peers in the court system, and they were involved in less-serious offences (Bergseth & Bouffard, 2007). Other studies of both adults and youth who have been involved in restorative justice practices have shown similar results, with those participating in restorative justice less likely to recidivate (reoffend) (Bradshaw & Roseborough, 2005; Latimer, Dowden, & Muise, 2005).

Lawyers in Youth Court

Before discussing the procedures in youth court, let us pause and consider the legal counsel who make arguments in youth court.

The Crown

The youth court is a formal adversarial process in which a lawyer for the state, known as the Crown, and a lawyer for the accused, known as defence counsel, present arguments in support of the accused's guilt or innocence. As in ordinary adult court, the primary role of the Crown prosecutor is to present the government's evidence about the accused's role in the alleged offences. Before the case goes to trial, the Crown must provide **disclosure** to the defence counsel of all the evidence and the names of witnesses that might be called. At trial, the Crown will outline both the substantive case against the young person and the procedures followed by the police at the time of arrest.

The Crown has to satisfy the court that the police considered the options of taking no further action, warning the accused, administering a police caution, and making a referral to a program; and that the circumstances of the case instead warrant a trial. The Crown also has to provide reasons for deciding that the case was not suitable for a Crown caution. It is the responsibility of the Crown to consider what would be in society's best interests when deciding to present the case to the court. If the offence is minor and the cost to the participants is high (for example, witnesses have to travel long distances), the Crown may drop the charges. It can also agree to reduce the charges, if the offender agrees to enter a guilty plea to a lesser offence (**plea bargain**).

Defence Counsel

The role of the defence is to argue on behalf of the legal interests of the young person. This may include actively presenting evidence in support of the accused's innocence by presenting a defence (mistaken identity, alibi, etc.), by challenging the evidence presented by the Crown, or by arguing that the police violated the accused's legal rights (including Charter rights) in the course of the investigation. Success in convincing the court that evidence was collected in violation of the young person's rights can lead to exclusion of that evidence; exclusion of evidence can make it difficult for the court to make a finding of guilt, which can lead to an acquittal.

In some cases, defence counsel and a young person's parents disagree about what the young person's best interests are, or about what is the best legal argument on behalf of the

disclosure
before trial, the release by the prosecutor to the defence of all evidence the prosecutor plans on using at trial

plea bargain
an agreement reached by the defendant and the prosecutor that both parties are satisfied with; must be approved by the court

accused. Where the parents have hired the defence counsel, this may pose a conflict of interest. For example, the parents may want their son or daughter to be "taught a lesson" and receive some form of sanction for their criminal behaviour. But this is not the job of the defence counsel; the defence is responsible for considering the accused as his or her sole client and representing his or her legal interests. The right to legal counsel is a *personal* right, spelled out in s. 25(8) of the YCJA. The youthful client enjoys the same rights as an adult client in his or her relationship with the lawyer. Significant among these rights is the client's entitlement to confidentiality, which means the lawyer is not permitted to reveal confidential information to the young person's parents.

The Right to Counsel

Under the welfare-oriented *Juvenile Delinquents Act* (JDA), the participation of lawyers in youth justice cases was strongly discouraged. While the legislation fell short of actually prohibiting the presence of lawyers, there was no mention of legal representation in the JDA because the court process called for "informality." Initially, even the majority of youth court judges lacked any legal training. The former *Young Offenders Act* and the enactment of the *Canadian Charter of Rights and Freedoms* introduced a right to counsel as one of the most fundamental rights accorded to youth.

The YCJA requires that young persons be reminded of their right to retain and instruct counsel repeatedly throughout their involvement with the youth criminal justice process (s. 25(3)). The judge is required to provide a youth with counsel either through legal aid mechanisms within the province (s. 25(4)) or, if not available, to direct that the attorney general (s. 5) appoint counsel to represent the youth. Lawyers being expensive, however, provincial governments became increasingly concerned about their own financial burden in providing legal services for young people in conflict with the law. In enacting s. 25(10), the legislature responded to pressure from the provinces to provide a mechanism for recovering legal costs from youth and their parents:

> **25**(10) Nothing in this Act prevents the lieutenant governor in council of a province … from establishing a program to authorize the recovery of the costs of a young person's counsel from the young person or the parents of the young person.

CASE IN POINT

R v. L.S., 2006 CanLII 40609 (Ont. CA)

There is little debate that young people who have to appear in a courtroom should be provided a lawyer if they cannot afford one. The question is: At what point in the process is the court mandated to direct **duty counsel**?

That question was explored in the case of *R v. L.S.* (2006). A 13-year-old appeared in court to answer a charge of uttering a threat of bodily harm. Neither he nor his parents were able to afford legal counsel, so he appeared before the court represented only by duty counsel. Because the Crown was planning to divert the charge using extrajudicial sanctions (EJS), the judge refused the youth's request for legal aid funding, arguing that there was "little consequence for the youth." After the hearing, the youth (via duty counsel) brought an application for **judicial review** to the Superior Court of Justice for a review of the decision of the youth court. He requested this review on the grounds that, in order to participate in the sanction program being offered by the Crown, he would be required to

duty counsel
a lawyer, either an employee of the court or working under contract for the court, who provides on-the-spot, no-charge (although there may be an eventual charge) advice to unrepresented accused

judicial review
a higher court's review, at a separate hearing, of aspects of a lower court proceeding (typically administrative or procedural aspects, not findings of fact or verdict/order)

accept responsibility for the alleged threat—equivalent to making an admission of guilt—and that he ought to have the right to counsel to make a decision about whether to make such an admission.

At the review hearing, the court overturned the lower court's ruling, stating that it is the court's obligation to direct the appointment of counsel whenever a youth or his or her family cannot provide for representation.

While the charge against the youth was ultimately dismissed, making the youth's right to counsel **moot**, the Crown appealed the decision to the Ontario Court of Appeal, asking the court to consider the issue in order to provide clarity for future decisions. The appeal court overturned the decision, explaining that, while the YCJA requires that counsel be provided for a youth who cannot afford one, this right is triggered only after the trial reaches a certain point: it is "only when there is a hearing related to the custody of the young person, including sentencing or when the young person is engaged in a trial that the youth may apply for publicly funded counsel. While a young person may require legal advice at the stage when he or she is considering whether to partake in EJS, that advice would be available through duty counsel" (*R v. L.S.*, 2006, para. 9).

QUESTIONS

1. What are your thoughts about the right to counsel and who should be required to pay for the services of a lawyer?

2. Do you have the same opinion with respect to the right to counsel and payment for services when the accused is an adult?

moot
the characteristic of a legal issue when it no longer requires a formal decision because intervening events have made it irrelevant

A large proportion of youthful accused are represented only by their parents or by duty counsel in criminal proceedings. While some parents believe that lawyers stand in the way of dealing with adolescents in a manner that serves their best interests, it is important to keep in mind that lawyers are "officers of the court" as well as representatives of their clients. They often help explain proceedings to youth and can hasten the processing of cases by acting for their clients in resolution meetings and other negotiations held with the Crown. In this way, defence counsel support the administration of justice, which suggests the need for more comprehensive and accessible legal aid programs across the country.

Inadequate legal representation is cause for concern, in light of the increased vulnerability of youth clients. Research has shown that while most young people have a basic understanding that defence counsel are there to be helpful, many do not understand that the role of counsel is to serve and support them personally (Schmidt, Reppucci, & Woolard, 2003). While youth may assume there is some agreed-on "privacy" in communications with their lawyer, they are often unaware that defence counsel are legally bound not to share confidences with parents or the judge. This may lead youth to withhold information important to their own defence (Viljoen, Klaver, & Roesch, 2005), which may actually impede the lawyer's ability to adequately fulfill his or her duty.

Research with youthful offenders about the lawyer–client relationship has shown that a young person's satisfaction with his or her lawyer depends on factors other than the extent to which they feel they have a direct say in their defence. Rather, youth reported that their lawyer's objectivity, trustworthiness, and respectfulness were far more important than whether the young person had a voice in the courtroom (Peterson-Badali, Care, & Broeking, 2007). While youth might be intimidated by lawyers and might have difficulty expressing wishes and giving specific instructions, lawyers working in the youth justice system have a duty to serve clients well, which includes making an extra effort to identify their wishes and best interests.

CHRIS, REVISITED (II): FIRING HIS LAWYER

You will recall that Chris fired his lawyer. In light of research on youth views of the court, what possible reasons might he have had?

Verdicts and Other Outcomes

Not all criminal trials continue through to conclusion and end in a verdict. Table 7.1 provides statistics about the outcome of criminal proceedings, comparing cases that appear before a judge in youth court with those cases in adult criminal court.

TABLE 7.1   Total Criminal Cases by Finding, Canada, 2011–12

	Adult cases		Youth cases	
	Number	Percentage	Number	Percentage
Total decisions	335,131	100.0	38,834	100.0
Guilty findings	214,825	64.1	21,256	54.7
Acquitted (not guilty)	11,345	3.4	582	1.5
Stayed or withdrawn	105,110	31.4	16,753	43.1
Other	3,851	1.1	243	0.6

SOURCE: Adapted from Statistics Canada (2014a, 2014b).

Review Table 7.1 and consider the differences in outcomes between the youth court and the adult court. What do you think might lead to the significant differences in the rate of proceedings stayed or withdrawn?

When reviewing Table 7.1, comparing the data in the categories "Stayed or withdrawn" and "Other" gives a better appreciation of the implications of the percentage of individuals actually found guilty. In addition to cases actually stayed or withdrawn, counted in this category are dismissals and discharges at the preliminary inquiry stage and court referrals to alternative or extrajudicial measures and restorative justice programs, which all involve the court stopping criminal proceedings against the accused.

The category "Other" includes cases in which the accused was found unfit to stand trial (which terminates the trial), or in which the final decision was a verdict of **not criminally responsible (NCR)**. A verdict of NCR means that while the accused was competent to stand trial at the time of the trial, at the time of the alleged offence he or she was not capable, for example, of distinguishing right from wrong (perhaps due to mental illness that is no longer present or has improved). Also counted under "other" are cases in which the court accepted a **special plea** (for example, *autrefois convict* [double jeopardy], which declares that the accused has already been tried and convicted on the same charge). Finally, if a case was removed from the docket for some other reason, it would also fit into the category of "other."

Table 7.1 shows that a very significant proportion of cases in both the adult and youth systems have an outcome other than an acquittal or a conviction (32.5 percent in adult court and 43.7 percent in youth court). When the outcomes other than acquittal and conviction are excluded—in other words, when the only cases considered are those that continue through a full trial, are adjudicated, and end in an acquittal or conviction—it

not criminally responsible (NCR)
a finding of the court about the status of an accused that is neither a conviction nor an acquittal, meaning that at the time of the alleged offence the accused could not form the intent to offend due to mental disorder

special plea
a plea other than guilty or not guilty; there are only a few recognized types

CHAPTER SUMMARY

Youth justice courts have exclusive jurisdiction over people who were between 12 and 17 years old when they allegedly committed a crime. The youth justice court not only upholds the administration of justice as in the adult court system, but also takes into account the YCJA procedural provisions designed for the unique needs of youth.

Once in the courtroom, the judge will advise youth on their right to counsel and ensure that a youth fully understands the charges. Once it is established that the youth is in full understanding of the charge and that a plea inquiry was held to ensure that the plea was voluntary, there are preliminary motions that may call for change of venue or disclosure orders. Here the mode of trial will also be examined; if a youth is charged with an offence that carries a maximum sentence of five years or more, he or she has the option of being tried either by judge alone or by judge and jury.

Even in cases in which formal charges have been laid, the YCJA allows for use of informal processes to resolve the issue. Youth justice committees and conferences can be employed, which bring together citizens that support various aspects of the youth justice system in order to explore a wrap-around approach to the specific youth and his or her needs. A conference may be held to discuss extrajudicial measures, sentencing, program availability, or restorative justice options.

Within the formal courtroom, the Crown and the defence counsel both have roles to fulfill. The Crown works on behalf of the state and is responsible for presenting the substantive case. The defence counsel argues on behalf of the legal interests of the young person. A large number of youthful accused are represented by their parents or duty counsel, which can be disconcerting because many youth have only a basic understanding of the criminal justice system.

Therapeutic jurisprudence, which bridges the law and the therapeutic needs of the accused, focuses on specialized accountability and treatment. For example, Toronto has introduced the Mental Health Court, which focuses on mental health and its link to criminality; and the First Nation community of Elsipogtog has developed the Healing to Wellness Court, which addresses the key areas of concern, such as mental health and substance abuse–related charges, in a culturally appropriate manner.

KEY TERMS

circle sentencing, 160

criminogenic needs, 160

disclosure, 154

duty counsel, 155

hybrid offence, 151

judicial review, 155

jurisdiction, 149

moot, 156

not criminally responsible (NCR), 157

plea bargain, 154

preliminary motions and applications, 150

procedural justice, 149

special plea, 157

stay of proceedings, 152

substantive justice, 149

therapeutic jurisprudence, 159

youth justice court, 148

REFERENCES

Applegate, B., & Santana, S. (2000). Intervening with youthful substance abusers: A preliminary analysis of juvenile drug court. *The Justice System Journal*, *21*(3), 281–300.

Bala, N., & Anand, S. (2012). *Youth criminal justice law* (3rd ed.). Toronto: Irwin Law.

Bergseth, K.J., & Bouffard, J.A. (2007). The long-term impact of restorative justice programming for juvenile offenders. *Journal of Criminal Justice*, *35*(4), 433–451.

Bradshaw, W., & Roseborough, D. (2005). Restorative justice dialogue: The impact of mediation and conferencing on juvenile recidivism. *Federal Probation*, *69*, 15–21.

Canadian Charter of Rights and Freedoms. (1982). Part I of the *Constitution Act, 1982*, being Schedule B to the *Canada Act 1982* (UK), 1982, c. 11.

CBC News. (2011, May 11). First Nation community to see new court system. *CBC News*. Retrieved from http://www.cbc.ca/news/canada/new-brunswick/first-nation-community -to-see-new-court-system-1.1037844.

Criminal Code. (1985). RSC 1985, c. C-46.

Davis, K., Peterson-Badali, M., & Skilling, T. (2014, June). *A process evaluation of Toronto's first youth mental health court* [PowerPoint presentation]. Canadian Youth Justice Conference, Toronto.

Davis-Barron, S. (2009). *Canadian youth and the criminal law.* Toronto: LexisNexis.

Elsipogtog Health and Wellness Centre. (2011). Elsipogtog Health and Wellness Centre. Retrieved from https://www .gnb.ca/0053/phc/presentations/Breakout%20session%20 presenters%20-%20HEALTHY%20LIVING/English/5%20 EN%20Eva%20Sock.pdf.

Foley, T. (2013). Restorative justice as a better practice for managing the need for rehabilitation in response to youth offending. Canberra, Australia: Australian Institute of Criminology. Retrieved from http://aic.gov.au/ media_library/conferences/2013-youthjustice/ presentations/foley-paper.pdf.

Greene, C., Sprott, J.B., Madon, N.S., & Jung, M. (2010). Punishing processes in youth court: Procedural justice, court atmosphere and youths' views of the legitimacy of the justice system. *Canadian Journal of Criminology and Criminal Justice, 52*(5), 527–544.

Hayes, H., & Daly, J. (2003). Youth justice conferencing and reoffending. *Justice Quarterly, 20*(3), 725–764.

K.P.H., R v. (2007). [2007] AJ No. 1467 (QB).

L.S., R v. (2006). 2006 CanLII 40609 (Ont. CA).

Latimer, J., Dowden, C., & Muise, D. (2005). The effectiveness of restorative justice practices: A meta-analysis. *The Prison Journal, 85*, 127–144.

Madell, D., Thom, K., & McKenna, B. (2013). A systematic review of literature relating to problem-solving youth courts. *Psychiatry, Psychology and Law, 20*(3), 412–422.

Peterson-Badali, M., Care, S., & Broeking, J. (2007). Young people's perceptions and experiences of the lawyer–client relationship. *Canadian Journal of Criminology and Criminal Justice, 49*(3), 375–401.

Safe Streets and Communities Act. (2012). SC 2012, c. 1.

Schmidt, M., Reppucci, N.D., & Woolard, J. (2003). Effectiveness of participation as a defendant: The attorney–juvenile client relationship. *Behavioral Sciences and the Law, 21*, 175–198.

Sloan, J.J., Smylka, J.O., & Rush, J.P. (2004). Do juvenile drug courts reduce recidivism? Outcomes of drug court and an adolescent substance abuse program. *American Journal of Criminal Justice, 29*(1), 96–115.

Statistics Canada. (2014a). Adult criminal courts, number of cases and charges by type of decision. CANSIM Table 252-0053. Retrieved November 17, 2014 from http://www5 .statcan.gc.ca/cansim/a05?lang=eng&id=2520053& pattern=2520053&searchTypeByValue=1&p2=35.

Statistics Canada. (2014b). Youth courts, number of cases and charges by type of decision. CANSIM Table 252-0064. Retrieved November 17, 2014 from http://www5.statcan .gc.ca/cansim/a05?lang=eng&id=2520064&pattern =2520064&searchTypeByValue=1&p2=35.

Viljoen, J., Klaver, J., and Roesch, R. (2005). Legal decisions of preadolescent and adolescent defendants: Predictors of confessions, pleas, communications with attorneys, and appeals. *Law and Human Behavior, 29*, 253–277.

Walgrave, L. (2006). Toward restoration as the mainstream in youth justice. In E. Elliott & R.M. Gordon (Eds.), *New directions in restorative justice: Issues, practice, evaluation* (pp. 3–25). Portland, OR: Willan.

Wiener, R.L., Winick, B.J., Skovran Georges, L., & Castro, A. (2010). A testable theory of problem solving courts: Avoiding past empirical and legal failures. *International Journal of Law and Psychiatry, 33*, 417–427.

York University. (2014, July 2). No one person can succeed alone, says former chief justice of Yukon court. *yFile*. Retrieved from http://yfile.news.yorku.ca/2014/07/02/ no-one-person-can-succeed-alone-hon-doc-tells -osgoode-grads.

Youth Criminal Justice Act. (2002). SC 2002, c. 1.

EXERCISES AND REVIEW

Review Questions

1. Is a youthful accused entitled to a trial by jury? Under what circumstances?

2. Can a youth bring an application under the Charter?

3. Can a youth be made to stand trial even after pleading guilty? Why or why not?

4. How are specialized courts organized differently from traditional criminal justice courtrooms in order to meet the needs of clientele and to reduce recidivism?

5. What has research shown about the relationship between a young person and his or her defence counsel?

6. What is the legal authority for requiring youth or their parents to repay the costs of duty counsel?

Discussion Questions

1. Imagine you are a 40-year-old male criminal defence lawyer hired by (or by the parents of) a 13-year-old girl charged with first-time arson. How might you treat this client differently from an adult repeat offender? How would you get representation instructions from her? Who is your client?

2. Can a youth be made to stand trial after partial completion or non-completion of an extrajudicial sanction (which requires an acknowledgment of responsibility for the act forming the basis of the charge)? Why or why not? How is a youth's right to be free from self-incrimination protected in this situation?

3. Alex, a 15-year-old male youth, was arrested for possession of illicit drugs. He was walking down the street when approached by police officers and asked to hand over the book bag he was carrying. Upon searching the bag the officers found the drugs, and Alex confessed they were his and had intent to sell them. When the police had approached Alex they had no grounds for detaining him or for conducting a search of his person. What kinds of questions will the defence want to raise about the collection of evidence? What Charter challenge might be presented? Examine this scenario from a procedural justice perspective and a substantive justice perspective. Should guilt outweigh violation of rights?

4. In a criminal trial the verdict must be reached so that it is beyond a reasonable doubt. What benefit is there for a youth charged with murder to choose to be tried by judge and jury, rather than by a judge alone?

PART IV

Meaningful Consequences

Sentencing

LEARNING OUTCOMES

After completing this chapter, you should be able to:

- Describe the philosophical and legislative principles that guide sentencing under the *Youth Criminal Justice Act* (YCJA).

- Describe the implications for young persons of the additional sentencing principles of denunciation and deterrence.

- Explain which element of the YCJA gives rise to an anti-custody presumption, and locate provisions designed to support that presumption.

- List the types of sentences that can be imposed under the YCJA and differentiate between community-based sanctions and custodial sanctions.

- Explain how and by whom the decision about the appropriate level of custody for a convicted youth is made.

- Discuss circumstances that might be defined as "exceptional" in terms of sentencing.

- Identify situations in which a youth might be sentenced as an adult under the YCJA.

- Discuss the implications of turning age 18 in custody.

- Describe the YCJA provisions for community reintegration and conditional supervision.

Introduction

The foregoing chapters focused on the ways youth are diverted from the formal justice system, even after they have made an appearance in court. Before 2012, the sentencing principles under the *Youth Criminal Justice Act* (YCJA) strongly discouraged custodial sentences (incarceration) for youth found guilty of offences. Amendments introduced in 2012 were intended to address criticisms about the handling of the most serious, repeat offenders while maintaining a preference for community-based options for minor offenders. The sentencing, custody, and supervision provisions that make up parts 4 and 5 of the YCJA, and that form nearly 50 percent of the total content of the legislation, are quite complicated to decipher and unique in their approach.

The issue of how best to deal with young persons convicted of criminal offences has been the topic of many debates over the years. One commentator wonders whether critics a hundred years from now will look back on our regime with the same shock and disbelief as we do at children being hanged for stealing a cow or jailed for stealing a gooseberry (Davis-Barron, 2009, p. 317). There has always been a significant political dimension to this debate. The YCJA's sentencing provisions are an attempt both to deal fairly with youth who offend and to enforce their accountability to the general public.

The sentencing provisions of the YCJA were originally created in response to public demands to reform the *Young Offenders Act* (YOA), which was perceived by many as too lenient despite evidence to the contrary. In 2006, when the Conservatives came into power, Prime Minister Stephen Harper was frequently quoted criticizing the YCJA as an "unmitigated failure" (*National Post*, 2008), particularly for its lack of attention to holding young people accountable. By 2012, when the Conservatives held a majority in Parliament, the *Safe Streets and Communities Act* was passed. The backgrounder to the bill explained that the government was committed to ensuring that "violent and repeat young offenders are held fully accountable" (Department of Justice, 2010). As part of the amendments introduced by this Act, the sentencing principles of the YCJA were revised in response to continued public and political concern about leniency in youth justice.

Let us begin with a case study, and then outline the principles and procedures for sentencing young people convicted of criminal offences.

SCHOOLYARD SCUFFLE LEADS TO CRIMINAL CHARGES

Jim has been found guilty of assault with a weapon. He is 14. The pre-sentence report indicates that his father recently passed away and his mother has been diagnosed with depression. Jim has pleaded guilty.

The facts on which Crown and defence counsel agree are that Jim struck a young girl, Terry, with his backpack as they were getting off the school bus. Unfortunately, the blow caused Terry to fall down the stairs of the bus and she broke her arm. Terry had previously been dating Jim, but they had broken up.

Jim has three prior guilty findings: one for theft under $5,000, one for mischief (making prank phone calls to Terry's house), and one for assault resulting from a schoolyard fight with Terry's older brother, Frank. Jim had been on probation for the prank calls when this last incident had occurred.

QUESTIONS

Read through the chapter to decide:

1. How should Jim be sentenced?

2. How should Jim's offence be characterized? (That is, is it a "violent" offence? Is it a "serious violent" offence?)

3. What sentencing principles should apply and in what ways?

4. Could Jim be sentenced to custody? Should he be?

5. Could Jim be sentenced as an adult? Should he be?

6. Looking at the list of all possible sentencing options, if you were the judge in his case, what sentence would you impose?

Purpose and Principles of Sentencing

In 1987, the Canadian Sentencing Commission identified the following as the purpose of sentencing:

> It is recognized and declared that in a free and democratic society peace and security can only be enjoyed through the due application of the principles of fundamental justice. In furtherance of the overall purpose of the criminal law of maintaining a just, peaceful and safe society, the fundamental purpose of sentencing is to preserve the authority of and promote respect for the law through the imposition of just sanctions. (Canadian Sentencing Commission, 1987, p. 51)

It is important to recognize, however, that the principles of youth sentencing derive from many sources: the common law, the *Criminal Code*, and the YCJA. The YCJA modifies the application of the Code to take into account its own preamble, declaration of principle, and sentencing principles specific to youth as found in s. 38.

Before moving on to the specific applications of principles, let us review the related provisions in the Code:

718. The fundamental purpose of sentencing is to contribute, along with crime prevention initiatives, to respect for the law and the maintenance of a just, peaceful and safe society by imposing just sanctions that have one or more of the following objectives:

    (a) to denounce unlawful conduct;

    (b) to deter the offender and other persons from committing offences;

    (c) to separate offenders from society, where necessary;

    (d) to assist in rehabilitating offenders;

    (e) to provide reparations for harm done to victims or to the community; and

    (f) to promote a sense of responsibility in offenders, and acknowledgment of the harm done to victims and to the community.

Think of some cases involving adults convicted of crimes and decide whether the sentences were in keeping with the above-mentioned purposes. What differences might there be in application of these principles to youth?

With regard to sentencing of young people, we need to begin with the preamble of the YCJA, which states:

AND WHEREAS Canadian society should have a youth criminal justice system that commands respect, takes into account the interests of victims, fosters responsibility and ensures accountability through meaningful consequences and effective rehabilitation and reintegration, and that reserves its most serious intervention for the most serious crimes and reduces the over-reliance on incarceration for non-violent young persons … .

> Compare the intentions expressed in this paragraph with the stated purposes of sentencing in s. 718 of the Code. What stands out as different?

As discussed throughout this book, the principles section (s. 3) of the YCJA is meant to guide all decisions related to the interpretation of the legislation. With respect to sentencing, the Act as proclaimed in 2003 spoke about the importance of ensuring that young persons are "subject to meaningful consequences" for their offence with a view that such consequences would "promote the long-term protection of the public" (s. 3(1)(a)(iii)). The Nunn Commission (2006), discussed in Chapter 6, recommended that there be an explicit principle within s. 3 that would help judges deal with problems presented by the small number of dangerous offenders and recidivists. The amendments brought about in the *Safe Streets and Communities Act* (2012) focused on public safety:

> **3**(1) The following principles apply in this Act:
> (a) the youth criminal justice system is intended to protect the public by
> (i) holding young persons accountable through measures that are proportionate to the seriousness of the offence and the degree of responsibility of the young person,
> (ii) promoting the rehabilitation and reintegration of young persons who have committed offences, and
> (iii) supporting the prevention of crime by referring young persons to programs or agencies in the community to address the circumstances underlying their offending behaviour.

As has been pointed out throughout this book, s. 3 is the guiding principle of the YCJA, used to interpret all other sections. However, because there had been issues in complying with the overriding principle of the *Young Offenders Act* when the YCJA was drafted, additional guiding principles were introduced in the sentencing provisions under part 4 (s. 38) of the Act:

> **38**(1) The purpose of sentencing under section 42 (youth sentences) is to hold a young person accountable for an offence through the imposition of just sanctions that have meaningful consequences for the young person and that promote his or her rehabilitation and reintegration into society, thereby contributing to the long-term protection of the public.

This "purpose" is relatively simply stated; but a review of other provisions makes it clear that the route to achieving the public-centred goal of protection must pass by several offender-centred signposts: accountability, meaningful consequences, rehabilitation, and supported reintegration. It should be noted that the idea of "meaningful consequences" was retained in the purpose of sentencing despite being removed from the overriding principle in s. 3 discussed above.

To help judges follow the prescribed route to public protection, the legislation provides "principles" in s. 38(2). These are complicated and warrant reference to the legislation itself. In summary:

- a youth sentence cannot be greater than the adult sentence for the same offence committed in similar circumstances;

- the sentence must be similar to others handed out to other youth in the same region for similar offences (that is, sentences are to be consistent);

- the sentence must be proportionate to the seriousness of the crime and the youth's degree of responsibility;

- the sentence should denounce the wrongful act being punished and seek to deter other people from committing a similar act while deterring the particular offender from committing the impugned act again; and

- the sentence must, subject to the proportionality issue, be the least restrictive one capable of satisfying the s. 38(1) purpose, be the most rehabilitative/reintegrative choice, and promote a sense of responsibility and acknowledgment of harm in the young person.

Besides these principles, s. 38(3) outlines **mitigating** and **aggravating factors**—ones that, respectively, decrease or increase the seriousness of the offence—that the judge should consider in determining the appropriate sentence. These factors include the young person's degree of participation in committing the crime, the harm done to the victim, anything the young person has done to repair the harm done to the victim and community, the time already spent in detention, prior criminal history, and any other relevant circumstances related to the purpose and principles of sentencing. Typical mitigating factors are that the accused cooperated with the police, showed remorse, or committed the act as a result of being provoked. Aggravating factors might be that the offence was motivated by bias, prejudice, or hate based on prohibited ground of discrimination, or that the accused abused a position of trust in relation to the victim.

mitigating factor
a circumstance or action taken by an offender during or after the commission of an offence that supports a lighter sentence

aggravating factor
a circumstance or action taken by an offender during or after the commission of an offence that supports a more onerous sentence

The Role of Deterrence and Denunciation in Youth Sentencing

As was discussed in the introduction to this chapter, when the public and the media cried out for "harsher" sentences under the YOA and the YCJA before 2012, they almost invariably demanded that offenders and youth at risk of offending need to be *specifically* and *generally* deterred from criminal behaviour. **Specific deterrence** aims to punish the individual offender just enough to stop him or her, but not necessarily anyone else, from committing offences in the future. **General deterrence** is aimed at the general public who, in seeing others suffer severe enough sanctions after being convicted of crimes, will themselves refrain from criminal behaviour.

Unfortunately, research has shown that the sentences that seem to most readily satisfy the demand for public accountability—typically custody—are not necessarily the same ones most likely to actually accomplish the goal of rehabilitation and the protection of society. The drafters of the YCJA's sentencing philosophy provided a set of principles that fostered a balance between the presumption against custodial sentences and a commitment to meaningful sentences.

The centre of gravity in this balance was thrown off by the amendments to the YCJA introduced by the *Safe Streets and Communities Act* (2012). The YCJA now includes specific deterrence and denunciation, which brings its sentencing principles significantly closer to those applied to adults, as provided in ss. 718(a) and (b) of the *Criminal Code*. The amendments still require the judge to consider a sentence that takes into account proportionality and the degree of responsibility of the young person for the offence (s. 38(2)(f)), but the judge "may" sentence the young person using the objective of "denouncing unlawful conduct" and "to deter the young person from committing offences" (ss. 38(2)(f)(i) and (ii)).

specific deterrence
the desired effect of a sentence consisting in prevention of a repeat of the offence by the convicted individual

general deterrence
the desired effect of a sentence consisting in prevention of a repeat of the offence like that of the convicted individual by any other member of the public

The balancing of principles required under s. 38 was also changed by another 2012 amendment to the YCJA to allow for a pattern of offending to be considered that also included the previous involvement with extrajudicial sanctions, which made it clear that protection of the public was the paramount objective.

CASE IN POINT

Denunciation

Municipal Court Judge Michael Cicconetti in Painesville, Ohio has received worldwide attention for his unconventional sentencing practices. He began handing down these sentences when he started seeing that traditional ones were not deterring certain crimes in his community.

Cicconetti sentenced one man to stand on a street corner with a live pig, holding a sign that read, "This is not a police officer," after the accused shouted obscenities at police officers and called them "pigs." And Cicconetti doesn't reserve these types of sentences for adults; youth are fair game as well. Two youth found guilty of stealing and defacing the baby Jesus from a church nativity scene were sentenced to dress as Mary and Joseph and walk the streets of their community with a donkey and a sign that read, "Sorry for the jackass offence" (Read, 2012).

QUESTIONS

Do you think these types of sentences meet the mandate of denunciation? Or has Cicconetti gone too far?

Not only the drafters of the YCJA, but also the justice system actors charged with administering the legislation—such as judges, Crown prosecutors, and police—must balance the goals of the YCJA with the needs and circumstances of particular offenders and the demands of victims and families. Remember too that, while a new set of amendments was passed in 2012, many of the people responsible for the implementation of the new law had been working with the previous law (YOA) before it was passed. The extent to which philosophical shifts in the approach to youth justice crafted by the drafters of the YCJA are actually reflected in the treatment of individual youths will depend on the actions of judges, lawyers, and police in each individual case.

The YOA recognized deterrence as a legitimate sentencing principle. When the YCJA was first introduced, it did *not* explicitly recognize a role for deterrence. Courts in different provinces dealt with the relevance of deterrence under the pre-2012 YCJA in different ways. The British Columbia Court of Appeal held that general deterrence remains a factor under the YCJA, albeit one of diminished importance (*R v. B.V.N.*, 2004). In contrast, the Manitoba Court of Appeal held that, although the judicial process may have a deterrent effect on the young person and others, neither general nor specific deterrence is a relevant YCJA sentencing principle (*R v. B.W.P.*, 2004).

In *R v. T.M.* (2003), one of the first decisions under the YCJA dealing with this issue, the Ontario Court of Appeal held that general deterrence has less importance but has not been entirely diminished. The court went on to ask: "What do accountability, meaningful consequences, and long-term protection of the public go to if not to specific deterrence?"

In 2005, the Supreme Court of Canada had resolved much of the controversy over the role of deterrence under the YCJA when it had heard appeals of two judgments—*B.V.N.* and *B.W.P.* (2006)—together. A majority held that the YCJA had introduced a new sentencing regime, and that its wording could only support the conclusion that Parliament had deliberately excluded general deterrence as a factor of youth sentencing. The court had therefore insisted that lower-level decision-makers focus on the young person before the court; general deterrence was no longer to be considered.

However, the 2012 amendments overrode this ruling. After all, judges—even judges of the Supreme Court—do not draft but only interpret legislation. Although general deterrence is now a valid consideration in youth sentencing, the question of whether it *should* be remains debatable, and will likely continue to be for years to come. More about the use of deterrence as a sanction will be taken up in Chapter 9 with regard to "what works" in offender rehabilitation.

> Deterrence is an uncontested aspect of adult sentencing principles. Why do you believe there is so much controversy over its inclusion in youth sentencing principles?

The Struggle to Define What Constitutes a "Violent Offence"

One reason why a youth might be sent into custody is that he or she has committed a **serious violent offence**. What constitutes such an offence has been one of the most hotly contested issues in youth criminal justice. Prior to the 2012 amendments to the YCJA, a serious violent offence was referred to as one in which the young person "causes or attempts to cause serious bodily harm." The Supreme Court of Canada, in *R v. C.D.; R v. C.D.K.* (2005), made it clear that the harm must be serious *bodily* harm and not merely psychological. The court held that the definition of "violent" under the YCJA should be interpreted narrowly, to give effect to the framers' intention of reducing Canada's overreliance on custodial sentences for young persons. The 2012 amendments defined "violent offence" in s. 2 of the YCJA as:

serious violent offence
an offence committed by a young person that includes an element of causing bodily harm, a threat or attempt to do so, or endangering the life and safety of another by creating the substantial likelihood of bodily harm

> (a) an offence committed by a young person that includes as an element the causing of bodily harm;
> (b) an attempt or a threat to commit an offence referred to in paragraph (a); or
> (c) an offence in the commission of which a young person endangers the life or safety of another person by creating a substantial likelihood of causing bodily harm.

You will recall from Chapter 6 that changes were also made to define "serious offence" as an indictable offence for which an adult would receive a maximum punishment of five years or more. In order to be specific about what constitutes a "serious violent offence," the amendments outlined the offences of murder, attempt to commit murder, manslaughter, and aggravated sexual assault. The clarification of these definitions was important with respect to the YCJA provisions regarding youth receiving adult sentences.

Reports Considered During Sentencing in Youth Court

The court may consider a report from the prosecution in the form of a **victim impact statement** (s. 50), as provided for by s. 722 of the *Criminal Code*. In some jurisdictions, police are instrumental in the preparation of such statements, because they will generally be the primary contact with victims. In other areas, the statements may be prepared by victim–offender reconciliation agencies. When victim impact statements are prepared by

victim impact statement
a written summary, authored by a victim, of the effects that an offence has had on his or her life, and of any ongoing problems that the incident can be expected to cause for him or her

police, they must form part of the disclosure given to the accused by the Crown. However, when they are prepared by third-party agencies, they need not be given to the accused before trial. In most cases, these statements will be filed with the court, but occasionally a victim may wish to read the statement aloud in court.

The court may also consider a medical or psychological report as provided for under s. 34 of the YCJA. At any stage of the proceedings a court may order, with consent of the young person, an assessment if there are "reasonable grounds" that the youth may be "suffering from a physical or mental illness or disorder, a psychological disorder, an emotional disturbance, a learning disability or a mental disability." In cases in which the youth has a pattern of repeated findings of guilt (s. 34(1)(b)(ii)), or if the youth has committed a serious violent offence, the court is more likely to order such a report.

Before sentencing, the judge should "consider a pre-sentence report and any sentencing proposal made by the young person or his or her counsel" (s. 39(6)) unless the use of a report is waived (declined) by the young person and/or his or her counsel and the court is satisfied that a report is not necessary.

A pre-sentence report *must* be admitted if the youth wants it to be, and if custody is being considered. If a non-custodial sentence is being considered, the court *may* order one prepared for consideration.

provincial director

a person or "a group or class of persons"—i.e., certain members of the provincial corrections administration—designated by a provincial government to perform a wide range of functions under the legislation (e.g., ensuring that pre-sentence reports are completed)

Section 40 provides for the preparation (by the **provincial director**) and admission into court of a "pre-sentence report"—a summary, usually in writing, of information relevant to the sentencing decision. This report can contain, among other things, information from interviews with the young person, the victim, and other interested parties; general information about the offender's background, character, living situation, and commitment to treatment and rehabilitation; school information; information about available rehabilitative/community programs; and a summary of the accused's criminal history (see s. 40(2)(d)(iii)).

CASE IN POINT

Media Access to Reports in Youth Court

In *Toronto Star Newspaper Ltd. v. Ontario* (2012), a reporter for the *Toronto Star* spent a number of months in youth court observing proceedings, including three in which the young accused were found guilty of serious criminal offences. The reporter applied to the youth court judge for access to the pre-sentence reports and victim impact statements filed as exhibits in the proceedings. The court dismissed the application.

As you will recall from Chapter 1, the general public receives most of their information about the court system through the news media, and while the reporter had provided a series of articles that may have shed light on the machinery of the youth justice system, there are still provisions within the YCJA to ban the publication of details surrounding the identity of young persons (see ss. 110, 111, 129).

In her reasons, Justice Cohen referred to the expert testimony of Dr. Alan Leschied, a psychologist with 34 years' experience dealing with the youth justice system. Leschied pointed out that allowing the media access to pre-sentence reports would adversely affect the quality of the information young people and their families would share with probation officers if they were not assured confidentiality. Such access, he argued, would jeopardize the quality of reports prepared and presented to the court and make it difficult for the judge to make a decision that "most fits the needs and circumstances of the young person because of the absence of important information in the pre-sentence report" (para. 58). Two probation officers agreed with Dr. Leschied and pointed out that, while the court may order such a report, the participation by the young person and his or her family is "voluntary" and it would be difficult to get accurate information from families. One of the officers suggested that not only are issues of family trauma involved, but the young person's personal information; "their secrets" and "their feelings about things that have happened in their families" are often part of a pre-sentence report (para. 63).

One of the young people affected by the application said that he was "desperate" to stop access because the report contained "a lot of really personal information" and he was losing sleep worrying about its possible publication. He and another youth affected by the application also expressed concern about the effects the publication of their reports would have on their families, saying their parents would be "humiliated, disgraced and ashamed." Youth had no faith in the idea that they might have their identities protected through *redactions* (censoring the text to obscure their identity) and were fearful of "dangerous people" who might come after them or "target their families." They also indicated that they "were trying very hard to change their lives" and the publication of information in the newspaper would set back their rehabilitation (at para 64).

QUESTIONS

1. Do you think the media should have access to pre-sentence reports of accused young persons in youth courts?

2. What benefit would there be for the reporter of having the actual document as compared with observing the presentation of the report in court?

3. What are the negative implications of having these reports?

The Imposition of Adult Sentences

Although all justice systems of the Western world deal with adolescents less severely than adults in general, they also allow for the prospect of treating as adults those who commit particularly heinous or shocking crimes. Some countries go to the extreme of imposing capital punishment. For example, the death penalty was available for adolescents in 20 American states until March 2005 when, in the case of *Roper v. Simmons* (2005), the US Supreme Court struck it down as an inappropriate sanction for "juveniles" (Associated Press, 2005)—a decision that commuted the sentences of 72 who were on death row.

While Canada does not allow capital punishment for either adolescent or adult offenders, we do allow some youth to be treated as seriously as adult offenders. Our system allows, under the YCJA, sentencing of certain youth as adults.

The adult sentencing provisions of the YCJA under s. 64 require the Crown to consider seeking an adult sentence for youth aged 14 or older who are charged with murder, attempted murder, manslaughter, or aggravated sexual assault. The provinces and territories have the discretion to set the age at which this applies at 14–16 years of age. The Crown is also required to give notice to the youth court if it chooses not to apply for an adult sentence in a case dealing with one of those serious violent offences.

Under both the *Juvenile Delinquents Act* and the *Young Offenders Act*, in cases where a youth had committed a serious offence, a "transfer hearing" took place before the actual trial to determine whether the youth should be transferred to adult court. The hearing was not to consider the young person's guilt or innocence, but rather to consider the appropriateness of adult court compared with youth court. The test for transfer sought to balance the best interests of the young person and the protection of the public. Evidence that would ordinarily be inadmissible at trial was permitted at this stage, including hearsay and opinions about the youth in the prosecutor's argument. (However, any such evidence could not be used later, regardless of whether the youth was transferred.) Although the burden of proof rested with the prosecutor (or the applicant for transfer), it was relatively easy to meet.

It was found, however, that young persons' right to a fair trial was violated by such hearings, and the drafters of the YCJA removed this provision. The main reason for transferring youth to adult court was to seek lengthier sentences than those available in youth court, and under the YCJA the youth court is able to hand out an adult sentence following specific procedures.

If the young person is over the age of 14 and has been convicted of a serious offence or a serious violent offence, the Crown must give notice to the youth court of its intention to seek an adult sentence before the young person enters a plea (s. 64(3)). In the case of a serious violent offence, the Crown is required to consider an adult sentence and make such an application to the court. The youth is given an opportunity to elect to be tried by a judge alone or a judge and jury if the application to seek an adult sentence is successful (s. 67). Following a hearing to determine whether to apply an adult sentence (s. 71), the court shall order an adult sentence if the presumption of moral blameworthiness of the young person is rebutted and the sentence provided for under s. 38 is not of sufficient length to hold the youth accountable (ss. 72(1)(a)–(b)). In other words, the court must be satisfied that the young person before the court is eligible to receive the more punitive adult sentence. In making such an order, the judge must consider a pre-sentence report (s. 72(3)). If the court does not find an adult sentence appropriate, he or she must deliver a youth sentence.

CASE IN POINT

Adult Sentencing: Accountability Is Key

In the rare cases in which imposing a youth custodial sentence would not hold a youth accountable, the Crown can apply for an adult sentence after a guilty verdict and if the offence would cause an adult to receive a sentence of more than two years.

Consider *R v. A.O.* (2007), in which two 16-year-olds, A.O. and J.M., committed six armed robberies at convenience stores. The crimes happened late at night when the store attendant was alone with the youth, who used knives or an imitation handgun. Four of the victims received knife wounds, another was seriously beaten and stabbed, and all six were "traumatized" (*R v. A.O.*, 2007, para. 9).

The Crown successfully argued that both young accused should receive adult sentences of eight years in prison (later reduced to five because they had already spent 2½ years in remand awaiting trial). Both youth appealed, but the Ontario Court of Appeal upheld the ruling, saying that an adult sentence was necessary in order to hold the youth accountable for their actions—the length of the maximum youth custodial sentence would not be sufficient.

QUESTION

What does it mean to cite "accountability" as a reason to issue an adult sentence to a young person?

Adult Custodial Facilities

Prior to the 2012 YCJA amendments, when available facilities made it impracticable for youth to be held separately, young persons could be housed in adult correctional facilities. The amendments ended that practice. Section 76(2) of the YCJA now states that regardless of whether a youth has received a youth sentence or an adult sentence, no young person under the age of 18 will serve his or her sentence in an adult prison or penitentiary.

Under s. 89, when a young person attains 20 years of age at the time of sentencing or while in custody, he or she is automatically ordered to serve the duration of the sentence in a provincial correctional facility for adults. (Adults sentenced after they turn 18 for crimes committed as youth are tried as young people but serve their sentences in adult facilities.) Section 89(2) enables the provincial director to apply to the youth justice court to transfer over-age young persons to a penitentiary for the remainder of their sentence if it would be in their or society's "best interests" and if there are at least two years left on the sentence.

Young persons who began their custodial sentence under 20 years of age may also be transferred to an adult facility. Section 92(1) enables a provincial director, upon application to the youth court, to transfer a young person who has attained the age of 18 to an adult correctional facility for the remainder of his or her sentence or to a penitentiary if there are more than two years remaining on the youth sentence.

> What "best interests" do you think are taken into account when transferring a young person to an adult facility to complete a sentence?

Sentences in Youth Justice Court

The youth justice court judge has a very wide range of sentencing options from which to choose. He or she must keep in mind the YCJA purpose and principles of sentencing and consider the pre-sentence report, victim impact statements, recommendations from counsel on both sides, and representations by parents. The possible sentences are described in s. 42(2).

SENTENCES FOR YOUNG PERSONS

Looking at the range of sentences in Table 8.1 for the years 2002–2012, you'll find that judges still seem to prefer community sanction over custody. As time has passed from the first year of the YCJA's implementation, judges have apparently become more familiar with new sanctions provided in the Act.

TABLE 8.1   Sentences for Young Persons, 2002–2012

	2002–3	2003–4	2004–5	2005–6	2006–7	2007–8	2008–9	2009–10	2010–11	2011–12
Custody										
Deferred custody	0	340	589	729	646	747	7 88	918	860	804
Custody	7,508	5,258	4,827	4,211	3,712	3,702	3,505	3,244	3,124	2,893
IRCS	0	0	3	6	3	1	6	6	3	2
Community										
Reprimand	0	162	274	365	353	301	324	420	452	0
Fine	2,232	1,654	1,414	1,358	1,326	1,319	1,393	1,026	905	688
Community service order	1,266	1,654	1,382	1,404	1,454	1,503	1,567	1,711	1,593	1,586
Conditional sentence	3	1	10	18	10	20	21	31	11	14
Probation	14,126	10,623	9,378	9,346	9,186	9,761	9,687	9,366	8,493	7,804
ISSP	0	84	116	134	141	131	170	188	146	124

SOURCE: Adapted from Statistics Canada (2014b).

Non-Custodial Sentences

The majority of youth under correctional supervision in 2012–13 were in a community program (Perreault, 2014) with 81 percent of all youth being sentenced to probation. Some of the non-custodial sanctions do not require community supervision; they will be outlined below.

Section 42(2)(a) provides for a *judicial reprimand* (a stern warning from the judge), which means a finding of guilt is entered, but the sentence is considered to have already been served. For a reprimand, the record is only accessible for two months from the time the guilty finding is entered (s. 119(2)(c)). The length of time during which the court can access the record is for the purpose of sentencing in a subsequent offence. As will be discussed later in this chapter, the length of time such access is available increases with each more onerous non-custodial sentence. The judge makes a such a reprimand when it is determined that the experience of the legal process thus far is thought to be punishment enough. In the case *R v. K.D.* (2003) from Chapter 3, the young person was given a judicial reprimand as follows: "I understand that the situation is not a good one at this point, but I want you to understand that these people do not deserve to be physically assaulted by you. Do you understand that? You have to use your best efforts, as it appears you have been trying to, to keep your anger under control."

In appropriate cases, typically involving young persons with no prior criminal history who have committed minor offences, the judge can order an *absolute discharge* if the court considers it in the best interests of the young person and not contrary to the public interest (s. 42(2)(b)). A finding of guilt will be recorded and the record will be able to be accessed for one year from the date of the finding. An absolute discharge is like a reprimand in that the processing of the young person through the formal court system is the sentence. And as in a reprimand, the young person is not required to disclose the fact of the discharge on any employment application (s. 82(3)(a)).

The judge may also order a *conditional discharge*. Here, the youth will be free of a criminal record after compliance with certain conditions. The available conditions are outlined in s. 55 of the YCJA. They include "keep the peace and be of good behaviour," report to the court when required, attend school, reside with a certain person, abide by curfews, and report to a probation officer. The conditions available for a conditional discharge are the same as those available when a judge is considering a probation order. (See below.) Once the conditions have been satisfied, the young person will be discharged. As with an absolute discharge, a finding of guilt will be recorded and the record can be accessed for a period of three years from the date of the guilty finding (s. 119(2)(f)). If the youth fails to fulfill the conditions, he or she can be charged under s. 137.

The youth court also has jurisdiction to impose a *fine* of up to $1,000 (s. 42(2)(d)). There are rules relating to such fines, and judges must not impose one when the youth has no realistic ability to pay without hardship. The same goes for orders of damages or restitution. If the young person is in possession of any person's property as a result of the offence, the judge can order him or her to return or replace the goods. Some courts are hesitant to give fines as a sentence because they are punitive with very little rehabilitative value, which is seen as contrary to the principle of the legislation. Further, courts are aware of the inequity for some young people who will have the fines paid by their parents.

A young person might be ordered to make *compensation* (payment, s. 42(2)(g)) or *restitution* (personal service, s. 42(2)(h)), for personal injury, loss of or damage to property, or loss of income or support. The judge cannot order personal service without the consent of the victim to be compensated, because not all victims may be open to contact or involvement with the young person. The judge might also order up to 240 hours of community service (s. 42(2)(i)) to be completed within one year of the date of order as a form of compensation to the community.

An order of *prohibition*, *seizure*, or *forfeiture* for at least two years relating, for example, to such items as firearms or other dangerous weapons can be ordered in accordance with s. 42(2)(j).

Probation, under s. 42(2)(k), has been one of the most preferred sanctions since inception of the *Juvenile Delinquents Act*. Judges have the option of putting youth on probation for up to two years. Probation orders might consist in the requirement to report periodically to a probation officer; to engage in community service; and to comply with other conditions meant to address the offence committed and respond in a meaningful manner, such as attending a non-residential program for support and supervision. As with adults under a probation order, youth on probation may be required to remain within a particular city, not associate with known youth or adult offenders, and make an effort to obtain and maintain suitable employment. However, as was discussed in Chapter 4, there is a provincial requirement that young persons attend school. The YCJA provides for the condition that the youth be required to "attend school or any other place of learning, training or recreation that is appropriate" (s. 55(2)(e)). Further, youth are required to live with their parents or some other adult the court considers "appropriate" and willing to "provide for the care and maintenance of the young person."

The court has considerable discretion to assign other conditions to a youth probation order, as follows (s. 55(2)(h)):

> comply with any other conditions set out in the order that the youth justice court considers appropriate, including conditions for securing the young person's good conduct and for preventing the young person from repeating the offence or committing other offences;

1. What kinds of conditions can you think of that might "secure a young person's good conduct"?
2. How would you define "good conduct"?
3. Do you believe it is reasonable to have a requirement such as this for youth and not for adults?

The *intensive support and supervision program* (ISSP), s. 42(2)(l), is a provision that calls for a more intensive probation order in those provinces where it is available. Rather than the young person having to serve a term in custody, he or she is kept in the community with support in the form of intensive monitoring and additional resources and referrals to community-based agencies. As in the case of a regular probation order, the imposition of ISSP cannot exceed two years.

As was discussed in Chapter 6 with respect to the number of conditions being set for pre-trial release and the inability of youth to comply with the orders, the same holds true for conditions of probation. When a young person is not able to comply with the conditions, the probation officer has the opportunity to seek a review of the conditions by making an application to the court under s. 59 (discussed below), or to charge the young person with a new offence under s. 137 of "wilfully failing or refusing to comply with the terms of an order." Under the *Young Offenders Act*, Sprott (2006), in her study of Ontario youth courts, reported that failure to comply with an order accounted for 13 percent of the cases in youth court and 23 percent of the cases sentenced to custody. Pulis (2014), in her study of 255 cases of breach of probation orders in 2005–2006 in Ontario, found that youth who received four or more conditions were more likely to be charged with breach of probation.

When a youth fails to comply, the probation officer should review the severity of the breach and the circumstances surrounding it. In addition, the progress a young person has made toward rehabilitation should also be reflected in a report to the court, which might also identify any change in circumstances since the sentence took effect. The YCJA provides for reviewing and altering the conditions if they are breached (s. 59); it does not require the laying of a new charge and the rigorous enforcement of conditions. This will be discussed below.

Review of a Non-Custodial Sentence

Section 59 of the YCJA provides that non-custodial sentences are subject to review at the request of the youth, the youth's parent, the attorney general, or the provincial director, six months following their imposition. With leave of the court, this review can come earlier. A youth sentence might be reviewed on any of several grounds: that the circumstances leading to the sentence have changed materially; that the youth is unable to perform or is having great difficulty performing the conditions; that the conditions are inhibiting positive opportunities available to the young person; and any other relevant factor at the discretion of the youth court. After such a review, the judge may order that the sentence continue unchanged, terminate the sentence, or change it. However, the court may not make the sentence more severe than it was.

> Bearing in mind the views of the courtroom expressed by some young people in Chapter 7, consider the kinds of issues that a sentence review might raise for a young person who would have to return to court. Might a negative experience put off a young person from asking to have his or her sentence reviewed?

Custodial Sentences

It has long been known that the incarceration of young people is more disruptive in their lives than it is in the lives of adults. This has been recognized by developmental psychologists, sociologists, and courts.

Removing adolescents from their communities and labelling them criminals by imposing custodial sentences presents unique problems for their development. Of course, it interrupts schooling and isolates from community supports. But also, psychological development in adolescence, including changes in cognitive development and the ability to make moral decisions, has not reached the level that adults may experience. For this reason, an assumption of reduced moral blameworthiness has been a cornerstone of juvenile justice since the inception of the juvenile justice system. Young people are still developing their identities and interruption in their lives due to incarceration can have serious negative effects on their psychological and social development (see, for example, Doob & Cesaroni, 2004, esp. pp. 30–31).

Many experts believe that custodial placements are in the best interests of young people only in certain narrow circumstances, and those who have studied youth criminal behaviour typically believe that "to not only effectively understand but to treat anti-social youth it is necessary to maintain them in their natural ecology" (Leschied, 1998, p. 4).

Negative peer relationships and experiences in custody can have a profound impact on a youth's long-term development. As a result, almost all social science researchers argue that custodial sentences, rather than fostering rehabilitation, can present significant barriers to positive change. This is why the YCJA has legally formalized a limitation on the use of custodial sentences.

"PRISONIZATION"

As this chapter has discussed, custody is reserved for only the most serious cases under the YCJA. Much research has demonstrated that placing a youth in custody does not necessarily rehabilitate him or her and may not be the best option for public safety either. But why?

There has been much research on the effects of custody. Closed custody facilities put young people together who have committed different crimes, so it may serve as a place where youth can learn new types of criminality. Labelling theorists have also found that putting a youth in custody causes him or her to be stigmatized after release, which can have devastating effects on reintegration.

One of the first researchers to examine the effects of imprisonment was Donald Clemmer (1940). In his book *The Prison Community* Clemmer coined the term "prisonization." He argued not only that the social and structural aspects of prisons predisposed inmates toward criminality, but also that the very nature of prison made it difficult for them to adjust to life on the outside. For these reasons and many more, we try to keep youth out of closed custody facilities unless absolutely necessary.

QUESTION

Knowing the harm that closed custody facilities can cause, how do you feel about sending youth to a facility for administration of justice offences (e.g., failing to appear in court, failing to abide by conditions of release)?

Limits on Custodial Sentences

As you will recall from the discussion in Chapter 6 about pre-trial detention, the rate of custodial sentences for young people has declined dramatically since the YCJA came into force in 2003.

As mentioned earlier, the YCJA, in both the preamble and s. 39, expresses the central goal of reducing the number and proportion of custodial sentences imposed on youth. The legislation also contains many provisions dealing with young persons' rights and responsibilities while serving a sentence. Section 83 sets out the purpose and principles of the youth custody and supervision system:

> **83**(1) The purpose of the youth custody and supervision system is to contribute to the protection of society by
> (a) carrying out sentences imposed by courts through the safe, fair and humane custody and supervision of young persons; and
> (b) assisting young persons to be rehabilitated and reintegrated into the community as law-abiding citizens, by providing effective programs to young persons in custody and while under supervision in the community.

Section 83(2) provides that, in addition to the general YCJA legislative principles set out in s. 3, several custody principles are to be followed, and lists first the "least restrictive measures" that provide appropriate protection for the public. Young persons in custody maintain the same rights as other young persons except those necessary for serving the sentence. Involvement of family and other members of the young person's community is to be encouraged.

To reach the goal of reducing custodial sentences, s. 39(1) of the YCJA limits the use of custody to circumstances that meet one of the following criteria:

- a youth has committed a violent offence;
- a youth has failed to comply with previous non-custodial sentences;
- a youth who has committed an indictable offence for which an adult would be liable to imprisonment for a term of more than two years and has a criminal history that indicates a pattern of either extrajudicial sanctions or of findings of guilt or both; and

- in exceptional cases, the evidence and the discretion of the sentencing judge deem a non-custodial sentence to be inconsistent with the stated purposes and principles of sentencing under s. 38 of the YCJA.

EXCEPTIONAL CASES

As has been explained throughout this text, under the YCJA, custody is reserved as a last resort, only to be imposed under specified conditions. One such condition is that the conviction is an "exceptional case," defined in s. 39(1)(d) as follows: "in exceptional cases where the young person has committed an indictable offence, the aggravating circumstances of the offence are such that the imposition of a non-custodial sentence would be inconsistent with the purpose and principles set out in section 38" (a section that, as you might recall, describes the accountability and meaningful consequences principles of sentencing). "Exceptional case" is not defined in the YCJA, but the findings in *R v. R.E.W.* (2006) have been used as a measure of exceptionalism. In that case, Justice Rosenberg defined exceptional cases as "those very rare [non-violent] cases where the circumstances of the crime are so extreme that anything less than custody would fail to reflect societal values" (para. 43). Let us examine a few cases that have been deemed exceptional since the YCJA came into effect.

R v. R.E.W.

In this case, a 14-year-old boy had been found guilty of being an accessory to murder after aiding in the disposal of bodies. The youth had befriended a man in his 30s, Douglas Moore, and when Moore had murdered two people, the youth had watched as the bodies were cut up with an electric saw. Afterward, the youth had helped the man dispose of the body parts and the blade. Important to the case was that the youth had been aware that Moore was going to murder the two because he, Moore, believed they had stolen drugs and money from him, when in fact the youth himself had taken them.

The youth was sentenced to four months in custody, two months of community supervision, and two years of probation. On appeal, the court was asked to consider whether the aggravating factors made this an "exceptional case" justifying custody under s. 38. Justice Rosenberg upheld the lower court's sentencing decision, ruling that custody was the only way to ensure that the public would maintain its confidence in the youth criminal justice system (*R.E.W.*, 2006, para. 52).

R v. L.B.

The application of "exceptional case" becomes less clear when the offence in question is not deemed violent, as in *R v. L.B.* (2007). This case concerned a young person involved in a "dial-a-dope" operation (in which the seller and dealer communicate via phone to make arrangements for a deal). The youth had been found with $480 worth of cocaine and charged with possession for the purpose of trafficking. It was the amount of cocaine, coupled with a report filed by the Crown, that led the court to consider this case "exceptional." The Crown argued that the community of Sunshine Coast, BC (where the crime took place) was being seriously impacted by cocaine, and this youth's actions would have added to the problem. The youth was sentenced to custody, in accordance with s. 39(1)(d), because sentencing this youth to a non-custodial sentence would not align with the purposes and principles of sentencing set out in s. 38.

R v. D.B.

In *R v. D.B.* (2007), three youth (two of whom were sisters) were charged with a minor assault (no injury) and six school break-ins. At two of the schools they had committed arson and caused $38,000 worth of property damage. The judge in *R v. D.B.* concluded that it qualified as an exceptional case because it was a "sustained, deliberate, concerted and repeated attack on schools." Further, he argued that "this was a course of criminal conduct conducted under the cover of darkness which could only be considered a rampage. Such attacks shock the community as schools are a valued community asset. They are institutions set apart for the special purpose of learning. … An attack against a school is an attack against learning and against civilization. … Such attacks impair the ability of others to learn, and deflect from the educative process. Hence they attack the community as a whole" (para. 17). Interestingly, the judge who sentenced D.B.'s sister for the same crimes did not find that the particulars of the case qualified it as an exceptional case.

QUESTION

Regarding the different outcomes of qualification as exceptional cases, what do the findings in *R v. D.B.* and in her sister's case say about sentencing disparity in the youth criminal justice system?

Even when these criteria are met, a youth court judge must always consider alternative sentencing measures and their likely effectiveness in the particular case before imposing a custodial sentence (ss. 39(2) and (3)). As at the pre-trial level, the court cannot commit a youth to custody for child protection, mental health, or social welfare purposes (s. 39(5)). One such alternative is the **deferred custody and supervision order (DCSO)**, which is a custodial sentence that the young person is permitted to serve in the community on conditions. It is only available for a maximum of six months, and if the youth does not comply with the conditions, he or she can be required to serve the remainder of the sentence as if it were a regular custody and supervision order under s. 42(2)(n). The DCSO is not available to someone sentenced for a serious violent offence, and the restrictions on the use of custody as will be discussed below apply.

deferred custody and supervision order (DCSO)
a sentencing option for youth convicted of offences not involving bodily harm or attempting to cause bodily harm; with a DCSO a youth can serve his or her sentence in the community, under conditions

Custody and Supervision

Every province is required, under s. 85, to establish at least two levels of youth facilities, which are usually described as "open" and "secure" custody and differentiated by degree of restraint. When a young person has been sentenced to serve time, the provincial director has the authority to determine the level at which the young person will be admitted. He or she also has the authority to transfer the young person to a different level if it would be in the interest of society and the young person.

Section 85(5) establishes the factors that the provincial director must consider in determining the level of custody or the appropriateness of a transfer. Placement should be the least restrictive to the young person having regard to the prescribed factors—namely, the seriousness of the offence and the circumstances surrounding it, the needs and circumstances of the youth, the safety of other young persons in custody, and societal interests. The decision on level of custody has to also take into account the appropriateness of programs available to the young person while in a particular facility or level of facility. The likelihood of escape is a relevant factor as well.

Consistently with the due process theme of the YCJA, several provisions protect the rights of a young person while he or she is serving a custodial sentence. Under s. 86, young persons are to be provided information throughout the process and given an opportunity to be heard. They also have the right to a review of decisions on initial placement or transfer under s. 87. Reviews are conducted by an independent review board.

The principles of rehabilitation and reintegration are central to a custodial disposition under the YCJA. Section 90(1) orders the provincial director to designate a youth worker to a young person in custody "without delay." A young person serving a sentence in the

reintegration leave
a period spent out of custody, with leave of the provincial director, for making arrangements or participating in activities that will facilitate the youth's reintegration into the community

conditional supervision
a portion of a custodial sentence that is served outside custody and during which a youth is subject to strict conditions of behaviour

community is also assigned a worker for support, supervision, and encouragement while completing the imposed conditions. Furthermore, s. 91 authorizes the provincial director to implement a **reintegration leave**, releasing the young person from custody for periods of time for the purposes of, among other things, attending school, obtaining employment, and attending community programs.

> What facilities are available in your province for youth to serve custodial sentences?

Section 42(2)(n) provides for a combined *custody and supervision order*. It specifies that, following custody, a young person is subject to supervision in the community, known as **conditional supervision**, for a period that is half the length of time of custody. The combined period cannot exceed two years for most offences. For offences that, under the Code, could lead to imprisonment for life, a three-year maximum custody and supervision order can be made. If the young person fails to comply with any conditions while under supervision, he or she may be ordered to serve the remainder of the sentence in custody (ss. 98, 104). This sentence is designed to contribute to the protection of society through safe, fair, and humane measures while at the same time assisting rehabilitation and reintegration into society. The focus of ss. 42(2)(n)–(o) is on following the principle of the least restrictive measure that would hold a young person accountable while recognizing his or her age and stage of development.

Section 42(2)(q) provides for the maximum custody and supervision orders that can be imposed on young persons for committing murder. In the case of first-degree murder, a young person can be sentenced for up to ten years—six years in custody and four years of conditional supervision served in the community. In the case of second-degree murder, the judge can order a maximum sentence of seven years—four years in custody and three years of conditional supervision.

The YCJA provides a list of *mandatory* conditions that apply to all young persons who are released on supervision into the community (s. 97(1)):

- keep the peace, be of good behaviour, and report to the assigned probation officer and police or any other named individual;
- abide by the weapons prohibition;
- report any changes of address, normal occupation, employment, educational training, or volunteer work; any changes in family or financial situation; and any other issues that might affect the person's ability to comply with the sentence conditions; and
- comply with any other conditions that support and address the needs of the young person, promote the reintegration of the him or her into the community, and offer adequate protection to the public.

> Having considered conditions of bail and conditions of probation, what kinds of conditions might you recommend that would be different for a young person being released from sentenced custody?

Unlike the sentences imposed under s. 42(2)(n), which state that the community conditional supervision must be at least half the length of the custody portion, in the case of murder the court determines what portion of the sentence will be spent in custody and what portion in the community.

In *R v. B.W.P.* (2004), the Manitoba Court of Appeal held that the court has complete discretion to determine the ratio of custody and supervision. In that case, the court found that the trial judge did not err in sentencing a young person to one day in custody and the remainder of 15 months' conditional supervision for manslaughter. The youth charged was Aboriginal and had, after killing another youth in a fight, pleaded guilty to manslaughter. The case was appealed to the Supreme Court of Canada, and the court upheld the lower court's decision to vary the proportion of time spent in a custodial setting under a custody and supervision sentence. The court made it clear that the trier of fact is entitled to impose a lesser amount of time in custody if he or she sees fit to do so. Unlike in the adult system, there is no mandatory minimum sentence to be served in youth court. There might be cases in which the young person serves the entire sentence in custody if he or she is thought to pose a risk of death or serious harm to another (s. 104(1)).

If it is suspected that a young person is about to breach or has breached a condition, the provincial director is empowered under s. 106 to suspend the supervision and place the young person in custody pending judicial review. When the suspension of conditional supervision is ordered, the youth may, if necessary, be apprehended by police pursuant to a warrant issued under s. 107. The youth court judge then has the option of cancelling suspension of the supervision, varying the existing conditions or creating new ones, or ordering the young person to remain in custody for a period (not exceeding his or her original sentence).

Factors that must be considered when a youth is brought before the court to review the application for continued custody are (s. 104(3)):

- a pattern of persistent violent behaviour, which may include use of weapons in the commission of the offence, the nature of the offence, evidence of difficulties in controlling violent impulses, explicit threats of violence, or a substantial degree of indifference to the consequences for others;

- psychiatric or psychological evidence of a physical or mental illness or disorder of such a nature that the person is likely to commit an offence causing death or serious harm to another; and

- the availability of supervision programs in the community that might provide adequate public protection.

Intensive Custody and Supervision

With the introduction of the *Youth Criminal Justice Act* came a new sentencing option: **intensive rehabilitative custody and supervision (IRCS)**. This option, prescribed under s. 42(2)(r), is available to some youth who are suffering psychological issues and have committed a serious offence. The IRCS program, which is specially funded by the federal government, is meant to provide specialized treatment to those youth most in need of rehabilitation due to their risk factors. What is most notable about the IRCS program is its focus on a "wraparound approach" to meet specific needs in all areas of the individual's life, helping the youth to develop pro-social behaviours that will support his or her reintegration back into society. An IRCS order includes a treatment plan in which the young person must participate while in custody and while being supervised during the community-based reintegrative portion of the sentence.

IRCS orders can be made only when all the following conditions are met: (1) the young person has committed a *presumptive offence* (first- or second-degree murder, attempted murder, manslaughter, aggravated sexual assault, or an offence deemed seriously violent); (2) he or she is suffering from a mental illness; (3) an effective treatment and supervision plan has been developed; and (4) consent has been obtained from the provincial director.

intensive rehabilitative custody and supervision (IRCS)
a sentence available for youth convicted of serious violent offences who are suffering from a mental illness or disorder, psychological disorder, or emotional disturbance where an intensive treatment plan is developed that is believed to reduce the risk of reoffence

An intensive rehabilitation and supervision sentence ordinarily cannot exceed two years. However, if the offence under the Code would lead to life imprisonment, a three-year rehabilitative custody order may be made. If the young person has been found guilty of first-degree murder, he or she may be subject to custody for intensive rehabilitation for six years and conditional supervision in the community for four. In the case of second-degree murder, the young person may face a maximum of four years of intensive rehabilitation in custody and three years' conditional supervision in the community.

CASE IN POINT

Young Girl Receives IRCS Order for Murder

An example of an IRCS order was discussed by Evans, Wong, and Van Harte (n.d.) of Kinark Child and Family Services in Ontario. The case referred to a 14-year-old girl who upon admission to foster care killed a three-year-old boy resident in the same home. She pleaded guilty to the offence and the court ordered a medical and psychological report.

The girl was diagnosed with multiple disorders: attention deficit hyperactivity disorder, pervasive developmental disorder, oppositional defiance disorder, chronic anxiety, depression, post-traumatic stress disorder, attachment disorder, mild mental retardation, and alcohol-related neurodevelopmental disorder. Her risk assessment showed that she was at high risk for violent recidivism. She was found to be eligible for an IRCS order and sentenced to four years' secure custody and three years' conditional supervision.

Youth who receive an IRCS order are eligible for up to $100,000 per year to access treatment and rehabilitative services. This girl was placed at Syl Apps Treatment Centre and assigned a youth worker to help with her daily compliance with the program. The treatment plan included cognitive behavioural play therapy, psychiatric monitoring, continual assessment, and annual updating of assessments.

QUESTIONS

1. If the young girl in this case received a youth sentence and was placed in a youth custodial facility, what issues would she face?

2. How does an IRCS order comply with s. 3 of the YCJA?

Review of Custodial Sentences

Section 94(1) of the YCJA provides that a review of a custodial sentence must take place before the youth court at least annually for the duration of the sentence. In addition, s. 94(3) enables the young person or his or her parent to request a review at any time on the grounds outlined as follows in s. 94(6):

94(6) A youth sentence imposed in respect of a young person may be reviewed …

(a) on the ground that the young person has made sufficient progress to justify a change in the youth sentence;

(b) on the ground that the circumstances that led to the youth sentence have changed materially;

(c) on the ground that new services or programs are available that were not available at the time of the youth sentence;

(d) on the ground that the opportunities for rehabilitation are now greater in the community; or

(e) on any other ground that the youth justice court considers appropriate.

After giving the young person, his or her parents, the attorney general, and the provincial director an opportunity to be heard at a custody review, the youth court judge renders a decision. The judge may order no changes or may release the young person from custody and put him or her under conditional supervision for a period not exceeding the remainder of the sentence.

Aboriginal Youth and Sentencing

The declaration of principle as outlined in s. 3 of the YCJA includes the requirement to respect and respond to the needs of Aboriginal young persons, which means that the sentence must also respond to their needs and special circumstances—that is, "respect gender, ethnic, cultural and linguistic differences and respond to the needs of aboriginal young persons and of young persons with special requirements" (s. 3(1)(c)(iv)). Further, under the sentencing provisions in s. 38(2)(d), judges are required to consider "all available sanctions other than custody that are reasonable in the circumstances … for all young persons, with particular attention to the circumstances of aboriginal young persons." This is similar to the provision for adults in the *Criminal Code* that was a result of the Supreme Court of Canada decision in *Gladue v. The Queen* (1999) (see box below). In 1997, according to the materials presented in *Gladue*, Aboriginal people made up about 3 percent of the population but amounted to 12 percent of federal adult inmates. In the provinces of Manitoba and Saskatchewan, reports indicated that Aboriginal adult offenders accounted for between 55 and 72 percent of all admissions to provincial corrections.

CASE IN POINT

Gladue v. The Queen, [1999] 1 SCR 688, 1999 CanLII 679

In its decision in *Gladue v. The Queen*, the Supreme Court of Canada endorsed the concept of restorative justice and the use of community-based alternatives to imprisonment. The court was asked to consider the meaning of s. 718.2(e) of the *Criminal Code*, which states that judges are to consider all reasonable alternatives to incarceration for all offenders, but "with particular attention to the circumstances of aboriginal offenders." The court ruled that this passage imposes a duty upon judges to recognize factors that affect offenders, particularly Aboriginal people, such as poverty, substance abuse, and lack of education or employment opportunities, and to consider the role these factors might play in bringing the offender before the courts. In determining a sentence, judges must consider the types of sanctions that might be appropriate for an offender given his or her heritage. Any sentencing decision should take into account whether there is community support for the offender and whether community programs exist that provide alternatives to incarceration. Although the *Gladue* case dealt specifically with Aboriginal offenders, the court clearly indicated that the aims of restorative justice should apply to all offenders. It also rejected the view that a restorative approach is more lenient, or that a sentence focusing on restorative justice is necessarily a lighter one. Restoring harmony involves determining sentences that respond to the needs of the victim, the community, and the offender.

QUESTIONS

1. What additional provisions are made in the YCJA for Aboriginal youth?

2. Do you think these provisions go far enough to support the *Gladue* decision? Why or why not?

The Department of Justice reported on a one-day snapshot of Aboriginal youth in custody and found that in 2001, they had represented about 7 percent of the juvenile population in select provinces and territories, but made up 25 percent of admissions to custodial facilities (Bittle, Hattem, Quann, & Muise, 2002). Latimer and Foss (2004, 2005) reported on a followup snapshot of Aboriginal youth in custody that, despite the YCJA being in effect, Aboriginal youth had continued to experience significantly higher incarceration rates; they accounted for 5 percent of the population but 33 percent of youth in custody. Yessine and Bonta (2009) reported that Aboriginal young offenders were nearly eight times more likely to be in custody than their non-Aboriginal counterparts.

Green (2012) reported that since the implementation of the YCJA, the number of Aboriginal youth in custody had increased from 28 percent in 2002–3 to 36 percent in 2008–9, despite Aboriginal youth representing only 6 percent of the youth population.

1. In Figure 8.1, what trends do you see in Aboriginal involvement in the youth criminal justice system?

2. What reasons might there be for the overrepresentation of Aboriginal youth in Canada's youth justice system?

3. With the ruling in *Gladue v. The Queen*, the Supreme Court stipulated that judges are to consider all reasonable alternatives to incarceration for all offenders, but "with particular attention to the circumstances of aboriginal offenders." Considering the information in Figure 8.1, have reasonable alternatives been sought?

FIGURE 8.1 Percentage of Youth of Aboriginal Identity Admitted to Custody and Community Services, 2011–12

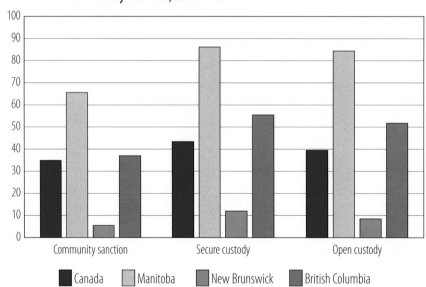

SOURCE: Adapted from Statistics Canada (2014c).

Aboriginal young offenders have much higher individual and environmental risk factors than their non-Aboriginal peers: higher levels of poverty, family conflict, substance abuse, fetal alcohol spectrum disorder, and mental illness, and low education (Corrado & Cohen, 2011). In a study of 404 incarcerated young serious offenders, Corrado, Kuehn, and Margaritescu (2014) looked at risk profiles, criminal histories, and offence profiles of two subsets of the sample; approximately two-thirds were Caucasian (250; 61.9 percent) and about one-third (154; 38.1 percent) were Aboriginal. The results indicated that both groups had very high risk profiles, including long histories of substance abuse problems and criminal activity, and poor family histories including physical and sexual abuse. However, the statistically significant difference between the two groups was the higher family profile index scores and higher number of foster care placements for the Aboriginal young offenders. In the explanation of this outcome, Corrado, Kuehn, and Margaritescu (2014, p. 53) suggested that these risk profiles are the result of broad socio-political issues and the "tragic multi-century history of colonialism" that has had severe adverse effects on Aboriginal families:

> [T]he expropriation of the land, disrupting Aboriginal communities, and the forced removal of Aboriginal children from their families and communities as well as cruel assimilation strategies that prohibited the practice of Aboriginal culture and language and the experienced abuse in Canadian residential schools have "broken" generations of Aboriginal families.

Alain, Corrado, and Reid (forthcoming) point out that a number of policies and practices have been put in place in all provinces and territories for judges and front-line youth justice practitioners. These policies and practices have enabled justice workers to adjust the criteria they use when dealing with Aboriginal youth at the pre-trial, sentencing, and treatment intervention stages. Despite these efforts and the focus on addressing Aboriginal young offenders through a more culturally sensitive lens, there are still issues relating to overrepresentation of Aboriginal youth in the system. Alain, Corrado, and Reid conclude there is a need to create explicit policies that not only consider Aboriginal cultural distinctiveness, but also include historical and intergenerational risk and need profiles to address the trauma and grief such communities continue to face. Further, they argue that the Aboriginal culture is not homogeneous in this country and solutions must be derived through multifaceted Aboriginal leadership and decision-making. While there have been attempts implement restorative justice approaches with First Nations communities (Corrado, Cohen, & Odgers, 2003), a lack of resources and the practical challenges of obtaining community involvement have meant that many of these programs have not been systematically implemented, despite their adherence to many of the key principles from Aboriginal cultures. Blagg (2012) suggests that, until such time as a framework for self-determination and implementation of programs developed by Aboriginal leaders is put in place, many First Nations communities will be reluctant to participate in programs controlled by the state.

Youth Records

When a young person is found guilty of a criminal offence, he or she will get a criminal record (YCJA, s. 119(2)). The period of time for which such a record may be accessed after a finding of guilt varies with the type of sentence. Generally, the more severe the offence, and therefore the more severe the sentence, the longer access is made available to police, victims, judges, courts of review, and persons carrying out criminal record checks. As has already been discussed, a judicial reprimand can only be accessed for two months, an absolute discharge for one year, and a conditional discharge for three years. For other sentences in youth court, the length of time during which a record can be accessed is dependent on whether the offence was a summary or indictable one. Summary conviction offences can be accessed for three years from the time the young person completes the sentence, while indictable offences can be accessed for five years.

Under s. 82(1), with certain exceptions, a youth's criminal record need not be disclosed for most purposes when he or she has been discharged absolutely or has completed the sentence. The record *can* be used within the youth criminal justice system—for example, for determining sentences and whether to sentence as a youth or as an adult; to decide whether a subsequent offence is a presumptive offence; or to decide whether pre-trial custody is appropriate.

The limitations on the public use of a young person's criminal record are intended to protect the youth and allow for easier reintegration into the community. Section 82(3), for example, specifically deals with public employment applications. It prohibits questions that relate to disclosure of a prior record.

If a young person is convicted of a subsequent offence, the access period is recalculated. Youth records are not protected from adult proceedings while the access period is still open, which means that a youth record can be brought forward at the time of sentencing as an adult. The fact that a young adult before the court has a youth record may also be published.

1. If a young person receives an absolute discharge at age 17½ years, will a criminal record check for a job at age 18 show that the youth has a criminal record?

2. What would a criminal record check show for the same individual if an extrajudicial sanction had been imposed instead?

3. Recall your response to the question about access to youth records in Chapter 3. Do you feel differently now that you have learned more about the youth justice process?

SCHOOLYARD SCUFFLE REVISITED

See again the case of Jim from the beginning of the chapter. Given what you have learned in this chapter, would you change your mind on how to deal with him?

QUESTIONS

1. How should Jim be sentenced?

2. How should Jim's offence be characterized? (That is, is it a "violent" offence? Is it a "serious violent" offence?)

3. What sentencing principles should apply and in what ways?

4. Could Jim be sentenced to custody? Should he be?

5. Could Jim be sentenced as an adult? Should he be?

6. Looking at the list of all possible sentencing options, if you were the judge in his case, what sentence would you impose?

CHAPTER SUMMARY

This chapter explored the many options available in the youth criminal justice system for sentencing a young person found guilty of a crime. Section 38 of the *Youth Criminal Justice Act* identifies the purpose of sentencing to be that of meaningful consequences and the promotion of rehabilitation and reintegration. Passage of the *Safe Streets and Communities Act* in 2012 introduced changes to youth sentencing, including deterrence and denunciation, and a focus on sentencing youth who commit serious offences and serious violent offences, with the ultimate goal of public safety.

When a youth commits a serious violent offence (murder, manslaughter, attempted murder, or aggravated sexual assault), the Crown may seek an adult sentence if the youth is over the age of 14. An adult sentence will be sought if it is believed such a sentence will hold the youth to a greater level of accountability and protect the public. No youth under 18 will serve his or her sentence in an adult prison or penitentiary even if given an adult sentence. At the age of 20, he or she will be automatically transferred to an adult institution.

Within youth justice court, many options are available for a convicted person. The majority of youth convicted of a criminal offence will receive a non-custodial sentence. Sentencing options include discharges, fines, restitution, and the most utilized option, probation. While non-custodial sentences are preferred, custodial options are sometimes required. Custody is reserved for youth who have been found guilty of a violent offence, have failed to comply with previous non-custodial sentences, or have been found guilty of an indictable offence for which an adult would be liable to a term of imprisonment greater than two years; and for exceptional cases. Because least-restrictive measures are preferable, a judge might choose a deferred custody and supervision order, under which a youth can serve his or her custodial sentence in the community. Or a youth might be sentenced to custody, open or closed. The newest option available is intensive rehabilitative custody and supervision (IRCS), which is for youth who suffer from a mental illness or disorder and have been found guilty of a presumptive offence. IRCS, which is considered therapeutic sentencing, allows for intensive support and treatment aimed at successfully rehabilitating the young person to allow reintegration into his or her community.

A final consideration of importance with regard to youth sentencing is ensuring that Aboriginal youth receive sentences that respect their cultural needs. Judges are required to use all available sanctions other than custody that focus on the individual and environmental risk factors particular to Aboriginal youth. Despite this focus in the YCJA, the number of Aboriginal youth in custody has continued to increase.

KEY TERMS

aggravating factor, 171
conditional supervision, 184
deferred custody and supervision order (DCSO), 183
general deterrence, 171
intensive rehabilitative custody and supervision (IRCS), 185
mitigating factor, 171

provincial director, 174
reintegration leave, 184
serious violent offence, 173
specific deterrence, 171
victim impact statement, 173

REFERENCES

A.O., R v. (2007). 2007 ONCA 144, 218 CCC (3d) 409.

Alain, A., Corrado, R., & Reid, S. (forthcoming). *Implementing and working with the YCJA across Canada: A view from the "ground."* Toronto: University of Toronto Press.

Associated Press. (2005, March 3). U.S. Supreme Court declares juvenile death penalty unconstitutional. Retrieved from http://www.legislationline.org/documents/id/2929.

B.V.N., R v. (2004). [2004] BCJ No. 974 (CA) (QL).

B.W.P., R v. (2004). [2004] MJ No. 267 (CA) (QL).

B.W.P., R v.; R v. B.V.N. (2006). 2006 SCC 27, [2006] 1 SCR 941.

Bittle, S., Hattem, T., Quann, N., & Muise, D. (2002). *A one-day snapshot of Aboriginal youth in custody across Canada.* Ottawa: Department of Justice.

Blagg, H. (2012). Re-imagining youth justice: Cultural contestation in the Kimberly Region of Australia since the 1991 Royal Commission into Aboriginal Deaths in Custody. *Theoretical Criminology, 16*(4), 481–498.

C.D., R v.; R v. C.D.K. (2005). 2005 SCC 78, [2005] 3 SCR 668.

Canadian Charter of Rights and Freedoms. (1982). Part I of the *Constitution Act, 1982,* being Schedule B to the *Canada Act 1982* (UK), 1982, c. 11.

Canadian Sentencing Commission. (1987). *Sentencing reform: A Canadian approach.* Report of the Canadian Sentencing Commission. Ottawa: Supply and Services Canada.

Clemmer, D. (1940). *The prison community.* Boston: Christopher Publishing House.

Corrado, R., & Cohen, I. (2011). Aboriginal youth at risk: The role of education, mobility, housing, employment, and language as protective factors for problem and criminal behaviours. In P. Dinsdale, J. White, & C. Hanselmann (Eds.), *Urban Aboriginal communities in Canada: Complexities, challenges, opportunities* (pp. 2–36). Toronto: Thomson Education.

Corrado, R., Cohen, I., & Odgers, C. (2003). Multi-problem violent youth: A challenge for the restorative justice paradigm. In E. Weitekamp & H. Kerner (Eds.), *Restorative justice in context: International practice and directions* (pp. 1–22). Cullompton, UK: Willan.

Corrado, R.R., Kuehn, S., & Margaritescu, I. (2014). Policy issues regarding the overrepresentation of incarcerated Aboriginal young offenders in a Canadian context. *Youth Justice, 14*(1), 40–62.

Criminal Code. (1985). RSC 1985, c. C-46.

D.B., R v. (2007). [2007] NJ No. 423 (Prov. Ct.) (QL).

Davis-Barron, S. (2009). *Canadian youth and the criminal law*. Toronto: LexisNexis.

Department of Justice Canada. (2010). Legislative summary of Bill C-4: An Act to amend the Youth Criminal Justice Act and to make consequential and related amendments to other acts—Sebastien's Law. Retrieved from http://www.parl.gc.ca/About/Parliament/LegislativeSummaries/bills_ls.asp?Language=E&ls=c4&Parl=40&Ses=3&source=library_prb.

Doob, A.N., & Cesaroni, C. (Eds.). (2004). *Responding to youth crime in Canada*. Toronto: University of Toronto Press.

Evans, E., Wong, J., & Van Harte, E. (n.d.). *Intensive rehabilitative custody and supervision orders: A case study of a female youth with mental disorders who committed murder*. Kinark Child and Family Services. Retrieved from http://www.kinark.on.ca.

Gladue v. The Queen. (1999). [1999] 1 SCR 688, 1999 CanLII 679.

Green, R. (2012). Explaining the Youth Criminal Justice Act. In J. Winterdyk & R. Smandych (Eds.), *Youth at risk and youth justice: A Canadian overview* (pp. 54–79). Toronto: Nelson.

K.D., R v. (2003). [2003] NSJ No. 165 (SC) (QL).

L.B., R v. (2007). [2007] BCJ No. 2921 (Prov. Ct.) (QL).

Latimer, J., & Foss, L.C. (2004). *A one-day snapshot of Aboriginal youth in custody across Canada: Phase II*. Ottawa: Youth Justice Policy, Department of Justice Canada.

Latimer, J., & Foss, L. (2005). The sentencing of Aboriginal and Non-Aboriginal youth under the Young Offenders Act: A multivariate analysis. *Canadian Journal of Criminology and Criminal Justice, 3*, 481–500.

Leschied, A.W. (1998, March). Implementing alternatives to custody in addressing youth crime: Applications of the multisystemic therapy approach in Canada. In *Beyond prisons*. Symposium hosted by Corrections Canada, CIDA, and Queen's University, Kingston, Ontario.

National Post. (2008, June 6). Harper vows changes to "failed" youth justice act. Retrieved from http://www.canada.com/theprovince/news/story.html?id=a69024fb-c635-4b23-af82-2ee5cb7ddea1.

Perreault, S. (2014). Correctional services key indicators, 2012–2013. *Juristat Bulletin*. Retrieved from http://www.statcan.gc.ca/pub/85-002-x/2014001/article/14007-eng.htm.

Pulis, J.E. (2014). *Set up for failure? Understanding probation orders and breaches of probation for youth in conflict with the law* (Doctoral dissertation). University of Waterloo. Retrieved from https://uwspace.uwaterloo.ca/bitstream/handle/10012/8475/Pulis_Jessica.pdf?sequence=5.

R.E.W., R v. (2006). 2006 CanLII 1761, 79 OR (3d) 1 (CA).

Read, T. (2012, January 31). Most influential: Judge Michael Cicconetti's alternative sentences leave impression. *The News Herald*. Retrieved from http://www.news-herald.com/general-news/20121231/most-influential-judge-michael-cicconettis-alternative-sentences-leave-impression-with-video.

Roper v. Simmons. (2005). 543 US 551.

Safe Streets and Communities Act. (2012). SC 2012, c. 1.

Sprott, J.B. (2006). The use of custody for failing to comply with a disposition cases under the Young Offenders Act. *Canadian Journal of Criminology and Criminal Justice, 48*(4), 609-622.

Statistics Canada. (2014a). Youth correctional services, average counts of young persons in provincial and territorial correctional services. CANSIM Table 251-0008. Retrieved November 20, 2014 from http://www5.statcan.gc.ca/cansim/a26?lang=eng&retrLang=eng&id=2510008&paSer=&pattern=&stByVal=1&p1=1&p2=37&tabMode=dataTable&csid=.

Statistics Canada. (2014b). Youth courts, guilty cases by most serious sentence. CANSIM Table 252-0068. Retrieved November 20, 2014 from http://www5.statcan.gc.ca/cansim/a05?lang=eng&id=2520068&pattern=2520068&searchTypeByValue=1&p2=35.

Statistics Canada. (2014c).Youth custody and community services (YCCS), admissions to correctional services, by sex and aboriginal identity. Retrieved November 20, 2014 from http://www5.statcan.gc.ca/cansim/a26?lang=eng&retrLang=eng&id=2510012&paSer=&pattern=&stByVal=1&p1=1&p2=37&tabMode=dataTable&csid=.

T.M., R v. (2003). [2003] OJ No. 4120 (CA) (QL).

Toronto Star Newspaper Ltd. v. Ontario. (2012). 2012 ONCJ 27.

Yessine, A., & Bonta, J. (2009). The offending trajectories of youthful Aboriginal offenders. *Canadian Journal of Criminology and Criminal Justice, 51*(4), 435–472.

Youth Criminal Justice Act. (2002). SC 2002, c. 1.

EXERCISES AND REVIEW

Review Questions

1. What are two new sentencing provisions introduced with the 2012 YCJA amendments?

2. What factors are taken into consideration when a judge is imposing an adult sentence?

3. Under what circumstances is it appropriate to sentence a youth to a closed custody facility?

4. What is the objective of an intensive rehabilitative custody and supervision sentence?

5. Once a youth is sentenced, can there ever be changes to his or her sentence? Explain.

6. Describe four community sentences and indicate the prevalence of each by referring to Table 8.1.

7. With respect to exceptional circumstances, outline the considerations designed to guide the sentencing of Aboriginal young persons.

Discussion Questions

1. Examine the list of available sentencing options for young people. Of these sentences, which do you feel best align with the goals of rehabilitation and reintegration? Explain your reasoning.

2. Have you ever heard people in your community complain that we are "too soft on youth crime" in Canada or that we do not send enough youth to "jail"? From what you now know about the nature of sentencing, do you agree or disagree with this viewpoint? How would you discuss this issue with a community member?

3. What do you anticipate will be the issues relating to custody and remand in 2024?

Prevention and Rehabilitation: What Works?

9

LEARNING OUTCOMES

After completing this chapter, you should be able to:

- Assess the effectiveness of deterrence strategies for preventing and controlling youth crime.

- Distinguish between primary, secondary, and tertiary prevention approaches and their application to young people, and explain what early intervention is and how it might prevent or reduce youth offending.

- Understand risk and protective factors and apply these to prevention, and rehabilitation approaches to youth crime.

- Explain the risk–needs–responsivity model of effective intervention with young persons at risk of criminal behaviour.

- Explain community policing and its approach to youth crime.

- Outline some of the factors that make it difficult to assess the effectiveness of rehabilitation and prevention programs.

- Consider the effects of prisonization on youth and identify strategies that might promote positive reintegration after release from custody.

Introduction

This chapter explains what researchers have discovered about what does and does not work to prevent youth crime and to rehabilitate youth who have been involved in criminal behaviour. In reading about the various approaches, you will note that some programs, such as probation and incarceration, are designed to treat the problem after it occurs; others, such as early intervention programs, are designed to prevent the problem from occurring in the first place.

It is somewhat difficult to assess whether a particular prevention program works at all, let alone works well, because many factors contribute to criminal behaviour. One leading scholar in the field has suggested that, in designing our policies and programs for youth who find themselves within the youth justice system, we should, above all, "do no harm" (Layton-MacKenzie, 2013, p. 1). She argues that in criminal justice policy, as in medicine, we have a social obligation not to harm either the individuals who come under the responsibility of the state or the society or communities from which they come.

Many people, when they think of sentences, think of punishment. Punishment of criminals can be thought of in three ways: (1) that it makes the community feel morally satisfied, (2) that it deters crime, and (3) that it may rehabilitate the criminal. Often, prevention is an afterthought, only considered in terms of specific and general deterrence provided by the punishment (Nagin, 2013).

What about the issue of rehabilitation? McNeill (2012) suggests that four forms of rehabilitation need to be considered: (1) psychological, (2) judicial, (3) moral, and (4) social. A good deal of the literature on correctional rehabilitation concerns individual-level, psychological rehabilitation, and this will be discussed with respect to the model of risk–needs–responsivity as well as the design and implementation of evidence-based programs.

Judicial rehabilitation is concerned with avoidance of labelling the offender in legal records so that he or she can go on to be a fully functioning member of society. For example, the *Youth Criminal Justice Act* (YCJA) has provisions for ensuring that the records of young persons who refrain from reoffending will not be available for scrutiny when they become adults. This chapter discusses the important role of **probation** and correctional officers in helping young people navigate the barriers they face when attempting to reintegrate.

probation
a period of supervision over an offender outside of incarceration

When we think about an "individual turning their lives around" through rehabilitation, this is seen as a form of moral rehabilitation, particularly when he or she has made reparation for the harm caused to the victim and the community. It is as though a restored social position is only achievable when an offender has paid back to the community (McNeill, 2004). Elements of restorative justice that have been discussed throughout this book would be examples of this perspective.

Social rehabilitation includes the elements of moral rehabilitation (that is, restoration of the citizen's formal social status) and whether the individual has the personal and social means to be able to reintegrate into the community. McNeill (2012, p. 18) suggests that social rehabilitation is more than individual psychological reform; it is achieved when there is an "informal social recognition and acceptance of the reformed ex-offender."

This chapter begins with an overview of programs based on the principles of deterrence, and offers insights about the value of deterrence for young people who commit crimes. The discussion then turns to primary, secondary, and tertiary crime prevention and to an outline of the approaches that have shown promise for the lives of young people based on risk and protective factors. A discussion of the risk–needs–responsivity model follows, building on our knowledge of "what works" to examine how we can ensure that the research findings are implemented in our programs for youth, through the use of evidence-based interventions. A discussion of probation and custodial sentences and the impact of officers' belief structures on the success of youth intervention illustrates these differing views. The view that "nothing works" to prevent crime is discussed, as are the results of research that strives instead to investigate "what works" in offender treatment.

Deterrence and Youth Justice

The concepts of deterrence suggest that people will be deterred from crime if

- they are *certain* they will be caught for the behaviour deemed criminal,
- they are apprehended *swiftly* after the offence, and
- the punishment is *severe* enough to offset the pleasure they might get from the offence.

In handing out a punishment, the judge who relies on deterrent value is aiming to not only deter the individual offender (*specific deterrence*) but also send a clear message to the rest of the community that this kind of behaviour will not be tolerated (*general deterrence*) (see Chapter 8).

Incarceration as a Deterrent

Incarceration is designed to deter the offender and, through example, deter others who might be contemplating similar behaviour. It also has another effect—it incapacitates him or her. Obviously, someone locked up is not free to commit more offences.

incarceration
imprisonment

But does the imprisonment of young offenders prevent crime? In the short term, the answer is yes for that particular person. But is the offender who has served time deterred as a result of being imprisoned, and are others deterred by his or her example?

Research has shown that youths who anticipate harsher punishment are not necessarily deterred from deviant acts. Also, it seems that adolescents' fear of punishment is diminished when certain lifestyle factors are present, among them poverty, elevated drug and alcohol use, and a lack of normative constraints such as parental rules (Johnson, Simons, & Conger, 2004; Clear, 2007).

Lipsey and Cullen (2007) did a **meta-analysis** (a summing-up of initial analyses) comparing those who received rehabilitative treatment with those who received a sanction without treatment. They found that recidivism was reduced by between 20 and 40 percent in those programs that incorporated a rehabilitation or treatment component. Apparently, the least successful rehabilitation program was still better than the most successful criminal sanction; moreover, in some cases sanction resulted in more recidivism. This implies that rehabilitation "works," and much better than conventional punitive sanctions.

meta-analysis
statistical method used to draw conclusions by analyzing a group of experimental studies

Prison is appropriate only for those who are the most violent or the most embedded in a criminal subculture. In fact, according to research by Andrews et al. (1990), overreliance on incarceration is one of the worst possible policy mistakes we can make. Because imprisonment provides opportunities for youth to make connections with the criminal subculture, weakens community ties, and affects employment prospects, incarceration itself can be said to increase the recidivism risk for low-risk, first-time offenders.

"Boot Camps": More Effective Than Other Types of Institutions?

The idea behind "boot camps" is that offenders will benefit from a highly structured program with military-style discipline. This kind of program, emphasizing discipline and obedience to superiors, is designed to deter offenders from further crime.

In 1995, the Ontario government announced its intention to establish a "strict discipline" boot camp–styled program with a military structure for young offenders in custody. In 1997, Project Turnaround opened its doors near Barrie, Ontario. Intended as a pilot project, Turnaround was contracted to a private, for-profit organization. The facility was to hold 12 young offenders, ages 16 and 17, with a history of difficult and defiant behaviour. However, after several offenders escaped from the program, admission was restricted to less-serious offenders serving a sentence of between four and six months.

Project Turnaround was not a success. Marred by escapes, underuse, and very high costs, it officially closed on January 31, 2004, the government of the day citing expenses (the annual operating budget was $2.3 million). Its failure to reduce recidivism rates, combined with a change in attitudes toward custody as a sentencing option ushered in by the YCJA, also likely contributed to its cancellation.

Despite additional evidence indicating that such programs are not successful, the concept remains popular with the public. *Brat Camp*, a reality television show created in the United Kingdom in 2005, ran for three seasons. It depicted a wilderness-style boot camp where parents sent their unruly children to seek correction of problems they were experiencing at home. Problem youth behaviours included "disobedience, acting spoilt, careless, anger issues and possible alcohol and drug problems." As the show gained popularity, it was copied and aired on US and Canadian television. An article about the series, when it aired in Canada, appeared in the front section of the *Toronto Star* under a headline that described the program as abusive (Menon, 2005). In Britain, when the show was released, the Barnardo charity wrote an opinion piece expressing concern that the show sent the wrong message to parents that a short period of "tough love" can resolve mental health and behaviour issues (Lee, 2004).

Cullen, Blevins, Trager, and Gendreau (2005, p. 68) note: "the consensus in the criminological community is that the evidence is persuasive that boot camps are largely a failed enterprise." Some studies have found that participation in boot camp may actually increase the likelihood of recidivism (MacKenzie, Wilson, & Kider, 2001; Meade & Steiner, 2010).

Latessa, Cullen, and Gendreau (2002) have noted that boot camps are also known in the profession as *correctional quackery*, because they satisfy the desire to punish but fail to produce a rehabilitative benefit.

"SCARED STRAIGHT" AS "CORRECTIONAL QUACKERY"

A number of individuals have suggested that young offenders can be deterred from further serious crime by subjecting them to a "scared straight" program—frightening them by having them tour a maximum-security prison and talk to inmates serving long sentences.

Two documentaries have been produced, in 1978 and in 1987, on a program operating in Rahway, New Jersey. It noted that 16 of the 17 persistent offenders had changed their ways and stayed out of trouble for at least three years, and that out of a further 9,000 who took part in this program at Rahway State Prison, 90 percent had stayed out of trouble.

Those in the program were exposed to the most negative aspects of imprisonment, including the unpleasant physical conditions, the threats of violence, and the noise, both by seeing the prison first-hand and by talking to inmates.

However, when James Finckenauer (1982) evaluated this program, he found that young offenders' encounters with prisoners did not alter their perception of the realities of prison as a form of punishment, nor did it reduce the delinquency of program participants. In fact, he found that those who had participated in the program actually committed further offences at a much higher rate (41.3 percent) than the control group (11.4 percent). The finding was supported by Canadian researchers Dowden and Andrews (1999), who found that such **shock incarceration** was associated with a *higher* recidivism rate than other approaches.

A meta-analysis of shock incarceration found that in all cases the effect was negative. This led the authors to conclude that such programs did not deter or scare kids at all; in fact, they seemed to encourage more offending (Petrosino, Turpin-Petrosino, & Buehler, 2003). Research since then has confirmed that the programs do not work (Drake, Aos, & Miller, 2009; Guerra & Williams, 2012).

The TV program *Beyond Scared Straight*, produced by Anthony Shapiro, who also produced the other two documentaries, focuses on a group of teens as they visit a prison and are confronted by inmates, and then follows up with them one month later to see if they've changed their ways. Critics argue that the tactics used on the program "don't make the kids more timid … it will 'harden their bravado'" and make them more likely to "want to affiliate with the nasty talking inmates who have the most power" (Lee, 2013).

Professor Dale Elliott of the Center for the Study and Prevention of Violence at the University of Colorado has suggested that there was a moral dilemma in airing a television program "promoting a program which is doing harm to our children," and called on the A&E network to take it off the air (Lee, 2013). Others have approached Walt Disney Corporation, which owns A&E, arguing that *Beyond Scared Straight* should be taken off because it "touts a program that does not work and also demeans the very children Disney claims to shower with wholesome programming" (Witt, 2011, 2013). In a report by Yu (2014), Anthony Petrosino, the researcher responsible for the meta-analysis of the Scared Straight program, discusses the issue of parents contacting him after they do a Google search of the program trying to get their sons and daughters into it. His response continues to be that he cannot in good conscience recommend that youth participate in this harmful program.

shock incarceration
an alternative to traditional incarceration in which youth are held for a short term in custody with a focus on rehabilitation by utilizing military discipline; often called *boot camp*

QUESTIONS

1. Watch an episode of *Beyond Scared Straight* and pick out three examples of scare tactics that are used. How do you feel about the program?
2. Which models (crime control, justice, welfare, community change, restorative justice) are represented in the episode you watched? Provide examples.

Having considered the foregoing deterrence-based approaches to youth crime, we have learned that measuring the effectiveness of deterrence is problematic. We can measure recidivism rates, but we can never be sure whether calculated deterrence in the form of incarceration, threats of it, or exposure to the conditions that characterize incarceration represent a significant motivation for youth who abandon crime after an initial experience. According to legal researcher Nicholas Bala (1997, p. 3), traits characteristic of adolescence (and particularly of those prone to offending)—immaturity, lack of foresight and judgment, and recklessness—make this group much less susceptible to deterrence than their more calculating adult counterparts.

As you learned in Chapter 8, the amendments to the YCJA in 2012 provided judges with the principle of deterrence as a reason for sentencing young persons convicted of crime. Discuss the literature you have read so far with your classmates and consider the impact of this change for youth receiving deterrence-based sentences.

Crime Prevention

Types of Crime Prevention Strategies

Crime prevention can be defined as "strategies and measures that seek to intervene on and modify identified risk factors in order to reduce the likelihood that a criminal act will be committed" (Brantingham, Brantingham, & Taylor, 2005).

primary crime prevention
crime prevention focusing on social and situational factors in order to reduce the opportunity for future crime and victimization

Primary crime prevention is directed at stopping the problem before it happens, either through reducing opportunities for crime or strengthening community and social structures. Primary prevention focuses on *social* and *situational* factors.

crime prevention through social development
crime prevention that addresses the social factors that underlie crime with the goal of reducing criminality

Social crime prevention, also referred to as **crime prevention through social development**, addresses factors that influence an individual's likelihood of committing a crime, such as poverty and unemployment, poor health, and low educational performance. Examples are school-based programs such as truancy initiatives, and community-based programs such as local resident action groups that promote shared community ownership and guardianship.

crime prevention through environmental design
crime prevention that addresses planning and development in a community with the goal of reducing crime

Situational crime prevention, also called **crime prevention through environmental design**, addresses the environment—for example, the design of buildings and landscapes and the products we purchase.

secondary crime prevention
crime prevention focusing on those considered at risk for committing crimes with the goal of eliminating opportunities that might foster criminal behaviour

Secondary crime prevention seeks to change people, typically those at high risk of embarking on a criminal career. It focuses on circumstances that might foster crime or on individuals identified as being at high risk to offend. Once we are able to identify potential places, people, situations, or opportunities that present risk for criminal activity, it might be possible to anticipate and prevent future crimes. Diversion programs are an example of a secondary prevention initiative, as discussed in Chapter 5 in the context of extrajudicial measures and extrajudicial sanctions.

tertiary crime prevention
crime prevention focusing on reducing recidivism and eliminating revictimization

Rehabilitation, also known as **tertiary crime prevention**, aims to reduce the recidivism rate and ensure that steps are taken so that a victim is not revictimized.

Evidence-Based Crime Prevention Programs

Scott Wortley and his colleagues, writing for the project *Roots of Youth Violence* (2008) in Toronto, have provided a good overview of the ways that crime prevention programs have come to be classified:

1. *Proven (model) programs.* Prevention programs that have been proven effective through numerous high-quality evaluations in different communities or settings. As established by the published literature, these programs have either directly or indirectly reduced violent or aggressive behaviour in youthful populations.

2. *Promising programs.* Prevention programs that have been subjected to limited evaluation and have shown positive results. However, unlike proven programs, promising programs may not have been evaluated using the most rigorous scientific standards, may have shown inconsistent results, or may not have been replicated in different types of communities. Such programs are thus endorsed with caution until they have been more fully evaluated.

3. *Ineffective programs.* Programs or strategies that have been subjected to high-quality evaluations and found to be ineffective—that is, results indicate that these programs have either no impact or a negative impact on violent behaviour and youth crime.

The National Crime Prevention Centre (NCPC) in Canada has created a list of evidence-based crime prevention programs that must to be implemented by agencies seeking funding to support crime prevention (Government of Canada, 2014a, 2014b).

Risk and Protective Factors for Youth Offending

You will recall that in Chapter 2 the concept of *risk factors* was introduced, and we discussed the importance of looking at the young person in the context of his or her social environment (for example, family, school, peer group).

A risk factor is anything that increases the probability that a person will suffer harm. The more risks a child or young person is exposed to, the greater the likelihood that healthy development will be compromised and problems will arise. **Static risk factors** are those we can do little if anything to change; **dynamic risk factors** are those amenable to treatment and intervention (Loeber & Farrington, 1998). Both types of risk factors for youth offending are listed in Table 9.1.

static risk factors
relatively unchangeable risk factors

dynamic risk factors
risk factors amenable to treatment and intervention

TABLE 9.1   Static and Dynamic Risk Factors

Static risk factors	Dynamic risk factors
• Being male • Neuropsychological characteristics and intelligence • Early age of onset of problem behaviour • Early age at first conviction • Length and intensity of delinquent careers • Parental neglect, physical maltreatment, conflicts with parents • Presence of a child protection order	• A number of personality characteristics • Substance abuse • Poor social and economic environment • Criminal peers • Truancy • Anti-social attitudes and beliefs • Living in disadvantaged neighbourhoods

SOURCE: Loeber & Farrington (1998).

1. What kinds of programs would you recommend as primary prevention strategies given the risk factors listed in Table 9.1?
2. Whom would you target?

The assessment of offenders for risk to reoffend has gained considerable research evidence over the past ten years. The **risk–needs–responsivity (RNR) model** (Andrews & Dowden, 2007) was designed to investigate the premise that, if we are able to effectively screen out low- to moderate-risk offenders using standardized assessment tools, we can then concentrate on the higher-risk offenders who will benefit from more intensive interventions.

One area of research useful in untangling the interplay between risk factors and outcomes is that on **resilience**, which is the quality that enables an individual at high risk for adverse outcomes not merely to survive, but to thrive under conditions of risk (Ungar, 2004).

risk–needs–responsivity (RNR) model
model that suggests that the best way to reduce recidivism is to assess the risks and needs of the individual and determine appropriate interventions that are responsive to the individual's criminogenic factors

resilience
the ability of an individual who has faced adversity, often through multiple risks, to thrive; cannot be present without risk

protective factors
circumstances and experiences that tend to shield people from involvement in behaviours that would be damaging to themselves and others

self-system beliefs
beliefs about one's attitudes, abilities, or cognitive skills

criminogenic needs
deficiencies in social cognition, problem-solving abilities, and sense of self-efficacy

Contributing to resilience are **protective factors**—those circumstances and experiences that buffer young people's involvement in behaviours that would be damaging to themselves and to others. Protective factors also come from the interaction of environmental processes (neighbourhood, school, peer group, community groups), family processes (family resources, parental characteristics, parental behaviour), and individual characteristics (self-beliefs, cognition).

Self-system beliefs (connectedness, competence) also have an impact on resilience. Research has shown that one of the hallmarks of a resilient youth is the presence of a close relationship with at least one caring, competent, reliable adult who recognizes, values, and rewards his or her pro-social behaviour (Resnick, Harris, & Blum, 1993; Ungar, 2004). Deficiencies in social cognition (understanding other people and social interactions), problem-solving abilities, and sense of self-efficacy (confidence in one's ability to perform a task in a specific situation) are all cognitive deficits or **criminogenic needs** found to be associated with criminal activity (MacKenzie, 2006; Serin et al., 2011).

There is a body of literature known as *positive youth development* that has shown youth–adult relationships are integral for the developmental transitions through adolescence to young adulthood (Zeldin, Larson, Camino, & O'Connor, 2005; Wong, Zimmerman, & Parker, 2010). Extrafamilial relationships (adult relatives, friends' parents, teachers, coaches) have also been shown to provide the young person with opportunities for extracurricular activities, social skill development, and other competencies that might not have been achieved given the young person's high-risk environment. These relationships are essential as a protective factor for youth who may be entangled in the youth justice system.

To sum up, for youth involved or at risk of involvement with the juvenile justice system, risk factors are those conditions or variables associated with a higher likelihood of juvenile justice system contact; protective factors are those conditions that lessen this likelihood. Perhaps the best way to prevent youth crime or other problematic outcomes is to reduce or eliminate risk factors and to increase or enhance protective factors.

Individual Domain

Research suggests that individual risk factors include such things as impulsivity, anti-social attitudes, continued contact with anti-social peers, and alcohol and other drug abuse (Lipsey, 2009).

Some studies suggest that children likely to become offenders can be identified at a relatively early age. A team of researchers in Montreal studied 295 students in the public school system who had been identified as disruptive in their kindergarten classes (Tremblay, 2010). Every spring until they reached age 17, the boys were asked to answer a questionnaire about their behaviour—for example, whether they had stolen, trespassed, taken alcohol or drugs, vandalized things, or been in fights.

At the end of the study, 13 percent more of those children who had received a treatment intervention graduated from high school. Those children identified in kindergarten received interventions for their aggression that focused on anger control and disruptive behaviour. Further, they were 11 percent less likely to have a criminal record by age 24. The study concluded that early intervention was warranted even before children reached school age.

EARLY INTERVENTION PROGRAM: SNAP®

One of the key indicators of risk to offend is the early onset of criminal behaviour.

Stop Now and Plan (SNAP®) was the first intervention program designed specifically to meet the needs of children under the age of 12 engaging in anti-social activities such as physical aggression/assault, break and enter, vandalism, and shoplifting/theft. The program, developed in Ontario in 1985, addresses such risk factors as poor self-control, poor problem solving, poor impulse control, bullying, delinquency, aggression and violence, anti-social values and conduct, cognitive distortions or thinking errors, problematic parent management strategies and parent–child interactions, authority contact, school failure, and isolation.

The "SNAP® technique" is a cognitive behavioural strategy intended to help children control impulsivity, think about the consequences of their behaviour, and develop a socially appropriate plan. Originally, the clinician would "snap her fingers" to cue a child to begin the SNAP® process. The program now uses coloured lights as a visual cue for the children: Red Light (STOP), Yellow Light (NOW AND), Green Light (PLAN). These steps are used to help children regulate angry feelings by helping them, first, to calm down, second, to use coping statements to remain calm, and, third, to generate effective solutions to make their problems smaller, so as to not hurt anyone, anything, or themselves.

As clinicians worked with the children, it became evident that girls were often withdrawn or not supportive of one another. Because there were additional risk factors for many of the girls, including high prevalence for risk for abuse, strained mother–daughter relationships, and difficult family dynamics, it was determined that there was a need for a gender-specific program based on feminist principles. The girls' program includes all the components of the original (social learning, self-control, and problem-solving), but also assertiveness and anti-oppression training to these largely mother-led families, as well as a focus on relationship building.

During the early 1990s, a risk–protective assessment tool was developed known as the Early Assessment Risk Lists (EARL). In one study, it was shown that 92 percent of at-risk boys and 95 percent of at-risk girls who had completed the SNAP® program had no history of criminal offences by age 15, and more than two-thirds were projected to not have a criminal record by age 19.

The developers of this program suggest that it costs about $110,000 per year to keep a youth in a secure custody facility in Canada, which would yield an estimated cost of $1,143,604 for a career criminal if no early intervention were provided. The SNAP® program estimates a cost savings of $7 for every dollar spent in the first year of the program.

For more information, see http://www.childdevelop.ca/snap/.

SOURCE: Augimeri, Farrington, Koegl, & Day (2007); Augimeri, Walsh, & Slater (2011); Pepler et al. (2010); Koegl, Farrington, Augimeri, & Day (2008).

QUESTION

The SNAP® program is sensitive to gender in its design. What kinds of things would you expect to notice in program participants that might alert you to the need to consider gender-specific programming?

Family Domain

Research has shown that family factors include such items as parenting styles, inconsistent and harsh discipline, parental criminality, and poor parental supervision. A review of research reports (Latimer, 2001; Henneberger, Durkee, Truong, Atkins, & Tolan, 2013) on the relationship between problem families and youth criminality notes:

- Families where there is no serious conflict between spouses are associated with lower rates of youth criminality.

- Single-parent families are associated with higher rates of youthful deviance. However, it is not the status of single-parenthood that is the predictor; it is the stresses often associated with this kind of family, such as family instability, economic deprivation, and reduction in parental supervision.

- Involvement in criminal behaviour by parents or by other children in the family is strongly associated with youthful criminality.

- Parental supervision and parental affection shown toward children during childhood appear to be the two most important positive family factors that deter later adult criminal behaviour.

There have been a number of sponsored general parenting "resource" programs based on the developmental importance of the very early childhood years. In recent years, programs have been developed to specifically teach parents how to work more effectively with their older children in the early adolescent years.

STRENGTHENING FAMILIES PROGRAM

The Strengthening Families Program (SFP) is an evidence-based 14-session family skills program. The youth and his or her parents come together for each of the sessions and at the outset a meal is served together with the counsellors and all participants. This is not only an incentive for families to participate, but also a venue for the families to observe communication strategies that are being modelled by the trainers and program staff, and to practise family communication skills in a group atmosphere.

After the meal, the group is split into two: the parents work with a trainer on parent skills, and the youth works with another trainer on a curriculum designed to enhance life skills, communication strategies, and problem-solving. This session lasts for about an hour, and then the two groups get back with the trainers as a large group to review and practise their skills.

A family history of alcoholism and substance abuse is a risk factor due to both the genetic dimension of addiction and the strained family relationships. Other family factors with an impact on youth are excessively high family conflict, low parent–child attachment, poor parenting skills, inappropriate discipline techniques, lack of pro-social role modelling, little supervision and monitoring of youth activities, and few if any opportunities to share family values and positive leisure activities. When these factors are present, family interaction has a negative impact.

It follows that such risk factors must be countered by protective factors. In well-functioning families, parents find opportunities to acknowledge achievements and talents and to offer critical insights about key life choices. When family values are promoted that draw attention to the skills, talents, and abilities of family members, it creates opportunities for pro-social connections outside the family with peers and community associations.

For more information, see http://www.strengtheningfamiliesprogram.org.

SOURCE: Kumpfer, Alvarado, & Whiteside (2003); Strengthening Families Program (2014).

QUESTIONS

1. What difficulties might there be in implementing the SFP crime prevention program for high-risk families?

2. What kinds of things (conditions, incentives, etc.) would you want to have in place to ensure high participation and retention over the 14-session program?

The Domain of Peers and School

Perhaps the most obvious risk factor for youth offending is affiliation with anti-social peers. Within the school domain, truancy, poor academic performance, lack of school engagement, and aggressive behaviour at school have been shown to relate to youth offending (Zimmerman & Rees, 2014). The lack of opportunities to engage with pro-social peers or rejection by peers also affects youthful offending (Carlo et al., 2014).

QUANTUM OPPORTUNITIES PROGRAM FOR HIGH-RISK YOUTH

Research has shown consistently that both academic failure and school dropout are risk factors highly correlated with criminal activity. The Quantum Opportunities Program (QOP), launched by the American Youth Policy Forum (AYPF) in 1989, is a long-term, multi-component intervention program that aims to reduce dropout rates, pregnancy, and delinquency among disadvantaged high school students. The program targets students entering grade 9 who come from low-income families, and supports them for the full four years they are in high school.

The interventions of QOP are made up of three general components: educational activities, developmental activities, and service activities. Students complete 250 hours of activity per year in each component, or 750 hours per year, and a total of 3,000 hours of participation over the four years of the project.

1. *Educational activities.* These are intended to improve academic achievement and increase the likelihood of graduation from high school and attending college or university. They normally consist in tutoring, homework help, computer skills training, learning skills and strategies (organization skills, time management, and effective study habits), and coaching to help overcome challenges posed by learning disabilities or low literacy skills.

2. *Developmental activities.* These are intended to reduce risky behaviours, problematic life choices, and anti-social, aggressive, or violent behaviour. They include training and coaching related to effective decision-making skills, employment skills, healthy lifestyles, relationship skills, social skills, and knowledge of how to access community resources.

3. *Service activities.* These are intended to help youth develop a sense of pride and responsibility for themselves and for others in their neighbourhood; feel a sense of belonging and ownership in their community; learn teamwork, planning, judgment, and social skills; develop interests leading to future education and employment choices; connect to resources that will be helpful in creating opportunities; and break down their social exclusion and marginalization through engagement in positive community activities and events. Activities can include volunteering, participating in community events, fundraising, participating in campaigns, neighbourhood cleanups and environmental improvements, sports teams, public speaking, team-building exercises, and other, similar activities.

An important element of QOP is reinforcing effort, progress, and achievement with incentives. As young persons achieve certain weekly, monthly, quarterly, or annual milestones (for example, completing 250 hours of annual activity in a particular component of their contract), they are offered rewards such as field trips to cultural or social events in the community, attendance at sports events, or enrollment in recreational and sports activities.

One of the essential ingredients of the program is continued involvement of the counsellors in the lives of the young people regardless of whether they have been removed from the formal school system through expulsion, are ill, are incarcerated, or have moved to a different neighbourhood.

Canadian Implementation of QOP

The Canadian implementation of QOP was funded through the National Crime Prevention Centre in New Brunswick and Ontario and run by the John Howard Society in two provinces. Youth were screened for entry using a risk assessment tool (JCP) that ensured that the participants in the program were indeed at high or very high risk for criminal involvement.

After four years in the program, there was a significant increase in protective factors and a reduction in risk factors. The youth referred to the program had not been considered likely to complete grade 9. But at the end of the four years more than half the active participants had graduated on time, and an additional group (about 20 percent) were set to graduate the following year. The 20 percent who were not in school at the end did continue to be engaged with the counsellors.

As you will see by Figure 9.1, from year 1 to year 2 and subsequent years, as the strengths scores increased and the youth began to feel connected to school and community, the risk scores for criminal and risky behaviour decreased.

FIGURE 9.1   Average Yearly Strength and Risk Scores (Quantum)

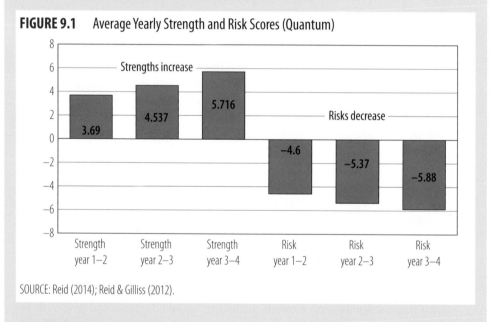

SOURCE: Reid (2014); Reid & Gilliss (2012).

QUESTIONS

1. What are the main risks and/or needs addressed by the Quantum program?
2. What components do you think are the most useful for reducing risk for criminal involvement?
3. Why do you think these components are so useful?

The Domain of Community and Society

Disorganized communities, the availability of drugs and alcohol, and a lack of amenities such as access to sports, leisure, and other activities are factors that contribute to youth feeling that they don't belong and to an increased risk of youth crime. As was discussed in Chapter 2, although some of these communities still experience many of the precursors to criminal behaviour such as unemployment, poverty, and family disruption, those that promote actions that value diversity, identity, and equality while supporting and encouraging youth to become contributing members of society appear to be most helpful in reducing the risks of living in such communities. The following section addresses various policing styles that focus on community problem solving.

Community and Problem-Oriented Policing

Many North American cities have developed community policing that gives officers a more visible presence by having them patrol on foot, get to know people in the neighbourhood, use neighbourhood substations, and involve themselves in community ventures and activities. One might assume that this kind of policing leads to more arrests and reduces street crime in the short run; but there is evidence that the criminals simply move somewhere else. When aggressive policing clears those people the police think likely to commit offences from an area, the crime rate in those areas certainly goes down, at least initially. But critics charge that the problem does not go away because the factors giving rise to it have not gone away (Wortley et al., 2008, p. 252).

One type of crime prevention policing strategy that attempts to both provide aggressive policing and attend to community needs has come to be known as the "weed and seed" program. This strategy takes a two-staged approach: law enforcement agencies and prosecutors cooperate in "weeding out" violent criminals, while community-based organizations work together to "seed" much-needed human services, including prevention, intervention, treatment, and neighbourhood restoration programs. Unfortunately, there has been a tendency for "weed" to overshadow "seed," because it gets more attention in terms of political will, enthusiasm from law enforcement agencies, and, most important, funding from federal agencies (Bridenball & Jesilow, 2005). The evidence so far on aggressive police strategies suggests that the approach is costly and does not, in fact, reduce crime—and may increase distrust between the community and the police.

Community policing includes three basic elements: (1) community partnership or engagement; (2) a problem-solving orientation; and (3) a focus on administrative decentralization (Skogan, 2006). However, when the police engage in community policing that focuses on relationship building as opposed to aggressive arresting, the results are more promising. While some law enforcement officials and academics view community policing as a *philosophy* to better explain police work, most in the field of policing view it as an actual policing *technique*. In any case, its fundamental principle is that police become an integral part of the community and the community assists in determining the priorities and goals and the allocation of resources.

One of the first Canadian police forces to adopt such a framework was the Halton Regional Police, in 1985. The "constable generalist" was primary, with a move away from specialized squads such as youth services bureaus. He or she was expected to spend at least half the time on duty in proactive community policing.

Another form of community policing has been adopted by the RCMP in New Brunswick. A civilian referred to as a *community programs officer* has the main responsibility of looking at issues of crime prevention. He or she also supports the work of community groups in creating programs to address social problems.

Schools have long sought to promote crime control indirectly, by reinforcing good manners and respect for authority. Some schools also take more direct crime control action—for example, by inviting law enforcement officers to participate as guest speakers—in an effort to dispel student mistrust of police and to educate students about the role of police in society. In some communities, police officers work out of substations located right inside high schools.

1. Does your local police force incorporate a community policing framework?

2. What kinds of questions would you ask police in your local community to better understand the concept of community policing?

3. Did your high school have a police officer in the school? What are the positive and negative features of this community policing model?

Predicting Highest-Risk Youth

So far in this chapter, we have reviewed the risk and protective factors introduced in Chapter 2 and noted that not all children and young people exposed to multiple risk factors become offenders (Steinberg, Blatt-Eisengart, & Cauffman, 2006).

How Many Youth Are High-Risk?

The evidence from many meta-analyses is clear (Andrews & Bonta, 2010): intervening with low-risk cases is likely to increase recidivism. First-time, minor offenders should not receive an intensive, rehabilitative sanction; however, if we provide the most intensive programming for the high-risk offenders, we are likely to reduce recidivism.

About 35 percent of Canadian youth are not involved in criminal behaviour of any sort, and would not come to the attention of the youth justice system or any other social service agency. They are engaged in school and recreation, and, emotionally and academically, are pro-social and well adjusted. An additional 25 percent of Canadian youth are at low risk for engaging in anti-social behaviour, but have shown some signs of defiance toward persons in authority, and may be showing early signs of problems with academic performance and/or affiliation with anti-social peers.

Moderate-risk youth account for about 20 percent of the total youth population, and are likely to be involved in some forms of conflict with the law or with school authorities. They may have been suspended or expelled from school, they may have had a family history of violence, they may have been victimized or bullied, and they may live in a disorganized neighbourhood.

Youth in the high-risk group account for about 15 percent of the youth population, and may have several of the risk factors acting upon them at the same time. Very high-risk youth account for about 5 percent of the youth population, and are responsible for most of the very serious crime or violence in the community. These persons are usually quite well known to police, social service agencies, and schools.

In other words, 80 percent of Canadian youth are at either no, low, or moderate risk for criminal offending. It is important to remember that no single risk factor leads a young person to commit crime, and that risk factors do not operate in isolation but depend on the context of a person's experiences. The more risk factors youth are exposed to, the greater the likelihood they will experience negative outcomes. When the risk factors that a youth is exposed to cross multiple domains, the likelihood of involvement in crime increases at an even greater rate.

1. Think of some people you may have gone to school with in your teen years. How does the breakdown of 35 percent no risk, 25 percent low risk, 20 percent moderate risk, 15 percent high risk, and 5 percent very high risk for criminal behaviour apply to them?

2. What kinds of behaviour were the high-risk ones you remember engaged in, and how were they dealt with at your school and in your community?

The Central Eight Predictors of Criminal Involvement

Andrews and Bonta (2010) have provided a summary of the meta-analyses in this area, and have found eight domains that have come to be referred to as the **central eight predictors**. The top four predictors of future offending include a history of criminal behaviour; anti-social personality pattern; anti-social attitudes, values, beliefs, and cognitive-emotional states; and anti-social associates. The other four domains are low levels of protective factors in the domains of family, school, and work, and the presence of substance abuse.

Perhaps the most widely used risk assessment tool is the *Youth Level of Service/Case Management Inventory* (YLS/CMI) (Hoge & Andrews, 2003), which includes the following eight domains in a 42-item assessment: criminal history, family circumstances, education and employment, peer group association, substance use, leisure or recreation, personality or behaviour, and attitudes or criminal orientation. The YLS/CMI has demonstrated its effectiveness in predicting overall rates of recidivism (Olver, Stockdale, & Wormith, 2009). However, it is not a diagnostic tool. If any one of the domains in the YLS/CMI is of clinical concern when assessing a young person, it is essential that a full assessment using other measures be conducted in order to determine appropriate interventions (Holsinger, Lowenkamp, & Latessa, 2006).

A screening version of the YLS/CMI was developed by Hoge and Andrews (2004) and is known as the *Youth Level of Service/Case Management Inventory: Screening Version* (YLS/CMI: SV). It is being used by front-line police in the New Brunswick RCMP and the Ottawa Police Services (Hall, Logue, & Shaw, 2011; Public Safety Canada, n.d.). Officers, in their initial interview with all chargeable youth, consider the central eight predictors. In this interview, officers are making a professional judgment to ensure that all low- to moderate-risk youth are being considered for extrajudicial measures.

In an analysis of the Ottawa Community Youth Diversion Program (OCYDP), which utilizes the YLS/CMI, those youth who completed the diversion program were much less likely to recidivate at 6, 12, or 18 months follow-up than their peers who either partially completed the program or did not comply (Wilson & Hoge, 2013).

A meta-analysis of youth diversion programs conducted by Wilson and Hoge (2012) revealed that programs that were primarily police cautions were more effective in reducing recidivism for low-risk offenders than ones that provided some form of intervention. The analysis concluded that "low-risk youth referred to caution programs were 2.44 times less likely to reoffend," while the same low-risk youth that were referred to an intervention program were only "1.49 times less likely to reoffend" (p. 507).

> Consider some of the challenges front-line officers might face when using a brief assessment to screen for the eight domains (prior criminal involvement, attending school/work, family involvement, recreation and leisure activities, alcohol or drug problems, pro-criminal friends, and pro-criminal attitudes) and make a decision on whether to charge a young person or administer a caution. What would encourage police to use this type of screening tool?

In a study of the highest-risk young offenders (that is, the top 5 percent) in the Netherlands (Mulder, Brand, Bullens, & Van Marle, 2011), it was found that while several of the static factors were present in the most **severe recidivists** (for example, early onset, poor parenting), a number of dynamic factors were present also: contact with criminal peers, lack of positive coping mechanisms, incidents or aggression at the youth custodial facility, and lack of adherence to a treatment program. For the violent recidivists, involvement in the criminal environment (measured at the start of treatment), lack of insight, lack of emotional support, lack of positive coping (defined as lack of help-seeking and support-seeking as a

central eight predictors
the eight predictors of criminal involvement: (1) a history of criminal behaviour; (2) anti-social personality pattern; (3) anti-social attitudes, values, beliefs, and cognitive-emotional states; (4) anti-social associates; low levels of protective factors in the domains (5) of family, (6) of school, and (7) of work; and (8) the presence of substance abuse

severe recidivists
the 5 percent of offenders with the highest recidivism rates

problem-solving strategy), escape, and lack of treatment adherence and motivation were the dynamic risk factors that were scored higher than they were for their non-violent peers. This suggests that it is essential to consider the impact of the correctional environment in which young people are placed to serve their sentences.

Effective Interventions and the Responsivity Principle

Individualized Programs Grounded in Cognitive Behavioural Theory

Bonta and Andrews (2007, p. 6) have provided a summary chart (Table 9.2) based on the central eight predictors of criminal involvement that outlines the risk factors, the indicators, and the most suitable intervention.

TABLE 9.2   Predictors of Criminal Involvement, Indicators, and Interventions

Major risk–need factor	Indicators	Intervention goals
Anti-social personality pattern	Impulsive, adventurous, pleasure seeking, restlessly aggressive and irritable	Build self-management skills, teach anger management
Pro-criminal attitudes	Rationalizations for crime, negative attitudes toward the law	Counter rationalizations with pro-social attitudes; build up a pro-social identity
Social supports for crime	Criminal friends, isolation from pro-social others	Replace pro-criminal friends and associates with pro-social friends and associates
Substance abuse	Abuse of alcohol and/or drugs	Reduce substance abuse, enhance alternatives to substance use
Family/marital relationships	Inappropriate parental monitoring and disciplining, poor family relationships	Teach parenting skills, enhance warmth and caring
School/work	Poor performance, low levels of satisfaction	Enhance work/study skills, nurture interpersonal relationships within the context of work and school
Pro-social recreational activities	Lack of involvement in pro-social recreational/leisure activities	Encourage participation in pro-social recreational activities, teach pro-social hobbies and sports

SOURCE: Adapted from Bonta & Andrews (2007, Table 1).

responsivity principle
the idea that in order to maximize the offender's ability to learn from a rehabilitative intervention, it is necessary to tie the program to the evidence that has been shown to be successful in reducing recidivism

bio-social
characterized by the interaction of biological and social factors

cognitive behavioural treatment
an effective form of intervention that helps patients to understand the thoughts and feelings that influence behaviours; focuses on how people think ("cognitive") and act ("behavioural")

The **responsivity principle** suggests that in order to maximize the offender's ability to learn from a rehabilitative intervention, it is necessary to tie the program to the evidence that has been shown to be successful in reducing recidivism. It is important to tailor the intervention to individuals in terms of their strengths, learning style, personality, and motivation for intervention. Further, effective responsivity interventions are careful to design gender-specific programming and adhere to cultural traditions based on race—the **bio-social** characteristics of the individual.

Cognitive behavioural treatment has been shown to be the most effective form of intervention provided that it is matched to the learning style, motivation, abilities, and strengths of the person (Dowden & Andrews, 2004). In the delivery of programs, it is important to establish a warm, respectful, and collaborative working relationship. How these relationships can be developed is discussed in the next section.

Research (Ezell & Cohen, 2005) has demonstrated that custodial programs (jail), their main concern being security and not treatment, have not shown much success in reducing recidivism, particularly when large and overcrowded. Greenwood and Turner (2011) identify three problems with institutional treatment. First, putting groups of serious-offending youth together makes it much more likely they will support each other in their offending behaviour. Second, institutional programs often create an artificial environment, making it difficult for youth to apply what they learn in real-world situations. Finally, residential treatment is expensive, costing "at least three times the cost of intensive non-residential programs" (p. 501).

For the small minority of serious youth offenders, there are empirically sound and convincing reports indicating that theoretically grounded, adequately staffed, and well-documented programs that involve institutional treatment can have impressive positive effects (Caldwell, Vitacco, & Van Rybroek, 2006). Institutional programs that rely on a cognitive behavioural approach have shown higher reductions in recidivism than programs that are not grounded in this theory (Lipsey & Cullen, 2007).

In summary, effective programs appear to have the following characteristics:

- They are designed to target crime-related characteristics that can be changed (dynamic factors) and that are predictive of future criminal activities.
- The requirements of the program are such that the individual must spend sufficient time considering the changes desired.
- The program is implemented in such a way that it is appropriate for the age and stage of development of the participant, and uses methods based on social learning or cognitive behavioural theories of change that emphasize positive reinforcement and provide contingencies for social behaviour.
- The program is delivered by well-trained staff who are knowledgeable and skilled.
- The most intensive programs are delivered to those at the highest risk of reoffending and are individualized as much as possible.

An emerging body of literature demonstrates that the social climate of an institutional setting (for example, its orderliness or harshness) affects the subsequent community outcomes of adolescent offenders in that setting (Schubert, Mulvey, Loughran, & Losoya, 2012).

Relationship Building with Probation Officers and Custodial Staff

The YCJA gives youth probation officers the freedom to decide which official methods to use in ensuring that the principle of the YCJA is reached. These methods might include referring youth to counselling services, encouraging parental involvement in the youth's life, and collaborating with schools to ensure the attendance of the probationer.

In a study of 308 probation officers, the researchers found that younger and high-risk youth with prior child welfare or social service involvement were more likely to receive more intensive interventions (Schwalbe & Maschi, 2009). These interventions included both the threat of breach of probation for those disobeying their order and more intensive counselling and referral to other service providers.

A more recent qualitative study of 20 youth probation officers in the Greater Toronto Area looked at the strategies the officers used in working with their probation case load. Almost all the officers reported the need to appear non-judgmental in order to gain the trust of their clients. Despite the severity of the offence committed, the officers reported that it was important to understand the difficult life circumstances the youth had been through and felt it essential to show empathy. Similarly, many of the officers reported that while the youth had made bad choices, they were not "bad people" and it was important to help guide the youth to capitalize on their "alternative stories" or the parts of their lives when they were not engaged in criminal behaviour. In order to fulfill their role as probation officers with youth, they reported the need to be both a support and an authority, and that while this was sometimes difficult to balance, it was essential for changing the young person (Umamaheswar, 2013).

The focus on the ability of the young person to make the needed changes to his or her patterns of behaviour has been shown in the research literature to be an effective strategy for reducing recidivism (Gottfredson, 2013). The majority of probation officers reported that this was done not only by holding the young people accountable, but also by celebrating small successes as the young person showed progress in changing behaviour.

Because probation officers are responsible for the preparation of pre-sentence reports (see Chapter 8), their role with respect to the young person is essential in gathering the necessary information to make an informed report to the court. When youth are sentenced to a term of probation, the research discussed above suggests that the quality of the relationship between the probation officer and the young person is an important consideration. It is equally important to consider this research in light of the fact that the YCJA has created a term of reintegration at the end of each custodial sentence that will be supervised by a probation officer. There is a strong likelihood that the highest-risk offenders come in contact with a probation officer at some point, either before sentencing, as a term of probation they are serving as a sentence, or upon completion of their term of custody.

CELLPHONE REMINDERS AND RECIDIVISM AMONG PROBATIONERS

While the research literature is clear that cognitive behavioural programs are the most successful in changing the thinking patterns of offenders, some have argued that it is equally important to supplement such programs with practice. The results of a study of 70 juvenile probationers given a cognitive training program for six weeks, followed by cellphone messages once a day for a year, indicated that not only did those given cognitive training do better than those who did not, but those given reminders on cellphones did best of all.

After a six-week in-class cognitive training program, the participants set personal goals with lists of specific activities that would help them accomplish both short- and long-term goals. After the goal setting, the youth decided how often they would be called. Each call consisted of three short questions: (1) whether they had followed their goal since the last call, (2) how much effort they had put toward achieving that goal, and (3) what results they got. The youth answered by text, and if there had been progress toward goals, a pre-recorded positive message was played at the end of the call. If help was required, a pre-recorded encouragement message was played. The messages could be recorded by friends, family, or anyone the participant invited and might be updated at any time, as suggested by participants or probation officers.

After one year of the cellphone messages, it was found that the median days to first arrest for the control group (that is, those who did not receive the cognitive training or the cellphone reminders) was 106 days. For the youth who received the cognitive behavioural training but did not have the cellphone messages, the figure was 191. For the group that received the cognitive training and the cellphone calls, the figure was 278. Ninety percent of the control participants had been rearrested, compared with 55 percent of the class-only group and 54 percent of the class-plus-cellphone group.

SOURCE: Burraston, Cherrington, & Bahr (2012).

QUESTIONS

1. What are some of the advantages of the cellphone reminders?

2. How, if in any way, do the automatic telephone calls enhance the relationship with the probation officer?

Positive relationships with adults are essential as a protective factor for youth who may be enmeshed in the youth justice system (Lipsey, 2009), and have become part of the **relationship custody framework** that guides the work with young persons in custody throughout the province of Ontario. The relationship custody approach requires staff not only to work from a strengths-based approach that reinforces the skills and talents of the young person, but also to engage young people, model appropriate behaviour to youth and other staff members, and develop a rapport that supports the young person to make more positive choices. It requires a balance between the dynamic security approaches (professional, positive relationships between youth and staff) and the static security approaches (physical barriers and surveillance).

Implementation of the framework has not been smooth. In 2009, a 192-bed secure custody facility called the Roy McMurtry Centre was opened in Brampton, Ontario. But soon, complaints made to the Office of the Child and Youth Advocate resulted in an investigation that uncovered numerous deficiencies. While the majority of young persons could identify at least one staff person who sufficiently embodied the philosophy behind the framework, 52 percent told of staff who left them feeling disrespected. They gave examples of rules being followed, changed, ignored, or disregarded depending on who was on shift (Provincial Advocate for Children and Youth, 2013).

Schubert et al. (2012) report that youth who do not feel they can turn to staff for help are more likely to have difficulty in post-release outcomes. Marsh and Evans (2009) found, as well, that when youth in a closed custody setting were asked to determine the qualities of staff members they respected, high levels of trust, positive affect for the youth, high levels of engagement, and effective problem-solving skills were cited. Those youth who spoke of staff having these qualities were also more likely to believe they would achieve significant success after their release.

> What qualities are necessary for correctional officers to maintain security while also encouraging youth to adopt more pro-social behaviour?

relationship custody framework

a balance between the dynamic security approaches (professional, positive relationships between youth and staff) and the static security approaches (physical barriers and surveillance) involved in correctional institutions

From "Nothing Works" to "What Works"

In 1974, authors Douglas Lipton, Robert Martinson, and J. Wilks, using meta-analysis, assessed all the evaluations of criminal rehabilitation programs between 1945 and 1967. They reached the following conclusion: "With few and isolated exceptions, the rehabilitative efforts that have been reported so far have had no appreciable effect on recidivism" (Martinson, 1974, p. 25). These results convinced them that not much works, and that no program seemed any more effective than any other. It did not seem to matter whether offenders were sentenced to prison or put on probation. Nor did it matter how long offenders were imprisoned, or what kind of prison-based programs they participated in, or whether they were in group-based or community-based programs.

Robert Martinson made this conclusion available much more widely when he published a short piece in *The Public Interest* (1974) asserting that "nothing works," and that phrase has been associated with his name ever since. Martinson's analysis has often been used to justify abandonment of rehabilitation in favour of classical deterrence. Using the rationale proposed by Martinson, many proponents of deterrence argue that if attempts to rehabilitate do not work, then we can at least jail offenders and, by doing so, incapacitate them. In a 1978 publication he admitted that they had left out of their study some pieces of research that might have shown rehabilitation to be more effective than they had publicly stated (Martinson, 1978). The phrase "nothing works," however, became the mantra of those opposed to rehabilitation and had some influence in moving the public away from programs of rehabilitation and toward retribution or deterrence as justifications for punishment.

Since the creation of the first juvenile justice system in Canada under the *Juvenile Delinquents Act* in 1908, preference has been given to the welfare model in working with young people who commit offences. Some critics of the system's reliance on this model argued the need to get tougher; however, return to the tenets of the adult system was contrary to the emerging literature, which argued convincingly that putting low-risk, low-need offenders in intensive rehabilitation programs might do more harm than good.

This finding led some advocates to propose a system of **radical non-intervention**. This approach is based on the belief that doing nothing at all is sometimes superior than using the machinery of the criminal justice system. The more intervention and labelling of low-risk youth, the theory goes, the more likely the net will be widened. This would mean we would have more offenders coming into the system rather than fewer.

One of the successes of the *Youth Criminal Justice Act* has been in its insistence on strategies outside the formal youth justice process, including extrajudicial measures and sanctions. However, there are times—and offenders—that call for some type of formal processing. When we intervene in the lives of young people, we need to be mindful of what approaches have been shown to work.

radical non-intervention

an approach to justice that advocates not intervening with a low-risk offender, to avoid having a young person labelled criminal by the criminal justice system; based on the belief that criminal justice processing of youth can lead to more offenders coming into the system

1. Where have you seen the mantra of "nothing works" portrayed in the media?

2. What provisions have been added to the YCJA on the basis of the minority of offenders who commit serious youth crime that reflect retribution and deterrence?

3. Given what you now know about the effectiveness of deterrence, what might you suggest as an alternative to these approaches?

CHAPTER SUMMARY

The underlying theme of the *Youth Criminal Justice Act* is that every young person can be rehabilitated, and as demonstrated in this chapter, the intervention options available are as varied as the youth themselves. Reserved for the smallest percentage of highest-risk youth are direct interventions such as probation and incarceration; but for the majority, a more complex process of understanding risk and protective factors is required. With this grasp of the factors involved, of the youth themselves, and of the social context, the most beneficial intervention can be applied (or even no intervention at all). While understanding youth criminality prevention and rehabilitation is not a one-size-fits-all science, what we have learned is that dealing with youth criminality is the responsibility of the entire community.

KEY TERMS

bio-social, 210
central eight predictors, 209
cognitive behavioural treatment, 210
crime prevention through environmental design, 200
crime prevention through social development, 200
criminogenic needs, 202
dynamic risk factors, 201
incarceration, 197
meta-analysis, 197
primary crime prevention, 200
probation, 196
protective factors, 202

radical non-intervention, 214
relationship custody framework, 213
resilience, 201
responsivity principle, 210
risk–needs–responsivity (RNR) model, 201
secondary crime prevention, 200
self-system beliefs, 202
severe recidivists, 209
shock incarceration, 199
static risk factors, 201
tertiary crime prevention, 200

REFERENCES

Andrews, D.A., & Bonta, J. (2010). *The psychology of criminal conduct* (5th ed.). New Providence, NJ: LexisNexis/Matthew Bender.

Andrews, D.A., & Dowden, C. (2007). The risk–need–responsivity model of assessment and human service in prevention and corrections: Crime-prevention jurisprudence. *Canadian Journal of Criminology and Criminal Justice, 49*, 439–464.

Andrews, D.A., Zinger, I., Hoge, R.D., Bonta, J., Gendreau, P., & Cullen, F.T. (1990). Does correctional treatment work? A clinically relevant and psychologically informed meta-analysis. *Criminology, 28*, 369–404.

Augimeri, L.K., Farrington, D.P., Koegl, C.J., & Day, D.M. (2007). The Under 12 Outreach Project: Effects of a community based program for children with conduct problems. *Journal of Child and Family Studies, 16*, 799–807.

Augimeri, L.K., Walsh, M., & Slater, N. (2011). Rolling out SNAP®: An evidence-based intervention: A summary of implementation, evaluation and research. *International Journal of Child, Youth and Family Studies, 2*(1), 330–352.

Bala, N. (1997). *Young offenders law*. Toronto: Irwin Law.

Bonta, J., & Andrews, D.A. (2007, June). *Risk–need–responsivity model for offender assessment and rehabilitation*. Ottawa: Public Safety Canada. Retrieved from http://www.publicsafety.gc.ca/cnt/rsrcs/pblctns/rsk-nd-rspnsvty/index-eng.aspx.

Brantingham, P., Brantingham, P.J., & Taylor, W. (2005). Situational crime prevention as a key component in embedded crime prevention. *Canadian Journal of Criminology & Criminal Justice, 47*(2), 271–292.

Bridenball, B., & Jesilow, P. (2005). Weeding criminals or planting fear: An evaluation of a weed and seed project. *Criminal Justice Review, 30*(1), 64–89.

Burraston, B.O., Cherrington, D.J., & Bahr, S.J. (2012). Reducing juvenile recidivism with cognitive training and a cell phone follow-up: An evaluation of the RealVictory Program. *International Journal of Offender Therapy and Comparative Criminology, 56*(1), 61–80.

Caldwell, M.F., Vitacco, M., & Van Rybroek, G.J. (2006). Are violent delinquents worth treating? A cost–benefit analysis. *Journal of Research in Crime and Delinquency, 43*(2), 148–168.

Carlo, G., Mestre, M.V., McGinley, M.M., Tur-Porcar, A., Samper, P., & Opal, D. (2014). The protective role of prosocial behaviors on antisocial behaviors: The mediating effects of deviant peer affiliation. *Journal of Adolescence, 37*(4), 359–366.

Clear, T. (2007). *Imprisoning communities: How mass incarceration makes disadvantaged neighborhoods worse*. New York: Oxford University Press.

Cullen, F.T., Blevins, K.R., Trager, J.S., & Gendreau, P. (2005). The rise and fall of boot camps: A case study in common sense corrections. *Journal of Offender Rehabilitation, 4*(3–4), 53–70.

Dowden, C., & Andrews, D.A. (1999). What works in young offender treatment: A meta-analysis. *Forum on Corrections Research, 11*(2), 21–24.

Dowden, C., & Andrews, D.A. (2004). The importance of staff practices in delivering effective correctional treatment: A meta-analysis of core correctional practices. *International Journal of Offender Therapy and Comparative Criminology, 48*, 203–214.

Drake, E.K., Aos, S., & Miller, M.G. (2009). Evidence-based public policy options to reduce crime and criminal justice costs: Implications in Washington State. *Victims and Offenders, 4*, 170–196.

Ezell, M.E., & Cohen, L.E. (2005). *Desisting from crime: Continuity and change in long-term crime patterns of serious chronic offenders*. New York: Oxford University Press.

Finckenauer, J. (1982). *Scared Straight and the panacea phenomenon* (Englewood Cliffs, NJ: Prentice Hall).

Gottfredson, G.D. (2013). What can schools do to help prevent gang-joining? In T.R. Simon, N.M. Ritter, & R.R. Mahendra (Eds.), *Changing course: Preventing gang membership* (pp. 89–104). Washington, DC: US Department of Justice, National Institute of Justice.

Government of Canada. (2014a). Model and promising crime prevention programs. Vol. 1. Retrieved from http://www.publicsafety.gc.ca/cnt/rsrcs/pblctns/prmsng-mdl-vlm1/index-eng.aspx.

Government of Canada. (2014b). Model and promising crime prevention programs. Vol. 2. Retrieved from http://www.publicsafety.gc.ca/cnt/rsrcs/pblctns/prmsng-mdl-vlm2/index-eng.aspx.

Greenwood, P.W., & Turner, S. (2011). Establishing effective community-based care in juvenile justice. *Juvenile Justice: Advancing Research, Policy, and Practice*, 477–504.

Guerra, N.G., & Williams, K.R. (2012). Implementing evidence-based practices for juvenile justice in communities (pp. 297–307). In E.L. Grigorenko (Ed.), *Handbook of juvenile forensic psychology and psychiatry*. New Haven, CT: Springer.

Hall, S., Logue, L., & Shaw, R. (2011). The rural approach to youth diversion, no easy fix. *Gazette, 74*(1), 15. Retrieved from http://www.rcmp-grc.gc.ca/gazette/vol74n1/coverstory-reportage-eng.htm#ops.

Henneberger, A.K., Durkee, M.I., Truong, N., Atkins, A., & Tolan, P.H. (2013). The longitudinal relationship between peer violence and popularity and delinquency in adolescent boys: Examining effects by family functioning. *Journal of Youth and Adolescence, 42*(11), 1651–1660.

Hoge, R.D., & Andrews, D.A. (2003). *Youth Level of Service/Case Management Inventory (YLS/CMI)*. Toronto: Multi-Health Systems.

Hoge, R.D., & Andrews, D.A. (2004). *Youth Level of Service/Case Management Inventory (YLS/CMI): Screening Version*. Toronto: Multi-Health Systems.

Holsinger, A.M., Lowenkamp, C.T., & Latessa, E.J. (2006). Predicting institutional misconduct using the Youth Level of Service/Case Management Inventory. *American Journal of Criminal Justice, 30*, 267–284.

Johnson, L.M., Simons, R.L., & Conger, R.D. (2004). Criminal justice system involvement and continuity of youth crime: A longitudinal analysis. *Youth and Society, 36*(1), 3–29.

Koegl, C.J., Farrington, D.P., Augimeri, L.K., & Day, D.M. (2008). Evaluation of a targeted cognitive-behavioural programme for children with conduct problems—The SNAP® Under 12 Outreach Project: Service intensity, age and gender effects on short- and long-term outcomes. *Clinical Child Psychology and Psychiatry, 13*(3), 419–434.

Kumpfer, K.L., Alvarado, R., & Whiteside, H.O. (2003). Family-based interventions for substance use and misuse prevention. *Substance Use and Misuse, 38*, 1759–1787.

Latessa, E.J., Cullen, F.T., & Gendreau, P. (2002). Beyond correctional quackery: Professionalism and the possibility of effective treatment. *Federal Probation, 66*(2), 43–49.

Latimer, J. (2001). A meta-analytical examination of youth delinquency, family treatment, and recidivism. *Canadian Journal of Criminology, 43*(2), 237–253.

Layton-MacKenzie. (2013). First do no harm: A look at correctional policies and programs today. *Journal of Experimental Criminology, 9*(1), 1–17.

Lee, D. (2004, March 25). Teenage fix. *The Guardian*. Retrieved from http://www.guardian.co.uk/education/2004/mar/25/schools.uk.

Lee, M. (2013, July 24). Scared Straight continues despite misgivings. *Juvenile Justice Hub*. Retrieved from http://jjie.org/scared-straight-continues-despite-misgivings/104977/.

Lipsey, M.W. (2009). The primary factors that characterize effective interventions with juvenile offenders: A meta-analytic overview. *Victims and Offenders, 4*, 124–147.

Lipsey, M.W., & Cullen, F.T. (2007). The effectiveness of correctional rehabilitation: A review of systematic reviews. *Annual Review of Law and Social Science, 3*, 297–320.

Lipton, D., Martinson, R., & Wilks, J. (1974). *The effectiveness of correctional treatment: A survey of treatment evaluation studies*. New York: Praeger.

Loeber, R., & Farrington, D.P. (1998). *Serious and violent juvenile offenders: Risk factors and successful interventions*. Thousand Oaks, CA: Sage.

MacKenzie, D., Wilson, D., & Kider, S. (2001). Effects of correctional boot camps on offending. *Annals of the American Academy of Political and Social Science, 578*, 126–143.

MacKenzie, D.L. (2006). *What works in corrections? Reducing the criminal activities of offenders and delinquents*. Cambridge: Cambridge University Press.

Marsh, S.C., & Evans, W.P. (2009). Youth perspectives on their relationships with staff in juvenile correction settings and perceived likelihood of success on release. *Youth Violence and Juvenile Justice, 7*(1), 46–67.

Martinson, R. (1974). What works? Questions and answers about prison reform. *The Public Interest*, (Spring), 22–54.

Martinson, R. (1978). New findings, new views: A note of caution regarding sentencing reform, *Hofstra Law Review, 7*, 242–258.

McNeill, F. (2004). Desistance, rehabilitation and correctionalism: Prospects and developments in Scotland. *Howard Journal of Criminal Justice, 43*, 420–436.

McNeill, F. (2012). Four forms of "offender" rehabilitation: Towards an interdisciplinary perspective. *Legal and Criminological Psychology, 17*(1), 18–36.

Meade, B., & Steiner, B. (2010). The total effects of boot camps that house juveniles: A systematic review of the evidence. *Journal of Criminal Justice, 38*(5), 841–853.

Menon, V. (2005, July 14). Boot camp for teens is abusive. *The Toronto Star*, p. A22.

Mulder, E., Brand, E., Bullens, R., & Van Marle, H. (2011). Risk factors for overall recidivism and severity of recidivism in serious juvenile offenders. *International Journal of Offender Therapy and Comparative Criminology, 55*(1), 118–135.

Nagin, D.S. (2013). Deterrence in the twenty-first century. *Crime and Justice, 42*(1), 199–263.

Olver, M.E., Stockdale, K.E., & Wormith, J.S. (2009). Risk assessment with young offenders: A meta-analysis of three assessment measures. *Criminal Justice and Behavior, 36*, 329–353.

Pepler, D., Walsh, M., Yuile, A., Levene, K., Vaughan, A., & Webber, J. (2010). Bridging the gender gap: Interventions with aggressive girls and their parents. *Prevention Science, 11*(3), 229–238.

Petrosino, A., Turpin-Petrosino, C., & Buehler, J. (2003). Scared Straight and other juvenile awareness programs for preventing delinquency: A systematic review of randomized experimental evidence. *The Annals of the American Academy of Political and Social Science, 589*(1), 41–62.

Provincial Advocate for Children and Youth. (2013). "It depends on who's working." The youth reality at the Roy McMurtry Youth Centre. Retrieved from http://provincialadvocate.on.ca/documents/en/RMYC_report_EN.pdf.

Public Safety Canada. (n.d.). Youth Intervention and Diversion Program (details), Royal Canadian Mounted Police (RCMP)—(J Division). Retrieved from http://www.publicsafety.gc.ca/cnt/cntrng-crm/plcng/cnmcs-plcng/ndx/dtls-eng.aspx?n=54.

Reid, S.A. (2014, June). Presentation to the Atlantic Crime Prevention Conference, Moncton, NB.

Reid, S.A., & Gilliss, S. (2012). Key challenges in hearing the voice of youth in the youth justice system. In J. Winterdyk & R. Smandych (Eds.), *Youth at risk and youth justice: A Canadian overview* (pp. 379–399). Toronto: Oxford University Press.

Resnick, M.D., Harris, I.J., & Blum, R.W. (1993). The impact of caring and connectedness on adolescent health and well-being. *Journal of Paediatric Child Health, 29*, 1–9.

Schubert, C.A., Mulvey, E.P., Loughran, T., & Losoya, S. (2012). Perceptions of institutional experience and community outcomes for serious adolescent offenders. *Criminal Justice and Behavior, 39*(1), 71–93.

Schwalbe, C.S., & Maschi, T. (2009). Investigating probation strategies with juvenile offenders: The influence of officers' attitudes and youth characteristics. *Law and Human Behavior, 33*(5), 357–367.

Serin, R., Forth, A., Brown, S., Nunes, K., Bennell, C., & Pozzula, J. (2011). *Psychology of criminal behaviour: A Canadian perspective*. Toronto: Pearson.

Skogan, W.G. (2006). *Police and community in Chicago: A tale of three cities*. New York: Oxford University Press.

Steinberg, L., Blatt-Eisengart, I., & Cauffman, E. (2006). Patterns of competence and adjustment among adolescents from authoritative, authoritarian, indulgent and neglectful homes: Replication in a sample of serious juvenile offenders. *Journal of Research on Adolescence, 16*, 47–58.

Strengthening Families Program. (2014). Program descriptions. Retrieved from http://www.strengtheningfamiliesprogram.org.

Tremblay, R. (2010). The Montreal Longitudinal Experimental Study: Tracing the developmental trajectories of behaviour problems and assessing their prevention. *International Society of the Study of Behavioural Development Bulletin, 57*(1), 21–24.

Umamaheswar, J. (2013). Bringing hope and change: A study of youth probation officers in Toronto. *International Journal of Offender Therapy and Comparative Criminology, 57*(9), 1158–1182.

Ungar, M. (2004). Resilience among children in child welfare, corrections, mental health and educational settings: Recommendations for service. *Child and Youth Care Forum, 34*(6), 445–464.

Wilson, H.A., & Hoge, R.D. (2012). The effect of youth diversion programs on recidivism: A meta-analytic review. *Criminal Justice and Behavior, 40*(5), 497–518.

Wilson, H.A., & Hoge, R.D. (2013). Diverting our attention to what works evaluating the effectiveness of a youth diversion program. *Youth Violence and Juvenile Justice, 11*(4), 313–331.

Witt, L. (2011, August 22). Disney, take "Beyond Scared Straight" off the air. *Juvenile Justice Information Exchange*. Retrieved from http://jjie.org/disney-take-beyond-scared -straight-off-air/comment-page-1/.

Witt, L. (2013, July 25). Shame on "Beyond Scared Straight" and shame on Douglas County, GA. *Juvenile Justice Information Exchange*. Retrieved from http://jjie.org/editorial-shame-on -beyond-scared-straight-and-shame-on-douglas-county -ga/105000/.

Wong, N.T., Zimmerman, M.A., & Parker, E.A. (2010). A typology of youth participation and empowerment for child and adolescent health promotion. *American Journal of Community Psychology, 46*, 100–114.

Wortley, S., Dorion, J., Levinsky, Z., Owusa-Bempuh, A., Marshall, L., Adhopa, R., Samuels, K., Cook, S., Roberts, S., & Boyce, S. (2008). Preventing youth crime and violence: A review of the literature. In *Review of the roots of violence: Vol. 1. Literature review*. Toronto: Ministry of Children Services. Available at http://www.children.gov.on.ca/ htdocs/English/topics/youthandthelaw/roots/volume5/ preventing01_introduction.aspx.

Youth Criminal Justice Act. (2002). SC 2002, c. 1.

Yu, E. (2014, May 19). At "wit's end": Scared Straight Programs remain popular among parents despite warnings. *Juvenile Justice Hub*. Retrieved from http://jjie.org/at-wits-end -scared-straight-programs-remain-popular-among-parents -despite-warnings/106811/.

Zeldin, S., Larson, R., Camino, L., & O'Connor, C. (2005). Intergenerational relationships and partnerships in community programs: Purpose, practice, and directions for research. *Journal of Community Psychology, 33*(1), 1–10.

Zimmerman, G.M., & Rees, C. (2014). Do school disciplinary policies have positive social impacts? Examining the attenuating effects of school policies on the relationship between personal and peer delinquency. *Journal of Criminal Justice, 42*(1), 54–65.

EXERCISES AND REVIEW

Review Questions

1. What is the difference between a rehabilitation and a prevention program?

2. How has the attitude toward offenders over time affected the types of programs developed to control youth crime?

3. Explain the extent to which the following programs are effective or ineffective in treating or preventing youth crime:

    a. purely punitive imprisonment

    b. "scared straight" programs

    c. custody-based rehabilitation programs

    d. probation

4. What is the basis for saying that, for some offences, the best rehabilitation and prevention is to do nothing?

5. Explain the risk–needs–responsivity model and how it is used to develop effective interventions for youth.

6. Suggest circumstances in which probation would be effective and circumstances in which it would not.

7. Explain what is meant by "criminogenic needs." Can you come up with a list of such needs?

8. Describe the profile of the kind of family most likely to encourage criminal behaviour.

9. Describe the profile of the kind of family least likely to encourage criminal behaviour.

Research Exercise

1. Project Venture, an outdoor experiential youth development intervention program developed by the National Indian Youth Leadership Project (NIYLP), has proven extremely effective in preventing substance abuse by Aboriginal youth. Learn more about Project Venture on the Public Safety Canada website at www.publicsafety.gc.ca and consider the following questions.

    a. What evidence is there to demonstrate that Project Venture is a proven model prevention program?

    b. How does the program promote change to negative self-system beliefs?

    c. If your community decided to implement Project Venture, what setting would be most effective? How would you make sure that you implemented the program with fidelity as prescribed by the program developers?

2. Find out whether there are any crime prevention programs directed at youth or children in your community. If so:

    a. List and describe them.

    b. How are these programs delivered—for example, through schools or community centres, or by referral?

    c. Who are the typical recipients of these programs? Are they youth identified as being "at risk" or youth in general? Which age groups are targeted by these programs?

    d. How are these programs funded, and how did they get started?

3. Do you believe your community is well served when it comes to prevention programs? Why or why not?

4. Can you come up with any ideas for programs that might benefit your community?

    a. List and describe each of these programs.

    b. How might the program(s) you describe be started? How might it or they be funded or staffed?

Discussion Questions

1. Identify what type of program might deflect the following individuals from continuing their criminal behaviour. Explain why it would likely be successful in doing this.

   a. Albert is a 13-year-old shoplifter. This is the second time he has been charged; the first time, he was put on probation. He lives at home with his parents, both of whom work. The family is stable and earns a middle-class family income, but the parents do not spend a lot of time with Albert or his 7-year-old brother, who is in school-age daycare after school. Neither child is notably disruptive in school, and both are in the middle of the pack academically.

   b. Jaspreet, a 16-year-old girl, assaulted her mother. She has no previous record, has done well in school, and is not known to have behavioural problems. Her mother is a single parent, and the assault followed the mother's attempt to prevent Jaspreet from going out on a school night at 11 p.m. to hang out with her friends.

   c. Charles, age 17, is charged with car theft. This is his fourth offence since he was 15. He comes from a two-parent family, but his parents are barely talking to him, and his father, on learning of the charges, has locked him out of the house and told him to live somewhere else. Both parents are clear that they have had enough of his behaviour and do not want him in the house.

   d. Ahmad, age 14, is charged with selling amphetamines. He has no previous record and comes from a stable family, although his father has a lengthy criminal record. Ahmad has a history of drug use, is disruptive at school, and is doing poorly academically.

   e. Edward, age 17, is charged with robbery. He has a police contact record going back to age 12 that includes sexual assault, other assaults, and various thefts. His last charge, which was for theft, resulted in three months' imprisonment. His academic record is quite good, but he is disruptive in school. A number of his friends have equally lengthy criminal histories.

2. "Schools are just as likely to encourage and foster criminal behaviour as discourage it." Discuss this statement, explaining why it is or is not accurate.

3. "Early intervention with a kindergarten kid to prevent criminal behaviour later is a lot of hooey. All the kid needs is a smack on the behind. The early interventionist stuff is just a lot of bleeding-heart nonsense." Can early intervention work, and in what circumstances?

4. Does anything work? List the "top five" programs you think are most likely to be successful with most young offenders.

5. Look at the list of model programs selected by the National Crime Prevention Centre and explore the evidence that is provided to show why it fits in this category of effectiveness.

PART V

Ongoing and Emerging Social Issues

Emerging Issues and Youth Crime: Continuities and Change

10

LEARNING OUTCOMES

After completing this chapter, you should be able to:

- Identify ongoing and emerging contextual factors relating to youth crime, particularly with respect to the changing demographic makeup and relationship patterns of Canada.

- Understand the importance of considering gender and gender-specific programing for young persons.

- Identify the changing nature of policing and enforcement with regard to cyberspace and cybercrime.

- Explain the specific challenges faced by youth who have fetal alcohol spectrum disorder in the criminal justice system.

- Understand the causes of overrepresentation of Aboriginal youth in the criminal justice system and explain how to reduce this problem.

- Identify some of the challenges related to mental health issues among young persons in conflict with the law.

- Discuss the impact living in poverty has on youth crime.

- Understand the role of gang culture in contributing to youth crime.

Introduction

As discussed in Chapter 1, youth crime and the nature of adolescence itself are issues with both ongoing and emerging dimensions. Certain aspects of adolescence as a developmental stage have not changed, and likely will not change over time (for example, puberty, cognitive development). Adolescents have always had certain attributes, such as physical and psychological immaturity and lack of experience, that lead them to take more risks than adults and to push social boundaries.

While adolescence as a phase of human development—and certain general patterns of adolescent offending—does not appear to have changed nearly as much as the media would lead us to believe, our social understanding of adolescence does change, as does our society. As a result, certain aspects of adolescence and youth crime do show historical changes. Also, recent social changes have altered both the public's perception of youth crime and the reality of that crime. Such changes, which have profound and far-reaching implications for the context in which criminal justice law is applied to youth, include: changing demographic patterns, shifting social relations between genders and about gender, a post-9/11 geopolitical context, an ever-escalating global trade in weapons and drugs, and the impact of the Internet and social media.

One enduring contextual factor related to youth crime in Canada is the marginalization of Aboriginal youth and how, despite changes to the *Youth Criminal Justice Act* (YCJA), they continue to be overrepresented at all stages of the youth criminal justice system.

Key Challenges for Youth Justice Today

The Overrepresentation of Aboriginal Youth in the Justice System

Research has shown that Aboriginal people are disproportionately involved in the criminal justice system. According to the Office of the Correctional Investigator, since 2000, the federal Aboriginal adult population has increased by 56.2 percent; Aboriginal offenders make up 23.2 percent of all incarcerated adults (Office of Correctional Investigator, 2013). It is very clear that the legacy of colonization continues, through the reserve system, and the repercussions of residential schools are felt by successive generations. As was pointed out in the case of *Gladue v. The Queen* (1999) (see Chapter 8) and reconfirmed by *R v. Ipeelee* (2012), the courts must take notice of such matters as "the history of colonialism, displacement, and residential schools and how that history continues to translate into lower educational attainment, lower incomes, higher unemployment, higher rates of substance abuse and suicide, and of course higher levels of incarceration for Aboriginal peoples" (para. 434).

This issue was brought to the fore in deliberations surrounding the drafting of the YCJA. Specific safeguards were added to the Act to help correct this dangerous trend. The YCJA's declaration of principle states that any measures imposed on young offenders should "respect gender, ethnic, cultural and linguistic differences and respond to the needs of aboriginal young persons and of young persons with special requirements" (s. 3(1)(c)(iv)). Not only does the YCJA provide alternatives to the youth justice system at all stages of the proceedings, but there are explicit provisions that direct youth court judges to consider the special needs of Aboriginal young offenders at the sentencing stage, including alternatives to prison (s. 38(2)).

Aboriginal children make up an increasing proportion of all children in Canada, but they are substantially overrepresented in statistics that reflect poor outcomes. While the number of Aboriginal young offenders sentenced to custody generally has been reduced, since the implementation of changes to the YCJA, the ratio of Aboriginal to non-Aboriginal young offenders has not decreased, and in several provinces it has even increased (Kong, 2009; Munch, 2012). Aboriginal youth account for 26 percent of the youth admitted to the correctional system, yet represent 6 percent of the general youth population (Calverley, Cotter, & Halla, 2010).

Indigenous children and youth in Canada are not only more likely to be involved in the youth justice system, but compared with their non-native peers, are more likely to be living in poverty and to be subject to debilitating personal and social risk factors (Corrado, Kuehn, & Margaritescu, 2014). When there is deep intergenerational poverty, the default response is to remove the child from the home into the child welfare system, exacerbating the problems already experienced through colonialism and residential schools. Cindy Blackstock, executive director of the First Nations Child and Family Caring Society of Canada, argues: "I made the pledge there that I would stand with this generation of children, in the company of many others … to ensure that this generation of children does not have to undergo the hardship of inequality like all the other generations that came before them. People are waking to the past injustices, but what they're not so aware of is that these injustices can continue to pan out in the lives of children today, and that's what we need to take action on" (Mark, 2013).

Fetal Alcohol Spectrum Disorder (FASD) and Young Offenders

Fetal alcohol spectrum disorder (FASD) is an umbrella term that describes a range of behavioural problems (lying, stealing), physical problems (growth delays), and cognitive deficits (problems with memory, understanding concepts, and decision-making) resulting from prenatal alcohol exposure. There is evidence that a disproportionate number of Aboriginal youth suffer from FASD (Corrado, Cohen, & Watkinson, 2008). Youth with FASD have a greater chance of becoming involved with the criminal justice system due to their underlying risk factors. Once within the system, corrective actions can amplify the problems, because these youth have difficulties understanding cause and effect (Fast, Conry, & Loock, 1999; Corrado, Cohen, & Watkinson, 2008).

Research has established that younger adolescents, particularly those with cognitive deficits, show high rates of impairment in legal capacities relevant to interrogation and adjudication. In a study of young offenders diagnosed with FASD, it was found that many of these young people had difficulty understanding their arrest rights and may have waived their rights to counsel without truly understanding what they were giving away (McLachlan, Roesch, Viljoen, & Douglas, 2014).

> In light of the evidence that Aboriginal youth have a higher incidence of FASD and involvement with the youth justice system, what kinds of safeguards need to be put in place to assist these vulnerable youth?

Research evidence shows that, despite policy changes and legislative enactments requiring youth justice personnel to reduce the impact of the justice system on Aboriginal youth, there is still substantial overrepresentation of young people from First Nations communities in the system (Alain, Corrado, & Reid, forthcoming). This makes it clear that we need to look at the kind of training provided to front-line responders. Given that Aboriginal young offenders are less likely to receive diversionary measures such as police cautions, conferencing, and other restorative justice options, perhaps it is within this realm that a training focus should be provided if we are serious about reducing the overrepresentation of Aboriginal youth in the system.

Changing Demographic Patterns

Patterns of immigration and birth rates have, in the past 30 or so years, dramatically altered Canada's demographic makeup. Young people make up a substantial proportion of Canada's population. However, the number of young people is declining. Thirty years ago, for every person between the ages of 55 and 64 there were two aged 15 to 24. However, according to census data, the ratio has fallen to just below one (Statistics Canada, 2014). According to Galarneau, Morissette, & Usalcas (2013), in 1971 youth between 15 and 24 years old represented 19 percent of the total Canadian population. However, by 2011, the proportion fell to 13 percent. They predict that the proportion of young people by the year 2031 could drop to 11 percent of the Canadian population.

These young people, as a group, are visibly and culturally different from Canadian youth of past generations. Visible minority populations and populations of Aboriginal people are increasing markedly relative to Caucasian Europeans.

Over time, patterns of immigration have shifted. Historically, most immigrants came from Europe. More recently, the largest group of newcomers to Canada has come from Asia and the Middle East. Foreign-born individuals in Canada represented 19.8 percent of the Canadian population in the 2006 Canadian census. This number increased to 20.6 percent in the 2011 National Household Survey. It is now estimated that one in five people living in Canada is foreign-born (Statistics Canada, 2013b). Accounting for 19.2 percent of the newcomer population were young people aged 14 and under, who came in the past five years. Another 14.5 percent of young immigrants were between the ages of 15 and 24. In 2011, 13 different ethnic origins surpassed the one million mark. Among these, while the majority of the respondents reported Canadian as their ethnic origin, English, French, Scottish, Irish, and German were also reported, either alone or in combination with Canadian origin. The other ethnic origins that surpassed the one million mark were Italian, Chinese, First Nations (North American Indian), Ukrainian, East Indian, Dutch, and Polish. One in five Canadians reported being a member of a visible minority, a group defined by the *Employment Equity Act* (1995, s. 3) as "persons, other than aboriginal peoples, who are non-Caucasian in race or non-white in colour." The visible minority population consisted mainly of the following groups: South Asian, Chinese, Black, Filipino, Latin American, Arab, Southeast Asian, West Asian, Korean, and Japanese.

As a consequence, we now have in Canadian society a large population of young people who are visibly, culturally, and racially different from the mainstream of adults of less than 20 years ago. Just as some 19th-century members of the Canadian public, referred to in Chapter 3 as the "child savers," worried that orphans and non-British immigrants were of lesser "stock," many writers believe these ethno-cultural differences contribute to racism and *xenophobia*—fear of strangers or the unknown—lurking beneath today's public perception that we are facing a crisis of ever-increasing youth crime (Chongatera, 2013; Wortley & Owusu-Bempah, 2012).

Research about immigrant youth and their involvement in the criminal justice system has suggested that a lack of personal and cultural identity, combined with a sense of powerlessness and hopelessness, may be key factors behind the higher likelihood that immigrant youth are attracted to youth gangs. According to research by Rossiter and Rossiter (2009), more than 80 percent of gang members identify as visible minorities and as either first- or second-generation immigrants. The research evidence, however, does not support the contention that immigrant youth are more involved in the criminal justice system than their non-immigrant counterparts (Bertrand, MacRae-Krisa, Costello, & Winterdyk, 2013). Immigrant youth who value education and have parents who encourage their sons and daughters to pursue educational and extracurricular activities seem to be protected from engaging in criminal behaviour. Research has also suggested that participation in intercultural peer programs helps give immigrant youth a sense of belonging and social acceptance.

EQUALITY IN THE RCMP

Baltej Singh Dhillon moved to Canada from Malaysia in 1983. As a Sikh, he is obligated by religious mandate to wear a turban and not shave, which presented a challenge when he decided to apply to the Royal Canadian Mounted Police in 1988. At that time the RCMP prohibited members from wearing turbans; they were required to conform to the official uniform of the organization, which included the iconic Stetson.

Dhillon, however, did not let this deter him from his goal of working for the RCMP, and proceeded to plead his case on the basis that this prohibition violated inalienable rights granted him by virtue of being on Canadian soil and thus under the protection of the *Canadian Charter of Rights and Freedoms*. He argued that by not allowing him to wear his turban the RCMP was violating his equality rights under s. 15, which states: "every individual is equal before and under the law and has the right to the equal protection and equal benefit of the law without discrimination"—in this case, without discrimination based on race or religion (Cahute & Desi, 2013).

In 1989, the RCMP commissioner recommended lifting the ban on turbans, and finally in 1990 Solicitor General Pierre Cadieux announced that this would be done, because the ban did, in fact, violate rights (CBC News, 1990). Dhillon went on to become the first, but not the last, member of the RCMP to proudly wear his turban in uniform. Today, he is the non-commissioned officer in charge of the RCMP's Federal and Serious Organized Crime Intelligence Unit and has also been active in working to educate Canadians about Sikh culture.

In 2014, Staff Sgt. Baltej Dhillon received an honorary degree from Kwantlen Polytechnic University in Vancouver, where he is a criminology alumnus (Woodin, 2014).

QUESTIONS

1. Why do you think there was resistance on the part of the RCMP to members' wearing turbans?

2. While this rights violation has been resolved, do you think there might be other challenges to police organizations on the basis of religious, racial, and cultural expression? Please investigate and explain.

Post-9/11 Geopolitical Context

Perhaps the most troubling difference between present-day and past perceptions of adolescent offending is in the context of international politics. The late 20th century saw the emergence of global tourism on an unprecedented scale, with international borders decreasing in significance and relaxed international travel. However, our confidence in our safety at home and abroad has now been seriously undermined. The **al-Qaeda** terrorist attacks of the early 21st century, most significantly those on September 11, 2001 in New York City but also those that followed in London, Madrid, and a series of other locations, led to America's "war on terror" and tremendous public xenophobia about potential "terrorists," particularly those perceived to be Islamic.

Although no al-Qaeda attacks have taken place in Canada at the time of writing, in June 2006 mass arrests were made in the Toronto area of 17 individuals who, as a "home-grown al-Qaeda cell," were allegedly planning a series of major terrorist assaults on targets in southern Ontario. Five of the 17 charged were youths at the time of their arrest. The arrests

al-Qaeda
international terrorist network that has claimed responsibility for several attacks on Western cities; "al-Qaeda" means "the base"

were preceded by 18 related arrests in the United States, Britain, Bosnia, Denmark, Sweden, and Bangladesh. Those arrested in Canada self-identified with al-Qaeda members abroad, had communicated via the Internet, and had even ordered explosives online. The case provides a significant example of technological changes and international politics as factors changing the nature of contemporary youth crime and public perception of it. The "Toronto 18" arrests exacerbated public fears about hostile, foreign youth living among us, and increased public perception that youth violence in Canada is on the rise. (For discussion of this case see, for example, Teotonio, 2010.)

Since the 9/11 attacks, many exceptions to the application of basic human rights law and procedural rights have been introduced for cases in which involvement with terrorist networks is suspected. Arguments in favour of denying an accused civil liberties have become commonplace when a person is suspected of committing a terror attack. In discussing the increased emphasis on racial profiling of Arabs and Muslims in Canada, despite legislation that does not allow such profiling, Bahdi (2003) argues that when decision-makers believe they are faced with an international conspiracy, they will likely interpret the facts before them through a "lens of fear" and adopt a "better safe than sorry" mentality whereby they feel it is better to violate someone's rights than risk a terrorist attack or incident.

The April 2013 Boston Marathon bombings provide a telling example of a situation in which a terror attack led to an entire city being put on lockdown, ending with a firefight, killing one suspect and severely wounding the other—a 19-year-old US citizen. Questions were raised about whether this surviving suspect, Dzhokhar Tsarnaev, should be tried in a US court or treated as an unlawful military combatant without rights. Ultimately, the US government decided to proceed against him under normal criminal law and appointed a public defender to represent him ("Criminal Complaint Against Dzhokhar Tsarnaev," 2013).

OMAR KHADR

In 2002, when he was 14, Omar Khadr was apprehended in Afghanistan by US forces as a "non-military combatant." He had been fighting on the side of the Taliban in a conflict alongside his father, who was killed in the battle. Khadr, born in Toronto and therefore a Canadian citizen, was held by the United States at Guantanamo Bay (GTMO) and only returned to Canada in 2012. He is currently incarcerated in Alberta.

During his time at Guantanamo, and while still an adolescent to whom the YCJA applied, Khadr was tortured by US officials and interrogated by CSIS without access to counsel. The US military held Khadr for two years without access to a lawyer, and it was another three years before any charges were laid. Khadr, despite being a Canadian citizen, was not repatriated to Canada for 12 years and was held without charge for much of that time. (For a timeline, see for example "Omar Khadr: A Chronology," 2012.)

While several hundred individuals were detained at GTMO, certain aspects made Khadr's case unique. During the time that the crimes occurred, he had been a "child soldier," and at GTMO he had been the only Western national whose government did not intervene to ensure his repatriation. Furthermore, Khadr's entire nuclear family (an al-Qaeda family) had been subjected to sensationalism and vilification in the Canadian media (Park, 2014). One of the most vocal advocates of Khadr was Roméo Dallaire, Canadian senator and retired general who served in Rwanda during the Rwandan genocide. Because of his experiences in Rwanda, Dallaire now focuses his efforts on raising awareness and bringing an end to the use of child soldiers in armed conflict. In a 2012 address, Dallaire raised the issue of Omar Khadr as the "the case of the only child soldier prosecuted for war crimes," which is in direct violation of the United Nations Convention on the Rights of the Child (Dallaire, 2012).

Almost apologetically, the mainstream media reported on Khadr's first appearance in court in Edmonton in September 2013 with phrases such as "he glanced around the courtroom," and "he appeared fit" (Copps, 2013). Kathleen Copps, a retired teacher, responded with a commentary on the mainstream media's portrayal, suggesting that the phrase "he glanced around the courtroom" did not include the information that Omar is blind in one eye due to shrapnel from the Delta Force bombing on the compound where he had been staying. And they didn't mention that during a decade in Guantanamo, he had not received any medical care to prevent total loss of vision, or that for most of those years Omar had been in solitary confinement and exposed 24 hours a day to fluorescent lighting, or that for years he had been denied sunglasses for "state security" reasons. Khadr launched a $20 million lawsuit in 2004 to seek damages from the federal government by arguing that Canada had conspired with the United States and breached his Charter rights when intelligence agents from the RCMP went to Guantanamo Bay and interviewed him in 2003 and 2004. US authorities allowed access to Khadr on the condition that the Canadian agents would share any information they gained. Following the agreement, Khadr was subjected to sleep deprivation in order to "soften him up" for the Canadian interrogation (CBC News, 2014a). Court documents have shown that the intelligence was shared. This conspiratorial claim would make Canada liable for the torture committed at Guantanamo Bay. In October 2014, federal Judge Richard Mosley ruled that Khadr's claim be allowed to go forward as part of the lawsuit (Perkel, 2014).

QUESTIONS

1. Do you think this was a unique event, or could this happen to a Canadian adolescent today?
2. What does this mean in terms of the provisions of the YCJA?
3. What kinds of issues can you identify with respect to the conspiracy claim in the lawsuit launched by Khadr against Ottawa?

As with other youth crime discussed in this chapter, adolescents are more likely to be victimized by people's fear of terrorism than they are to perpetrate it. Hate crime directed against youth perceived to be Islamic has increased since September 11, 2001, with young people at greater risk than adults of victimization, such as assaults and bullying (Statistics Canada, 2001). Immediately following the 2006 "Toronto 18" arrests discussed above, a Toronto-area mosque was vandalized in an act characterized by many as a response to the arrests (CBC News, 2006a). Further, in all of the reported cases of planned terrorist attacks in New York, London, and Boston, and most recently in Canada, whether linked to al-Qaeda or not, the planning process involved one or more adults influencing impressionable adolescents and exploiting them to commit the crimes (CBC News, 2006b). This suggests that it might be more appropriate to focus on preventing the exploitation of adolescent alienation by adults than to concentrate on harsh consequences for adolescents who do offend.

In July 2014, a 20-year-old York University student went missing. His family, when they had traced him to Turkey on his cellphone, contacted the Canadian Security Intelligence Service (CSIS) and the RCMP to report that their son may have taken up arms with the Islamic State of Iraq and Syria (ISIS). In September, CSIS reported to the family that their son had been killed by the anti-ISIS military campaign, apparently dying during attacks from Kurdish forces in northern Syria. Mohamud Mohamed Mohamud was reportedly the first Canadian to die since the United States had launched airstrikes to combat ISIS. The family reported that their son had shown changes in behaviour, devoting almost all his time to his Internet community, becoming harsher in his views on events in the world, and making claims about weak members within his own Muslim community (CBC News, 2014b).

Shifting Social Relations Between Genders and About Gender

Changing relations between genders and power inequalities relating to gender continue to present challenges in the youth criminal justice context. Feminism and the notion that women and men should be equal are no longer new ideas. What is more novel is a growing awareness that the gender "binary" that forces boys into one box and girls into another—in which girls are expected to like pink toys, especially dolls, and boys are expected to like hockey—can have very negative consequences. With the legality of same-sex marriage and a general liberalization in Canadian society of attitudes toward a wide range of family forms, issues relating to gender identity and expression are a social reality with ramifications for youth criminal justice law. For example, it raises questions about where adolescents can be held in custody if they self-identify as transgender or as a different gender from that which they are identified as in official documents (Peterson & Panfil, 2014).

hate crime
illegal activity motivated by prejudice against an identifiable group

Changing definitions of what constitutes bullying and **hate crime**, and the growing awareness of the issues around homophobic bullying, affect the lives both of adolescent bullying victims and of those charged with offences (see ss. 318–319 of the *Criminal Code*).

HOMOPHOBIA AND HARASSMENT: LGBTQ YOUTH

Throughout most of the world, lesbian, gay, bisexual, transgender, queer, and questioning (LGBTQ) youth experience health inequities, including self-harm, suicide, and substance misuse, mostly because societal stigma targets them for harassment, discrimination, violence, and rejection. LGBTQ youth and adults experience higher rates of violent victimization, including sexual assault, robbery, and physical assault, and general rates of discrimination "higher than that of heterosexuals" (MacCreary Centre Society, 2007; Saewyc, 2011). As part of a five-year research study through Dalhousie University, researchers are conducting youth advisories and forums with young people in both gender-segregated and gender-mixed groups in order to create a safe space for discussing gender-specific experience and to elicit each gender's perceptions of their own and others' experiences of homophobia and harassment (Saewyc et al., 2012).

QUESTIONS

1. What kind of climate would need to be in place to ensure a "safe space" for youth to discuss these issues?

2. How would training about safe spaces and the issues facing LGBTQ youth assist police in better responding to young people in conflict with the law?

Despite statistics showing no scientific basis in fact for the contention, it remains commonly believed by the Canadian public that adolescent girls have become more criminally active generally, and more prone to violent behaviour specifically, than girls in generations past (Canadian Women's Foundation, 2012). Newspapers and TV newscasts regularly report on young girls involved in violence. For example, there was nationwide media coverage of the 2003 murder by two adolescent girls of their mother in her bathtub, which led to their convictions for first-degree murder and receipt of ten-year jail sentences in June 2006 (CBC News, 2006d). In June 2005, *Newsweek* ran a story entitled "Bad Girls Go Wild" that referred to a significant increase in girls committing crime, calling it a "burgeoning national crisis" (Scelfo, 2005).

Zahn (2009) reports that while girls' involvement in the youth justice system has increased over the past decade, there is no evidence of an increase in violent acts. Arrest, victimization, and self-report data suggest that while girls may be arrested more for simple assaults than previously, this may be explained better by changes in police enforcement than by dramatic changes in girls' behaviour. She concludes that there is "no burgeoning national crisis" of serious violence among adolescent girls. If girls were committing more serious crimes, this would likely be reflected in a change in admissions to all forms of correctional services. As noted in Figure 10.1, the percentage of female youth entering any form of correctional service post-adjudication has remained around 20 percent over the past ten years.

FIGURE 10.1   Admissions to Correctional Services Youth, 2002–2012

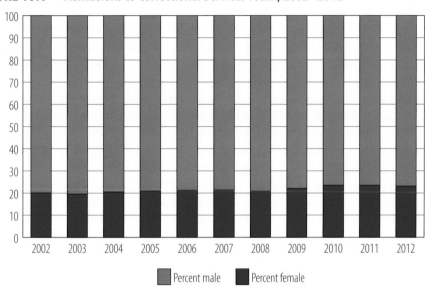

SOURCE: Statistics Canada, CANSIM Table 251-0012.

Since girls still make up such a small minority of youth charged and convicted of criminal offences, particularly violent offences, the perception by police and the public that girls are "out of control" is not easily explained. However, other factors, such as changes in gender roles, may shed some light.

What our society expects of, and accepts from, women and girls has changed markedly over the past 30 years or so. The overwhelming majority of females two generations ago were not educated to the same extent as males and were expected to have roles primarily in the home. As a result of cultural changes and feminist activism, women now enter the paid labour force in ever-increasing numbers, even taking on combat roles in the military. Females in Canada are entitled to equal treatment in education and under the law, and no longer expect to be treated as inferior. So, too, have the expectations of behaviour of adolescent girls changed. This change in female roles and behaviour stands in contrast not only to Canada's past, but also to the expectations many new Canadians bring from their cultures of origin. Arguably, perfectly legal but assertive behaviour of young women can be surprising to some older adult members of our communities. It is likely at least in part as a result of these factors that the public increasingly perceives female youth to be unmanageable.

At least publicly and politically, most Canadians view women's advances toward equality in a positive light. Status of Women Canada, a federal agency devoted to promoting gender equality and full participation of women in national life (www.swc-cfc.gc.ca), receives a good deal of public funding toward its goal, as do many similarly focused women's groups. Canada sees itself as an international leader in this respect. However, many display varying levels of discomfort with women's new roles, and this may underlie the expressed sentiments that teenage girls are "out of control." Especially because women were historically primarily responsible for rearing children at home and have now moved on to broader roles, some people blame changing gender roles not only for a perceived increase in offending by girls, but also for an increase in youth crime in general.

Even though crime by girls still constitutes a small proportion of overall offending by youth, it is significant and bears close consideration. Female youth crime poses unique problems for the Canadian justice and corrections systems, which are tailored primarily to male offenders. Rehabilitation programs, for example, are generally based on research about what treatments are most effective in controlling *male* violence. Custody facilities are generally not set up for handling inmates of both sexes. Needed are systems to meet females' **gender-specific** rehabilitative needs.

gender-specific
associated with persons of one gender to the exclusion of the other

The province of Ontario considers female young offenders to be a special population, so the Youth Justice Services Division has attempted to incorporate gender considerations into policy development, programming, facility planning, and staff training since the proclamation of the YCJA in 2003.

Regarding custody/detention, gender-dedicated services are seen as the ideal; however, the numbers are so low that finances do not permit the provision of completely separate facilities. Gender-specific programs have been among the first to be terminated under austerity budgets. For example, in British Columbia, the Vancouver Island Victoria Youth Detention Centre no longer accepts females sentenced to custody; instead, they are sent to the mainland Burnaby Youth Detention Centre. Co-located facilities have separate programming and accommodation for male and female youth, whereas co-ed facilities have separate accommodation but resident youth participate in shared programming and activities.

---

1. What kinds of issues can you think of that may influence the decision to hold young persons in pre-trial detention if they are female?

2. What does gender-specific housing mean for young persons held in police lockup?

3. What are the added implications for police lockup of dealing with a young person who is female in light of the provisions in the UN Convention on the Rights of the Child, which requires young offenders to be housed separately from adults?

On the basis of evidence now available, it appears that the most worrisome role that young women play in violence is not that of perpetrator, but that of victim. It is particularly troubling that the public perceives young women to be increasingly the perpetrators of violent behaviour, when in fact not only are they far less likely to commit crime than males, but they are far more likely to be victimized by both crime and violence than male youth. It is hypothesized that this is attributable to females' greater risk of sexual assault. Female youth aged 12 through 17 years were the primary victims in both sexual and physical family assaults.

These statistics speak to the continuing vulnerability of teenage females in the face of the growing social power of women in general. Despite the gains attained by Canadian women in the past half-century, violence against women remains a serious impediment to women's equality that needs to be addressed (Smith, Leve, & Chamberlain, 2006).

Mental Health Problems and Youth in Conflict with the Law

The previous section showed that, despite anecdotal comments from the police and the public, female youth crime is not increasing at an alarming rate as some would have us believe. Issues that affect young women more than young men may also lead to different kinds of responses in females to risk-taking behaviour.

For example, a number of studies have shown that a history of sexual abuse is more likely among girls who engage in anti-social behaviour, particularly violent behaviour, than among their male counterparts (Smith, Leve, & Chamberlain, 2006; Podgurski, Lyons, Kisiel, & Griffin, 2014). Some research has indicated that a history of childhood abuse co-occurs with delinquency in adolescent girls as often as 80 percent of the time (Smith, Leve, & Chamberlain, 2006).

Boys and girls in the youth justice system appear to be equally exposed to physical abuse (Henggeler, Edwards, & Borduin, 1987). Research has shown that adolescents who come into conflict with the law have experienced a much higher rate of abuse than the general population.

In addition to gender differences in exposure to certain risk factors or stressors, girls and boys may also vary in their sensitivity to the same stressor. For example, there is evidence that girls may be more sensitive to dysfunction and trauma within the home (Hennessey, Ford, Mahoney, Ko, & Siegfried, 2004), which may predispose them to anti-social behaviour through truancy and running away from the family environment. In a recent study of co-occurring trauma, rates of childhood abuse, trauma, and substance use were as high as 90 percent in adolescent girls within the juvenile justice system (Smith & Saldana, 2013).

In terms of mental health disorders, boys outnumber girls by 3 to 1 in the diagnoses of attention deficit/hyperactivity disorder (ADHD) and conduct disorder, while girls are diagnosed at a much higher rate for depression, anxiety, and post-traumatic stress disorder (Teplin, Abram, McClelland, Dulcan, & Mericle, 2002). Although these disorders are also associated with delinquency among boys, the relationship appears to be much stronger for girls (Teplin et al., 2002). Despite considerable literature on the mental health challenges facing young people in the criminal justice system, particularly girls, there is little evidence of a concerted effort to ensure that mental health challenges are being adequately addressed in youth justice centres (Marston, Russell, Obsuth, & Watson, 2012).

In a recent Canadian study in which youth with mental health challenges accessing services in the community were compared with similar youth inside the youth justice system, those in the justice system reported lower levels of interaction with health services, mental health services, and educational support. Further, it was found that the history of involvement with mental health support was sorely lacking for those within the juvenile justice system, and that this may be indicative of a lack of a prevention focus for youth in conflict with the law (Liebenberg & Ungar, 2014).

ASHLEY SMITH

Ashley Smith, a 19-year-old woman from Moncton, New Brunswick, died by self-induced asphyxiation while in an adult penitentiary after being transferred from the youth system less than one year before. Ashley's trouble with the law began in March 2002, at the age of 14, with offences related to public disturbances, trespass or violence (harassing telephone calls to unknown persons, assaulting strangers on the street, insulting passengers and drivers on public transportation, insulting a parking attendant).

Ashley was referred by the province's Youth Treatment Program team for a 34-day assessment at a six-bed residential program, Pierre Caissie Centre, in Moncton. The psychiatrist ruled out depression but added "narcissistic personality traits" in an addendum to the report. The psychiatric assessment stated under the category of "diagnostic impressions" that Ashley suffered from "learning disorder, ADHD, borderline personality disorder." The psychological assessment recommended that her parents receive counselling sessions on how to deal with an "oppositional defiant youth" and that everyone work together in dealing with Ashley's behaviour. While she was resident at the Pierre Caissie Centre, the behaviour escalated and police were called twice for her assaults on staff.

Ashley was remanded to the New Brunswick Youth Centre (NBYC), a closed custody facility, for one month. During that time she was charged with a number of offences relating to not following orders and threatening self-harm. In less than three months, Ashley was in and out of the NBYC five times. She would be released on community supervision and then either breach her conditions or commit a new offence, which would send her back to remand at the youth jail. She spent approximately three years in the youth jail. During that time, there were hundreds of institutional charges, 50 criminal charges, and over 150 self-harm incidents.

With the promise of more gender-specific programming and therapeutic mental health treatment offered through the Correctional Services of Canada, the superintendent of the NBYC made an application under s. 92 of the *Youth Criminal Justice Act* to transfer Ashley to the adult system. During the year she was housed in the federal system, she spent all her time in administrative segregation and was transferred 17 times between four different provinces, three federal penitentiaries, two treatment facilities, two external hospitals, and one provincial correctional facility.

According to the correctional investigator following her death, "In the end, Ms. Smith was identified by an institutional psychologist as being highly suicidal. … With misinformed and poorly communicated decisions as a backdrop, Ms. Smith died—wearing nothing but a suicide smock, lying on the floor of her segregation cell, with a ligature tied tightly around her neck—under the direct observation of several correctional staff."

A high-profile coroner's inquest returned a verdict on December 19, 2013, ruling Ashley's death a homicide. The report provided over 100 recommendations for an overhaul of the correctional system and its treatment of female young adult offenders, the treatment protocols for inmates with mental health challenges, and clearer guidelines for administration and training.

For further information, see Reid (2013) and Canadian Press (2013).

QUESTIONS

1. In view of Ashley Smith's case, what should a police officer do if confronted with the case of minor offending by an adolescent girl?

2. What kinds of issues might a police officer have to deal with when presented with a youth with mental health challenges?

Impact of Poverty on Youth Crime

Over 25 years have passed since the House of Commons passed a resolution to eliminate child poverty by the year 2000 (unanimous resolution passed in November 1989). The number of children living in poverty in Canada has increased from 15.8 percent of all children in 1989 to 19.1 percent in 2012 (Campaign 2000, 2014). Child poverty has particularly significant impacts on health, developmental delays, and behaviour disorders. In July 2013, the Canadian Medical Association released its report *Health Care in Canada: What Makes Us Sick*, indicating that the majority of Canadians recognize a pressing need to address the issue of poverty if we want to enhance health and well-being of Canadians (Matusicky, 2014).

There are many theories on the relationship between growing up in poverty and how cultural values related to deprivation are transmitted to the next generation. These theories suggest that the transmission makes it likely the cycle will repeat. Other circumstances also make it more likely that the effects of poverty will enhance the likelihood of both committing crime and being the victim of crime. Eisler and Schissel (2004) suggest that poverty disposes children to various forms of disadvantage, one of the most debilitating of which is victimization, both actual and expected. In a study of 2,605 Saskatchewan school children, they found that youth who fell into the "poor" income category were more likely to be afraid in school, to be hurt at school, to be victims of attacks outside school, and to be victims of crime. There were also gender distinctions, with poor boys being more vulnerable to fear and attack in schools than poor girls, relative to their wealthier peers.

The media has reported on the role of poverty in creating disorganized communities ripe for proliferation of youth gangs. In their analysis of the impact of poverty on crime and victimization, Eisler and Schissel (2004) also considered the impact of geography, and found that living in rural areas appeared to protect youth from the damaging effects of poverty, especially school-context victimization. However, somewhat ironically, they report that for criminal victimization, poor urban youth are at no greater risk than their wealthier urban counterparts. In other words, crime and victimization in urban centres is not dependent upon whether the target is rich or poor.

BOOMTOWNS AND CRIME

Given the research that rural geography appears to have a buffering effect on the potential for crime and victimization, what might one expect of rural communities that experience economic gain and expansion? Some research evidence indicates that rapid population increases following from economic gain in small boomtowns are related to higher rates of crime, victimization, and disorder.

In recent years, development and spending in the Alberta oil sands has led to rapid population growth in and around Fort McMurray. One Edmonton paper reported that it was *easier to buy cocaine than pizza* in reference to the changing dynamics of the area. From 2000 to 2009, the number of *Criminal Code* offences in the city of Fort McMurray increased from 24,896 to 39,488.

Increases in crime, whether real or a product of media sensationalism, shape the perceptions of boomtown residents about their safety and risks of victimization and have implications for how police deliver services. Between 2008 and 2012, the local government contracted with a private research firm to conduct telephone surveys of 1,000 residents of the area and asked them to comment on quality-of-life indicators since the infusion of new moneys from the oil sands. One of the questions asked participants to identify the top ten neighbourhood concerns. Not in keeping with the expectation that participants would cite increasing levels of violent crime, the top three perceived problems were all non-violent offences: drug use, speeding/aggressive driving, and residential burglaries. Respondents also indicated that property damage, youth behaviour (for example, loitering or being noisy), and other thefts were troubling. No violent offences were of concern, although the ninth- and tenth-most-important issues were gangs and guns. In all five years of the survey, residents expressed concern about youth anti-social behaviour, despite the fact that those who had migrated into the community to work were over the age of 18 years.

For further information, see Carrington and Pereira (2011) and Ruddell (2011).

QUESTIONS

1. Why would boomtown residents perceive crime and victimization differently than previously?

2. Given that rural communities were seen as a buffer against crime and victimization in the earlier literature, what is different about rural communities when economic vitality enters into the landscape?

Gangs, Guns, and Drugs

Certain high-profile cases of gun violence have given rise to a great deal of public concern about increases in the use of guns and the proliferation of youth gangs in Canada. Much of this concern was led by media reports about Toronto, Canada's largest city.

Toronto's rate of gun-related homicides increased rapidly in the early years of the 21st century, reaching a record year in 2005. (See, for example, Lamberti, 2003.) The shooting death of a 15-year-old girl, Jane Creba, and injuries suffered by six other bystanders struck by stray bullets in a gang shooting on Yonge Street on Boxing Day 2005 gave rise to a media and political outcry, with 2005 being referred to in Toronto media as "the year of the gun" (CBC News, 2006c).

The outcry resulted in gun control becoming a major issue in the debates leading up to the 2006 federal election. Toronto's mayor led the call to ban handguns (CBC News, 2005). On May 23, 2007, a 15-year-old boy, Jordan Manners, was shot and killed in a Toronto high school. This was reported in the media as gang-related, despite police insistence to the contrary. More recently, a mass shooting at Toronto's Eaton Centre in June 2012 injured 12 people, killing one, and caused a resurgence in public anxiety about gun violence in Toronto (CBC News, 2012).

Clearly the media has played a substantial role in promoting the suggestion that youth gangs are getting increasingly violent. It has been shown that interest in youth gangs goes up with incidents identified in the news media as gang-related, even if there is no evidence to support such a relation. Most of the ideas the public has about gangs are based on anecdotal evidence, perceptions, myths, stereotypes, and media reporting.

A troubling aspect of Canada's youth gang membership is the disproportionately high representation of visible minority youth—particularly black Canadian—and Aboriginal youth in the gangs. Media commentators focus on economic disadvantage and social marginalization suffered by minority youth, particularly black youth, as a key cause of gang activity. (See, for example, "After Jane, a Rallying Cry," 2006). In the Jordan Manners shooting, the media began its coverage of the event as another school shooting and made a number of references to the well-known Columbine, Taber, and Virginia Tech shootings. Without any evidence of the nature of the incident, the media switched its focus from school shootings to the possibility of gang involvement with one notable story from the *Toronto Star*: "Who and why would somebody hunt down and kill 15-year-old Jordan Manners in broad daylight inside his Toronto high school?" (Marlo, Huffman, & Kassam, 2007, p. B1). Despite increased attention to video surveillance and additional police presence, in the fall of 2014—seven years after the Jordan Manners shooting—there was another incident, a stabbing, in the same area. A lawyer who had represented students, Mr. Selwyn Pieters, reportedly tweeted after the stabbing as follows: "Two more young people gone. Grave and jail. We really need to teach our young people proper dispute resolution skills. Knives + guns solves nothing" (Brown & Rushowy, 2014).

As pointed out by O'Grady, Parnaby, and Schikschneit (2010), the media discourse on the Jordan Manners school shooting emphasized a gang culture framework supplemented with explanatory references to Toronto's "underclass" primarily located in the Jane–Finch corridor. Despite a press conference from the Toronto Police Service strongly indicating that the youth's death was not gang-related, the way the media discussed it was couched in terms suggesting that a dysfunctional, low-income, primarily black community was the root cause. Missing from the media accounts was the public outrage that normally accompanies school shootings, suggesting that gang culture was to blame and thereby making this case out to be an exception to the "normal" school shootings. Khenti (2013) argues that the high rate of homicide among black Canadians is really an "unrecognized major public health crisis" and more a consequence of income inequality, poverty, poor quality of life, mental health risks, and sustained racism.

Reliable information about youth gangs in Canada is relatively scarce. The 2002 Canadian Police Survey on Youth Gangs, which was the first survey of its kind conducted on a national scale, is still being relied upon as the main source (Astwood Strategy Corporation, 2002). The existence of 434 youth gangs was reported, with a membership of 7,071 adolescents, making up only 0.24 percent of the youth population. According to Toronto Police statistics, in 2010, Toronto had the fourth-highest rate of gang-related homicides per capita of any major Canadian city after Winnipeg, Vancouver, and Montreal. According to Statistics Canada, the rate of gang-related homicide steadily increased from the early 1990s until 2008, before declining in both 2009 and 2010 (Statistics Canada, 2012).

Research has shown that gang-involved youth tend to have elevated profiles of personal and contextual risk compared with youth not involved in gangs, but most are not "super-predators" and, as Howell (2012) argues, actually spend much of their time on the same mundane, everyday activities as uninvolved youth (O'Brien, Daffern, Chu, & Thomas, 2013). Factors linked to gang involvement among youth supports an **enhancement model**, suggesting that gang-involved youth have the highest levels of risk. However, we do not necessarily understand the relationships between anti-social youth forming friendship groups without becoming "gangs" or merging with gangs and those groups that attract members specifically to become gang-involved (Boxer, Veysey, Ostermann, & Kubik, 2014). Research has explored the notion of whether youth gang members who carried a weapon considered guns to be a status symbol, and found that the complex process of peer influence in these friendship networks, combined with individual aggressive tendencies, led to more use of weapons over time (Dijkstra et al., 2010). Further, structural inequalities (for example, inadequate housing, education, or social welfare initiatives) led to a greater likelihood of marginalization among disadvantaged social groups, which might contribute to gang formation and increased violence (Thompson, 2009).

Concerns about youth being actively recruited into youth gangs have been fuelled by the concept of **cyberbanging**. While social media is being used by individuals to display their involvement with various gangs, there is no evidence that such sites are being used to actively recruit members. While social media has created a new venue for people who share the values underlying street-gang lifestyle to be reinforced for their commitment to the subculture, these sites are more providing intelligence to police personnel about individual affiliations than encouraging recruitment (Morselli, 2010).

Data from the National Gang Center in the United States suggests that youth gangs are associated with increased availability of guns and drugs in schools, and that these youth are responsible for a large proportion of criminal incidents (Arciaga, Sakamoto, & Jones, 2010). In an international study comparing youth in Amsterdam, Philadelphia, Toronto, and Montreal, Korf, Brochu, Benschop, Harrison, & Erickson (2008) found that carrying a weapon and associated violence were related to drug-dealing activities and that the rate of gun ownership varied with the drugs that were sold. Research has shown that gun crime in some Canadian urban communities is quite a serious problem whose victims in Toronto were primarily young, male, and disproportionately from ethnic minority or other socially marginal groups (Ezeonu, 2010). As has been already discussed, being young and black in Toronto may be indicative not only of weapon involvement but also of links with other background risk factors including poverty, family instability, and poor school performance. Whether a young person has attitudes favourable to weapon acquisition cannot really determine the availability of guns. However, despite strict gun control legislation in Canada and the fact that it is illegal to own a firearm under the age of 18, youth in Toronto and Montreal indicated that they could obtain firearms quite readily (Butters, Sheptycki,

enhancement model
a theory that suggests that youth already engaging in anti-social behaviour are more likely to join gangs, and that, in turn, this elevates their involvement in further anti-social activity facilitated by the gangs

cyberbanging
the use of social media to showcase images and exploits of various street gangs

Brochu, & Erickson, 2011). Further, if youth report being able to access a gun quickly, they are more likely to report using guns to threaten or harm others.

WEAPON VIOLENCE/AVAILABILITY AND GEOGRAPHY

In their study examining youth gang involvement, Butters et al. (2011) looked at a sample of over 600 youth aged 14–17 years in Toronto and Montreal who were either detained in custody or had dropped out of school. Of the total sample, 60 percent of the Toronto group indicated that they had threatened or tried to hurt someone with a gun compared with only 43 percent of youth in Montreal. Similarly, 46 percent of Toronto youth as against 27 percent of Montreal youth reported that they had hurt someone with a weapon.

QUESTIONS

1. What might account for these statistically significant differences between the two cities?

2. Table 10.1 describes the characteristics of those youth who reported that they had either threatened someone with a gun or had actually hurt someone with a weapon in each of the two cities. Looking at the variables in the left column, consider the profiles of the youth in each of the two groups and attempt to account for the differences in the two cities.

TABLE 10.1   Percentage of Youth at Risk Who Report Threatening or Actually Hurting Someone with a Weapon

	Threaten or try to hurt with gun		Hurt someone with a weapon	
	Toronto	Montreal	Toronto	Montreal
Witnessing drug use and selling 50+ times	72	74	64	66
Personal drug selling activity	94	84	84	78
Any lifetime gang fighting	77	88	69	87
Report able to get gun in 3 hours or less	63	49	52	43
More than 5 symptoms of conduct disorder	63	68	57	55
More than 3 delinquent behaviours in last year	66	66	64	68

SOURCE: Butters, Sheptycki, Brochu, & Erickson (2011, p. 414).

It is probably safe to say that you cannot arrest your way out of a gun violence problem. A balanced approach that addresses the underlying factors associated with gun violence is necessary. As has been pointed out, many of the risk factors associated with gun violence are ongoing ones for youth who live in poverty, have low educational achievements, and lack meaningful employment. Once we address some of these root causes at the systemic level, we have hope of reducing the numbers of young people turning to gangs.

According to Criminal Intelligence Service Canada (CISC) (2010), there is considerable variation in the structure, composition, and membership of street gangs from one region to the next across Canada. The descriptors "urban," "Aboriginal," "rural," "hybrid," and "ethnic" applied to gangs all denote some aspect of what is generally referred to as a *street gang*. Definitions of what constitutes a street gang vary considerably among academics, policymakers, and criminal justice personnel. Some criteria that have been used are: (1) youthful age; (2) a group name; (3) distinctive symbols or insignia; (4) control of a certain area or "turf"; (5) level of organization, durability, and stability; (6) number of members; (7) formal and/or informal rules; (8) initiation rituals; (9) regular and/or continuous involvement of members in crime and violence; and (10) common ethnic or racial background of members (Wortley, 2010).

The *Criminal Code* defines a gang under the provisions of criminal organization; various police agencies have operationalized this definition as follows:

1. There is information from a reliable source (for example, inside gang member/rival gang member, legitimate community resources such as schools, business, citizen).

2. Police information is provided as a result of observed association with known gang members.

3. An individual admits to gang membership.

4. There is involvement (direct/indirect) in gang-motivated crime.

5. Previous court findings identify a person as gang member.

6. A person has or participates in common and/or symbolic gang identifiers such as paraphernalia (tattoos, weapons, poems, clothing) and induction rituals (Hemmati, 2006).

The most common response to violence perpetrated by members of youth gangs is suppression by focusing on persistent offenders and aggressively enforcing laws as they apply to these individuals. These types of enforcement strategies have little effect on the rates of crime and victimization, and lead to a series of unintended consequences that may increase the cohesiveness of the gang and its attractiveness to vulnerable youth. Further, high-profile and aggressive police activity, while leading to few arrests that can turn into serious charges, may undermine the reputation and legitimacy of the police and create a damaging cycle of release and re-incarceration of known gang members (Chettleburgh, 2007).

Since 2007, the National Crime Prevention Centre through the Canadian Department of Public Safety has operated the Youth Gang Prevention Fund to provide funding for programs that reduce the number of gang-involved youth in communities with a known or emerging gang problem. Fourteen impact assessments were conducted, and it was found that those programs using a "wrap-around" approach were best at attracting and retaining these high-risk youth; that is, youth with multiple risk factors were better served through a multidisciplinary service group of partners.

Research in Britain has indicated that gang affiliation leads to a weakening of social bonds to conventional institutions, a development, learning, and strengthening of deviant values and self-concepts, and a change in routine activities of young people (Melde & Finn-Age, 2011). The involvement of youth who have gang affiliation tends to increase the use and abuse of psychoactive drugs (Ariza, Cebulla, Aldridge, Shute, & Ross, 2014).

Psychoactive substances (with the exception of alcohol and tobacco) are regulated through the federal *Controlled Drugs and Substances Act* (1996). However, the range of drugs, including prescription drugs, available for illicit sale in Canada is ever-expanding. Health Canada conducts the Canadian Alcohol and Drug Use Monitoring Survey (CADUMS), and in 2012 reported that there were no significant increases from 2011 in the rates of use by Canadians 15 years and older, but that abuse of psychoactive prescription drugs had increased from 3.2 percent in 2011 to 6.5 percent in 2012 (Nasr & Phillips, 2014).

bath salts

drugs containing one or more synthetic chemicals related to an amphetamine (cathinone)

New drugs such as **bath salts** emerge on the streets periodically, and are not always illegal at first. Use of psychoactive substances by adolescents is widespread, with alcohol and cannabis being the most common; and research has shown that upwards of 80 percent of incarcerated youth have problematic substance use (Brochu, 2006). The progression of more serious involvement with drugs follows a pattern similar to that discussed with gang involvement. The more youth use and abuse drugs, the more the nature of the drug–crime relationship emerges. The progression begins with occasional use and gradually escalates to regular use. Adolescents on limited incomes report that they commit delinquent acts in order to have the income necessary to feed their addiction and this becomes what is referred to as an *economic-compulsive stage*—that is, substantial abuse and psychoactive drug addiction (Brunelle, Tremblay, Blanchette-Martin, Gendron, & Tessier, 2014).

PRESCRIPTION DRUG ABUSE: THE CASE OF NEIL

This case study from the National Advisory Council on Prescription Drug Abuse is illustrative of the issues related to the abuse of prescription medication.

> I stole from my parents, my grandmother, my uncle … everyone. I took money, necklaces and a camcorder to get money for drugs. I was arrested trying to sell a hand gun. I went to jail that night and then to court. At court, I still had drugs hidden in my winter coat. I asked for a magazine and a pencil and used that to crush up the drugs. I snorted them off a magazine in my courthouse holding cell. The only thing I wanted was that drug. Nothing else mattered to me.

For further information, see Canadian Centre on Substance Abuse (2013).

QUESTIONS

1. How does this case study relate to the issues discussed around substance abuse?
2. What do you think should be the strategy for dealing with prescription drug abuse?

At the same time, perceptions about drug use are changing, at least for certain substances. While recreational marijuana use remains illegal in Canada, the admission by Justin Trudeau that he had smoked marijuana while in office is just the latest step toward normalizing marijuana consumption, and calls for the legalization of marijuana continue to grow. Recall that in Chapter 2 this issue was considered in "To Pot or Not." Despite input from a number of groups, at this point, the Canadian government has shown no interest in legalizing marijuana. However, as evidenced by legalization proclamations in various US states in 2012 and 2014, it is likely that the federal government will feel additional pressure on this issue.

LEGAL MARIJUANA: A FICTITIOUS ACCOUNT

Jon Walker (2014), in his book *After Legalization*, considers the various possibilities of how individuals would purchase legal marijuana. Here is an excerpt:

> It is 2030, you're at least 21 years of age, and you want to acquire some marijuana. If you live in part of the vast majority of the country that is "green," meaning it allows marijuana to be sold, you simply head to your nearest marijuana retailer. It is likely to be a small, nondescript store with very minimal advertising on the exterior—the type of place you would miss if you weren't looking for it.

QUESTIONS

1. What is your impression of the ways legalized marijuana will be available?
2. How will the police be able to control the consumption of marijuana by young people under the age of 19?
3. What would the legalization of marijuana mean for the lives of young offenders?

The Internet and Social Media

The **globalization** of youth culture has led to technological changes that play a significant role in altering the nature of youth crime. The importance of cyberspace through the Internet, social media, and other global telecommunications technologies in changing Western society cannot be overestimated. In 2012, 83 percent of Canadian households had access to the Internet at home, 97 percent of households with Internet reporting a high-speed connection (Statistics Canada, 2013a). While laptops and computers remain the most common form of Internet use, 59 percent of those surveyed indicated using the Internet at home on their smartphone in 2012. The consequences of these changes are not all socially beneficial; new technologies have also made new kinds of crime possible and offered new ways for people to commit existing crimes worldwide. Law enforcement officials refer to these new types of criminal behaviour as **cybercrime**. Special units have been set up in police forces worldwide, including those in Canada, to deal with cybercrime.

In chat rooms, on blogs, on social media like Twitter, Facebook, Instagram, LinkedIn, and Pinterest, and by email, people now communicate with each other instantaneously around the globe. The Canadian Internet Registration Authority (CIRA) and the Office of the Privacy Commissioner, together with MediaSmarts, surveyed over 5,000 Canadian students ages 9–17 in a multi-year study to determine the Internet use by young people in Canada. The report reveals that Internet use is universal, with 99 percent of students indicating that they access it outside school. Students report using a portable device more regularly than a laptop or desktop; students as young as grade 5 preferred a tablet over a desktop. One-quarter of students in grade 4, 52 percent of students in grade 7, and 85 percent of students in grade 11 report having their own cellphone with which they can access the Internet.

globalization

the increasing economic interdependence of countries worldwide through a growing quantity and variety of cross-border transactions in goods and services, free international capital flows, and rapid, widespread distribution of technology

cybercrime

criminal activity committed on computers over the Internet

WHAT ARE YOUTH DOING ON THE INTERNET?

According to the MediaSmarts report *Young Canadians in a Wired World* (Steeves, 2014, p. 13), young people reported the following as their most frequent online activities:

Playing online games	59%
Downloading or streaming music, TV shows, or movies	51%
Reading or posting on someone else's social network site	52%
Posting on own social networking site	41%
Posting on own Twitter profile	21%
Following friends and family on Twitter	21%
Following celebrities on Twitter	20%
Pranking or trolling someone	20%

As for their favourite sites, students in 2013 listed more than 3,000 different ones. However, YouTube got the most votes (75 percent), followed by Facebook (57 percent). Seven of the top ten favourite sites are ones that allow users to post and share information and content (YouTube, Facebook, Twitter, Tumblr, Instagram, Minecraft, and Hotmail), underscoring the need for young people to have digital-literacy skills so that they understand the concepts of digital permanence, ethical decision-making, and protecting personal information.

QUESTION

Given the kinds of activities that young people report engaging in online, what are the threats of victimization or potential problems for them?

As a result of the rapid development of new information and computer technologies, some have argued that there is a large technological "generation gap." Prensky (2001) coined the term *digital natives* to describe members of the generation born after computers were invented; these youth feel at home in an environment consisting of Internet, social networks, online media, and games. In contrast, previous generations (*digital immigrants*), born in the analog age or printed text/paper era, struggle to make sense of the new technologies. By virtue of their high computer literacy, adolescents have become involved in new types of criminal activity of surprising sophistication and dramatic consequences.

Police officers report the Internet has made it easy for alienated young people to connect with other disenfranchised youth and track down potentially harmful information. When online conversations between alienated young people focus on violent fantasies, the participants can get the impression that these acts are acceptable or justifiable because so many people seem to be agreeing.

One good thing is that when young people commit crimes of extreme violence, they often leave behind an electronic paper trail. For example, after 25-year-old Kimveer Gill embarked on a shooting spree at Dawson College in Montreal in 2006, killing one teenager and wounding 19 other people, his diary on a "goth" website—where he posted photographs of himself pointing guns at the camera and wrote that he wanted to die in a hail of gunfire—was widely publicized by the media (CBC News, 2006e).

In reality, a more compelling concern than adolescents using the Internet to commit crimes is that adolescents, by virtue of their computer literacy and frequent Internet use, are more likely than adults to fall victim to cybercrime. For example, adult sexual predators can gain access to young victims through Internet chat rooms. Another concern is that the Internet has brought hate speech and literature to an audience who would not otherwise be exposed to it. Alienated adolescents who surf the Web will almost invariably come across hate sites, and they are especially vulnerable to the messages there because their lack of life experience makes them less critical. The influence of Internet hate speech on adolescents has even been linked to school shootings: Columbine students Dylan Klebold and Eric Harris's killing spree was linked to their Internet use, particularly their interest in neo-Nazi hate websites. (For a discussion of Internet use by adolescent offenders, see Verton, 2002.)

Although originally developed by the American military, the Internet has become a democratic information source and communication system. This, while exciting and positive, has also enabled the international organization of criminal activity on a large scale. Symantec, a US-based software security company that makes the popular Norton anti-virus computer application, reported in 2013 that about 7 million people in Canada had been victims of cybercrime in the past 12 months, with the average cost per victim being $380. Further, it reported that the cost of cybercrime has risen to more than $100 billion (Symantec, 2013).

According to a recent report by five of the major Internet security firms, it is anticipated that in 2014 cybercriminals will target five main areas: (1) smart appliances such as refrigerators through which attackers might determine not only personal details but whether a house is empty; (2) social networks including smaller ones with only a few members (LinkedIn is predicted to be a strong target for hackers interested in details about executives); (3) the cloud, where many businesses are storing information away from secure onsite servers; (4) Android smartphones (evidence suggests that Google has experienced increased cybercrime over the past year); and (5) Java plug-ins that have been the gateway for large cyberattacks over the past few years (CBC News, 2014c).

Cybercrime Offences

There are difficulties with enforcing laws in cyberspace because, under s. 6(2) of the *Criminal Code*, people cannot be convicted of an offence that took place outside Canada (with the exceptions of torture, terrorism, and child sex tourism). In the case of cybercrime, international cooperation is facilitated through the Convention on Cybercrime (Council of Europe, 2001), requiring each state party to prosecute cybercrimes committed within its territory. (Canada signed the convention in 2001 but has not yet ratified it.) The *Criminal Code* outlines the following cyber offences:

- *Viruses.* Includes disseminating or attempting to disseminate computer viruses (as well as other malicious code such as worms and Trojan horses).
- *Child pornography.* Includes producing, possessing, accessing, and making available such material. A recent amendment requires Internet service providers to report any incidents of child pornography.
- *Identity theft.* Includes both fraud and trafficking in identity theft.
- *Spam.* Includes unsolicited email including identity theft, phishing, spyware, botnets, and viruses.

In several high-profile cases, **hackers**—individuals who write malicious code to break into and damage others' computers—have turned out to be adolescents. For example, German youth Sven Juergens caused worldwide havoc with his "Sasser" worm virus, bringing banks, airlines, military bases, hospitals, and government buildings to a halt in 2004 ("Teenage Hacker Faces Jail for Global Net Virus," 2004). Juergens was relatively lucky to get only jail time; in 1997, two young Chinese hackers were sentenced to death.

While teenage hackers have committed high-profile mischief using malicious code, this often has had playful dimensions and was not generally intended to harm. For example, the Sasser worm, according to its inventor, was not intended to actually hurt anyone but rather to counter existing viruses. However, many adult career criminal entrepreneurs use the Internet for illicit purposes. Credit card fraud is one example; others are hacking, development of computer viruses, identity theft, and child pornography. In all of these, adult career criminals engage in lucrative black market entrepreneurship electronically, gaining access to victims with whom they would not otherwise have contact. Despite public perception that adolescents are behind most cybercrime, evidence indicates it is actually adults who are responsible for much, if not the vast majority, of its more damaging varieties.

hackers
individuals who, by means of programming skills, gain illegal access to computer files or networks

Cyberbullying

The Internet has also become a tool used by adolescents to bully, harass, and stalk other youth. *Cyberbullying* is generally defined as aggression that is intentionally and repeatedly carried out in an electronic context (for example, email, blogs, instant messages, text messages) against a person who cannot easily defend himself or herself (Kowalski, Giumetti, Schroeder, & Lattanner, 2014). While this broad definition provides an overview of the general state of bullying through electronic means, there are a number of different forms of cyberbullying or *cyberthreats*:

- *Flaming.* Refers to extreme online verbal battles.
- *Harassment.* Refers to repetitive offensive messages sent to the same individual target.
- *Outing and trickery.* Refers to the solicitation of personal information from someone through electronic means and then sharing that information without the individual's consent.
- *Exclusion.* Refers to blocking an individual from "friend" lists.
- *Impersonation.* Refers to pretending to be the victim and then communicating negative information with others as if it were coming from him or her.

- *Cyberstalking.* Refers to the use of electronic communication to "follow" and harass another person by sending repetitive threatening communications.
- *Sexting.* Refers to the distribution of nude pictures of another person without his or her consent (Willard, 2007).

---

1. Review the list and consider what criminal implications there are for participating in cyberbullying, referring to the present offences available in the *Criminal Code*.
2. Do you think all of these "offences" are criminal?
3. If not, which are and which aren't?

A meta-analysis of 131 studies found that those who cyberbully tend to also engage in traditional, face-to-face bullying (Willard, 2007). Further, those who cyberbully are more likely to have been a victim of cyberbullying. The amount of time one spends online and risky behaviour online are also linked to cyberbullying. A lack of parental supervision, poor academic performance, raised anxiety, loneliness, and depression were all linked to being a victim or a perpetrator of cyberbullying.

A recent study of police perceptions of cyberbullying included in-depth interviews with 12 officers from southwestern Ontario, including general patrol officers and school resource officers. Most of the officers indicated that parents' expectation that police should handle cases of bullying has escalated and that they didn't believe all cases were criminal in nature. One officer reported that he felt like a "well-paid babysitter" in dealing with some cases of cyberbullying name-calling that he felt could have been better dealt with by parents or the school.

All of the officers spoke of the need to provide specific guidance, in legislation, not only to define what cyberbullying is, but also to distinguish minor offences from more serious behaviours. Most felt that the current provisions in the *Criminal Code* were sufficient to handle the more serious offences, and cited criminal harassment, uttering threats, and mischief as the most suitable charges to be laid (Broll & Huey, 2014).

CYBERBULLYING: THE CASE OF REHTAEH PARSONS

In 2012, 15-year-old Nova Scotia teenager Rehtaeh Parsons and a close friend attended a small house party where, despite being under the legal age to consume alcohol, Rehtaeh became intoxicated and passed out. While she was passed out, four boys took turns having sex with her without consent. One of the boys took photographs on his cellphone that he sent to his friends. A week later, Rehtaeh found out about the photographs, and a number of peers began to harass her online with repeated comments referring to her as a "slut."

After a police investigation failed to result in charges, Rehtaeh felt unable to return to school and face her attackers, so her parents transferred her to a new school. Despite attending counselling, she was unable to cope with suicidal depression, and on April 4, 2013 she attempted suicide by hanging. She fell into a coma and was taken off life support three days later.

In April 2014, the police laid charges against two of the boys, now 18 years of age. One was accused of two counts of distributing child pornography, the other with making and distributing child pornography. The other was charged with uttering death threats and criminal harassment after Rehtaeh's father received threats on YouTube and his blog.

As a result of this case, anti-cyberbullying legislation was passed in Nova Scotia (*Cyber-Safety Act*, 2013). It allows victims to get protection orders and includes provisions for victims to sue the parents of young cyberbullies. Several municipal governments have passed bylaws prohibiting bullying, including cyberbullying, with fines ranging from $2,000 to $10,000 available for repeat offences. The federal government is now contemplating cyberbullying legislation in an attempt at prevention.

A publication ban was imposed in this case in order to protect the identity of the young persons involved, as discussed in Chapter 3. The ban was lifted when the parents sought public support to honour the memory of their daughter.

The young person who took the photos pleaded guilty to making child pornography in November 2014 and was given a conditional discharge, which included an order to apologize to the Parsons family in writing and provide a DNA sample for the national sex offender registry. The other young person was sentenced to 12 months' probation in January 2015, while still facing separate charges of assault and making death threats.

QUESTIONS

1. Are new laws necessary? Could justice for Rehtaeh have been achieved by existing laws? Could police have done anything differently in her case, and, if so, what?

2. The Nova Scotia *Cyber-Safety Act* defines cyberbullying as "any electronic communication through the use of technology … typically repeated or with continuing effect, that is intended or ought reasonably [to] be expected to cause fear, intimidation, humiliation, distress or other damage or harm to another person's health, emotional well-being, self-esteem or reputation, and includes assisting or encouraging such communication in any way." The term "sexting" does not appear in this definition, yet the Act was implemented in response to the Rehtaeh Parsons case. How might this definition be interpreted to cover cases of sexting?

3. What is your opinion of the sentences the young men received?

This is the brave new world of social interaction, in which existing ways of supervising teens and legal frameworks regulating their behaviour are inadequate and need to be adapted. Things like cyberbullying and "sexting" present serious challenges to the youth criminal justice system with respect to regulating young people's actions on social media and the Internet in ways that protect teens without unduly criminalizing others. It is perhaps more appropriate to focus on ways of protecting adolescents from cybercrime rather than to crack down on their electronic offending.

CHAPTER SUMMARY

While minor offending remains a normal part of adolescence, young people are not more likely to commit serious crimes than adults. Youth crime and violence are not on the rise in Canada, even when emerging factors such as gangs and guns, drugs, globalization, shifting immigration patterns, tensions in international politics, changing understandings of gender and gender roles, social media, and other technological changes are considered. The influence of the media on public perceptions of these issues, however, has left most people misinformed, anxious, and fearful.

Adolescents are especially vulnerable and are more likely to be victimized than adults. For Aboriginal adolescents, additional risk factors—the preponderance of fetal alcohol spectrum disorder and other mental health challenges—predispose them to be involved in the criminal justice system, and they make up far more than their statistical share of the population of adolescents charged and sentenced for crimes despite provisions in the law to utilize alternative methods.

Of course, when adolescents offend, this must be addressed. It is evident that youth offending takes place in a complex social context, and should be approached with insight about that context. Police, together with lawyers, judges, courts, community groups, social advocates, and politicians, should seek to act thoughtfully in the moment and to implement programs and initiatives that focus more on addressing the underlying social causes of youth crime than on forcefully "solving" the problem with arrest, detention, conviction, and incarceration.

KEY TERMS

al-Qaeda, 227
bath salts, 240
cyberbanging, 237
cybercrime, 241
enhancement model, 237

gender-specific, 232
globalization, 241
hackers, 243
hate crime, 230

REFERENCES

After Jane, a rallying cry. (2006, June 18). *Toronto Star*.

Alain, A., Corrado, R., & Reid, S. (forthcoming). *Implementing and working with the YCJA across Canada: A view from the "ground."* Toronto: University of Toronto Press.

Arciaga, M., Sakamoto, W., & Jones, E.F. (2010). Responding to gangs in the school setting. National Gang Center Bulletin. Retrieved from http://www.nationalgangcenter.gov/Content/Documents/Bulletin-5.pdf.

Ariza, J.J.M., Cebulla, A., Aldridge, J., Shute, J., & Ross, A. (2014). Proximal adolescent outcomes of gang membership in England and Wales. *Journal of Research in Crime and Delinquency*, *51*(2), 168–199.

Astwood Strategy Corporation. (2002). *Canadian police survey on youth gangs*. Catalogue No. PS4-4/2002. Ottawa: Solicitor General of Canada.

Bahdi, R. (2003). No exit: Racial profiling and Canada's war against terrorism. *Osgoode Hall Law Journal*, *41*, 293–316.

Bertrand, L.D., MacRae-Krisa, L.D., Costello, M., & Winterdyk, J. (2013). Ethnic diversity and youth offending: An examination of risk and protective factors. *International Journal of Child, Youth and Family Studies*, *4*(1), 166–188.

Boxer, P., Veysey, B., Ostermann, M., & Kubik, J. (2014). Measuring gang involvement in a justice-referred sample of youth in treatment. *Youth Violence and Juvenile Justice*, 1–19.

Brochu, S. (2006). *Drogue et criminalité* [Drugs and criminality] (2nd ed.). Montreal: Les Presses de l'Université de Montréal.

Broll, R., & Huey, L. (2014). "Just being mean to somebody isn't a police matter": Police perspectives on policing cyberbullying. *Journal of School Violence*, *13*, 1–22. doi:10.1080/15388220.2013.879367.

Brown, L., & Rushowy, K. (2014, September 23). School stabbing revives trauma of Jordan Manners shooting. *Toronto Star*. Retrieved from http://www.thestar.com/yourtoronto/education/2014/09/23/toronto_school_stabbing_death_deja_vu_seven_years_later.html.

Brunelle, N., Tremblay, J., Blanchette-Martin, N., Gendron, A., & Tessier, M. (2014). Relationships between drugs and delinquency in adolescence: Influence of gender and victimization experiences. *Journal of Child and Adolescent Substance Abuse*, *23*(1), 19–28.

Butters, J.E., Sheptycki, J., Brochu, S., & Erickson, P.G. (2011). Guns and sublethal violence: A comparative study of at-risk youth in two Canadian cities. *International Criminal Justice Review*, *21*(4), 402–426.

Cahute, L., & Desi, V. (2013). Sikh heritage museum tells of turban's troubled times in B.C. Retrieved from http://www.vancouverdesi.com/news/nridiaspora/exhibit-sikh-heritage-museum-tells-of-turbans-troubled-times-in-b-c/466404/.

Calverley, D., Cotter, A., & Halla, E. (2010). Youth custody and community services in Canada, 2008/2009. *Juristat*, *30*(1). Catalogue No. 85-002-X. Ottawa: Statistics Canada.

Campaign 2000. (2014). Child poverty 25 years later: We can fix this. Retrieved from http://www.campaign2000.ca/anniversaryreport/CanadaRC2014EN.pdf.

Canadian Centre on Substance Abuse. (2013, March). *First do no harm: Responding to Canada's prescription drug crisis*. Ottawa: Canadian Centre on Substance Abuse. Retrieved from http://www.ccsa.ca.

Canadian Charter of Rights and Freedoms. (1982). Part I of the *Constitution Act, 1982*, being Schedule B to the *Canada Act 1982* (UK), 1982, c. 11.

Canadian Press. (2013, December 19). Ashley Smith death ruled a homicide by inquest jury. Retrieved from http://news.nationalpost.com/2013/12/19/ashley-smith-death-ruled-a-homicide-by-inquest-jury/.

Canadian Women's Foundation. (2012). Moving girls into confidence [Fact sheet]. Retrieved from http://canadianwomen.org/sites/canadianwomen.org/files//FactSheet-Girls-ACTIVE_2.pdf.

Carrington, K., & Pereira, M. (2011). Assessing the social impacts of the resources boom on rural communities. *Rural Society*, *21*(1), 2–20.

CBC News. (1990, March 15). Sikh Mounties permitted to wear turbans [Broadcast]. Retrieved from http://www.cbc.ca/archives/categories/society/crime-justice/mounties-on-duty-a-history-of-the-rcmp/sikh-mounties-permitted-to-wear-turbans.html.

CBC News. (2005, December 31). Support ban on handguns, Toronto's mayor urges. Retrieved from http://www.cbc.ca/story/canada/national/2005/12/30/mayor_shootings051230.html.

CBC News. (2006a, June 4). Mosque vandalized after bomb-plot sweep. Retrieved from http://www.cbc.ca/story/canada/national/2006/06/04/mosque-vandalized.html.

CBC News. (2006b, June 12). In depth: Toronto bomb plot profiles of the suspects. Retrieved from http://www.cbc.ca/news/background/toronto-bomb-plot/suspects.html.

CBC News. (2006c, June 13). 8 arrested in Jane Creba shooting death. Retrieved from http://www.cbc.ca/toronto/story/to-creba20060613.html.

CBC News. (2006d, June 20). 2 sisters get maximum penalty in mother's drowning. Retrieved from http://www.cbc.ca/news/canada/toronto/2-sisters-get-maximum-youth-penalty-in-mother-s-drowning-1.601264.

CBC News. (2006e, September 15). College shooter Gill obsessed with guns. Retrieved from http://www.cbc.ca/news/canada/montreal/college-shooter-gill-obsessed-with-guns-1.589809.

CBC News. (2012, June 2). Toronto Eaton Centre shooting kills 1, injures 7. Retrieved from http://www.cbc.ca/news/canada/toronto/toronto-eaton-centre-shooting-kills-1-injures-7-1.1160460.

CBC News. (2014a, September 3). Omar Khadr reattempts to sue Canada for $20M. Retrieved from http://www.cbc.ca/news/world/omar-khadr-reattempts-to-sue-canada-for-20m-1.2753689.

CBC News. (2014b, September 24). Mohamud Mohamed Mohamud: Hamilton youth reported killed as ISIS fighter "not the son they knew." Retrieved from http://www.cbc.ca/news/canada/hamilton/news/mohamud-mohamed-mohamud-hamilton-youth-reported-killed-as-isis-fighter-not-the-son-they-knew-1.2776246.

CBC News. (2014c, January 2). Cybercriminals are eyeing these 5 targets in 2014. Retrieved from http://www.cbc.ca/news/technology/cybercriminals-are-eyeing-these-5-targets-in-2014-1.2475721.

Chettleburgh, M.C. (2007). *Young thugs: Inside the dangerous world of Canadian street gangs*. Toronto: HarperCollins.

Chongatera, G. (2013). Hate-crime victimization and fear of hate crime among racially visible people in Canada: The role of income as a mediating factor. *Journal of Immigrant and Refugee Studies*, *11*(1), 44–64.

Controlled Drugs and Substances Act. (1996). SC 1996, c. 19.

Copps, K. (2013, October 13). Omar Khadr in court: Eight ways the mainstream media missed the real story. Retrieved from http://freeomarakhadr.com/articles/omar-khadr-in-court-eight-ways-the-mainstream-media-missed-the-real-story/.

Corrado, R., Cohen, I., & Watkinson, A. (2008). The over-representation of Aboriginal youth in custody: Policy challenges. *Horizons, Policy Research Initiative*, *10*(1), 70–87.

Corrado, R.R., Kuehn, S., & Margaritescu, I. (2014). Policy issues regarding the overrepresentation of incarcerated aboriginal young offenders in a Canadian context. *Youth Justice*, *14*(1), 40–62.

Council of Europe. (2001, November 23). *Convention on cybercrime*. ETS No. 185.

Criminal Code. (1985). RSC 1985, c. C-46.

Criminal complaint against Dzhokhar Tsarnaev. (2013, April 21). US District Court, Massachusetts. Retrieved from http://online.wsj.com/articles/SB10001424127887324235304578438930168800650.

Criminal Intelligence Service Canada (CISC). (2010). *Report on organized crime*. Ottawa: CISC. Retrieved from http://www.cisc.gc.ca/media/2014/2014-08-22-eng.htm.

Cyber-Safety Act. (2013). SNS 2013, c. 2.

Dallaire, R. (2012, June 29). Speech on Omar Khadr. Speech to the Senate of Canada. Retrieved from http://romeodallaire.sencanada.ca/en/p103115/.

Dijkstra, J.K., Lindenberg, S., Veenstra, R., Steglich, C., Isaacs, J., Card, N.S., & Hodges, E.V.E. (2010). Influence and selection processes in weapon carrying during adolescence: The roles of status, aggression and vulnerability. *Criminology*, *48*, 187–220.

Eisler, L., & Schissel, B. (2004). Privation and vulnerability to victimization for Canadian youth: The contexts of gender, race, and geography. *Youth Violence and Juvenile Justice*, *2*(4), 359–373.

Employment Equity Act. (1995). SC 1995, c. 44.

Ezeonu, I. (2010). Gun violence in Toronto: Perspectives from the police. *The Howard Journal*, *49*, 147–165.

Fast, D.K., Conry, J., & Loock, C.A. (1999). Identifying fetal alcohol syndrome among youth in the criminal justice system. *Journal of Developmental and Behavioral Pediatrics*, *20*(5), 370–372.

Galarneau, D., Morissette, R., & Usalcas, J. (2013). What has changed for young people in Canada? Statistics Canada, Catalogue No. 75-006-X. Retrieved from http://www.statcan .gc.ca/pub/75-006-x/2013001/article/11847-eng.pdf.

Hemmati, T. (2006). *The nature of Canadian urban gangs and their use of firearms: A review of the literature and police survey*. Ottawa: Department of Justice Canada. Retrieved from http://www.justice.gc.ca/eng/rp-pr/csj-sjc/crime/ rr07_1/rr07_1.pdf.

Henggeler, S.W., Edwards, J., & Borduin, C.M. (1987). The family relations of female juvenile delinquents. *Journal of Abnormal Child Psychology*, *15*, 199–209.

Hennessey, M., Ford, J.D., Mahoney, K., Ko, S.J., & Siegfried, C.B. (2004). *Trauma among girls in the juvenile justice system*. Los Angeles: National Child Traumatic Stress Network.

Howell, J.C. (2012). *Gangs in America's communities*. Thousand Oaks, CA: Sage.

Ipeelee, R v. (2012). 2012 SCC 13, [2012] 1 SCR 433.

Khenti, A.A. (2013). Homicide among young black men in Toronto: An unrecognized public health crisis? *Canadian Journal of Public Health*, *104*(1), 12–14.

Kong, R. (2009). Youth custody and community services in Canada, 2007/2008. *Juristat*. Ottawa: Statistics Canada.

Korf, D., Brochu, S., Benschop, A., Harrison, L., & Erickson, P.G. (2008). Teen drug sellers: A cross national study of segregated drug markets and related violence. *Contemporary Drug Problems*, *35*, 153–176.

Kowalski, R.M., Giumetti, G.W., Schroeder, A.N., & Lattanner, M.R. (2014, February 10). Bullying in the digital age: A critical review and meta-analysis of cyberbullying research among youth. *Psychological Bulletin*. Advance online publication. Retrieved from http://dx.doi.org/ 10.1037/a0035618.

Lamberti, R. (2003, December 31). Gun violence is way up in Toronto this year. *Toronto Sun*.

Liebenberg, L., & Ungar, M. (2014). A comparison of service use among youth involved with juvenile justice and mental health. *Children and Youth Services Review*, *39*, 117–122.

MacCreary Centre Society. (2007). Not yet equal: The health of lesbian, gay, & bisexual youth in BC. Retrieved from http://www.mcs.bc.ca/pdf/not_yet_equal_web.pdf.

Mark, M. (2013). Cindy Blackstock: Fighting for the vulnerable. *Vue Weekly*. Retrieved from http://www.vueweekly.com/ cindy-blackstock-fighting-for-the-vulnerable.

Marlow, I., Huffman, T., & Kassam, T. (2007, May 25). Police mum on shooting motive. *Toronto Star*. Retrieved from http://www.thestar.com/news/2007/05/25/police_mum _on_shooting_motive.html.

Marston, E.G., Russell, M.A., Obsuth, I., & Watson, G.K. (2012). Dealing with double jeopardy: Mental health disorders among girls in the juvenile justice system. In S. Miller, L.D. Leve, & P.K. Kerig (Eds.), *Delinquent girls: Contexts, relationships, and adaptation* (pp. 105–118). New York: Springer.

Matusicky, C. (2014). Wealth and well-being among Canada's children. *Transition*, *43*(4), 15.

McLachlan, K., Roesch, R., Viljoen, J.L., & Douglas, K.S. (2014). Evaluating the psycholegal abilities of young offenders with fetal alcohol spectrum disorder. *Law and Human Behavior*, *38*(1), 10–22.

Melde, C., & Finn-Age, E. (2011). Gang membership as a turning point in the life course. *Criminology*, *49*, 513–552.

Morselli, C. (2010). *Crime facilitation purposes of social networking sites: A review and analysis of the "cyberbanging" phenomenon*. Ottawa: Public Safety Canada.

Munch, C. (2012). Youth correctional statistics in Canada, 2010/2011. *Juristat*. Ottawa: Statistics Canada.

Nasr, W., & Phillips, K. (2014). Current issues in mental health in Canada: Directions in federal substance abuse policy. Publication No. 2014-06-E. Ottawa: Library of Parliament. Retrieved from http://www.parl.gc.ca/Content/LOP/ ResearchPublications/2014-06-e.pdf.

O'Brien, K., Daffern, M., Chu, C.M., & Thomas, S.D.M. (2013). Youth gang affiliation, violence, and criminal activities: A review of motivational, risk, and protective factors. *Aggression and Violent Behavior*, *18*, 417–425.

Office of the Correctional Investigator. (2013). Aboriginal offenders: A critical situation. Retrieved from http://www.oci-bec.gc.ca/cnt/rpt/oth-aut/ oth-aut20121022info-eng.aspx.

O'Grady, W., Parnaby, P.F., & Schikschneit, J. (2010). Guns, gangs, and the underclass: A constructionist analysis of gun violence in a Toronto high school. *Canadian Journal of Criminology and Criminal Justice*, *52*(1), 55–77.

Omar Khadr: A chronology. (2012, September 29). *Toronto Star*. Retrieved from http://www.thestar.com/news/world/2012/09/29/omar_khadr_a_chronology.html.

Park, A.S. (2014). Constituting Omar Khadr: Cultural racism, childhood, and citizenship. *International Political Sociology*, *8*(1), 43–62.

Perkel, C. (2014, October 23). Omar Khadr wins right to expand lawsuit against Ottawa. *Toronto Star*. Retrieved from http://www.thestar.com/news/canada/2014/10/23/omar_khadr_wins_right_expand_lawsuit_against_ottawa.html.

Peterson, D., & Panfil, V.R. (2014). Introduction: Reducing the invisibility of sexual and gender identities in criminology and criminal justice. In D. Peterson & V.R. Panfil (Eds.), *Handbook of LGBT communities, crime, and justice* (pp. 3–13). New York: Springer.

Podgurski, I., Lyons, J.S., Kisiel, C., & Griffin, G. (2014). Understanding bad girls: The role of trauma in antisocial behavior among female youth. *Residential Treatment for Children and Youth*, *31*(1), 80–88.

Prensky, M. (2001). Digital natives, digital immigrants. *On the Horizon*, *9*(5), 1–6.

Reid, S. (2013). Ashley Smith case study. In K. O'Regan & S. Reid (Eds.), *Thinking about criminal justice in Canada* (pp. 325–332). Toronto: Emond Montgomery.

Rossiter, M.J., & Rossiter, K.R. (2009). Diamonds in the rough: Bridging gaps in supports for at-risk immigrant and refugee youth. *International Migration and Immigration*, *10*(4), 409–429.

Ruddell, R. (2011). Boomtown policing: Responding to the dark side of resource development. *Policing*, *5*(4), 328–342.

Saewyc, E.M. (2011). Research on adolescent sexual orientation: Development, health disparities, stigma, and resilience. *Journal of Research on Adolescence*, *21*(1), 256–272.

Saewyc, E., Gahagan, J., Austin, B., Beaulieu-Prevost, D., Chaberland, L., Emond, G., Grace, A., Peter, T., Rose, H., Russell, S., Smith, A., Taylor, C., Travers, R., Wells, K., & Marshall, S. (2012). Reducing stigma, promoting resilience: Population health interventions for LGBTQ youth. Dalhousie University multi-year study. http://www.dal.ca/diff/gahps/research-projects/reducing-stigma-promoting-resilience.html.

Scelfo, J. (2005, June 13). Bad girls go wild. *Newsweek*, p. 2.

Smith, D.K., Leve, L.D., and Chamberlain, P. (2006). Adolescent girls' offending and health risking sexual behavior: The predictive role of trauma. *Child Maltreatment*, *11*, 346–353.

Smith, D.K., & Saldana, L. (2013). Trauma, delinquency, and substance use: Co-occurring problems for adolescent girls in the juvenile justice system. *Journal of Child and Adolescent Substance Abuse*, *22*(5), 450–465.

Statistics Canada. (2001). *Hate crime in Canada: An overview of issues and data sources*. Canadian Centre for Justice Statistics. Catalogue No. 85-551-XIE. Ottawa: Statistics Canada.

Statistics Canada. (2011). National Household Survey, Data profile. Retrieved from http://www12.statcan.gc.ca/nhs-enm/2011.

Statistics Canada. (2012). Homicide in Canada, 2011. *Juristat*. Retrieved from http://www.statcan.gc.ca/pub/85-002-x/2012001/article/11738-eng.htm.

Statistics Canada. (2013a, November 26). Canadian Internet use survey 2012. *The Daily*.

Statistics Canada. (2013b). *Immigration and ethnocultural diversity in Canada: National household survey, 2011*. Catalogue No. 99-010-X2011001. Ottawa: Statistics Canada.

Statistics Canada. (2014, September 26). Canada's population estimates: Age and sex, 2014. *The Daily*. Retrieved from http://www.statcan.gc.ca/daily-quotidien/140926/dq140926b-eng.htm.

Steeves, V. (2014). *Young Canadians in a wired world: Phase III—Life online*. Ottawa: MediaSmarts. Retrieved from http://mediasmarts.ca/research-policy.

Symantec. (2013). *Norton report*. Retrieved from http://www.symantec.com/about/news/resources/press_kits/detail.jsp?pkid=norton-report-2013.

Teenage hacker faces jail for global net virus. (2004, May 10). *The Scotsman*. Retrieved from http://www.scotsman.com/news/sci-tech/teenage-hacker-faces-jail-for-global-net-virus-1-530328.

Teotonio, I. (2010). Toronto 18. *Toronto Star*. Retrieved from http://www3.thestar.com/static/toronto18/.

Teplin, L.A., Abram, K.M., McClelland, G.M., Dulcan, M.K., & Mericle, A.A. (2002). Psychiatric disorders in youth in juvenile detention. *Archives of General Psychiatry*, *59*, 1133–1143.

Thompson, S.K. (2009). *The social ecology and spatial distribution of lethal violence in Toronto, 1988–2003* [Doctoral dissertation]. University of Toronto.

Totten and Associates. (2011, March). Final evaluation report for the Regina Anti-Gang Services (RAGS) project. Gatineau, QC. Retrieved from http://www.nccaregina.ca/wp-content/uploads/2011/11/RAGS_YGPF_Final_Evaluation_Report_Totten_March_24_2011.pdf.

Verton, D. (2002). *The hacker diaries: Confessions of teenage hackers*. Berkeley, CA: McGraw-Hill/Osborne.

Walker, J. (2014). *After legalization: Understanding the future of marijuana policy*. Washington, DC: FDL Writers Foundation.

Willard, N.E. (2007). *Cyberbullying and cyberthreats: Responding to the challenge of online social aggression, threats, and distress*. Champaign, IL: Research Press.

Woodin, H. (2014). First Sikh RCMP officer to wear turban will receive honorary degree from KPU. Retrieved from http://www.kpu.ca/news/first-sikh-rcmp-officer-wear-turban-will-receive-honorary-degree-kpu.

Wortley, S. (2010). *Identifying street gangs: Definitional dilemmas and their policy implications*. Ottawa: Public Safety Canada.

Wortley, S., & Owusu-Bempah, A. (2012). Race, ethnicity, crime and criminal justice in Canada. In A. Kalunta-Crumpton (Ed.), *Race, ethnicity, crime and criminal justice in the Americas* (pp. 11–40). New York: Palgrave Macmillan.

Youth Criminal Justice Act. (2002). SC 2002, c. 1.

Zahn, M.A. (Ed.). (2009). *The delinquent girl*. Philadelphia: Temple University Press.

EXERCISES AND REVIEW

Gangster Finally Makes an Exit

The following vignette is taken from Totten and Associates (2011, p. 2). The original words of the participant have been maintained for this case study.

Anthony was a 26-year-old who, after participating in the Regina Anti-Gang Services (RAGS) project, had finally left his gang. At the time of his writing this case study, he had been out of his gang for 22 weeks. He explains his circumstances below:

> My mom passed away last month, my dad is in jail looking at a Dangerous Offender status. I was raised by foster homes and my grandma. I quit 3 months into grade 12 because I wanted to be a gangster, be cool. I got more hard into it. That's when drugs came in. Started off smoking weed then to harder ones, coke and mo. Started off somewhat positive with my friends then we all started taking off from school. Getting high then started off into drugs, violence, selling drugs then in and out of jail, after grade nine. I was doing missions for my gang, scamming and taxing people. Basically all drug dealers, doing armed robberies. I made the paper a couple of times. Even when I stayed in (city) I made the paper there—stabbing. I got a thrill outta that.
>
> Twelve years of my life a gang member—half of my life. I am out now. I dropped my rag because of family life. I have three kids. I started basically seeing the better side of life, having friends who actually cared. Like when I was in the hospital, I found out who my friends really were, who my true friends were.
>
> It wasn't easy getting out. Not just takin' a lickin', but I still got problems. I don't answer to anyone but myself. The hardest part was abandoning them. When I needed them they were there. But when I really needed them they were nowhere to be found. Having people like you guys [RAGS staff] around, for showing the positive side, what I never seen. There's more to life than that. Someone listening to you and you being heard. 'Cause I know I don't have to answer to anyone, I am in charge now.

What activities reported on by this former gang member have you read about in this chapter?

Sexting: Hypothetical—Jane's Case

Jane, a 14-year-old girl, sent a nude photo of herself in a smartphone message to her boyfriend, John. Two weeks later, the two broke up, and John angrily forwarded the photo to his friend Jim, who then passed it along. In short order, the photo "went viral" in their high school.

Should John be charged with child pornography offences? Should Jim? Should Jane? How might police called to the school to deal with this situation address the circumstances appropriately?

Review Questions

1. Describe what aspects of the nature of adolescence have not changed, and probably will not change, over time.

2. Describe some effects of economic globalization on the public's perceptions of, and realities in relation to, adolescent offending.

3. What might account for the continuing perception of the public and police that offending by adolescent females is increasing?

4. Describe the different varieties of cybercrime and discuss ways adolescents are involved in, or affected by, each.

5. How are international tensions affecting public perceptions and realities about youth crime?

6. What role does increased digital literacy have on youth's potential for the commission of crime? What has changed and what has stayed the same in terms of technology and youth, and what methods should be employed to prevent youth from becoming victims of cybercrime?

Discussion Question

Using an Internet search engine, look up the terms "youth," "crime," and "violence" in combination. Conduct a review of the first ten search results. Analyze the articles in terms of whether the article is concerned with, alludes to, mentions, or cites the following:

   a. gang activity

   b. race or ethnicity

   c. gender

   d. poverty

   e. social values

   f. adequacy of the law

   g. terrorism

   h. violence

   i. positive or negative views about youth

What terms came up most frequently in your search? Were there some terms that you were not able to find in any news articles? Were there certain times of the year that seemed to have more articles? What was most surprising to you?

Youth Criminal Justice Act

SC 2002, c. 1, as amended
Retrieved from http://laws.justice.gc.ca

An Act in respect of criminal justice for young persons and to amend and repeal other Acts

PREAMBLE

WHEREAS members of society share a responsibility to address the developmental challenges and the needs of young persons and to guide them into adulthood;

WHEREAS communities, families, parents and others concerned with the development of young persons should, through multidisciplinary approaches, take reasonable steps to prevent youth crime by addressing its underlying causes, to respond to the needs of young persons, and to provide guidance and support to those at risk of committing crimes;

WHEREAS information about youth justice, youth crime and the effectiveness of measures taken to address youth crime should be publicly available;

WHEREAS Canada is a party to the United Nations Convention on the Rights of the Child and recognizes that young persons have rights and freedoms, including those stated in the *Canadian Charter of Rights and Freedoms* and the *Canadian Bill of Rights*, and have special guarantees of their rights and freedoms;

AND WHEREAS Canadian society should have a youth criminal justice system that commands respect, takes into account the interests of victims, fosters responsibility and ensures accountability through meaningful consequences and effective rehabilitation and reintegration, and that reserves its most serious intervention for the most serious crimes and reduces the over-reliance on incarceration for non-violent young persons;

NOW, THEREFORE, Her Majesty, by and with the advice and consent of the Senate and House of Commons of Canada, enacts as follows:

SHORT TITLE

Short title

1. This Act may be cited as the *Youth Criminal Justice Act.*

INTERPRETATION

Definitions

2. (1) The definitions in this subsection apply in this Act.

"adult" means a person who is neither a young person nor a child.

"adult sentence", in the case of a young person who is found guilty of an offence, means any sentence that could be imposed on an adult who has been convicted of the same offence.

"Attorney General" means the Attorney General as defined in section 2 of the *Criminal Code*, read as if the reference in that definition to "proceedings" were a reference to "proceedings or extrajudicial measures", and includes an agent or delegate of the Attorney General.

"child" means a person who is or, in the absence of evidence to the contrary, appears to be less than twelve years old.

"conference" means a group of persons who are convened to give advice in accordance with section 19.

"confirmed delivery service" means certified or registered mail or any other method of service that provides proof of delivery.

"custodial portion", with respect to a youth sentence imposed on a young person under paragraph 42(2)(n), (o), (q) or (r), means the period of time, or the portion of the young person's youth sentence, that must be served in custody before he or she begins to serve the remainder under supervision in the community subject to conditions under paragraph 42(2)(n) or under conditional supervision under paragraph 42(2)(o), (q) or (r).

"disclosure" means the communication of information other than by way of publication.

"extrajudicial measures" means measures other than judicial proceedings under this Act used to deal with a young person alleged to have committed an offence and includes extrajudicial sanctions.

"extrajudicial sanction" means a sanction that is part of a program referred to in section 10.

"offence" means an offence created by an Act of Parliament or by any regulation, rule, order, by-law or ordinance made under an Act of Parliament other than a law of the Legislature of Yukon, of the Northwest Territories or for Nunavut.

"parent" includes, in respect of a young person, any person who is under a legal duty to provide for the young person or any person who has, in law or in fact, the custody or control of the young person, but does not include a person who has the custody or control of the young person by reason only of proceedings under this Act.

"pre-sentence report" means a report on the personal and family history and present environment of a young person made in accordance with section 40.

"presumptive offence" [Repealed, 2012, c. 1, s. 167]

"provincial director" means a person, a group or class of persons or a body appointed or designated by or under an Act of the legislature of a province or by the lieutenant governor in council of a province or his or her delegate to perform in that province, either generally or in a specific case, any of the duties or functions of a provincial director under this Act.

"publication" means the communication of information by making it known or accessible to the general public through any means, including print, radio or television broadcast, telecommunication or electronic means.

"record" includes any thing containing information, regardless of its physical form or characteristics, including microform, sound recording, videotape, machine-readable record, and any copy of any of those things, that is created or kept for the purposes of this Act or for the investigation of an offence that is or could be prosecuted under this Act.

"review board" means a review board referred to in subsection 87(2).

"serious offence" means an indictable offence under an Act of Parliament for which the maximum punishment is imprisonment for five years or more.

"serious violent offence" means an offence under one of the following provisions of the *Criminal Code*:

(a) section 231 or 235 (first degree murder or second degree murder);

(b) section 239 (attempt to commit murder);

(c) section 232, 234 or 236 (manslaughter); or

(d) section 273 (aggravated sexual assault).

"violent offence" means

(a) an offence committed by a young person that includes as an element the causing of bodily harm;

(b) an attempt or a threat to commit an offence referred to in paragraph (a); or

(c) an offence in the commission of which a young person endangers the life or safety of another person by creating a substantial likelihood of causing bodily harm.

"young person" means a person who is or, in the absence of evidence to the contrary, appears to be twelve years old or older, but less than eighteen years old and, if the context requires, includes any person who is charged under this Act with having committed an offence while he or she was a young person or who is found guilty of an offence under this Act.

"youth custody facility" means a facility designated under subsection 85(2) for the placement of young persons and, if so designated, includes a facility for the secure restraint of young persons, a community residential centre, a group home, a child care institution and a forest or wilderness camp.

"youth justice court" means a youth justice court referred to in section 13.

"youth justice court judge" means a youth justice court judge referred to in section 13.

"youth sentence" means a sentence imposed under section 42, 51 or 59 or any of sections 94 to 96 and includes a confirmation or a variation of that sentence.

"youth worker" means any person appointed or designated, whether by title of youth worker or probation officer or by any other title, by or under an Act of the legislature of a province or by the lieutenant governor in council of a province or his or her delegate to perform in that province, either generally or in a specific case, any of the duties or functions of a youth worker under this Act.

Words and expressions

(2) Unless otherwise provided, words and expressions used in this Act have the same meaning as in the *Criminal Code*.

Descriptive cross-references

(3) If, in any provision of this Act, a reference to another provision of this Act or a provision of any other Act is followed by words in parentheses that are or purport to be descriptive of the subject-matter of the provision referred to, those words form no part of the provision in which they occur but are inserted for convenience of reference only.

DECLARATION OF PRINCIPLE

Policy for Canada with respect to young persons

3. (1) The following principles apply in this Act:

(a) the youth criminal justice system is intended to protect the public by

(i) holding young persons accountable through measures that are proportionate to the seriousness of the offence and the degree of responsibility of the young person,

(ii) promoting the rehabilitation and reintegration of young persons who have committed offences, and

(iii) supporting the prevention of crime by referring young persons to programs or agencies in the community to address the circumstances underlying their offending behaviour;

(b) the criminal justice system for young persons must be separate from that of adults, must be based on the principle of diminished moral blameworthiness or culpability and must emphasize the following:

(i) rehabilitation and reintegration,

(ii) fair and proportionate accountability that is consistent with the greater dependency of young persons and their reduced level of maturity,

(iii) enhanced procedural protection to ensure that young persons are treated fairly and that their rights, including their right to privacy, are protected,

(iv) timely intervention that reinforces the link between the offending behaviour and its consequences, and

(v) the promptness and speed with which persons responsible for enforcing this Act must act, given young persons' perception of time;

(c) within the limits of fair and proportionate accountability, the measures taken against young persons who commit offences should

(i) reinforce respect for societal values,

(ii) encourage the repair of harm done to victims and the community,

(iii) be meaningful for the individual young person given his or her needs and level of development and, where appropriate, involve the parents, the extended family, the community and social or other agencies in the young person's rehabilitation and reintegration, and

(iv) respect gender, ethnic, cultural and linguistic differences and respond to the needs of aboriginal young persons and of young persons with special requirements; and

(d) special considerations apply in respect of proceedings against young persons and, in particular,

(i) young persons have rights and freedoms in their own right, such as a right to be heard in the course of and to participate in the processes, other than the decision to prosecute, that lead to decisions that affect them, and young persons have special guarantees of their rights and freedoms,

(ii) victims should be treated with courtesy, compassion and respect for their dignity and privacy and should suffer the minimum degree of inconvenience as a result of their involvement with the youth criminal justice system,

(iii) victims should be provided with information about the proceedings and given an opportunity to participate and be heard, and

(iv) parents should be informed of measures or proceedings involving their children and encouraged to support them in addressing their offending behaviour.

Act to be liberally construed

(2) This Act shall be liberally construed so as to ensure that young persons are dealt with in accordance with the principles set out in subsection (1).

PART 1
EXTRAJUDICIAL MEASURES

PRINCIPLES AND OBJECTIVES

Declaration of principles

4. The following principles apply in this Part in addition to the principles set out in section 3:

(a) extrajudicial measures are often the most appropriate and effective way to address youth crime;

(b) extrajudicial measures allow for effective and timely interventions focused on correcting offending behaviour;

(c) extrajudicial measures are presumed to be adequate to hold a young person accountable for his or her offending behaviour if the young person has committed a non-violent offence and has not previously been found guilty of an offence; and

(d) extrajudicial measures should be used if they are adequate to hold a young person accountable for his or her offending behaviour and, if the use of extrajudicial measures is consistent with the principles set out in this section, nothing in this Act precludes their use in respect of a young person who

(i) has previously been dealt with by the use of extrajudicial measures, or

(ii) has previously been found guilty of an offence.

Objectives

5. Extrajudicial measures should be designed to

(a) provide an effective and timely response to offending behaviour outside the bounds of judicial measures;

(b) encourage young persons to acknowledge and repair the harm caused to the victim and the community;

(c) encourage families of young persons—including extended families where appropriate—and the community to become involved in the design and implementation of those measures;

(d) provide an opportunity for victims to participate in decisions related to the measures selected and to receive reparation; and

(e) respect the rights and freedoms of young persons and be proportionate to the seriousness of the offence.

WARNINGS, CAUTIONS AND REFERRALS

Warnings, cautions and referrals

6. (1) A police officer shall, before starting judicial proceedings or taking any other measures under this Act against a young person alleged to have committed an offence, consider whether it would be sufficient, having regard to the principles set out in section 4, to take no further action, warn the young person, administer a caution, if a program has been established under section 7, or, with the consent of the young person, refer the young person to a program or agency in the community that may assist the young person not to commit offences.

Saving

(2) The failure of a police officer to consider the options set out in subsection (1) does not invalidate any subsequent charges against the young person for the offence.

Police cautions

7. The Attorney General, or any other minister designated by the lieutenant governor of a province, may establish a program authorizing the police to administer cautions to young persons instead of starting judicial proceedings under this Act.

Crown cautions

8. The Attorney General may establish a program authorizing prosecutors to administer cautions to young persons instead of starting or continuing judicial proceedings under this Act.

Evidence of measures is inadmissible

9. Evidence that a young person has received a warning, caution or referral mentioned in section 6, 7 or 8 or that a police officer has taken no further action in respect of an offence, and evidence of the offence, is inadmissible for the purpose of proving prior offending behaviour in any proceedings before a youth justice court in respect of the young person.

EXTRAJUDICIAL SANCTIONS

Extrajudicial sanctions

10. (1) An extrajudicial sanction may be used to deal with a young person alleged to have committed an offence only if the young person cannot be adequately dealt with by a warning, caution or referral mentioned in section 6, 7 or 8 because of the seriousness of the offence, the nature and number of previous offences committed by the young person or any other aggravating circumstances.

Conditions

(2) An extrajudicial sanction may be used only if

(a) it is part of a program of sanctions that may be authorized by the Attorney General or authorized by a person, or a member of a class of persons, designated by the lieutenant governor in council of the province;

(b) the person who is considering whether to use the extrajudicial sanction is satisfied that it would be appropriate, having regard to the needs of the young person and the interests of society;

(c) the young person, having been informed of the extrajudicial sanction, fully and freely consents to be subject to it;

(d) the young person has, before consenting to be subject to the extrajudicial sanction, been advised of his or her right to be represented by counsel and been given a reasonable opportunity to consult with counsel;

(e) the young person accepts responsibility for the act or omission that forms the basis of the offence that he or she is alleged to have committed;

(f) there is, in the opinion of the Attorney General, sufficient evidence to proceed with the prosecution of the offence; and

(g) the prosecution of the offence is not in any way barred at law.

Restriction on use

(3) An extrajudicial sanction may not be used in respect of a young person who

(a) denies participation or involvement in the commission of the offence; or

(b) expresses the wish to have the charge dealt with by a youth justice court.

Admissions not admissible in evidence

(4) Any admission, confession or statement accepting responsibility for a given act or omission that is made by a young person as a condition of being dealt with by extrajudicial measures is inadmissible in evidence against any young person in civil or criminal proceedings.

No bar to judicial proceedings

(5) The use of an extrajudicial sanction in respect of a young person alleged to have committed an offence is not a bar to judicial proceedings under this Act, but if a charge is laid against the young person in respect of the offence,

(a) the youth justice court shall dismiss the charge if it is satisfied on a balance of probabilities that the young person has totally complied with the terms and conditions of the extrajudicial sanction; and

(b) the youth justice court may dismiss the charge if it is satisfied on a balance of probabilities that the young person has partially complied with the terms and conditions of the extrajudicial sanction and if, in the opinion of the court, prosecution of the charge would be unfair having regard to the circumstances and the young person's performance with respect to the extrajudicial sanction.

Laying of information, etc.

(6) Subject to subsection (5) and section 24 (private prosecutions only with consent of Attorney General), nothing in this section shall be construed as preventing any person from laying an information or indictment, obtaining the issue or confirmation of any process or proceeding with the prosecution of any offence in accordance with law.

Notice to parent

11. If a young person is dealt with by an extrajudicial sanction, the person who administers the program under which the sanction is used shall inform a parent of the young person of the sanction.

Victim's right to information

12. If a young person is dealt with by an extrajudicial sanction, a police officer, the Attorney General, the provincial director or any organization established by a province to provide assistance to victims shall, on request, inform the victim of the identity of the young person and how the offence has been dealt with.

PART 2
ORGANIZATION OF YOUTH CRIMINAL JUSTICE SYSTEM

YOUTH JUSTICE COURT

Designation of youth justice court

13. (1) A youth justice court is any court that may be established or designated by or under an Act of the legislature of a province, or designated by the Governor in Council or the lieutenant governor in council of a province, as a youth justice court for the purposes of this Act, and a youth justice court judge is a person who may be appointed or designated as a judge of the youth justice court or a judge sitting in a court established or designated as a youth justice court.

Deemed youth justice court

(2) When a young person elects to be tried by a judge without a jury, the judge shall be a judge as defined in section 552 of the *Criminal Code*, or if it is an offence set out in section 469 of that Act, the judge shall be a judge of the superior court of criminal jurisdiction in the province in which the election is made. In either case, the judge is deemed to be a youth justice court judge and the court is deemed to be a youth justice court for the purpose of the proceeding.

Deemed youth justice court

(3) When a young person elects or is deemed to have elected to be tried by a court composed of a judge and jury, the superior court of criminal jurisdiction in the province in which the election is made or deemed to have been made is deemed to be a youth justice court for the purpose of the proceeding, and the superior court judge is deemed to be a youth justice court judge.

Court of record

(4) A youth justice court is a court of record.

Exclusive jurisdiction of youth justice court

14. (1) Despite any other Act of Parliament but subject to the *Contraventions Act* and the *National Defence Act*, a youth justice court has exclusive jurisdiction in respect of any offence alleged to have been committed by a person while he or she was a young person, and that person shall be dealt with as provided in this Act.

Orders

(2) A youth justice court has jurisdiction to make orders against a young person under sections 810 (recognizance—fear of injury or damage), 810.01 (recognizance—fear of criminal organization offence) and 810.2 (recognizance—fear of serious personal injury offence) of the *Criminal Code*. If the young person fails or refuses to enter into a recognizance referred to in any of those sections, the court may impose any one of the sanctions set out in subsection 42(2) (youth sentences) except that, in the case of an order under paragraph 42(2)(n) (custody and supervision order), it shall not exceed thirty days.

Prosecution prohibited

(3) Unless the Attorney General and the young person agree, no extrajudicial measures shall be taken or judicial proceedings commenced under this Act in respect of an offence after the end of the time limit set out in any other Act of Parliament or any regulation made under it for the institution of proceedings in respect of that offence.

Continuation of proceedings

(4) Extrajudicial measures taken or judicial proceedings commenced under this Act against a young person may be continued under this Act after the person attains the age of eighteen years.

Young persons over the age of eighteen years

(5) This Act applies to persons eighteen years old or older who are alleged to have committed an offence while a young person.

Powers of youth justice court judge

(6) For the purpose of carrying out the provisions of this Act, a youth justice court judge is a justice and a provincial court judge and has the jurisdiction and powers of a summary conviction court under the *Criminal Code*.

Powers of a judge of a superior court

(7) A judge of a superior court of criminal jurisdiction, when deemed to be a youth justice court judge for the purpose of a proceeding, retains the jurisdiction and powers of a superior court of criminal jurisdiction.

Contempt against youth justice court

15. (1) Every youth justice court has the same power, jurisdiction and authority to deal with and impose punishment for contempt against the court as may be exercised by the superior court of criminal jurisdiction of the province in which the court is situated.

Jurisdiction of youth justice court

(2) A youth justice court has jurisdiction in respect of every contempt of court committed by a young person against the youth justice court whether or not committed in the face of the court, and every contempt of court committed by a young person against any other court otherwise than in the face of that court.

Concurrent jurisdiction of youth justice court

(3) A youth justice court has jurisdiction in respect of every contempt of court committed by a young person against any other court in the face of that court and every contempt of court committed by an adult against the youth justice court in the face of the youth justice court, but nothing in this subsection affects the power, jurisdiction or authority of any other court to deal with or impose punishment for contempt of court.

Youth sentence—contempt

(4) When a youth justice court or any other court finds a young person guilty of contempt of court, it may impose as a youth sentence any one of the sanctions set out in subsection 42(2) (youth sentences), or any number of them that are not inconsistent with each other, but no other sentence.

Section 708 of *Criminal Code* applies in respect of adults

(5) Section 708 (contempt) of the *Criminal Code* applies in respect of proceedings under this section in youth justice court against adults, with any modifications that the circumstances require.

Status of offender uncertain

16. When a person is alleged to have committed an offence during a period that includes the date on which the person attains the age of eighteen years, the youth justice court has jurisdiction in respect of the offence and shall, after putting the person to their election under section 67 (adult sentence) if applicable, and on finding the person guilty of the offence,

(a) if it has been proven that the offence was committed before the person attained the age of eighteen years, impose a sentence under this Act;

(b) if it has been proven that the offence was committed after the person attained the age of eighteen years, impose any sentence that could be imposed under the *Criminal Code* or any other Act of Parliament on an adult who has been convicted of the same offence; and

(c) if it has not been proven that the offence was committed after the person attained the age of eighteen years, impose a sentence under this Act.

Youth justice court may make rules

17. (1) The youth justice court for a province may, subject to the approval of the lieutenant governor in council of the province, establish rules of court not inconsistent with this Act or any other Act of Parliament or with any regulations made under section 155 regulating proceedings within the jurisdiction of the youth justice court.

Rules of court

(2) Rules under subsection (1) may be made

(a) generally to regulate the duties of the officers of the youth justice court and any other matter considered expedient to attain the ends of justice and carry into effect the provisions of this Act;

(b) subject to any regulations made under paragraph 155(b), to regulate the practice and procedure in the youth justice court; and

(c) to prescribe forms to be used in the youth justice court if they are not otherwise provided for by or under this Act.

Publication of rules

(3) Rules of court that are made under the authority of this section shall be published in the appropriate provincial gazette.

YOUTH JUSTICE COMMITTEES

Youth justice committees

18. (1) The Attorney General of Canada or a province or any other minister that the lieutenant governor in council of the province may designate may establish one or more committees of citizens, to be known as youth justice committees, to assist in any aspect of the administration of this Act or in any programs or services for young persons.

Role of committee

(2) The functions of a youth justice committee may include the following:

(a) in the case of a young person alleged to have committed an offence,

(i) giving advice on the appropriate extrajudicial measure to be used in respect of the young person,

(ii) supporting any victim of the alleged offence by soliciting his or her concerns and facilitating the reconciliation of the victim and the young person,

(iii) ensuring that community support is available to the young person by arranging for the use of services from within the community, and enlisting members of the community to provide short-term mentoring and supervision, and

(iv) when the young person is also being dealt with by a child protection agency or a community group, helping to coordinate the interaction of the agency or group with the youth criminal justice system;

(b) advising the federal and provincial governments on whether the provisions of this Act that grant rights to young persons, or provide for the protection of young persons, are being complied with;

(c) advising the federal and provincial governments on policies and procedures related to the youth criminal justice system;

(d) providing information to the public in respect of this Act and the youth criminal justice system;

(e) acting as a conference; and

(f) any other functions assigned by the person who establishes the committee.

Conferences may be convened

19. (1) A youth justice court judge, the provincial director, a police officer, a justice of the peace, a prosecutor or a youth worker may convene or cause to be convened a conference for the purpose of making a decision required to be made under this Act.

Mandate of a conference

(2) The mandate of a conference may be, among other things, to give advice on appropriate extrajudicial measures, conditions for judicial interim release, sentences, including the review of sentences, and reintegration plans.

Rules for conferences

(3) The Attorney General or any other minister designated by the lieutenant governor in council of a province may establish rules for the convening and conducting of conferences other than conferences convened or caused to be convened by a youth justice court judge or a justice of the peace.

Rules to apply

(4) In provinces where rules are established under subsection (3), the conferences to which those rules apply must be convened and conducted in accordance with those rules.

JUSTICES OF THE PEACE

Certain proceedings may be taken before justices

20. (1) Any proceeding that may be carried out before a justice under the *Criminal Code*, other than a plea, a trial or an adjudication, may be carried out before a justice in respect of an offence alleged to have been committed by a young person, and any process that may be issued by a justice under the *Criminal Code* may be issued by a justice in respect of an offence alleged to have been committed by a young person.

Orders under section 810 of *Criminal Code*

(2) A justice has jurisdiction to make an order under section 810 (recognizance—fear of injury or damage) of the *Criminal Code* in respect of a young person. If the young person fails or refuses to enter into a recognizance referred to in that section, the justice shall refer the matter to a youth justice court.

CLERKS OF THE COURT

Powers of clerks

21. In addition to any powers conferred on a clerk of a court by the *Criminal Code*, a clerk of the youth justice court may exercise the powers ordinarily exercised by a clerk of a court, and, in particular, may

(a) administer oaths or solemn affirmations in all matters relating to the business of the youth justice court; and

(b) in the absence of a youth justice court judge, exercise all the powers of a youth justice court judge relating to adjournment.

PROVINCIAL DIRECTORS

Powers, duties and functions of provincial directors

22. The provincial director may authorize any person to exercise the powers or perform the duties or functions of the provincial director under this Act, in which case the powers, duties or functions are deemed to have been exercised or performed by the provincial director.

PART 3
JUDICIAL MEASURES

CONSENT TO PROSECUTE

Pre-charge screening

23. (1) The Attorney General may establish a program of pre-charge screening that sets out the circumstances in which the consent of the Attorney General must be obtained before a young person is charged with an offence.

Pre-charge screening program

(2) Any program of pre-charge screening of young persons that is established under an Act of the legislature of a province or by a directive of a provincial government, and that is in place before the coming into force of this section, is deemed to be a program of pre-charge screening for the purposes of subsection (1).

Private prosecutions

24. No prosecutions may be conducted by a prosecutor other than the Attorney General without the consent of the Attorney General.

RIGHT TO COUNSEL

Right to counsel

25. (1) A young person has the right to retain and instruct counsel without delay, and to exercise that right personally, at any stage of proceedings against the young person and before and during any consideration of whether, instead of starting or continuing judicial proceedings against the young person under this Act, to use an extrajudicial sanction to deal with the young person.

Arresting officer to advise young person of right to counsel

(2) Every young person who is arrested or detained shall, on being arrested or detained, be advised without delay by the arresting officer or the officer in charge, as the case may be, of the right to retain and instruct counsel, and be given an opportunity to obtain counsel.

Justice, youth justice court or review board to advise young person of right to counsel

(3) When a young person is not represented by counsel

(a) at a hearing at which it will be determined whether to release the young person or detain the young person in custody prior to sentencing,

(b) at a hearing held under section 71 (hearing—adult sentences),

(c) at trial,

(d) at any proceedings held under subsection 98(3) (continuation of custody), 103(1) (review by youth justice court), 104(1) (continuation of custody), 105(1) (conditional supervision) or 109(1) (review of decision),

(e) at a review of a youth sentence held before a youth justice court under this Act, or

(f) at a review of the level of custody under section 87,

the justice or youth justice court before which the hearing, trial or review is held, or the review board before which the review is held, shall advise the young person of the right to retain and instruct counsel and shall give the young person a reasonable opportunity to obtain counsel.

Trial, hearing or review before youth justice court or review board

(4) When a young person at trial or at a hearing or review referred to in subsection (3) wishes to obtain counsel but is unable to do so, the youth justice court before which the hearing, trial or review is held or the review board before which the review is held

(a) shall, if there is a legal aid program or an assistance program available in the province where the hearing, trial or review is held, refer the young person to that program for the appointment of counsel; or

(b) if no legal aid program or assistance program is available or the young person is unable to obtain counsel through the program, may, and on the request of the young person shall, direct that the young person be represented by counsel.

Appointment of counsel

(5) When a direction is made under paragraph (4)(b) in respect of a young person, the Attorney General shall appoint counsel, or cause counsel to be appointed, to represent the young person.

Release hearing before justice

(6) When a young person, at a hearing referred to in paragraph (3)(a) that is held before a justice who is not a youth justice court judge, wishes to obtain counsel but is unable to do so, the justice shall

(a) if there is a legal aid program or an assistance program available in the province where the hearing is held,

(i) refer the young person to that program for the appointment of counsel, or

(ii) refer the matter to a youth justice court to be dealt with in accordance with paragraph (4)(a) or (b); or

(b) if no legal aid program or assistance program is available or the young person is unable to obtain counsel through the program, refer the matter without delay to a youth justice court to be dealt with in accordance with paragraph (4)(b).

Young person may be assisted by adult

(7) When a young person is not represented by counsel at trial or at a hearing or review referred to in subsection (3), the justice before whom or the youth justice court or review board before which the proceedings are held may, on the request of the young person, allow the young person to be assisted by an adult whom the justice, court or review board considers to be suitable.

Counsel independent of parents

(8) If it appears to a youth justice court judge or a justice that the interests of a young person and the interests of a parent are in conflict or that it would be in the best interests of the young person to be represented by his or her own counsel, the judge or justice shall ensure that the young person is represented by counsel independent of the parent.

Statement of right to counsel

(9) A statement that a young person has the right to be represented by counsel shall be included in

(a) any appearance notice or summons issued to the young person;

(b) any warrant to arrest the young person;

(c) any promise to appear given by the young person;

(d) any undertaking or recognizance entered into before an officer in charge by the young person;

(e) any notice given to the young person in relation to any proceedings held under subsection 98(3) (continuation of custody), 103(1) (review by youth justice court), 104(1) (continuation of custody), 105(1) (conditional supervision) or 109(1) (review of decision); or

(f) any notice of a review of a youth sentence given to the young person.

Recovery of costs of counsel

(10) Nothing in this Act prevents the lieutenant governor in council of a province or his or her delegate from establishing a program to authorize the recovery of the costs of a young person's counsel from the young person or the parents of the young person. The costs may be recovered only after the proceedings are completed and the time allowed for the taking of an appeal has expired or, if an appeal is taken, all proceedings in respect of the appeal have been completed.

Exception for persons over the age of twenty

(11) Subsections (4) to (9) do not apply to a person who is alleged to have committed an offence while a young person, if the person has attained the age of twenty years at the time of his or her first appearance before a youth justice court in respect of the offence; however, this does not restrict any rights that a person has under the law applicable to adults.

NOTICES TO PARENTS

Notice in case of arrest or detention

26. (1) Subject to subsection (4), if a young person is arrested and detained in custody pending his or her appearance in court, the officer in charge at the time the young person is detained shall, as soon as possible, give or cause to be given to a parent of the young person, orally or in writing, notice of the arrest stating the place of detention and the reason for the arrest.

Notice in other cases

(2) Subject to subsection (4), if a summons or an appearance notice is issued in respect of a young person, the person who issued the summons or appearance notice, or, if a young person is released on giving a promise to appear or entering into an undertaking or recognizance, the officer in charge, shall, as soon as possible, give or cause to be given to a parent of the young person notice in writing of the summons, appearance notice, promise to appear, undertaking or recognizance.

Notice to parent in case of ticket

(3) Subject to subsection (4), a person who serves a ticket under the *Contraventions Act* on a young person, other than a ticket served for a contravention relating to parking a vehicle, shall, as soon as possible, give or cause to be given notice in writing of the ticket to a parent of the young person.

Notice to relative or other adult

(4) If the whereabouts of the parents of a young person are not known or it appears that no parent is available, a notice under this section may be given to an adult relative of the young person who is known to the young person and is likely to assist the young person or, if no such adult relative is available, to any other adult who is known to the young person and is likely to assist the young person and who the person giving the notice considers appropriate.

Notice on direction of youth justice court judge or justice

(5) If doubt exists as to the person to whom a notice under this section should be given, a youth justice court judge or, if a youth justice court judge is, having regard to the circumstances, not reasonably available, a justice may give directions as to the person to whom the notice should be given, and a notice given in accordance with those directions is sufficient notice for the purposes of this section.

Contents of notice

(6) Any notice under this section shall, in addition to any other requirements under this section, include

(a) the name of the young person in respect of whom it is given;

(b) the charge against the young person and, except in the case of a notice of a ticket served under the *Contraventions Act*, the time and place of appearance; and

(c) a statement that the young person has the right to be represented by counsel.

Notice of ticket under *Contraventions Act*

(7) A notice under subsection (3) shall include a copy of the ticket.

Service of notice

(8) Subject to subsections (10) and (11), a notice under this section that is given in writing may be served personally or be sent by confirmed delivery service.

Proceedings not invalid

(9) Subject to subsections (10) and (11), failure to give a notice in accordance with this section does not affect the validity of proceedings under this Act.

Exception

(10) Failure to give a notice under subsection (2) in accordance with this section in any case renders invalid any subsequent proceedings under this Act relating to the case unless

(a) a parent of the young person attends court with the young person; or

(b) a youth justice court judge or a justice before whom proceedings are held against the young person

(i) adjourns the proceedings and orders that the notice be given in the manner and to the persons that the judge or justice directs, or

(ii) dispenses with the notice if the judge or justice is of the opinion that, having regard to the circumstances, the notice may be dispensed with.

Where notice is not served

(11) Where there has been a failure to give a notice under subsection (1) or (3) in accordance with this section and none of the persons to whom the notice may be given attends court with the young person, a youth justice court judge or a justice before whom proceedings are held against the young person may

(a) adjourn the proceedings and order that the notice be given in the manner and to the persons that the judge or justice directs; or

(b) dispense with the notice if the judge or justice is of the opinion that, having regard to the circumstances, the notice may be dispensed with.

Exception for persons over the age of twenty

(12) This section does not apply to a person who is alleged to have committed an offence while a young person, if the person has attained the age of twenty years at the time of his or her first appearance before a youth justice court in respect of the offence.

Order requiring attendance of parent

27. (1) If a parent does not attend proceedings held before a youth justice court in respect of a young person, the court may, if in its opinion the presence of the parent is necessary or in the best interests of the young person, by order in writing require the parent to attend at any stage of the proceedings.

No order in ticket proceedings

(2) Subsection (1) does not apply in proceedings commenced by filing a ticket under the *Contraventions Act*.

Service of order

(3) A copy of the order shall be served by a peace officer or by a person designated by a youth justice court by delivering it personally to the parent to whom it is directed, unless the youth justice court authorizes service by confirmed delivery service.

Failure to attend

(4) A parent who is ordered to attend a youth justice court under subsection (1) and who fails without reasonable excuse, the proof of which lies on the parent, to comply with the order

(a) is guilty of contempt of court;

(b) may be dealt with summarily by the court; and

(c) is liable to the punishment provided for in the *Criminal Code* for a summary conviction offence.

Warrant to arrest parent

(5) If a parent who is ordered to attend a youth justice court under subsection (1) does not attend when required by the order or fails to remain in attendance as required and it is proved that a copy of the order was served on the parent, a youth justice court may issue a warrant to compel the attendance of the parent.

DETENTION BEFORE SENTENCING

Application of Part XVI of *Criminal Code*

28. Except to the extent that they are inconsistent with or excluded by this Act, the provisions of Part XVI (compelling appearance of an accused and interim release) of the *Criminal Code* apply to the detention and release of young persons under this Act.

Detention as social measure prohibited

29. (1) A youth justice court judge or a justice shall not detain a young person in custody prior to being sentenced as a substitute for appropriate child protection, mental health or other social measures.

Justification for detention in custody

(2) A youth justice court judge or a justice may order that a young person be detained in custody only if

(a) the young person has been charged with

(i) a serious offence, or

(ii) an offence other than a serious offence, if they have a history that indicates a pattern of either outstanding charges or findings of guilt;

(b) the judge or justice is satisfied, on a balance of probabilities,

(i) that there is a substantial likelihood that, before being dealt with according to law, the young person will not appear in court when required by law to do so,

(ii) that detention is necessary for the protection or safety of the public, including any victim of or witness to the offence, having regard to all the circumstances, including a substantial likelihood that the young person will, if released from custody, commit a serious offence, or

(iii) in the case where the young person has been charged with a serious offence and detention is not justified under subparagraph (i) or (ii), that there are exceptional circumstances that warrant detention and that detention is necessary to maintain confidence in the administration of justice, having regard to the principles set out in section 3 and to all the circumstances, including

(A) the apparent strength of the prosecution's case,

(B) the gravity of the offence,

(C) the circumstances surrounding the commission of the offence, including whether a firearm was used, and

(D) the fact that the young person is liable, on being found guilty, for a potentially lengthy custodial sentence; and

(c) the judge or justice is satisfied, on a balance of probabilities, that no condition or combination of conditions of release would, depending on the justification on which the judge or justice relies under paragraph (b),

(i) reduce, to a level below substantial, the likelihood that the young person would not appear in court when required by law to do so,

(ii) offer adequate protection to the public from the risk that the young person might otherwise present, or

(iii) maintain confidence in the administration of justice.

Onus

(3) The onus of satisfying the youth justice court judge or the justice as to the matters referred to in subsection (2) is on the Attorney General.

Designated place of temporary detention

30. (1) Subject to subsection (7), a young person who is arrested and detained prior to being sentenced, or who is detained in accordance with a warrant issued under subsection 59(6) (compelling appearance for review of sentence), shall be detained in any place of temporary detention that may be designated by the lieutenant governor in council of the province or his or her delegate or in a place within a class of places so designated.

Exception

(2) A young person who is detained in a place of temporary detention under subsection (1) may, in the course of being transferred from that place to the court or from the court to that place, be held under the supervision and control of a peace officer.

Detention separate from adults

(3) A young person referred to in subsection (1) shall be held separate and apart from any adult who is detained or held in custody unless a youth justice court judge or a justice is satisfied that, having regard to the best interests of the young person,

(a) the young person cannot, having regard to his or her own safety or the safety of others, be detained in a place of detention for young persons; or

(b) no place of detention for young persons is available within a reasonable distance.

Transfer to adult facility

(4) When a young person is detained under subsection (1), the youth justice court may, on application of the provincial director made at any time after the young person attains the age of eighteen years, after giving the young person an opportunity to be heard, authorize the provincial director to direct, despite subsection (3), that the young person be temporarily detained in a provincial correctional facility for adults, if the court considers it to be in the best interests of the young person or in the public interest.

When young person is twenty years old or older

(5) When a young person is twenty years old or older at the time his or her temporary detention under subsection (1) begins, the young person shall, despite subsection (3), be temporarily detained in a provincial correctional facility for adults.

Transfer by provincial director

(6) A young person who is detained in custody under subsection (1) may, during the period of detention, be transferred by the provincial director from one place of temporary detention to another.

Exception relating to temporary detention

(7) Subsections (1) and (3) do not apply in respect of any temporary restraint of a young person under the supervision and control of a peace officer after arrest, but a young person who is so restrained shall be transferred to a place of temporary detention referred to in subsection (1) as soon as is practicable, and in no case later than the first reasonable opportunity after the appearance of the young person before a youth justice court judge or a justice under section 503 of the *Criminal Code*.

Authorization of provincial authority for detention

(8) In any province for which the lieutenant governor in council has designated a person or a group of persons whose authorization is required, either in all circumstances or in circumstances specified by the lieutenant governor in council, before a young person who has been arrested may be detained in accordance with this section, no young person shall be so detained unless the authorization is obtained.

Determination by provincial authority of place of detention

(9) In any province for which the lieutenant governor in council has designated a person or a group of persons who may determine the place where a young person who has been arrested may be detained in accordance with this section, no young person may be so detained in a place other than the one so determined.

Placement of young person in care of responsible person

31. (1) A young person who has been arrested may be placed in the care of a responsible person instead of being detained in custody if a youth justice court or a justice is satisfied that

(a) the young person would, but for this subsection, be detained in custody under section 515 (judicial interim release) of the *Criminal Code*;

(b) the person is willing and able to take care of and exercise control over the young person; and

(c) the young person is willing to be placed in the care of that person.

Inquiry as to availability of a responsible person

(2) If a young person would, in the absence of a responsible person, be detained in custody, the youth justice court or the justice shall inquire as to the availability of a responsible person and whether the young person is willing to be placed in that person's care.

Condition of placement

(3) A young person shall not be placed in the care of a person under subsection (1) unless

(a) that person undertakes in writing to take care of and to be responsible for the attendance of the young person in court when required and to comply with any other conditions that the youth justice court judge or the justice may specify; and

(b) the young person undertakes in writing to comply with the arrangement and to comply with any other conditions that the youth justice court judge or the justice may specify.

Removing young person from care

(4) A young person, a person in whose care a young person has been placed or any other person may, by application in writing to a youth justice court judge or a justice, apply for an order under subsection (5) if

(a) the person in whose care the young person has been placed is no longer willing or able to take care of or exercise control over the young person; or

(b) it is, for any other reason, no longer appropriate that the young person remain in the care of the person with whom he or she has been placed.

Order

(5) When a youth justice court judge or a justice is satisfied that a young person should not remain in the custody of the person in whose care he or she was placed under subsection (1), the judge or justice shall

(a) make an order relieving the person and the young person of the obligations undertaken under subsection (3); and

(b) issue a warrant for the arrest of the young person.

Effect of arrest

(6) If a young person is arrested in accordance with a warrant issued under paragraph (5)(b), the young person shall be taken before a youth justice court judge or a justice without delay and dealt with under this section and sections 28 to 30.

APPEARANCE

Appearance before judge or justice

32. (1) A young person against whom an information or indictment is laid must first appear before a youth justice court judge or a justice, and the judge or justice shall

(a) cause the information or indictment to be read to the young person;

(b) if the young person is not represented by counsel, inform the young person of the right to retain and instruct counsel; and

(c) if notified under subsection 64(2) (intention to seek adult sentence) or if section 16 (status of accused uncertain) applies, inform the young person that the youth justice court might, if the young person is found guilty, order that an adult sentence be imposed.

(d) [Repealed, 2012, c. 1, s. 170]

Waiver

(2) A young person may waive the requirements of subsection (1) if the young person is represented by counsel and counsel advises the court that the young person has been informed of that provision.

Young person not represented by counsel

(3) When a young person is not represented by counsel, the youth justice court, before accepting a plea, shall

(a) satisfy itself that the young person understands the charge;

(b) if the young person is liable to an adult sentence, explain to the young person the consequences of being liable to an adult sentence and the procedure by which the young person may apply for an order that a youth sentence be imposed; and

(c) explain that the young person may plead guilty or not guilty to the charge or, if subsection 67(1) (election of court for trial—adult sentence) or (3) (election of court for trial in Nunavut—adult sentence) applies, explain that the young person may elect to be tried by a youth justice court judge

without a jury and without having a preliminary inquiry, or to have a preliminary inquiry and be tried by a judge without a jury, or to have a preliminary inquiry and be tried by a court composed of a judge and jury and, in either of the latter two cases, a preliminary inquiry will only be conducted if requested by the young person or the prosecutor.

If youth justice court not satisfied

(4) If the youth justice court is not satisfied that a young person understands the charge, the court shall, unless the young person must be put to his or her election under subsection 67(1) (election of court for trial—adult sentence) or, with respect to Nunavut, subsection 67(3) (election of court for trial in Nunavut—adult sentence), enter a plea of not guilty on behalf of the young person and proceed with the trial in accordance with subsection 36(2) (young person pleads not guilty).

If youth justice court not satisfied

(5) If the youth justice court is not satisfied that a young person understands the matters set out in subsection (3), the court shall direct that the young person be represented by counsel.

RELEASE FROM OR DETENTION IN CUSTODY

Application for release from or detention in custody

33. (1) If an order is made under section 515 (judicial interim release) of the *Criminal Code* in respect of a young person by a justice who is not a youth justice court judge, an application may, at any time after the order is made, be made to a youth justice court for the release from or detention in custody of the young person, as the case may be, and the youth justice court shall hear the matter as an original application.

Notice to prosecutor

(2) An application under subsection (1) for release from custody shall not be heard unless the young person has given the prosecutor at least two clear days notice in writing of the application.

Notice to young person

(3) An application under subsection (1) for detention in custody shall not be heard unless the prosecutor has given the young person at least two clear days notice in writing of the application.

Waiver of notice

(4) The requirement for notice under subsection (2) or (3) may be waived by the prosecutor or by the young person or his or her counsel, as the case may be.

Application for review under section 520 or 521 of *Criminal Code*

(5) An application under section 520 or 521 of the *Criminal Code* for a review of an order made in respect of a young person

by a youth justice court judge who is a judge of a superior court shall be made to a judge of the court of appeal.

Nunavut

(6) Despite subsection (5), an application under section 520 or 521 of the *Criminal Code* for a review of an order made in respect of a young person by a youth justice court judge who is a judge of the Nunavut Court of Justice shall be made to a judge of that court.

No review

(7) No application may be made under section 520 or 521 of the *Criminal Code* for a review of an order made in respect of a young person by a justice who is not a youth justice court judge.

Interim release by youth justice court judge only

(8) If a young person against whom proceedings have been taken under this Act is charged with an offence referred to in section 522 of the *Criminal Code*, a youth justice court judge, but no other court, judge or justice, may release the young person from custody under that section.

Review by court of appeal

(9) A decision made by a youth justice court judge under subsection (8) may be reviewed in accordance with section 680 of the *Criminal Code* and that section applies, with any modifications that the circumstances require, to any decision so made.

MEDICAL AND PSYCHOLOGICAL REPORTS

Medical or psychological assessment

34. (1) A youth justice court may, at any stage of proceedings against a young person, by order require that the young person be assessed by a qualified person who is required to report the results in writing to the court,

(a) with the consent of the young person and the prosecutor; or

(b) on its own motion or on application of the young person or the prosecutor, if the court believes a medical, psychological or psychiatric report in respect of the young person is necessary for a purpose mentioned in paragraphs (2)(a) to (g) and

(i) the court has reasonable grounds to believe that the young person may be suffering from a physical or mental illness or disorder, a psychological disorder, an emotional disturbance, a learning disability or a mental disability,

(ii) the young person's history indicates a pattern of repeated findings of guilt under this Act or the *Young Offenders Act*, chapter Y-1 of the Revised Statutes of Canada, 1985, or

(iii) the young person is alleged to have committed a serious violent offence.

Purpose of assessment

(2) A youth justice court may make an order under subsection (1) in respect of a young person for the purpose of

(a) considering an application under section 33 (release from or detention in custody);

(b) making its decision on an application heard under section 71 (hearing—adult sentences);

(c) making or reviewing a youth sentence;

(d) considering an application under subsection 104(1) (continuation of custody);

(e) setting conditions under subsection 105(1) (conditional supervision);

(f) making an order under subsection 109(2) (conditional supervision); or

(g) authorizing disclosure under subsection 127(1) (information about a young person).

Custody for assessment

(3) Subject to subsections (4) and (6), for the purpose of an assessment under this section, a youth justice court may remand a young person to any custody that it directs for a period not exceeding thirty days.

Presumption against custodial remand

(4) A young person shall not be remanded in custody in accordance with an order made under subsection (1) unless

(a) the youth justice court is satisfied that

(i) on the evidence custody is necessary to conduct an assessment of the young person, or

(ii) on the evidence of a qualified person detention of the young person in custody is desirable to conduct the assessment of the young person, and the young person consents to custody; or

(b) the young person is required to be detained in custody in respect of any other matter or by virtue of any provision of the *Criminal Code*.

Report of qualified person in writing

(5) For the purposes of paragraph (4)(a), if the prosecutor and the young person agree, evidence of a qualified person may be received in the form of a report in writing.

Application to vary assessment order if circumstances change

(6) A youth justice court may, at any time while an order made under subsection (1) is in force, on cause being shown, vary the terms and conditions specified in the order in any manner that the court considers appropriate in the circumstances.

Disclosure of report

(7) When a youth justice court receives a report made in respect of a young person under subsection (1),

(a) the court shall, subject to subsection (9), cause a copy of the report to be given to

(i) the young person,

(ii) any parent of the young person who is in attendance at the proceedings against the young person,

(iii) any counsel representing the young person, and

(iv) the prosecutor; and

(b) the court may cause a copy of the report to be given to

(i) a parent of the young person who is not in attendance at the proceedings if the parent is, in the opinion of the court, taking an active interest in the proceedings, or

(ii) despite subsection 119(6) (restrictions respecting access to certain records), the provincial director, or the director of the provincial correctional facility for adults or the penitentiary at which the young person is serving a youth sentence, if, in the opinion of the court, withholding the report would jeopardize the safety of any person.

Cross-examination

(8) When a report is made in respect of a young person under subsection (1), the young person, his or her counsel or the adult assisting the young person under subsection 25(7) and the prosecutor shall, subject to subsection (9), on application to the youth justice court, be given an opportunity to cross-examine the person who made the report.

Non-disclosure in certain cases

(9) A youth justice court shall withhold all or part of a report made in respect of a young person under subsection (1) from a private prosecutor, if disclosure of the report or part, in the opinion of the court, is not necessary for the prosecution of the case and might be prejudicial to the young person.

Non-disclosure in certain cases

(10) A youth justice court shall withhold all or part of a report made in respect of a young person under subsection (1) from the young person, the young person's parents or a private prosecutor if the court is satisfied, on the basis of the report or evidence given in the absence of the young person, parents or private prosecutor by the person who made the report, that disclosure of the report or part would seriously impair the treatment or recovery of the young person, or would be likely to endanger the life or safety of, or result in serious psychological harm to, another person.

Exception—interests of justice

(11) Despite subsection (10), the youth justice court may release all or part of the report to the young person, the young person's parents or the private prosecutor if the court is of the opinion that the interests of justice make disclosure essential.

Report to be part of record

(12) A report made under subsection (1) forms part of the record of the case in respect of which it was requested.

Disclosure by qualified person

(13) Despite any other provision of this Act, a qualified person who is of the opinion that a young person held in detention or committed to custody is likely to endanger his or her own life or safety or to endanger the life of, or cause bodily harm to, another person may immediately so advise any person who has the care and custody of the young person whether or not the same information is contained in a report made under subsection (1).

Definition of "qualified person"

(14) In this section, "qualified person" means a person duly qualified by provincial law to practice medicine or psychiatry or to carry out psychological examinations or assessments, as the circumstances require, or, if no such law exists, a person who is, in the opinion of the youth justice court, so qualified, and includes a person or a member of a class of persons designated by the lieutenant governor in council of a province or his or her delegate.

REFERRAL TO CHILD WELFARE AGENCY

Referral to child welfare agency

35. In addition to any order that it is authorized to make, a youth justice court may, at any stage of proceedings against a young person, refer the young person to a child welfare agency for assessment to determine whether the young person is in need of child welfare services.

ADJUDICATION

When young person pleads guilty

36. (1) If a young person pleads guilty to an offence charged against the young person and the youth justice court is satisfied that the facts support the charge, the court shall find the young person guilty of the offence.

When young person pleads not guilty

(2) If a young person charged with an offence pleads not guilty to the offence or pleads guilty but the youth justice court is not satisfied that the facts support the charge, the court shall proceed with the trial and shall, after considering the matter, find the young person guilty or not guilty or make an order dismissing the charge, as the case may be.

APPEALS

Appeals

37. (1) An appeal in respect of an indictable offence or an offence that the Attorney General elects to proceed with as an indictable offence lies under this Act in accordance with Part XXI (appeals—indictable offences) of the *Criminal Code*, which Part applies with any modifications that the circumstances require.

Appeals for contempt of court

(2) A finding of guilt under section 15 for contempt of court or a sentence imposed in respect of the finding may be appealed as if the finding were a conviction or the sentence were a sentence in a prosecution by indictment.

Appeal

(3) Section 10 of the *Criminal Code* applies if a person is convicted of contempt of court under subsection 27(4) (failure of parent to attend court).

Appeals heard together

(4) An order under subsection 72(1) or (1.1) (adult or youth sentence), 75(2) (lifting of ban on publication) or 76(1) (placement when subject to adult sentence) may be appealed as part of the sentence and, unless the court to which the appeal is taken otherwise orders, if more than one of these is appealed they must be part of the same appeal proceeding.

Appeals for summary conviction offences

(5) An appeal in respect of an offence punishable on summary conviction or an offence that the Attorney General elects to proceed with as an offence punishable on summary conviction lies under this Act in accordance with Part XXVII (summary conviction offences) of the *Criminal Code*, which Part applies with any modifications that the circumstances require.

Appeals where offences are tried jointly

(6) An appeal in respect of one or more indictable offences and one or more summary conviction offences that are tried jointly or in respect of which youth sentences are jointly imposed lies under this Act in accordance with Part XXI (appeals—indictable offences) of the *Criminal Code*, which Part applies with any modifications that the circumstances require.

Deemed election

(7) For the purpose of appeals under this Act, if no election is made in respect of an offence that may be prosecuted by indictment or proceeded with by way of summary conviction, the Attorney General is deemed to have elected to proceed with the offence as an offence punishable on summary conviction.

If the youth justice court is a superior court

(8) In any province where the youth justice court is a superior court, an appeal under subsection (5) shall be made to the court of appeal of the province.

Nunavut

(9) Despite subsection (8), if the Nunavut Court of Justice is acting as a youth justice court, an appeal under subsection (5) shall be made to a judge of the Nunavut Court of Appeal, and an appeal of that judge's decision shall be made to the Nunavut Court of Appeal in accordance with section 839 of the *Criminal Code*.

Appeal to the Supreme Court of Canada

(10) No appeal lies under subsection (1) from a judgment of the court of appeal in respect of a finding of guilt or an order dismissing an information or indictment to the Supreme Court of Canada unless leave to appeal is granted by the Supreme Court of Canada.

No appeal from youth sentence on review

(11) No appeal lies from a youth sentence under section 59 or any of sections 94 to 96.

PART 4
SENTENCING

PURPOSE AND PRINCIPLES

Purpose

38. (1) The purpose of sentencing under section 42 (youth sentences) is to hold a young person accountable for an offence through the imposition of just sanctions that have meaningful consequences for the young person and that promote his or her rehabilitation and reintegration into society, thereby contributing to the long-term protection of the public.

Sentencing principles

(2) A youth justice court that imposes a youth sentence on a young person shall determine the sentence in accordance with the principles set out in section 3and the following principles:

(a) the sentence must not result in a punishment that is greater than the punishment that would be appropriate for an adult who has been convicted of the same offence committed in similar circumstances;

(b) the sentence must be similar to the sentences imposed in the region on similar young persons found guilty of the same offence committed in similar circumstances;

(c) the sentence must be proportionate to the seriousness of the offence and the degree of responsibility of the young person for that offence;

(d) all available sanctions other than custody that are reasonable in the circumstances should be considered for all young persons, with particular attention to the circumstances of aboriginal young persons;

(e) subject to paragraph (c), the sentence must

(i) be the least restrictive sentence that is capable of achieving the purpose set out in subsection (1),

(ii) be the one that is most likely to rehabilitate the young person and reintegrate him or her into society, and

(iii) promote a sense of responsibility in the young person, and an acknowledgement of the harm done to victims and the community; and

(f) subject to paragraph (c), the sentence may have the following objectives:

(i) to denounce unlawful conduct, and

(ii) to deter the young person from committing offences.

Factors to be considered

(3) In determining a youth sentence, the youth justice court shall take into account

(a) the degree of participation by the young person in the commission of the offence;

(b) the harm done to victims and whether it was intentional or reasonably foreseeable;

(c) any reparation made by the young person to the victim or the community;

(d) the time spent in detention by the young person as a result of the offence;

(e) the previous findings of guilt of the young person; and

(f) any other aggravating and mitigating circumstances related to the young person or the offence that are relevant to the purpose and principles set out in this section.

Committal to custody

39. (1) A youth justice court shall not commit a young person to custody under section 42 (youth sentences) unless

(a) the young person has committed a violent offence;

(b) the young person has failed to comply with non-custodial sentences;

(c) the young person has committed an indictable offence for which an adult would be liable to imprisonment for a term of more than two years and has a history that indicates a pattern of either extrajudicial sanctions or of findings of guilt or of both under this Act or the *Young Offenders Act*, chapter Y-1 of the Revised Statutes of Canada, 1985; or

(d) in exceptional cases where the young person has committed an indictable offence, the aggravating circumstances of the offence are such that the imposition of a non-custodial sentence would be inconsistent with the purpose and principles set out in section 38.

Alternatives to custody

(2) If any of paragraphs (1)(a) to (c) apply, a youth justice court shall not impose a custodial sentence under section 42 (youth sentences) unless the court has considered all alternatives to custody raised at the sentencing hearing that are reasonable in the circumstances, and determined that there is not a reasonable alternative, or combination of alternatives, that is in accordance with the purpose and principles set out in section 38.

Factors to be considered

(3) In determining whether there is a reasonable alternative to custody, a youth justice court shall consider submissions relating to

(a) the alternatives to custody that are available;

(b) the likelihood that the young person will comply with a non-custodial sentence, taking into account his or her compliance with previous non-custodial sentences; and

(c) the alternatives to custody that have been used in respect of young persons for similar offences committed in similar circumstances.

Imposition of same sentence

(4) The previous imposition of a particular non-custodial sentence on a young person does not preclude a youth justice court from imposing the same or any other non-custodial sentence for another offence.

Custody as social measure prohibited

(5) A youth justice court shall not use custody as a substitute for appropriate child protection, mental health or other social measures.

Pre-sentence report

(6) Before imposing a custodial sentence under section 42 (youth sentences), a youth justice court shall consider a pre-sentence report and any sentencing proposal made by the young person or his or her counsel.

Report dispensed with

(7) A youth justice court may, with the consent of the prosecutor and the young person or his or her counsel, dispense with a pre-sentence report if the court is satisfied that the report is not necessary.

Length of custody

(8) In determining the length of a youth sentence that includes a custodial portion, a youth justice court shall be guided by the purpose and principles set out in section 38, and shall not take into consideration the fact that the supervision portion of the sentence may not be served in custody and that the sentence may be reviewed by the court under section 94.

Reasons

(9) If a youth justice court imposes a youth sentence that includes a custodial portion, the court shall state the reasons why it has determined that a non-custodial sentence is not adequate to achieve the purpose set out in subsection 38(1), including, if applicable, the reasons why the case is an exceptional case under paragraph (1)(d).

PRE-SENTENCE REPORT

Pre-sentence report

40. (1) Before imposing sentence on a young person found guilty of an offence, a youth justice court

(a) shall, if it is required under this Act to consider a pre-sentence report before making an order or a sentence in respect of a young person, and

(b) may, if it considers it advisable,

require the provincial director to cause to be prepared a pre-sentence report in respect of the young person and to submit the report to the court.

Contents of report

(2) A pre-sentence report made in respect of a young person shall, subject to subsection (3), be in writing and shall include

the following, to the extent that it is relevant to the purpose and principles of sentencing set out in section 38 and to the restrictions on custody set out in section 39:

(a) the results of an interview with the young person and, if reasonably possible, the parents of the young person and, if appropriate and reasonably possible, members of the young person's extended family;

(b) the results of an interview with the victim in the case, if applicable and reasonably possible;

(c) the recommendations resulting from any conference referred to in section 41;

(d) any information that is applicable to the case, including

(i) the age, maturity, character, behaviour and attitude of the young person and his or her willingness to make amends,

(ii) any plans put forward by the young person to change his or her conduct or to participate in activities or undertake measures to improve himself or herself,

(iii) subject to subsection 119(2) (period of access to records), the history of previous findings of delinquency under the *Juvenile Delinquents Act*, chapter J-3 of the Revised Statutes of Canada, 1970, or previous findings of guilt for offences under the *Young Offenders Act*, chapter Y-1 of the Revised Statutes of Canada, 1985, or under this or any other Act of Parliament or any regulation made under it, the history of community or other services rendered to the young person with respect to those findings and the response of the young person to previous sentences or dispositions and to services rendered to him or her,

(iv) subject to subsection 119(2) (period of access to records), the history of alternative measures under the *Young Offenders Act*, chapter Y-1 of the Revised Statutes of Canada, 1985, or extrajudicial sanctions used to deal with the young person and the response of the young person to those measures or sanctions,

(v) the availability and appropriateness of community services and facilities for young persons and the willingness of the young person to avail himself or herself of those services or facilities,

(vi) the relationship between the young person and the young person's parents and the degree of control and influence of the parents over the young person and, if appropriate and reasonably possible, the relationship between the young person and the young person's extended family and the degree of control and influence of the young person's extended family over the young person, and

(vii) the school attendance and performance record and the employment record of the young person;

(e) any information that may assist the court in determining under subsection 39(2) whether there is an alternative to custody; and

(f) any information that the provincial director considers relevant, including any recommendation that the provincial director considers appropriate.

Oral report with leave

(3) If a pre-sentence report cannot reasonably be committed to writing, it may, with leave of the youth justice court, be submitted orally in court.

Report forms part of record

(4) A pre-sentence report shall form part of the record of the case in respect of which it was requested.

Copies of pre-sentence report

(5) If a pre-sentence report made in respect of a young person is submitted to a youth justice court in writing, the court

(a) shall, subject to subsection (7), cause a copy of the report to be given to

(i) the young person,

(ii) any parent of the young person who is in attendance at the proceedings against the young person,

(iii) any counsel representing the young person, and

(iv) the prosecutor; and

(b) may cause a copy of the report to be given to a parent of the young person who is not in attendance at the proceedings if the parent is, in the opinion of the court, taking an active interest in the proceedings.

Cross-examination

(6) If a pre-sentence report made in respect of a young person is submitted to a youth justice court, the young person, his or her counsel or the adult assisting the young person under subsection 25(7) and the prosecutor shall, subject to subsection (7), on application to the court, be given the opportunity to cross-examine the person who made the report.

Report may be withheld from private prosecutor

(7) If a pre-sentence report made in respect of a young person is submitted to a youth justice court, the court may, when the prosecutor is a private prosecutor and disclosure of all or part of the report to the prosecutor might, in the opinion of the court, be prejudicial to the young person and is not, in the opinion of the court, necessary for the prosecution of the case against the young person,

(a) withhold the report or part from the prosecutor, if the report is submitted in writing; or

(b) exclude the prosecutor from the court during the submission of the report or part, if the report is submitted orally in court.

Report disclosed to other persons

(8) If a pre-sentence report made in respect of a young person is submitted to a youth justice court, the court

(a) shall, on request, cause a copy or a transcript of the report to be supplied to

(i) any court that is dealing with matters relating to the young person, and

(ii) any youth worker to whom the young person's case has been assigned; and

(b) may, on request, cause a copy or a transcript of all or part of the report to be supplied to any person not otherwise authorized under this section to receive a copy or a transcript of the report if, in the opinion of the court, the person has a valid interest in the proceedings.

Disclosure by the provincial director

(9) A provincial director who submits a pre-sentence report made in respect of a young person to a youth justice court may make all or part of the report available to any person in whose custody or under whose supervision the young person is placed or to any other person who is directly assisting in the care or treatment of the young person.

Inadmissibility of statements

(10) No statement made by a young person in the course of the preparation of a pre-sentence report in respect of the young person is admissible in evidence against any young person in civil or criminal proceedings except those under section 42 (youth sentences), 59 (review of non-custodial sentence) or 71 (hearing—adult sentences) or any of sections 94 to 96 (reviews and other proceedings related to custodial sentences).

Youth Sentences

Recommendation of conference

41. When a youth justice court finds a young person guilty of an offence, the court may convene or cause to be convened a conference under section 19 for recommendations to the court on an appropriate youth sentence.

Considerations as to youth sentence

42. (1) A youth justice court shall, before imposing a youth sentence, consider any recommendations submitted under section 41, any pre-sentence report, any representations made by the parties to the proceedings or their counsel or agents and by the parents of the young person, and any other relevant information before the court.

Youth sentence

(2) When a youth justice court finds a young person guilty of an offence and is imposing a youth sentence, the court shall, subject to this section, impose any one of the following sanctions or any number of them that are not inconsistent with each other and, if the offence is first degree murder or second degree murder within the meaning of section 231 of the *Criminal Code*, the court shall impose a sanction set out in paragraph (q) or subparagraph (r)(ii) or (iii) and may impose any other of the sanctions set out in this subsection that the court considers appropriate:

(a) reprimand the young person;

(b) by order direct that the young person be discharged absolutely, if the court considers it to be in the best interests of the young person and not contrary to the public interest;

(c) by order direct that the young person be discharged on any conditions that the court considers appropriate and

may require the young person to report to and be supervised by the provincial director;

(d) impose on the young person a fine not exceeding $1,000 to be paid at the time and on the terms that the court may fix;

(e) order the young person to pay to any other person at the times and on the terms that the court may fix an amount by way of compensation for loss of or damage to property or for loss of income or support, or an amount for, in the Province of Quebec, pre-trial pecuniary loss or, in any other province, special damages, for personal injury arising from the commission of the offence if the value is readily ascertainable, but no order shall be made for other damages in the Province of Quebec or for general damages in any other province;

(f) order the young person to make restitution to any other person of any property obtained by the young person as a result of the commission of the offence within the time that the court may fix, if the property is owned by the other person or was, at the time of the offence, in his or her lawful possession;

(g) if property obtained as a result of the commission of the offence has been sold to an innocent purchaser, where restitution of the property to its owner or any other person has been made or ordered, order the young person to pay the purchaser, at the time and on the terms that the court may fix, an amount not exceeding the amount paid by the purchaser for the property;

(h) subject to section 54, order the young person to compensate any person in kind or by way of personal services at the time and on the terms that the court may fix for any loss, damage or injury suffered by that person in respect of which an order may be made under paragraph (e) or (g);

(i) subject to section 54, order the young person to perform a community service at the time and on the terms that the court may fix, and to report to and be supervised by the provincial director or a person designated by the youth justice court;

(j) subject to section 51 (mandatory prohibition order), make any order of prohibition, seizure or forfeiture that may be imposed under any Act of Parliament or any regulation made under it if an accused is found guilty or convicted of that offence, other than an order under section 161 of the *Criminal Code*;

(k) place the young person on probation in accordance with sections 55 and 56 (conditions and other matters related to probation orders) for a specified period not exceeding two years;

(l) subject to subsection (3) (agreement of provincial director), order the young person into an intensive support and supervision program approved by the provincial director;

(m) subject to subsection (3) (agreement of provincial director) and section 54, order the young person to attend a non-residential program approved by the provincial director, at the times and on the terms that the court may fix, for a maximum of two hundred and forty hours, over a period not exceeding six months;

(n) make a custody and supervision order with respect to the young person, ordering that a period be served in custody and that a second period—which is one half as long as the first—be served, subject to sections 97 (conditions to be included) and 98 (continuation of custody), under supervision in the community subject to conditions, the total of the periods not to exceed two years from the date of the coming into force of the order or, if the young person is found guilty of an offence for which the punishment provided by the *Criminal Code* or any other Act of Parliament is imprisonment for life, three years from the date of coming into force of the order;

(o) in the case of an offence set out in section 239 (attempt to commit murder), 232, 234 or 236 (manslaughter) or 273 (aggravated sexual assault) of the *Criminal Code*, make a custody and supervision order in respect of the young person for a specified period not exceeding three years from the date of committal that orders the young person to be committed into a continuous period of custody for the first portion of the sentence and, subject to subsection 104(1) (continuation of custody), to serve the remainder of the sentence under conditional supervision in the community in accordance with section 105;

(p) subject to subsection (5), make a deferred custody and supervision order that is for a specified period not exceeding six months, subject to the conditions set out in subsection 105(2), and to any conditions set out in subsection 105(3) that the court considers appropriate;

(q) order the young person to serve a sentence not to exceed

(i) in the case of first degree murder, ten years comprised of

(A) a committal to custody, to be served continuously, for a period that must not, subject to subsection 104(1) (continuation of custody), exceed six years from the date of committal, and

(B) a placement under conditional supervision to be served in the community in accordance with section 105, and

(ii) in the case of second degree murder, seven years comprised of

(A) a committal to custody, to be served continuously, for a period that must not, subject to subsection 104(1) (continuation of custody), exceed four years from the date of committal, and

(B) a placement under conditional supervision to be served in the community in accordance with section 105;

(r) subject to subsection (7), make an intensive rehabilitative custody and supervision order in respect of the young person

(i) that is for a specified period that must not exceed

(A) two years from the date of committal, or

(B) if the young person is found guilty of an offence for which the punishment provided by the *Criminal Code* or any other Act of Parliament is imprisonment for life, three years from the date of committal,

and that orders the young person to be committed into a continuous period of intensive rehabilitative custody for the first portion of the sentence and, subject to subsection 104(1) (continuation of custody), to serve the remainder under conditional supervision in the community in accordance with section 105,

(ii) that is for a specified period that must not exceed, in the case of first degree murder, ten years from the date of committal, comprising

(A) a committal to intensive rehabilitative custody, to be served continuously, for a period that must not exceed six years from the date of committal, and

(B) subject to subsection 104(1) (continuation of custody), a placement under conditional supervision to be served in the community in accordance with section 105, and

(iii) that is for a specified period that must not exceed, in the case of second degree murder, seven years from the date of committal, comprising

(A) a committal to intensive rehabilitative custody, to be served continuously, for a period that must not exceed four years from the date of committal, and

(B) subject to subsection 104(1) (continuation of custody), a placement under conditional supervision to be served in the community in accordance with section 105; and

(s) impose on the young person any other reasonable and ancillary conditions that the court considers advisable and in the best interests of the young person and the public.

Agreement of provincial director

(3) A youth justice court may make an order under paragraph (2)(l) or (m) only if the provincial director has determined that a program to enforce the order is available.

Youth justice court statement

(4) When the youth justice court makes a custody and supervision order with respect to a young person under paragraph (2)(n), the court shall state the following with respect to that order:

You are ordered to serve (*state the number of days or months to be served*) in custody, to be followed by (*state one-half of the number of days or months stated above*) to be served under supervision in the community subject to conditions.

If you breach any of the conditions while you are under supervision in the community, you may be brought back into custody and required to serve the rest of the second period in custody as well.

You should also be aware that, under other provisions of the *Youth Criminal Justice Act*, a court could require you to serve the second period in custody as well.

The periods in custody and under supervision in the community may be changed if you are or become subject to another sentence.

Deferred custody and supervision order

(5) The court may make a deferred custody and supervision order under paragraph (2)(p) if

(a) the young person is found guilty of an offence other than one in the commission of which a young person causes or attempts to cause serious bodily harm; and

(b) it is consistent with the purpose and principles set out in section 38 and the restrictions on custody set out in section 39.

Application of sections 106 to 109

(6) Sections 106 to 109 (suspension of conditional supervision) apply to a breach of a deferred custody and supervision order made under paragraph (2)(p) as if the breach were a breach of an order for conditional supervision made under subsection 105(1) and, for the purposes of sections 106 to 109, supervision under a deferred custody and supervision order is deemed to be conditional supervision.

Intensive rehabilitative custody and supervision order

(7) A youth justice court may make an intensive rehabilitative custody and supervision order under paragraph (2)(r) in respect of a young person only if

(a) either

(i) the young person has been found guilty of a serious violent offence, or

(ii) the young person has been found guilty of an offence, in the commission of which the young person caused or attempted to cause serious bodily harm and for which an adult is liable to imprisonment for a term of more than two years, and the young person had previously been found guilty at least twice of such an offence;

(b) the young person is suffering from a mental illness or disorder, a psychological disorder or an emotional disturbance;

(c) a plan of treatment and intensive supervision has been developed for the young person, and there are reasonable grounds to believe that the plan might reduce the risk of the young person repeating the offence or committing a serious violent offence; and

(d) the provincial director has determined that an intensive rehabilitative custody and supervision program is available and that the young person's participation in the program is appropriate.

Safeguard of rights

(8) Nothing in this section abrogates or derogates from the rights of a young person regarding consent to physical or mental health treatment or care.

(9) and (10) [Repealed, 2012, c. 1, s. 174]

Inconsistency

(11) An order may not be made under paragraphs (2)(k) to (m) in respect of an offence for which a conditional discharge has been granted under paragraph (2)(c).

Coming into force of youth sentence

(12) A youth sentence or any part of it comes into force on the date on which it is imposed or on any later date that the youth justice court specifies.

Consecutive youth sentences

(13) Subject to subsections (15) and (16), a youth justice court that sentences a young person may direct that a sentence imposed on the young person under paragraph (2)(n), (o), (q) or (r) be served consecutively if the young person

(a) is sentenced while under sentence for an offence under any of those paragraphs; or

(b) is found guilty of more than one offence under any of those paragraphs.

Duration of youth sentence for a single offence

(14) No youth sentence, other than an order made under paragraph (2)(j), (n), (o), (q) or (r), shall continue in force for more than two years. If the youth sentence comprises more than one sanction imposed at the same time in respect of the same offence, the combined duration of the sanctions shall not exceed two years, unless the sentence includes a sanction under paragraph (2)(j), (n), (o), (q) or (r) that exceeds two years.

Duration of youth sentence for different offences

(15) Subject to subsection (16), if more than one youth sentence is imposed under this section in respect of a young person with respect to different offences, the continuous combined duration of those youth sentences shall not exceed three years, except if one of the offences is first degree murder or second degree murder within the meaning of section 231 of the *Criminal Code*, in which case the continuous combined duration of those youth sentences shall not exceed ten years in the case of first degree murder, or seven years in the case of second degree murder.

Duration of youth sentences made at different times

(16) If a youth sentence is imposed in respect of an offence committed by a young person after the commencement of, but before the completion of, any youth sentences imposed on the young person,

(a) the duration of the sentence imposed in respect of the subsequent offence shall be determined in accordance with subsections (14) and (15);

(b) the sentence may be served consecutively to the sentences imposed in respect of the previous offences; and

(c) the combined duration of all the sentences may exceed three years and, if the offence is, or one of the previous offences was,

(i) first degree murder within the meaning of section 231 of the *Criminal Code*, the continuous combined duration of the youth sentences may exceed ten years, or

(ii) second degree murder within the meaning of section 231 of the *Criminal Code*, the continuous combined duration of the youth sentences may exceed seven years.

Sentence continues when adult

(17) Subject to sections 89, 92 and 93 (provisions related to placement in adult facilities) of this Act and section 743.5 (transfer of jurisdiction) of the *Criminal Code*, a youth sentence imposed on a young person continues in effect in accordance with its terms after the young person becomes an adult.

Additional youth sentences

43. Subject to subsection 42(15) (duration of youth sentences), if a young person who is subject to a custodial sentence imposed under paragraph 42(2)(n), (o), (q) or (r) that has not expired receives an additional youth sentence under one of those paragraphs, the young person is, for the purposes of the *Corrections and Conditional Release Act*, the *Criminal Code*, the *Prisons and Reformatories Act* and this Act, deemed to have been sentenced to one youth sentence commencing at the beginning of the first of those youth sentences to be served and ending on the expiry of the last of them to be served.

Custodial portion if additional youth sentence

44. Subject to subsection 42(15) (duration of youth sentences) and section 46 (exception when youth sentence in respect of earlier offence), if an additional youth sentence under paragraph 42(2)(n), (o), (q) or (r) is imposed on a young person on whom a youth sentence had already been imposed under one of those paragraphs that has not expired and the expiry date of the youth sentence that includes the additional youth sentence, as determined in accordance with section 43, is later than the expiry date of the youth sentence that the young person was serving before the additional youth sentence was imposed, the custodial portion of the young person's youth sentence is, from the date the additional sentence is imposed, the total of

(a) the unexpired portion of the custodial portion of the youth sentence before the additional youth sentence was imposed, and

(b) the relevant period set out in subparagraph (i), (ii) or (iii):

(i) if the additional youth sentence is imposed under paragraph 42(2)(n), the period that is two thirds of the period that constitutes the difference between the expiry of the youth sentence as determined in accordance with section 43 and the expiry of the youth sentence that the young person was serving before the additional youth sentence was imposed,

(ii) if the additional youth sentence is a concurrent youth sentence imposed under paragraph 42(2)(o), (q) or (r), the custodial portion of the youth sentence imposed under that paragraph that extends beyond the expiry date of the custodial portion of the sentence being served before the imposition of the additional sentence, or

(iii) if the additional youth sentence is a consecutive youth sentence imposed under paragraph 42(2)(o), (q) or (r), the custodial portion of the additional youth sentence imposed under that paragraph.

Supervision when additional youth sentence extends the period in custody

45. (1) If a young person has begun to serve a portion of a youth sentence in the community subject to conditions under paragraph 42(2)(n) or under conditional supervision under paragraph 42(2)(o), (q) or (r) at the time an additional youth sentence is imposed under one of those paragraphs, and, as a result of the application of section 44, the custodial portion of the young person's youth sentence ends on a day that is later than the day on which the young person received the additional youth sentence, the serving of a portion of the youth sentence under supervision in the community subject to conditions or under conditional supervision shall become inoperative and the young person shall be committed to custody under paragraph 102(1)(b) or 106(b) until the end of the extended portion of the youth sentence to be served in custody.

Supervision when additional youth sentence does not extend the period in custody

(2) If a youth sentence has been imposed under paragraph 42(2)(n), (o), (q) or (r) on a young person who is under supervision in the community subject to conditions under paragraph 42(2)(n) or under conditional supervision under paragraph 42(2)(o), (q) or (r), and the additional youth sentence would not modify the expiry date of the youth sentence that the young person was serving at the time the additional youth sentence was imposed, the young person may be remanded to the youth custody facility that the provincial director considers appropriate. The provincial director shall review the case and, no later than forty-eight hours after the remand of the young person, shall either refer the case to the youth justice court for a review under section 103 or 109 or release the young person to continue the supervision in the community or the conditional supervision.

Supervision when youth sentence additional to supervision

(3) If a youth sentence has been imposed under paragraph 42(2)(n), (o), (q) or (r) on a young person who is under conditional supervision under paragraph 94(19)(b) or subsection 96(5), the young person shall be remanded to the youth custody facility that the provincial director considers appropriate. The provincial director shall review the case and, no later than forty-eight hours after the remand of the young person, shall either

refer the case to the youth justice court for a review under section 103 or 109 or release the young person to continue the conditional supervision.

Exception when youth sentence in respect of earlier offence

46. The total of the custodial portions of a young person's youth sentences shall not exceed six years calculated from the beginning of the youth sentence that is determined in accordance with section 43 if

(a) a youth sentence is imposed under paragraph 42(2)(n), (o), (q) or (r) on the young person already serving a youth sentence under one of those paragraphs; and

(b) the later youth sentence imposed is in respect of an offence committed before the commencement of the earlier youth sentence.

Committal to custody deemed continuous

47. (1) Subject to subsections (2) and (3), a young person who is sentenced under paragraph 42(2)(n) is deemed to be committed to continuous custody for the custodial portion of the sentence.

Intermittent custody

(2) If the sentence does not exceed ninety days, the youth justice court may order that the custodial portion of the sentence be served intermittently if it is consistent with the purpose and principles set out in section 38.

Availability of place of intermittent custody

(3) Before making an order of committal to intermittent custody, the youth justice court shall require the prosecutor to make available to the court for its consideration a report of the provincial director as to the availability of a youth custody facility in which an order of intermittent custody can be enforced and, if the report discloses that no such youth custody facility is available, the court shall not make the order.

Reasons for the sentence

48. When a youth justice court imposes a youth sentence, it shall state its reasons for the sentence in the record of the case and shall, on request, give or cause to be given a copy of the sentence and the reasons for the sentence to

(a) the young person, the young person's counsel, a parent of the young person, the provincial director and the prosecutor; and

(b) in the case of a committal to custody under paragraph 42(2)(n), (o), (q) or (r), the review board.

Warrant of committal

49. (1) When a young person is committed to custody, the youth justice court shall issue or cause to be issued a warrant of committal.

Custody during transfer

(2) A young person who is committed to custody may, in the course of being transferred from custody to the court or from the court to custody, be held under the supervision and control of a peace officer or in any place of temporary detention referred to in subsection 30(1) that the provincial director may specify.

Subsection 30(3) applies

(3) Subsection 30(3) (detention separate from adults) applies, with any modifications that the circumstances require, in respect of a person held in a place of temporary detention under subsection (2).

Application of Part XXIII of *Criminal Code*

50. (1) Subject to section 74 (application of *Criminal Code* to adult sentences), Part XXIII (sentencing) of the *Criminal Code* does not apply in respect of proceedings under this Act except for paragraph 718.2(e) (sentencing principle for aboriginal offenders), sections 722 (victim impact statements), 722.1 (copy of statement) and 722.2 (inquiry by court), subsection 730(2) (court process continues in force) and sections 748 (pardons and remissions), 748.1 (remission by the Governor in Council) and 749 (royal prerogative) of that Act, which provisions apply with any modifications that the circumstances require.

Section 787 of *Criminal Code* does not apply

(2) Section 787 (general penalty) of the *Criminal Code* does not apply in respect of proceedings under this Act.

Mandatory prohibition order

51. (1) Despite section 42 (youth sentences), when a young person is found guilty of an offence referred to in any of paragraphs 109(1)(a) to (d) of the *Criminal Code*, the youth justice court shall, in addition to imposing a sentence under section 42 (youth sentences), make an order prohibiting the young person from possessing any firearm, cross-bow, prohibited weapon, restricted weapon, prohibited device, ammunition, prohibited ammunition or explosive substance during the period specified in the order as determined in accordance with subsection (2).

Duration of prohibition order

(2) An order made under subsection (1) begins on the day on which the order is made and ends not earlier than two years after the young person has completed the custodial portion of the sentence or, if the young person is not subject to custody, after the time the young person is found guilty of the offence.

Discretionary prohibition order

(3) Despite section 42 (youth sentences), where a young person is found guilty of an offence referred to in paragraph 110(1)(a) or (b) of the *Criminal Code*, the youth justice court shall, in addition to imposing a sentence under section 42 (youth sentences), consider whether it is desirable, in the interests of the safety of the young person or of any other person, to

make an order prohibiting the young person from possessing any firearm, cross-bow, prohibited weapon, restricted weapon, prohibited device, ammunition, prohibited ammunition or explosive substance, or all such things, and where the court decides that it is so desirable, the court shall so order.

Duration of prohibition order

(4) An order made under subsection (3) against a young person begins on the day on which the order is made and ends not later than two years after the young person has completed the custodial portion of the sentence or, if the young person is not subject to custody, after the time the young person is found guilty of the offence.

Reasons for the prohibition order

(5) When a youth justice court makes an order under this section, it shall state its reasons for making the order in the record of the case and shall give or cause to be given a copy of the order and, on request, a transcript or copy of the reasons to the young person against whom the order was made, the counsel and a parent of the young person and the provincial director.

Reasons

(6) When the youth justice court does not make an order under subsection (3), or when the youth justice court does make such an order but does not prohibit the possession of everything referred to in that subsection, the youth justice court shall include in the record a statement of the youth justice court's reasons.

Application of *Criminal Code*

(7) Sections 113 to 117 (firearm prohibition orders) of the *Criminal Code* apply in respect of any order made under this section.

Report

(8) Before making an order referred to in section 113 (lifting firearms order) of the *Criminal Code* in respect of a young person, the youth justice court may require the provincial director to cause to be prepared, and to submit to the youth justice court, a report on the young person.

Review of order made under section 51

52. (1) A youth justice court may, on application, review an order made under section 51 at any time after the end of the period set out in subsection 119(2) (period of access to records) that applies to the record of the offence that resulted in the order being made.

Grounds

(2) In conducting a review under this section, the youth justice court shall take into account

(a) the nature and circumstances of the offence in respect of which the order was made; and

(b) the safety of the young person and of other persons.

Decision of review

(3) When a youth justice court conducts a review under this section, it may, after giving the young person, a parent of the young person, the Attorney General and the provincial director an opportunity to be heard,

(a) confirm the order;

(b) revoke the order; or

(c) vary the order as it considers appropriate in the circumstances of the case.

New order not to be more onerous

(4) No variation of an order made under paragraph (3)(c) may be more onerous than the order being reviewed.

Application of provisions

(5) Subsections 59(3) to (5) apply, with any modifications that the circumstances require, in respect of a review under this section.

Funding for victims

53. (1) The lieutenant governor in council of a province may order that, in respect of any fine imposed in the province under paragraph 42(2)(d), a percentage of the fine as fixed by the lieutenant governor in council be used to provide such assistance to victims of offences as the lieutenant governor in council may direct from time to time.

Victim fine surcharge

(2) If the lieutenant governor in council of a province has not made an order under subsection (1), a youth justice court that imposes a fine on a young person under paragraph 42(2)(d) may, in addition to any other punishment imposed on the young person, order the young person to pay a victim fine surcharge in an amount not exceeding fifteen per cent of the fine. The surcharge shall be used to provide such assistance to victims of offences as the lieutenant governor in council of the province in which the surcharge is imposed may direct from time to time.

Where a fine or other payment is ordered

54. (1) The youth justice court shall, in imposing a fine under paragraph 42(2)(d) or in making an order under paragraph 42(2)(e) or (g), have regard to the present and future means of the young person to pay.

Discharge of fine or surcharge

(2) A young person on whom a fine is imposed under paragraph 42(2)(d), including any percentage of a fine imposed under subsection 53(1), or on whom a victim fine surcharge is imposed under subsection 53(2), may discharge the fine or surcharge in whole or in part by earning credits for work performed in a program established for that purpose

(a) by the lieutenant governor in council of the province in which the fine or surcharge was imposed; or

(b) by the lieutenant governor in council of the province in which the young person resides, if an appropriate agreement is in effect between the government of that province and the government of the province in which the fine or surcharge was imposed.

Rates, crediting and other matters

(3) A program referred to in subsection (2) shall determine the rate at which credits are earned and may provide for the manner of crediting any amounts earned against the fine or surcharge and any other matters necessary for or incidental to carrying out the program.

Representations respecting orders under paragraphs 42(2)(e) to (h)

(4) In considering whether to make an order under any of paragraphs 42(2)(e) to (h), the youth justice court may consider any representations made by the person who would be compensated or to whom restitution or payment would be made.

Notice of orders under paragraphs 42(2)(e) to (h)

(5) If the youth justice court makes an order under any of paragraphs 42(2)(e) to (h), it shall cause notice of the terms of the order to be given to the person who is to be compensated or to whom restitution or payment is to be made.

Consent of person to be compensated

(6) No order may be made under paragraph 42(2)(h) unless the youth justice court has secured the consent of the person to be compensated.

Orders under paragraph 42(2)(h), (i) or (m)

(7) No order may be made under paragraph 42(2)(h), (i) or (m) unless the youth justice court is satisfied that
(a) the young person against whom the order is made is a suitable candidate for such an order; and
(b) the order does not interfere with the normal hours of work or education of the young person.

Duration of order for service

(8) No order may be made under paragraph 42(2)(h) or (i) to perform personal or community services unless those services can be completed in two hundred and forty hours or less and within twelve months after the date of the order.

Community service order

(9) No order may be made under paragraph 42(2)(i) unless
(a) the community service to be performed is part of a program that is approved by the provincial director; or
(b) the youth justice court is satisfied that the person or organization for whom the community service is to be performed has agreed to its performance.

Application for further time to complete youth sentence

(10) A youth justice court may, on application by or on behalf of the young person in respect of whom a youth sentence has been imposed under any of paragraphs 42(2)(d) to (i), allow further time for the completion of the sentence subject to any regulations made under paragraph 155(b) and to any rules made by the youth justice court under subsection 17(1).

Conditions that must appear in orders

55. (1) The youth justice court shall prescribe, as conditions of an order made under paragraph 42(2)(k) or (l), that the young person
(a) keep the peace and be of good behaviour; and
(b) appear before the youth justice court when required by the court to do so.

Conditions that may appear in orders

(2) A youth justice court may prescribe, as conditions of an order made under paragraph 42(2)(k) or (l), that a young person do one or more of the following that the youth justice court considers appropriate in the circumstances:
(a) report to and be supervised by the provincial director or a person designated by the youth justice court;
(b) notify the clerk of the youth justice court, the provincial director or the youth worker assigned to the case of any change of address or any change in the young person's place of employment, education or training;
(c) remain within the territorial jurisdiction of one or more courts named in the order;
(d) make reasonable efforts to obtain and maintain suitable employment;
(e) attend school or any other place of learning, training or recreation that is appropriate, if the youth justice court is satisfied that a suitable program for the young person is available there;
(f) reside with a parent, or any other adult that the youth justice court considers appropriate, who is willing to provide for the care and maintenance of the young person;
(g) reside at a place that the provincial director may specify;
(h) comply with any other conditions set out in the order that the youth justice court considers appropriate, including conditions for securing the young person's good conduct and for preventing the young person from repeating the offence or committing other offences; and
(i) not own, possess or have the control of any weapon, ammunition, prohibited ammunition, prohibited device or explosive substance, except as authorized by the order.

Communication of order

56. (1) A youth justice court that makes an order under paragraph 42(2)(k) or (l) shall
(a) cause the order to be read by or to the young person bound by it;

(b) explain or cause to be explained to the young person the purpose and effect of the order, and confirm that the young person understands it; and

(c) cause a copy of the order to be given to the young person, and to any parent of the young person who is in attendance at the sentencing hearing.

Copy of order to parent

(2) A youth justice court that makes an order under paragraph 42(2)(k) or (l) may cause a copy to be given to a parent of the young person who is not in attendance at the proceedings if the parent is, in the opinion of the court, taking an active interest in the proceedings.

Endorsement of order by young person

(3) After the order has been read and explained under subsection (1), the young person shall endorse on the order an acknowledgement that the young person has received a copy of the order and had its purpose and effect explained.

Validity of order

(4) The failure of a young person to endorse the order or of a parent to receive a copy of the order does not affect the validity of the order.

Commencement of order

(5) An order made under paragraph 42(2)(k) or (l) comes into force

(a) on the date on which it is made; or

(b) if a young person receives a sentence that includes a period of continuous custody and supervision, at the end of the period of supervision.

Effect of order in case of custody

(6) If a young person is subject to a sentence that includes both a period of continuous custody and supervision and an order made under paragraph 42(2)(k) or (l), and the court orders under subsection 42(12) a delay in the start of the period of custody, the court may divide the period that the order made under paragraph 42(2)(k) or (l) is in effect, with the first portion to have effect from the date on which it is made until the start of the period of custody, and the remainder to take effect at the end of the period of supervision.

Notice to appear

(7) A young person may be given notice either orally or in writing to appear before the youth justice court under paragraph 55(1)(b).

Warrant in default of appearance

(8) If service of a notice in writing is proved and the young person fails to attend court in accordance with the notice, a youth justice court may issue a warrant to compel the appearance of the young person.

Transfer of youth sentence

57. (1) When a youth sentence has been imposed under any of paragraphs 42(2)(d) to (i), (k), (l) or (s) in respect of a young person and the young person or a parent with whom the young person resides is or becomes a resident of a territorial division outside the jurisdiction of the youth justice court that imposed the youth sentence, whether in the same or in another province, a youth justice court judge in the territorial division in which the youth sentence was imposed may, on the application of the Attorney General or on the application of the young person or the young person's parent, with the consent of the Attorney General, transfer to a youth justice court in another territorial division the youth sentence and any portion of the record of the case that is appropriate. All subsequent proceedings relating to the case shall then be carried out and enforced by that court.

No transfer outside province before appeal completed

(2) No youth sentence may be transferred from one province to another under this section until the time for an appeal against the youth sentence or the finding on which the youth sentence was based has expired or until all proceedings in respect of any such appeal have been completed.

Transfer to a province when person is adult

(3) When an application is made under subsection (1) to transfer the youth sentence of a young person to a province in which the young person is an adult, a youth justice court judge may, with the consent of the Attorney General, transfer the youth sentence and the record of the case to the youth justice court in the province to which the transfer is sought, and the youth justice court to which the case is transferred shall have full jurisdiction in respect of the youth sentence as if that court had imposed the youth sentence. The person shall be further dealt with in accordance with this Act.

Interprovincial arrangements

58. (1) When a youth sentence has been imposed under any of paragraphs 42(2)(k) to (r) in respect of a young person, the youth sentence in one province may be dealt with in any other province in accordance with any agreement that may have been made between those provinces.

Youth justice court retains jurisdiction

(2) Subject to subsection (3), when a youth sentence imposed in respect of a young person is dealt with under this section in a province other than that in which the youth sentence was imposed, the youth justice court of the province in which the youth sentence was imposed retains, for all purposes of this Act, exclusive jurisdiction over the young person as if the youth sentence were dealt with within that province, and any warrant or process issued in respect of the young person may be executed or served in any place in Canada outside the province where the youth sentence was imposed as if it were executed or served in that province.

Waiver of jurisdiction

(3) When a youth sentence imposed in respect of a young person is dealt with under this section in a province other than the one in which the youth sentence was imposed, the youth justice court of the province in which the youth sentence was imposed may, with the consent in writing of the Attorney General of that province and the young person, waive its jurisdiction, for the purpose of any proceeding under this Act, to the youth justice court of the province in which the youth sentence is dealt with, in which case the youth justice court in the province in which the youth sentence is dealt with shall have full jurisdiction in respect of the youth sentence as if that court had imposed the youth sentence.

Review of youth sentences not involving custody

59. (1) When a youth justice court has imposed a youth sentence in respect of a young person, other than a youth sentence under paragraph 42(2)(n), (o), (q) or (r), the youth justice court shall, on the application of the young person, the young person's parent, the Attorney General or the provincial director, made at any time after six months after the date of the youth sentence or, with leave of a youth justice court judge, at any earlier time, review the youth sentence if the court is satisfied that there are grounds for a review under subsection (2).

Grounds for review

(2) A review of a youth sentence may be made under this section

(a) on the ground that the circumstances that led to the youth sentence have changed materially;

(b) on the ground that the young person in respect of whom the review is to be made is unable to comply with or is experiencing serious difficulty in complying with the terms of the youth sentence;

(c) on the ground that the young person in respect of whom the review is to be made has contravened a condition of an order made under paragraph 42(2)(k) or (l) without reasonable excuse;

(d) on the ground that the terms of the youth sentence are adversely affecting the opportunities available to the young person to obtain services, education or employment; or

(e) on any other ground that the youth justice court considers appropriate.

Progress report

(3) The youth justice court may, before reviewing under this section a youth sentence imposed in respect of a young person, require the provincial director to cause to be prepared, and to submit to the youth justice court, a progress report on the performance of the young person since the youth sentence took effect.

Subsections 94(10) to (12) apply

(4) Subsections 94(10) to (12) apply, with any modifications that the circumstances require, in respect of any progress report required under subsection (3).

Subsections 94(7) and (14) to (18) apply

(5) Subsections 94(7) and (14) to (18) apply, with any modifications that the circumstances require, in respect of reviews made under this section and any notice required under subsection 94(14) shall also be given to the provincial director.

Compelling appearance of young person

(6) The youth justice court may, by summons or warrant, compel a young person in respect of whom a review is to be made under this section to appear before the youth justice court for the purposes of the review.

Decision of the youth justice court after review

(7) When a youth justice court reviews under this section a youth sentence imposed in respect of a young person, it may, after giving the young person, a parent of the young person, the Attorney General and the provincial director an opportunity to be heard,

(a) confirm the youth sentence;

(b) terminate the youth sentence and discharge the young person from any further obligation of the youth sentence; or

(c) vary the youth sentence or impose any new youth sentence under section 42, other than a committal to custody, for any period of time, not exceeding the remainder of the period of the earlier youth sentence, that the court considers appropriate in the circumstances of the case.

New youth sentence not to be more onerous

(8) Subject to subsection (9), when a youth sentence imposed in respect of a young person is reviewed under this section, no youth sentence imposed under subsection (7) shall, without the consent of the young person, be more onerous than the remainder of the youth sentence reviewed.

Exception

(9) A youth justice court may under this section extend the time within which a youth sentence imposed under paragraphs 42(2)(d) to (i) is to be complied with by a young person if the court is satisfied that the young person requires more time to comply with the youth sentence, but in no case shall the extension be for a period of time that expires more than twelve months after the date the youth sentence would otherwise have expired.

Provisions applicable to youth sentences on review

60. This Part and Part 5 (custody and supervision) apply with any modifications that the circumstances require to orders made in respect of reviews of youth sentences under sections 59 and 94 to 96.

ADULT SENTENCE AND ELECTION

61. [Repealed, 2012, c. 1, s. 175]

62. [Repealed, 2012, c. 1, s. 175]

63. [Repealed, 2012, c. 1, s. 175]

Application by Attorney General

64. (1) The Attorney General may, before evidence is called as to sentence or, if no evidence is called, before submissions are made as to sentence, make an application to the youth justice court for an order that a young person is liable to an adult sentence if the young person is or has been found guilty of an offence for which an adult is liable to imprisonment for a term of more than two years and that was committed after the young person attained the age of 14 years.

Obligation

(1.1) The Attorney General must consider whether it would be appropriate to make an application under subsection (1) if the offence is a serious violent offence and was committed after the young person attained the age of 14 years. If, in those circumstances, the Attorney General decides not to make an application, the Attorney General shall advise the youth justice court before the young person enters a plea or with leave of the court before the commencement of the trial.

Order fixing age

(1.2) The lieutenant governor in council of a province may by order fix an age greater than 14 years but not greater than 16 years for the purpose of subsection (1.1).

Notice of intention to seek adult sentence

(2) If the Attorney General intends to seek an adult sentence for an offence by making an application under subsection (1), the Attorney General shall, before the young person enters a plea or with leave of the youth justice court before the commencement of the trial, give notice to the young person and the youth justice court of the intention to seek an adult sentence.

Included offences

(3) A notice of intention to seek an adult sentence given in respect of an offence is notice in respect of any included offence of which the young person is found guilty for which an adult is liable to imprisonment for a term of more than two years.

(4) and (5) [Repealed, 2012, c. 1, s. 176]

65. [Repealed, 2012, c. 1, s. 177]

66. [Repealed, 2012, c. 1, s. 177]

Election—adult sentence

67. (1) The youth justice court shall, before a young person enters a plea, put the young person to his or her election in the words set out in subsection (2) if

(a) [Repealed, 2012, c. 1, s. 178]

(b) the Attorney General has given notice under subsection 64(2) of the intention to seek an adult sentence for an offence committed after the young person has attained the age of fourteen years;

(c) the young person is charged with having committed first or second degree murder within the meaning of section 231 of the *Criminal Code* before the young person has attained the age of fourteen years; or

(d) the person to whom section 16 (status of accused uncertain) applies is charged with having, after attaining the age of fourteen years, committed an offence for which an adult would be entitled to an election under section 536 of the *Criminal Code*, or over which a superior court of criminal jurisdiction would have exclusive jurisdiction under section 469 of that Act.

Wording of election

(2) The youth justice court shall put the young person to his or her election in the following words:

You have the option to elect to be tried by a youth justice court judge without a jury and without having had a preliminary inquiry; or you may elect to be tried by a judge without a jury; or you may elect to be tried by a court composed of a judge and jury. If you do not elect now, you are deemed to have elected to be tried by a court composed of a judge and jury. If you elect to be tried by a judge without a jury or by a court composed of a judge and jury or if you are deemed to have elected to be tried by a court composed of a judge and jury, you will have a preliminary inquiry only if you or the prosecutor requests one. How do you elect to be tried?

Election—Nunavut

(3) In respect of proceedings in Nunavut, the youth justice court shall, before a young person enters a plea, put the young person to his or her election in the words set out in subsection (4) if

(a) [Repealed, 2012, c. 1, s. 178]

(b) the Attorney General has given notice under subsection 64(2) of the intention to seek an adult sentence for an offence committed after the young person has attained the age of fourteen years;

(c) the young person is charged with having committed first or second degree murder within the meaning of section 231 of the *Criminal Code* before the young person has attained the age of fourteen years; or

(d) the person to whom section 16 (status of accused uncertain) applies is charged with having, after attaining the age of fourteen years, committed an offence for which an adult would be entitled to an election under section 536.1 of the *Criminal Code*.

Wording of election

(4) The youth justice court shall put the young person to his or her election in the following words:

You have the option to elect to be tried by a judge of the Nunavut Court of Justice alone, acting as a youth justice court without a jury and without a preliminary inquiry; or you may elect to be tried by a judge of the Nunavut Court of Justice, acting as a youth justice court without a jury; or you may elect to be tried by a judge of the Nunavut Court of Justice, acting as a youth justice court with a jury. If you elect to be tried by a judge without a jury or by a judge, acting as a youth justice court, with a jury or if you are deemed to have elected to be tried by a judge, acting as a youth justice court, with a jury, you will have a preliminary inquiry only if you or the prosecutor requests one. How do you elect to be tried?

Mode of trial where co-accused are young persons

(5) When two or more young persons who are charged with the same offence, who are jointly charged in the same information or indictment or in respect of whom the Attorney General seeks joinder of counts that are set out in separate informations or indictments are put to their election, then, unless all of them elect or re-elect or are deemed to have elected, as the case may be, the same mode of trial, the youth justice court judge

(a) may decline to record any election, re-election or deemed election for trial by a youth justice court judge without a jury, a judge without a jury or, in Nunavut, a judge of the Nunavut Court Justice without a jury; and

(b) if the judge declines to do so, shall hold a preliminary inquiry, if requested to do so by one of the parties, unless a preliminary inquiry has been held prior to the election, re-election or deemed election.

Attorney General may require trial by jury

(6) The Attorney General may, even if a young person elects under subsection (1) or (3) to be tried by a youth justice court judge without a jury or a judge without a jury, require the young person to be tried by a court composed of a judge and jury.

Preliminary inquiry

(7) When a young person elects to be tried by a judge without a jury, or elects or is deemed to have elected to be tried by a court composed of a judge and jury, the youth justice court referred to in subsection 13(1) shall, on the request of the young person or the prosecutor made at that time or within the period fixed by rules of court made under section 17 or 155 or, if there are no such rules, by the youth justice court judge, conduct a preliminary inquiry and if, on its conclusion, the young person is ordered to stand trial, the proceedings shall be conducted

(a) before a judge without a jury or a court composed of a judge and jury, as the case may be; or

(b) in Nunavut, before a judge of the Nunavut Court of Justice acting as a youth justice court, with or without a jury, as the case may be.

Preliminary inquiry if two or more accused

(7.1) If two or more young persons are jointly charged in an information and one or more of them make a request for a preliminary inquiry under subsection (7), a preliminary inquiry must be held with respect to all of them.

When no request for preliminary inquiry

(7.2) If no request for a preliminary inquiry is made under subsection (7), the youth justice court shall fix the date for the trial or the date on which the young person must appear in the trial court to have the date fixed.

Preliminary inquiry provisions of *Criminal Code*

(8) The preliminary inquiry shall be conducted in accordance with the provisions of Part XVIII (procedure on preliminary inquiry) of the *Criminal Code*, except to the extent that they are inconsistent with this Act.

Parts XIX and XX of *Criminal Code*

(9) Proceedings under this Act before a judge without a jury or a court composed of a judge and jury or, in Nunavut, a judge of the Nunavut Court of Justice acting as a youth justice court, with or without a jury, as the case may be, shall be conducted in accordance with the provisions of Parts XIX (indictable offences—trial without jury) and XX (procedure in jury trials and general provisions) of the *Criminal Code*, with any modifications that the circumstances require, except that

(a) the provisions of this Act respecting the protection of privacy of young persons prevail over the provisions of the *Criminal Code*; and

(b) the young person is entitled to be represented in court by counsel if the young person is removed from court in accordance with subsection 650(2) of the *Criminal Code*.

68. [Repealed, 2012, c. 1, s. 179]

69. (1) [Repealed, 2012, c. 1, s. 180]

Included offences

(2) If the Attorney General has given notice under subsection 64(2) of the intention to seek an adult sentence and the young person is found guilty of an included offence for which an adult is liable to imprisonment for a term of more than two years, committed after he or she has attained the age of 14 years, the Attorney General may make an application under subsection 64(1) (application for adult sentence).

70. [Repealed, 2012, c. 1, s. 181]

Hearing—adult sentences

71. The youth justice court shall, at the commencement of the sentencing hearing, hold a hearing in respect of an application under subsection 64(1) (application for adult sentence), unless the court has received notice that the application is not opposed. Both parties and the parents of the young person shall be given an opportunity to be heard at the hearing.

Order of adult sentence

72. (1) The youth justice court shall order that an adult sentence be imposed if it is satisfied that

(a) the presumption of diminished moral blameworthiness or culpability of the young person is rebutted; and

(b) a youth sentence imposed in accordance with the purpose and principles set out in subparagraph 3(1)(b)(ii) and section 38 would not be of sufficient length to hold the young person accountable for his or her offending behaviour.

Order of youth sentence

(1.1) If the youth justice court is not satisfied that an order should be made under subsection (1), it shall order that the young person is not liable to an adult sentence and that a youth sentence must be imposed.

Onus

(2) The onus of satisfying the youth justice court as to the matters referred to in subsection (1) is on the Attorney General.

Pre-sentence report

(3) In making an order under subsection (1) or (1.1), the youth justice court shall consider the pre-sentence report.

Court to state reasons

(4) When the youth justice court makes an order under this section, it shall state the reasons for its decision.

Appeal

(5) For the purposes of an appeal in accordance with section 37, an order under subsection (1) or (1.1) is part of the sentence.

Court must impose adult sentence

73. (1) When the youth justice court makes an order under subsection 72(1) in respect of a young person, the court shall, on a finding of guilt, impose an adult sentence on the young person.

Court must impose youth sentence

(2) When the youth justice court makes an order under subsection 72(1.1) in respect of a young person, the court shall, on a finding of guilt, impose a youth sentence on the young person.

Application of Parts XXIII and XXIV of *Criminal Code*

74. (1) Parts XXIII (sentencing) and XXIV (dangerous and long-term offenders) of the *Criminal Code* apply to a young person in respect of whom the youth justice court has ordered that an adult sentence be imposed.

Finding of guilt becomes a conviction

(2) A finding of guilt for an offence in respect of which an adult sentence is imposed becomes a conviction once the time allowed for the taking of an appeal has expired or, if an appeal is taken, all proceedings in respect of the appeal have been completed and the appeal court has upheld an adult sentence.

Interpretation

(3) This section does not affect the time of commencement of an adult sentence under subsection 719(1) of the *Criminal Code.*

Decision regarding lifting of publication ban

75. (1) When the youth justice court imposes a youth sentence on a young person who has been found guilty of a violent offence, the court shall decide whether it is appropriate to make an order lifting the ban on publication of information that would identify the young person as having been dealt with under this Act as referred to in subsection 110(1).

Order

(2) A youth justice court may order a lifting of the ban on publication if the court determines, taking into account the purpose and principles set out in sections 3and 38, that the young person poses a significant risk of committing another violent offence and the lifting of the ban is necessary to protect the public against that risk.

Onus

(3) The onus of satisfying the youth justice court as to the appropriateness of lifting the ban is on the Attorney General.

Appeals

(4) For the purposes of an appeal in accordance with section 37, an order under subsection (2) is part of the sentence.

Placement when subject to adult sentence

76. (1) Subject to subsections (2) and (9) and sections 79 and 80 and despite anything else in this Act or any other Act of Parliament, when a young person who is subject to an adult sentence in respect of an offence is sentenced to a term of imprisonment for the offence, the youth justice court shall order that the young person serve any portion of the imprisonment in

(a) a youth custody facility separate and apart from any adult who is detained or held in custody;

(b) a provincial correctional facility for adults; or

(c) if the sentence is for two years or more, a penitentiary.

Young person under age of 18

(2) No young person who is under the age of 18 years is to serve any portion of the imprisonment in a provincial correctional facility for adults or a penitentiary.

Opportunity to be heard

(3) Before making an order under subsection (1), the youth justice court shall give the young person, a parent of the young person, the Attorney General, the provincial director and representatives of the provincial and federal correctional systems an opportunity to be heard.

Report necessary

(4) Before making an order under subsection (1), the youth justice court shall require that a report be prepared for the purpose of assisting the court.

Appeals

(5) For the purposes of an appeal in accordance with section 37, an order under subsection (1) is part of the sentence.

Review

(6) On application, the youth justice court shall review the placement of a young person under this section and, if satisfied that the circumstances that resulted in the initial order have changed materially, and after having given the young person, a parent of the young person, the Attorney General, the provincial director and the representatives of the provincial and federal correctional systems an opportunity to be heard, the court may order that the young person be placed in

(a) a youth custody facility separate and apart from any adult who is detained or held in custody;

(b) a provincial correctional facility for adults; or

(c) if the sentence is for two years or more, a penitentiary.

Who may make application

(7) An application referred to in this section may be made by the young person, one of the young person's parents, the provincial director, representatives of the provincial and federal correctional systems and the Attorney General, after the time for all appeals has expired.

Notice

(8) When an application referred to in this section is made, the applicant shall cause a notice of the application to be given to the other persons referred to in subsection (7).

Limit—age twenty

(9) No young person shall remain in a youth custody facility under this section after the young person attains the age of twenty years, unless the youth justice court that makes the order under subsection (1) or reviews the placement under subsection (6) is satisfied that remaining in the youth custody facility would be in the best interests of the young person and would not jeopardize the safety of others.

Obligation to inform—parole

77. (1) When a young person is ordered to serve a portion of a sentence in a youth custody facility under paragraph 76(1)(a) (placement when subject to adult sentence), the provincial director shall inform the appropriate parole board.

Applicability of *Corrections and Conditional Release Act*

(2) For greater certainty, Part II of the *Corrections and Conditional Release Act* applies, subject to section 78, with respect to a young person who is the subject of an order under subsection 76(1) (placement when subject to adult sentence).

Appropriate parole board

(3) The appropriate parole board for the purposes of this section is

(a) if subsection 112(1) of the *Corrections and Conditional Release Act* would apply with respect to the young person but for the fact that the young person was ordered into a youth custody facility, the parole board mentioned in that subsection; and

(b) in any other case, the Parole Board of Canada.

Release entitlement

78. (1) For greater certainty, section 6 of the *Prisons and Reformatories Act* applies to a young person who is ordered to serve a portion of a sentence in a youth custody facility under paragraph 76(1)(a) (placement when subject to adult sentence) only if section 743.1 (rules respecting sentences of two or more years) of the *Criminal Code* would direct that the young person serve the sentence in a prison.

Release entitlement

(2) For greater certainty, section 127 of the *Corrections and Conditional Release Act* applies to a young person who is ordered to serve a portion of a sentence in a youth custody facility under paragraph 76(1)(a) (placement when subject to adult sentence) only if section 743.1 (rules respecting sentences of two or more years) of the *Criminal Code* would direct that the young person serve the sentence in a penitentiary.

If person convicted under another Act

79. If a person who is serving all or a portion of a sentence in a youth custody facility under paragraph 76(1)(a) (placement when subject to adult sentence) is sentenced to a term of imprisonment under an Act of Parliament other than this Act, the remainder of the portion of the sentence being served in the youth custody facility shall be served in a provincial correctional facility for adults or a penitentiary, in accordance with section 743.1 (rules respecting sentences of two or more years) of the *Criminal Code*.

If person who is serving a sentence under another Act is sentenced to an adult sentence

80. If a person who has been serving a sentence of imprisonment under an Act of Parliament other than this Act is sentenced to an adult sentence of imprisonment under this Act, the sentences shall be served in a provincial correctional facility for adults or a penitentiary, in accordance with section 743.1 (rules respecting sentences of two or more years) of the *Criminal Code*.

Procedure for application or notice

81. An application or a notice to the court under section 64 or 76 must be made or given orally, in the presence of the other party, or in writing with a copy served personally on the other party.

Effect of absolute discharge or termination of youth sentence

82. (1) Subject to section 12 (examination as to previous convictions) of the *Canada Evidence Act*, if a young person is found guilty of an offence, and a youth justice court directs under paragraph 42(2)(b) that the young person be discharged absolutely, or the youth sentence, or any disposition made under the *Young Offenders Act*, chapter Y-1 of the Revised Statutes of Canada, 1985, has ceased to have effect, other than an order under section 51 (mandatory prohibition order) of this Act or section 20.1 (mandatory prohibition order) of the *Young Offenders Act*, the young person is deemed not to have been found guilty or convicted of the offence except that

(a) the young person may plead *autrefois convict* in respect of any subsequent charge relating to the offence;

(b) a youth justice court may consider the finding of guilt in considering an application under subsection 64(1) (application for adult sentence);

(c) any court or justice may consider the finding of guilt in considering an application for judicial interim release or in considering what sentence to impose for any offence; and

(d) the Parole Board of Canada or any provincial parole board may consider the finding of guilt in considering an application for conditional release or for a record suspension under the *Criminal Records Act*.

Disqualifications removed

(2) For greater certainty and without restricting the generality of subsection (1), an absolute discharge under paragraph 42(2)(b) or the termination of the youth sentence or disposition in respect of an offence for which a young person is found guilty removes any disqualification in respect of the offence to which the young person is subject under any Act of Parliament by reason of a finding of guilt.

Applications for employment

(3) No application form for or relating to the following shall contain any question that by its terms requires the applicant to disclose that he or she has been charged with or found guilty of an offence in respect of which he or she has, under this Act or the *Young Offenders Act*, chapter Y-1 of the Revised Statutes of Canada, 1985, been discharged absolutely, or has completed the youth sentence under this Act or the disposition under the *Young Offenders Act*:

(a) employment in any department, as defined in section 2 of the *Financial Administration Act*;

(b) employment by any Crown corporation, as defined in section 83 of the *Financial Administration Act*;

(c) enrolment in the Canadian Forces; or

(d) employment on or in connection with the operation of any work, undertaking or business that is within the legislative authority of Parliament.

Finding of guilt not a previous conviction

(4) A finding of guilt under this Act is not a previous conviction for the purposes of any offence under any Act of Parliament for which a greater punishment is prescribed by reason of previous convictions, except for

(a) [Repealed, 2012, c. 1, s. 188]

(b) the purpose of determining the adult sentence to be imposed.

PART 5
CUSTODY AND SUPERVISION

Purpose

83. (1) The purpose of the youth custody and supervision system is to contribute to the protection of society by

(a) carrying out sentences imposed by courts through the safe, fair and humane custody and supervision of young persons; and

(b) assisting young persons to be rehabilitated and reintegrated into the community as law-abiding citizens, by providing effective programs to young persons in custody and while under supervision in the community.

Principles to be used

(2) In addition to the principles set out in section 3, the following principles are to be used in achieving that purpose:

(a) that the least restrictive measures consistent with the protection of the public, of personnel working with young persons and of young persons be used;

(b) that young persons sentenced to custody retain the rights of other young persons, except the rights that are necessarily removed or restricted as a consequence of a sentence under this Act or another Act of Parliament;

(c) that the youth custody and supervision system facilitate the involvement of the families of young persons and members of the public;

(d) that custody and supervision decisions be made in a forthright, fair and timely manner, and that young persons have access to an effective review procedure; and

(e) that placements of young persons where they are treated as adults not disadvantage them with respect to their eligibility for and conditions of release.

Young person to be held apart from adults

84. Subject to subsection 30(3) (pre-trial detention), paragraphs 76(1)(b) and (c) (placement in adult facilities with adult sentence) and sections 89 to 93 (placement in adult facilities with youth sentence), a young person who is committed to custody shall be held separate and apart from any adult who is detained or held in custody.

Levels of custody

85. (1) In the youth custody and supervision system in each province there must be at least two levels of custody for young persons distinguished by the degree of restraint of the young persons in them.

Designation of youth custody facilities

(2) Every youth custody facility in a province that contains one or more levels of custody shall be designated by

(a) in the case of a youth custody facility with only one level of custody, being the level of custody with the least degree of restraint of the young persons in it, the lieutenant governor in council or his or her delegate; and

(b) in any other case, the lieutenant governor in council.

Provincial director to specify custody level—committal to custody

(3) The provincial director shall, when a young person is committed to custody under paragraph 42(2)(n), (o), (q) or (r) or an order is made under subsection 98(3), paragraph 103(2)(b), subsection 104(1) or paragraph 109(2)(b), determine the level of custody appropriate for the young person, after having taken into account the factors set out in subsection (5).

Provincial director to specify custody level—transfer

(4) The provincial director may determine a different level of custody for the young person when the provincial director is satisfied that the needs of the young person and the interests of society would be better served by doing so, after having taken into account the factors set out in subsection (5).

Factors

(5) The factors referred to in subsections (3) and (4) are

(a) that the appropriate level of custody for the young person is the one that is the least restrictive to the young person, having regard to

(i) the seriousness of the offence in respect of which the young person was committed to custody and the circumstances in which that offence was committed,

(ii) the needs and circumstances of the young person, including proximity to family, school, employment and support services,

(iii) the safety of other young persons in custody, and

(iv) the interests of society;

(b) that the level of custody should allow for the best possible match of programs to the young person's needs and behaviour, having regard to the findings of any assessment in respect of the young person; and

(c) the likelihood of escape.

Placement and transfer at appropriate level

(6) After the provincial director has determined the appropriate level of custody for the young person under subsection (3) or (4), the young person shall be placed in the youth custody facility that contains that level of custody specified by the provincial director.

Notice

(7) The provincial director shall cause a notice in writing of a determination under subsection (3) or (4) to be given to the young person and a parent of the young person and set out in that notice the reasons for it.

Procedural safeguards

86. (1) The lieutenant governor in council of a province shall ensure that procedures are in place to ensure that the due process rights of the young person are protected with respect to a determination made under subsection 85(3) or (4), including that the young person be

(a) provided with any relevant information to which the provincial director has access in making the determination, subject to subsection (2);

(b) given the opportunity to be heard; and

(c) informed of any right to a review under section 87.

Withholding of information

(2) Where the provincial director has reasonable grounds to believe that providing the information referred to in paragraph (1)(a) would jeopardize the safety of any person or the security of a facility, he or she may authorize the withholding from the young person of as much information as is strictly necessary in order to protect such safety or security.

Review

87. (1) A young person may apply for a review under this section of a determination

(a) under subsection 85(3) that would place the young person in a facility at a level of custody that has more than a minimal degree of restraint; or

(b) under subsection 85(4) that would transfer a young person to a facility at a level of custody with a higher degree of restraint or increase the degree of restraint of the young person in the facility.

Procedural safeguards

(2) The lieutenant governor in council of a province shall ensure that procedures are in place for the review under subsection (1), including that

(a) the review board that conducts the review be independent;

(b) the young person be provided with any relevant information to which the review board has access, subject to subsection (3); and

(c) the young person be given the opportunity to be heard.

Withholding of information

(3) Where the review board has reasonable grounds to believe that providing the information referred to in paragraph (2)(b) would jeopardize the safety of any person or the security of a facility, it may authorize the withholding from the young

person of as much information as is strictly necessary in order to protect such safety or security.

Factors

(4) The review board shall take into account the factors referred to in subsection 85(5) in reviewing a determination.

Decision is final

(5) A decision of the review board under this section in respect of a particular determination is final.

Functions to be exercised by youth justice court

88. The lieutenant governor in council of a province may order that the power to make determinations of the level of custody for young persons and to review those determinations be exercised in accordance with the *Young Offenders Act*, chapter Y-1 of the Revised Statutes of Canada, 1985. The following provisions of that Act apply, with any modifications that the circumstances require, to the exercise of those powers:

(a) the definitions "review board" and "progress report" in subsection 2(1);

(b) section 11;

(c) sections 24.1 to 24.3; and

(d) sections 28 to 31.

Exception if young person is twenty years old or older

89. (1) When a young person is twenty years old or older at the time the youth sentence is imposed on him or her under paragraph 42(2)(n), (o), (q) or (r), the young person shall, despite section 85, be committed to a provincial correctional facility for adults to serve the youth sentence.

If serving youth sentence in a provincial correctional facility

(2) If a young person is serving a youth sentence in a provincial correctional facility for adults pursuant to subsection (1), the youth justice court may, on application of the provincial director at any time after the young person begins to serve a portion of the youth sentence in a provincial correctional facility for adults, after giving the young person, the provincial director and representatives of the provincial and federal correctional systems an opportunity to be heard, authorize the provincial director to direct that the young person serve the remainder of the youth sentence in a penitentiary if the court considers it to be in the best interests of the young person or in the public interest and if, at the time of the application, that remainder is two years or more.

Provisions to apply

(3) If a young person is serving a youth sentence in a provincial correctional facility for adults or a penitentiary under subsection (1) or (2), the *Prisons and Reformatories Act* and the *Corrections and Conditional Release Act*, and any other statute, regulation or rule applicable in respect of prisoners or offenders within the meaning of those Acts, statutes, regulations and

rules, apply in respect of the young person except to the extent that they conflict with Part 6 (publication, records and information) of this Act, which Part continues to apply to the young person.

Youth worker

90. (1) When a youth sentence is imposed committing a young person to custody, the provincial director of the province in which the young person received the youth sentence and was placed in custody shall, without delay, designate a youth worker to work with the young person to plan for his or her reintegration into the community, including the preparation and implementation of a reintegration plan that sets out the most effective programs for the young person in order to maximize his or her chances for reintegration into the community.

Role of youth worker when young person in the community

(2) When a portion of a young person's youth sentence is served in the community in accordance with section 97 or 105, the youth worker shall supervise the young person, continue to provide support to the young person and assist the young person to respect the conditions to which he or she is subject, and help the young person in the implementation of the reintegration plan.

Reintegration leave

91. (1) The provincial director of a province may, subject to any terms or conditions that he or she considers desirable, authorize, for a young person committed to a youth custody facility in the province further to an order under paragraph 76(1)(a) (placement when subject to adult sentence) or a youth sentence imposed under paragraph 42(2)(n), (o), (q) or (r),

(a) a reintegration leave from the youth custody facility for a period not exceeding thirty days if, in the opinion of the provincial director, it is necessary or desirable that the young person be absent, with or without escort, for medical, compassionate or humanitarian reasons or for the purpose of rehabilitating the young person or reintegrating the young person into the community; or

(b) that the young person be released from the youth custody facility on the days and during the hours that the provincial director specifies in order that the young person may

(i) attend school or any other educational or training institution,

(ii) obtain or continue employment or perform domestic or other duties required by the young person's family,

(iii) participate in a program specified by the provincial director that, in the provincial director's opinion, will enable the young person to better carry out employment or improve his or her education or training, or

(iv) attend an out-patient treatment program or other program that provides services that are suitable to addressing the young person's needs.

Renewal of reintegration leave

(2) A reintegration leave authorized under paragraph (1)(a) may be renewed by the provincial director for one or more thirty-day periods on reassessment of the case.

Revocation of authorization

(3) The provincial director of a province may, at any time, revoke an authorization made under subsection (1).

Arrest and return to custody

(4) If the provincial director revokes an authorization under subsection (3) or if a young person fails to comply with any term or condition of a reintegration leave or a release from custody under this section, the young person may be arrested without warrant and returned to custody.

Transfer to adult facility

92. (1) When a young person is committed to custody under paragraph 42(2)(n), (o), (q) or (r), the youth justice court may, on application of the provincial director made at any time after the young person attains the age of eighteen years, after giving the young person, the provincial director and representatives of the provincial correctional system an opportunity to be heard, authorize the provincial director to direct that the young person, subject to subsection (3), serve the remainder of the youth sentence in a provincial correctional facility for adults, if the court considers it to be in the best interests of the young person or in the public interest.

If serving youth sentence in a provincial correctional facility

(2) The youth justice court may authorize the provincial director to direct that a young person, subject to subsection (3), serve the remainder of a youth sentence in a penitentiary

  (a) if the youth justice court considers it to be in the best interests of the young person or in the public interest;

  (b) if the provincial director applies for the authorization at any time after the young person begins to serve a portion of a youth sentence in a provincial correctional facility for adults further to a direction made under subsection (1);

  (c) if, at the time of the application, that remainder is two years or more; and

  (d) so long as the youth justice court gives the young person, the provincial director and representatives of the provincial and federal correctional systems an opportunity to be heard.

Provisions to apply

(3) If the provincial director makes a direction under subsection (1) or (2), the *Prisons and Reformatories Act* and the *Corrections and Conditional Release Act*, and any other statute, regulation or rule applicable in respect of prisoners and offenders within the meaning of those Acts, statutes, regulations and rules, apply in respect of the young person except to the extent that they conflict with Part 6 (publication, records and informa-tion) of this Act, which Part continues to apply to the young person.

Placement when adult and youth sentences

(4) If a person is subject to more than one sentence, at least one of which is a youth sentence imposed under paragraph 42(2)(n), (o), (q) or (r) and at least one of which is a sentence referred to in either paragraph (b) or (c), he or she shall serve, in a provincial correctional facility for adults or a penitentiary in accordance with section 743.1 (rules respecting sentences of two or more years) of the *Criminal Code*, the following:

  (a) the remainder of any youth sentence imposed under paragraph 42(2)(n), (o), (q) or (r);

  (b) an adult sentence to which an order under paragraph 76(1)(b) or (c) (placement in adult facility) applies; and

  (c) any sentence of imprisonment imposed otherwise than under this Act.

Youth sentence and adult sentence

(5) If a young person is committed to custody under a youth sentence under paragraph 42(2)(n), (o), (q) or (r) and is also already subject to an adult sentence to which an order under paragraph 76(1)(a) (placement when subject to adult sentence) applies, the young person may, in the discretion of the provincial director, serve the sentences, or any portion of the sentences, in a youth custody facility, in a provincial correctional facility for adults or, if the unexpired portion of the sentence is two years or more, in a penitentiary.

When young person reaches twenty years of age

93. (1) When a young person who is committed to custody under paragraph 42(2)(n), (o), (q) or (r) is in a youth custody facility when the young person attains the age of twenty years, the young person shall be transferred to a provincial correctional facility for adults to serve the remainder of the youth sentence, unless the provincial director orders that the young person continue to serve the youth sentence in a youth custody facility.

If serving youth sentence in a provincial correctional facility

(2) If a young person is serving a portion of a youth sentence in a provincial correctional facility for adults pursuant to a transfer under subsection (1), the youth justice court may, on application of the provincial director after the transfer, after giving the young person, the provincial director and representatives of the provincial and federal correctional systems an opportunity to be heard, authorize the provincial director to direct that the young person serve the remainder of the youth sentence in a penitentiary if the court considers it to be in the best interests of the young person or in the public interest and if, at the time of the application, that remainder is two years or more.

Provisions to apply

(3) If the provincial director makes the direction, the *Prisons and Reformatories Act* and the *Corrections and Conditional*

Release Act, and any other statute, regulation or rule applicable in respect of prisoners and offenders within the meaning of those Acts, statutes, regulations and rules, apply in respect of the young person except to the extent that they conflict with Part 6 (publication, records and information) of this Act, which Part continues to apply to the young person.

Annual review

94. (1) When a young person is committed to custody pursuant to a youth sentence under paragraph 42(2)(n), (o), (q) or (r) for a period exceeding one year, the provincial director of the province in which the young person is held in custody shall cause the young person to be brought before the youth justice court without delay at the end of one year from the date of the most recent youth sentence imposed in respect of the offence—and at the end of every subsequent year from that date—and the youth justice court shall review the youth sentence.

Annual review

(2) When a young person is committed to custody pursuant to youth sentences imposed under paragraph 42(2)(n), (o), (q) or (r) in respect of more than one offence for a total period exceeding one year, the provincial director of the province in which the young person is held in custody shall cause the young person to be brought before the youth justice court without delay at the end of one year from the date of the earliest youth sentence imposed—and at the end of every subsequent year from that date—and the youth justice court shall review the youth sentences.

Optional review

(3) When a young person is committed to custody pursuant to a youth sentence imposed under paragraph 42(2)(n), (o), (q) or (r) in respect of an offence, the provincial director may, on the provincial director's own initiative, and shall, on the request of the young person, the young person's parent or the Attorney General, on any of the grounds set out in subsection (6), cause the young person to be brought before a youth justice court to review the youth sentence,

(a) when the youth sentence is for a period not exceeding one year, once at any time after the expiry of the greater of

(i) thirty days after the date of the youth sentence imposed under subsection 42(2) in respect of the offence, and

(ii) one third of the period of the youth sentence imposed under subsection 42(2) in respect of the offence; and

(b) when the youth sentence is for a period exceeding one year, at any time after six months after the date of the most recent youth sentence imposed in respect of the offence.

Time for optional review

(4) The young person may be brought before the youth justice court at any other time, with leave of the youth justice court judge.

Review

(5) If a youth justice court is satisfied that there are grounds for review under subsection (6), the court shall review the youth sentence.

Grounds for review

(6) A youth sentence imposed in respect of a young person may be reviewed under subsection (5)

(a) on the ground that the young person has made sufficient progress to justify a change in the youth sentence;

(b) on the ground that the circumstances that led to the youth sentence have changed materially;

(c) on the ground that new services or programs are available that were not available at the time of the youth sentence;

(d) on the ground that the opportunities for rehabilitation are now greater in the community; or

(e) on any other ground that the youth justice court considers appropriate.

No review if appeal pending

(7) Despite any other provision of this section, no review of a youth sentence in respect of which an appeal has been taken shall be made under this section until all proceedings in respect of any such appeal have been completed.

Youth justice court may order appearance of young person for review

(8) When a provincial director is required under subsections (1) to (3) to cause a young person to be brought before the youth justice court and fails to do so, the youth justice court may, on application made by the young person, his or her parent or the Attorney General, or on its own motion, order the provincial director to cause the young person to be brought before the youth justice court.

Progress report

(9) The youth justice court shall, before reviewing under this section a youth sentence imposed in respect of a young person, require the provincial director to cause to be prepared, and to submit to the youth justice court, a progress report on the performance of the young person since the youth sentence took effect.

Additional information in progress report

(10) A person preparing a progress report in respect of a young person may include in the report any information relating to the personal and family history and present environment of the young person that he or she considers advisable.

Written or oral report

(11) A progress report shall be in writing unless it cannot reasonably be committed to writing, in which case it may, with leave of the youth justice court, be submitted orally in court.

Subsections 40(4) to (10) to apply

(12) Subsections 40(4) to (10) (procedures respecting pre-sentence reports) apply, with any modifications that the circumstances require, in respect of progress reports.

Notice of review from provincial director

(13) When a youth sentence imposed in respect of a young person is to be reviewed under subsection (1) or (2), the provincial director shall cause any notice that may be directed by rules of court applicable to the youth justice court or, in the absence of such a direction, at least five clear days notice of the review to be given in writing to the young person, a parent of the young person and the Attorney General.

Notice of review from person requesting it

(14) When a review of a youth sentence imposed in respect of a young person is requested under subsection (3), the person requesting the review shall cause any notice that may be directed by rules of court applicable to the youth justice court or, in the absence of such a direction, at least five clear days notice of the review to be given in writing to the young person, a parent of the young person and the Attorney General.

Statement of right to counsel

(15) A notice given to a parent under subsection (13) or (14) shall include a statement that the young person whose youth sentence is to be reviewed has the right to be represented by counsel.

Service of notice

(16) A notice under subsection (13) or (14) may be served personally or may be sent by confirmed delivery service.

Notice may be waived

(17) Any of the persons entitled to notice under subsection (13) or (14) may waive the right to that notice.

If notice not given

(18) If notice under subsection (13) or (14) is not given in accordance with this section, the youth justice court may

(a) adjourn the proceedings and order that the notice be given in the manner and to the persons that it directs; or

(b) dispense with the notice if, in the opinion of the court, having regard to the circumstances, notice may be dispensed with.

Decision of the youth justice court after review

(19) When a youth justice court reviews under this section a youth sentence imposed in respect of a young person, it may, after giving the young person, a parent of the young person, the Attorney General and the provincial director an opportunity to be heard, having regard to the needs of the young person and the interests of society,

(a) confirm the youth sentence;

(b) release the young person from custody and place the young person under conditional supervision in accordance with the procedure set out in section 105, with any modifications that the circumstances require, for a period not exceeding the remainder of the youth sentence that the young person is then serving; or

(c) if the provincial director so recommends, convert a youth sentence under paragraph 42(2)(r) to a youth sentence under paragraph 42(2)(q) if the offence was murder or to a youth sentence under paragraph 42(2)(n) or (o), as the case may be, if the offence was an offence other than murder.

Orders are youth sentences

95. Orders under subsections 97(2) (conditions) and 98(3) (continuation of custody), paragraph 103(2)(b) (continuation of custody), subsections 104(1) (continuation of custody) and 105(1) (conditional supervision) and paragraph 109(2)(b) (continuation of suspension of conditional supervision) are deemed to be youth sentences for the purposes of section 94 (reviews).

Recommendation of provincial director for conditional supervision of young person

96. (1) When a young person is held in custody pursuant to a youth sentence under paragraph 42(2)(n), (o), (q) or (r), the provincial director may, if satisfied that the needs of the young person and the interests of society would be better served by doing so, make a recommendation to the youth justice court that the young person be released from custody and placed under conditional supervision.

Notice

(2) If the provincial director makes a recommendation, the provincial director shall cause a notice to be given in writing that includes the reasons for the recommendation and the conditions that the provincial director would recommend be set under section 105 to the young person, a parent of the young person and the Attorney General and give a copy of the notice to the youth justice court.

Application to court for review of recommendation

(3) If notice of a recommendation is made under subsection (2) with respect to a youth sentence imposed on a young person, the youth justice court shall, if an application for review is made by the young person, the young person's parent or the Attorney General within ten days after service of the notice, review the youth sentence without delay.

Subsections 94(7), (9) to (12) and (14) to (19) apply

(4) Subject to subsection (5), subsections 94(7) (no review of appeal pending), (9) to (12) (progress reports) and (14) to (19) (provisions respecting notice and decision of the youth justice court) apply, with any modifications that the circumstances require, in respect of reviews made under this section and any notice required under subsection 94(14) shall also be given to the provincial director.

If no application for review made under subsection (3)

(5) A youth justice court that receives a notice under subsection (2) shall, if no application for a review is made under subsection (3),

(a) order the release of the young person and place the young person under conditional supervision in accordance with section 105, having regard to the recommendations of the provincial director; or

(b) if the court considers it advisable, order that the young person not be released.

For greater certainty, an order under this subsection may be made without a hearing.

Notice when no release ordered

(6) When a youth justice court orders that the young person not be released under paragraph (5)(b), it shall cause a notice of its order to be given to the provincial director without delay.

Provincial director may request review

(7) When the provincial director is given a notice under subsection (6), he or she may request a review under this section.

When provincial director requests a review

(8) When the provincial director requests a review under subsection (7),

(a) the provincial director shall cause any notice that may be directed by rules of court applicable to the youth justice court or, in the absence of such a direction, at least five clear days notice of the review to be given in writing to the young person, a parent of the young person and the Attorney General; and

(b) the youth justice court shall review the youth sentence without delay after the notice required under paragraph (a) is given.

Conditions to be included in custody and supervision order

97. (1) Every youth sentence imposed under paragraph 42(2)(n) shall contain the following conditions, namely, that the young person, while serving the portion of the youth sentence under supervision in the community,

(a) keep the peace and be of good behaviour;

(b) report to the provincial director and then be under the supervision of the provincial director;

(c) inform the provincial director immediately on being arrested or questioned by the police;

(d) report to the police, or any named individual, as instructed by the provincial director;

(e) advise the provincial director of the young person's address of residence and report immediately to the provincial director any change

(i) in that address,

(ii) in the young person's normal occupation, including employment, vocational or educational training and volunteer work,

(iii) in the young person's family or financial situation, and

(iv) that may reasonably be expected to affect the young person's ability to comply with the conditions of the sentence; and

(f) not own, possess or have the control of any weapon, ammunition, prohibited ammunition, prohibited device or explosive substance, except as authorized in writing by the provincial director for the purposes of the young person participating in a program specified in the authorization.

Other conditions

(2) The provincial director may set additional conditions that support and address the needs of the young person, promote the reintegration of the young person into the community and offer adequate protection to the public from the risk that the young person might otherwise present. The provincial director shall, in setting the conditions, take into account the needs of the young person, the most effective programs for the young person in order to maximize his or her chances for reintegration into the community, the nature of the offence and the ability of the young person to comply with the conditions.

Communication of conditions

(3) The provincial director shall

(a) cause the conditions to be read by or to the young person bound by them;

(b) explain or cause to be explained to the young person the purpose and effect of the conditions, and confirm that the young person understands them; and

(c) cause a copy of the conditions to be given to the young person, and to a parent of the young person.

Provisions to apply

(4) Subsections 56(3) (endorsement of order by young person) and (4) (validity of order) apply, with any modifications that the circumstances require, in respect of conditions under this section.

Application for continuation of custody

98. (1) Within a reasonable time before the expiry of the custodial portion of a young person's youth sentence, the Attorney General or the provincial director may apply to the youth justice court for an order that the young person remain in custody for a period not exceeding the remainder of the youth sentence.

Continuation of custody

(2) If the hearing for an application under subsection (1) cannot be completed before the expiry of the custodial portion of the youth sentence, the court may order that the young person remain in custody pending the determination of the application if the court is satisfied that the application was made in a reasonable time, having regard to all the circumstances, and that there are compelling reasons for keeping the young person in custody.

Decision

(3) The youth justice court may, after giving both parties and a parent of the young person an opportunity to be heard, order that a young person remain in custody for a period not exceeding the remainder of the youth sentence, if it is satisfied that there are reasonable grounds to believe that

    (a) the young person is likely to commit a serious violent offence before the expiry of the youth sentence he or she is then serving; and

    (b) the conditions that would be imposed on the young person if he or she were to serve a portion of the youth sentence in the community would not be adequate to prevent the commission of the offence.

Factors

(4) For the purpose of determining an application under subsection (1), the youth justice court shall take into consideration any factor that is relevant to the case of the young person, including

    (a) evidence of a pattern of persistent violent behaviour and, in particular,

        (i) the number of offences committed by the young person that caused physical or psychological harm to any other person,

        (ii) the young person's difficulties in controlling violent impulses to the point of endangering the safety of any other person,

        (iii) the use of weapons in the commission of any offence,

        (iv) explicit threats of violence,

        (v) behaviour of a brutal nature associated with the commission of any offence, and

        (vi) a substantial degree of indifference on the part of the young person as to the reasonably foreseeable consequences, to other persons, of the young person's behaviour;

    (b) psychiatric or psychological evidence that a physical or mental illness or disorder of the young person is of such a nature that the young person is likely to commit, before the expiry of the youth sentence the young person is then serving, a serious violent offence;

    (c) reliable information that satisfies the youth justice court that the young person is planning to commit, before the expiry of the youth sentence the young person is then serving, a serious violent offence;

    (d) the availability of supervision programs in the community that would offer adequate protection to the public from the risk that the young person might otherwise present until the expiry of the youth sentence the young person is then serving;

    (e) whether the young person is more likely to reoffend if he or she serves his or her youth sentence entirely in custody without the benefits of serving a portion of the youth sentence in the community under supervision; and

    (f) evidence of a pattern of committing violent offences while he or she was serving a portion of a youth sentence in the community under supervision.

Report

99. (1) For the purpose of determining an application under section 98 (application for continuation of custody), the youth justice court shall require the provincial director to cause to be prepared, and to submit to the youth justice court, a report setting out any information of which the provincial director is aware with respect to the factors set out in subsection 98(4) that may be of assistance to the court.

Written or oral report

(2) A report referred to in subsection (1) shall be in writing unless it cannot reasonably be committed to writing, in which case it may, with leave of the youth justice court, be submitted orally in court.

Provisions apply

(3) Subsections 40(4) to (10) (procedures respecting presentence reports) apply, with any modifications that the circumstances require, in respect of a report referred to in subsection (1).

Notice of hearing

(4) When an application is made under section 98 (application for continuation of custody) in respect of a young person, the provincial director shall cause to be given, to the young person and to a parent of the young person, at least five clear days notice of the hearing in writing.

Statement of right to counsel

(5) Any notice given to a parent under subsection (4) shall include a statement that the young person has the right to be represented by counsel.

Service of notice

(6) A notice under subsection (4) may be served personally or may be sent by confirmed delivery service.

When notice not given

(7) When notice under subsection (4) is not given in accordance with this section, the youth justice court may

    (a) adjourn the hearing and order that the notice be given in any manner and to any person that it directs; or

    (b) dispense with the giving of the notice if, in the opinion of the youth justice court, having regard to the circumstances, the giving of the notice may be dispensed with.

Reasons

100. When a youth justice court makes an order under subsection 98(3) (decision for continued custody), it shall state its reasons for the order in the record of the case and shall provide, or cause to be provided, to the young person in respect of whom the order was made, the counsel and a parent of the young person, the Attorney General and the provincial director

(a) a copy of the order; and

(b) on request, a transcript or copy of the reasons for the order.

Review of youth justice court decision

101. (1) An order made under subsection 98(3) (decision for continued custody) in respect of a young person, or the refusal to make such an order, shall, on application of the young person, the young person's counsel, the Attorney General or the provincial director made within thirty days after the decision of the youth justice court, be reviewed by the court of appeal, and that court may, in its discretion, confirm or reverse the decision of the youth justice court.

Extension of time to make application

(2) The court of appeal may, at any time, extend the time within which an application under subsection (1) may be made.

Notice of application

(3) A person who proposes to apply for a review under subsection (1) shall give notice of the application in the manner and within the period of time that may be directed by rules of court.

Breach of conditions

102. (1) If the provincial director has reasonable grounds to believe that a young person has breached or is about to breach a condition to which he or she is subject under section 97 (conditions to be included in custody and supervision orders), the provincial director may, in writing,

(a) permit the young person to continue to serve a portion of his or her youth sentence in the community, on the same or different conditions; or

(b) if satisfied that the breach is a serious one that increases the risk to public safety, order that the young person be remanded to any youth custody facility that the provincial director considers appropriate until a review is conducted.

Provisions apply

(2) Sections 107 (apprehension) and 108 (review by provincial director) apply, with any modifications that the circumstances require, to an order under paragraph (1)(b).

Review by youth justice court

103. (1) When the case of a young person is referred to the youth justice court under section 108 (review by provincial director), the provincial director shall, without delay, cause the young person to be brought before the youth justice court, and the youth justice court shall, after giving the young person an opportunity to be heard,

(a) if the court is not satisfied on reasonable grounds that the young person has breached or was about to breach one of the conditions under which he or she was being supervised

in the community, order that the young person continue to serve a portion of his or her youth sentence in the community, on the same or different conditions; or

(b) if the court is satisfied on reasonable grounds that the young person has breached or was about to breach one of the conditions under which he or she was being supervised in the community, make an order under subsection (2).

Order

(2) On completion of a review under subsection (1), the youth justice court

(a) shall order that the young person continue to serve the remainder of the youth sentence the young person is then serving in the community, and when the court does so, the court may vary the existing conditions or impose new conditions; or

(b) shall, despite paragraph 42(2)(n) (custody and supervision order), order that the young person remain in custody for a period that does not exceed the remainder of the youth sentence the young person is then serving, if the youth justice court is satisfied that the breach of the conditions was serious.

Provisions apply

(3) Subsections 109(4) to (8) apply, with any modifications that the circumstances require, in respect of a review under this section.

Continuation of custody

104. (1) When a young person on whom a youth sentence under paragraph 42(2)(o), (q) or (r) has been imposed is held in custody and an application is made to the youth justice court by the Attorney General, within a reasonable time before the expiry of the custodial portion of the youth sentence, the provincial director of the province in which the young person is held in custody shall cause the young person to be brought before the youth justice court and the youth justice court may, after giving both parties and a parent of the young person an opportunity to be heard and if it is satisfied that there are reasonable grounds to believe that the young person is likely to commit an offence causing the death of or serious harm to another person before the expiry of the youth sentence the young person is then serving, order that the young person remain in custody for a period not exceeding the remainder of the youth sentence.

Continuation of custody

(2) If the hearing of an application under subsection (1) cannot be completed before the expiry of the custodial portion of the youth sentence, the court may order that the young person remain in custody until the determination of the application if the court is satisfied that the application was made in a reasonable time, having regard to all the circumstances, and that there are compelling reasons for keeping the young person in custody.

Factors

(3) For the purpose of determining an application under subsection (1), the youth justice court shall take into consideration any factor that is relevant to the case of the young person, including

(a) evidence of a pattern of persistent violent behaviour and, in particular,

(i) the number of offences committed by the young person that caused physical or psychological harm to any other person,

(ii) the young person's difficulties in controlling violent impulses to the point of endangering the safety of any other person,

(iii) the use of weapons in the commission of any offence,

(iv) explicit threats of violence,

(v) behaviour of a brutal nature associated with the commission of any offence, and

(vi) a substantial degree of indifference on the part of the young person as to the reasonably foreseeable consequences, to other persons, of the young person's behaviour;

(b) psychiatric or psychological evidence that a physical or mental illness or disorder of the young person is of such a nature that the young person is likely to commit, before the expiry of the youth sentence the young person is then serving, an offence causing the death of or serious harm to another person;

(c) reliable information that satisfies the youth justice court that the young person is planning to commit, before the expiry of the youth sentence the young person is then serving, an offence causing the death of or serious harm to another person; and

(d) the availability of supervision programs in the community that would offer adequate protection to the public from the risk that the young person might otherwise present until the expiry of the youth sentence the young person is then serving.

Youth justice court to order appearance of young person

(4) If a provincial director fails to cause a young person to be brought before the youth justice court under subsection (1), the youth justice court shall order the provincial director to cause the young person to be brought before the youth justice court without delay.

Provisions to apply

(5) Sections 99 to 101 apply, with any modifications that the circumstances require, in respect of an order made, or the refusal to make an order, under this section.

If application denied

(6) If an application under this section is denied, the court may, with the consent of the young person, the Attorney General

and the provincial director, proceed as though the young person had been brought before the court as required under subsection 105(1).

Conditional supervision

105. (1) The provincial director of the province in which a young person on whom a youth sentence under paragraph 42(2)(o), (q) or (r) has been imposed is held in custody or, if applicable, with respect to whom an order has been made under subsection 104(1) (continuation of custody), shall cause the young person to be brought before the youth justice court at least one month before the expiry of the custodial portion of the youth sentence. The court shall, after giving the young person an opportunity to be heard, by order, set the conditions of the young person's conditional supervision.

Conditions to be included in order

(2) The youth justice court shall include in the order under subsection (1) the following conditions, namely, that the young person

(a) keep the peace and be of good behaviour;

(b) appear before the youth justice court when required by the court to do so;

(c) report to the provincial director immediately on release, and then be under the supervision of the provincial director or a person designated by the youth justice court;

(d) inform the provincial director immediately on being arrested or questioned by the police;

(e) report to the police, or any named individual, as instructed by the provincial director;

(f) advise the provincial director of the young person's address of residence on release and after release report immediately to the clerk of the youth justice court or the provincial director any change

(i) in that address,

(ii) in the young person's normal occupation, including employment, vocational or educational training and volunteer work,

(iii) in the young person's family or financial situation, and

(iv) that may reasonably be expected to affect the young person's ability to comply with the conditions of the order;

(g) not own, possess or have the control of any weapon, ammunition, prohibited ammunition, prohibited device or explosive substance, except as authorized by the order; and

(h) comply with any reasonable instructions that the provincial director considers necessary in respect of any condition of the conditional supervision in order to prevent a breach of that condition or to protect society.

Other conditions

(3) In setting conditions for the purposes of subsection (1), the youth justice court may include in the order the following conditions, namely, that the young person

(a) on release, travel directly to the young person's place of residence, or to any other place that is noted in the order;

(b) make reasonable efforts to obtain and maintain suitable employment;

(c) attend school or any other place of learning, training or recreation that is appropriate, if the court is satisfied that a suitable program is available for the young person at such a place;

(d) reside with a parent, or any other adult that the court considers appropriate, who is willing to provide for the care and maintenance of the young person;

(e) reside in any place that the provincial director may specify;

(f) remain within the territorial jurisdiction of one or more courts named in the order;

(g) comply with conditions set out in the order that support and address the needs of the young person and promote the reintegration of the young person into the community; and

(h) comply with any other conditions set out in the order that the court considers appropriate, including conditions for securing the young person's good conduct and for preventing the young person from repeating the offence or committing other offences.

Temporary conditions

(4) When a provincial director is required under subsection (1) to cause a young person to be brought before the youth justice court but cannot do so for reasons beyond the young person's control, the provincial director shall so advise the youth justice court and the court shall, by order, set any temporary conditions for the young person's conditional supervision that are appropriate in the circumstances.

Conditions to be set at first opportunity

(5) When an order is made under subsection (4), the provincial director shall bring the young person before the youth justice court as soon after the order is made as the circumstances permit and the court shall then set the conditions of the young person's conditional supervision.

Report

(6) For the purpose of setting conditions under this section, the youth justice court shall require the provincial director to cause to be prepared, and to submit to the youth justice court, a report setting out any information that may be of assistance to the court.

Provisions apply

(7) Subsections 99(2) to (7) (provisions respecting reports and notice) and 104(4) (ordering appearance of young person) apply, with any modifications that the circumstances require, in respect of any proceedings held under subsection (1).

Provisions apply

(8) Subsections 56(1) to (4) (provisions respecting probation orders), (7) (notice to appear) and (8) (warrant in default) and section 101 (review of youth justice court decision) apply, with any modifications that the circumstances require, in respect of an order made under subsection (1).

Suspension of conditional supervision

106. If the provincial director has reasonable grounds to believe that a young person has breached or is about to breach a condition of an order made under subsection 105(1), the provincial director may, in writing,

(a) suspend the conditional supervision; and

(b) order that the young person be remanded to any youth custody facility that the provincial director considers appropriate until a review is conducted under section 108 and, if applicable, section 109.

Apprehension

107. (1) If the conditional supervision of a young person is suspended under section 106, the provincial director may issue a warrant in writing, authorizing the apprehension of the young person and, until the young person is apprehended, the young person is deemed not to be continuing to serve the youth sentence the young person is then serving.

Warrants

(2) A warrant issued under subsection (1) shall be executed by any peace officer to whom it is given at any place in Canada and has the same force and effect in all parts of Canada as if it had been originally issued or subsequently endorsed by a provincial court judge or other lawful authority having jurisdiction in the place where it is executed.

Peace officer may arrest

(3) If a peace officer believes on reasonable grounds that a warrant issued under subsection (1) is in force in respect of a young person, the peace officer may arrest the young person without the warrant at any place in Canada.

Requirement to bring before provincial director

(4) If a young person is arrested under subsection (3) and detained, the peace officer making the arrest shall cause the young person to be brought before the provincial director or a person designated by the provincial director

(a) if the provincial director or the designated person is available within a period of twenty-four hours after the young person is arrested, without unreasonable delay and in any event within that period; and

(b) if the provincial director or the designated person is not available within that period, as soon as possible.

Release or remand in custody

(5) If a young person is brought before the provincial director or a person designated by the provincial director under subsection (4), the provincial director or the designated person

(a) if not satisfied that there are reasonable grounds to believe that the young person is the young person in respect of whom the warrant referred to in subsection (1) was issued, shall release the young person; or

(b) if satisfied that there are reasonable grounds to believe that the young person is the young person in respect of whom the warrant referred to in subsection (1) was issued, may remand the young person in custody to await execution of the warrant, but if no warrant for the young person's arrest is executed within a period of forty-eight hours after the time the young person is remanded in custody, the person in whose custody the young person then is shall release the young person.

Review by provincial director

108. Without delay after the remand to custody of a young person whose conditional supervision has been suspended under section 106, or without delay after being informed of the arrest of such a young person, the provincial director shall review the case and, within forty-eight hours, cancel the suspension of the conditional supervision or refer the case to the youth justice court for a review under section 109.

Review by youth justice court

109. (1) If the case of a young person is referred to the youth justice court under section 108, the provincial director shall, without delay, cause the young person to be brought before the youth justice court, and the youth justice court shall, after giving the young person an opportunity to be heard,

(a) if the court is not satisfied on reasonable grounds that the young person has breached or was about to breach a condition of the conditional supervision, cancel the suspension of the conditional supervision; or

(b) if the court is satisfied on reasonable grounds that the young person has breached or was about to breach a condition of the conditional supervision, review the decision of the provincial director to suspend the conditional supervision and make an order under subsection (2).

Order

(2) On completion of a review under subsection (1), the youth justice court shall order

(a) the cancellation of the suspension of the conditional supervision, and when the court does so, the court may vary the conditions of the conditional supervision or impose new conditions;

(b) in a case other than a deferred custody and supervision order made under paragraph 42(2)(p), the continuation of the suspension of the conditional supervision for any period of time, not to exceed the remainder of the youth

sentence the young person is then serving, that the court considers appropriate, and when the court does so, the court shall order that the young person remain in custody; or

(c) in the case of a deferred custody and supervision order made under paragraph 42(2)(p), that the young person serve the remainder of the order as if it were a custody and supervision order under paragraph 42(2)(n).

Custody and supervision order

(3) After a court has made a direction under paragraph (2)(c), the provisions of this Act applicable to orders under paragraph 42(2)(n) apply in respect of the deferred custody and supervision order.

Factors to be considered

(4) In making its decision under subsection (2), the court shall consider the length of time the young person has been subject to the order, whether the young person has previously contravened it, and the nature of the contravention, if any.

Reasons

(5) When a youth justice court makes an order under subsection (2), it shall state its reasons for the order in the record of the case and shall give, or cause to be given, to the young person in respect of whom the order was made, the counsel and a parent of the young person, the Attorney General and the provincial director,

(a) a copy of the order; and

(b) on request, a transcript or copy of the reasons for the order.

Report

(6) For the purposes of a review under subsection (1), the youth justice court shall require the provincial director to cause to be prepared, and to submit to the youth justice court, a report setting out any information of which the provincial director is aware that may be of assistance to the court.

Provisions apply

(7) Subsections 99(2) to (7) (provisions respecting reports and notice) and 105(6) (report for the purpose of setting conditions) apply, with any modifications that the circumstances require, in respect of a review under this section.

Provisions apply

(8) Section 101 (review of youth justice court decision) applies, with any modifications that the circumstances require, in respect of an order made under subsection (2).

PART 6
PUBLICATION, RECORDS AND INFORMATION

PROTECTION OF PRIVACY OF YOUNG PERSONS

Identity of offender not to be published

110. (1) Subject to this section, no person shall publish the name of a young person, or any other information related to a young person, if it would identify the young person as a young person dealt with under this Act.

Limitation

(2) Subsection (1) does not apply

(a) in a case where the information relates to a young person who has received an adult sentence;

(b) in a case where the information relates to a young person who has received a youth sentence for a violent offence and the youth justice court has ordered a lifting of the publication ban under subsection 75(2); and

(c) in a case where the publication of information is made in the course of the administration of justice, if it is not the purpose of the publication to make the information known in the community.

Exception

(3) A young person referred to in subsection (1) may, after he or she attains the age of eighteen years, publish or cause to be published information that would identify him or her as having been dealt with under this Act or the *Young Offenders Act*, chapter Y-1 of the Revised Statutes of Canada, 1985, provided that he or she is not in custody pursuant to either Act at the time of the publication.

Ex parte application for leave to publish

(4) A youth justice court judge shall, on the *ex parte* application of a peace officer, make an order permitting any person to publish information that identifies a young person as having committed or allegedly committed an indictable offence, if the judge is satisfied that

(a) there is reason to believe that the young person is a danger to others; and

(b) publication of the information is necessary to assist in apprehending the young person.

Order ceases to have effect

(5) An order made under subsection (4) ceases to have effect five days after it is made.

Application for leave to publish

(6) The youth justice court may, on the application of a young person referred to in subsection (1), make an order permitting the young person to publish information that would identify him or her as having been dealt with under this Act or the *Young Offenders Act*, chapter Y-1 of the Revised Statutes of Canada, 1985, if the court is satisfied that the publication would not be contrary to the young person's best interests or the public interest.

Identity of victim or witness not to be published

111. (1) Subject to this section, no person shall publish the name of a child or young person, or any other information related to a child or a young person, if it would identify the child or young person as having been a victim of, or as having appeared as a witness in connection with, an offence committed or alleged to have been committed by a young person.

Exception

(2) Information that would serve to identify a child or young person referred to in subsection (1) as having been a victim or a witness may be published, or caused to be published, by

(a) that child or young person after he or she attains the age of eighteen years or before that age with the consent of his or her parents; or

(b) the parents of that child or young person if he or she is deceased.

Application for leave to publish

(3) The youth justice court may, on the application of a child or a young person referred to in subsection (1), make an order permitting the child or young person to publish information that would identify him or her as having been a victim or a witness if the court is satisfied that the publication would not be contrary to his or her best interests or the public interest.

Non-application

112. Once information is published under subsection 110(3) or (6) or 111(2) or (3), subsection 110(1) (identity of offender not to be published) or 111(1) (identity of victim or witness not to be published), as the case may be, no longer applies in respect of the information.

FINGERPRINTS AND PHOTOGRAPHS

Identification of Criminals Act applies

113. (1) The *Identification of Criminals Act* applies in respect of young persons.

Limitation

(2) No fingerprint, palmprint or photograph or other measurement, process or operation referred to in the *Identification of Criminals Act* shall be taken of, or applied in respect of, a young person who is charged with having committed an offence except in the circumstances in which an adult may, under that Act, be subjected to the measurements, processes and operations.

RECORDS THAT MAY BE KEPT

Youth justice court, review board and other courts

114. A youth justice court, review board or any court dealing with matters arising out of proceedings under this Act may keep a record of any case that comes before it arising under this Act.

Police records

115. (1) A record relating to any offence alleged to have been committed by a young person, including the original or a copy of any fingerprints or photographs of the young person, may be kept by any police force responsible for or participating in the investigation of the offence.

Extrajudicial measures

(1.1) The police force shall keep a record of any extrajudicial measures that they use to deal with young persons.

Police records

(2) When a young person is charged with having committed an offence in respect of which an adult may be subjected to any measurement, process or operation referred to in the *Identification of Criminals Act*, the police force responsible for the investigation of the offence may provide a record relating to the offence to the Royal Canadian Mounted Police. If the young person is found guilty of the offence, the police force shall provide the record.

Records held by R.C.M.P.

(3) The Royal Canadian Mounted Police shall keep the records provided under subsection (2) in the central repository that the Commissioner of the Royal Canadian Mounted Police may, from time to time, designate for the purpose of keeping criminal history files or records of offenders or keeping records for the identification of offenders.

Government records

116. (1) A department or an agency of any government in Canada may keep records containing information obtained by the department or agency

(a) for the purposes of an investigation of an offence alleged to have been committed by a young person;

(b) for use in proceedings against a young person under this Act;

(c) for the purpose of administering a youth sentence or an order of the youth justice court;

(d) for the purpose of considering whether to use extrajudicial measures to deal with a young person; or

(e) as a result of the use of extrajudicial measures to deal with a young person.

Other records

(2) A person or organization may keep records containing information obtained by the person or organization

(a) as a result of the use of extrajudicial measures to deal with a young person; or

(b) for the purpose of administering or participating in the administration of a youth sentence.

Exception—adult sentence

117. Sections 118 to 129 do not apply to records kept in respect of an offence for which an adult sentence has been imposed once the time allowed for the taking of an appeal has expired or, if an appeal is taken, all proceedings in respect of the appeal have been completed and the appeal court has upheld an adult sentence. The record shall be dealt with as a record of an adult and, for the purposes of the *Criminal Records Act*, the finding of guilt in respect of the offence for which the record is kept is deemed to be a conviction.

No access unless authorized

118. (1) Except as authorized or required by this Act, no person shall be given access to a record kept under sections 114 to 116, and no information contained in it may be given to any person, where to do so would identify the young person to whom it relates as a young person dealt with under this Act.

Exception for employees

(2) No person who is employed in keeping or maintaining records referred to in subsection (1) is restricted from doing anything prohibited under subsection (1) with respect to any other person so employed.

Persons having access to records

119. (1) Subject to subsections (4) to (6), from the date that a record is created until the end of the applicable period set out in subsection (2), the following persons, on request, shall be given access to a record kept under section 114, and may be given access to a record kept under sections 115 and 116:

(a) the young person to whom the record relates;

(b) the young person's counsel, or any representative of that counsel;

(c) the Attorney General;

(d) the victim of the offence or alleged offence to which the record relates;

(e) the parents of the young person, during the course of any proceedings relating to the offence or alleged offence to which the record relates or during the term of any youth sentence made in respect of the offence;

(f) any adult assisting the young person under subsection 25(7), during the course of any proceedings relating to the offence or alleged offence to which the record relates or during the term of any youth sentence made in respect of the offence;

(g) any peace officer for

(i) law enforcement purposes, or

(ii) any purpose related to the administration of the case to which the record relates, during the course of proceedings against the young person or the term of the youth sentence;

(h) a judge, court or review board, for any purpose relating to proceedings against the young person, or proceedings against the person after he or she becomes an adult, in respect of offences committed or alleged to have been committed by that person;

(i) the provincial director, or the director of the provincial correctional facility for adults or the penitentiary at which the young person is serving a sentence;

(j) a person participating in a conference or in the administration of extrajudicial measures, if required for the administration of the case to which the record relates;

(k) a person acting as ombudsman, privacy commissioner or information commissioner, whatever his or her official designation might be, who in the course of his or her duties under an Act of Parliament or the legislature of a province is investigating a complaint to which the record relates;

(l) a coroner or a person acting as a child advocate, whatever his or her official designation might be, who is acting in the course of his or her duties under an Act of Parliament or the legislature of a province;

(m) a person acting under the *Firearms Act*;

(n) a member of a department or agency of a government in Canada, or of an organization that is an agent of, or under contract with, the department or agency, who is

(i) acting in the exercise of his or her duties under this Act,

(ii) engaged in the supervision or care of the young person, whether as a young person or an adult, or in an investigation related to the young person under an Act of the legislature of a province respecting child welfare,

(iii) considering an application for conditional release, or for a record suspension under the *Criminal Records Act*, made by the young person, whether as a young person or an adult,

(iv) administering a prohibition order made under an Act of Parliament or the legislature of a province, or

(v) administering a youth sentence, if the young person has been committed to custody and is serving the custody in a provincial correctional facility for adults or a penitentiary;

(o) a person, for the purpose of carrying out a criminal record check required by the Government of Canada or the government of a province or a municipality for purposes of employment or the performance of services, with or without remuneration;

(p) an employee or agent of the Government of Canada, for statistical purposes under the *Statistics Act*;

(q) an accused or his or her counsel who swears an affidavit to the effect that access to the record is necessary to make a full answer and defence;

(r) a person or a member of a class of persons designated by order of the Governor in Council, or the lieutenant governor in council of the appropriate province, for a purpose and to the extent specified in the order; and

(s) any person or member of a class of persons that a youth justice court judge considers has a valid interest in the record, to the extent directed by the judge, if the judge is satisfied that access to the record is

(i) desirable in the public interest for research or statistical purposes, or

(ii) desirable in the interest of the proper administration of justice.

Period of access

(2) The period of access referred to in subsection (1) is

(a) if an extrajudicial sanction is used to deal with the young person, the period ending two years after the young person consents to be subject to the sanction in accordance with paragraph 10(2)(c);

(b) if the young person is acquitted of the offence otherwise than by reason of a verdict of not criminally responsible on account of mental disorder, the period ending two months after the expiry of the time allowed for the taking of an appeal or, if an appeal is taken, the period ending three months after all proceedings in respect of the appeal have been completed;

(c) if the charge against the young person is dismissed for any reason other than acquittal, the charge is withdrawn, or the young person is found guilty of the offence and a reprimand is given, the period ending two months after the dismissal, withdrawal, or finding of guilt;

(d) if the charge against the young person is stayed, with no proceedings being taken against the young person for a period of one year, at the end of that period;

(e) if the young person is found guilty of the offence and the youth sentence is an absolute discharge, the period ending one year after the young person is found guilty;

(f) if the young person is found guilty of the offence and the youth sentence is a conditional discharge, the period ending three years after the young person is found guilty;

(g) subject to paragraphs (i) and (j) and subsection (9), if the young person is found guilty of the offence and it is a summary conviction offence, the period ending three years after the youth sentence imposed in respect of the offence has been completed;

(h) subject to paragraphs (i) and (j) and subsection (9), if the young person is found guilty of the offence and it is an indictable offence, the period ending five years after the youth sentence imposed in respect of the offence has been completed;

(i) subject to subsection (9), if, during the period calculated in accordance with paragraph (g) or (h), the young person is found guilty of an offence punishable on summary conviction committed when he or she was a young person, the latest of

(i) the period calculated in accordance with paragraph (g) or (h), as the case may be, and

(ii) the period ending three years after the youth sentence imposed for that offence has been completed; and

(j) subject to subsection (9), if, during the period calculated in accordance with paragraph (g) or (h), the young person is found guilty of an indictable offence committed when he or she was a young person, the period ending five years after the sentence imposed for that indictable offence has been completed.

Prohibition orders not included

(3) Prohibition orders made under an Act of Parliament or the legislature of a province, including any order made under section 51, shall not be taken into account in determining any period referred to in subsection (2).

Extrajudicial measures

(4) Access to a record kept under section 115 or 116 in respect of extrajudicial measures, other than extrajudicial sanctions, used in respect of a young person shall be given only to the following persons for the following purposes:

(a) a peace officer or the Attorney General, in order to make a decision whether to again use extrajudicial measures in respect of the young person;

(b) a person participating in a conference, in order to decide on the appropriate extrajudicial measure;

(c) a peace officer, the Attorney General or a person participating in a conference, if access is required for the administration of the case to which the record relates; and

(d) a peace officer for the purpose of investigating an offence.

Exception

(5) When a youth justice court has withheld all or part of a report from any person under subsection 34(9) or (10) (nondisclosure of medical or psychological report) or 40(7) (nondisclosure of pre-sentence report), that person shall not be given access under subsection (1) to that report or part.

Records of assessments or forensic DNA analysis

(6) Access to a report made under section 34 (medical and psychological reports) or a record of the results of forensic DNA analysis of a bodily substance taken from a young person in execution of a warrant issued under section 487.05 of the *Criminal Code* may be given only under paragraphs (1)(a) to (c), (e) to (h) and (q) and subparagraph (1)(s)(ii).

Introduction into evidence

(7) Nothing in paragraph (1)(h) or (q) authorizes the introduction into evidence of any part of a record that would not otherwise be admissible in evidence.

Disclosures for research or statistical purposes

(8) When access to a record is given to a person under paragraph (1)(p) or subparagraph (1)(s)(i), the person may subsequently disclose information contained in the record, but shall not disclose the information in any form that would reasonably be expected to identify the young person to whom it relates.

Application of usual rules

(9) If, during the period of access to a record under any of paragraphs (2)(g) to (j), the young person is convicted of an offence committed when he or she is an adult,

(a) section 82 (effect of absolute discharge or termination of youth sentence) does not apply to the young person in respect of the offence for which the record is kept under sections 114 to 116;

(b) this Part no longer applies to the record and the record shall be dealt with as a record of an adult; and

(c) for the purposes of the *Criminal Records Act*, the finding of guilt in respect of the offence for which the record is kept is deemed to be a conviction.

Records of offences that result in a prohibition order

(10) Despite anything in this Act, when a young person is found guilty of an offence that results in a prohibition order being made, and the order is still in force at the end of the applicable period for which access to a record kept in respect of the order may be given under subsection (2),

(a) the record kept by the Royal Canadian Mounted Police pursuant to subsection 115(3) may be disclosed only to establish the existence of the order for purposes of law enforcement; and

(b) the record referred to in section 114 that is kept by the youth justice court may be disclosed only to establish the existence of the order in any offence involving a breach of the order.

Access to R.C.M.P. records

120. (1) The following persons may, during the period set out in subsection (3), be given access to a record kept under subsection 115(3) in respect of an offence set out in the schedule:

(a) the young person to whom the record relates;

(b) the young person's counsel, or any representative of that counsel;

(c) an employee or agent of the Government of Canada, for statistical purposes under the *Statistics Act*;

(d) any person or member of a class of persons that a youth justice court judge considers has a valid interest in the record, to the extent directed by the judge, if the judge is satisfied that access is desirable in the public interest for research or statistical purposes;

(e) the Attorney General or a peace officer, when the young person is or has been charged with another offence set out in the schedule or the same offence more than once, for the purpose of investigating any offence that the young person is suspected of having committed, or in respect of which the young person has been arrested or charged, whether as a young person or as an adult;

(f) the Attorney General or a peace officer to establish the existence of an order in any offence involving a breach of the order; and

(g) any person for the purposes of the *Firearms Act*.

Access for identification purposes

(2) During the period set out in subsection (3), access to the portion of a record kept under subsection 115(3) that contains the name, date of birth and last known address of the young person to whom the fingerprints belong, may be given to a person for identification purposes if a fingerprint identified as that of the young person is found during the investigation of an offence or during an attempt to identify a deceased person or a person suffering from amnesia.

Period of access

(3) For the purposes of subsections (1) and (2), the period of access to a record kept under subsection 115(3) in respect of an offence is the following:

(a) if the offence is an indictable offence, other than an offence referred to in paragraph (b), the period starting at the end of the applicable period set out in paragraphs 119(2)(h) to (j) and ending five years later; and

(b) if the offence is a serious violent offence for which the Attorney General has given notice under subsection 64(2) (intention to seek adult sentence), the period starting at the end of the applicable period set out in paragraphs 119(2)(h) to (j) and continuing indefinitely.

Subsequent offences as young person

(4) If a young person was found guilty of an offence set out in the schedule is, during the period of access to a record under subsection (3), found guilty of an additional offence set out in the schedule, committed when he or she was a young person, access to the record may be given to the following additional persons:

(a) a parent of the young person or any adult assisting the young person under subsection 25(7);

(b) a judge, court or review board, for a purpose relating to proceedings against the young person under this Act or any other Act of Parliament in respect of offences committed or alleged to have been committed by the young person, whether as a young person or as an adult; or

(c) a member of a department or agency of a government in Canada, or of an organization that is an agent of, or is under contract with, the department or agency, who is

(i) preparing a report in respect of the young person under this Act or for the purpose of assisting a court in sentencing the young person after the young person becomes an adult,

(ii) engaged in the supervision or care of the young person, whether as a young person or as an adult, or in the administration of a sentence in respect of the young person, whether as a young person or as an adult, or

(iii) considering an application for conditional release, or for a record suspension under the *Criminal Records Act*, made by the young person after the young person becomes an adult.

Disclosure for research or statistical purposes

(5) A person who is given access to a record under paragraph (1)(c) or (d) may subsequently disclose information contained in the record, but shall not disclose the information in any form that would reasonably be expected to identify the young person to whom it relates.

Subsequent offences as adult

(6) If, during the period of access to a record under subsection (3), the young person is convicted of an additional offence set out in the schedule, committed when he or she was an adult,

(a) this Part no longer applies to the record and the record shall be dealt with as a record of an adult and may be included on the automated criminal conviction records retrieval system maintained by the Royal Canadian Mounted Police; and

(b) for the purposes of the *Criminal Records Act*, the finding of guilt in respect of the offence for which the record is kept is deemed to be a conviction.

Deemed election

121. For the purposes of sections 119 and 120, if no election is made in respect of an offence that may be prosecuted by indictment or proceeded with by way of summary conviction, the Attorney General is deemed to have elected to proceed with the offence as an offence punishable on summary conviction.

Disclosure of information and copies of record

122. A person who is required or authorized to be given access to a record under section 119, 120, 123 or 124 may be given any information contained in the record and may be given a copy of any part of the record.

Where records may be made available

123. (1) A youth justice court judge may, on application by a person after the end of the applicable period set out in subsection 119(2), order that the person be given access to all or part of a record kept under sections 114 to 116 or that a copy of the record or part be given to that person,

(a) if the youth justice court judge is satisfied that

(i) the person has a valid and substantial interest in the record or part,

(ii) it is necessary for access to be given to the record or part in the interest of the proper administration of justice, and

(iii) disclosure of the record or part or the information in it is not prohibited under any other Act of Parliament or the legislature of a province; or

(b) if the youth court judge is satisfied that access to the record or part is desirable in the public interest for research or statistical purposes.

Restriction for paragraph (1)(a)

(2) Paragraph (1)(a) applies in respect of a record relating to a particular young person or to a record relating to a class of

young persons only if the identity of young persons in the class at the time of the making of the application referred to in that paragraph cannot reasonably be ascertained and the disclosure of the record is necessary for the purpose of investigating any offence that a person is suspected on reasonable grounds of having committed against a young person while the young person is, or was, serving a sentence.

Notice

(3) Subject to subsection (4), an application for an order under paragraph (1)(a) in respect of a record shall not be heard unless the person who makes the application has given the young person to whom the record relates and the person or body that has possession of the record at least five days notice in writing of the application, and the young person and the person or body that has possession have had a reasonable opportunity to be heard.

Where notice not required

(4) A youth justice court judge may waive the requirement in subsection (3) to give notice to a young person when the judge is of the opinion that

(a) to insist on the giving of the notice would frustrate the application; or

(b) reasonable efforts have not been successful in finding the young person.

Use of record

(5) In any order under subsection (1), the youth justice court judge shall set out the purposes for which the record may be used.

Disclosure for research or statistical purposes

(6) When access to a record is given to any person under paragraph (1)(b), that person may subsequently disclose information contained in the record, but shall not disclose the information in any form that would reasonably be expected to identify the young person to whom it relates.

Access to record by young person

124. A young person to whom a record relates and his or her counsel may have access to the record at any time.

DISCLOSURE OF INFORMATION IN A RECORD

Disclosure by peace officer during investigation

125. (1) A peace officer may disclose to any person any information in a record kept under section 114 (court records) or 115 (police records) that it is necessary to disclose in the conduct of the investigation of an offence.

Disclosure by Attorney General

(2) The Attorney General may, in the course of a proceeding under this Act or any other Act of Parliament, disclose the following information in a record kept under section 114 (court reports) or 115 (police records):

(a) to a person who is a co-accused with the young person in respect of the offence for which the record is kept, any information contained in the record; and

(b) to an accused in a proceeding, if the record is in respect of a witness in the proceeding, information that identifies the witness as a young person who has been dealt with under this Act.

Information that may be disclosed to a foreign state

(3) The Attorney General or a peace officer may disclose to the Minister of Justice of Canada information in a record that is kept under section 114 (court records) or 115 (police records) to the extent that it is necessary to deal with a request to or by a foreign state under the *Mutual Legal Assistance in Criminal Matters Act*, or for the purposes of any extradition matter under the *Extradition Act*. The Minister of Justice of Canada may disclose the information to the foreign state in respect of which the request was made, or to which the extradition matter relates, as the case may be.

Disclosure to insurance company

(4) A peace officer may disclose to an insurance company information in a record that is kept under section 114 (court records) or 115 (police records) for the purpose of investigating a claim arising out of an offence committed or alleged to have been committed by the young person to whom the record relates.

Preparation of reports

(5) The provincial director or a youth worker may disclose information contained in a record if the disclosure is necessary for procuring information that relates to the preparation of a report required by this Act.

Schools and others

(6) The provincial director, a youth worker, the Attorney General, a peace officer or any other person engaged in the provision of services to young persons may disclose to any professional or other person engaged in the supervision or care of a young person—including a representative of any school board or school or any other educational or training institution—any information contained in a record kept under sections 114 to 116 if the disclosure is necessary

(a) to ensure compliance by the young person with an authorization under section 91 or an order of the youth justice court;

(b) to ensure the safety of staff, students or other persons; or

(c) to facilitate the rehabilitation of the young person.

Information to be kept separate

(7) A person to whom information is disclosed under subsection (6) shall

(a) keep the information separate from any other record of the young person to whom the information relates;

(b) ensure that no other person has access to the information except if authorized under this Act, or if necessary for the purposes of subsection (6); and

(c) destroy their copy of the record when the information is no longer required for the purpose for which it was disclosed.

Time limit

(8) No information may be disclosed under this section after the end of the applicable period set out in subsection 119(2) (period of access to records).

Records in the custody, etc., of archivists

126. When records originally kept under sections 114 to 116 are under the custody or control of the Librarian and Archivist of Canada or the archivist for any province, that person may disclose any information contained in the records to any other person if

(a) a youth justice court judge is satisfied that the disclosure is desirable in the public interest for research or statistical purposes; and

(b) the person to whom the information is disclosed undertakes not to disclose the information in any form that could reasonably be expected to identify the young person to whom it relates.

Disclosure with court order

127. (1) The youth justice court may, on the application of the provincial director, the Attorney General or a peace officer, make an order permitting the applicant to disclose to the person or persons specified by the court any information about a young person that is specified, if the court is satisfied that the disclosure is necessary, having regard to the following circumstances:

(a) the young person has been found guilty of an offence involving serious personal injury;

(b) the young person poses a risk of serious harm to persons; and

(c) the disclosure of the information is relevant to the avoidance of that risk.

Opportunity to be heard

(2) Subject to subsection (3), before making an order under subsection (1), the youth justice court shall give the young person, a parent of the young person and the Attorney General an opportunity to be heard.

Ex parte application

(3) An application under subsection (1) may be made *ex parte* by the Attorney General where the youth justice court is satisfied that reasonable efforts have been made to locate the young person and that those efforts have not been successful.

Time limit

(4) No information may be disclosed under subsection (1) after the end of the applicable period set out in subsection 119(2) (period of access to records).

DISPOSITION OR DESTRUCTION OF RECORDS AND PROHIBITION ON USE AND DISCLOSURE

Effect of end of access periods

128. (1) Subject to sections 123, 124 and 126, after the end of the applicable period set out in section 119 or 120 no record kept under sections 114 to 116 may be used for any purpose that would identify the young person to whom the record relates as a young person dealt with under this Act or the *Young Offenders Act*, chapter Y-1 of the Revised Statutes of Canada, 1985.

Disposal of records

(2) Subject to paragraph 125(7)(c), any record kept under sections 114 to 116, other than a record kept under subsection 115(3), may, in the discretion of the person or body keeping the record, be destroyed or transmitted to the Librarian and Archivist of Canada or the archivist for any province, at any time before or after the end of the applicable period set out in section 119.

Disposal of R.C.M.P. records

(3) All records kept under subsection 115(3) shall be destroyed or, if the Librarian and Archivist of Canada requires it, transmitted to the Librarian and Archivist, at the end of the applicable period set out in section 119 or 120.

Purging CPIC

(4) The Commissioner of the Royal Canadian Mounted Police shall remove a record from the automated criminal conviction records retrieval system maintained by the Royal Canadian Mounted Police at the end of the applicable period referred to in section 119; however, information relating to a prohibition order made under an Act of Parliament or the legislature of a province shall be removed only at the end of the period for which the order is in force.

Exception

(5) Despite subsections (1), (2) and (4), an entry that is contained in a system maintained by the Royal Canadian Mounted Police to match crime scene information and that relates to an offence committed or alleged to have been committed by a young person shall be dealt with in the same manner as information that relates to an offence committed by an adult for which a record suspension ordered under the *Criminal Records Act* is in effect.

Authority to inspect

(6) The Librarian and Archivist of Canada may, at any time, inspect records kept under sections 114 to 116 that are under the control of a government institution as defined in section 2 of the *Library and Archives of Canada Act*, and the archivist for a

province may at any time inspect any records kept under those sections that the archivist is authorized to inspect under any Act of the legislature of the province.

Definition of "destroy"

(7) For the purposes of subsections (2) and (3), "destroy", in respect of a record, means

(a) to shred, burn or otherwise physically destroy the record, in the case of a record other than a record in electronic form; and

(b) to delete, write over or otherwise render the record inaccessible, in the case of a record in electronic form.

No subsequent disclosure

129. No person who is given access to a record or to whom information is disclosed under this Act shall disclose that information to any other person unless the disclosure is authorized under this Act.

PART 7
GENERAL PROVISIONS

DISQUALIFICATION OF JUDGE

Disqualification of judge

130. (1) Subject to subsection (2), a youth justice court judge who, prior to an adjudication in respect of a young person charged with an offence, examines a pre-sentence report made in respect of the young person in connection with that offence or has, after a guilty plea or a finding of guilt, heard submissions as to sentence and then there has been a change of plea, shall not in any capacity conduct or continue the trial of the young person for the offence and shall transfer the case to another judge to be dealt with according to law.

Exception

(2) A youth justice court judge may, in the circumstances referred to in subsection (1), with the consent of the young person and the prosecutor, conduct or continue the trial of the young person if the judge is satisfied that he or she has not been predisposed by a guilty plea or finding of guilt, or by information contained in the pre-sentence report or submissions as to sentence.

SUBSTITUTION OF JUDGE

Powers of substitute youth justice court judge

131. (1) A youth justice court judge who acts in the place of another youth justice court judge under subsection 669.2(1) (continuation of proceedings) of the *Criminal Code* shall

(a) if an adjudication has been made, proceed to sentence the young person or make the order that, in the circumstances, is authorized by law; or

(b) if no adjudication has been made, recommence the trial as if no evidence had been taken.

Transcript of evidence already given

(2) A youth justice court judge who recommences a trial under paragraph (1)(b) may, if the parties consent, admit into evidence a transcript of any evidence already given in the case.

EXCLUSION FROM HEARING

Exclusion from hearing

132. (1) Subject to subsection (2), a court or justice before whom proceedings are carried out under this Act may exclude any person from all or part of the proceedings if the court or justice considers that the person's presence is unnecessary to the conduct of the proceedings and the court or justice is of the opinion that

(a) any evidence or information presented to the court or justice would be seriously injurious or seriously prejudicial to

(i) the young person who is being dealt with in the proceedings,

(ii) a child or young person who is a witness in the proceedings, or

(iii) a child or young person who is aggrieved by or the victim of the offence charged in the proceedings; or

(b) it would be in the interest of public morals, the maintenance of order or the proper administration of justice to exclude any or all members of the public from the court room.

Exception

(2) Subject to section 650 (accused to be present) of the *Criminal Code* and except if it is necessary for the purposes of subsection 34(9) (nondisclosure of medical or psychological report) of this Act, a court or justice may not, under subsection (1), exclude from proceedings under this Act

(a) the prosecutor;

(b) the young person who is being dealt with in the proceedings, the counsel or a parent of the young person or any adult assisting the young person under subsection 25(7);

(c) the provincial director or his or her agent; or

(d) the youth worker to whom the young person's case has been assigned.

Exclusion after adjudication or during review

(3) A youth justice court, after it has found a young person guilty of an offence, or a youth justice court or a review board, during a review, may, in its discretion, exclude from the court or from a hearing of the review board any person other than the following, when it is being presented with information the knowledge of which might, in its opinion, be seriously injurious or seriously prejudicial to the young person:

(a) the young person or his or her counsel;

(b) the provincial director or his or her agent;

(c) the youth worker to whom the young person's case has been assigned; and

(d) the Attorney General.

Exception

(4) The exception set out in paragraph (3)(a) is subject to subsection 34(9) (nondisclosure of medical or psychological report) of this Act and section 650 (accused to be present) of the *Criminal Code*.

TRANSFER OF CHARGES

Transfer of charges

133. Despite subsections 478(1) and (3) of the *Criminal Code*, a young person charged with an offence that is alleged to have been committed in one province may, if the Attorney General of the province consents, appear before a youth justice court of any other province and

(a) if the young person pleads guilty to that offence and the youth justice court is satisfied that the facts support the charge, the court shall find the young person guilty of the offence alleged in the information or indictment; and

(b) if the young person pleads not guilty to that offence, or pleads guilty but the court is not satisfied that the facts support the charge, the young person shall, if he or she was detained in custody prior to the appearance, be returned to custody and dealt with according to law.

FORFEITURE OF RECOGNIZANCES

Applications for forfeiture of recognizances

134. Applications for the forfeiture of recognizances of young persons shall be made to the youth justice court.

Proceedings in case of default

135. (1) When a recognizance binding a young person has been endorsed with a certificate under subsection 770(1) of the *Criminal Code*, a youth justice court judge shall

(a) on the request of the Attorney General, fix a time and place for the hearing of an application for the forfeiture of the recognizance; and

(b) after fixing a time and place for the hearing, cause to be sent by confirmed delivery service, not less than ten days before the time so fixed, to each principal and surety named in the recognizance, directed to his or her latest known address, a notice requiring him or her to appear at the time and place fixed by the judge to show cause why the recognizance should not be forfeited.

Order for forfeiture of recognizance

(2) When subsection (1) is complied with, the youth justice court judge may, after giving the parties an opportunity to be heard, in his or her discretion grant or refuse the application and make any order with respect to the forfeiture of the recognizance that he or she considers proper.

Judgment debtors of the Crown

(3) If, under subsection (2), a youth justice court judge orders forfeiture of a recognizance, the principal and his or her sureties become judgment debtors of the Crown, each in the amount that the judge orders him or her to pay.

Order may be filed

(4) An order made under subsection (2) may be filed with the clerk of the superior court or, in the province of Quebec, the prothonotary and, if an order is filed, the clerk or the prothonotary shall issue a writ of *fieri facias* in Form 34 set out in the *Criminal Code* and deliver it to the sheriff of each of the territorial divisions in which any of the principal and his or her sureties resides, carries on business or has property.

If a deposit has been made

(5) If a deposit has been made by a person against whom an order for forfeiture of a recognizance has been made, no writ of *fieri facias* shall issue, but the amount of the deposit shall be transferred by the person who has custody of it to the person who is entitled by law to receive it.

Subsections 770(2) and (4) of *Criminal Code* do not apply

(6) Subsections 770(2) (transmission of recognizance) and (4) (transmission of deposit) of the *Criminal Code* do not apply in respect of proceedings under this Act.

Sections 772 and 773 of *Criminal Code* apply

(7) Sections 772 (levy under writ) and 773 (committal when writ not satisfied) of the *Criminal Code* apply in respect of writs of *fieri facias* issued under this section as if they were issued under section 771 (proceedings in case of default) of that Act.

OFFENCES AND PUNISHMENT

Inducing a young person, etc.

136. (1) Every person who

(a) induces or assists a young person to leave unlawfully a place of custody or other place in which the young person has been placed in accordance with a youth sentence or a disposition imposed under the *Young Offenders Act*, chapter Y-1 of the Revised Statutes of Canada, 1985,

(b) unlawfully removes a young person from a place referred to in paragraph (a),

(c) knowingly harbours or conceals a young person who has unlawfully left a place referred to in paragraph (a),

(d) wilfully induces or assists a young person to breach or disobey a term or condition of a youth sentence or other order of the youth justice court, or a term or condition of a disposition or other order under the *Young Offenders Act*, chapter Y-1 of the Revised Statutes of Canada, 1985, or

(e) wilfully prevents or interferes with the performance by a young person of a term or condition of a youth sentence or other order of the youth justice court, or a term or condition of a disposition or other order under the *Young Offenders Act*, chapter Y-1 of the Revised Statutes of Canada, 1985,

is guilty of an indictable offence and liable to imprisonment for a term not exceeding two years or is guilty of an offence punishable on summary conviction.

Absolute jurisdiction of provincial court judge

(2) The jurisdiction of a provincial court judge to try an adult charged with an indictable offence under this section is absolute and does not depend on the consent of the accused.

Failure to comply with sentence or disposition

137. Every person who is subject to a youth sentence imposed under any of paragraphs 42(2)(c) to (m) or (s) of this Act, to a victim fine surcharge ordered under subsection 53(2) of this Act or to a disposition made under any of paragraphs 20(1)(a.1) to (g), (j) or (l) of the *Young Offenders Act*, chapter Y-1 of the Revised Statutes of Canada, 1985, and who wilfully fails or refuses to comply with that sentence, surcharge or disposition is guilty of an offence punishable on summary conviction.

Offences

138. (1) Every person who contravenes subsection 110(1) (identity of offender not to be published), 111(1) (identity of victim or witness not to be published), 118(1) (no access to records unless authorized) or 128(3) (disposal of R.C.M.P. records) or section 129 (no subsequent disclosure) of this Act, or subsection 38(1) (identity not to be published), (1.12) (no subsequent disclosure), (1.14) (no subsequent disclosure by school) or (1.15) (information to be kept separate), 45(2) (destruction of records) or 46(1) (prohibition against disclosure) of the *Young Offenders Act*, chapter Y-1 of the Revised Statutes of Canada, 1985,

(a) is guilty of an indictable offence and liable to imprisonment for a term not exceeding two years; or

(b) is guilty of an offence punishable on summary conviction.

Provincial court judge has absolute jurisdiction on indictment

(2) The jurisdiction of a provincial court judge to try an adult charged with an offence under paragraph (1)(a) is absolute and does not depend on the consent of the accused.

Offence and punishment

139. (1) Every person who wilfully fails to comply with section 30 (designated place of temporary detention), or with an undertaking entered into under subsection 31(3) (condition of placement),

(a) is guilty of an indictable offence and liable to imprisonment for a term not exceeding two years; or

(b) is guilty of an offence punishable on summary conviction.

Offence and punishment

(2) Every person who wilfully fails to comply with section 7 (designated place of temporary detention) of the *Young Offenders Act*, chapter Y-1 of the Revised Statutes of Canada, 1985, or with an undertaking entered into under subsection 7.1(2) (condition of placement) of that Act is guilty of an offence punishable on summary conviction.

Punishment

(3) Any person who uses or authorizes the use of an application form in contravention of subsection 82(3) (application for employment) is guilty of an offence punishable on summary conviction.

APPLICATION OF CRIMINAL CODE

Application of *Criminal Code*

140. Except to the extent that it is inconsistent with or excluded by this Act, the provisions of the *Criminal Code* apply, with any modifications that the circumstances require, in respect of offences alleged to have been committed by young persons.

Sections of *Criminal Code* applicable

141. (1) Except to the extent that they are inconsistent with or excluded by this Act, section 16 (defence of mental disorder) and Part XX.1 (mental disorder) of the *Criminal Code* apply, with any modifications that the circumstances require, in respect of proceedings under this Act in relation to offences alleged to have been committed by young persons.

Notice and copies to counsel and parents

(2) For the purposes of subsection (1),

(a) wherever in Part XX.1 (mental disorder) of the *Criminal Code* a reference is made to a copy to be sent or otherwise given to an accused or a party to the proceedings, the reference shall be read as including a reference to a copy to be sent or otherwise given to

(i) any counsel representing the young person,

(ii) a parent of the young person who is in attendance at the proceedings against the young person, and

(iii) a parent of the young person not in attendance at the proceedings who is, in the opinion of the youth justice court or Review Board, taking an active interest in the proceedings; and

(b) wherever in Part XX.1 (mental disorder) of the *Criminal Code* a reference is made to notice to be given to an accused or a party to proceedings, the reference shall be read as including a reference to notice to be given to a parent of the young person and any counsel representing the young person.

Proceedings not invalid

(3) Subject to subsection (4), failure to give a notice referred to in paragraph (2)(b) to a parent of a young person does not affect the validity of proceedings under this Act.

Exception

(4) Failure to give a notice referred to in paragraph (2)(b) to a parent of a young person in any case renders invalid any subsequent proceedings under this Act relating to the case unless

(a) a parent of the young person attends at the court or Review Board with the young person; or

(b) a youth justice court judge or Review Board before whom proceedings are held against the young person

(i) adjourns the proceedings and orders that the notice be given in the manner and to the persons that the judge or Review Board directs, or

(ii) dispenses with the notice if the youth justice court or Review Board is of the opinion that, having regard to the circumstances, the notice may be dispensed with.

(5) [Repealed, 2005, c. 22, s. 63]

Considerations of court or Review Board making a disposition

(6) Before making or reviewing a disposition in respect of a young person under Part XX.1 (mental disorder) of the *Criminal Code*, a youth justice court or Review Board shall consider the age and special needs of the young person and any representations or submissions made by a parent of the young person.

(7) to (9) [Repealed, 2005, c. 22, s. 63]

Prima facie case to be made every year

(10) For the purpose of applying subsection 672.33(1) (fitness to stand trial) of the *Criminal Code* to proceedings under this Act in relation to an offence alleged to have been committed by a young person, wherever in that subsection a reference is made to two years, there shall be substituted a reference to one year.

Designation of hospitals for young persons

(11) A reference in Part XX.1 (mental disorder) of the *Criminal Code* to a hospital in a province shall be construed as a reference to a hospital designated by the Minister of Health for the province for the custody, treatment or assessment of young persons.

Definition of "Review Board"

(12) In this section, "Review Board" has the meaning assigned by section 672.1 of the *Criminal Code*.

Part XXVII and summary conviction trial provisions of *Criminal Code* to apply

142. (1) Subject to this section and except to the extent that they are inconsistent with this Act, the provisions of Part XXVII (summary conviction offences) of the *Criminal Code*, and any other provisions of that Act that apply in respect of summary conviction offences and relate to trial proceedings, apply to proceedings under this Act

(a) in respect of an order under section 810 (recognizance—fear of injury or damage), 810.01 (recognizance—fear of criminal organization offence) or 810.2 (recognizance—fear of serious personal injury offence) of that Act or an offence under section 811 (breach of recognizance) of that Act;

(b) in respect of a summary conviction offence; and

(c) in respect of an indictable offence as if it were defined in the enactment creating it as a summary conviction offence.

Indictable offences

(2) For greater certainty and despite subsection (1) or any other provision of this Act, an indictable offence committed by a young person is, for the purposes of this Act or any other Act of Parliament, an indictable offence.

Attendance of young person

(3) Section 650 of the *Criminal Code* applies in respect of proceedings under this Act, whether the proceedings relate to an indictable offence or an offence punishable on summary conviction.

Limitation period

(4) In proceedings under this Act, subsection 786(2) of the *Criminal Code* does not apply in respect of an indictable offence.

Costs

(5) Section 809 of the *Criminal Code* does not apply in respect of proceedings under this Act.

PROCEDURE

Counts charged in information

143. Indictable offences and offences punishable on summary conviction may under this Act be charged in the same information or indictment and tried jointly.

Issue of subpoena

144. (1) If a person is required to attend to give evidence before a youth justice court, the subpoena directed to that person may be issued by a youth justice court judge, whether or not the person whose attendance is required is within the same province as the youth justice court.

Service of subpoena

(2) A subpoena issued by a youth justice court and directed to a person who is not within the same province as the youth justice court shall be served personally on the person to whom it is directed.

Warrant

145. A warrant issued by a youth justice court may be executed anywhere in Canada.

EVIDENCE

General law on admissibility of statements to apply

146. (1) Subject to this section, the law relating to the admissibility of statements made by persons accused of committing offences applies in respect of young persons.

When statements are admissible

(2) No oral or written statement made by a young person who is less than eighteen years old, to a peace officer or to any other person who is, in law, a person in authority, on the arrest or detention of the young person or in circumstances where the peace officer or other person has reasonable grounds for believing that the young person has committed an offence is admissible against the young person unless

(a) the statement was voluntary;

(b) the person to whom the statement was made has, before the statement was made, clearly explained to the young person, in language appropriate to his or her age and understanding, that

(i) the young person is under no obligation to make a statement,

(ii) any statement made by the young person may be used as evidence in proceedings against him or her,

(iii) the young person has the right to consult counsel and a parent or other person in accordance with paragraph (c), and

(iv) any statement made by the young person is required to be made in the presence of counsel and any other person consulted in accordance with paragraph (c), if any, unless the young person desires otherwise;

(c) the young person has, before the statement was made, been given a reasonable opportunity to consult

(i) with counsel, and

(ii) with a parent or, in the absence of a parent, an adult relative or, in the absence of a parent and an adult relative, any other appropriate adult chosen by the young person, as long as that person is not a co-accused, or under investigation, in respect of the same offence; and

(d) if the young person consults a person in accordance with paragraph (c), the young person has been given a reasonable opportunity to make the statement in the presence of that person.

Exception in certain cases for oral statements

(3) The requirements set out in paragraphs (2)(b) to (d) do not apply in respect of oral statements if they are made spontaneously by the young person to a peace officer or other person in authority before that person has had a reasonable opportunity to comply with those requirements.

Waiver of right to consult

(4) A young person may waive the rights under paragraph (2)(c) or (d) but any such waiver

(a) must be recorded on video tape or audio tape; or

(b) must be in writing and contain a statement signed by the young person that he or she has been informed of the right being waived.

Waiver of right to consult

(5) When a waiver of rights under paragraph (2)(c) or (d) is not made in accordance with subsection (4) owing to a technical irregularity, the youth justice court may determine that the waiver is valid if it is satisfied that the young person was informed of his or her rights, and voluntarily waived them.

Admissibility of statements

(6) When there has been a technical irregularity in complying with paragraphs (2)(b) to (d), the youth justice court may admit into evidence a statement referred to in subsection (2), if satisfied that the admission of the statement would not bring into disrepute the principle that young persons are entitled to enhanced procedural protection to ensure that they are treated fairly and their rights are protected.

Statements made under duress are inadmissible

(7) A youth justice court judge may rule inadmissible in any proceedings under this Act a statement made by the young person in respect of whom the proceedings are taken if the young person satisfies the judge that the statement was made under duress imposed by any person who is not, in law, a person in authority.

Misrepresentation of age

(8) A youth justice court judge may in any proceedings under this Act rule admissible any statement or waiver by a young person if, at the time of the making of the statement or waiver,

(a) the young person held himself or herself to be eighteen years old or older;

(b) the person to whom the statement or waiver was made conducted reasonable inquiries as to the age of the young person and had reasonable grounds for believing that the young person was eighteen years old or older; and

(c) in all other circumstances the statement or waiver would otherwise be admissible.

Parent, etc., not a person in authority

(9) For the purpose of this section, a person consulted under paragraph (2)(c) is, in the absence of evidence to the contrary, deemed not to be a person in authority.

Statements not admissible against young person

147. (1) Subject to subsection (2), if a young person is assessed in accordance with an order made under subsection 34(1) (medical or psychological assessment), no statement or reference to a statement made by the young person during the course and for the purposes of the assessment to the person who conducts the assessment or to anyone acting under that person's direction is admissible in evidence, without the consent of the young person, in any proceeding before a court, tribunal, body or person with jurisdiction to compel the production of evidence.

Exceptions

(2) A statement referred to in subsection (1) is admissible in evidence for the purposes of

(a) making a decision on an application heard under section 71 (hearing—adult sentences);

(b) determining whether the young person is unfit to stand trial;

(c) determining whether the balance of the mind of the young person was disturbed at the time of commission of the alleged offence, if the young person is a female person charged with an offence arising out of the death of her newly-born child;

(d) making or reviewing a sentence in respect of the young person;

(e) determining whether the young person was, at the time of the commission of an alleged offence, suffering from automatism or a mental disorder so as to be exempt from criminal responsibility by virtue of subsection 16(1) of the *Criminal Code*, if the accused puts his or her mental capacity for criminal intent into issue, or if the prosecutor raises the issue after verdict;

(f) challenging the credibility of a young person in any proceeding if the testimony of the young person is inconsistent in a material particular with a statement referred to in subsection (1) that the young person made previously;

(g) establishing the perjury of a young person who is charged with perjury in respect of a statement made in any proceeding;

(h) deciding an application for an order under subsection 104(1) (continuation of custody);

(i) setting the conditions under subsection 105(1) (conditional supervision);

(j) conducting a review under subsection 109(1) (review of decision); or

(k) deciding an application for a disclosure order under subsection 127(1) (information about a young person).

Testimony of a parent

148. (1) In any proceedings under this Act, the testimony of a parent as to the age of a person of whom he or she is a parent is admissible as evidence of the age of that person.

Evidence of age by certificate or record

(2) In any proceedings under this Act,

(a) a birth or baptismal certificate or a copy of it purporting to be certified under the hand of the person in whose custody those records are held is evidence of the age of the person named in the certificate or copy; and

(b) an entry or record of an incorporated society that has had the control or care of the person alleged to have committed the offence in respect of which the proceedings are taken at or about the time the person came to Canada is evidence of the age of that person, if the entry or record was made before the time when the offence is alleged to have been committed.

Other evidence

(3) In the absence of any certificate, copy, entry or record mentioned in subsection (2), or in corroboration of that certificate, copy, entry or record, the youth justice court may receive and act on any other information relating to age that it considers reliable.

When age may be inferred

(4) In any proceedings under this Act, the youth justice court may draw inferences as to the age of a person from the person's appearance or from statements made by the person in direct examination or cross-examination.

Admissions

149. (1) A party to any proceedings under this Act may admit any relevant fact or matter for the purpose of dispensing with proof of it, including any fact or matter the admissibility of which depends on a ruling of law or of mixed law and fact.

Other party may adduce evidence

(2) Nothing in this section precludes a party to a proceeding from adducing evidence to prove a fact or matter admitted by another party.

Material evidence

150. Any evidence material to proceedings under this Act that would not but for this section be admissible in evidence may, with the consent of the parties to the proceedings and if the young person is represented by counsel, be given in such proceedings.

Evidence of a child or young person

151. The evidence of a child or a young person may be taken in proceedings under this Act only after the youth justice court judge or the justice in the proceedings has

(a) if the witness is a child, instructed the child as to the duty to speak the truth and the consequences of failing to do so; and

(b) if the witness is a young person and the judge or justice considers it necessary, instructed the young person as to the duty to speak the truth and the consequences of failing to do so.

Proof of service

152. (1) For the purposes of this Act, service of any document may be proved by oral evidence given under oath by, or by the affidavit or statutory declaration of, the person claiming to have personally served it or sent it by confirmed delivery service.

Proof of signature and official character unnecessary

(2) If proof of service of any document is offered by affidavit or statutory declaration, it is not necessary to prove the signature or official character of the person making or taking the affidavit or declaration, if the official character of that person appears on the face of the affidavit or declaration.

Seal not required

153. It is not necessary to the validity of any information, indictment, summons, warrant, minute, sentence, conviction, order or other process or document laid, issued, filed or entered in any proceedings under this Act that any seal be attached or affixed to it.

Forms

154. (1) The forms prescribed under section 155, varied to suit the case, or forms to the like effect, are valid and sufficient in the circumstances for which they are provided.

If forms not prescribed

(2) In any case for which forms are not prescribed under section 155, the forms set out in Part XXVIII of the *Criminal Code*, with any modifications that the circumstances require, or other appropriate forms, may be used.

Regulations

155. The Governor in Council may make regulations

(a) prescribing forms that may be used for the purposes of this Act;

(b) establishing uniform rules of court for youth justice courts across Canada, including rules regulating the practice and procedure to be followed by youth justice courts; and

(c) generally for carrying out the purposes and provisions of this Act.

AGREEMENTS WITH PROVINCES

Agreements with provinces

156. Any minister of the Crown may, with the approval of the Governor in Council, enter into an agreement with the government of any province providing for payments by Canada to the province in respect of costs incurred by the province or a municipality in the province for care of and services provided to young persons dealt with under this Act.

PROGRAMS

Community-based programs

157. The Attorney General of Canada or a minister designated by the lieutenant governor in council of a province may establish the following types of community-based programs:

(a) programs that are an alternative to judicial proceedings, such as victim-offender reconciliation programs, mediation programs and restitution programs;

(b) programs that are an alternative to detention before sentencing, such as bail supervision programs; and

(c) programs that are an alternative to custody, such as intensive support and supervision programs, and programs to carry out attendance orders.

PART 8
TRANSITIONAL PROVISIONS

Prohibition on proceedings

158. On and after the coming into force of this section, no proceedings may be commenced under the *Young Offenders Act*, chapter Y-1 of the Revised Statutes of Canada, 1985, in respect of an offence within the meaning of that Act, or under the *Juvenile Delinquents Act*, chapter J-3 of the Revised Statutes of Canada, 1970, in respect of a delinquency within the meaning of that Act.

Proceedings commenced under *Young Offenders Act*

159. (1) Subject to section 161, where, before the coming into force of this section, proceedings are commenced under the *Young Offenders Act*, chapter Y-1 of the Revised Statutes of Canada, 1985, in respect of an offence within the meaning of that Act alleged to have been committed by a person who was at the time of the offence a young person within the meaning of that Act, the proceedings and all related matters shall be dealt with in all respects as if this Act had not come into force.

Proceedings commenced under *Juvenile Delinquents Act*

(2) Subject to section 161, where, before the coming into force of this section, proceedings are commenced under the *Juvenile Delinquents Act*, chapter J-3 of the Revised Statutes of Canada, 1970, in respect of a delinquency within the meaning of that Act alleged to have been committed by a person who was at the time of the delinquency a child as defined in that Act, the proceedings and all related matters shall be dealt with under this Act as if the delinquency were an offence that occurred after the coming into force of this section.

160. [Repealed, 2012, c. 1, s. 193]

Applicable sentence

161. (1) A person referred to in section 159 who is found guilty of an offence or delinquency, other than a person convicted of an offence in ordinary court, as defined in subsection 2(1) of the *Young Offenders Act*, chapter Y-1 of the Revised Statutes of Canada, 1985, shall be sentenced under this Act, except that

(a) paragraph 110(2)(b) does not apply in respect of the offence or delinquency; and

(b) paragraph 42(2)(r) applies in respect of the offence or delinquency only if the young person consents to its application.

The provisions of this Act applicable to sentences imposed under section 42 apply in respect of the sentence.

Dispositions under paragraph 20(1)(k) or (k.1) of *Young Offenders Act*

(2) Where a young person is to be sentenced under this Act while subject to a disposition under paragraph 20(1)(k) or (k.1) of the *Young Offenders Act*, chapter Y-1 of the Revised Statutes of Canada, 1985, on the application of the Attorney General or the young person, a youth justice court shall, unless to do so would bring the administration of justice into disrepute, order that the remaining portion of the disposition made under that Act be dealt with, for all purposes under this Act or any other Act of Parliament, as if it had been a sentence imposed under paragraph 42(2)(n) or (q) of this Act, as the case may be.

Review of sentence

(3) For greater certainty, for the purpose of determining when the sentence is reviewed under section 94, the relevant date is the one on which the disposition came into force under the *Young Offenders Act*, chapter Y-1 of the Revised Statutes of Canada, 1985.

Commencement of proceedings

162. For the purposes of sections 158 and 159, proceedings are commenced by the laying of an information or indictment.

Application to delinquency and other offending behaviour

163. Sections 114 to 129 apply, with any modifications that the circumstances require, in respect of records relating to the offence of delinquency under the *Juvenile Delinquents Act*, chapter J-3 of the Revised Statutes of Canada, 1970, and in respect of records kept under sections 40 to 43 of the *Young Offenders Act*, chapter Y-1 of the Revised Statutes of Canada, 1985.

Agreements continue in force

164. Any agreement made under the *Young Offenders Act*, chapter Y-1 of the Revised Statutes of Canada, 1985, remains in force until it expires, unless it is amended or a new agreement is made under this Act.

Designation of youth justice court

165. (1) Any court established or designated as a youth court for the purposes of the *Young Offenders Act*, chapter Y-1 of the Revised Statutes of Canada, 1985, is deemed, as of the coming into force of this section, to have been established or designated as a youth justice court for the purposes of this Act.

Designation of youth justice court judges

(2) Any person appointed to be a judge of the youth court for the purposes of the *Young Offenders Act*, chapter Y-1 of the Revised Statutes of Canada, 1985, is deemed, as of the coming into force of this section, to have been appointed as a judge of the youth justice court for the purposes of this Act.

Designation of provincial directors and youth workers

(3) Any person, group or class of persons or body appointed or designated as a provincial director for the purposes of the *Young Offenders Act*, chapter Y-1 of the Revised Statutes of Canada, 1985, and any person appointed or designated as a youth worker for the purposes of that Act is deemed, as of the coming into force of this section, to have been appointed or designated as a provincial director or youth worker, as the case may be, for the purposes of this Act.

Designation of review boards and youth justice committees

(4) Any review board established or designated for the purposes of the *Young Offenders Act*, chapter Y-1 of the Revised Statutes of Canada, 1985, and any youth justice committee established for the purposes of that Act is deemed, as of the coming into force of this section, to have been established or designated as a review board or a youth justice committee, as the case may be, for the purposes of this Act.

Alternative measures continued as extrajudicial sanctions

(5) Any program of alternative measures authorized for the purposes of the *Young Offenders Act*, chapter Y-1 of the Revised Statutes of Canada, 1985, is deemed, as of the coming into force of this section, to be a program of extrajudicial sanctions authorized for the purposes of this Act.

Designation of places of temporary detention and youth custody

(6) Subject to subsection (7), any place that was designated as a place of temporary detention or open custody for the purposes of the *Young Offenders Act*, chapter Y-1 of the Revised Statutes of Canada, 1985, and any place or facility designated as a place of secure custody for the purposes of that Act is deemed, as of the coming into force of this section, to have been designated for the purposes of this Act as

(a) in the case of a place of temporary detention, a place of temporary detention; and

(b) in the case of a place of open custody or secure custody, a youth custody facility.

Exception

(7) If the lieutenant governor in council of a province makes an order under section 88 that the power to make determinations of the level of custody for young persons and to review those determinations be exercised in accordance with the *Young Offenders Act*, chapter Y-1 of the Revised Statutes of Canada, 1985, the designation of any place as a place of open custody or secure custody for the purposes of that Act remains in force for the purposes of section 88, subject to revocation or amendment of the designation.

Designation of other persons

(8) Any person designated as a clerk of the youth court for the purposes of the *Young Offenders Act*, chapter Y-1 of the Revised Statutes of Canada, 1985, or any person or group of persons who were designated under that Act to carry out specified functions and duties are deemed, as of the coming into force of this section, to have been designated as a clerk of the youth justice court, or to carry out the same functions and duties, as the case may be, under this Act.

PART 9
CONSEQUENTIAL AMENDMENTS, REPEAL AND COMING INTO FORCE

Consequential Amendments

166. to 198. [Amendments]

REPEAL

199. [Repeal]

COMING INTO FORCE

Coming into force

*200. The provisions of this Act come into force on a day or days to be fixed by order of the Governor in Council.

* [Note: Act in force April 1, 2003, *see* SI/2002-91.]

SCHEDULE *(Subsections 120(1), (4) and (6))*

1. An offence under any of the following provisions of the *Criminal Code*:

(a) paragraph 81(2)(a) (using explosives);

(b) subsection 85(1) (using firearm in commission of offence);

(c) section 151 (sexual interference);

(d) section 152 (invitation to sexual touching);

(e) section 153 (sexual exploitation);

(f) section 155 (incest);

(g) section 159 (anal intercourse);

(h) section 170 (parent or guardian procuring sexual activity by child);

(i) subsection 212(2) (living off the avails of prostitution by a child);

(j) subsection 212(4) (obtaining sexual services of a child);

(k) section 231 or 235 (first degree murder or second degree murder within the meaning of section 231);

(l) section 232, 234 or 236 (manslaughter);

(m) section 239 (attempt to commit murder);

(n) section 267 (assault with a weapon or causing bodily harm);

(o) section 268 (aggravated assault);

(p) section 269 (unlawfully causing bodily harm);

(q) section 271 (sexual assault);

(r) section 272 (sexual assault with a weapon, threats to a third party or causing bodily harm);

(s) section 273 (aggravated sexual assault);

(t) section 279 (kidnapping);

(u) section 344 (robbery);

(v) section 433 (arson—disregard for human life);

(w) section 434.1 (arson—own property);

(x) section 436 (arson by negligence); and

(y) paragraph 465(1)(a) (conspiracy to commit murder).

2. An offence under any of the following provisions of the *Criminal Code*, as they read immediately before July 1, 1990:

(a) section 433 (arson);

(b) section 434 (setting fire to other substance); and

(c) section 436 (setting fire by negligence).

3. An offence under any of the following provisions of the *Criminal Code*, chapter C-34 of the Revised Statutes of Canada, 1970, as they read immediately before January 4, 1983:

(a) section 144 (rape);

(b) section 145 (attempt to commit rape);

(c) section 149 (indecent assault on female);

(d) section 156 (indecent assault on male); and

(e) section 246 (assault with intent).

4. An offence under any of the following provisions of the *Controlled Drugs and Substances Act*:

(a) section 5 (trafficking);

(b) section 6 (importing and exporting); and

(c) section 7 (production of substance).

Convention on the Rights of the Child

B

Adopted and opened for signature, ratification and accession by General Assembly resolution 44/25 of 20 November 1989

Entry into force 2 September 1990, in accordance with article 49

Retrieved from http://www.ohchr.org

PREAMBLE

The States Parties to the present Convention,

Considering that, in accordance with the principles proclaimed in the Charter of the United Nations, recognition of the inherent dignity and of the equal and inalienable rights of all members of the human family is the foundation of freedom, justice and peace in the world,

Bearing in mind that the peoples of the United Nations have, in the Charter, reaffirmed their faith in fundamental human rights and in the dignity and worth of the human person, and have determined to promote social progress and better standards of life in larger freedom,

Recognizing that the United Nations has, in the Universal Declaration of Human Rights and in the International Covenants on Human Rights, proclaimed and agreed that everyone is entitled to all the rights and freedoms set forth therein, without distinction of any kind, such as race, colour, sex, language, religion, political or other opinion, national or social origin, property, birth or other status,

Recalling that, in the Universal Declaration of Human Rights, the United Nations has proclaimed that childhood is entitled to special care and assistance,

Convinced that the family, as the fundamental group of society and the natural environment for the growth and well-being of all its members and particularly children, should be afforded the necessary protection and assistance so that it can fully assume its responsibilities within the community,

Recognizing that the child, for the full and harmonious development of his or her personality, should grow up in a family environment, in an atmosphere of happiness, love and understanding,

Considering that the child should be fully prepared to live an individual life in society, and brought up in the spirit of the ideals proclaimed in the Charter of the United Nations, and in particular in the spirit of peace, dignity, tolerance, freedom, equality and solidarity,

Bearing in mind that the need to extend particular care to the child has been stated in the Geneva Declaration of the Rights of the Child of 1924 and in the Declaration of the Rights of the Child adopted by the General Assembly on 20 November 1959 and recognized in the Universal Declaration of Human Rights, in the International Covenant on Civil and Political Rights (in particular in articles 23 and 24), in the International Covenant on Economic, Social and Cultural Rights (in particular in article 10) and in the statutes and relevant instruments of specialized agencies and international organizations concerned with the welfare of children,

Bearing in mind that, as indicated in the Declaration of the Rights of the Child, "the child, by reason of his physical and mental immaturity, needs special safeguards and care, including appropriate legal protection, before as well as after birth",

Recalling the provisions of the Declaration on Social and Legal Principles relating to the Protection and Welfare of Children, with Special Reference to Foster Placement and Adoption Nationally and Internationally; the United Nations Standard Minimum Rules for the Administration of Juvenile Justice (The Beijing Rules) ; and the Declaration on the Protection of Women and Children in Emergency and Armed Conflict, Recognizing that, in all countries in the world, there are children living in exceptionally difficult conditions, and that such children need special consideration,

Taking due account of the importance of the traditions and cultural values of each people for the protection and harmonious development of the child, Recognizing the importance of international co-operation for improving the living conditions of children in every country, in particular in the developing countries,

Have agreed as follows:

PART I

Article 1

For the purposes of the present Convention, a child means every human being below the age of eighteen years unless under the law applicable to the child, majority is attained earlier.

Article 2

1. States Parties shall respect and ensure the rights set forth in the present Convention to each child within their jurisdiction without discrimination of any kind, irrespective of the child's or his or her parent's or legal guardian's race, colour, sex, language, religion, political or other opinion, national, ethnic or social origin, property, disability, birth or other status.

2. States Parties shall take all appropriate measures to ensure that the child is protected against all forms of discrimination or punishment on the basis of the status, activities, expressed opinions, or beliefs of the child's parents, legal guardians, or family members.

Article 3

1. In all actions concerning children, whether undertaken by public or private social welfare institutions, courts of law, administrative authorities or legislative bodies, the best interests of the child shall be a primary consideration.

2. States Parties undertake to ensure the child such protection and care as is necessary for his or her well-being, taking into account the rights and duties of his or her parents, legal guardians, or other individuals legally responsible for him or her, and, to this end, shall take all appropriate legislative and administrative measures.

3. States Parties shall ensure that the institutions, services and facilities responsible for the care or protection of children shall conform with the standards established by competent authorities, particularly in the areas of safety, health, in the number and suitability of their staff, as well as competent supervision.

Article 4

States Parties shall undertake all appropriate legislative, administrative, and other measures for the implementation of the rights recognized in the present Convention. With regard to economic, social and cultural rights, States Parties shall undertake such measures to the maximum extent of their available resources and, where needed, within the framework of international co-operation.

Article 5

States Parties shall respect the responsibilities, rights and duties of parents or, where applicable, the members of the extended family or community as provided for by local custom, legal guardians or other persons legally responsible for the child, to provide, in a manner consistent with the evolving capacities of the child, appropriate direction and guidance in the exercise by the child of the rights recognized in the present Convention.

Article 6

1. States Parties recognize that every child has the inherent right to life. 2. States Parties shall ensure to the maximum extent possible the survival and development of the child.

Article 7

1. The child shall be registered immediately after birth and shall have the right from birth to a name, the right to acquire a nationality and. as far as possible, the right to know and be cared for by his or her parents.

2. States Parties shall ensure the implementation of these rights in accordance with their national law and their obligations under the relevant international instruments in this field, in particular where the child would otherwise be stateless.

Article 8

1. States Parties undertake to respect the right of the child to preserve his or her identity, including nationality, name and family relations as recognized by law without unlawful interference.

2. Where a child is illegally deprived of some or all of the elements of his or her identity, States Parties shall provide appropriate assistance and protection, with a view to re-establishing speedily his or her identity.

Article 9

1. States Parties shall ensure that a child shall not be separated from his or her parents against their will, except when competent authorities subject to judicial review determine, in accordance with applicable law and procedures, that such separation is necessary for the best interests of the child. Such determination may be necessary in a particular case such as one involving abuse or neglect of the child by the parents, or one where the parents are living separately and a decision must be made as to the child's place of residence.

2. In any proceedings pursuant to paragraph 1 of the present article, all interested parties shall be given an opportunity to participate in the proceedings and make their views known.

3. States Parties shall respect the right of the child who is separated from one or both parents to maintain personal relations and direct contact with both parents on a regular basis, except if it is contrary to the child's best interests.

4. Where such separation results from any action initiated by a State Party, such as the detention, imprisonment, exile, deportation or death (including death arising from any cause while the person is in the custody of the State) of one or both parents or of the child, that State Party shall, upon request, provide the parents, the child or, if appropriate, another member of the family with the essential information concerning the whereabouts of the absent member(s) of the family unless the provision of the information would be detrimental to the well-being of the child. States Parties shall further ensure that the submission of such a request shall of itself entail no adverse consequences for the person(s) concerned.

Article 10

1. In accordance with the obligation of States Parties under article 9, paragraph 1, applications by a child or his or her parents to enter or leave a State Party for the purpose of family reunification shall be dealt with by States Parties in a positive, humane and expeditious manner. States Parties shall further ensure that the submission of such a request shall entail no adverse consequences for the applicants and for the members of their family.

2. A child whose parents reside in different States shall have the right to maintain on a regular basis, save in exceptional circumstances personal relations and direct contacts with both parents. Towards that end and in accordance with the obligation of States Parties under article 9, paragraph 1, States Parties shall respect the right of the child and his or her parents to leave any country, including their own, and to enter their own country. The right to leave any country shall be subject only to such restrictions as are prescribed by law and which are necessary to protect the national security, public order (*ordre public*), public health or morals or the rights and freedoms of others and are consistent with the other rights recognized in the present Convention.

Article 11

1. States Parties shall take measures to combat the illicit transfer and non-return of children abroad.

2. To this end, States Parties shall promote the conclusion of bilateral or multilateral agreements or accession to existing agreements.

Article 12

1. States Parties shall assure to the child who is capable of forming his or her own views the right to express those views freely in all matters affecting the child, the views of the child being given due weight in accordance with the age and maturity of the child.

2. For this purpose, the child shall in particular be provided the opportunity to be heard in any judicial and administrative proceedings affecting the child, either directly, or through a representative or an appropriate body, in a manner consistent with the procedural rules of national law.

Article 13

1. The child shall have the right to freedom of expression; this right shall include freedom to seek, receive and impart information and ideas of all kinds, regardless of frontiers, either orally, in writing or in print, in the form of art, or through any other media of the child's choice.

2. The exercise of this right may be subject to certain restrictions, but these shall only be such as are provided by law and are necessary:

(a) For respect of the rights or reputations of others; or

(b) For the protection of national security or of public order (*ordre public*), or of public health or morals.

Article 14

1. States Parties shall respect the right of the child to freedom of thought, conscience and religion.

2. States Parties shall respect the rights and duties of the parents and, when applicable, legal guardians, to provide direction to the child in the exercise of his or her right in a manner consistent with the evolving capacities of the child.

3. Freedom to manifest one's religion or beliefs may be subject only to such limitations as are prescribed by law and are necessary to protect public safety, order, health or morals, or the fundamental rights and freedoms of others.

Article 15

1. States Parties recognize the rights of the child to freedom of association and to freedom of peaceful assembly.

2. No restrictions may be placed on the exercise of these rights other than those imposed in conformity with the law and which are necessary in a democratic society in the interests of national security or public safety, public order (*ordre public*), the protection of public health or morals or the protection of the rights and freedoms of others.

Article 16

1. No child shall be subjected to arbitrary or unlawful interference with his or her privacy, family, home or correspondence, nor to unlawful attacks on his or her honour and reputation.

2. The child has the right to the protection of the law against such interference or attacks.

Article 17

States Parties recognize the important function performed by the mass media and shall ensure that the child has access to information and material from a diversity of national and international sources, especially those aimed at the promotion of his or her social, spiritual and moral well-being and physical and mental health.

To this end, States Parties shall:

(a) Encourage the mass media to disseminate information and material of social and cultural benefit to the child and in accordance with the spirit of article 29;

(b) Encourage international co-operation in the production, exchange and dissemination of such information and material from a diversity of cultural, national and international sources;

(c) Encourage the production and dissemination of children's books;

(d) Encourage the mass media to have particular regard to the linguistic needs of the child who belongs to a minority group or who is indigenous;

(e) Encourage the development of appropriate guidelines for the protection of the child from information and material injurious to his or her well-being, bearing in mind the provisions of articles 13 and 18.

Article 18

1. States Parties shall use their best efforts to ensure recognition of the principle that both parents have common responsibilities for the upbringing and development of the child. Parents or, as the case may be, legal guardians, have the primary responsibility for the upbringing and development of the child. The best interests of the child will be their basic concern.

2. For the purpose of guaranteeing and promoting the rights set forth in the present Convention, States Parties shall render appropriate assistance to parents and legal guardians in the performance of their child-rearing responsibilities and shall ensure the development of institutions, facilities and services for the care of children.

3. States Parties shall take all appropriate measures to ensure that children of working parents have the right to benefit from child-care services and facilities for which they are eligible.

Article 19

1. States Parties shall take all appropriate legislative, administrative, social and educational measures to protect the child from all forms of physical or mental violence, injury or abuse, neglect or negligent treatment, maltreatment or exploitation, including sexual abuse, while in the care of parent(s), legal guardian(s) or any other person who has the care of the child.

2. Such protective measures should, as appropriate, include effective procedures for the establishment of social programmes to provide necessary support for the child and for those who have the care of the child, as well as for other forms of prevention and for identification, reporting, referral, investigation, treatment and follow-up of instances of child maltreatment described heretofore, and, as appropriate, for judicial involvement.

Article 20

1. A child temporarily or permanently deprived of his or her family environment, or in whose own best interests cannot be allowed to remain in that environment, shall be entitled to special protection and assistance provided by the State.

2. States Parties shall in accordance with their national laws ensure alternative care for such a child.

3. Such care could include, *inter alia*, foster placement, *kafalah* of Islamic law, adoption or if necessary placement in suitable institutions for the care of children. When considering solutions, due regard shall be paid to the desirability of continuity in a child's upbringing and to the child's ethnic, religious, cultural and linguistic background.

Article 21

States Parties that recognize and/or permit the system of adoption shall ensure that the best interests of the child shall be the paramount consideration and they shall:

(a) Ensure that the adoption of a child is authorized only by competent authorities who determine, in accordance with applicable law and procedures and on the basis of all perti-

nent and reliable information, that the adoption is permissible in view of the child's status concerning parents, relatives and legal guardians and that, if required, the persons concerned have given their informed consent to the adoption on the basis of such counselling as may be necessary;

(b) Recognize that inter-country adoption may be considered as an alternative means of child's care, if the child cannot be placed in a foster or an adoptive family or cannot in any suitable manner be cared for in the child's country of origin;

(c) Ensure that the child concerned by inter-country adoption enjoys safeguards and standards equivalent to those existing in the case of national adoption;

(d) Take all appropriate measures to ensure that, in inter-country adoption, the placement does not result in improper financial gain for those involved in it;

(e) Promote, where appropriate, the objectives of the present article by concluding bilateral or multilateral arrangements or agreements, and endeavour, within this framework, to ensure that the placement of the child in another country is carried out by competent authorities or organs.

Article 22

1. States Parties shall take appropriate measures to ensure that a child who is seeking refugee status or who is considered a refugee in accordance with applicable international or domestic law and procedures shall, whether unaccompanied or accompanied by his or her parents or by any other person, receive appropriate protection and humanitarian assistance in the enjoyment of applicable rights set forth in the present Convention and in other international human rights or humanitarian instruments to which the said States are Parties.

2. For this purpose, States Parties shall provide, as they consider appropriate, co-operation in any efforts by the United Nations and other competent intergovernmental organizations or non- governmental organizations co-operating with the United Nations to protect and assist such a child and to trace the parents or other members of the family of any refugee child in order to obtain information necessary for reunification with his or her family. In cases where no parents or other members of the family can be found, the child shall be accorded the same protection as any other child permanently or temporarily deprived of his or her family environment for any reason , as set forth in the present Convention.

Article 23

1. States Parties recognize that a mentally or physically disabled child should enjoy a full and decent life, in conditions which ensure dignity, promote self-reliance and facilitate the child's active participation in the community.

2. States Parties recognize the right of the disabled child to special care and shall encourage and ensure the extension, subject to available resources, to the eligible child and those responsible for his or her care, of assistance for which application

is made and which is appropriate to the child's condition and to the circumstances of the parents or others caring for the child.

3. Recognizing the special needs of a disabled child, assistance extended in accordance with paragraph 2 of the present article shall be provided free of charge, whenever possible, taking into account the financial resources of the parents or others caring for the child, and shall be designed to ensure that the disabled child has effective access to and receives education, training, health care services, rehabilitation services, preparation for employment and recreation opportunities in a manner conducive to the child's achieving the fullest possible social integration and individual development, including his or her cultural and spiritual development.

4. States Parties shall promote, in the spirit of international cooperation, the exchange of appropriate information in the field of preventive health care and of medical, psychological and functional treatment of disabled children, including dissemination of and access to information concerning methods of rehabilitation, education and vocational services, with the aim of enabling States Parties to improve their capabilities and skills and to widen their experience in these areas. In this regard, particular account shall be taken of the needs of developing countries.

Article 24

1. States Parties recognize the right of the child to the enjoyment of the highest attainable standard of health and to facilities for the treatment of illness and rehabilitation of health. States Parties shall strive to ensure that no child is deprived of his or her right of access to such health care services.

2. States Parties shall pursue full implementation of this right and, in particular, shall take appropriate measures:

(a) To diminish infant and child mortality;

(b) To ensure the provision of necessary medical assistance and health care to all children with emphasis on the development of primary health care;

(c) To combat disease and malnutrition, including within the framework of primary health care, through, inter alia, the application of readily available technology and through the provision of adequate nutritious foods and clean drinking-water, taking into consideration the dangers and risks of environmental pollution;

(d) To ensure appropriate pre-natal and post-natal health care for mothers;

(e) To ensure that all segments of society, in particular parents and children, are informed, have access to education and are supported in the use of basic knowledge of child health and nutrition, the advantages of breastfeeding, hygiene and environmental sanitation and the prevention of accidents;

(f) To develop preventive health care, guidance for parents and family planning education and services.

3. States Parties shall take all effective and appropriate measures with a view to abolishing traditional practices prejudicial to the health of children.

4. States Parties undertake to promote and encourage international co-operation with a view to achieving progressively the full realization of the right recognized in the present article. In this regard, particular account shall be taken of the needs of developing countries.

Article 25

States Parties recognize the right of a child who has been placed by the competent authorities for the purposes of care, protection or treatment of his or her physical or mental health, to a periodic review of the treatment provided to the child and all other circumstances relevant to his or her placement.

Article 26

1. States Parties shall recognize for every child the right to benefit from social security, including social insurance, and shall take the necessary measures to achieve the full realization of this right in accordance with their national law.

2. The benefits should, where appropriate, be granted, taking into account the resources and the circumstances of the child and persons having responsibility for the maintenance of the child, as well as any other consideration relevant to an application for benefits made by or on behalf of the child.

Article 27

1. States Parties recognize the right of every child to a standard of living adequate for the child's physical, mental, spiritual, moral and social development.

2. The parent(s) or others responsible for the child have the primary responsibility to secure, within their abilities and financial capacities, the conditions of living necessary for the child's development.

3. States Parties, in accordance with national conditions and within their means, shall take appropriate measures to assist parents and others responsible for the child to implement this right and shall in case of need provide material assistance and support programmes, particularly with regard to nutrition, clothing and housing.

4. States Parties shall take all appropriate measures to secure the recovery of maintenance for the child from the parents or other persons having financial responsibility for the child, both within the State Party and from abroad. In particular, where the person having financial responsibility for the child lives in a State different from that of the child, States Parties shall promote the accession to international agreements or the conclusion of such agreements, as well as the making of other appropriate arrangements.

Article 28

1. States Parties recognize the right of the child to education, and with a view to achieving this right progressively and on the basis of equal opportunity, they shall, in particular:

(a) Make primary education compulsory and available free to all;

(b) Encourage the development of different forms of secondary education, including general and vocational education, make them available and accessible to every child, and take appropriate measures such as the introduction of free education and offering financial assistance in case of need;

(c) Make higher education accessible to all on the basis of capacity by every appropriate means;

(d) Make educational and vocational information and guidance available and accessible to all children;

(e) Take measures to encourage regular attendance at schools and the reduction of drop-out rates.

2. States Parties shall take all appropriate measures to ensure that school discipline is administered in a manner consistent with the child's human dignity and in conformity with the present Convention.

3. States Parties shall promote and encourage international cooperation in matters relating to education, in particular with a view to contributing to the elimination of ignorance and illiteracy throughout the world and facilitating access to scientific and technical knowledge and modern teaching methods. In this regard, particular account shall be taken of the needs of developing countries.

Article 29

1. States Parties agree that the education of the child shall be directed to:

(a) The development of the child's personality, talents and mental and physical abilities to their fullest potential;

(b) The development of respect for human rights and fundamental freedoms, and for the principles enshrined in the Charter of the United Nations;

(c) The development of respect for the child's parents, his or her own cultural identity, language and values, for the national values of the country in which the child is living, the country from which he or she may originate, and for civilizations different from his or her own;

(d) The preparation of the child for responsible life in a free society, in the spirit of understanding, peace, tolerance, equality of sexes, and friendship among all peoples, ethnic, national and religious groups and persons of indigenous origin;

(e) The development of respect for the natural environment.

2. No part of the present article or article 28 shall be construed so as to interfere with the liberty of individuals and bodies to establish and direct educational institutions, subject always to the observance of the principle set forth in paragraph 1 of the present article and to the requirements that the education given in such institutions shall conform to such minimum standards as may be laid down by the State.

Article 30

In those States in which ethnic, religious or linguistic minorities or persons of indigenous origin exist, a child belonging to such a minority or who is indigenous shall not be denied the right, in community with other members of his or her group, to enjoy his or her own culture, to profess and practise his or her own religion, or to use his or her own language.

Article 31

1. States Parties recognize the right of the child to rest and leisure, to engage in play and recreational activities appropriate to the age of the child and to participate freely in cultural life and the arts.

2. States Parties shall respect and promote the right of the child to participate fully in cultural and artistic life and shall encourage the provision of appropriate and equal opportunities for cultural, artistic, recreational and leisure activity.

Article 32

1. States Parties recognize the right of the child to be protected from economic exploitation and from performing any work that is likely to be hazardous or to interfere with the child's education, or to be harmful to the child's health or physical, mental, spiritual, moral or social development.

2. States Parties shall take legislative, administrative, social and educational measures to ensure the implementation of the present article. To this end, and having regard to the relevant provisions of other international instruments, States Parties shall in particular:

(a) Provide for a minimum age or minimum ages for admission to employment;

(b) Provide for appropriate regulation of the hours and conditions of employment;

(c) Provide for appropriate penalties or other sanctions to ensure the effective enforcement of the present article.

Article 33

States Parties shall take all appropriate measures, including legislative, administrative, social and educational measures, to protect children from the illicit use of narcotic drugs and psychotropic substances as defined in the relevant international treaties, and to prevent the use of children in the illicit production and trafficking of such substances.

Article 34

States Parties undertake to protect the child from all forms of sexual exploitation and sexual abuse. For these purposes, States Parties shall in particular take all appropriate national, bilateral and multilateral measures to prevent:

(a) The inducement or coercion of a child to engage in any unlawful sexual activity;

(b) The exploitative use of children in prostitution or other unlawful sexual practices;

(c) The exploitative use of children in pornographic performances and materials.

Article 35

States Parties shall take all appropriate national, bilateral and multilateral measures to prevent the abduction of, the sale of or traffic in children for any purpose or in any form.

Article 36

States Parties shall protect the child against all other forms of exploitation prejudicial to any aspects of the child's welfare.

Article 37

States Parties shall ensure that:

(a) No child shall be subjected to torture or other cruel, inhuman or degrading treatment or punishment. Neither capital punishment nor life imprisonment without possibility of release shall be imposed for offences committed by persons below eighteen years of age;

(b) No child shall be deprived of his or her liberty unlawfully or arbitrarily. The arrest, detention or imprisonment of a child shall be in conformity with the law and shall be used only as a measure of last resort and for the shortest appropriate period of time;

(c) Every child deprived of liberty shall be treated with humanity and respect for the inherent dignity of the human person, and in a manner which takes into account the needs of persons of his or her age. In particular, every child deprived of liberty shall be separated from adults unless it is considered in the child's best interest not to do so and shall have the right to maintain contact with his or her family through correspondence and visits, save in exceptional circumstances;

(d) Every child deprived of his or her liberty shall have the right to prompt access to legal and other appropriate assistance, as well as the right to challenge the legality of the deprivation of his or her liberty before a court or other competent, independent and impartial authority, and to a prompt decision on any such action.

Article 38

1. States Parties undertake to respect and to ensure respect for rules of international humanitarian law applicable to them in armed conflicts which are relevant to the child.

2. States Parties shall take all feasible measures to ensure that persons who have not attained the age of fifteen years do not take a direct part in hostilities.

3. States Parties shall refrain from recruiting any person who has not attained the age of fifteen years into their armed forces. In recruiting among those persons who have attained the age of fifteen years but who have not attained the age of eighteen years, States Parties shall endeavour to give priority to those who are oldest.

4. In accordance with their obligations under international humanitarian law to protect the civilian population in armed conflicts, States Parties shall take all feasible measures to ensure protection and care of children who are affected by an armed conflict.

Article 39

States Parties shall take all appropriate measures to promote physical and psychological recovery and social reintegration of a child victim of: any form of neglect, exploitation, or abuse; torture or any other form of cruel, inhuman or degrading treatment or punishment; or armed conflicts. Such recovery and reintegration shall take place in an environment which fosters the health, self-respect and dignity of the child.

Article 40

1. States Parties recognize the right of every child alleged as, accused of, or recognized as having infringed the penal law to be treated in a manner consistent with the promotion of the child's sense of dignity and worth, which reinforces the child's respect for the human rights and fundamental freedoms of others and which takes into account the child's age and the desirability of promoting the child's reintegration and the child's assuming a constructive role in society.

2. To this end, and having regard to the relevant provisions of international instruments, States Parties shall, in particular, ensure that:

(a) No child shall be alleged as, be accused of, or recognized as having infringed the penal law by reason of acts or omissions that were not prohibited by national or international law at the time they were committed;

(b) Every child alleged as or accused of having infringed the penal law has at least the following guarantees:

(i) To be presumed innocent until proven guilty according to law;

(ii) To be informed promptly and directly of the charges against him or her, and, if appropriate, through his or her parents or legal guardians, and to have legal or other appropriate assistance in the preparation and presentation of his or her defence;

(iii) To have the matter determined without delay by a competent, independent and impartial authority or judicial body in a fair hearing according to law, in the presence of legal or other appropriate assistance and, unless it is considered not to be in the best interest of the child, in particular, taking into account his or her age or situation, his or her parents or legal guardians;

(iv) Not to be compelled to give testimony or to confess guilt; to examine or have examined adverse witnesses and to obtain the participation and examination of witnesses on his or her behalf under conditions of equality;

(v) If considered to have infringed the penal law, to have this decision and any measures imposed in consequence thereof reviewed by a higher competent, independent and impartial authority or judicial body according to law;

(vi) To have the free assistance of an interpreter if the child cannot understand or speak the language used;

(vii) To have his or her privacy fully respected at all stages of the proceedings.

3. States Parties shall seek to promote the establishment of laws, procedures, authorities and institutions specifically applicable to children alleged as, accused of, or recognized as having infringed the penal law, and, in particular:

(a) The establishment of a minimum age below which children shall be presumed not to have the capacity to infringe the penal law;

(b) Whenever appropriate and desirable, measures for dealing with such children without resorting to judicial proceedings, providing that human rights and legal safeguards are fully respected. 4. A variety of dispositions, such as care, guidance and supervision orders; counselling; probation; foster care; education and vocational training programmes and other alternatives to institutional care shall be available to ensure that children are dealt with in a manner appropriate to their well-being and proportionate both to their circumstances and the offence.

Article 41

Nothing in the present Convention shall affect any provisions which are more conducive to the realization of the rights of the child and which may be contained in:

(a) The law of a State party; or

(b) International law in force for that State.

PART II

Article 42

States Parties undertake to make the principles and provisions of the Convention widely known, by appropriate and active means, to adults and children alike.

Article 43

1. For the purpose of examining the progress made by States Parties in achieving the realization of the obligations undertaken in the present Convention, there shall be established a Committee on the Rights of the Child, which shall carry out the functions hereinafter provided.

2. The Committee shall consist of ten experts of high moral standing and recognized competence in the field covered by this Convention. The members of the Committee shall be elected by States Parties from among their nationals and shall serve in their personal capacity, consideration being given to equitable geographical distribution, as well as to the principal legal systems.

3. The members of the Committee shall be elected by secret ballot from a list of persons nominated by States Parties. Each State Party may nominate one person from among its own nationals.

4. The initial election to the Committee shall be held no later than six months after the date of the entry into force of the present Convention and thereafter every second year. At least four months before the date of each election, the Secretary-General of the United Nations shall address a letter to States Parties inviting them to submit their nominations within two months. The Secretary-General shall subsequently prepare a list in alphabetical order of all persons thus nominated, indicating States Parties which have nominated them, and shall submit it to the States Parties to the present Convention.

5. The elections shall be held at meetings of States Parties convened by the Secretary-General at United Nations Headquarters. At those meetings, for which two thirds of States Parties shall constitute a quorum, the persons elected to the Committee shall be those who obtain the largest number of votes and an absolute majority of the votes of the representatives of States Parties present and voting.

6. The members of the Committee shall be elected for a term of four years. They shall be eligible for re-election if renominated. The term of five of the members elected at the first election shall expire at the end of two years; immediately after the first election, the names of these five members shall be chosen by lot by the Chairman of the meeting.

7. If a member of the Committee dies or resigns or declares that for any other cause he or she can no longer perform the duties of the Committee, the State Party which nominated the member shall appoint another expert from among its nationals to serve for the remainder of the term, subject to the approval of the Committee.

8. The Committee shall establish its own rules of procedure.

9. The Committee shall elect its officers for a period of two years.

10. The meetings of the Committee shall normally be held at United Nations Headquarters or at any other convenient place as determined by the Committee. The Committee shall normally meet annually. The duration of the meetings of the Committee shall be determined, and reviewed, if necessary, by a meeting of the States Parties to the present Convention, subject to the approval of the General Assembly.

11. The Secretary-General of the United Nations shall provide the necessary staff and facilities for the effective performance of the functions of the Committee under the present Convention.

12. With the approval of the General Assembly, the members of the Committee established under the present Convention shall receive emoluments from United Nations resources on such terms and conditions as the Assembly may decide.

Article 44

1. States Parties undertake to submit to the Committee, through the Secretary-General of the United Nations, reports on the measures they have adopted which give effect to the rights recognized herein and on the progress made on the enjoyment of those rights

(a) Within two years of the entry into force of the Convention for the State Party concerned;

(b) Thereafter every five years.

2. Reports made under the present article shall indicate factors and difficulties, if any, affecting the degree of fulfilment of the obligations under the present Convention. Reports shall also contain sufficient information to provide the Committee

with a comprehensive understanding of the implementation of the Convention in the country concerned.

3. A State Party which has submitted a comprehensive initial report to the Committee need not, in its subsequent reports submitted in accordance with paragraph 1 (b) of the present article, repeat basic information previously provided.

4. The Committee may request from States Parties further information relevant to the implementation of the Convention.

5. The Committee shall submit to the General Assembly, through the Economic and Social Council, every two years, reports on its activities.

6. States Parties shall make their reports widely available to the public in their own countries.

Article 45

In order to foster the effective implementation of the Convention and to encourage international co- operation in the field covered by the Convention:

(a) The specialized agencies, the United Nations Children's Fund, and other United Nations organs shall be entitled to be represented at the consideration of the implementation of such provisions of the present Convention as fall within the scope of their mandate. The Committee may invite the specialized agencies, the United Nations Children's Fund and other competent bodies as it may consider appropriate to provide expert advice on the implementation of the Convention in areas falling within the scope of their respective mandates. The Committee may invite the specialized agencies, the United Nations Children's Fund, and other United Nations organs to submit reports on the implementation of the Convention in areas falling within the scope of their activities;

(b) The Committee shall transmit, as it may consider appropriate, to the specialized agencies, the United Nations Children's Fund and other competent bodies, any reports from States Parties that contain a request, or indicate a need, for technical advice or assistance, along with the Committee's observations and suggestions, if any, on these requests or indications;

(c) The Committee may recommend to the General Assembly to request the Secretary-General to undertake on its behalf studies on specific issues relating to the rights of the child;

(d) The Committee may make suggestions and general recommendations based on information received pursuant to articles 44 and 45 of the present Convention. Such suggestions and general recommendations shall be transmitted to any State Party concerned and reported to the General Assembly, together with comments, if any, from States Parties.

PART III

Article 46

The present Convention shall be open for signature by all States.

Article 47

The present Convention is subject to ratification. Instruments of ratification shall be deposited with the Secretary-General of the United Nations.

Article 48

The present Convention shall remain open for accession by any State. The instruments of accession shall be deposited with the Secretary-General of the United Nations.

Article 49

1. The present Convention shall enter into force on the thirtieth day following the date of deposit with the Secretary-General of the United Nations of the twentieth instrument of ratification or accession.

2. For each State ratifying or acceding to the Convention after the deposit of the twentieth instrument of ratification or accession, the Convention shall enter into force on the thirtieth day after the deposit by such State of its instrument of ratification or accession.

Article 50

1. Any State Party may propose an amendment and file it with the Secretary-General of the United Nations. The Secretary-General shall thereupon communicate the proposed amendment to States Parties, with a request that they indicate whether they favour a conference of States Parties for the purpose of considering and voting upon the proposals. In the event that, within four months from the date of such communication, at least one third of the States Parties favour such a conference, the Secretary-General shall convene the conference under the auspices of the United Nations. Any amendment adopted by a majority of States Parties present and voting at the conference shall be submitted to the General Assembly for approval.

2. An amendment adopted in accordance with paragraph 1 of the present article shall enter into force when it has been approved by the General Assembly of the United Nations and accepted by a two- thirds majority of States Parties.

3. When an amendment enters into force, it shall be binding on those States Parties which have accepted it, other States Parties still being bound by the provisions of the present Convention and any earlier amendments which they have accepted.

Article 51

1. The Secretary-General of the United Nations shall receive and circulate to all States the text of reservations made by States at the time of ratification or accession.

2. A reservation incompatible with the object and purpose of the present Convention shall not be permitted.

3. Reservations may be withdrawn at any time by notification to that effect addressed to the Secretary-General of the United Nations, who shall then inform all States. Such notification shall take effect on the date on which it is received by the Secretary-General.

Article 52

A State Party may denounce the present Convention by written notification to the Secretary-General of the United Nations. Denunciation becomes effective one year after the date of receipt of the notification by the Secretary-General.

Article 53

The Secretary-General of the United Nations is designated as the depositary of the present Convention.

Article 54

The original of the present Convention, of which the Arabic, Chinese, English, French, Russian and Spanish texts are equally authentic, shall be deposited with the Secretary-General of the United Nations.

IN WITNESS THEREOF the undersigned plenipotentiaries, being duly authorized thereto by their respective governments, have signed the present Convention.

Glossary

A

absolute discharge a type of judgment of a criminal case, in which a finding of guilt is obtained but no conviction is registered and no conditions are imposed

absolute liability offence an offence of which an accused can be found guilty if the prosecution proves that the accused committed the act or omission that constitutes the offence, regardless of the presence or absence of intent or of any particular state of mind

administration of justice offence violation of court-ordered conditions such as curfew, non-association with criminals, attendance at school or mandated treatment, showing up in court, etc.

aggravating factor a circumstance or action taken by an offender during or after the commission of an offence that supports a more onerous sentence

al-Qaeda international terrorist network that has claimed responsibility for several attacks on Western cities; "al-Qaeda" means "the base"

appearance notice a notice given to an accused by police after being charged, telling him or her to appear in court on a specific day/time to answer to a criminal charge

arrest police control of the movement of a person by some demand or direction on the basis of probable cause, in order for the person to answer for a criminal charge

assault level 1 assaults that cause little to no physical harm to victims; can include such acts as pushing and shoving

B

bath salts drugs containing one or more synthetic chemicals related to an amphetamine (cathinone)

best interests of the child a guiding principle of the UNCRC that, in all matters affecting children, care must be taken to consider what decision would best protect the child's physical, psychological, and emotional safety, security, and well-being

bio-social characterized by the interaction of biological and social factors

C

car surfing a thrill-seeking activity consisting in riding the exterior of a moving vehicle while another person drives; the term was introduced in the mid-1980s

central eight predictors the eight predictors of criminal involvement: (1) a history of criminal behaviour; (2) anti-social personality pattern; (3) anti-social attitudes, values, beliefs, and cognitive-emotional states; (4) anti-social associates; low levels of protective factors in the domains (5) of family, (6) of school, and (7) of work; and (8) the presence of substance abuse

certificate of offence an unsworn, formulaic document (in a specific format and with specific content) prepared for proceedings having to do with less serious offences

certificate of parking infraction a parking ticket or "tag"

child abuse physically harming, sexually molesting, or sexually exploiting a child

child in need of protection legal definition/determination, based on an established set of criteria and evidence, that forms the basis of a protective order in child welfare proceedings

circle sentencing a First Nations form of restorative justice that brings together the offender, the victim, and the community

cognitive behavioural treatment an effective form of intervention that helps patients to understand the thoughts and feelings that influence behaviours; focuses on how people think ("cognitive") and act ("behavioural")

collective response focuses on broader issues in society that affect an individual (e.g., poverty)

community change model a model of justice that stresses the importance of the broader community in looking after members of the community and addressing the root causes of crime to ensure that all people have an opportunity to do well

conditional discharge a type of judgment of a criminal case, in which a finding of guilt is obtained but no conviction is registered, but a set of conditions is imposed in the form of a probation order

conditional supervision a portion of a custodial sentence that is served outside custody and during which a youth is subject to strict conditions of behaviour

conferences meetings that can occur at various stages of a criminal matter that bring together interested parties (judge, accused, lawyers, parents, others) in an attempt to resolve an issue related to the charge or trial

conflict theory an approach to how societies work that emphasizes conflict, power relations, differences among groups, and social change resulting from group conflict

crime control model a model of justice that is largely concerned with the protection of society and with assuring the public that crime will not be tolerated, and will be severely punished

crime funnel the reduction in the number of individuals involved at each stage of the decision-making process in the criminal justice system

crime myth distorted conceptions of issues related to crime and criminal justice policy that have come to be accepted because they have been relied on in public forums, debates, and personal conversations

crime prevention through environmental design crime prevention that addresses planning and development in a community with the goal of reducing crime

crime prevention through social development crime prevention that addresses the social factors that underlie crime with the goal of reducing criminality

crime rate ratio of police-reported crimes in an area to the population of that area

Crime Severity Index (CSI) system for measuring the severity of police-reported crimes each year, and the change in severity year to year; created to alleviate some of the problems in determining the crime rate

criminogenic needs deficiencies in social cognition, problem-solving abilities, and sense of self-efficacy

Crown brief the document or file that contains the important information about a charge (for what offences, name of accused, summary of evidence, details of prior criminal record, etc.)

custodial sentence a judicial sentence that requires a term of either open or secure imprisonment of the offender

cyberbanging the use of social media to showcase images and exploits of various street gangs

cybercrime criminal activity committed on computers over the Internet

D

dark figure of crime the number of crimes that do not come to the attention of the criminal justice system

deferred custody and supervision order (DCSO) a sentencing option for youth convicted of offences not involving bodily harm or attempting to cause bodily harm; with a DCSO a youth can serve his or her sentence in the community, under conditions

denunciation a way to communicate disapproval of a young person's actions as "wrong" through punishment

detention being stopped by police on the basis of a reasonable suspicion; includes not only physical but also psychological restraint, as when the individual believes he or she is not free to go

deterrence a philosophy of justice that holds that individual offenders choose to commit crime on the basis of their own personal gain

disclosure before trial, the release by the prosecutor to the defence of all evidence the prosecutor plans on using at trial

doli incapax a Latin term for the notion that young children are not capable of distinguishing between right and wrong

due diligence the taking of reasonable steps to avoid committing an offence

due process the doctrine that the state must respect all rights owed to a person under the *Canadian Charter of Rights and Freedoms*

duty counsel a lawyer, either an employee of the court or working under contract for the court, who provides on-the-spot, no-charge (although there may be an eventual charge) advice to unrepresented accused

duty to report a statutorily or legally explicit (as opposed to moral/ethical) requirement to report qualifying incidents or observations

dynamic risk factors risk factors amenable to treatment and intervention

E

enhancement model a theory that suggests that youth already engaging in anti-social behaviour are more likely to join gangs, and that, in turn, this elevates their involvement in further anti-social activity facilitated by the gangs

extrajudicial measure a way of dealing with offenders outside the formal justice system

extrajudicial sanction a more formal counterpart of extrajudicial measures

F

fiduciary duty the duty of adults to meet a higher standard of care when entrusted with the responsibility of protecting children

functionalist theory an approach to how societies work that emphasizes the way various parts of society function and interact to produce social harmony or equilibrium

G

gender-specific associated with persons of one gender to the exclusion of the other

general deterrence the desired effect of a sentence consisting in prevention of a repeat of the offence like that of the convicted individual by any other member of the public

globalization the increasing economic interdependence of countries worldwide through a growing quantity and variety of cross-border transactions in goods and services, free international capital flows, and rapid, widespread distribution of technology

H

hackers individuals who, by means of programming skills, gain illegal access to computer files or networks

hacking a breach of a database security system to destroy or damage information by introducing a computer virus into the data system

hate crime illegal activity motivated by prejudice against an identifiable group

hidden delinquency undetected rule-breaking behaviour

hybrid offence a type of offence that can be dealt with either as a summary conviction offence or as an indictable offence, at the discretion of the Crown; for arrest purposes, police treat all hybrid offences as indictable

I

ideology a set of general and abstract beliefs or assumptions about the proper state of things that shapes one's position on specific issues

incarceration imprisonment

indictable offence the most serious of offences, which carries a maximum penalty of life imprisonment

individual response focuses on factors and behaviour related to a single person (e.g., mental illness)

information a statement sworn, typically before a justice of the peace, for the purpose of laying a more serious charge

intensive rehabilitative custody and supervision (IRCS) a sentence available for youth convicted of serious violent offences who are suffering from a mental illness or disorder, psychological disorder, or emotional disturbance where an intensive treatment plan is developed that is believed to reduce the risk of reoffence

J

judicial interim release (bail) pre-trial release of an individual accused of a crime after he or she has appeared before the court in a show-cause hearing

judicial reprimand a stern warning from a judge

judicial review a higher court's review, at a separate hearing, of aspects of a lower court proceeding (typically administrative or procedural aspects, not findings of fact or verdict/order)

jurisdiction the scope of authority of a court; can be based on a defined territory (Ontario court), a defined age range (youth court), a defined class of offences (small claims court), a defined area of law (family court), and so on

justice model a model of justice that focuses on the protection of society through deterrence principles; those upholding this model believe young people should be accorded the same rights to legal protection as adults

L

labelling theory a subtheory of symbolic interactionism that suggests that individuals will "live up to" stereotypical labels—e.g., "delinquent"—ascribed to them by others

M

medical model a model of justice that focuses on intervention based on the belief that criminal behaviour is a sign of illness

meta-analysis statistical method used to draw conclusions by analyzing a group of experimental studies

mitigating factor a circumstance or action taken by an offender during or after the commission of an offence that supports a lighter sentence

moot the characteristic of a legal issue when it no longer requires a formal decision because intervening events have made it irrelevant

moral panic extreme social response to the belief that the moral condition of society is deteriorating rapidly; may be directed against targeted groups to justify harsh and oppressive treatment

N

neglect failure to meet a child's basic needs, such as health care, supervision, and nutrition, and psychological, educational, or housing needs

not criminally responsible (NCR) a finding of the court about the status of an accused that is neither a conviction nor an acquittal, meaning that at the time of the alleged offence the accused could not form the intent to offend due to mental disorder

novice driver in Ontario, someone who has a G1 or G2 licence (or an M1 or M2 motorcycle licence)

P

pacifism ideology or movement that consists in being opposed to war or violence

paradigm a pattern to explain phenomena

parens patriae the doctrine that the state has the responsibility to look after the well-being of vulnerable persons, such as youth, and to step in as parent if necessary

penology the study of corrections and control of criminal offenders

person in authority for the purposes of the YCJA, any person a reasonable young person might think to be an agent of the criminal justice system

plea bargain an agreement reached by the defendant and the prosecutor that both parties are satisfied with; must be approved by the court

police (or Crown) caution an extrajudicial measure that consists of a formal warning, which might include a letter to the youth (and parents) and/or a dedicated meeting at a police station to discuss the incident

positivist school of thought a branch of social sciences that argues that human behaviour is a product of social, biological, or psychological forces

preamble an introduction that explains the intent and philosophy of a piece of legislation

preliminary motions and applications mini-hearings, separate from the main trial, to resolve preliminary, usually procedural, issues

prescriptive standard with respect to child welfare, a standard that requires a person responsible for a child to do something (e.g., provide shelter)

primary crime prevention crime prevention focusing on social and situational factors in order to reduce the opportunity for future crime and victimization

pro-social intended to help others; a characteristic of behaviours

probation a period of supervision over an offender outside of incarceration

procedural fairness a general legal principle that exists to help children and youth exercise their rights regardless of what others might assert to be in their best interests

procedural justice ensures that the administration of justice and fair processes are upheld in the courtroom

promise to appear a notice signed by an accused promising that he or she will appear before the court for trial on the specific date

proscriptive standard with respect to child welfare, a standard that prohibits a person from doing something to or in respect of a child (e.g., selling tobacco to him or her)

protective factors circumstances and experiences that tend to shield people from involvement in behaviours that would be damaging to themselves and to others

provincial director a person or "a group or class of persons"—i.e., certain members of the provincial corrections administration—designated by a provincial government to perform a wide range of functions under the legislation (e.g., ensuring that pre-sentence reports are completed)

R

radical non-intervention an approach to justice that advocates not intervening with a low-risk offender, to avoid having a young person labelled criminal by the criminal justice system; based on the belief that criminal justice processing of youth can lead to more offenders coming into the system

reasonable grounds facts or circumstances, used as justification for police action, that to a reasonable person are beyond mere suspicions

recognizance a formal agreement by an accused after being charged that requires an acknowledgment of a debt to the Crown for an amount up to $500, which may require a deposit, in order to be released prior to trial

reintegration leave a period spent out of custody, with leave of the provincial director, for making arrangements or participating in activities that will facilitate the youth's reintegration into the community

relationship custody framework a balance between the dynamic security approaches (professional, positive relationships between youth and staff) and the static security approaches (physical barriers and surveillance) involved in correctional institutions

remand to put (a defendant) on bail or in custody, especially when a trial is adjourned; committal to custody

reparation a way for a young person to alleviate the harm he or she caused to either the victim or the community, by such means as a letter of apology or community service

reservation a statement made to the United Nations that limits how the government accepts a part of a treaty or convention (e.g., the UN Convention on the Rights of the Child)

resilience the ability of an individual who has faced adversity, often through multiple risks, to thrive; cannot be present without risk

responsible person an individual willing and able to exercise control over a young person in order for him or her to be released prior to trial

responsivity principle the idea that in order to maximize the offender's ability to learn from a rehabilitative intervention, it is necessary to tie the program to the evidence that has been shown to be successful in reducing recidivism

restitution financial reparations owed by an offender to a crime victim who suffers a financial loss as a result of the crime

restorative justice model an approach to justice that characterizes crime as harm done to people and relationships, and that encourages responses to crime that help repair that harm

reverse onus the burden of proof being shifted from the Crown to a defendant in either a criminal offence or tort claim; e.g., the burden of proof resting on defence counsel to show cause why a youth should be released

risk factors negative influences or circumstances in the lives of individuals, groups of persons, or communities that may increase the presence of crime, victimization, and/or fear of crime in a given community

risk–needs–responsivity (RNR) model model that suggests that the best way to reduce recidivism is to assess the risks and needs of the individual and determine appropriate interventions that are responsive to the individual's criminogenic factors

S

sanction a penalty that requires a young offender to accept responsibility for the act that forms the basis of the offence and to comply with certain terms and conditions, failure to comply with which can result in prosecution of the offence

secondary crime prevention crime prevention focusing on those considered at risk for committing crimes with the goal of eliminating opportunities that might foster criminal behaviour

self-report studies method of data collection that relies on self-administered surveys or questionnaires given to a target group in order to obtain a group profile of the identified behaviours in which the researcher is interested

self-system beliefs beliefs about one's attitudes, abilities, or cognitive skills

serious offence any indictable offence for which the maximum punishment for an adult is imprisonment for five years or more, including violent offences, some property offences (e.g., auto theft), and offences that might endanger the public (e.g., dangerous driving, murder)

serious violent offence an offence committed by a young person that includes an element of causing bodily harm, a threat or attempt to do so, or endangering the life and safety of another by creating the substantial likelihood of bodily harm

severe recidivists the 5 percent of offenders with the highest recidivism rates

shock incarceration an alternative to traditional incarceration in which youth are held for a short term in custody with a focus on rehabilitation by utilizing military discipline; often called *boot camp*

show-cause hearing another name for a bail or judicial interim release hearing; the burden of proof is on the Crown to "show cause" why the accused should be detained pending trial

social learning theory a social psychological approach that holds that behaviour is learned by observing and modelling those around one

special plea a plea other than guilty or not guilty; there are only a few recognized types

specific deterrence the desired effect of a sentence consisting in prevention of a repeat of the offence by the convicted individual

spontaneous statement a statement offered by a youth without his or her being prompted by police questions or comments, and before police have had a chance to advise the youth of his or her s. 146 rights

static risk factors relatively unchangeable risk factors

status offence a genre of criminal offence that is based not on the committing in the past of a particular prohibited action or inaction but on the allegation that the offender has a certain personal condition or is of a specified character

statutory prioritization the organization of statutory provisions in order of priority of their application

stay of proceedings a dismissal of further legal proceedings

strict liability offence an offence that does not require proof of intent, but to which the accused may have a defence (e.g., the defence of due diligence)

substantive justice ensures that the application of law is fair and just

summary conviction offence a minor offence carrying a maximum penalty of six months in jail, or a fine

surety a person who agrees to vouch for the accused's return to court for a trial, and to pay a certain sum if the accused does not show

symbolic interactionist theory an approach that holds that individual behaviour is influenced by people's interaction with others, and that self-image is constructed by a conscious reading of the symbolic meaning of these interactions

T

tertiary crime prevention crime prevention focusing on reducing recidivism and eliminating revictimization

therapeutic jurisprudence a type of jurisprudence that merges the law with a variety of therapeutic techniques, without compromising the values of justice and due process

truancy not attending school (without a legally acceptable excuse) when school attendance is required by law for a child of the truant's age in the truant's province

U

undertaking conditions set out on a promise to appear or a recognizance when the youth agrees to such things as a curfew, parental supervision, or other such requirement(s)

Uniform Crime Reporting (UCR) Survey system for classifying reported incidents by type of crime, on the basis of crime detected by police and reported by the public

V

vandalism destruction of, or damage to, private property

victim impact statement a written summary, authored by a victim, of the effects that an offence has had on his or her life, and of any ongoing problems that the incident can be expected to cause for him or her

victim–offender mediation negotiation between a victim and an offender, facilitated by a trained mediator, with the goal of resolving the conflict and constructing their own approach to justice as it relates to the specific crime

victimization surveys crime surveys based on incidents of crime (either reported to police or unreported) as described by self-identified victims

W

waiver the oral or written giving up or dispensing with the exercise of a legal right

ward a legally protected individual, usually either a child or an incapacitated person

wardship the legal status of an individual that consists of being a ward of the state

welfare model a model of justice that stresses the importance of looking after the needs of the offender to ensure that his or her problems are treated so that crime will not recur

Y

young driver any driver under the age of 22, regardless of his or her class of licence

youth justice court (1) a court specifically constituted for the purpose of hearing youth trials; (2) an existing adult court designated (temporarily or permanently) for that purpose

Index